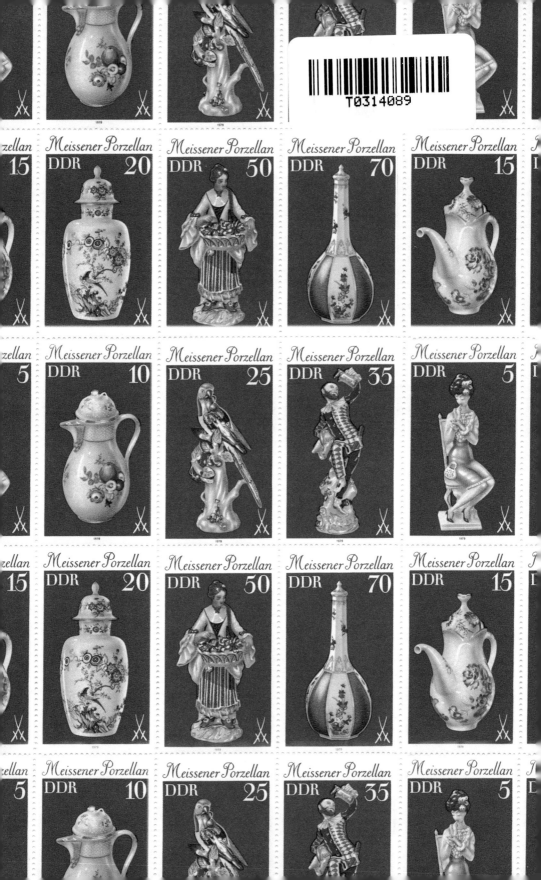

Porcelaín

Por

celain

A History from the
Heart of Europe

Suzanne L. Marchand

PRINCETON UNIVERSITY PRESS

Princeton and Oxford

Published by Princeton University Press
41 William Street, Princeton, New Jersey 08540
6 Oxford Street, Woodstock, Oxfordshire OX20 1TR

press.princeton.edu

All Rights Reserved
ISBN 978-0-691-18233-9
ISBN (e-book) 978-0-691-20198-6

British Library Cataloging-in-Publication Data is available

Editorial: Eric Crahan and Thalia Leaf
Production Editorial: Mark Bellis
Text Design: C. Alvarez-Gaffin
Jacket Design: Jason Alejandro
Production: Jacqueline Poirier
Publicity: Maria Whelan and Kate Farquhar-Thomson
Copyeditor: Kathleen Kageff

Jacket Credit: from the Onion Pattern "Style" dish; ® Meissen

This book has been composed in Sabon LT Std and Ogg

Printed on acid-free paper. ∞

Printed in the United States of America

10 9 8 7 6 5 4 3 2 1

To all the women—and men!—who gather
around my family table:

Betsy, Victor, Jean, JoAnn and Nia,
Jeannie and Sotiros, Paul and Beth,
and Charles and Henry

Contents

Illustrations and Tables

Figures

Plates (between pages 264 and 265)

Maps

Tables

German economic history is a very complicated subject, which this author cannot claim to have fully mastered. Some of the complexities include the multiple currencies used by inhabitants of the myriad states of central Europe until the later nineteenth century (when these were at least stabilized, though not united), the changing of units of exchange over time, and the very different "real" value of coins, especially before 1815. Although an agreement was made in the mid-sixteenth century that all states of the Holy Roman Empire that issued reichstaler would maintain its silver content at 25.98 grams of silver,[1] in practice these were often clipped or the silver or gold mixed with cheaper alloys. A taler being a relatively large coin, each state could also issue its own smaller coins, in amounts left to their own discretion, making for a proliferation of fractional currencies (the most common being the groschen and the pfennig; twelve pfennig were equal to one groschen, and twenty-four groschen made up the taler). Between 1754 and 1892, Austria denominated its currency in florins (F), often called gulden, which were further divided into one hundred heller; after 1892, the Austrian currency became the krone, worth .5 of a florin. The schilling (S) was introduced in 1924 and divided into one hundred groschen; this gave way to the reichsmark after Germany's annexation of Austria in 1938 but was reinstated in 1945. Some of the southern states, such as Bavaria, traded in gulden (G). As the distinguished economic historians Hans-Jürgen Gerhard and Karl Heinrich Kaufhold noted on this subject: "Through the hands of wholesalers and retailers, of workers, shopkeepers, and women operating market stalls passed a great quantity of completely different and frequently changing coins from every possible princely domain, the value of each changing from year to year."[2] This—plus enormous fluctuations in the price of the grains that fed, or failed to feed, most of the population—makes it very hard to estimate the "real" value of wages or prices for the eighteenth century in particular, and what we have available for the porcelain industry are mostly nominal wages or prices, which might have meant quite different things to the persons who earned or paid these at the time. In chapters 1–3 I have tried to introduce some figures simply to get a sense of the costs and values attached to particular occupations or items, but none of these is fully meaningful without closer analysis of local currency values and food prices, and contrasts to later wage figures or commodity prices must be contextualized to ascertain their significance. I have converted figures given in florins or gulden to taler to make comparison easier.

As we get to the modern period, this problem is less severe as the silver content of the reichstaler (T) stabilized, and this unit of currency began to be used in many northern German states. The southern states, including Austria, however, continued to use florins (the name adapted from the Italians, who used it for their gold coins) or gulden, usually worth about two-thirds of a taler, but also varying from one another and in value over time. In currency conventions established by the Zollverein (Customs Union) in the 1830s, the currencies were linked to a fixed amount of silver, such that 1 T was equivalent to .57 gulden. In 1857, the Austrian florin (F) was pegged at 1 T = .66 F.[3] After Bismarck's unification, the new German Empire created a single currency, the mark, to be used across all its states and valued at .33 of a taler; it was subdivided into one hundred pfenning. The mark survived the German Empire but not the great financial crisis of the early Weimar Republic; in order to end the hyperinflation of 1922–23, the Weimar regime issued a new currency, the rentenmark (RtM), backed by a massive mortgage on land. By the summer of 1924, sufficient stability had been achieved that a new, gold-backed reichsmark (RM) could be introduced (1 RtM = 1 RM). In 1948, the reichsmark was replaced in West Germany with the deutschmark (DM) and in the East with the ostmark (OM), which was not officially exchangeable into western currencies. When the bureaucrats of the German Democratic Republic estimated the value of the goods they exchanged with the West, they did so in a fictional currency called the valutamark (VM), with the same value as the DM. In 2002, after a transitional period, the reunited Germany gave up its deutschmark in favor of the euro at the rate of about 1.96 DM = 1 E; the Austrian schilling was exchanged for euros at the rate of 13.76 S = 1 E. For the reader's assistance, here is a brief list of currency abbreviations and exchanges:

DM   deutschmark; introduced as West Germany's currency in 1948
E   euro; introduced at about 1.98 DM in 2002
F   florin; used in Austria and some southern states; value set in 1857 at .66 = 1 T
G   gulden (guilder) used in some southern German states, value set in 1838 at .57 of a taler
M   mark; replaces the taler in 1873 at the rate of 3 M = 1 T
OM   ostmark; East German currency after 1948
RM   reichsmark; introduced in 1924 to replace the rentenmark (RtM); indexed to the market price of gold
S   schilling; Austrian currency used between 1924 and 1938 and again 1945–2002
T   reichstaler; set in 1566 at 25.98 grams of silver
VM   valutamark; fictional currency name used in the GDR to estimate value of sales or purchases from the West; equivalent to 1 DM

The following abbreviations have been used for manufacturers:

KGGM Königliche Gesundheitsgeschirr Manufaktur
KPM   Königliche Porzellanmanufaktur
WPM   Wiener Porzellan Manufaktur

A list of archival abbreviations appears at the end of the bibliography.

Acknowledgments

*W*hen one sets out to write a book in a new field, one incurs even more debts to friends, colleagues, and new contacts than when one excavates in familiar terrain. At all stages of this project I have needed, and found, a great deal of help. My first conversations about the project were with my emeritus colleague and beloved friend, the quantitative historian Paul Paskoff, who encouraged me to pursue a business history, and over the years has given me endless references and good advice. Perhaps second to hear about the "porcelain book" (other than, of course, my long-suffering husband and children) was James Brophy, whose unflagging friendship and excellent critiques of each and every chapter have guided me throughout; I am very much looking forward to seeing Jim's deeply researched and critically important history of the German publishing industry—with which this study has some fascinating parallels—in print as well. Margaret Lavinia Anderson took a great deal of time out of her busy retirement to go over several chapters with a fine-toothed comb and improved them immensely with her incisive questioning and surgical strikes on my embarrassingly vague phrasings. Mary Lindemann endured a barrage of questions about the complexities of the early modern German economy, which she understands better than anyone else I know; Frank Trentmann, author of the best recent global history of consumption, offered exceptionally helpful comments, especially on some of the middle chapters and the introduction. Having presented versions of this project in many conference papers or visiting lectures, I fear I have forgotten many of those I ought to thank for their helpful comments: among those I can remember as most inspiring were questions asked by Jonathan Sperber, Simone Lässig, Glenn Penny, Till van Rahden, Jesse Sponholz, Rebekka Habermas, Dror Wahrman, and Alice Goff. Finally, when the manuscript was (supposedly!) done, the anonymous readers for Princeton University Press also prompted me to really clarify why this story was worth telling, and to inject it with as much firsthand testimony as possible. If I have failed on either of those points, it is certainly not for lack of trying to respond to their critically important suggestions.

A large number of other interlocutors have helped me find materials or understand particular aspects of a subject that just kept getting more complicated the longer I pursued it. I am so fortunate to count as a friend Katherine Aaslestad, whose expertise on matters Napoleonic has been invaluable; together we have cultivated a shared interest in commemorative military memorabilia. I also learned a great deal about monarchical commemorations from my student (or I like to claim her, anyway) Eva Giloi, whose book about the Wilhelmine royal image broke new ground in this field. Another recent PhD (this time from Emory University), Claudia Kreklau, kindly shared her fascinating work on middle-class German foodways, which helped enhance my understanding of this field, also being ploughed by my longtime friend Corinna Treitel. Corinna's training in the history of science makes her work all the stronger; and indeed, other friends and colleagues in that field have proved greatly helpful in pursuing some aspects of this project. Thanks to a fellowship in fall 2018 at the Max Planck Institut für Wissenschaftsgeschichte, I was able to discuss my writing at a critical stage with Lorraine Daston, Joan Richards, Christine von Oertzen, Sebastian Felten, and Ursula Klein, among others. Last minute help came from Gabriella Szalay, now curating porcelain at the Busch-Reisinger Museum in Cambridge, Massachusetts.

I was lucky to follow up this semester in the company of historians of science with several months among the (mostly) art historians at Villa I Tatti, the Harvard Center for Italian Renaissance Studies. There, director Alina Payne and I had enlightening conversations about the history of German (and European) art theory and design, and I met many wonderful interlocutors, among them Thomas Gruber and Alexandra Enzensberger. An evening presentation of a spin-off essay—on porcelain and the classical tradition—offered a cornucopia of fascinating questions and comments to follow up on. Last but far from least, my colleagues and students at Louisiana State University have been extremely helpful and supportive throughout, and I would most of all like to thank my colleague in art history Darius Spieth, who, having grown up visiting Rosenthal Studio-Häuser and German flea markets, knows much more about recent porcelain making than I could learn from books, and John Pojman, a chemist specializing in polymers, who shares my fascination with ceramic recipes and happily answered my technical questions. My last-minute undergraduate research assistant Timothy Kemp did a terrific job turning up some secondary literature and proofing all my chapters for typos. Finally, it is with pride in his accomplishments that I thank Christopher Mapes—whose honors thesis I supervised many years ago—for providing me with archival scans and for making the maps for this book; now that he has earned his PhD (at Vanderbilt), I look forward to watching his own scholarly career flourish.

A crucial aspect of the research undertaken for this book was the visiting of dozens of museums, where I learned invaluable lessons by looking and reading. Among those that made a special impact I would like to acknowledge the Porzellanikon museums in Hohenberg an der Eger and Selb (Bavaria), Meissen Porzellan Manufaktur und Museum, Musée de Sèvres, Kunstgewerbe Museum (Berlin), Charlottenburg Palace (Berlin), Porzellansammlung (Dresden), Silberkabinett (Vienna), Augarten Museum (Vienna), Museum of Nymphenburg Porcelain (Nymphenburg Palace), Villeroy & Boch Museum (Mettlach), Museum für Kunst und Industrie (Vienna), Musée des Arts Décoratifs (Paris), Museo di Capodimonte (Naples), Museo Nazionale della Ceramica (Naples), Victoria and Albert Museum (London), Treasury of the Grand Dukes, Pitti Palace (Florence), Royal Delft Factory and Museum (Netherlands), Friedenstein Palace and Herzogliches Museum (Gotha), Thüringer Landesmuseum Heidecksburg (Rudolstadt), Museum

Leuchtenburg/Porzellanwelten (Kahla), Museum Künstlerkolonie (Darmstadt), Reiss-Engelhorn-Museen and Mannheimer Schloss (Mannheim), Musée Carnavalet (Paris), and Thüringer Museum (Eisenach).

This project was also made possible by archivists, administrators, and of course Princeton University Press personnel who have helped me make this book a reality. The receipt of a Boyd (University) professorship from Louisiana State University in 2014 has made possible a great deal of travel as well as purchases of books and images that would have become overwhelming without these research funds. I am enormously grateful to my chair (Aaron Sheehan-Dean), my dean (Troy Blanchard), and my provost (Stacia Haynie), as well as my former chair and dean (Gaines Foster), and the all-wise associate dean and grants coordinator (Ann Whitmer) for making possible a leave in 2018–19 without which this book would have been several years more in the making. I am also very much in debt to the librarians and archivists who have helped me find materials over the years, most especially the staff at the Max Planck Institut für Wissenschaftsgeschichte (Berlin) and the Villa I Tatti (Florence). The archives themselves are listed in the bibliography, but I should like to personally thank Eva Wollschläger at the KPM archive, Agnes Müller at the Villeroy & Boch Unternehmensarchiv, Peter Braun at Meissen, and most especially Rüdiger Barth and Petra Werner at the Porzellanikon Archiv in Selb for their assistance. I am very grateful to Michaela Howse and Ortwin Knorr for permission to publish family photos, and for further information about their family histories. At Princeton, I will be eternally grateful to Brigitta van Rheinberg for her immediate embrace of this project at an early stage of its inception, and to Eric Crahan, Thalia Leaf, Mark Bellis, and Kathleen Kageff for their careful tending of the whole process.

It is hard to let go of a manuscript, but my friends and above all my beloved family tell me it is time. My husband, Victor, and my sons, Charles and Henry, have had their fill of porcelain talk and are ready for me to importune them with my next subject. I am eager, too, to have a bound copy to give to my mother, Betsy; my mother-in-law, Jean; my sister and brother-in-law, Jeannie and Sotiri; my aunt and cousin-in-law, JoAnn and Nia; and our great friends Paul and Beth, all of whom have been part of *my* porcelain experience for decades. Porcelain was once about aristocratic display but then became a powerful symbol of family, and home. It is to those who gather around my holiday table that I dedicate this book.

Porcelain

There is something magical, collectors and holiday hosts agree, about porcelain. It is the finest, whitest, and most difficult to make form of ceramics, and it enraptured Chinese emperors long before the first pieces made their way to Europe in the fourteenth century. For four centuries, European royals and rich merchants cherished their imported porcelains, and entrepreneurial craftsmen mixed endless concoctions in the hopes of cutting in on this lucrative luxury trade. When a desperate Saxon alchemist finally hit upon an approximation of the Chinese recipe, his vessels were dubbed "white gold": and in the small Saxon town of Meissen, in the heart of Europe, an industry, and obsession, was born.

The book tells the story of Europe's reinvention of porcelain and concludes with the state of the fine ceramics industry today. It is a rich and complicated adventure, in which we not only visit lavishly decorated palaces but also linger in blisteringly hot craft workshops and spartan working-class homes. Though actual porcelain objects in all their splendor and strangeness play a central role, the focus is really on the people who made, marketed, and purchased them, whether they were princes, or peddlers, or middle-class housewives. While originally its uses were purely ornamental and decorative, over time, porcelain became a kind of "plastic," one that could be molded to please any palate or pocketbook. A number of large-scale manufactories—some state sponsored, many not—offered busts of Frederick the Great and Napoleon, as well as Zeus and figures from the commedia dell'arte, classicizing toast racks, and "orientalizing" inkwells. Centuries later, under the Nazi regime, one whole factory devoted itself to SS paraphernalia. Porcelains were made to imitate Parian marble, lapis lazuli, or, as in the case of the many dolls' heads made from the mixture, human flesh. And then there were the less visible uses of porcelain: in telegraph insulator tubes, in doorknobs and floor tiles, in false teeth. Across three centuries, from the eighteenth to the twentieth, in its central European birthplace *porcelain* has been a word to conjure with, and an everyday part of life. This, then, is the story of the rich and complicated lives people and porcelain have shared—down to the present moment, when the European chapter of this tale, at least, seems to be drawing to a close.

When I began this inquiry, I conceived of it as a part of my work on the modern afterlives of classical antiquity and the biblical Orient. My eye was caught by the spectacular confections that fill German (and non-German) decorative arts museums and so many exquisitely illustrated and researched exhibition catalogs. I owe most of what I know about porcelain as an art form to these sources.[1] In those pages I discovered a world of vast diversity—of styles, of objects, of uses—and began to be intrigued by the business history side of the story: who were these manufacturers, and who bought all this stuff, from squirrel-shaped teapots to semipornographic porcelain pipes? How were Rembrandt's masterpieces reproduced on tiny teacups, and just how did Meissen—originally founded by King Augustus II—survive and even flourish during the era of East German communist rule? Intrigued, I pursued my interests by delving into manufactory histories and then archival documents, and as I turned this material on my historian's wheel, I increasingly found that I had a wonderful means to tell a story about people, about states and markets, and about the changing nature of work and consumption over the last three centuries. This was, perhaps most importantly, the story of the struggle between a long-surviving mercantile economy and the arrival of new forms of capitalist production and management, and the story of the transformation of an aristocratic obsession into a bourgeois necessity—and finally into an unloved white elephant. Much more than describing the imagery and artistry of porcelains, I discovered I wanted to tell these wider stories, stories that offer us a fresh way not only to grasp porcelain's unique and fascinating trajectory, but also to narrate German and central European history as a whole.

In keeping with this attempt to fuse porcelain's story together with the history of central Europeans since about 1700, this book does not pretend to be a commodity history of the sort that has taught us so much about the trades in coffee, tea, salt, sugar, and other transnational substances. Here, porcelain is featured, but firmly rooted in the wider context of economic and cultural developments, and treated as part of a network of other commodities, both those that competed with it (such as fine-grade earthenware, or faience, and much cheaper stoneware) and those that enabled its spread (such as coffee, tea, and etageres for its display).[2] By no means is this a truly transnational study, like the wonderful, related works of Robert Finlay, whose *The Pilgrim Art* tells the story of the earlier East Asian and Near Eastern traffic in porcelains, and of Erika Rappaport, whose work describes the British Empire's commandeering of the tea trade.[3] I do, however, emphasize the reality that central European developments were very much shaped by consumption and production patterns elsewhere, including those in China, England, France, the Ottoman Empire, and the United States. Similarly, though informed and inspired by the now-extensive literature on material culture and consumption, most of which focuses on Britain, France, and the United States, I am not deeply concerned with porcelain as a "thing" or with theories of materiality.[4] My method is rather guided by Daniel Roche's insistence that historians ought to pay more attention to "the real world of objects without high aesthetic value," and by Leora Auslander's advice that the best writing about material culture is that which "seeks to grasp how the large-scale transformations of the world are crystallized, reproduced, and changed in the small gestures of the everyday."[5]

This focus on porcelain and material goods generally is not an approach familiar to most historians of Germany, who, for understandable reasons, typically feel obliged to treat more serious, often political, subjects. While historians of Britain, America, France, and the Netherlands have shown us the great value and delight offered by histories of consumer goods, central Europeanists have been slow to devote attention to objects of minor aesthetic value, or even to the history of consumption itself.[6] Perhaps the presumption that a consumer culture did not exist even in West Germany until the 1950s—and arrived in other parts of central Europe only after 1989—has stifled interest in consumption in earlier periods.[7] In Marx's homeland, too, the *critique* of consumption has seemed more important to study than consumption itself.[8] But times are changing. The study of food cultures—again mostly emerging from the United States, Britain, and France—is now attracting German historians as well, and innovative cultural histories have demonstrated the ways in which central Europe's monarchies and regional states won nineteenth-century hearts and minds, partly through their inhabitants' consumption of commemorative goods.[9]

Yet we still have a need for some close studies of courtly and urban consumption in the eighteenth century and especially for work that helps us understand the ups and downs of the transition from courtly to middle-class consumption across the "saddle period" of 1780 to 1830 or 1840.[10] Even if consumption and material objects—as opposed to status, education, political party, or ethnicity—did not define central Europeans' social roles until quite recently (and one may still debate how much of a part it plays today), it can nevertheless be held that consumer goods such as silk hats or porcelain have played an important role in shaping Germanness (as well as Czech and Hungarian identities, of which this author can say little but that they too need investigation). It would be wonderful to have studies of the Wilhelmine household as evocative and detailed as some of the recent works on the Victorian home.[11] I hope that this book may help to promote interest in this sort of inquiry for this region.

The biggest difference between this study and previous books on the subject, however, is that while it is partly a cultural history, *Porcelain* is also an economic and business history, one that illuminates German-speaking central Europe's transition from a plurality of mercantile states to its imbrication in a globalizing capitalist economy. The book's focus, then, is on porcelain as an *industry*, one in which German princes as well as private entrepreneurs from the outset have played a major role. Economic history, so profoundly important for understanding both cultural and political developments, has been neglected by German and Austrian historians for some time and is in need of revival and reemphasis. By using some of its tools and rephrasing its questions, we can comprehend developments that still resonate strongly in our time. In the porcelain industry, for example, competition on price had already begun by the 1760s, and makers regularly committed what we would today call "industrial espionage." Here we can see the special challenges faced by would-be private entrepreneurs in central European conditions, and how they responded—not always successfully— to the more advanced industrial societies to the west. *Porcelain* relates in concrete detail the particular history of central European industrialization and gives us a glimpse of the evolution of the highly skilled workforce and the elegantly designed consumer goods for which Germany, in particular, remains famous today. Economic histories do not need to be dry, and this one, it is hoped, makes it all the easier to understand the origins of the European consumer marketplace by coating the tale in the translucent splendor of porcelain.

Of course, there are many excellent economic histories of central Europe, and one might rightly ask: why does porcelain matter, as compared to iron, coal, steel, cotton, or beer, all commodities of greater consequence for the economy as a whole? Social historians might wonder why one should focus on employees in this semiluxury industry—who never numbered more than one hundred thousand—rather than on the millions of workers in other branches of manufacturing? Porcelain may have played a smallish part in gross national output, but it was a highly visible, mercantile product, for centuries mass-produced with large inputs of skilled artisanal labor but without the stereotypical steam-powered machines, making porcelain's history a window on the trades and production practices of the Old Regime. Porcelain played a central role in putting the previously "backward" German states on Europe's luxury-making map and, as one of the commodities first exported en masse, it helped to integrate the states that produced it into the wider global marketplace. Founded in 1710, Augustus II's Meissen manufactory earned itself one of the first internationally admired "brand" names, and the strategies this and other mercantile makers developed to protect the

brand's reputation while also attempting to turn a profit foreshadow in remarkable ways the operations of luxury makers today. As a non-necessary
consumer good, one associated primarily with women and family life, porcelain also takes us into the world of bourgeois self-presentation and individual (and especially female) choice, something impossible for historians of
the coal or steel industries. And finally, the history of porcelain illuminates
the many strategies state officials and business owners have attempted to
tame the unpredictable capitalist marketplace, made more volatile by Germany's history of internal fragmentation, warfare, and dictatorship. Most
economic histories do not emphasize the contingencies that make or break
an entrepreneur, or an entire industry; this one—I hope readers will pardon
the pun!—is all about that fragility.

Finally, perhaps the most unconventional aspect of this book is that its
center of gravity lies not in the period usually identified as the heyday of central European porcelain production, the eighteenth century, but in the nineteenth and twentieth centuries.[12] Many connoisseurs regard this period as
one that—aside from a few Jugendstil masterpieces—produced only "flea
market trash."[13] But it is in the post-1800 era that the history of the porcelain industry offers us real insight into the very long afterlives of mercantile
economies and of forms of craft production, even as capitalist markets and
mass production begin to take hold. Of course, porcelain is much too frail a
foundation on which to build a comprehensive history of political and economic developments in Germany and Austria since about 1700. But time and
again fascinating moments in this history flash past, illuminating in new ways
familiar developments such as the rise of the nation-state and the ravages
of the Great Depression, the power of cartels and the increasing centrality
of advertising. I hope readers will be convinced that while there are other
stories to be told through porcelain, the history of this industry tells us a
great deal about the peculiarities of central European capitalism that have
shaped German and European culture and economic development down to
the present day.

At the end of this story, however, we find ourselves at a crossroads, at
which porcelain and central Europeans seem to be parting ways. In the last

thirty years, and especially since the economic downturn beginning in 2008, the European porcelain industry has entered a period of severe crisis. This has to do partly with global competition and the relentless pressure underselling exerts on small, artisanal businesses, and partly with the lapsing of state subsidies for the arts and crafts. But lifestyle changes are also afoot, and for younger Europeans and Americans—many of whom are growing up without porcelain in their lives—the magical ambience of "white gold" has almost entirely vanished.

My own biography illustrates just how recently this special commodity lost its international allure. Although I grew up in a middle-class Californian household, from the time I was small I knew that one used the "fine china" for holidays and that grandmother's porcelain figurines were to be admired only in their glass cabinet. When I married, I picked out a "china" pattern—in my case, a Viennese Secession pattern made by a Japanese firm—and now we use that set only for guests and holidays. We store our own motley collection of other porcelain pieces in my husband's grandmother's breakfront; this includes some coffee cups hand painted by my grandmother and my great aunt, but no figurines (I have always disliked those). All are terribly dusty and neglected; I suspect my children have never even noticed them. We eat our meals from mismatched earthenware dishes—some of them printed with the ubiquitous "blue willow" pattern, and others made by the Welsh Portmeiron factory. Had we come from more affluent families, or families with central European heritages, we might have chosen, or inherited, porcelain pieces made by Meissen, the oldest and most prestigious, German manufacturer, or Rosenthal, the masterful adapter of modern designs. Had we been married not in 1989 but in 2009, we might not have put any "china" at all on our wedding registry. Americans have traditionally cared less about the quality of their tableware than Europeans have, yet until very recently, porcelain was very much part of our cultural and economic history too. *Porcelain* thus ends with a poignant question: Has this story, which began with an alchemical miracle at Europe's heart, and eventually embraced by so many, come to an end? I would hope not; but porcelain's fate will be decided beyond these pages; perhaps, even, in the readers' dining rooms.

Chapter 1

Reinventing the Recipe

In 1976, in the waters around the lonely island of St. Helena, the Dutch underwater archaeologist Robert Sténuit made a remarkable find: the wreckage of the Dutch East Indiaman the *White Lion*. Portuguese warships had sunk the ship in 1613, as the two trading powers vied for control of shipping routes to the East Indies. The *White Lion*'s cargo gives us a snapshot of the commodities Europeans were willing to risk multiyear voyages, hard-won capital, and perilous seas to obtain: pepper and diamonds, but also barrel after barrel of another commodity: blue-and-white Ming porcelains.[1] Like pepper and diamonds, Chinese porcelain was a luxury good, before 1600 owned chiefly by Ottoman, Iberian, and Italian elites. But when, in 1602, the Dutch captured and auctioned off their first Portuguese boatload of porcelain, they discovered that northern Europeans, too, were willing to pay a premium for this delicate commodity, which, moreover, made an ideal, waterproof ballast. By the time Dutch East India Company merchants loaded up the *White Lion*, it had become quite conventional to fill holds with porcelains of many sizes and shapes, some of them quite humble (fig. 1.1). Northern Europe's love affair with porcelain had begun.

The *White Lion*'s porcelains never made it to Amsterdam. But this ill-fated commercial voyage and the ship's sunken cargo tip us off to two important realities about porcelain's history that will resound through this book. The first is that while made in China

1.1. *White Lion* teacup

This humble teacup made up part of the salable ballast discovered in the hold of the shipwrecked *White Lion*. Intended for the Dutch market, this mass-produced Chinese vessel never made it to Amsterdam.

since at least the Song Dynasty (960–1279 CE), porcelain soon became a commodity sought after by consumers of and traders in luxuries across the world. The second is that all porcelains are not created equal; there are exquisitely made grand vases and one-of-a-kind novelties, and there are modestly decorated, often almost invisible, utilitarian vessels—the ones whose sales often sustain the production of more "artistic" forms. As porcelain's history is usually told as a tale either of luxury pieces or of single or regional manufactories, it is useful for us to begin by invoking this international commercial context and the long history of stylistic diversity and widely divergent price points. The *White Lion* reminds us to think globally, even as we focus on the central European chapters of this story, and not to forget the role played by ordinary household consumers in the sustaining of the luxury trades. This case, too, will not be the last of porcelain's "shipwrecks," reminding us that commercial success is generally fleeting, whether we are describing a single manufactory, a particular commodity, a fashionable style, a nation's prosperity, or even the endurance of an entire industry. It is in the nature of commerce to be perpetually one *White Lion* away from ruin.

Properly, porcelain's history, like the *White Lion*'s voyage, begins in China, and the centers of dispersion into northern Europe were England and the Netherlands. Both of these nations subsequently developed thriving ceramics industries of their own, though neither they nor the more elegant Italian and French makers of "soft-paste" porcelain or "faience" (named after Faenza, Italy, one of the early centers of production) were able to replicate the Chinese recipe for the highest-quality, "hard-paste" porcelains.[2] That distinction goes to Saxony, where in 1708 a would-be alchemist first made a translucent, white vessel comparable to those of the East Asian makers. Saxony's state sponsorship of the industry generated a model imitated by princes across the Holy Roman Empire for whom porcelain making quickly became, as Duke Carl Eugen of Württemberg described in 1758, "a necessary aspect of splendor [Glanz] and prestige [Würde]."[3]

By the third quarter of the eighteenth century, a special relationship had developed between porcelain and central Europe, previously weakly integrated into the luxury markets to the west. That relationship would flourish and embrace an ever-widening consumer base, even as most state manufactories closed or were transferred into private hands, rendering central Europe, in the words of historian Friedrich Hofmann, "the classical land of porcelain making."[4]

The story of central Europe's passion for porcelain and the translation of that passion into an industry is the one told in this book. Porcelain making offered central European princes and states a means to demonstrate to the wealthier and more cultured Italian, French, Dutch, and English elites that they too could create elegant wares. For centuries it tantalized entrepreneurs in a generally low-consuming, war-torn region with hopes that a stable market for luxury goods might materialize. If dreams of prosperity through porcelain making were often dashed, the industry's endless attempts to produce the most refined of all ceramics and to please buyers of all sorts entwined the commodity in the lives and hearts of central Europeans. This book will follow our commodity over time, as it made its way into the homes of more and more consumers, and as symbolic meanings changed. In the eighteenth century, porcelain served as a princely proof of *Glanz*; in the nineteenth, it bound itself up with regional pride, with bourgeois respectability, and with hygiene; in the twentieth century, porcelain became, especially for women, part of an indestructible sense of "home," security, and continuity in the face of political upheaval and total war—even as it was also mobilized to make munitions and to embellish dictatorships. The central European entanglement with porcelain is not one we can grasp without delving deeply into the past and ranging across almost all aspects of life.

The foregoing may help to explain why this book, written by a historian, emphasizes porcelain's production, consumption, and cultural significance rather than its artistry. Porcelain's artistic masterpieces have been well studied by connoisseurs and museum curators; but to this author, the non-artistic aspects of porcelain's history—its relationship to advances in mineralogy, chemistry, and marketing, for example, and its complicated relationship to state power—are as interesting as the history of its marketing and its use by consumers. These avenues of inquiry allow us to investigate, by a less usual route, the histories of industrialization, of commerce and consumption, of style and fashion, and of science. For porcelain came to central Europe as a scientific breakthrough that followed a cascade of other experiments and improvements, and its manufacture was propelled forward by political and economic concerns as well as aesthetic longings. It is a commodity that richly deserves a "total" history, or as "total" a history as this author can hope to conjure. Embarking at St. Helena with the *White Lion*, we have an eventful voyage—including many shipwrecks—ahead.

European Ceramics before Porcelain

Long before the *White Lion* took on its cargo in Java, elegant porcelains had been produced for centuries in various parts of East Asia. Production probably began first in Jingdezhen, China, where a translucent, green ceramic form was sought to mimic the highly prized "imperial gem," jade. Although we cannot establish precisely the date of the first "discovery" of Chinese porcelain, the production of exquisite vessels for the emperor's table was already a major industry in the eleventh century. The making of pottery is of course a much older activity, practiced the world over by prehistoric humans. But Chinese porcelain production at Jingdezhen was different in several ways: first of all, it was an industry so important to the ruling elites that it was owned and overseen by the imperial state. Secondly, it was already an industry that featured an extensive division of labor, including skilled and unskilled clay mixers, modelers, painters, and kiln tenders. It was said that seventy-two hands went into making a single pot.[5] Thirdly, in a world in which virtually all production and consumption was local, here was an industry geared to exporting its products, in this case, chiefly to the court in Kaifeng and then (under the Yuan Dynasty) Beijing, which monopolized the purchase of the finest, all-white, line. In China, as in Europe for many centuries, porcelain was not for commoners.

Admirers in the Islamic world soon began to import Chinese porcelain, or to make their own imitations. Moving in the opposite direction were techniques and materials: the blue-and-white patterns that became so strongly associated with Chinese porcelain were enabled by the importing of Persian cobalt to China and Chinese adapting of Persian methods of painting in the fourteenth century. Blue-and-white porcelain was also cheaper to produce and easier to fire than the previously favored celadon imitations of jade, adding a pecuniary incentive for makers to switch styles.[6] The addition of tin oxide to lead glazes—also pioneered in Asia Minor—made possible the opaque, white glazing of lesser-grade ceramics, such as "Iznik" wares, made in Anatolia from the fifteenth century, and "majolica" (named after the island of Majorca, where Italian traders acquired tin-glazed earthenwares from

Andalusian makers). Usually decorated in strong blues, yellows, and reds, majolica, by the later fifteenth century, had already diffused northward with other Renaissance arts. As would be the case for European ceramics, experimentation never stopped, and recipes always varied, depending on local clays and other ingredients.

Before East Asian porcelain began to circulate widely in Europe, Europeans could make or purchase many other forms of ceramics. The most humble were unglazed earthenware vessels; stoneware, a more durable form of ceramics that can withstand firing at 1,000–1,200°C, and does not require a glaze, was a bit more costly. At the higher end, craftsmen labored to please noble patrons with ceramics that were also works of art, such as the majolica platters that depicted classical or biblical tales, or reproduced famous works of art, and were intended for show, not for daily use. Innovation— prompted by competition between craftsmen and by the scientific trends of the day—did not cease; in France, the Huguenot polymath Bernard Palissy made heroic, but unsuccessful, attempts to fire true porcelain, succeeding, however, in making majolica featuring a new palette of colors and unique, naturalistic designs. Meanwhile, in Faenza in northeastern Italy, another version of tin-glazed earthenware, subsequently known as "faience," went into large-scale production. Faience was difficult and expensive to make, as kilns had to be stoked with precious wood to reach the firing temperature of 1,000°C. But there were great advantages. Faience's smooth surface allows for elaborate overpainting with paints that do not bleed or smear, as was often true of majolica, or melt, as in the case of most early porcelain glazes. It too would quickly diffuse to the north and west, spurring a demand for ceramics that remained, however, pieces for display rather than tableware for regular use.

If majolica and faience were admired, East Asian porcelain retained the highest rank in luxury ceramics.[7] It was more delicate, translucent, and glassy—but required whiter clays than southern Europe possessed and even higher firing temperatures (1,400°C) to produce. Southern princes found it irresistible, and as in painting, architecture, sculpture, music, and food, so too in ceramics, northern princes adopted southerners' tastes. The Medici were the first great collectors, followed by Philip II of Spain, whose household by the time of his death in 1598 boasted some three thousand porcelains. Thanks to Sir Francis Drake's raiding of Spanish ships, Elizabeth I acquired more than fifteen hundred blue-and-white pieces for her "Jewel House" in the Tower of London; the Holy Roman Emperor Ferdinand II (r. 1619–37) owned only half as much.[8] Commerce, too, first focused on Mediterranean markets, but soon shifted northward where the Dutch found new buyers. In 1608, the Dutch East India company (VOC) imported one hundred thousand pieces of Chinese porcelain, selling some of it domestically, and exporting the rest to continental markets; by the 1630s, the Dutch imports were exceeding two hundred thousand pieces per year.[9] Despite the disruptions of the Thirty Years' War and the many other religious and civil conflicts of the period, the volume of the Dutch porcelain trade burgeoned during the next decades, reaching by one estimate more than three million pieces imported between 1604 and 1656 for the VOC alone.[10]

This surge in European purchases benefited Chinese producers, who had suffered a downturn in domestic orders thanks to the Ming Empire's attempts at economizing. The Chinese ceramicists, who had been catering to the tastes of Ottoman and South Asian buyers for centuries, now varied their production methods to suit the Dutch and English East India Companies. Europeans could order particular designs or shapes from Chinese makers, though misunderstandings often took place. But just as European demand rose in the wake of the Thirty Years' War (1618–48), political conflicts resulting in the fall of the Ming and the rise of the Qing Empire interrupted supply. More severe disruptions occurred in the period 1662–84, when the Qing closed ports and evacuated coastal areas. This shortage in supply led to rising prices for porcelains on the European market and the search for substitutes, which were found in fine ceramics made in Japan, Vietnam, and Persia, and in Dutch delftware.

Although the Chinese "china" trade made a powerful recovery in the later 1680s, the hiatus provided the context in which a flurry of new efforts to duplicate Asian recipes commenced.[11] Predictably, the Italians produced the first, best, imitations, generating large quantities of faience by the late sixteenth century. Under the patronage of the Medici, Florentine ceramicists also successfully fired a type of ceramics we now call "soft-paste porcelain," because it is fired at a lower temperature than "true" or hard-paste porcelain, and has a stronger tendency to slump in the kiln.[12] "Soft-paste" shapes and colors (mostly blue and white) usually imitated the prized Mamluk and Chinese forms already owned by the Medici. It would be this form of porcelain that spread to France by the later seventeenth century, and inspired many of the Germans' first efforts at porcelain making.

If the Italians succeeded in making the first European proto-porcelains, just as predictably, it was the Dutch who made porcelain imitations a commercial success. Already in 1614 Claes Jansen Sytmans in The Hague received a patent for making porcelain "like that that comes from foreign lands."[13] Working undoubtedly from Chinese models, Sytmans pioneered the firing of a form of blue-and-white tin-glazed earthenware that quickly spread to several locations in the United Provinces. After a gunpowder explosion destroyed much of Delft in 1654, many new potteries set up here, making it the center of Dutch production, and bequeathing the name "delftware" to the blue-and-white earthenware style. Delftware had the advantage over Medici porcelain or Italian faience of being more easily accessible to northern Europeans, and much less expensive; the Dutch rapidly developed the art of something like mass production, at least for their widely admired tiles.[14] By 1670, delftware had become sufficiently desirable to support the operation of thirty large, and many more small, workshops in the United Provinces.[15]

Naturally, delftware too was imitated. Its success seems to have spurred the development of a much wider network of faience factories in the later seventeenth century, many of them started by Dutch craftsmen. Wherever consumers had a bit more disposable income, in England and the Netherlands in particular, ceramics making boomed. In Staffordshire, England, the number of potteries tripled between the 1680s and 1750s, and middling Dutch households in the later seventeenth century already contained relatively large supplies of delftware and "Kraak."[16] The continent followed suit, though more slowly. Some of the most famous producers were the French firms operating in Rouen, Moustiers, Nevers, Marseilles, and

St. Cloud near Paris, but there were also faience and fine earthenware makers in Spain, Portugal, Sweden, Russia, and the German states. These potters already offered a wide selection of wares, from lavishly decorated grand platters to more modest tableware, and competed with the import market for commissions and sales.

Central Europe's cultural, as well as commercial, debts to the Dutch often go unstated, but in this case it seems clear that the taste for blue-and-white ceramics was spread to German courts chiefly by Dutch princesses such as Louise Henriette of Nassau, wife of Elector Frederick William of Brandenburg-Prussia, who began serious porcelain collecting already in 1652, and a decade later designed central Europe's first "porcelain chamber" in her Oranienburg Palace near Berlin.[17] Louise's sister, Henriette Catherine, married a lesser German prince but also insisted on a Dutch-style palace at Oranienbaum near Dessau, where she installed a Dutch-tiled summer dining room. (This is by no means the last time that we will find women acting as tastemakers.) It would be Dutch importers, who began selling East Asian porcelains at the biannual Leipzig fair sometime after 1650, who stocked Augustus the Strong's porcelain cabinet.[18] And it would be two Calvinist refugees from the Spanish Netherlands skilled in the making of delftware who founded the first German faience factory in the town of Hanau in 1661.

The story of this first founding is instructive, as it demonstrates the interwovenness of "industry" with geography, politics, and religious matters in the Holy Roman Empire, and sets out a pattern that would be followed by many entrepreneurs and their princely patrons when porcelain making came to the Germanys. Hanau, situated on the Main River near the commercial center of Frankfurt, was at the time legally two cities, one of which had been settled by Calvinist craftsmen, including goldsmiths; our faienciers chose to set up shop among their coreligionists as well as other high-end tradesmen. As was the common practice of the time, they first had to request an official "privilege" from their sovereign—in this case the Count of Hanau-Münzenberg—to ply their trade; we must remember that in early modern Europe, there was no freedom of labor, or of speech, or of movement, as such. Most legal entitlements came in the form of such "privileges," given to particular individuals or groups to perform particular duties in particular places according to particular specifications. In this case, the count was agreeable, undoubtedly hoping that the new business would produce taxable exports and artisanal prestige for his realm. Our craftsmen received a document giving them a twenty-five-year monopoly on faience making in the microstate and tariff-free imports of raw materials. By 1675, their workshop employed thirty, an exceptionally large number of craftsmen for the day.[19] In 1678, the Elector of Brandenburg bestowed a privilege on another Dutchman, Fransen van der Lee, to establish Berlin's first faiencerie.[20] By 1721, there were factories in Ansbach, Nurnberg, Bayreuth, and Strassbourg.[21]

Faience sold wonderfully, and throughout the period covered by this book its producers competed with the porcelain makers for customers and always took the larger market share. In this parallel industry, too, many techniques that would be transferred to porcelain making were pioneered. But faience was not porcelain: it was clunkier; it was not translucent; its bodies were not perfectly white. And thus, even the success of the faienceries did not slow Europeans' purchases from Asia, or their search for the secret to making "true" porcelain.

Who "Needs" Porcelain?

It is commonly, and rightly, said that the demand for porcelain in the eighteenth century was closely related to Europe's rising consumption of exotic hot beverages such as tea, coffee, and chocolate. But it does not follow that utility was the mother of invention, and in fact, the reinvention of porcelain had little to do with eating and drinking at all. In 1708, when porcelain was first fired in Dresden, only a handful of central Europeans had tasted coffee, and only the Dutch and the Ottomans drank theirs in porcelain cups; others used silver, as befit a luxury beverage.[22] Ordinary people in the seventeenth century, and in some rural areas as late as the 1880s, ate their meals from one common pot (often iron or copper), dunking their fingers or hunks of bread into the soup, or using "trenchers" hewn out of wood instead of bowls or plates.[23] Jugs and some cooking vessels might have been made of earthenware. Taverns and inns generally chose pewter—which did not break—for individual plates and serving dishes or used wood or tin to serve the cheapest meals. Middling persons who could afford to abandon wood also stocked their kitchens with a combination of pewter, copper, tin, and earthenware, and in early modern depictions we typically find a combination of earthenware jugs, copper molds, and pewter platters arrayed on walls and shelves (see ahead to fig. 2.1). Stout stoneware tankards or jugs might be used by those able to invest in longer-lasting drinking vessels; faience began to creep in for elite diners from the seventeenth century. But even the nobility did not at first consider porcelain desirable for the serving of meals. Silver remained de rigueur for most feasts, whose purpose, after all, was chiefly to impress the guests with the hosts' wealth and generosity; at most, porcelain might be used for fruit or desserts, or for coffee and tea after an elite meal. Eighteenth-century Europeans, then, did not "need" porcelain, at least not for dining. We must look elsewhere to explain the factors that led to its invention and rise in popularity, and then trace its adoption for domestic uses.[24]

What the nobility—virtually the only central Europeans capable of purchasing porcelain in the later seventeenth century—wanted porcelain for was for display, and as a sort of architectural feature, complementing their tapestries, parquet floors, and elaborate mirrors. There was precedent for this: majolica platters, for example, were for display on buffet racks or walls, not for serving food, and at banquets, the prince's very best silver and gold pieces were regularly displayed on shelves to show off his wealth to diners. Similarly, what early noble collectors did with the porcelain vases, pots, or platters was to put them in their cabinets of curiosity, or place them on specially made shelves in specially designed porcelain rooms. That Louise Henriette of Brandenburg-Prussia, Austria's Maria Theresa, the Dukes of Saxe-Gotha-Altenburg, and the Margrave of Brandenburg-Ansbach—to cite just a few tastemakers—built such rooms indicates that for them, porcelain was an object of admiration and curiosity; its purpose was less to keep tea warm than to complement a world of splendor that included crystal chandeliers, gilded molding, and intricately carved ivories.

Porcelain's appeal and functions, then, differed entirely from those of earthenware, and we should not expect potters per se—with the possible exception of a few faience manufacturers—to have been the ones in hottest pursuit of the "secret recipe." For the most part, making pottery was a *local* industry, for transporting heavy, breakable, and inexpensive vessels by wagons over Europe's rutted roads or treacherous (and tariff-ridden) rivers made little sense. In towns and cities guilds determined production, but "Töpfer" or "Hafner" were never among the most highly respected of guildsmen, for making an earthenware pot is not a terribly difficult exercise and the materials neither scarce nor costly. A determined layperson with a stout stick could extract clay from the ground—well-traveled roadways were favored spots to dig, as they revealed the patches of clay clearly; hence our term "pot hole."[25] Along with earthenware jugs and bowls, skilled potters did make more sophisticated decorative items such as beer steins and pharmaceutical jars, and a few makers, such as the stoneware masters of the Westerwald region, were known for their high-quality products throughout Europe. But these ceramics makers operated in markets catering to the everyday needs of peasants, innkeepers, brewers, middling townspersons; they had little hope, or ambition, to rival Chinese porcelain makers, with whom, at least until the later eighteenth century, they were not in competition.

Rather than look to the suppliers, then, we need to look to the patrons, and the potential customers for the luxury wares to be produced if the recipe could finally be found: and this, in central Europe in particular, meant the Holy Roman Empire's many princes, and their courts.

Court Culture at the Dawn of the Porcelain Age

As James Sheehan has beautifully described it, the social experience of living in the early modern Holy Roman Empire was one of extreme social fragmentation; language, customs, styles of dress, diets, and, after the 1520s, religious beliefs varied so much between regions that as late as 1765, in traveling the approximately 250 miles from his native Frankfurt to the city of Leipzig, Goethe's clothes, manners, and speech made him seem to locals to have "dropped down out of another world."[26] The vast majority of the Empire's inhabitants, moreover, made their living from agriculture and, at least until the dawn of the nineteenth century, survived, if they did, in producing for and buying from highly localized markets. No one would have dreamed that these central Europeans would have the means, taste, or opportunity to purchase porcelain.

On the other hand, thanks to its political fragmentation, the Holy Roman Empire was also home to many wealthy (and many more not so wealthy) princes. Rich Renaissance-era German rulers, high-ranking noblemen, and bankers—Emperor Rudolf II, for example, or the Fuggers—could and did commission intricate masterpieces made by local craftsmen as well as purchase imported luxury goods from Dutch and Armenian traders, and from agents located in Rome, Amsterdam, and Paris. The sixteenth-century wars of religion, however, and even more importantly, the devastating Thirty Years' War decimated sources of income and budgets for many central European nobles. While France, England, and the Netherlands were able to recover quickly from these midcentury bloodlettings, it took central Europe, where some areas had lost nearly half their prewar population, considerably longer to rebound. In the era when Charles II and above all Louis XIV began investing huge sums in luxurious living and display, central European princes put their fortunes chiefly into building standing armies. Only in the very late seventeenth and early eighteenth centuries were most able to think seriously about renovating their palaces or offering new entertainments at court.

This does not mean, however, that German princes were not carefully watching what was happening elsewhere, in Italy, France, and the Netherlands. Medici princes and the Spanish kings, as we have seen, already had large porcelain collections, and intermarriages between German nobles and princesses from the house of Orange-Nassau spread the taste for blue-and-white ceramics to central European palaces. Those who visited Versailles—including the young Augustus the Strong, Elector of Saxony (and also king of Poland, 1697–1706 and 1709–33)—had the opportunity to see a great deal of porcelain, including Louis le Vau's "Trianon de Porcelaine," built in

the 1670s as a private rendezvous for Louis XIV and Madame de Montespan, and decorated with blue-and-white tiles as well as Asian porcelains.[27]
By the seventeenth century's close it had become de rigueur to sprinkle stately
rooms with Chinese lidded jars and elaborate delftware tulip vases. Sophie
Charlotte, Electress of Brandenburg (and after 1701, queen of Prussia), took
this much further and used her predecessor's collection to wallpaper a whole
room (plate 1).[28]

Completed in 1695, Charlottenburg Palace, built by Frederick III, soon
to be Frederick I, king in Prussia, was one of the first of the new German
royal "residences." The early eighteenth century saw the widespread building of similar baroque palaces in locations such as Ansbach and Würzburg
and the appearance of a string of new Versailles knock-offs such as Nymphenburg, near Munich, and Schönbrunn, near Vienna. The Holy Roman
Empire, after all, had 330 or so affiliated states, ruled by electors, prince-
bishops, dukes, free knights, and other princelings, all of whom wanted their
own, estimable residences. Political, cultural, and economic centers, their new
palaces, moreover, increasingly came to be divided into more specialized and
more private rooms, with symbolic or fashionable décor. There were Chinese
murals in several rooms at the Oranienbaum Palace near Halle, and dedicated
porcelain rooms at Nymphenburg, Schönbrunn, and Friedenstein (Gotha),
among others, updating the centuries' old practice of displaying silver and
gold vessels in feasting locations. Augustus II, who visited Versailles in the late
1680s and the Prussian palaces at Charlottenburg and Oranienburg in 1709,
would take this conceit to a new level of extravagance in the plans for his
"Japanese" Palace (see below) and in the many Asian details carried out in
his pleasure gardens at Pillnitz. Frederick the Great, for his part, would later
turn the convention inside out, putting the chinoiseries on the exterior of his
teahouse at Sans Souci. Royal architects such as Johann Bernhard Fischer
von Erlach in Austria and Mattäus Daniel Pöppelmann in Prussia would also
include Chinese motifs among their designs. The imitation of Chinese porcelains was deeply linked to this courtly decorative fad.

As the number of new palaces grew, so too did the quantity of courtiers
and the luxuriousness of their accommodations and entertainments. In the

course of the early eighteenth century, staff and supplicants at German-speaking courts increased appreciably, with Augustus's Saxon entourage, for example, doubling in size from 460 in 1700 to more than seven hundred in 1730. Augustus periodically treated his courtiers and guests to great feasts, where spectators, too, were invited to watch the king strengthen himself with food and drink. Augustus kept a menagerie and held lavish horse and animal parades known as "carousel," as well as barbaric bouts of "fox tossing," in which courtiers holding the ends of large cloths threw foxes and other animals into the air until they expired—or, uncomfortably, landed on one of the tossers.[29] Like other princes, Augustus bought rich clothing, books, imported furnishings, clocks, works of art, exotic foodstuffs—and ceramics, chiefly, it seems, from Dutch importers,[30] notorious for their willingness to please all palates.

Expenses at the court consumed a goodly portion of state budgets—12.4 percent of the Habsburg budget in 1700, and a whopping 36 percent of the Electoral Palatinate's expenses a bit later in the century.[31] Banquets for weddings, coronations, festivals, and royal visits—which could sometimes last for days—became more habitual and more lavish. At such banquets, it was customary to advertise the host's wealth and power by displaying the household's silver on dining-room shelves; at Joseph II's coronation banquet in 1764, as Martin von Meytens's beautiful painting shows, the room was wallpapered with silver and gold vessels. The emperor and family dined on gold, their guests on silver; although the tables were set in the newly fashionable à la française manner (see chapter 3), porcelain was not yet good enough for such a grand occasion (plate 2). As Daniel Roche—and Norbert Elias before him—emphasized, this form of luxury consumption had primarily political functions: to display the monarch's power and to reinforce respect for authority.[32] This was, after all, the age of "absolutism." And if one could show oneself a great prince through display rather than warfare, that was an appealing alternative.

Thus the expansion of courtly luxury in the era of absolutism provides the most important context for new attempts to imitate East Asian porcelain, a luxury good chiefly used for display. But the absolutist state had another urgent imperative to accomplish: the creation of new revenue streams that would support the replacement of mercenaries with standing armies. Standing armies were extremely costly, as they required perpetual upkeep as well as provisioning with standard-issue weapons, uniforms, and powder; new bureaucracies were needed to manage the budgets and coordinate conscription, training, and the distribution of supplies. To fill their coffers, the states of central Europe adopted what was to be the first form of national economic policy, known as mercantilism. Associated with Louis XIII's finance minister, Jean-Baptiste Colbert, mercantilism, a philosophy as well as a policy, aspired to keep liquid currency—silver and gold—within the prince's borders. The appeal of such a policy accelerated in the later seventeenth century as the need for expensive armies increased. Colbert's policy called for discouraging imports and encouraging the production of commodities, and especially luxury goods, at home. Overseas colonies were to be founded to produce raw materials and to provide markets for finished goods. Very high tariffs were to be applied to imports, and more efficient taxation exerted so that the state could fund its army and subsidize industries or trading enterprises that the prince wanted to keep at home, such as the manufacturing of armaments—or porcelain.

Porcelain in the Age of Mercantilist Modernization

It would be a fool's errand to generalize about "the" economy of the Holy Roman Empire in the early modern period, as each of the 330-odd principalities had its own peculiarities, dependent on size, location (with respect to rivers, raw materials, and bordering states), number of urban areas, and political and religious configurations.[33] In the later seventeenth century, Saxony—blessed with rich mines; important trading centers such as Leipzig, Dresden, and Pirna; and a powerful monarch—played in an entirely different economic league than did the much poorer and more rural Eastern Pomerania, or the tiny and powerless Lordship of Eglofs. We can say that the Empire was overwhelmingly a world of peasants—only about 2 percent of the population lived in towns over ten thousand, and even by 1800 only

4 percent did so: quite a contrast with the United Provinces, where urbanization had already topped 40 percent in the seventeenth century.[34] Many of these peasants remained en-serfed, and the large majority lived at subsistence levels, especially after 1550, as too much Spanish silver chased too few loaves of bread.

Just as most central Europeans were peasants, most of the region's capital was in land, or in servants and serfs, although there were rich court cities such as Vienna, Dresden, Prague, and Braunschweig, thick with artisans, clergymen, and nobles. The Holy Roman Empire was also home to some successful commercial entrepôts, such as Hamburg, Frankfurt, and Leipzig, whose annual Easter fair featured goods from Asia and the Americas as well as from western Europe and Russia. In glassmaking, mining, and metalworking, central Europeans could even rival peers in England, Italy, and France. Yet in its level of investment in agricultural improvements or in small industries such as silk weaving or shipbuilding, the region as a whole was already behind the Low Countries, England, and France when the Thirty Years' War commenced in 1618. In this terrible conflict, bad weather, disease, and the depredations of mercenaries exacerbated the horrors of a war fought mostly on central European territory. When peace finally arrived in 1648, hundreds of villages and towns had been decimated, their princes now staggering under enormous debts, incurred in part by the hiring of so many mercenaries. It was time to get the states' finances in order, if only to be able to afford a standing army for the next time around.

Here we can identify the importance of state building and army building in the wake of the Thirty Years' War even to such a seemingly remote issue as the search for a European porcelain recipe. For it was that devastating war and its dislocations that inspired the German princes of central Europe to adopt their own versions of Colbert's mercantilism. Although Colbert's policy was originally a wartime measure, it made sense after the war ended too. At a time in which speculators with spare cash were few, and largely confined their interests to currency trading or overseas ventures, state investment in manufacturing was one way to get local production moving, in the directions and places the prince thought it should move. The furthering of home "manufactures" or "Industrie," by which officials meant small-scale, low-tech, and unguilded workshop production, was also a way to put impoverished people to work and to reduce their dependence on their local lords, the church, or state charity. Prussia's state-subsidized wool-making factory, for example, employed soldiers during peacetime to provide them with the means of subsistence.[35] Central European states in particular found this modernizing method appealing—although applying French policies would have unintended consequences.

Farming, animal husbandry, and metalworking formed especially important sectors of the economy and were everywhere subsidized or subjected to state intervention or both to a greater or lesser extent. But the first two of these sectors were too large and diverse to be completely state dominated or funded, and the latter was controlled by a variety of guilds, silversmiths, clockmakers, armaments producers, and so on. The luxury trades, on the other hand, were especially favored in these state business ventures, for they did double duty. Not only did making luxuries at home reduce costly imports, but their production reflected the refinement of the prince's court and could be touted as providing domestic artisans and consumers a series of lessons in good taste.[36] Moreover, the luxury trade was smaller, more concentrated, and easier to control. Many of the luxuries—silk, velvet, coffee, sugar—were purchased almost exclusively by courtiers, and sometimes even forbidden to commoners by sumptuary laws, which limited non-noble purchasing of some goods, partly in paternalist attempts to prevent reckless spending on non-necessities and partly to maintain boundaries between status groups. As such laws lapsed, however, and German nobles accumulated the funds to procure more luxury items, producing these commodities at home became more and more attractive.

Introducing mercantile policies into central Europe, however, was no easy matter. Mercantile measures that sought to pull money and power to the state center flew in the face of a decentralized "Society of Orders," in which nobles, towns, and ecclesiastical institutions jealously guarded their time-honored legal privileges and local economic power. Landlords lived off land rents and the labor of their serfs, and only a few were willing or able to consider investing in new industries. There were plenty of small workshops, but few with sufficient capital or legal status to expand without state assistance. Local guilds stood in their way; it is estimated that as late as 1800, half of western German output was still controlled by guildsmen,[37] and they continued to be hostile to would-be entrepreneurs. The guilds did not control labor in the countryside, however, which partly explains why mercantile manufacturing began there, either in small factories making, for example, glass or iron, or in the form of "cottage" textile production.

Moreover, the vital mercantile tactic of establishing overseas colonies was largely closed to central European states, which entered the race late, and without much verve. This was perhaps the result of geographical fragmentation, a lack of deep-pocketed speculators, or simply princes whose ambitions ran only to continental power and influence. A few of the Hanseatic cities did have ships and trading expertise, most noteworthy among which was the imperial free city of Hamburg. But Hamburg was too small to compete with Great Britain, or France. The gigantic Habsburg Empire did not have a major seaport until the annexation of Trieste after the Napoleonic Wars; and Trieste was a Mediterranean port, more suited to trading with the Ottomans and North Africans than with the Atlantic or Pacific worlds. Prussia spent much of the eighteenth century trying to establish and consolidate its territorial holdings to the east. There were a few tepid attempts at founding East or West India companies, but most fizzled; Denmark, with holdings in the Indian Ocean and the West Indies, was perhaps the most successful of the Germanic colonizers. But only the post-1871 German Empire would succeed in developing the long-range maritime commerce and naval power sufficient to sustain a major colonial empire.

Within the Holy Roman Empire, commerce was complicated and the application of mercantile modernizing strategies halting. Rivers there were plentiful; but without canals to connect them, many of them were difficult to navigate. Roads and bridges, too, were in poor shape, and they were riddled with an estimated eighteen hundred tollbooths—sixty-seven in Prussia alone! The states employed different weights and measures and extracted their fees in a dizzying array of local currencies.[38] All these factors made it difficult for states to regulate trade; the many smaller and larger wars of the period simply exacerbated the problem. Given the impossibility of policing so many borders, smuggling of all sorts was ubiquitous, especially as the German-speaking nobility, although relatively poor, was eager to purchase French, English, and Italian luxuries. All these factors—the Empire's comparative infrastructural inferiority, the small scale of its enterprises, the difficulty of accumulating liquid capital, the extreme diversity of its measurements, and its porous borders—made getting a toehold in the global marketplace difficult even for central Europe's larger and richer states.

And yet, by the mid-eighteenth century central European princes had indeed set about introducing modernizing plans on the mercantilist model—which went hand in hand with political absolutism—into their domains. Taxes and tariffs were reformed in order to protect domestic wares from foreign competition, and in many cases their collection was taken over by the state, to the dissatisfaction of local officials and smugglers. Recognizing that most nobles were land rich and cash poor, German princes founded enterprises themselves, or bribed, cajoled, or even strong-armed their courtiers into doing so. To sweeten the pot, would-be entrepreneurs or investors were offered special privileges, including monopolies on domestic sales and reduced materials or transportation costs. Rather frequently these efforts backfired when those same courtiers dumped their unprofitable enterprises back in the prince's lap.[39] To encourage manufacturing, German princes also lured skilled craftsmen from France, Switzerland, and the Low Countries, regardless of their religious affiliations, to their domains—we can recall here the experience of our Hanau faienciers. Skilled labor, after all, produced items of higher value, which could be more profitably taxed. The general effect was indeed to increase manufacturing and commerce in selected spheres, but also to diminish the local economic autonomy of towns and guilds for the benefit of the princely states. On the other hand, sometimes in order to win cooperation with these new forms of taxation, conscription, and regulation, princes were forced to renew some local privileges, to limit cross-border trade, and in the East, to give landlords expanded rights over their serfs.[40]

Mercantilism was by no means an ideal way to modernize the economy. Increased taxes squelched private investment from non-state-funded actors, even as they took money away from lower-end buyers who might otherwise have been able to consume more.[41] The mercantile system subsidized ventures that now seem slightly silly—such as Carolus Linnaeus's forlorn attempts to grow pineapples in Sweden. Some of these experiments proved to be exorbitantly expensive, such as Prussia's attempts to found a silk industry. They also might have downstream consequences for those tasked with administering them. Thus when an unusually daring state official reported to Frederick the Great that Prussian silk was of poor quality and wouldn't sell, the king was sufficiently incensed to put the hapless truth teller in Spandau prison.[42] Heavy-handed state interventions into the marketplace often resulted in fraud, mismanagement, and the artificial protection and preservation of obsolete or unprofitable industries long after free-market forces would have killed them off. But the historical reality is that state-led modernization was what the decision makers of the day believed was necessary, and for better and for worse that is the direction they chose.

Albeit in a piecemeal and halting fashion, mercantilism did help to modernize central Europe—naturally in its own way. Tax revenues increased, and princes built new fortifications, standing armies, and palaces intended to display their wealth and power. In a world where most wealthy persons still put their capital into land, serfs, horses, and banquets rather than into the founding of commercial or manufacturing enterprises, state intervention did introduce some new liquidity, even as it tended to corrode local economic privileges—such the "closed shop" enforced by the guilds, the long-standing consumption taxes exacted by the towns, and the domination of the labor market by the nobles. State officials found themselves, unwittingly, furthering religious toleration when, in cajoling foreign craftsmen to relocate into German lands, they extended privileges, if not rights, to minority populations. And although it disrupted older patterns of employment, state-led investment provided jobs at a time of population growth and made some regions exporters of finished goods, allowing a rise in the standard of living and the purchasing of new consumer items in return.[43] Mercantilism also stimulated competition between states, which, at least in some cases, produced innovation. In the end, we cannot say that mercantilism was the best choice for the princes' bottom line: but the bottom line was not, for these rulers, the be all and end all. For most, showing oneself to be in command of a "refined" state with a sufficient army and an obedient, tax-paying population mattered more.

Could the recipe for porcelain have been discovered, and an industry founded, without the support of princes? The answer to the first part of this hypothetical question is a clear yes, and to the second, a provisional no. Artisans working without state support had made many smaller and larger technical discoveries over the centuries, perfecting glass-bead making, for example, or grinding better and better optical lenses. Craft practices had always depended on an unstable combination of secrecy and sharing of information, and "invention" could be a matter of serendipity. One English potter's son described his sudden insight, in applying to his horse's infected eye a white powder given to him by a stable boy: this substance might make a wonderful faience glaze![44] This is probably an apocryphal story, but it draws on the reality that there were plenty of people tinkering with clay recipes and glazes long before porcelain makers came on the scene. It is not impossible that a Dutch, French, or English artisan might have hit on a workable recipe. In fact, in the case of some craftsmen at work in the small states that now make up Thuringia, it seems that several did (see chapter 2). The magic "recipe" was, in any case, not just a simple list of ingredients; in addition to specifying the components of the paste and the glaze, the Arcanum included the know-how necessary to build a kiln able to fire at a steady, very high temperature. As clay, water, pebbles, and sand varied across regions, mixtures always required tinkering. Contrary to its reputation, there was, in the end, no single, secret formula for porcelain, and many different recipes could and did succeed.[45]

But could a recipe, once fired successfully, have been parlayed into an *industry* without state support? By industry here one would have to mean the continuous production of a single commodity, especially as pursued by more than one workshop, and in pursuit of a translocal market. Founding an industry of this sort might have been possible in the Netherlands or England, places where the guilds were now defunct, where direct state intervention into the economy was minor, and where producers enjoyed relatively large and wealthy consumer bases. In fact, both places *did* have their own comparable industries, which employed many, and did not need state support: delftware on the one hand, and Staffordshire fine earthenware on the other. When porcelain came along, it had to compete with these other, established ceramic products for esteem as well as for resources. These states, too, had long traditions of importing Asian wares, at low prices, and their aristocracies seem to have been less desperate to imitate the excesses of the French court. The Dutch did establish two porcelain manufactories, at Weesp and The Hague, but neither had much success. The English eventually founded numerous private firms making "bone china" or porcelain with a different clay mixture, but these firms were never so profitable as the Staffordshire potteries (which would include Wedgwood), nor so closely linked to courtly self-representation as were the German firms. Thus was porcelain, as a product and as an industry, quite a different animal than it would be in central Europe.

It is difficult to see how the Holy Roman Empire might have broken into the international market for fine ceramics without the patronage of deep-pocketed princes. Indeed, given the political and economic conditions described above, it is hard to imagine how that would have been possible. Only a few states had the wherewithal to support the vital, and as it turned out, lengthy, experiments necessary to discover the recipe, and to cover the start-up costs of an industry in which there was, especially at the outset, much wastage. Among the Empire's polities, Electoral Saxony had great advantages; boasting long traditions of mining and assaying, glassmaking and alchemy, it was home to many craftsmen skilled in working at high temperatures, something vital to making hard-paste porcelain, which needed to be fired first at about 900°C and then again (after glazing) at 1,400–1,500°C, for as long as two days' time. This largest Saxon state was also abundantly endowed with crucial raw materials—kaolin clay, alabaster, and wood. Finally, most of Saxony's wealth and resources lay in the hands of its prince, Elector Augustus II (r. 1694–1733), who was also titular king of Poland from

1697 to 1706, and again from 1709 until his death in 1733. Augustus was already a great collector of exotic luxuries—including jeweled drinking vessels in the shape of stags, intricately carved cherry pits, and an enormous collection of Asian porcelain.[46] Yet the birth of the Saxon porcelain industry was not in the first instance the result of an attempt to take advantage of Augustus's self-confessed "porcelain sickness." It was the result, in fact, of the prince's longing to bring an even more lucrative industry to his state: the making of gold.

The Saxon Success Story

In the social world of the Old Regime, Johann Friedrich Böttger (1682–1719) was a nobody, one of the members of the Third Estate who, as the French reformer Abbé Emmanuel de Sieyès would later complain, counted for nothing even though their work formed the foundation for the state's wealth. Yet Böttger was lucky enough to have been born the son of the mintkeeper in Schleiz (then one of the Empire's tiniest microstates), and to have relatives willing and able to help him; in early modern society, family resources were crucial to individuals' success. When Johann's father lost his job, the family moved to the Prussian town of Magdeburg, to share quarters with his brother, a prosperous goldsmith. After his father's death, Johann was again fortunate in his stepfather, a well-to-do engineer and bureaucrat who could afford to give Johann what was for the time a very good bourgeois education and pay for his apprenticeship to an apothecary in Berlin. Here the ambitious teenager demonstrated an aptitude for experiment—and a penchant for ignoring rules. His apprenticeship brought him into contact with a number of men engaged in the alchemical search for the philosopher's stone, the mineral compound that, it was believed, could be combined with base metals to make gold. Böttger, too, became obsessed with this quest. Having received some ingredients and instructions from a mysterious, wandering Greek monk, this swaggering nobody made a fateful boast: while the wisest of scholars for centuries had failed in this esoteric endeavor, *he* had discovered the secret to making gold.[47]

Böttger's boast was not so implausible at the time. Suffused with mystical and magical elements, alchemy nonetheless counted as a "science," and like Böttger's Berlin friends, many of the leading scientists of the day, including Sir Isaac Newton, expended much energy and effort in the hopes that their alchemical experiments would succeed. Moreover, investment in alchemical research made sense, above all for nations experienced in smelting precious metals, but also for poorer states seeking a quick fix for depleted treasuries.[48] Evidently Böttger's demonstrations were convincing enough that rumors began to spread, and in 1701 they reached the ears of the Prussian elector (soon to become Frederick I, king in Prussia), eager to employ an alchemist to help him make more gold to finance his lavish tastes, his sizable army, and his big debts. Frederick commanded Böttger to report to him in Berlin.

Fearful he would be punished for his magic tricks, Böttger abandoned his apprenticeship and went into hiding—and then made a dash for the border. This put him beyond the long arm of the Prussian elector but regrettably delivered him into the clutches of Saxony's elector Augustus the Strong, who was also in great need of funds, to feed his collecting habits as well as to keep himself on the Polish throne. On learning that an alchemist had entered his territory, Augustus promptly had Böttger arrested, with the same aims as those of his Hohenzollern neighbor. To prevent the young alchemist from being kidnapped by Prussian soldiers or from running away, Augustus now locked him in a Saxon prison. The prisoner was comfortably accommodated and provided with materials, books, and lavish meals; he was allowed to entertain many of the state's leading scholars, including the senior scientist and courtier Ehrenfried Walther von Tschirnhaus. Meanwhile, the Saxon elector impatiently awaited news that his real-life Rumpelstiltskin had turned dross into gold.[49]

Augustus wanted Böttger to succeed. Perhaps, as the fictional porcelain fancier of Bruce Chatwin's novel *Utz* claims, the elector credited some of the more esoteric alchemical theories and hoped his prisoner would discover the secret of immortality.[50] The evidence, however, suggests that Augustus simply wanted Böttger to make him piles of gold. But making gold, it turned out, required steep initial investments, and by 1703, Augustus had already plunged forty thousand taler into this endeavor: the equivalent of a very respectable annual wage for some four thousand men.[51] It was only in this year, however, perhaps thanks to Tschirnhaus's intervention, that Böttger was allowed to depart his gilded cage, and move operations to the Goldhaus, a fully equipped alchemist's laboratory just meters from the electoral palace in Dresden. Here Böttger had access to the latest equipment and to a fully stocked scientific library; he was also allowed to hire some skilled craftsmen to assist him. He moved into apartments in the palace and was given space for a billiards room and freedom to walk in the palace gardens, although if he got too close to the gate, his guards were instructed to shoot pellets at him from a blowpipe.[52]

Böttger's move to the Goldhaus enabled him to do better science, but it was his collaboration with the much older Tschirnhaus (1651–1708) that was crucial to his scholarly success, and saved him from execution for having perpetrated a fraud. A skilled mathematician and chemist, the Silesian-born Tschirnhaus had studied medicine, mineralogy, chemistry, and philosophy at the University of Leiden. He had then proceeded to Paris, where he took a job as tutor to Colbert's son, fell under the spell of mercantilist ideas, and was introduced to experiments in porcelain making. In Louis XIV's capital and in the course of his travels he had also befriended experts in the chemical properties of glass. He had made intensive studies of burning mirrors, which enabled the melting and assaying of materials at high temperatures. Linked to the Saxon court by his wife's connections, the cosmopolitan Tschirnhaus had settled in Dresden, and become one of a number of scholars at Augustus's court. Like the leading scientists of the day, Tschirnhaus was interested in alchemy, but he prioritized the practical, political aim of improving Saxon industries such as marble polishing, glassblowing, and, if possible, porcelain making. By 1694 at the latest he was using his burning lenses to melt delftware and Chinese porcelain in pursuit of its recipe. In 1701–2, he arranged visits to St. Cloud in France and to delftware workshops in the Netherlands, and he learned about French experiments with mixtures using eggshells, snail shells, and chalk. Tschirnhaus himself pioneered a process to fuse chalk and quartz, a process at the heart of porcelain making,[53] and he was unhappy to leave aside his own projects when Augustus tasked him with speeding up Böttger's science. But assisting this "nobody" gave him the opportunity to explore high-temperature firing, and the development of ceramic crucibles for gold making was an enterprise this odd couple could work on in tandem. When, in May 1706, they succeeded in turning out a hard, red ceramic paste that resembled the Yixing porcelains already in Augustus's and other princely collections, it was surely Tschirnhaus who recognized that the right recipe for the most desired white porcelain was within reach, and who persuaded both Böttger and the elector to pursue this more probable concoction while putting the longer-term project of making gold on the back burner.[54]

We should not, however, diminish the contributions made by our nobody. As Ursula Klein has shown, most apothecary shops contained something known even in the later seventeenth century as "laboratories," and pharmaceutical production in these shops overlapped a great deal with academic chemistry.[55] Böttger, by all accounts, was a chemical prodigy and, by dint of many failed efforts, became an expert kiln builder, a highly important part of his "magic." Thus Böttger was the inventive technician and hands-on experimenter, Tschirnhaus, his scholarly consultant. They set to work, officially in pursuit of gold, but increasingly of the porcelain recipe. Augustus allowed them the assistance of five craftsmen from Freiburg im Breisgau, experienced in mining and assaying, who tested compound after compound.[56] Their work was interrupted by Böttger's removal to the Königstein prison in 1706–7, when Saxony was occupied by the Swedes; Augustus did not want his Rumpelstiltskin captured by another greedy king. But when in 1707 work commenced again in Dresden, the team devoted itself to perfecting the vitrified red stoneware that would subsequently be known as Böttger stoneware, as well as to formulating the elusive recipe for the most coveted *white* porcelain.

At this point it was perhaps the input of the chemist and mining expert Gottfried Pabst von Ohaim, another courtier Augustus had assigned to the gold-making project, that mattered most. Böttger and Tschirnhaus had been using good quality clay from Colditz, near Leipzig; Pabst suggested seeking calcified clay and pebbles to make a white paste, and he is probably the one who located a viable clay near the town of Aue in the Erzgebirge, on the estate of one Veit Hans Schnorr von Scheeberg.[57] This very white clay—kaolin, composed heavily of aluminum silicate—was already known to courtiers, as it had been marketed as a wig powder. When combined with Colditz clay (43 percent each) and alabaster (14 percent) it proved plastic enough to form a proper "paste."[58] This, then, was finally the "Arcanum," whose name carried with it strong whiffs of magic, and whose mixing could be accomplished only by the few initiates who came to be called "arcanists." But the paste recipe was not the only part of the Arcanum. The other parts, how to build a proper kiln and to mix a glaze that would not melt away at 1,400°C, were still mysterious. Tragically, on October 11, 1708, on the eve of the first successful firings of the new white paste, Tschirnhaus died, leaving Böttger to complete this final, crucial step. In March 1709, Böttger was confident enough to announce to the king that he was now able to make porcelain "as good as that of the Chinese, if not better."[59] Notwithstanding subsequent monumentalizations of this moment (fig. 1.2). this remained a premature boast. Only in 1713 could the Saxons more or less reliably fire white porcelains, and it took much longer to perfect the glazes and underglaze enamels that could rival East Asian wares.

Böttger's claim—to have made porcelain "as good as that of the Chinese"—should remind us that this "invention" was in fact an imitation—of the Chinese and Japanese porcelains already owned by Augustus and other princes.[60] Augustus, as we have seen, had long been buying vast quantities of imported porcelain; Böttger's findings simply enabled Saxony to replicate these imports, something that is clearly evident in our real-life Rumpelstiltskin's first products, which initially copied Asian shapes as exactly as possible; Böttger, after all, was a chemist, not a potter. But imitations were welcome, both to the porcelain-mad prince and to the minders of the royal treasury. The elector longed to enhance his own collection, as well as to demonstrate his state's artistic and technological prowess; his financial advisers welcomed the reduction of the king's expenditures on costly imports. Thus Augustus moved Böttger and his operations to the old Wettin castle in Saxony's former capital

1.2. Böttger presents the Arcanum
This idealized mural recreating J. G. Böttger's presentation of the Arcanum
to King Augustus II captures Augustus's keen interest in the discovery as
well as Böttger's status as a gentleman-prisoner. Its unusual shape is the
result of the mural's placement on a wall in the Gothic Albrechtsburg
Palace.

of Meissen, about fifteen miles from Dresden, where production could begin
in earnest, and perhaps more than ever, in secret.

The "factory" Augustus bestowed on Böttger was in fact the disused
Albrechtsburg Castle, walled and sited on the top of a hill overlooking the
Elbe River. Here Böttger once again built a kiln and set up a horse mill to
grind paste and glaze materials. At first production was devoted to the
more easily fired red "Böttger Steingut," shaped after Yixing models from

the elector's collection. In 1710, many pieces of this "stoneware" and sam-ples of white porcelain could be exhibited at the Easter fair in Leipzig, though, somewhat ominously, only about half the inventory sold. A master silver-smith was hired to oversee the artistic side of production and soon added pieces made after baroque silver. Böttger also secured exclusive rights from Aue to its all-important kaolin clay, which was sent in boxes marked with crossed swords and the letters A and R (Augustus Rex), the first appearance of what would evolve into Meissen's trademark. By 1711, the Meissen works employed more than thirty men and had produced more than twelve thousand pieces ready for sale, virtually all of them made of red "Böttger" stoneware.[61] A mercantile industry had been born.

This was, however, not an "industry" in the nineteenth-century sense, and if money making was its object, the whole enterprise was a laughable disaster, at least during Böttger's lifetime. Böttger was paid a princely 50 T a month and, from 1715 until his death in early 1719, served as the manufactory's leaseholder. But frequently ill and falling ever deeper into alcoholism, he now lived in Dresden and visited the works irregularly. Above him, and receiving triple Böttger's monthly salary, was a courtier who showed up even more rarely. The court's lacquer master was seconded to the manufactory at 100 T a month, and there were other high salaries for craftsmen and administra-tors, of 16–20 T a month. But workers frequently went for long periods with-out pay, which inspired them to theft, flight, or intrigue; production was sporadic owing to Böttger's haphazard management, debts, and distraction by other schemes, such as the manufacturing of artificial borax (at which he failed) or ruby glass (at which he succeeded). Wood costs during the experi-mental phase were already at 1,400 T per year and surged thereafter. And the firm paid so much for exhibiting at the Leipzig fair that it wiped out all its profits.[62] Industrial production in the Manchester mode this was not.

Augustus was vexed by Böttger's failure to make gold and by the enor-mous expenses of the manufactory. In 1712, the elector proclaimed that the manufactory needed to cultivate sales beyond the Saxon elite, to target for-eign courts and "leading Standes-Personen" (persons of rank), but without forgetting the desires of the "Mittel-Mann."[63] Even so, production for the market was never a major goal of the enterprise. For Augustus, it was *Glanz*, and one-upping other princes, that mattered. He clearly aimed to make a big show of his porcelain, as the plans for his never-completed "Japanese Palace" indicate. This structure, across the Elbe from his Dresden residence, was to feature at least eighteen lavish rooms; the lower level was to be wallpapered with thousands of imported Chinese and Japanese porcelains, the upper to be plastered in Meissen products, one room celadon and gold, the next purple and gold, others gray and blue.[64] Augustus's porcelain menagerie of life-sized birds and animals was also to reside on the top floor. If he found porcelains endlessly delightful, Augustus would discover that they also made excellent gifts, cheaper than jeweled swords, and versatile enough to employ both in charming foreign princes and in rewarding domestic officials. Augustus himself would become the firm's best, and worst, customer; "best" in terms of his enormous number of orders, "worst" in that he failed to pay the manufactory for most of them. Accustomed to spending absurd sums on fox tossing and emollients to Polish nobles, Augustus and his ministers, for all their complaints, were not terribly bothered by Meissen's (red) bottom line.

In 1714, Böttger officially received his freedom, on the condition that he remain in Saxony and keep the Arcanum a secret. His health was poor, his alcoholism ever more pronounced, his finances chaotic. He was still closely watched by Augustus's spies. It is one of the signs of Böttger's artisanal and scientific curiosity and ambition that he continued to innovate, working out techniques of glazing and underglaze painting, both technically difficult processes. It was hard enough to heat a kiln to 900°C for the first firing; but once glazed, porcelain needed a second baking at the extremely high temperature of 1400°C, which caused many vessels to crack and most glaze mixtures to run. By 1717, Böttger and his staff were working hard on blue underglaze paintings and the application of gold and silver decoration to their vessels, but the arcanist was too ill to do much, or to care much, about the conditions of the factory, where pay continued to be in arrears and morale low. This was a dangerous situation, as some of these men now knew the Arcanum, in whole or in part, a very valuable bargaining chip, as they well knew. Poisoned both by drink and by the substances with which he tinkered, Böttger expired in March 1719. At his death he owed 8,564 T in personal obligations, and his manufactory had outstanding debts of nearly three times that amount, not including back wages owed to his workers.[65]

Why did Böttger remain more or less the elector's prisoner even after he had invented what came to be called "white gold"? The answer is that Böttger's recipe for porcelain paste remained a secret, except to a few initiates on his staff. That secret officially belonged not to the scientist, but to his lord and patron, Augustus, and Augustus wanted to keep that knowledge inside his own realm and to exploit it for his own, exclusive, gain. As an absolutist prince, the elector could command his subjects to do his bidding, on pain of death. On the other hand, workers were often kept on the state payroll even when they proved ineffective or unneeded. Arcanists, like other persons thought indispensable for running the state, used their privileged positions to command high wages and other perks (see chapter 3). The immense effort to keep secret the means of producing a luxury good that promised the sovereign prestige, if not profit, would shape the industry in both obvious and not so obvious ways down to the monopoly's official abolition in 1810.

Keeping—and Stealing—the Secret

Keeping the secret had been part of the reason in 1710 for moving Böttger's operations from Dresden, the residence of the elector and center of court sociability, to the old Wettin stronghold of Meissen, a short distance to the southeast. In Meissen, Böttger's operations could be safely housed, as we have seen, on the top of the hill overlooking the Elbe River in the little-used Albrechtsburg Castle, easy to wall off from prying eyes. Augustus claimed that the move had been motivated by his desire to help the town, which had suffered "misfortune in many forms," to recover by returning the "blessed nourishment and trade to the land, chiefly through manufacturing and commerce."[66] The Meisseners, however, were not so sure they were being blessed. In order to claim his crown as king of Poland, Augustus had converted to Roman Catholicism, and the Protestant inhabitants of Meissen looked on the founding of the prince's factory in their town as an attempt to force Catholicism down their throats. In Saxony, the heartland of the Reformation, and home to a nearly 100 percent Protestant population, Catholics were most unwelcome, and Meisseners were offended to have even seven Catholics among the 380 or so porcelain workers in 1752. Moreover, the townsmen objected to the importing of foreign craftsmen—imperiling their own guild privileges—as well as the housing and food shortages that ensued as the factory grew. Pub proprietors viewed with particular hostility the workers' habit of crossing the Elbe to the neighboring towns of Vorbrücke and Cölln to do their drinking.[67] Eventually, the porcelain works brought prosperity and fame to Meissen, but it took some time for the locals to appreciate its contribution. What looked like economic "progress" to Augustus was not welcomed with open arms by people suspicious of outsiders and accustomed to having a large degree of control over their local affairs.[68]

Just as Tschirnhaus—and his team of kiln hands and other craftsmen—had assisted in the original discovery of the Arcanum, so too would Böttger's work involve from the outset a variety of other artisans, without whose assistance the Meissen manufactory would not have endured and, eventually, prospered. Division of labor coupled with teamwork would characterize European porcelain making from the first—as it had defined production already in eleventh-century Jingdezhen. Porcelain making depends on a series of stages, from mining and mixing to forming, firing, and glazing (and firing once more), each of which requires particular artisanal knowledge. Böttger needed helpers to feed and tend the wood-burning kilns and to develop forms, glazes, and decorative elements. We have noted the presence of Freiburg experts in smelting; but from early on, various other technology and craft transfers would be important catalysts of innovation in the porcelain industry. In the early years, Böttger hired Delft-trained potters and ceramicists from the town of Pirna, who almost certainly had glassmaking experience, given that town's proximity to Bohemia. J. J. Irminger, silversmith to the Saxon court, was instrumental in designing tasteful shapes for Meissen products and by 1710 had become something like the artistic director of the works.[69] Information on other manufacturers, whether stolen or shared, was always highly sought after and valued. When the Jesuit missionary Father Xavier d'Entrecolles published two letters describing porcelain making in China in 1717, his eyewitness account was devoured by the Meisseners as well as by other would-be factory founders.[70] This account did not, however, provide a replicable recipe for making porcelain, much less the necessary tacit artisanal knowledge, in part because, *pace* Voltaire, nature, or at least geology, is nowhere *exactly* the same. Clay, wood, sand, even water have slightly different chemical and mineral components across the earth, and the very tricky art, and science, of making fine porcelain had to be adjusted to the ingredients, climate, and workforce at hand. And nowhere was the mixing, shaping, and firing of translucent, elegant, and perfectly white porcelain easy to do.

Meissen's recipe was a trade secret in the classic sense. But the problem with trade secrets is that humans are the ones who must keep them. As soon as word spread that the Saxons had made true porcelain, other sovereigns, eager to establish their own manufactories and keep cash in their own dominions, began scheming to steal Böttger's Arcanum. Or others schemed on their behalf, attempting to extract secrets from runaway arcanists—of whom there were a number—by bribery, strong drink, or tricking a daughter into betraying a father's secret. Böttger's illnesses and unpaid salaries, especially in the year of his death (1719), made the future of the manufactory uncertain, and the extraction of its secrets easier. Suborned by the Habsburg courtier Innocent du Paquier, Christoph Hunger, for example, left Meissen for Vienna. When he failed to mix the clay properly, he fled back to Meissen, where he was kept on costly retainer for fear that next time he *would* reveal the secret.[71] Du Paquier then recruited another Meissener, Samuel Stöltzel, offering him a lavish 1,000 T salary. In 1719, Stöltzel, in Vienna, fired the first true European porcelain outside of Saxony.[72]

By the 1720s, the Holy Roman Empire had become awash in "itinerant ceramicists" (*Keramiker Vaganten*), fast-talkers of dubious character trying to convince German princes that they could, naturally for a price, make porcelain for the *Hof*. As the recipe—or the purported recipe—spread, other sovereigns too compelled their arcanists to swear oaths of loyalty and secrecy, binding themselves to the prince, and his factory, for life.[73] But many were willing to break these oaths for the right price. Claiming that he had extracted the Arcanum from a former Meissen employee "in a tragic hour in Vienna," one of these wandering potters duped the Elector of Bavaria in 1729: after many attempted firings, it became clear that his "secret recipe" didn't work. The boondoggle made the Bavarians hesitant to try again; the next attempt did not commence until 1747.[74]

Some of these shady characters, however, actually did possess the secret and were willing to sell their services, while keeping the secret to themselves. Employed as a painter at the Viennese manufactory, J. J. Ringler seems to have extracted the Arcanum from the director's daughter. He then spread the secret or improvements to it to Fürstenberg and then to Karl Hannong's factory (Strassbourg), Höchst, and Neudeck (predecessor to Nymphenburg), where the first true Bavarian porcelain was made under his supervision in 1754. He was fired in 1757 for the irregularities in his paste, which led to enormous wastage, and received a farewell payment "to seek his luck elsewhere." His "luck" took him first to a faience factory in Uzmemmingen and then to the Duke of Württemberg's manufactory at Ludwigsburg, where he would finally settle until his retirement in 1802.[75] But even those fortunate enough to win Ringler's services needed the right clay, a complication that foxed many first efforts, as Meissen had purchased monopoly rights on Schnorr von Scheeberg's kaolin from Aue. Schnorr was not above taking bribes himself, but importing large quantities from this source was difficult and expensive. Eventually avid prospectors located new sources at Passau, in Bavaria, and then at St. Yrieix, near Limoges, France (see map 1). Kiln designs and glaze recipes were also smuggled and shared. Although he did not possess the Arcanum, the former Meissen painter Adam Friedrich von Löwenfinck was willing to share something else, his unique Japanese-style painting techniques, and these too, were copied by porcelain and faience makers across Europe.

It did not take long, in the end, for the "secret" recipe to spread across the Germanys and across Europe. The Viennese courtier du Paquier, as we have seen, had the recipe by 1719; by 1744, however, du Paquier was in debt,

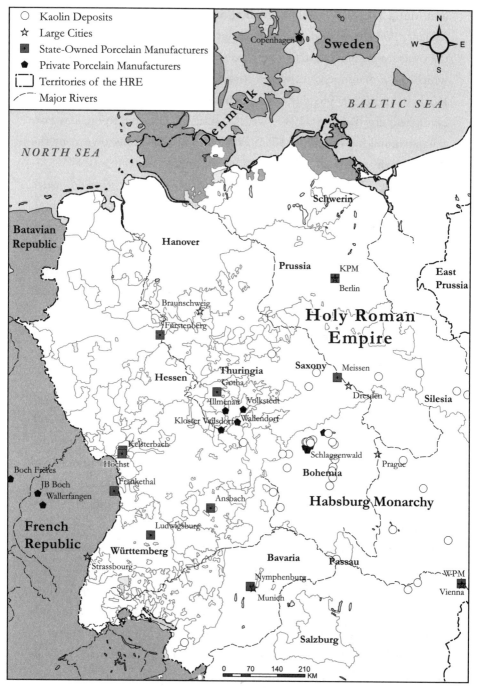

Map 1.

Porcelain manufacturers in central Europe, ca. 1800.

and Maria Theresa agreed to buy him out for 51,543 florins, making the "Wiener Porzellanmanufaktur" (hereafter WPM) a state firm.[76] Then came the others, the founding dates not necessarily coinciding with the dates at which these manufactories were actually able to produce true porcelain: Höchst (Mainz), 1746; Fürstenberg (Braunschweig-Wolfenbüttel), 1747; Nymphenburg (Bavaria), 1747; Wegeley (Prussia; later the Königliche Porzellanmanufaktur, or KPM), 1751; Frankenthal, 1754 (fully owned by the Palatinate elector after 1762), 1754; Ludwigsburg (Württemberg), 1758. Already by the 1760s, there were far too many such firms for us to do justice to the intricacies of each one's history. We will have to be content with an overview, first, of the intertwined histories of the two longest-lived and most successful German firms, Meissen and the manufactory that came to be known as the KPM, the Königliches Porzellan Manufaktur, headquartered in Berlin, and then an even more cursory treatment of the other European firms. For already by 1750, porcelain making had become a pan-European, and not just a German, industry.

Meissen: The First Years, 1720-63

In the 1720s and 1730s, while others were absorbed in stealing its secret, Meissen prospered, improving its bookkeeping and expanding its workforce from thirty-three in 1720 to forty-nine in 1740, and making a leap to 218 in 1745.[77] Augustus II's orders, for his porcelain menagerie and his planned Japanese Palace among other smaller commissions, were gigantic; by 1735, the factory had by no means delivered all the animals ordered but had succeeded in making thirteen lions and lionesses, five elephants, twenty-six apes, eight sphinxes, and nine peacocks, among many other beasts and birds.[78] Valuing each lion, for example, at 106 taler (an amount exceeding a skilled worker's yearly salary at the time[79]), the Meissen workshop would have made a very fat profit indeed on the menagerie alone had Augustus not perpetually raided his own stocks, commandeering by one estimate, over 1.6 million T worth of china, and returning to the enterprise only about 500,000 T.[80] After his death in 1733, his successor, Frederick Augustus II, continued the

Japanese Palace project but devoted more funds to opera and old master paintings and left the running of the factory to the aristocratic courtiers he chose as his advisers. In an era predating the existence of a professional bu-reaucracy, this was all a prince could do; but it made his enterprises depen-dent on the competence and probity of his courtiers. When the clever and conniving Count Heinrich von Brühl took charge of the firm in 1738, he and his friends regularly followed Augustus the Strong's example by helping themselves to large quantities of ceramics, with minimal reimbursements to the factory. By 1753, von Brühl owned 623 pieces of tableware, 868 table decorations, and 2,676 figurines, including his famous absurdity, a porce-lain rendering of his tailor riding a goat (plate 3).[81] It is a tribute to Meissen porcelain's growing appeal that even in the age of Brühl the firm turned small profits, rising gently from its small proceeds of 130 T in 1720. Between 1733 and 1742, the firm's profits amounted to a little over 50,000 T; the warehouse stock was valued (probably overvalued) at just over 225,000 T. Some years were far better than others, with the firm making, for example, 14,440 T in 1733, and losing more than 5,000 T in 1736.[82] Even in this period, when Meissen was virtually alone in the market, porcelain selling was never a sure thing.

Once introduced, white porcelain soon drove out red Böttger stoneware, and the factory stopped producing it entirely after 1728. Beginning in 1723, the polychrome enamel overglaze painting pioneered by the former wallpaper painter Johann Gregor Höroldt contributed significantly to Meissen's mar-ket success—and his own. Höroldt wangled for himself a special position as a subcontractor, paid by the piece, and delegated work to his own workshop, an arrangement that netted him the enormous income of 3,000 to 4,000 T per year until Augustus insisted his salary be capped at a still-lavish 1,000 T. Höroldt's specialty was Chinese motifs, adapted from illustrated travel ac-counts, but he and his team of painters also adopted designs from the Dutch and French, adding harbor scenes, hunts, and then Watteau-esque pastoral scenes in the 1730s and 1740s.[83] Orders from home and abroad were brisk. Already in 1732 Meissen had filled an order for two thousand dozens of "Türkenköppchen" or small, handleless cups, from a Turkish merchant;

in 1734 this coup turned into a standing order for three thousand dozens per year.[84]

Even more important to Meissen's flourishing was the modeler Johann Joachim Kändler, who arrived in 1731. Meissen had produced figurines before Kändler's arrival; Böttger himself had made statuettes of figures from the commedia dell'arte, though most of the first forms tended to chinoiserie, including incense burners called "pagodes," modeled precisely on items in the elector's possessions (see ahead to fig. 3.4). But production quickly moved to Christian saints, dogs, dwarves, and frogs.[85] Trained as a sculptor, Kändler was hired to help design animals for the menagerie. He struggled at first with the technical challenges of making near life-sized goats and slender-necked herons, and he blamed Höroldt, probably unfairly, for intentionally misfiring his creations.[86] Once he got used to the medium's particularities, however, Kändler expanded Meissen's repertoire enormously, inventing thousands of designs for allegorical, pastoral, humorous, and religious figures and groups. His "monkey orchestra," his harlequins, and his muses became almost synonymous with "Meissen" and today continue to be hailed as the perfect adaptation of sculptural content and style to the medium of porcelain.[87]

Kändler and Höroldt differed fiercely on the firm's priorities, with Höroldt insisting that it should focus on brightly colored salable goods, and Kändler siding with Frederick Augustus II in plumping for the production of one-of-a-kind, prestige items, such as the twenty-two-hundred-piece "Swan Service" modeled for von Brühl, or the eight-meter-tall mirror made for Louis XV, so delicate that Kändler had to travel with it to Paris to install it in the Palace of Versailles.[88] But the expanding firm was able to continue along both lines, and its volume of production increased exponentially, from sales amounting to 9,694 T in 1720 and 82,330 T in 1742.[89] Meissen was turning good profits, even with von Brühl's pilferings, when calamity struck, in the form of the Prussian army, led by that enlightened bully, Frederick the Great.

In 1740, the Saxons had sided with Prussia in the First Silesian War against Maria Theresa, hoping to be rewarded with territory. But when in the Second

Silesian War (1744–45) they switched sides, Frederick took the opportunity to occupy and pillage Meissen, extracting wood, clay, cash, and thousands of pieces of porcelain, which the manufactory later valued at just under 44,000 T.[90] Ahead of the invasion the Meisseners had sent their arcanists and account books across the Saxon border. Höroldt, the master painter, escaped to Frankfurt, where he enjoyed a comfortable exile. Some other craftsmen also fled, spreading the now not so arcane Arcanum to Ansbach and Kelsterbach, near Mainz. Meissen model master Kändler, who apparently did not know the secret paste recipe, stayed, and together with the accountant G. M. Helbig, got the factory up and running after peace came in January 1746.

Frederick once claimed that Saxony, Prussia's rich neighbor, was like a flour sack: no matter how many times you beat it, something always came out.[91] Thus when Prussia went to war again in 1756, he was eager to shake down Saxony, and its Meissen factory, once more. This much wider and longer war—eventually to be known as the Seven Years' War in Europe, and the French and Indian Wars in North America—saw Meissen ransacked again, and occupied from November 1760 until March 1763. Frederick, who visited the manufactory numerous times, seized the factory and sold the whole of Meissen's backlog, now valued at 300,000 T, to a wealthy merchant for 120,000 T—though the faithful accountant Helbig, fearful that porcelains would be sold to the Prussian maker Wegeley (see below), bought most of it back. Helbig was compelled to pay the Prussian king 2,000 T a month to lease the Meissen works and to provide him with the finest goods.[92] As manufactory owner, Frederick reduced wages by 30 percent and then debased the currency, further diminishing workers' buying power.

According to a later summary, the firm handed over to Frederick a total of more than 550,000 T in cash and porcelain during these two wars.[93] These depredations did not, however, idle production. Meissen was still churning out record amounts of porcelain when the war ended, and in 1763 it reached its peak number of employees at 731, not bested until the late nineteenth century, making it one of the largest employers in central Europe at the time.[94] These early years established Meissen as the manufactory to imitate, and to beat; to its owners' perpetual regret, although it would continue to be respected, copied, and envied, it would never enjoy the same sort of market dominance again.

The KPM

The Berlin-based firm that would later be known as the Royal Prussian Manufactory (Königliches Porzellan Manufaktur, or KPM) was not, originally, directly financed by the Hohenzollerns. Augustus II's younger Prussian contemporary Frederick William I was not a man to covet a porcelain factory; his tastes ran, rather, to soldiers and hunting dogs, and he had actually taken steps to restrict luxury production in favor of the manufacturing of goods for his beloved army. His son, however, later Frederick II ("the Great"), had evidently explored possibilities as early as 1737, and between 1740 and 1746 he spent 6,000 T commissioning chemists to find the secret; some thirty thousand trials later, they admitted failure.[95]

The idea of founding a Prussian porcelain manufactory lay dormant until revived by Wilhelm Caspar Wegeley (1714–64), whose father, a Swiss emigrant, had made a fortune in the wool industry and had long experience in wringing concessions from the Prussian state. Wilhelm Caspar had no background in ceramics, but as a partner in the family firm, Wegeley did have capital, connections, and political clout. Perhaps looking to diversify the family's portfolio, he promised in 1751 to make wares as beautiful as but cheaper than those of Meissen, and also "to bring many people into the state and provide bread and sustenance for them." With arguments like these, Wegeley convinced Frederick to give him a centrally located building and a fifty-year privilege for the making and selling of porcelain in Prussia.[96] The next year, Wegeley obtained the Arcanum, apparently from craftsmen who had recently left the Höchst manufactory in Mainz.[97]

Wegeley did make some porcelain, but by the time production really began in 1755, Prussia was on the eve of another war with Saxony, and Frederick had lost interest. Incensed that Frederick had sold off Meissen wares at home, violating Wegeley's privilege, and seeing much more chance for profit in woolens, the entrepreneur closed shop and auctioned off his plant.

In 1761, a sculptor named E. H. Reichard, who had worked for Wegeley, sold the secret and his porcelain stock to Johann Ernst Gotzkowsky, an extremely wealthy and well-connected dealer in luxury goods, for a reported sum of 4,000 T.[98] This acquisition was almost surely not Gotzkowsky's idea, but that of one of his best customers: Frederick the Great. Frederick had previously saddled his dealer with a wobbly silk enterprise that had to be artificially sustained with royal gifts and loans and, in 1760, gave him a 50,000 T bonus, partly as a reward for diplomatic endeavors Gotzkowsky had undertaken with the Russians on behalf of Berlin's merchants, but probably mostly intended as seed money to entice Gotzkowsky to establish a Prussian porcelain factory.[99] Wholly unfamiliar with the ceramic arts, chemistry, or manufacturing, Gotzkowsky immediately turned operations over to the Saxon Kommerzienrat J. G. Grieninger and a staff of exceptionally highly paid craftsmen. They began churning out porcelains in large numbers, their sale enhanced by the fact that at a time of devalued currency, those who had made money on the wars put cash into luxury items as a way of storing value.

The war's end, however, brought a deep dip in consumption, a terrible credit crunch, the collapse of numerous Dutch and Hamburgian lenders, bankruptcies, and the first of many reversals of fortune in the history of Prussian porcelain making. Gotzkowsky had grossly overextended himself and could not meet his obligations. He sold his silk works to a pair of Jewish merchants and in 1765 sold his porcelain factory as well, complete with 146 workers, the firm's tools and supplies, and over forty thousand pieces of porcelain in various stages of completion, to Frederick himself, for the bargain price of 225,000 T. Never able to reestablish Frederick's trust, Gotzkowsky in 1775 died a pauper.[100]

Perhaps Frederick's renewed interest in porcelain had been awakened by his seizure of the Meissen works or by many months of living in Count von Brühl's well-stocked Dresden palace during Prussia's occupation of Saxony. In 1760 the king had already made the first of several sketches for tableware services that drew heavily on Saxon models. Tellingly, the enlightened warrior-king ordered a service with plates featuring allegories of music and warfare and tureens bearing an inscription from Descartes: *Dubium initium sapientiae (est)*: doubt is the beginning of wisdom.[101] But Frederick certainly did not doubt his own taste, or his conviction that the new "Königliches Porzellan Manufaktur" would pay. As we will see in the next chapter, after 1765, he looked on his royal manufactory with a mixture of princely pride and fiscal rapacity. Longing to outdo the hated Saxons, Frederick took charge of the firm's finances and would micromanage the KPM down to the time of his death in 1786. He changed the manufactory's trademark from a G (for Gotzkowsky) to a Prussian scepter but kept on Gotzkowsky's manager Grieninger, who ran the manufactory until his death in 1798.[102]

Successes and Failures: Some Other German Stories

The fortunes—in purely economic terms—of other early German firms were certainly mixed. In the early success column, we can place Austria's Viennese Porcelain Manufactory (WPM), which, as we have seen, became a state industry when Innocent du Paquier went bankrupt in 1744. In 1745, the WPM moved to cut in on Meissen's Turkish sales by making a self-interested gift of some of its wares to the Ottomans; in 1749 it was rewarded with a large order for *Türkenkoppchen*. The Turkish market would continue to be lucrative for the Viennese down to the end of the century, when a rash of private makers shouldered in (see chapter 2). In 1755, the WPM was able to employ a staff of 105 and operate two branch shops, in Trieste and Karlsbad. But by the early 1760s, sales fell so low that Maria Theresa considered privatizing the firm. The WPM rebounded, however, from the Seven Years' War with Prussia, and by 1775 it had tripled in size, to three hundred workers.[103]

Another relative success story in the early years was the Fürstenberg manufactory, founded by Duke Carl I of Braunschweig-Wolfenbüttel. An enlightened man, Carl aspired to develop cottage industries that would take advantage of the one resource he had in abundance—wood. It is not surprising that the duke's thoughts turned to porcelain, as his ancestral summer palace, Salzdalum, yet another Versailles knockoff, already boasted a collection of more than eight thousand pieces of East Asian ceramics. By the 1740s, he also had Meissen's accomplishments before his eyes. In 1747, the duke donated not Salzdalum but his hunting lodge at Fürstenberg, on the Weser River, to the cause of porcelain making and put his hunting master in charge. The first arcanist that Carl I hired fiddled for six years without success. Finally the gamekeeper-director bribed the arcanist at Höchst, Johann Benckgraff, offering him 1,320 T for the secret, along with a princely annual salary of 790 T, plus free lodging and wood, emoluments to continue for Benckgraff's wife after his death—which, as it turned out, proved to be almost immediate.[104]

Even with the Arcanum, all did not proceed smoothly at Fürstenberg. Throughout the eighteenth century, the factory had an extraordinarily high rate of misfirings; between 1775 and 1777, for example, only about one in ten of the pieces fired came out of the kilns unblemished. Still, Fürstenberg could offer porcelains at prices cheaper than those of Meissen, and in 1756, it added a faience factory to increase its range of affordable objects for sale (it too began producing *Türkenkoppchen*). The firm enjoyed its heyday after the 1760s, as a result of its relatively inexpensive pricing and its innovations in neoclassical design, and would survive longer than most state firms. Only in 1859 was it leased to a private proprietor.[105]

Survival, however, did not mean that Fürstenberg was an economic success. Something similar can be said of Nymphenburg, in Bavaria, and many of the other smaller firms. As we have seen, the Bavarians were also duped at first by an imposter who could not make good on his claim to produce "white gold." The inspiration to try again came from Electress Maria Anna Sophia, daughter of Frederick Augustus II. Maria Anna Sophia collected porcelain and surely pressed her husband, Elector Maximillian III Joseph (r. 1745–77), to make this one of the industries he patronized—along with silk, stocking, and canvas factories—after the War of the Austrian Succession.[106] The elector donated a small residence on the Isar canal, but the works were soon moved to the Bavarian summer palace compound known as Nymphenburg, and the manufactory would subsequently be known by that name. In 1747 the elector's ministers ventured to Vienna to seek Catholic potters, but Nymphenburg did not possess the Arcanum until after the arrival of J. J. Ringler in 1753. Ringler made possible the production of true porcelain at Nymphenburg, but within three years he had departed for Württemberg, where he finally settled in as director of its Ludwigsburg factory—and he took his precious secrets with him. The Bavarian elector, now cautious, insisted that his next arcanist, P. R. Haertl, write down the secret recipe and give it to the state in exchange for giving him the status of a *Beamter*, a position with tenure. Haertl reluctantly agreed, swapping his secret for a secure salary and pension. Production expanded, and the rococo confections of Nymphenburg's master modeler, Franz Anton Bustelli, earned renown across the continent. By 1761, Nymphenburg could boast 171 employees, making it the fourth-largest firm behind Meissen, the KPM, and the WPM.

Yet Bustelli's fame and the employment numbers of 1761 tell us little about Nymphenburg's more general economic well-being.[107] In the year of its relocation, the factory, unusually, posted a profit: but this amounted to less than one taler, and it had also received a loan from its ducal director that year. It received another loan in 1762, and then a series of subsidies. From 1747 to 1766, in addition to covering its wood and transport costs, the electoral mint (*Münzamt*), which had formal supervision over the manufactory, provided financial assistance to the tune of more than 150,000 T.[108] The firm's sales, too, fell off steeply in 1765–66, in the wake of Bustelli's early death (1763), the devaluation of the Bavarian florin, and a more general crisis in the industry to be detailed in chapter 2. By 1767, the factory had laid off 111 of its workers, leaving only sixty. The Bavarian elector, who was expecting to end subsidies in 1767, had to fork over additional thousands to keep the factory from closing, and by 1771, the firm employed only twenty-eight demoralized ceramicists.[109]

Other cases give us similar examples of financial turmoil. The now-forgotten Kelsterbach manufactory in Hesse-Darmstadt was founded in 1760 on the Main River between Frankfurt and Mainz, home of its main competitor, the Höchst factory (see chapter 4). Perhaps to other men the

bankruptcies of the two previous endeavors founded on the site—one a faiencerie, one a porcelain works—might have been a warning; but Landgrave Ludwig VIII founded a porcelain works there anyway, stipulating
that it would be his own personal property, so that his cabinet ministers
could not complain about the subsidies it received.[110] As arcanist he hired
one Christian Daniel Busch, who had been employed, alongside his father,
at Meissen, but had fled to Vienna, then worked for the Bavarians and in
Paris. For a time, the rococo shepherdesses and cupids made by the master
modeler Vogelmann sold well, but in 1764, both Vogelmann and Busch
left the firm, and budget cuts resulted in the firing of skilled painters. Attempts to continue producing in the rococo style—but with less skill and
cheaper materials—sunk the manufactory, which faced especial challenges
as tiny Hesse-Darmstadt failed to generate appreciable domestic demand.
After Ludwig VIII's death in 1768, the Kelsterbach factory devoted itself
chiefly to faience production—funded by an oddly constructed joint-stock
company—which continued on the same spot until 1840.[111] In the next
chapter, we will follow subsequent attempts at reviving Kelsterbach porcelain, all of which failed.

There were many others—at Rudolstadt, Ludwigsburg, and Frankenthal.
The important story of the private, but usually state-protected firms in the
kaolin-rich towns that cluster in what are now Thuringia and Upper Franconia will occupy us in later chapters. All these firms survived at least a short
while; other start-ups, at Augsburg, Durlach, and Bremen, seem to have succeeded only in producing faience. In any event, the large number of foundings
and failures tells us something important: early eighteenth-century entrepreneurs and statesmen were extremely eager to bring porcelain making to
their regions, both for the purposes of *Glanz*, and in the expectation of en-
ergizing their mercantile economies.

Although this book cannot survey them all, these narratives were replicated across the continent and are in many cases intertwined with our central European stories. For example, Doccia, established near Florence by the
enterprising aristocrat Carlo Ginori, was born in the wake of the passage
of the Grand Duchy of Tuscany into Habsburg hands in 1737.[112] As the

Medici's consul in Lisbon, Ginori's father had procured East Asian treasures for Cosimo III's collections and knew well the value of porcelain imports. The new political relationship enabled Ginori not only to visit Vienna and the Du Paquier manufactory, but also to entice a Viennese arcanist to Florence. There, employing highly skilled Italian craftsmen and casts from bronze and marble workshops, the Doccia manufactory began firing artistic masterpieces, including grand-scale copies of famous sculptures in Roman and Florentine collections, works as technically sophisticated as Kändler's porcelain animals. Ginori, like so many early German makers, lost money for all of the founder's lifetime; only when his more economically minded son Lorenzo took over the manufactory in 1757 and added a line of inexpensive majolica did the firm begin, at last, to make profits.[113]

It is useful to mention another "Italian" firm, as German historians often overlook the marital and sometimes territorial linkages that made for considerable north-south cultural traffic in the eighteenth and nineteenth centuries. Women of royal blood, often forced by incest laws and diplomatic deals to marry abroad—and to take their entourages with them—were important transporters of taste. The founding of Capodimonte in Naples, for example, was surely inspired by the Saxon princess Maria Amalia, granddaughter of Augustus II and sister of Maria Anna Sophia, whom we have met as the wife of Bavaria's elector Maximilian III Joseph, and the patroness of Bavaria's porcelain collection at Nymphenburg.[114] Maria Amalia married Charles VII, king of the Two Sicilies in 1738, and production of soft-paste wares began on the grounds of their new palace at Capodimonte, on the outskirts of Naples, a decade later. The palace itself was equipped with an elaborate porcelain room, modeled on the scores of others now gracing Germanic palaces. But when Charles inherited the Spanish throne in 1759, he moved to Madrid and took his porcelain factory with him, establishing a new manufactory at Buen Retiro. The Capodimonte factory was ordered disbanded and razed, though Charles's son and successor in Naples, Ferdinand IV, would found a new royal Neapolitan factory at Portici, site of the magnificent collections from Herculaneum, in 1771. The factory moved back to Naples in 1773 but apparently garnered no profits.[115] Neither Joseph Bonaparte nor his queen consort, Julie Clary, cared much about porcelain, and after 1806, production fizzled, but the firm's exquisite early wares testify to the artistry it was able to command, and its stylistic linkages with Meissen and the other central European manufactories.

In Russia, czars from the time of Ivan the Terrible had been trying, to no avail, to get central Asian caravan leaders to extract the porcelain secret from their Chinese trading partners. Lacking a competent arcanist, Elizabeth I nonetheless founded an imperial manufactory in St. Petersburg in 1744, giving it the exclusive right, and obligation, to produce for the crown. Petersburg's supposed monopoly did not prevent Catherine I from also giving the English banker Frances Gardner a privilege to set up a manufactory at Verbliki, near Russia's earlier capital city, Moscow. This enterprise also served the court and nobility but like so many others may never have made a profit.[116] The Swedes and Danes also founded privileged factories, although they did not enter the hard-paste market until the 1770s. The Czechs and Hungarians might also have had their manufactories—but they were forbidden to compete with the Habsburg's WPM. Their porcelain ambitions would have to wait.

The most important, and longest-lasting, of the Germans' continental competitors, not surprisingly, were the French. It is worth tracing in a bit more detail the evolution of that rival mercantile effort, for a number of factors—the much deeper pockets of the king, the greater orientation to artistry, and the much larger and less fragmented French aristocratic market—made for important differences in the framework of France's porcelain industry. We have already met the French as early experts in faience making, and as is well known, it was the French who, by the time of Böttger's discovery, had already wrested the lead in cultural trendsetting away from the Italians in spheres such as theater, painting, architecture, and science. French pride in its artistic leadership would shape the nation's porcelain industry as well. It was here, too, that new eating and dining habits were evolving, such as the serving of elaborate breakfasts and dining "à la française," with a full, matching place setting allotted to each individual diner (see chapter 3). Faience, or imported Asian wares, would have sufficed for this, but the Bourbons had observed Meissen's achievements and did not wish to be outdone.

In 1740, the king's chief financial adviser and director of the French East India Company, Jean-Henry-Louis Orry de Fulvy, settled a group of elite craftsmen on the grounds of the royal hunting lodge at Vincennes and provided them with ten thousand livres from Louis XV's purse to make Saxon-style porcelain for the crown. They succeeded in making high-quality soft-paste wares, and in 1745, Fulvy's manufactory received a privilege confirming its *exclusive* right to manufacture porcelain after the "façon de Saxe" in France. The firm was now incorporated, and financed with the enormous sum of eight hundred thousand livres by seven wealthy backers, including several "tax farmers" and members of the guild of traders in luxury goods, the *marchands-merciers*.[117] At Vincennes, too, potters had difficulty in actually making hard-paste porcelain and in obtaining the highest-quality clay. Until 1769, in fact, when kaolin deposits were found in France, the French royal makers had to depend on clay imports from the area around Passau, in Bavaria, a dangerous dependency for a mercantile firm![118]

Vincennes's porcelain recipe did produce shimmering white wares, and the French manufactory excelled in design and artistry. It grew famous for the quality of its painting and for its charming pastoral figurines after the hugely popular rococo artist François Boucher, as well as for its imitations of Japanese Imari wares. With the help of chemists from the Académie des Sciences, it was able to fire appealing new colors (such as "bleu du roi" and "rose Pompadour"). The king and his mistresses were pleased, and in 1745 His Majesty decreed that only Vincennes was allowed to produce porcelain with colored decoration or gilding. Louis would later ban the production of all painted white ceramics elsewhere in France.[119] In 1751, after the death of Orry de Fulvy, the king dissolved the corporation and took a quarter of the stock. Two years later, he assumed full ownership, partly to please his mistress, France's now-reigning tastemaker Jeanne Antoinette Poisson, Madame de Pompadour. La Pompadour would take a keen interest in porcelain, bolstering the commodity's association with intimate female spaces and the fashionable home furnishings of courtesans. In addition to making many purchases, Madame de Pompadour bestowed on the factory a more suitable property in the town of Sèvres, on the road between Paris and Versailles, and the works and workers were relocated from Vincennes. By 1760, Louis had forced out the last remaining shareholder, and declared himself the sole owner of the Manufacture Royale de Porcelains de France à Sèvres, the new name by which the French royal manufactory would be known.[120]

Sèvres, it should be noted, had from the beginning advantages that our German firms did not. Its royal patrons were extremely wealthy and extravagant connoisseurs. The French manufactory could draw on scientists and artists from a kingdom with an enormous, highly skilled population. Its privilege provided for a monopoly on sales throughout Louis's realm, where, especially in Paris, the market for household luxuries was booming. In fact, however, even under such conditions, porcelain making never proved to be a surefire investment. Labor and materials costs were astronomical, and the French aristocracy, kings included, never restricted their purchases to Sèvres. Sèvres later experienced competition, hardships, and periods of tighter budgets—during the revolution, not surprisingly, and afterward as well. But for the French, the profitability of the royal manufactory would always be far less significant than its artistic leadership, a hierarchy of values that our German firms, especially by the nineteenth century, could not afford (see chapters 4–6). This emphasis on artistry would give the French royal manufactory a specific cultural significance, and do much to shape the European porcelain marketplace, for all.

A brief survey of one last national "industry" offers us the opportunity to reflect, again, on the unique patterns developing in central Europe. The English porcelain industry is perhaps least like any of the continental manufacturers, with the exception of the Dutch, whose efforts were similarly directed at the less exalted forms of ceramics production. The English had only one court, but a large quantity of rich, middling, and upper-middling non-nobles, who also wanted to set a fine table or serve tea in style. A few entrepreneurs sought to introduce porcelain making, beginning with Chelsea, a pottery founded in 1745 by French Huguenots in what was then London's outskirts. Chelsea adopted continental soft-paste recipes to make, first, copies of oriental porcelains, and then imitations of Meissen wares. Chelsea, however, had no royal privileges or monopolistic rights, and very shortly afterward, the Bow works in East London and a factory in Bristol (1749) started production. When the Bristol firm folded in 1752, its stock and molds were taken over by the Worcester "Tonquin" manufactory, which originated in a partnership between a doctor and an apothecary. Worcester's founders claimed to have developed their recipe by experimenting in a makeshift furnace at the back of the apothecary's shop. In fact they probably took their recipe from Bristol, for it included the use of the mineral talc steatite, commonly found in soapstone, which provided a white color, but also made teapots susceptible to cracking when filled with boiling water. The founders obtained capital for their venture from thirteen private investors by showing off samples of their work. Entering a market suffused with inexpensive Chinese wares, Worcester experimented with shapes not made in Asia, such as gravy boats, and by 1750 it had halted production of chinoiserie in favor of producing imitations of Meissen. Worcester's most important contribution to the making of affordable porcelain lay in its being the first to adopt transfer printing to ceramics, a process in which a copperplate etching was inked, and then the pattern stamped on special paper. This in turn was pasted on ceramic vessels; during firing the paper burned away, leaving a standardized image on the piece. Worcester first used transfer printing for black overglaze designs, such as their famous "King of Prussia" mugs, and then, beginning in 1757, for blue underglaze printing.[121]

Already some characteristic patterns can be seen in the Worcester experience that will later prove important in British porcelain making more generally: the absence of monopolies, the pooling of familial capital, the adoption of technologies to speed and cheapen production. These stand in sharp contrast to the forms of financing and patronage employed on the continent—at Sèvres, for example. In fact, the respective business models adopted by these manufactories differed more than did their styles, marketing ploys, or conditions inside the factory, which displayed remarkable similarities across the European board—probably because all the firms spent so much time and effort in copying each other.

What had uncertain and dangerous overseas commercial ventures in the ceramics trade such as that of the ill-starred *White Lion* wrought? By the mid-eighteenth century, imitations and elaborations of Chinese porcelain had created new forms of artistry, production, and consumption in Europe in general and central Europe in particular. In Saxony, the recipe that allowed these developments (the Arcanum) had been discovered, or, more properly, reinvented, and a means discovered by which central Europe might distinguish itself as a place where tasteful luxury goods were made. "Germany is properly regarded as the country of beautiful porcelain," stated the Italo-French nobleman Cosimo Alessandro Collini in his *Lettres sur les Allemandes* (1790). "Every prince of this country seems to have invested his hopes for glory, so to speak, in having his own manufactory."[122] Mercantilism, the philosophy and policy that gave ambitious and jealous princes incentives beyond *Glanz* and glory to subsidize these developments, did not always—or even often—operate according to plan. But by the 1760s, aesthetic obsession, cultural competition, and economic *Staatsräson* had made porcelain a must-have for members of Germandom's courts, and a must-make for princes aspiring to demonstrate their good taste and command of the marketplace. The table had been set, as it were, for the deep entanglement of porcelain and "national" pride.

Chapter 2

The Challenge of Wedgwood and the Rise of the Private Firm

When Friedrich von Hohenzollern, later to be known as Frederick the Great, was born in 1712, Prussia was something of a marshy backwater. Frederick's great grandfather Frederick William (r. 1640–99), the so-called Great Elector of Brandenburg-Prussia, had begun building a large army, a tradition his successors continued.[1] But in other respects, the kingdom remained weaker and poorer than many of its neighbors to the west and south. Geographically, Prussia could not boast the hexagonal regularity of France and resembled instead an unfinished jigsaw puzzle, its non-contiguous territories a cartographer's nightmare (see map 1). Still recovering from the demographic devastations of the Thirty Years' War, it remained overwhelmingly rural and subject to periodic famine. Prussia's commerce was heavily taxed, limited by guild and travel restrictions, and overwhelmingly local. Its roads were deplorable, and its towns were small and inward looking. Only 5 percent of the population lived in cities over five thousand, and 80 percent of the remainder lived in the countryside.[2] The nobility was not very wealthy or cultivated, and most townsmen lived in small, dark, unadorned rooms, often carpeted with sand. This was no place for a modern luxury industry to thrive.

When Frederick died in 1786, however, Prussia was a quite different kingdom, thanks partly to his wars, partly to his reforms, and partly to the abatement of the plague and a gradual improvement of agricultural yields. Immediately upon his ascension to the throne in 1740, the young king declared war on Austria and managed to grab the coal-rich and strategically vital territory of Silesia, an annexation confirmed by his victory in the Seven Years' War (1756–63). Prussia's population thereby tripled, and several million more subjects were added when the kingdom shared in the first partition of Poland in 1772. By the time of Frederick's death in 1786, the population had grown from a bit under 2.8 million in 1740 to a bit over 5.6 million; the kingdom now boasted an army five times larger than it had been in 1713.[3] But Frederick had also been active in the support of commerce, small industries, and agricultural improvement; notoriously, he championed the cultivation of potatoes, which were much more nutritious than traditional grains. He founded a Royal Bank (1765) and an Overseas Trading Corporation (Seehandlung; 1772), and funded canal building and land reclamation. Not all his economic activities were wise, and none of them was selfless; of his 2,775,000 T total expenditures on manufactures, some 1,840,000 T was devoted to a largely failed attempt to found a silk industry able to best the French, and he regularly strong-armed wealthy civilians, especially Jews and émigrés, into operating businesses he wished to see flourish.[4] He was not trying to destroy the feudal order, or to advance capitalist practices, but rather to strengthen his own autocratic state. Even so, he laid the foundations for a particular form of Prussian economic modernization, one in which luxury making was expected to play a central role.

Frederick's cultural policies contributed equally to opening up Prussia to foreign ideas and influences. A man of enlightened and libertine tastes, Frederick made it clear that the churches would no longer dominate cultural matters. Extending his predecessors' policies of rewarding Huguenot entrepreneurs willing to establish trades in Prussian lands, he encouraged skilled foreign workers to settle in his domains, whatever their religious convictions. He built a new summer palace, Sans Souci, outside of Berlin and filled it with secular art, some of it rather risqué; he wrote treatises in French and invited Voltaire, the great critic of Christian cruelties and superstitions, to stay at his palace; he put another Frenchman in charge of the Berlin Academy of Sciences. His capital city also began, finally, to grow, and by 1786, Berlin was approaching the population levels of Rome, Madrid, and Vienna (150,000). Although it still lagged far behind Paris (400,000) and London (800,000), and its cultural treasures could not yet rival those of Dresden, Vienna, and Munich, Berlin now signaled its aspiration to become a city of culture as well as of commerce.

What was true of Prussia was true to a greater or lesser degree of a number of central Europe's larger states. Just after midcentury, these economies began to expand, thanks to the opening of a new era of sustained population growth and to the beginnings of proto-industrialization and production for the market. The Seven Years' War interrupted this evolution, and a banking crisis and economic downturn rippled across central Europe in its wake. But agricultural production and trade rebounded quickly, aided by a new generation of reform-minded rulers and ministers who began to see the benefits of improving land, dissolving local privileges (often so that the states could issue their own), easing transport, and introducing "manufactures" of different kinds into their domains. Cultural changes came here, too, as German merchants, artists, scholars, and nobles became more mobile, venturing to Italy to revel in the arts, to France to enjoy theater and cuisine, to England to study technological advances. Dutch traders, in particular, made deeper inroads into the Empire, offering German consumers access to "colonial" commodities such as sugar, coffee, tea, and cotton textiles. Courtiers seem to have remained the chief consumers of such products, but in the century's last decades we see demand increasing for a few more modestly priced non-necessities such as playing cards, straw hats, or umbrellas, which Cissie Fairchild has memorably dubbed "populuxe" items.[5] Although it is hard to track this process, porcelain, one of the region's most widely available and symbolically resonant commodities, opens a window into the gradual integration of more and more central European consumers into this dynamic commercial and cultural world.

By examining the new economy in the making during Frederick's reign through the prism of the porcelain industry we will surely neglect some of the crucial aspects of this change, including increasing agricultural yields and the expansion of textile manufacturing. But perhaps by focusing our attention on porcelain we can obtain a better view of other aspects of central Europe's economic modernization that are often left out. Domestically made porcelain, as we have seen, began as a courtly luxury but very quickly also began to be sold as one of the Germanys' most widely desired "populuxe" commodities. If princes first commanded its making chiefly to advertise their refinement, they very soon began to wish, too, for sales and profits; and as many states and a few private producers entered the market, intense rivalry between neighboring firms for exports generated competitions based not only on quality, but also on price. In the porcelain industry, we see the increasing integration of courtly and middle-class markets and firms beginning to seek the means to reduce production costs and consumer prices. And we see large numbers of goods of many styles being made by non-mechanized manufactories, a phenomena we might call artisanal mass production. These features do not capture the central European economy as a whole, but they do nicely illuminate the particular ways in which this region began its evolution away from mercantile and court-dominated consumption toward a freer and wider marketplace, a patchy and fitful process that helped to shape the cultural as well as economic history of the region.

By focusing on the evolution of this particular commodity, too, we can see how German statesmen, artisans, and entrepreneurs sought to make their way in a wider global and especially European economy, into which the British and Dutch, in particular, had introduced capitalist aspirations, financial instruments, and forms of behavior. It is senseless to define capitalism, historically, as a system of perfectly "free" markets, as nowhere has trade ever been entirely free of restrictions or protections for certain products or persons. The British and Dutch systems certainly were not "free markets," and indeed the lucrative British and Dutch East and West India Companies not only were trading monopolies but could also count on state military support for their adventures overseas. But in the eighteenth century, the Netherlands and Great Britain came closest to possessing "capitalist" marketplaces, in which private individuals or corporations were expected to control the nation's means of production and to engage in commerce for the purposes of profit. In neither country did private individuals need a privilege to risk their money on ventures of their choosing and spend their profits as they liked. By contrast, central Europe's many economies were restricted by the system of legal privileges—including the guild system—and by the fact that most "capital" was held in the form of land or in serfs and was thus unavailable for investment in trade or manufacturing. Those who held privileges did not wish to lose them, and as we saw in chapter 1, princes attempting to found new industries often opted simply to bypass such local barriers and set up their own mercantile operations. By the century's end, most rulers and higher officials remained committed to state-backed modernization, but some, at least, began to take note of the benefits the Britons and Dutch had reaped by promoting "free" trade. For many reasons, central Europeans could not develop capitalist systems exactly like those of Britain or the Netherlands, nor did they want to do so; but these systems did impinge, increasingly, on their economies and force them to respond.

Exemplary of this process is the enormous impact made on the central European porcelain industry by the efforts and successes of the English entrepreneurial genius Josiah Wedgwood (1730–95). Wedgwood, who very nearly realized his aspiration to become "Vase Maker to the Universe," showed continental porcelain makers that marketing and salesmanship mattered; he also demonstrated the benefits of ceaseless R&D to perfect both products and the efficiency of their manufacture. The huge popularity of his modestly priced wares overseas compelled local makers to move, gradually, from bespoke commissions to semistandardized products, advertised in catalogs. In surveying Wedgwood's impact in the Germanys, we can see just how difficult it was for court-oriented, mercantile makers to negotiate this transition; in fact, ministerial pressure was often necessary to make changes happen. In the final section of the chapter, we will also survey the challenges the entrepreneurial ceramicists of the Thuringian forests faced in attempting to imitate Wedgwood's entrepreneurial successes. Discerning a market for lower-quality porcelains, and seeking to lower labor and materials costs in order to undersell the state manufactories, these firms extended the reach of capitalist competition into the porcelain industry. If such competition proved, in the longer run, unstoppable, this does not mean that anyone—entrepreneurs, artisans, state officials, or consumers—adjusted to it quickly or cheerfully. Capitalism did not conquer central Europe without a fight—indeed, in some cases, it did not conquer at all, and the shades of mercantilism linger today in some of its economies' little-studied corners.

In this chapter, we, along with our porcelain makers, will begin to confront an intrinsic tension in the industry that was already dimly visible in Augustus II's time, but became ever more pronounced as the market widened: the desire to create the sort of artistic objects that reflected the splendor of the prince and his realm versus the need to produce a profit for the state's coffers. This tension will accompany us throughout the book. It would prove especially painful for state-sponsored porcelain makers, for whom *Glanz* had been, as it were, baked into the recipe from the start. Even in porcelain's "golden age," manufacturers scrambled not only to please the changeable palates of princely patrons (chapter 3), but also to establish businesses that could weather the eighteenth century's political and economic upheavals. It was not so easy, after all, to produce "white gold."

Transformations and Continuities in the Mercantile Economy after 1763

Although much less studied than the French Revolution and Napoleonic Wars, the Seven Years' War was, for European geopolitics, arguably just as important a turning point. Crucially, the war confirmed Britain's ascendancy in overseas trade, significantly increasing at France's expense its colonial holdings in North America and the Caribbean as well as in India. The war embarrassed the French monarchy and left it in deeper economic distress. For central Europe, the conflict marked the first real intervention of Russia into continental events; Austria was compelled to recognize formally its loss of Silesia and to endure the new military clout exercised by Bavaria, Saxony, and Hanover. For Frederick the Great, it was a make-or-break war; in its course the Prussian king came very close indeed to earning the title "Frederick the

Loser" rather than "Frederick the Great." As it happened, however, Frederick emerged from the war a victor, and Prussia earned the right to be counted among the European great powers. This crucial change in the Germanic balance of power proved permanent and prepared the way for Prussia's later leading role in German and continental politics. Taking Silesia also offered the Prussians a new source of cheap labor and raw materials, including wood, coal, and good clays, all of which would prove very important in the German porcelain industry's nineteenth-century transformations.

Frederick was by no means the only German sovereign to take a deeper interest in economic matters after 1763. In the short term, the Seven Years' War had done considerable damage to continental economies and currencies. The ripple of bank failures and bankruptcies in Hamburg and Amsterdam that arrived on the heels of the war further disrupted trade by severely tightening credit at a time of skyrocketing food costs.[6] But in the longer term, the war spurred rulers to intervene more actively in their economies, to put people to work—in workhouses if not elsewhere—and to establish a secure tax base and dependable food supplies.

In the war's wake, a new generation of reform-minded princes and ministers began to absorb physiocratic doctrines, which taught that economic improvement began with the more efficient cultivation of land and the elimination of spending that did not lead to greater national productivity. To make the appropriate reforms, close study of the state's resources and practices was needed, as was ministerial oversight and steering to ensure that changes were actually implemented. These aspirations drove the development of what was known as cameralism, a kind of expertise in state administration that played an essential role in professionalizing German bureaucracies and convincing rulers to undertake reforms. Although many princes continued to spend a great deal on the court and to worry about keeping cash inside their borders, increasingly physiocratic thinking and cameralist practices ate away at mercantilist systems and inclined both rulers and their advisers to think differently about their states: less as the monarch's patrimony, an assemblage of his and other nobles' estates, and more as economic entities composed of resources (land, people, salt, wood, precious metals) that needed to be enumerated and managed by competent state officials. We can see here the groundwork being laid for the proto-industrial development of central Europe's economies and, politically, for what, in the nineteenth century, would be called "nation-states."

How much reformist princes shaped the economy and how much the economic transformations shaped princely reform we need not here debate; the two clearly went hand in hand. The foundations of both lay in the fact that though smaller wars continued to rage, the famines and plagues of the past had abated, and population growth was sustained, as the sixteen to eighteen million estimated inhabitants in 1750 of the territory that would later make up Bismarck's German Empire grew to about twenty-four million by 1800.[7] More people and better management helped to expand market-oriented agriculture (as opposed to cultivation merely to maintain the lord and his manor at customary levels). More people also meant that some could be spared farming duties to engage in manufacturing, which princes encouraged by relaxing guild bans on finishing products in the non-guilded countryside. In response, cottage cloth production surged. By the 1770s, Silesia alone had 230,000 rural linen makers, and Austria's state-owned woolen manufactory headquartered in the town of Linz farmed out tasks to thirty-five thousand workers, of whom four-fifths worked at home.[8]

Encouraged by the rising volume of global trade, private entrepreneurship expanded in the second half of the eighteenth century. All kinds of people founded firms—merchants (including Jews), moonlighting officials, even pastors—and set about all manner of operations, weaving silk, refining sugar, printing wallpaper. In Electoral Saxony, blessed with a comparatively prosperous and highly skilled population, risk takers like these managed to establish some 150 new businesses between 1763 and 1800. Although that averaged only about four foundings a year (in a state of about two million inhabitants),[9] within central Europe these were remarkable numbers—a propitious omen for a future in which Saxony would boast the most industrialized population in the German states. Elsewhere, too, princes proved willing to offer gifts or loans to those willing to start up businesses in their domains and increasingly preferred supporting others to assuming full ownership.[10]

They aided employers—and angered clergymen and guildsmen—by eliminating religious holidays and attempting to restrict the privileges of the urban guilds, incentives Prussia had employed as early as 1731.[11] In imitation of the French, many German princes, including the Habsburg rulers Joseph II and his mother, Maria Theresa, attempted to reduce and centralize the collection of internal tariffs. Confronting these and other new claims on the public purse, cities and states also began to repeal paternalist social policies and curtail poor relief, "one of the basic preconditions," Ernst Schubert argues, "for economic liberalization, or, more precisely, the transfer of social problems to a self-organizing economy."[12]

Here, then, we find a kind of enlightened, ministerial absolutism and the first forms of economic liberalization emerging in tandem, the states acting to speed up the disintegration of the old "Society of Orders" with its particularistic privileges and paternalist customs. In another way, too, the princes of this period accelerated social and cultural changes by means of their increasingly secular inclinations and often libertine tastes. Frederick is again a good example here, as he stocked his palaces with French books and Italian art and much preferred playing the flute to prayer. Some of his noble contemporaries, such as Count Johann Karl Philipp von Cobenzl, plenipotentiary to Maria Theresa in the Austrian Netherlands, were equally worldly in their affairs and equally dedicated to expanding their collections—of books, paintings, and exotic "curiosities." Committed to a mercantile belief in the need to encourage the arts in his Habsburgian province, Cobenzl was instrumental in obtaining state protection for his local porcelain manufactory (Tournai), saving it from almost certain closure; regrettably, his passion for porcelain contributed greatly to his own bankruptcy in 1764.[13] The patronage and consumption patterns of these greater nobles sanctioned and stimulated lesser princes and *their* courtiers to expand purchases of non-necessary commodities just as townsmen, too, began to consume more goods that contributed to individual comfort or pleasure.[14] In this way, German forms of social emulation contributed to the modernization of Old Regime society.[15]

How much consumption of non-necessities occurred beyond the upper reaches of central European society is a subject that still needs study.

Unquestionably, even by 1750, middling-level consumption here lagged behind Dutch and British levels. But after that time, we can, perhaps, see signs of change. Often the first "luxury" that consumers allowed themselves was more and better food, and indeed, statistics show a significant increase in food imports into Prussia's core lands between 1720 and 1781, including a 79.1 percent increase in per capita sugar imports and a whopping 835 percent increase in coffee imports.[16] The rising number of coffee roasters, refiners of sugar, and pastry chefs (Konditoren) in Prussia between 1750 and 1801 offers a picture of the expansion of professionals who specialized in the preparation of coffee and sweets (see chapter 3).[17] Fashion sensitivity and with it, the purchasing of non-essential clothing—often the next luxury consumers chose—gradually increased.[18] Tablewares and cooking utensils came further down in the list of consumers' desires, and their ownership is difficult to gauge, in part because many were too trivial to be mentioned in inventories. In the absence of good data for central Europe, and judging from the cross-national comparisons we have for other consumer items, we can guess that the statistics for middle-class ownership of earthenware in 1725 for England (57 percent of the population) and for France (44 percent) were probably much too high for central Europe even in 1765.[19] Pictorial evidence suggests that most central Europeans continued to equip their kitchens with non-breakable pewter, tin, and wood items, adding earthenware jugs as needed; note that the image of the typical kitchen depicted in figure 2.1 was probably made in the 1820s, and does not yet feature any fine ceramics at all. But the household's more precious vessels were probably on display elsewhere, and we can guess that a family able to afford so many servants and copper molds probably did own at least some faience or porcelain by this time.

There are faint signs that a "retailing revolution," well underway in England, had also begun in the Empire's larger towns.[20] At the beginning of the century, courtiers seem to have purchased their luxuries directly from artisanal workshops, or from a small number of high-end luxury merchants. Augustus the Strong, for example, purchased the lion's share of his East Asian porcelain "and other Indian lacquered things" from a Dutch widow named

2.1. German kitchen, ca. 1820

Quite typically, this southern German illustration of the proper kitchen features earthenware vessels, pewter platters, and copper molds affixed to the walls. Not an item of porcelain is visible in this clearly upper-middle-class kitchen.

Elisabeth de Bassetouche, who in turn acquired them either from the Leipzig fair, or, more probably, directly from Dutch merchants.[21] After her passing in 1730, Bassetouche's heirs continued selling from a well-stocked shop in Dresden, close to the palace and the Saxon court. In 1731 Augustus II purchased some 4,970 T worth of Japanese porcelain here, and a little over a quarter century later, in 1757, his son bought out the store—at a discount—for 6,754 T.[22] Bassetouche's business was exceptional in dealing in finished goods and foreign products; most other luxury suppliers were the artisans themselves, and guild restrictions generally limited their workshops to one master and one apprentice, which made capital formation difficult. The average furniture painter for example, employed in decorative work similar to that of ceramics makers, had little hope of commercial success. Such a painter, according to Wilhelm Treue, "without a groschen saved or any start-up capital for a larger workshop, died where and in the same condition as he had lived."[23] But as the century waned, a few wealthy artisans proved willing and able to try their hands at retail sales. One of the earliest successes, the Mainz furniture maker David Röntgen, obtained permission to employ a remarkably large staff (twelve to fifteen in 1770) and was reputedly selling 100,000 T in furnishings annually by the 1780s. Regrettably, by 1794, he was broke.[24] But others, too, came along, and in cities and larger towns, market squares increasingly became home to small retailers of glass, plaster casts, and porcelains.[25]

One challenge to the entrepreneur of that day would have been the difficulty of generalizing about who, exactly, the new consumers in this world might be, and how much money they might be willing to spend on luxury items. Sèvres is ahead of us, argued one would-be director of Prussia's Royal Porcelain Manufacture (the KPM) in 1788, "because we don't have anything like a public that is prepared to pay 30 or 40 écus for a cup."[26] But while it was true that central Europe had fewer persons than France who were willing to pay the equivalent of two months' wages for a skilled workman for a coffee cup, with so many states with so many capitals (*Residenzen*), it *could* boast a significant number of courtiers and a rising number of well-paid bureaucrats. In Württemberg, for example, the court numbered 1,130 in 1807, and 1,510 by 1812; in Saxony, twelve hundred nobles and functionaries were in attendance at court.[27] It was in such circles that the *Journal des Luxus und der Moden*—founded in 1785—was being read, and it was among such folk that credit was available for purchasing luxuries. We must not forget that consumption of most goods was extremely uneven; if the exceptionally rich were already consuming more than 1.5 kilograms of sugar a year in the sixteenth century, this average was not reached for the German population as a whole until 1860.[28] The urban or semi-urban "residence" towns were much bigger consumers of luxury goods than were the more numerous smaller villages and rural manors of the Empire. Thus coffee consumption in the Habsburg capital of Vienna was three times the Austrian average.[29]

Finally, in spite of some attempts at the liberalization of the economy on the part of individual states, central Europe remained largely devoted to mercantile and protectionist practices. In response to rising imports, many businesses lobbied for, and received, tariff protections or even full bans on the import of specific commodities. Coffee, a highly relevant commodity for our story, is a good example. As imports rose steeply after midcentury, many princes slapped on high tariffs or tried to ban the commodity entirely, even threatening to smash coffeepots and cups. In 1764, motivated by rising food costs brought on by the Seven Years' War, the Duke of Braunschweig banned the sale of coffee (along with wine, tea, and sugar) to commoners; innkeepers along major roads were to keep diaries recording use of such commodities, and to be fined 20 T if they served local or foreign "Landleute." The decree did reduce consumption somewhat, though every locality asked for an exception.[30] Frederick the Great, typically, went further. In 1766 he made coffee imports a state monopoly and in 1777 importuned his subjects to start their days not with coffee but with a much more nutritious beer soup, as had His Majesty in his childhood. When these efforts failed to reduce sales, in 1781 he declared a state monopoly on roasting and hired four hundred "invalids" from the state hospital as "Kaffeeriecher," or coffee smellers, tasked with sniffing Berlin and Potsdam breezes to root out rogue roasters. Prices of coffee beans, accordingly, rose out of the reach of the average consumer, at about 1 T for ten ounces of coffee.[31]

Like other bans during the period, however, Frederick's coffee laws did not work. They simply led to increased smuggling and to the development of a bewildering array of substitutes and additives. The most palatable were roasted malt (making for *Malzkaffee* or *Bauernkaffee*) and chicory (*Preussische Kaffee*), sometimes mixed with small quantities of real coffee beans. Probably without these cheaper substitutes, coffee drinking would not have caught on as it did, and the substitutes themselves became big business. Frederick's successor did away with the ban, and coffee drinking became a German habit. In 1790, a foreign traveler reported that "in Germany, everyone, from the beggar to the super rich, drinks coffee, once, twice, three or four times a day, with or without milk. . . . It is the nectar of the Germans."[32] By 1797, in Prussia alone, 1,228 people were employed in roasting chicory,[33] while sugar refining and the making of porcelain coffee wares, along with the other industries that supported the coffee habit and its surrogates, experienced a related surge.

In 1798 the yearbook of the Prussian monarchy dealt a blow to the country's state-supported entrepreneurs by declaring Prussia's decision to discontinue the subsidizing of factories—perhaps gladdening the hearts of their would-be competitors.[34] But the state's parallel desire to keep businesses operating and workers employed meant that in practice the system changed relatively little. Subsidies to favored employers continued, although often at levels insufficient to enable—and oversight inadequate to compel—modernization. In 1782, for example, Prussian glassmakers had been commanded by the Forestry Bureau to stop using the king's wood and were given subsidies to transition to the use of coal. Workers resisted, arguing that coal soot contaminated the quality of their products. Four years later the factories were still operating exclusively with wood. Frustrated, the state allowed the glassmakers another decade of privileges and dispensations, thereby discouraging private firms—but then began resisting requests for subsidies and perks.[35] It would be decades before Prussian glassmaking completed a full transition to coal, and it eventually did so, perhaps, more in response to competition from Bohemian rivals than in response to ministerial nagging.

The travails of late eighteenth-century glassmaking mirrored those of the porcelain industry in Prussia and the other German states. Both industries' histories illustrate the difficulties and contradictions that accompanied the efforts of these relatively small and poor monarchical states to extricate themselves from mercantile practices. In the case of porcelain, the retreat from mercantilism and forced embrace of new production and marketing practices was bound up with the attempt of state firms to face their most severe market challenge yet, that posed by the Staffordshire hustler, Josiah Wedgwood.

The Challenge of Wedgwood

This is not the place, and I am not the historian, to offer an in-depth portrait of the "Potteries," the eighteenth-century term for the many English ceramics makers clustered in northern Staffordshire, around the town of Stoke-on-Trent.[36] But this region and its most famous innovator and entrepreneur, Josiah Wedgwood, play a key role in our Central European story too. As suggested in chapter 1, ceramics making here had different social and economic foundations from central Europe's, and we can learn much from the contrast. On the production end, England had no guild restrictions or royal monopolies in ceramics making, and Staffordshire in particular was chock full of potters. These skilled craftsmen belonged to a world of literate and ambitious English tinkerers, whose proximity and access to information allowed them both to adopt others' innovations and to add their own improvements.[37] They had already entered the age of artisanal mass production by dividing labor internally and between workshops and had pioneered techniques, such as slip casting, press molding, stamping, and lathe turning, to speed the making of identical wares.[38] Josiah Wedgwood had served two apprenticeships to potters who believed in scientific experimentation, investment in the latest technologies, and workplace discipline.[39] When he struck out on his own in 1759, he was one among many of Staffordshire's modernizing potters.

Wedgwood's location gave him a number of natural as well as commercial and technological advantages. Burslem, where he began his life and career, was located near the River Weaver, navigable after 1733 to the busy port of Liverpool. Distances between population centers were shorter in England than in central Europe, and roads were much better, especially by the later eighteenth century. Although Staffordshire clay was good for earthenware products, local potteries had already begun aspiring higher, importing whiter clay from southwest England. Wedgwood would himself—briefly—use imperial connections to extract white "Cherokee Clay" from North Carolina, turning back to British sources only after America's independence was won in 1783. Coal, which Wedgwood would use to fire his pottery and stoke his steam engines, was nearby, plentiful, and cheap. His adoption of this more efficient energy source decades ahead of continental makers would demonstrate his technological virtuosity as well as give him a marked competitive advantage in the global ceramics market.

If continental producers benefited from proximity to their princes, Wedgwood's success owed much to his family: the uncle who trained him, and then rented him his first workshop; his wife, Sally, who brought considerable wealth into the marriage at a crucial moment (1764) and shared his work until his death in 1795; his cousin, tellingly nicknamed "Useful Tom," who managed the works when Josiah was away.[40] As Leonore Davidoff and Catherine Hall showed long ago, this pooling of family resources was essential to middle-class capital formation after 1750,[41] but Wedgwood was most certainly one of those who knew best how to enroll his extended household in his operations.

Josiah also profited from Britain's much larger market for moderately priced household goods, and, thanks to a drop in the price of tea after about 1720, a huge demand for tea sets. Women, even poorer women, wanted serviceable and if possible fashionable sets and seem to have found the wherewithal to buy them.[42] The period's teapots were also susceptible to cracking and breakage, which meant a frequent turnover in each household's wares. Moreover, thanks to the Navigation Laws and the expansion of its empire, England's share in world trade burgeoned. Exports of glass and earthenware, Maxine Berg notes, rose from 785,975 pieces in 1700 to well over thirty *million* pieces in 1800.[43] Wedgwood's products, after the 1760s, contributed much to this export success, although they were not, of course, the whole of it.

In 1765, at about the time this chapter begins, Wedgwood had just perfected his recipe for a fine, light-colored stoneware he called "creamware" and had completed his first major commission—a tea service featuring green flowers against a gold background—for the queen consort. Hearing that Queen Charlotte was pleased, he then sent a box of other vessels as a gift and by 1766, Wedgwood was advertising his creamware as "Queen's Ware" and himself as "Potter to the Queen"[44]—which meant only that he received commissions from the queen, not that she subsidized his manufactory. His cultivation of the court was not, then, a bid for direct support, but a marketing strategy. And it worked.

While other Staffordshire potters believed that making "uniques" would never cover costs, Wedgwood understood the value of making a splash. In his view, tastes flowed downward, from the "head" to the "inferior members," and thus producers ought first to please princes and aristocrats, even when commissions were difficult to execute and the likelihood of nonpayment strong. He cultivated the friendship of the well-educated shipping agent Thomas Bentley, who alerted him to the fact that aristocratic tastes in the mid-1760s were evolving away from rococo and chinoiserie toward neoclassicism. Through Bentley, Wedgwood met other tastemakers, including Lady Jane Cathcart, sister of Sir William Hamilton, Britain's ambassador to Naples, who was a passionate student of volcanoes and collector of classical art. Lady Cathcart gave Wedgwood prepublication copies of images from her brother's catalog of his Greek and Roman vases (published in 1766–67), and the potter committed himself to the campaign, promoted especially by the libertine Society of Dilettanti, to revive the arts in England through the imitation of classical antiquities.[45] Bentley and Wedgwood formed a partnership, with Bentley's networks and commercial savvy complementing Wedgwood's technological and artistic skills. In 1767 they opened a new factory dubbed "Etruria" in Newcastle upon Tyne and began producing copies of the black basalt wares and red- and black-figure classical vases featured in Hamilton's catalog.[46] They were immediately successful, earning profits as well as connoisseurs' esteem. But Wedgwood wisely recognized that fashions are fleeting, and in the early 1770s, the potter turned his attention to the reproduction of Roman cameo gems, seeking to set a very white biscuit off against a deeply colored background.[47] By 1776 he was ready to market "Jasperware" gems, reliefs in yellow, black, green, and lilac, and then in what became his iconic combination of white on blue. By the time he produced his last major artistic and commercial coup, Jasperware copies of the Portland Vase, Wedgwood's signature style had already give rise to numerous British and continental copyists (fig. 2.2).[48]

2.2. Imitation Wedgwood medallion
This Wedgwoodian medallion featuring a maenad was produced by the private Thuringian manufacturer Ilmenau in about 1800.

Wedgwood's sophisticated understanding of chemistry and his participation in the scientific world of his day are sometimes underestimated. He was a member of numerous scientific societies, including the Lunar Society of Birmingham, and in touch with many fellows of the Royal Society. His scientific attitude revealed itself in his ceaseless experiments with glazes and pastes and his willingness to adopt new technologies. In his drive to perfect Jasperware, for example, he logged upward of five thousand experiments, and he spent nearly four years in his effort to duplicate that much-admired masterpiece of Roman glassmaking, the Portland Vase. His "creamware" was already more resistant to cracking than most, and he worked hard to further strengthen his pastes against breakage during firing and transport. In 1782, he took the guesswork out of assessing temperatures in the kiln by developing a pyrometer, a gadget into which small, standard-sized clay cylinders could be inserted to test their shrinkage. (Entrepreneur that he was, by 1786, he was offering pyrometer *sets* for sale to other potters!)[49] We have seen how far ahead he was in coal firing; by 1782, he was also using steam power in his workshop, whereas the earliest continental firm to apply it, Frederick the Great's KPM, did not employ steam until 1799, and many other firms continued to use only water- or animal-driven power into the 1850s. Wedgwood also tinkered with labor-saving machinery and introduced new forms of workplace oversight to keep his workers constantly occupied. Ever in search of new models, he drew on Sèvres and Meissen, but also set up a studio in Rome so that his artists could copy classical bas-reliefs, gems, and friezes.

Wedgwood, then, was a scientific tinkerer and a technological innovator. But perhaps more importantly, he was a pioneer in salesmanship.[50] Even if some of his marketing ploys—the creation of showrooms and traveling agents, the goosing of demand by giving gifts, the taking on of difficult commissions to generate fame—had been attempted before his day, Wedgwood went the extra mile. He sold tickets to curious Londoners to inspect his 952-piece Frog service (named for its frog medallion motif) before it was sent to Catherine the Great, and to see his replica of the Portland Vase. He cultivated fashion leaders from heads of state to artists and paid special attention to women's tastes, noting in a letter that he never made a pot without the approbation of his wife, Sally.[51] Together with Thomas Bentley in 1773 he produced one of the first illustrated sales catalogs. New ones followed in 1774 and 1779.

For Wedgwood, the potter's business was to please as many customers as possible. Even after Jasperware took off, he continued producing Queen's Ware adorned with romantic, transfer-printed flowers and Italian scenery for customers whose tastes had not yet shifted to neoclassical austerity. Among the thousands of medallions depicted in his catalog, Wedgwood, an ardent Methodist in his private life, included a series of all 253 popes. He was even willing to reproduce a pot he thought ugly if a customer wished it. Like Meissen's managers, his original aim had been to produce quality wares rather than to compete on price; but much more, and much earlier, than Meissen and the other royal firms, he understood the market potential offered by "populuxe" products and embraced salesmanship and the vicissitudes of fashion.[52] After his entry, the market for fine ceramics would never be the same.

As early as the late 1760s Wedgwood was selling outside of Britain; he cultivated, and won, hefty sales by sending materials to heads of state in Turkey, Russia, Poland, Portugal, Spain, and Sweden. Seeing an opportunity, after 1770 Wedgwood made "something beyond a *Gentle push*" to sell in the Germanys, expressing a forward-thinking hope "that we shall have no cause to treat the Majority of German Princes in the end, as Hereticks, goths, or Vandals."[53] Here, Wedgwood tried something new: he sent out one thousand parcels of ceramics, valued at about £20 each (no small sum in those days), in order to beguile minor nobles; these prospective customers, he assured Bentley, were "waiting with so much impatience for their turns to be served with our fine things."[54] These tactics worked: by the 1780s, exports abroad formed some 80 percent of his firm's business. The popularity of his wares cut deeply into sales of delftware, so much so that of the twenty-three potteries operating in Delft in 1764, by 1804 only six remained.[55] Wedgwood had realized, at least in part, his aspiration to become "Vase Maker General to the Universe."

For the Germanys, Wedgwood's products arrived just as neoclassicism began to sweep through intellectual circles.[56] Enlightened, and especially Anglophile, aristocrats on the continent began buying. As early as 1768, the soon-to-be Duke Ernst II of Saxe-Gotha-Altenburg, related by various family intermarriages to the British royals, returned from a visit to England with an extensive Wedgwood creamware service for his father to use at the Friedenstein Palace in Gotha.[57] The eccentric and well-traveled Prince Franz of Anhalt-Dessau accumulated the largest collection of Wedgwood's neoclassical wares outside England for display in his Wörlitz palace, perhaps the first neoclassical building in the Germanys.[58] Even before Wedgwood's creamware took off, continental porcelain makers had begun to worry about English competition; Frederick the Great had already banned English stoneware in

1765. As Wedgwood's exports surged, others followed suit, crosshatching central Europe with new trade barriers. But, as usual, protection did not work. By the 1780s, virtually "everyone" was buying Wedgwood, and even the elite manufactories—including Meissen and Sèvres—were imitating it.[59]

What these firms were imitating, above all, was Jasperware neoclassicism, a leaner, simpler, and more exacting rendering of classical motifs than previous treatments of mythological scenes had allowed. In chapter 3, we will examine more fully the social and cultural backdrop to the efflorescence of this style. What should be noted here is that if our German firms copied Wedgwood's products, they were less able and willing to imitate his marketing techniques and his eager adaptation of new technologies and practices, including his application of consistent (some would say draconian) workplace discipline. That they did not imitate him more closely in these ways owed partly to the shortage of capital, partly to their reluctance to give up artisanal and courtly ideals, and partly to the traditions of the Empire's artisanal workplaces, where technical processes were jealously guarded and skilled labor hard to lay off. It is hard to imagine an unapologetic salesman like Wedgwood rubbing shoulders with central Europe's educated and moneyed elites. With the possible exception of some of Thuringia's entrepreneurs (see below), it would be another two generations before we find on the continent ceramic makers to equal his enthusiasm for new research and technologies.

But just because "Etruria" was successful during Josiah's lifetime does not mean that his was the only way to operate a fine ceramics business, or that his skills ensured the firm's eternal success; in fact, after Josiah's death Wedgwood floundered for some time, and the company would never develop a product line whose success equaled that of Jasperware. If it is often easy enough to copy another's products, it is another matter to copy business practices across cultures or across generations, and chances of similar success are small. In ceramics as in the industrial revolution more generally: the English model was not and could not be the only model for everyone's modernization.

We have focused our discussion on Wedgwood, but we should not forget that there were many other English firms, some of them making true porcelain: Chelsea, founded in 1743; Worcester, on the banks of the River Severn; Bow, in East London (and bankrupt in 1763); and Derby, in Staffordshire, to name a few. Their works were cheaper than those of Meissen; this would especially be true of vessels produced by manufacturers such as Minton and Spode, who perfected the making of "bone china"—stretching kaolin with bone ash. Some English makers even undersold Wedgwood, which in 1787 goaded the manufacturer into denouncing those consumers "who buy, for the sake of a fallacious [sic] Saving," making it "impossible for Manufacturers either to improve or keep up the Quality of their Works."[60] These lower-cost English firms produced chiefly for the domestic or colonial markets and so did not worry the continental makers nearly so much. They belonged, however, to a rapidly expanding and diversifying marketplace, one in which porcelain was becoming a common rather than a rare commodity, putting old monopolies under ever-greater strain.

Meissen Confronts the New Market

After Frederick II's armies departed from Saxony in 1763, the electorate was forced to adopt austerity policies in order to recover from the economic and physical depredations visited upon it by the Prussian army.[61] Under the very long reign of Elector Frederick Augustus III (r. 1763–1806; in 1806 he would become king of Saxony and rule for a further twenty-one years), a much more efficient cameralist bureaucracy took over the promotion of trade and manufacturing, emphasizing the improvement of agriculture and of forestry. Saxony also invested additional sums in the education of miners and in mathematical and mechanical training. These efforts would contribute to the state's economic rebound by 1774, and make early nineteenth-century Saxony, in the words of a local historian, "a pioneering nation of the industrial revolution."[62] Meissen was part of this mixture, at least for a time. But as officials with new priorities arrived, and profits rose and fell, it became more and more clear that this mercantile manufactory, too, would have to find ways to adjust to the new economic conditions in the century's second half.

In 1764–65, the Meissen works churned out porcelain at a remarkable rate. At first it was pent-up aristocratic demand that caused sales to surge, in 1766 topping 220,000 T.[63] These successes, however, masked underlying problems, which soon became evident. Meissen was overstocked with expensive artisans, and especially painters, and labor costs were exorbitant. Other firms had already begun copying Meissen's styles in the 1750s, and now Doccia, the Marchese Ginori's Florentine firm, France's Sèvres, and Vienna's Wiener Porzellanmanufaktur (WPM) were improving on them. Subtle price wars were also beginning, with the Frankenthal manufactory advertising, as early as 1760, that its prices were one-third lower than those of Sèvres and Meissen.[64] Having had no opportunity to invest in R&D, or to take stock of aesthetic changes, and no Wedgwood to push the envelope, the Meissen works had stagnated, both technologically and artistically.

In 1764 and 1766, Meissen organized auctions in an attempt to jettison its enormous, outdated inventory, but much remained in the warehouse unsold.[65] Buyers began to complain that Meissen's "customer service," to use a modern term, was poor: the firm was slow to deliver on commissions, and the shops had very limited stocks for consumers to examine in person. Merchants insisted on returning items that didn't sell, and the factory often felt duty bound to reabsorb this overstock, or to compensate commissioned sellers for their losses.[66] Retaliating for Saxony's embargo on Prussian porcelains, Frederick the Great banned not just Meissen imports, but even their transshipment across his domains, which effectively and disastrously cut the Saxons off from their outlets in Hamburg and Amsterdam. Although Meissen, the first manufactory, still wished to squeeze everyone else, and especially its central European competitors, out of the market, that prospect grew more and more distant.

The steps the firm took to address these problems are instructive and suggest that a shift was underway in the fine porcelain market, and perhaps in the luxury market as a whole. In his analysis of Meissen's change in orientation after 1763, Alessandro Monti argues,

Here for the first time we see a break from the traditional merchant's credo that had existed since the Renaissance. Up to this point, the conviction held that the product alone was the guarantee for sales and profitability. [Meissen's manager] Helbig now recognized that unless market considerations were taken into account, production itself was unlikely to be successful. Trends, waves of fashion, taste, and artistic styles, especially in the case of an artistically sophisticated product like porcelain, could no longer be dismissed. . . . Satisfying the customer's desire became a focus 250 years ago almost as much as today.[67]

Monti's analysis of this shift from the reckoning of value based on a product's intrinsic properties to an assessment based on its marketability captures a very important moment of transformation in the history of the luxury trades,[68] though his concluding sentence strikes me as an anachronistic overstatement. For centuries thereafter, as we will see over the course of this book, Meissen resisted the pressure to cater only to public taste. In fact, one of the campaigns it launched immediately upon the end of the Seven Years' War was aimed at recapturing Meissen's artistic leadership rather than at pleasing customers. In February 1764 the firm founded its own art school to train future painters and modelers and offered high salaries to lure craftsmen away from Frankenthal, Vienna, and Paris. In that same year, the Saxons hired the twenty-eight-year-old Michel Victor Acier, a French sculptor who had studied at the Académie Royale. Hoping that Acier would bring French panache to Meissen, the firm appointed him a second master modeler, provoking the fury of the long-serving J. J. Kändler. Meissen then sent artistic delegations to other factories to study (and steal) their secrets; two painters, for example, spent a full three years at Sèvres improving their tastes to suit "modern fancies."[69]

But as Monti has also shown, Meissen did now attempt a more efficient production of salable wares. First, the firm undertook to get its labor costs under control, examining wages in the context of workers' living expenses and reducing the salaries of some of its skilled artisans. Others were laid off, so that by 1770 the number of employees had dropped to 606, more than one hundred fewer than just five years earlier. Among the remaining employees were Meissen's first women, surely hired to reduce labor costs, as they were paid one-third to one-half the wages paid to men. The manufactory also introduced new forms of bookkeeping to reduce theft and waste; artisans were no longer to fulfill independent commissions using company materials. Finally, especially after Kändler's death in 1775, Meissen reduced production of figurines—costly to mold and fire and never making up a large portion of sales—and began producing more cups and saucers. Cup buyers could choose from fourteen different painting designs, across a wide price range.[70] One can see here the beginnings of a double-pronged strategy to compete on the one hand with Wedgwood and the private firms in the market for ordinary goods (see below), and on the other, with Sèvres, for the high-end trade. In practice, this would mean that sales from Meissen's "ordinary" branch subsidized the much less profitable artistic endeavors—a strategy that today much more self-consciously operates to sustain many of our luxury "brands."

Central Europe's midcentury market for semiluxury goods such as fine china was not terribly large, however, and was already dominated by French faience and English earthenware. Thus the most lucrative of Meissen's post-1763 initiatives were its new efforts to create demand beyond Saxony's borders. They began in 1764 when two of the firm's officials ventured abroad to scout out the commercial landscape. But the more extensive travels of the porcelain painter and auctioneer J. F. Otto to the Netherlands, Italy, Switzerland, Russia, and elsewhere in the period 1765–70 were more fruitful, resulting in intelligence about foreign markets and manufactories, as well as in new orders worth hundreds of thousands of taler. Meissen had previously sold its wares from the factory itself or from factory-owned shops in Dresden, Leipzig, and Warsaw; it had also commissioned a few established international dealers to sell abroad. Otto elaborated this system, organizing deals with existing luxury shops to sell Meissen wares, at marked-up prices and with the promise that unsold wares could be returned to the factory. In 1774, one such shop in Constantinople alone sold 9,000 T worth of goods for the manufacturer.[71] Sales in Turkey and Russia, in particular, helped keep the budget relatively healthy—although the Viennese were strong competitors, and after the first partition of Poland in 1772, Saxony lost even more of its influence in the East, and Meissen's Warsaw shop was forced to close. A further complication of increasing international sales was that dealers here, as at home, were permitted to take wares on credit, meaning that by 1774 Meissen was trying to collect payments from agents in Krakow, Smolensk, Rotterdam, and Cadiz.[72]

What the manufactory did *not* invest in, importantly, was new technology and scientific research, and by the early 1770s, Meissen was in financial trouble. Aside from new kilns, it introduced no labor-saving tools, and certainly not machines. Unlike the Prussian KPM, Meissen was also slow to seek out new recipes and processes. Even artistic change came too slowly, in a market crowded with other highly talented ceramicists. Both Acier and Kändler continued to produce works in the midcentury form of "soft" neoclassicism (see plate 7) borrowed from Italian firms, and Meissen thus was slow to respond to the new taste for Wedgwoodian wares. Kändler, too, continued to favor the production of commissioned masterworks, although he also consented to making smaller-sized objects to appeal to a wider range of consumers. In 1773 a fire damaged the works, and the next year Meissen posted a major (7 percent, or about 10,500 T) loss.[73] Then in 1775 Kändler died, leaving shoes too big for any new modeler to fill. Meissen now had to ask for increased tariff protection and a state subsidy, and in 1790 it needed another 30,000 T bailout plus a 9,000 T loan and permission to hold lotteries to stay afloat.[74] As the firm's share of sales to western nations dropped, it was forced to focus on supplying its still-lively eastern markets—in Russia, the Ottoman Empire, and central Europe. Sales in these regions would be essential in keeping the factory going until 1806, the firm's last good year before sales fell off the table.

Only sixty-odd years after Johann Friedrich Böttger's pathbreaking reinvention, the Saxons had lost market leadership—it turned out, for good. By 1810, despite the eloquent tributes paid to the factory at its centenary celebrations, Meissen's continued existence was by no means ensured.

The Monopolies and the Widening Market

Other firms, too, struggled with the new competitive landscape of the late 1760s and 1770s. The Duchy of Braunschweig's Fürstenberg manufactory had employed 130 workers, the highest number ever, in 1762 and even in 1767 had boasted 141 employees. But only two years later these numbers had fallen to 104. Competition coupled with poor financial management had forced severe cuts and necessitated bailouts.[75] In 1768, state officials gave the factory an ultimatum to produce a profit in two years' time, or close. In fact, although sales remained poor, the duke couldn't face closing his beloved manufactory and offered it first a subsidy (2,000 T) and then a 12,000 T loan. When hard times hit again in 1773, the factory director blamed the other manufactories for dumping their wares at cheap prices, especially on the Dutch marketplace. Nevertheless, although the director consented to reduce staff by nearly 40 percent,[76] his ultimate answer to the unfair competition was to recommend a "beggar thy neighbor" approach: he would now sell Fürstenberg's own wares at a loss, forcing competitors to even greater price cuts: "Dumping their wares will force most porcelain firms out of business," he wrote.

> Those who endure through bad periods will later have success. . . . It is thus vital that it [our factory] follow [the strategy of the] others and sell at a loss. With God's help, however, it can expect to obtain rising prosperity and respectable prices soon.[77]

The Fürstenberg director's gamble paid off: this first period of intense competition on price proved bruising, if not disastrous, to many firms. But the duke's manufactory survived.

In an increasingly "enlightened" age, the rapidity with which information jumped borders meant that it was harder than ever to protect trade secrets. Many people, especially those one might call amateur scientists and businessmen, were curious about how porcelain was made, by the Chinese as well as by their European imitators, and press notices about porcelain abounded, especially in the century's second half.[78] In 1771, the comte de Milly presented a paper to the French Academy of Sciences on porcelain making at Meissen, derived in part from observations he had made at the factory during the Seven Years' War; this material went into his illustrated book *L'Art de la porcelain* (1771), translated into German as *Die Kunst Porcelain zu Machen* in 1774. Milly's treatise was full of recipes for paste and glaze mixtures and kiln designs. Actual firing, of course, remained difficult, but this and other similar publications began to threaten the older firms' monopoly on information, and more imitators entered the marketplace.

The threat of too many producers vying for the same international buyers and producing very similar goods now became evident. Firms weaker in quality or with flimsier state backing now began to flounder. Producing Meissen-style rococo wares, the Höchst and Kelsterbach factories were briefly successful in the 1760s but by the 1770s were running at a loss. Frankenthal, founded by a private maker in 1755, had to be sold to the Palatine elector Carl Theodore in 1762 to cover its debts; it does not seem to have ever made much money. Founded in 1766, the Kassel porcelain factory, in the words of Charles Ingrao, "proved wholly unable to compete abroad with better-quality products, or even to find a sufficiently large captive domestic market. By 1770 it was forced to liquidate its unsold inventory through porcelain lotteries and auctions, where it could be purchased for as low as one-seventh of the actual cost."[79] The effects of this increased competition were felt beyond the Germanys. Having only started production in 1775, by 1779, F. H. Müller's Copenhagen manufactory was nearly bankrupt and had to be taken over entirely by the crown.[80] Even Sèvres lost its stranglehold in France, as so many illegal porcelain makers set up shop that the state ceased trying to enforce the firm's monopoly rights.[81]

By the 1770s all those who remained in the market were resorting to the classic mercantilist tactic: the tariff. Austria, Prussia, Denmark, Portugal, and Sweden banned the buying of wares from Meissen; Russia imposed customs duties of 40 percent on imports, and France, England, and Spain taxed them at 55–60 percent.[82] In 1775, Meissen asked for a total ban on English imports, in retaliation for English duties of 65 percent on the Saxon manufactory's wares. Elector Frederick Augustus did not agree to the ban, but he did double the price of English stoneware for Saxon purchasers, and Saxon exporters received a rebate for English tariff costs so that they could sell at continental prices.[83] Protection shielded preferred local makers from dumping and underselling. But in a market with too many high-end producers chasing too few consumers, tariffs could not rescue everyone's profitability.

In Austria, Bavaria, and to a lesser extent Prussia, the costly wars of the Bavarian Succession (1778–79)—in which Joseph II was prevented from adding Bavaria to his territories—depressed consumption and increased cameralist critiques of extravagant courtly expenditures. Now even some of the richest princes curtailed state investment in the manufactories and contemplated their sale. By 1782, Nymphenburg employed only twenty-eight artisans and laborers, and its finances did not permit it to purchase even necessary materials. The Bavarian elector wanted to sell the manufactory but found no buyer. In hopes of reforming the factory, he turned operations over to a commission headed by Matthias Flurl, a professor of physics and chemistry. Unfortunately, this undiplomatic move caused the factory's aggrieved arcanist to quit, and he had to be lured back with a hefty payment, as he alone knew the "secret."[84]

Committed to making his kingdom more productive and efficient, in 1783 Joseph II of Austria also tried in sell off his manufactory but, similarly, found no takers. He then appointed Conrad von Sorgenthal, a freemason and formerly the director of the Linz woolen factory, to overhaul porcelain production, promising him 10 percent of the profits. Sorgenthal launched a classic mercantile defense of the manufactory, claiming that it remained "a powerful means of preventing Austrian money from being spent abroad and of promoting the influx of foreign monies as payment for its products." He also supported the artisans' view that reducing wages would "drive away geniuses and attract cheap imitators. Inauthentic, imitative production would in a few years so weaken the credit of the factory that it would find itself compelled to degrade its most beautiful wares by producing them in faience and earthenware."[85] Sorgenthal introduced more transparent accounting practices so that prices could be properly calculated; he adopted new forms of work discipline and added new models and styles. But the director's reforms met with fierce resistance from some of the "geniuses" at his factory and ended in tepid success, provoking one insider to compare his difficulty in modernizing the firm to the backlash Joseph himself was receiving in his attempts to impose religious reforms on the Habsburg Empire.[86]

The story of the KPM in this period is also one of some modernization, but certainly not an embrace of market-oriented mass production. Naturally, this manufactory's peculiarities reflect those of Prussia and its rulers. Having taken control of the firm in 1763, Frederick the Great micromanaged his manufactory with a characteristic combination of megalomania and enlightened efficiency. In some ways, however, he proved to be quite typical of other monarchical operators, serving as the factory's best customer and spending upward of two million taler on porcelain.[87] One service alone—partly of his own design—was made in 1761 for his general Wichard Joachim Heinrich von Möllendorff and valued by the manufactory at 9,412 T.[88]

But Frederick also wanted the factory to make money, and he devoted unusual energy and authoritarian methods to those ends. In addition to his bans on Saxon and English wares, in 1769 he decreed that KPM prices should be set at 4 percent below those of the hated Saxons. He insisted on reviewing monthly statements and made regular visits to the factory; he issued pronouncements on how workers should be paid and overseen. To prompt sales, Frederick also compelled those who leased the rights to conduct the Prussian lottery to purchase 6,000 talers' worth of KPM wares, which he then increased by a further 3,600 T.[89] Finally, and notoriously, he instituted a requirement that all Jews seeking concessions from the state—including the permission to set up a new household or to accept a title—had to purchase 300–500 T worth of KPM porcelain. A list compiled by the Prussian state archives shows that between 1769 and 1788, 1,377 Jewish Prussians made such purchases. Officials were permitted to allow hardship cases to buy as little as 30 T worth of goods, but even that amounted to a sizable sum, almost a half year's salary for a journeyman.[90] Although legend has it that Moses Mendelssohn himself was compelled to buy a set of porcelain apes from the KPM, his name does not appear on this list.[91]

In a set of instructions to the firm in 1775, Frederick explicitly articulated his demand that production be oriented to the wider market:

> The chief long-term goal is to widen and broaden sales of porcelain. Thus it is important that the manufactory constantly maintain a satisfactory array of all sorts of beautiful and tasteful porcelains, of the exquisite sort, which will be found by the public to be in the best taste, and are of the type most frequently sold, and that orders be filled as quickly as possible; also [it is important] that the prices not be set too high, that in special circumstances discounts be offered, so that the manufactory promotes itself continuously, and especially abroad, and is able to draw in ever more orders.[92]

Indeed, the KPM did begin to sell more broadly, opening outlet stores in Breslau, Königsberg, Stettin, Magdeburg, Halle, Minden, and Emmerich, and increasing the variety of its offerings. But, like Meissen, it struggled to turn a profit, and what profits it made were probably the result of squeezing a workforce that included children seconded from the state orphanage. Between 1763 and 1769 KPM employees were working twelve hours a day; by 1779, Frederick had commanded the workday be increased to fourteen hours, including Sundays.[93] The factory first turned a profit of 12,000 T in 1769 and reported 50,000 T in revenues in 1779—but we ought not to assume that this achievement was necessarily a marketing triumph, as one-fourth of the sales that year were to Jews, who were forced to buy.[94]

Yet even Frederick the Great could not force the market to do his bidding. Average annual profits during his tenure came only to 19,335 T. After his death, his successor, Frederick William II (r. 1786–97), continued to make extensive orders (averaging nearly 17,000 T a year) but, much more importantly, opted for policies that initiated the KPM's transition from a courtly mercantile firm, dependent on the privileges the king bestowed on it and hostage to his dictates and whims, toward one managed for the sake of profits and sales. The king appointed a manufacturing commission, which insisted on immediate reforms. First of all, it recommended that the firm stop making the "old, tasteless, heavily decorated items" that Frederick had liked, but which were clogging warehouses, in favor of producing imitations of the market leader, Wedgwood.[95] It also permitted the Jewish community to buy out its porcelain purchasing obligation for a lump sum of 40,000 T. The king then put the commission and the KPM under the supervision of the forward-looking minister Friedrich Anton Freiherr von Heinitz, who introduced new efficiencies and a new line of modestly priced white wares (see chapter 4). At the same time, other reform-minded officials persuaded Frederick William to surrender the crown's tobacco and coffee monopolies, driving down prices for these commodities and increasing demand for pipes and coffee cups. All these reforms benefited the KPM's bottom line, resulting in proceeds of some 40,839 T by the time Frederick William died in 1797.[96]

Over the next two decades—that is, even before the French revolutionary wars commenced—the royal manufactories of numerous other central European monarchs faced closure. As losses mounted and other businesses demanded their support, the princes lost faith in the mercantile promise of porcelain. At Ansbach (founded in 1757), quality declined when supplies of good clay ran out in 1763 and the arcanist was jailed for deception. Thereafter, the young Alexander von Humboldt lamented, the manufactory suffered from "miserable artists, the absence of innovative ideas in selling the wares, and a constantly growing backlog of bad dishes!"[97] The Fulda manufactory, founded in 1764 by the region's prince-bishop, closed with the death of its patron in 1788; Zurich's porcelain manufactory closed in 1790. In Mainz, the prince-archbishop tried to find new investors for his porcelain manufactory, Höchst, turning it into one of central Europe's first joint-stock companies (*Aktiengesellschaft*). But as none stepped forward, in 1778 the archbishop was forced to buy all the shares himself to keep the workers employed and to save face among his fellow electors. He continued to sink thousands of florins every year into the economic albatross until it was finally knocked out of commission by French troops in 1792.[98] The Ludwigsburg manufactory cut its staff from a high of 154 in 1766 to seventy-eight by 1778; in 1801 it was subjected to an official inquiry, "due to the tragic and wholly dysfunctional condition of the porcelain factory," and saved, in the end, only by the personal intervention of the Duke of Württemberg.[99]

Perhaps flagging princely taste in porcelain had something to do with its increasing circulation and affordability; as prices fell and shapes and styles on offer multiplied, porcelain began to seem an ordinary, rather than a special, material. Howard Coutts claims that already by 1781, when the porcelain collection exhibited in Dresden's Japanese Palace was placed in the cellar, to make way for exhibitions of books, coins, and plaster casts, the "death-knell of the respect for porcelain as a material" had already begun to toll.[100] As porcelain's *Glanz* began to fade, state manufactories could no longer be sure of the princes' commitment to their survival.

Faced with this threat, arcanists and artisans continued to emphasize the mercantile as well as artistic attributes of the state firms. We have heard Conrad Sorgenthal promise to revive commerce by keeping quality high; the archives are full of other manufacturers' promises to reform and to innovate. Many of them did that, and the late eighteenth century saw the production of some magnificent pieces of art, as well as the expansion and diversification of offerings for consumers. Some factories returned to profitability, at least on and off. And many princes, loathe to relinquish the prestige of owning a porcelain works and not yet ready to leave mercantilism and courtly consumption behind, did what was easiest, and least likely to shame them in the view of their fellow rulers. Rather than shuttering factories, they provided further subsidies or loans. They also kept in place, or created, new paternalist funds to support widows, orphans, or invalided workers, into which both workers and employers paid (see chapter 3). From keeping skilled workers in the state to maintaining a supply of available gifts that might grease the wheels of diplomacy, sovereigns had good reasons to keep porcelain factories afloat. As it happens, they were not alone in believing in porcelain's promise, for by the 1780s, there was a considerable number of not-so-princely Germans pursuing their own—more practical—porcelain-making dreams.

The Birth of the "Private" Firm

If we now turn our attention away from larger, richer German states such as Prussia, Austria, and Electoral Saxony and toward some of the smaller principalities so characteristic of the Holy Roman Empire, we find other models for ceramics production, including manufactories operated by private owners. The locations in which most of these were founded are instructive: in addition to the region we will refer to as "Thuringia" (see below), we can list: in the west, the Empire's French borderlands, now part of Luxembourg or the Saarland; and in the east, northeastern Bavaria or Franconia; Bohemia, until 1918 a kingdom belonging to the Habsburg Empire; and Prussian Silesia. All these territories were alike in having water transport, an impoverished, though often skilled, workforce, and good supplies of wood and clay. None of them had large or wealthy domestic markets, which meant that producing for export, and for middle-range buyers, was crucial. As the manufactories in the Saar region, Silesia, and Upper Franconia would play a minor role in German markets until after 1815, we will postpone a discussion of them for the present, and focus here on the "private" firms of Thuringia, turning thereafter to start-ups elsewhere in the Sudeten borderlands, most especially Bohemia.[101] Our sample here cannot hope to be exhaustive, as there were almost certainly scores of entrepreneurs who set themselves up to make porcelain, but who either never succeeded in obtaining the recipe (and so continued to make stoneware or faience) or survived only briefly and then folded, leaving little trace. But the story of German porcelain making cannot be told without putting these firms in the picture, for it was here that the first post-mercantilist templates for porcelain making and selling were forged.

The Mixed Models of Thuringia

The German federal state now known as Thuringia was in the eighteenth century no single entity, but a region divided into several Saxon duchies, each belonging to a duke from one of the two lines of the Wettin dynasty of Saxon princes (see map 1). The area, abutting Electoral Saxony to the north, Bavarian Upper Franconia to the south, and the Bohemian Sudetenland to the east, was blessed with thick forests, good clay, and numerous streams and waterways. The dukes who ruled these microstates were timber rich, but land poor, with domains often scarcely extending beyond their capital cities. They had privileges in their gift, but their pockets were not deep enough to support major manufactories, nor were their domestic courts and markets large enough to sustain inwardly focused firms. Each principality had its share of artisans, especially men skilled in industries requiring the management of heat such as glassmaking and iron making. And all had undernourished populations scratching out a living on heavily forested, rocky, and sandy soils, and desperate for gainful employment. In many respects, this, too, was an unlikely place for a semiluxury industry to thrive.

In the following section it will be best for us to temper our discussion of "private" entrepreneurship with the recognition that even in Thuringia, porcelain makers typically asked for, and received, some special perks from their local princes. All makers still required the ruler's permission to produce and sell porcelain in his or her realm, and all, probably, hoped to be given additional privileges. Princes here, too, wanted to advertise their refinement, as well as bring foreign silver into their territories, and were often willing to help, providing small loans or subsidies. Many were persuaded to purchase shares in fledgling joint-stock companies, only one of the "mixed models" of private and public proprietorship we will encounter below. But the "mixed models" did operate differently, given that they evolved in a context in which a princely bailout could not be counted on, and court purchases were likely to be small. Firms here could not afford to hire expensive artisanal modelers and painters and thus oriented themselves much more readily to middling markets than did manufactories in Prussia or Saxony. Unlike those who saw themselves competing with Sèvres, Thuringian producers were quick to push down prices and expand production to make ends meet. Thuringian makers also tended to engage in shady business practices, perhaps the only way they felt they could compete with firms whose state subsidies, protections, and privileges the private makers considered unfair. To be clear, these entrepreneurs acted differently than did state producers not out of the conviction that a "free market" was best, but simply because they lacked the clout and resources to constrict the market for *their own* benefit.

Porcelain Making Comes to Thuringia: Four Stories

There is considerable mystery about how the secret recipe came to some of our Thuringian factories; if the first regional manufactory to make hard-paste porcelain—the manufactory at Gotha—learned it from the Berlin ar-canist Nikolaus Paul, subsequent formulas seem to have been independently discovered in several places at almost exactly the same time, enabled by the local glassmaking and iron-making expertise and apparently spurred on by alchemical aspirations. Thuringia, indeed, seems to have been home to more than the usual number of amateur alchemists, possibly the Holy Roman Empire's equivalents of Britain's pre-industrial tinkerers.[102] The fact that in 1760 there were *three* would-be arcanists applying to the Duke of Schwarzburg-Rudolstadt for porcelain-making privileges suggests a leak or foul play. But whatever the reason for the recipe's quick spread, by 1800, at least thirteen factories capable of producing hard-paste porcelain of varying quality dotted the region; of these we will take a representative sample, fo-cusing on the histories of the factories at Gotha (founded in 1757), Volk-stedt (founded in 1760), Kloster Veilsdorf (founded in 1760), and Wallendorf (founded in 1764) (see table 2.1).

The honor of founding Thuringia's first porcelain works goes to the Gotha Porzellan Manufaktur—the bold name initially boasting more promise than reality, as the factory was not able to make true porcelain for almost a de-cade after its founding in 1757. The story of the Gotha manufactory typifies the struggles private owners faced in finding what we might call a workable business model. The founder was Wilhelm Theodor von Rotberg, formerly a tutor at the libertine and art-loving court of Duke Frederick III of Saxe-Gotha-Altenburg. He had undoubtedly seen, and been inspired by, the duke's extensive collection of East Asian porcelains and soapstone figurines at the Friedenstein castle. Von Rotberg did eventually obtain the Arcanum from Nikolaus Paul, who had been previously employed by Wegeley in Berlin's first factory and then by the Fürstenberg manufactory. It is unclear if von Rotberg's works ever produced a profit, and by 1782 he was forced to lease

TABLE 2.1. Firm Foundings in Thuringia, Eighteenth Century

	Date of Founding	Original Owner/ Leaseholder	Location
Gotha Porzellan Manufaktur	1757	Theodor von Rotberg	Saxe-Gotha-Altenstadt
Volkstedt	1760	G. H. Macheleid and others	Schwarzburg-Rudolstadt
Kloster Veilsdorf	1760	Johann Hermann Meyer; after 1797, Johann Gotthelf Greiner and sons	Saxe-Hilburghausen
Wallendorf	1764	Johann Gotthelf and Johann Gottfried Greiner, J. W. Hamman; after 1772 Anna Margarete Hamann (née Greiner)	Saxe-Coburg-Saalfeld
Limbach	1772	Johann Gotthelf Greiner	Saxe-Meiningen
Ilmenau	1777	C. Z. Gräbner; after 1786: Johann Gotthelf Greiner	Saxe-Weimar-Eisenach

his little factory to a local businessman, who created a consortium to-gether with five skilled workers, all entitled to a share of the proceeds. When Rotberg died, however, his widow claimed full ownership and demanded that other consortium members pay her an enormous leasing fee. The result was a lawsuit. Not wishing to see the firm go under, Augustus of Saxe-Gotha-Altenburg—who would succeed to the title of duke in 1804—poured 13,000 T into the business and handed it over to a favorite courtier, Friedrich Egidius Henneberg, to manage. This solution kept the workers employed, making, among other things, a set of teacups decorated with phalluses that the libertine Augustus brought out for parties with his closest confidantes.[103] In 1807, Henneberg changed the firm's name to F. E. Henneberg & Co., and in 1814 he succeeded in buying out the other leaseholders. Until 1840, his heirs continued to enjoy the privileges the founding duke had bestowed so long before on his beloved tutor.[104]

The tale of the next Thuringian foundings is more complicated but involves in all cases a blend of notable features: artisanal sciences and skills, the pooling of family capital and effort, and the procurement of minor princely perks. The focal point of the story is the pocket-sized principality of Schwarzburg-Rudolstadt, where between 1760 and 1762, Prince Johann Friedrich was presented with three separate applications for porcelain-making privileges. The one that would eventually succeed was submitted by a theologian named Georg Heinrich Macheleid, who had abandoned a career in the church to devote himself to dabbling in his father's alchemy lab.[105] Two years later, he evidently hit on a workable Arcanum, and in 1760, Macheleid began producing porcelain at a former enamel works in the town of Sitzendorf.

A royal privilege, however, that might offer some hope of financial security, was slow in coming. For nearly two years, Macheleid's petition still lay on the prince's desk, together with two similar appeals, one from the cousins Johann Gotthelf and Johann Gottlieb Greiner, who belonged to a well-known glassmaking family, and the other from Johann Hermann Meyer, yet another "itinerant ceramicist." At last the prince's counselors tested the recipes, and in 1762 the ruler bestowed the porcelain-making privilege on Macheleid.[106] Macheleid received exclusive rights to use local raw materials and to buy wood from the prince's forests at a good price; otherwise, his manufactory was financed by way of a primitive joint-stock company, in which the duke was one of eight stockholders. The firm now moved from Sitzendorf to Volkstedt, setting up on the grounds of a former faience manufactory in order to be closer to Ludwigsburg castle, the prince's *Residenz* in Rudolstadt, on the Saale River.

Macheleid proved a better chemist than man of business, for even with these advantages, by 1765 his "Volkstedt Porcelain Manufactory" was facing bankruptcy. The prince then intervened and leased the firm to Christian Nonne, a clever entrepreneur who succeeded in breaking into Turkish and Polish markets. Nonne slyly adopted a trademark of crossed forks, which looked so suspiciously like Meissen's that the Elector of Saxony retaliated by confiscating the firm's wares at the 1775 Leipzig *Messe*. The elector could take these steps in Leipzig, within his own domains, but in the absence of a pan-imperial commercial code, the Meisseners could not enforce their priority outside of Electoral Saxony, and Volkstedt continued to use this mark for

2.3. Gotthelf Greiner and sons

Thuringian artisan and entrepreneur Johann Gotthelf Greiner bequeathed his dedication to porcelain making to his five sons, pictured here in an 1820 family portrait by Gottwald Kühn.

another twelve years.[107] When the manufactory fell into arrears once more, a prominent local merchant advised Rudolstadt's now-reigning prince, Louis Günther II, to throw in the towel: "If princely operations actually do bring advantages—a rare occurrence—then onerous monopolies arise, which inhibit [individual] subjects and bring the interests of the prince into unpleasant collisions with the industries of [his] subjects."[108] For once, a German princeling listened to sound business advice and unloaded the firm on his peer, Wilhelm of Hesse-Philippsthal. In 1799, Wilhelm, too, sold the firm, still running at a loss, to two members of the same Greiner family whose competing application for a royal privilege had lost out to Macheleid's bid thirty-seven years earlier. Greiner descendants would manage to keep the Volkstedt manufactory alive, under a variety of names, for the next sixty years.[109]

Of all the early Thuringian porcelain makers, Johann Gotthelf Greiner (1732–97) was perhaps most important, not only for getting several private manufactories up and running, but also for having sired five sons, all of whom—in addition to several daughters and sons-in-law—went into the porcelain business (fig. 2.3).[110] Johann Gotthelf also offers us a model of the artisan turned entrepreneur, made possible by the pooling of family skills and capital. It appears, in fact, that the person who hit on a successful porcelain recipe at almost the same moment as Macheleid was Johann Gotthelf's cousin Johann Gottfried, a glass painter keen on experimenting who had begun tinkering with alchemical and porcelain recipes in about 1760. But it was Johann Gotthelf, now the chief leaseholder of his father's successful glass-works, who fronted the cash for his relative to do a year's worth of experiments, and also brought in a potter to help with the glazes. In 1761 a workable recipe was discovered, and Johann Gotthelf rode off to convince his prince—the same Johann Friedrich of Schwarzburg-Rudolstadt—to give him a privilege. The story of his protracted and humiliating negotiations—including being once compelled to dine with the prince's children and servants—along with his endless fights with other local manufacturers over wood tell us a great deal about how hard it was for even a successful craftsman to become an entrepreneur in this period.[111] In the end the Greiners had to partner with a capital-rich foundry owner, J. W. Hamann, husband to their kinswoman Anna Margarethe Greiner, and to apply to the ruler of the principality next door to Schwarzburg-Rudolstadt, Duke Josias of Saxe-Coburg-Saalfeld, for permission to make porcelain in his town of Wallendorf. They received a privilege, at last, in 1764.

Wallendorf's proprietors began making porcelain, but their partnership did not last long. Johann Gottfried died in 1768, and four years later, unhappy with his financial arrangements, Johann Gotthelf sold his share and moved to Limbach in the Duchy of Saxe-Meiningen, where, at one of the family's glass factories, he again began porcelain production. Financial security at last in reach, in 1786 he also took over the leasehold for a porcelain works in yet *another* small Saxon duchy, the Ilmenau factory, which had just been saved from bankruptcy by the intervention of Duke Carl August of Saxe-Weimar-Eisenach and his favorite courtier, the poet Johann Wolfgang von Goethe.[112] Anna Margarethe, now J. W. Hamann's widow, was also on secure footing. She seems to have managed the Wallendorf firm until 1811, when her son took over. In 1829, this son leased the Wallendorf Porzellanmanufaktur to another relative, Johann Heinrich Hutschenreuther, the father

2.4. Turkish cup

This Meissen "Turkish cup" (ca. 1725–30) imitates the shape desired by Ottoman coffee and tea drinkers. By the 1790s, Thuringian private firms such as Wallendorf were making cheaper versions of these cups by the tens of thousands.

of Carolus Magnus Hutschenreuther, who will play a leading role in the later history of private porcelain making (see chapters 4 and on).[113] Statistics show that by the later 1790s the firm employed some fifty workers and was producing more than one thousand "Turkish cups" in every firing, as well as dozens of teapots, saucers, and sugar bowls, suitable for smaller budgets (fig. 2.4).[114] During and after the upheavals of the French Revolution and Napoleonic Wars, Wallendorf continued to cultivate export markets for its useful and inexpensive goods; in 1818 alone it sent thirty thousand "Turkish" cups to Cairo, Aleppo, Jaffa, and Damiette.[115]

The Volkstedt (Macheleid) and Wallendorf (Greiner/Hamann) stories, with their intermittent bankruptcies, princely rescues, and flashes of entrepreneurial brilliance or chicanery or both, are echoed in the story of the founding of yet another Thuringian firm: Kloster Veilsdorf. This firm owes its birth to Johann Hermann Meyer, who had been the third applicant in the quest to obtain the concession for Schwarzburg-Rudolstadt. When Macheleid prevailed, Meyer turned to the nearby Duchy of Saxe-Hildburghausen, where Prince Eugen promptly gave him a ruined Benedictine abbey (Kloster Veilsdorf) in which to experiment. Meyer proved to be an inept or fraudulent arcanist, however, and this fourth Thuringian factory, like the Gotha manufactory, did not succeed in making anything better than faience until 1763, at which point Meyer received the technical assistance of Nikolaus Paul, the younger, the Arcanum having evidently passed from father to son.[116]

Here, too, costs—including about 1,700 T spent to refurbish the cloister—began to mount. Prince Eugen, however, could not convince his brother (who was the actual sovereign) to buy his pet project, and it continued to drain Prince Eugen's purse down to the time of his death in 1795. In the meantime, he undertook several desperate, and rather dicey, schemes to make his manufactory successful, including the hiring of Jewish merchants to sell his wares; some of these merchants balked when he suggested staging a lottery for "Saxon pottery," intended to mislead customers seeking to buy Meissen at bargain prices. (Kloster Veilsdorf was also accused—apparently with good reason—of trying to deceive consumers by—following in Nonne's footsteps—using a mark very like the crossed swords of Meissen.) Prince Eugen finally bequeathed Meyer's money pit to his nephew, who promptly sold it—to Johann Gotthelf Greiner. Two of Greiner's sons, F. C. Greiner and J. F. Greiner, operated Kloster Veilsdorf until 1822, when they sold it to another member of the family.[117] Thus by the century's end, Greiners owned or operated Wallendorf, Limbach, Ilmenau, Volkstedt, Kloster Veilsdorf, and two other factories—though by no means did this make them all rich, or ensure the long-term success of any of these still-fragile "private" enterprises.

To summarize: Well before the Old Regime's end, we find in Thuringia models of provincial, familial entrepreneurship coupled with orientation to the wider market that would become more and more general half a century later. We find princely assistance entering the picture in the form of official "privileges," but also private risk taking in the form of noble and bourgeois investments in early forms of stock companies. Rather than the cultivation of *Glanz* that would reflect glory on a royal patron, here we find rampant competition for an emerging export market in low-priced wares, and the emergence of provincial manufactories that were relatively large for the day, with Volkstedt employing as many as one hundred workers in the 1780s and Rauenstein, another Greiner family enterprise, boasting as many as 124 in 1794.[118] Large numbers of these employees were not skilled male craftsmen, but women, working at home, as handle fitters or *Hausmalerinnen*. These ceramicists were devoting themselves to the making of simple consumer articles such as pipes and teacups, rather than grand dining services. But the Thuriginians, at the time, were below the notice of the state porcelain makers, who did not really consider themselves to be operating in the same marketplace. No one would at the time would have guessed that Thuringia's "mixed" models would help define the German semiluxury industry for the post-mercantilist future.

The Wider Central European Landscape

Less is known, at least in sources available to this author, about some of the faience and soft-paste firms in the *eastern* reaches of central Europe, but by the mid-eighteenth century, they too were enjoying a burgeoning trade. According to Anna Szkurlat, at least three workshops had been established in Poland by the 1740s, again mostly by former glassmakers. A royal faience factory had operated at the Belvedere Palace in Warsaw, although it ceased production in 1780.[119] A more long-lived firm, Korzec, was founded in 1783 in the once-wealthy town of Korets in Volhynia (then part of the Polish Lithuanian Commonwealth, now Ukraine) by the son of the royal hunt master, Prince Jozef Klemens Czartoryzski, and seems to have begun making porcelain in 1790. Korzec, like the Greiners' Volkstedt, was founded as a joint-stock company, in which the prince held the majority of the shares. The firm employed as many as three hundred workers in 1794 and began to show profits by 1796, but dividends were paid only beginning in 1804, which meant that stockholders had a long time to wait to see their investments rewarded. Like the German firms, the Polish one had its own outlet stores and sold its ready-made goods at fairs. In 1814, after one of these fairs, a representative of the firm reported: "On this occasion it was observed that modestly decorated products of average quality were the easiest to sell, while buyers for exquisitely ornamented services and products of lower quality were the hardest to find."[120] Acceding to this logic, the Korzec firm developed a strong trade in lightly decorated, moderately priced services and managed to survive until 1832.

Glassmaking, as we have seen, often provided a point of departure for entry into the porcelain business, and Bohemia was *the* northern European glassmaking hub. Meissen had from the beginning drawn on the talents and sophisticated techniques of Bohemia's glassmakers, located only a few miles down the Elbe, and by the later eighteenth century, the industry was flourishing as never before. Moreover, like its Thuringian neighbors, Bohemia possessed thick forests, cheap as well as skilled laborers, major deposits of kaolin, and—importantly for the later development of the industry—an abundance of coal. Bohemia also had an aristocracy, some of it German, a great city (Prague), and an emerging spa culture, centered around the hot springs of Karlsbad (today's Kalovy Vary).

The Czech lands, then, would have been perfectly positioned to found porcelain manufactories—except that the Kingdom of Bohemia at the time belonged to the Habsburgs, who had given the Viennese WPM a monopoly on the making of hard-paste wares in their hereditary domains. Nonetheless, in 1792 J. G. Paulus set to work at Schlaggenwald (Horní Slavkov), nestled in the heavily forested region on what is now the far western edge of the Czech Republic, producing what was not yet, but he hoped would be, true porcelain. The WPM protested vigorously, warning that such a factory would only corrupt public taste and put the jobs of 350 Viennese workers at risk. But protests, in those days, did not necessarily bring action, and in this case the state evidently took none, for in 1799 the WPM director issued yet another complaint about rogue Bohemian porcelain factories.[121]

In 1800, Paulus sold his workshop to Sophie Luise Greiner, yet another member of the Thuringian porcelain clan. Her son managed to obtain the recipe at just about the moment that the secret itself was lifted, and French occupiers forced the Austrians to dissolve the Old Regime's monopolies. By 1820, the Schlaggenwald factory was churning out middling-priced hardpaste wares featuring landscapes and sentimental subjects, and offering stiff competition to the royal German firms.[122]

Another Bohemian factory was founded in about 1792 or 1793 at Klösterle, with the support of the very rich landowner, Josef Johann, Count of Thun und Hohenstein. Klösterle was leased to a Thuringian in 1797, but the Thun family took over ownership in 1820. By 1822, its works were of sufficient quality to obtain the now non-exclusive title of "*k. und k. priviligierte Fabrik*" (Imperial and Royal Privileged Factory), improving its brand.[123] The Thun family continued to own the works until after 1945, when it—along with Schlaggenwald—was nationalized under the postwar communist regime. A third major Bohemian firm—reorganized several times but, like Klösterle, still in business today—was the Pirkenhammer manufactory, whose production really began only after 1815, but which soon became a major producer. A fourth, Elbogen (later Haidinger Brothers Porcelain), also took off quickly and by 1823 could boast two hundred workers at a time when the royal firms were in financial crisis.[124] By then the Hungarians, too, had gotten into the business—founding the Herend Manufactory in 1826. The Hólloháza works, originally established in 1777 to make glass, began producing porcelains as well. Soon manufactories would be established in Austrian Silesia (that part of the Habsburg province that Austria had retained after Frederick II had annexed most of it), where labor and coal were cheap. By the 1830s, Habsburg central Europe had begun to pose just as important a set of competitors to the German firms as had the English in the later eighteenth century. From this time on, the bitter commercial as well as political rivalries that characterized the Sudeten borderlands will haunt us throughout this book.

The expansion of the luxury market in the second half of the eighteenth century offered new opportunities for both state and private porcelain makers. Meissen and the KPM, as well as the "privates," such as Wedgwood and

Wallendorf, were able to expand operations and, periodically, to pull in profits. But the fluctuations of the markets, thanks especially to the period's many wars, disrupted steady periods of improvement, and the rush of so many competitors into fine ceramics making generated an oversupply of goods that relatively poor central European consumers did not need and could not afford. In retrospect, this era has often been treated as the "golden age" of porcelain manufacturing, and indeed, magnificent (as well as humble) works of many different types were made (see chapter 3). But those engaged in the business had little time to rest on their laurels, if they ever did so. And if Wedgwood, ministerial reforms, and the rise of the private firms had posed a major challenge to the princely firms, they would soon face another challenge even more daunting: Napoleon.

Chapter 3

Making, Marketing, and Consuming in the "Golden Age"

O*ne* of the well-worn stories about the evolution of German nationalist sentiment in the later eighteenth century narrates the rising tide of critiques of the "Frenchified" court societies of the Holy Roman Empire. German intellectuals—some of them courtiers or officials themselves—did attack libertine manners and excessive, non-utilitarian consumption in the name of civic, Christian, and "German" values such as simplicity, chastity, and sincerity.[1] But focusing on their critiques of courtly luxury leaves out an analysis of which commodities aristocratic Germans in this period were actually consuming, and how those commodities were made, marketed, and sold. Thus this chapter departs from the usual cultural histories of the period by examining not the critiques, but the inner workings of a luxury industry. It describes what it was like to perform the actual work of designing and making our delicate commodity and of selling it in the premodern marketplace, and it details the ways in which consumers put porcelain to use. It concludes with a longer section on style, which embeds this unique commodity in the artistic and artisanal contexts of the day, and shows that even in porcelain's early years, diversity in design and in pricing was one of the hallmarks of this industry.

By investigating these practices, the chapter deepens a business history story that runs the risk of leaving out individual skills and decision making as well as the aesthetic considerations that have always been important to porcelain makers and buyers. It also tells us more about the meanings and internal contradictions of the early modern German market for luxury goods by offering some concrete examples of how it worked—and when it failed. As it happens, investigating the manufacturing, marketing, and consuming of porcelain gives us a wide window into the social world of the Old Regime in its last decades, for the manufactories employed day laborers and a few women as well as highly paid artisans and artists, and the selling of ceramics involved state officials as well as illegal hawkers. If the consumers at midcentury were chiefly courtiers and wealthy townspersons, by the century's end many middling Germans were addicted to coffee and eager to own a presentable pot and cups to serve it in. Domestic interiors and women's roles did not change much, but there are signs that transformations lay ahead. By surveying these changes in consumption and behavior as well as production—with proper cautions as to their limited scope—we can perhaps grasp a bit more concretely what role this specific luxury good played in the lives of various members of the population.[2]

Finally, perhaps by throwing some light on consumption itself rather than critiques of it we can understand from a new direction the gradual breaking down of the central European Society of Orders. Without invoking the market directly, Alexis de Tocqueville long ago sagely listed among the revolution's preconditions the fact that by the 1770s or so, the French were becoming more like one another than ever before, in their behavior, their patterns of consumption, and even their dress, even as the system of privileges policed status divides.[3] Cautiously, and allowing for enormous regional differences, we might pose the question: can the same be said about the Germans? Were they too becoming more like one another, in their everyday customs and their accoutrements? Fleshing out consumption patterns—a much larger project of which this book is only a small part—might help us to get a bit closer to an answer.

In response to the many recent works in the field of the history of science that focus on the *practices* of production, learning, and the distribution of knowledge and know-how, I will devote much of this chapter to an

examination of how the business of porcelain making, selling, and displaying worked in this period. That we have to do already with an "industry" has
been demonstrated. But how did the work actually get done, and how did all
those luxurious items make it to princely banquet tables? It is time to pull
back the curtain, as it were, to look inside the manufactories, and, to the extent that we are able, to reconstruct what porcelain purchasers in this era
wanted for their money. After all, even "useless" things do have social functions, and in many respects their making and display tell us as much about
the period as do inquiries into the production of necessities.[4] Once again,
porcelain does not tell us *everything* about Old Regime society and culture;
but it opens a valuable window into a world very different from our own.

Fashions and Food Cultures of the Old Regime

"At the Old Regime's close, the majority of German families lived at the edge
of subsistence," the economic historian Diedrich Saalfeld concluded many
years ago.[5] The approximately 20 percent of the population inhabiting towns
by 1800 had become a bit richer than their country cousins, but by one estimate, the average German town dweller in the 1750s still spent a whopping
81.7 percent of his wages on food and an additional 11.3 percent on firewood, leaving only 7 percent for other consumer goods, much of which must
have gone to other necessities such as candles and clothing.[6] That their consumption patterns were changing, above all to accommodate small purchases
of "colonial commodities" such as coffee, tea, and tobacco, is certain; Beverly Lemire is right to challenge older claims that the material world of the
lower orders "stood still" as European exploration, trade, and colonization
proceeded.[7] Yet, for most, disposable income remained minuscule, and social sanctions against acquiring luxury commodities such as porcelain only
gradually relaxed. The vast majority would have confined their housewares
purchases to earthenware, or invested in unbreakable tin, pewter, or wood.
Despite the fact that the nobility constituted only about 1 percent of the population or approximately 250,000 people in the eighteenth century,[8] it was

this social group whose customs and tastes shaped the production and use of porcelains, at least for most of this "golden age."

Despite its relatively small size, it is difficult to generalize about the central European nobility. The image conjured by period-drama movies of an unchanging world of identically bewigged ladies and gentlemen politely lifting a delicate Meissen chocolate cup certainly does not do this status group justice. Eighteenth-century aristocratic society was anything but uniform and stagnant. There were richer and poorer nobles; some were highly educated, others virtually illiterate. Some lived in rural Prussia or Hungary and experienced little "society"; others married foreign princes or princesses and traveled a great deal. Some were Catholic and some Protestant, some pious and some, after midcentury, inclined to libertinism. Each had his or her own domain to tend and did so according to custom, legal privileges, income, competence, and whim. But they watched wealthier French and Italian nobles, and one another, carefully; after all, those who claimed the right to occupy the highest rank in society were expected to "live nobly," even as noble lifestyles changed.

Indeed, over the course of the eighteenth century, the occupations and income streams of the central European nobility had begun to change, although most continued to have the majority of their wealth invested in that quintessentially noble and non-liquid asset, land. Gradually, however, nobles began to orient agricultural production toward the market and to convert personal service and payments in kind into money rents, generating a bit more liquidity to be used for the purposes of consumption. Following princely upgrading of palaces and accoutrements, lesser nobles too began to change their diets, habits, and living spaces. And although these processes began later in central Europe than further west, they were certainly palpable by the 1740s, and in some places, such as Saxony, a bit earlier. The wealthier noble families, of which there were an estimated fifty thousand in the Empire at the time,[9] began to frequent "residence" cities and gather at summer palaces. In Vienna, Berlin, Munich, and Dresden, but also Würzburg, Kassel, and Braunschweig, increased expenditure on fashionable goods and changes in manners began at court, but then radiated outward, abetted by and, in turn, accelerating transformations in commerce and in social life more generally.

"Fashion," especially in clothing, was not new to the eighteenth century. Italians in particularly had been making and wearing lighter, cheaper, and more various textiles by the fifteenth century, and rich Renaissance Germans, too, liked to dress in style,[10] though pious "reformed" persons frowned on bright colors and extravagant jewelry. While the Italians went in for luxurious textiles—silks, damasks—the weavers of the Low Countries increased, cheapened, and diversified their production of more utilitarian broadcloths. By the 1670s, "good" society, especially in France, was awash in discussions of "la mode," and the Parisians had appointed themselves the arbiters of a fashion cycle that changed annually, to the benefit of French textile producers. The English reciprocated by demanding that East India Company factors in Bengal "change the fashion and flower as much as you can every yeare" in order to sell at exorbitant prices to novelty-hungry English continental ladies.[11] Note that in cloth production, too, a form of early mercantilist competition drove trade and diversification, and that the French seized control of and systematized a luxury market that had begun in the Italian states. The Dutch dominated the market for more durable and less costly stuffs, replicating the relationship between delftware and Italian and French soft-paste porcelain. The English sought to undercut the market with colonial wares. Less well informed, and less well heeled, consumers in the provinces, Latin America, and central Europe could purchase last year's styles—if, that is, they were not still constrained by sumptuary laws.

For consumers, fashion in the seventeenth and eighteenth centuries was not just about changing one's taste, but about the pursuit of distinction. Louis XIV made his dressing and undressing a major court ritual and annually renewed his wardrobe; his courtiers were supposed to follow suit, not, however, upstaging the king.[12] As Ulinka Rublack and Daniel Roche have emphasized, clothing, intimately linked to the individual's appearance, was the most direct means to display superiority in birth and standing, at court and beyond. The wearing of costly materials, velvet, brocade, fur, and silk, for example, demonstrated the status, real, or aspirational, of the individual and his or her family.[13] Similarly, the possession of plenty of clean, white linen was a proof of status: only the well-off could manage to wear white in an age before detergents and machines. In addition, clothes stored value and were regularly sold or pawned when families were short on cash. Thus, extra clothing was usually the first durable purchase "industrious" Europeans made with their savings, and by the time of the revolution, virtually all Frenchmen, and probably most Europeans, especially in the upwardly mobile middling ranks, were devoting a larger portion of their incomes to this commodity.[14]

Clothing was a huge market—Roche reminds us that in the age of Louis XVI, twenty-eight million French subjects alone had to dress and undress daily[15]—but fashion affected other commodities and behaviors as well. To maintain one's rank, eighteenth-century aristocrats also needed horses, carriages, and jewelry. For entertaining at home, they needed proper furnishings, including tapestries, clocks, and tableware. Houses themselves began to change. Those who could afford to do so now aspired to divide up their living spaces into rooms with specific functions—bedrooms, kitchens, dining rooms, music rooms, libraries—and to choose furnishings and decorations proper to each. Porcelains, with different functions, were accordingly sprinkled throughout the household. Courtesans and royal mistresses such as Madame de Pompadour ordered elaborate déjeuner or dressing-table sets for their boudoirs, powerfully associating the most delicate porcelains with intimacy, and female spaces.[16] But male courtiers too purchased writing sets, snuffboxes, clocks, candelabra, and mirrors, and fashioned their own libraries, and later billiard rooms. Naturally all these purchases supported the work of mirror makers, bookbinders, and porcelain producers—at least when the nobles paid their bills, which was by no means all the time.

Dining and behavior at table was also changing. Medieval and early modern banquets were generally served on long, rectangular or U-shaped tables, with guests seated only along the outer side (so that they could be served from the inside, and so that any viewers could "read" their ranks). Conversation as well as access to the best dishes was regulated by strict codes of precedence. The best tables offered the most elegant and succulent delicacies, on silver (kings and emperors alone ate from gold salvers); the next ranks might dine on majolica or faience, and the next-best meats; should some lower orders be served, their tables might be set with tin or wood. Partakers used knives, bread, or fingers, and only later forks. Spectators considered themselves fortunate just to watch the proceedings, and to see the silver and gold displayed on walls and sideboards.

Gradually, however, French and then central European elite eaters began to replace heavily spiced meat dishes with lighter, fresher fare. Hosts increasingly frowned on using fingers and introduced forks, individual place settings, and more intimate round or rectangular tables. Dishes were displayed *à la française*, which meant that each course's fare was served on specially shaped platters, placed on these smaller tables according to a rational, symmetrical design (see plate 4; see also the table in the foreground in plate 2). Guests were now expected to converse together, across the tables, rather than only with a neighbor to the side. Thus were medieval displays of the prince's virility—demonstrated in the game he had captured and the meat he could consume—replaced by displays of the prince's refinement, shown in his selection of delicacies, the elegance of his table settings, and his guests' repartee.

We find porcelain entering into this new "table culture" in an unexpected way: as a complement to or substitute for the sugar sculptures long used to adorn Italian banqueting tables. Sugar remained an expensive commodity long into the eighteenth century, but it could be molded into almost any shape, making it ideal for ostentatious displays. The spread of sugar fashions occasioned the rising status of the court confectioner (*Konditor*), often an Italian or Frenchman, whose job entailed the decoration of tables as well as the introduction of new desserts.[17] The Konditor became the impresario of the banquet, making his name by way of elaborate confections intended to be admired rather than eaten. But sugar or marzipan sculptures were time-consuming to fashion, and leftovers lost their luster once they yellowed or were nibbled by servants or rats. Thus hosts hit on the notion of replacing them with delicate porcelain baskets, figurines, saltcellars, condiment trays, and centerpieces meant to be seen from all sides known by the French name "surtouts." In 1763, on the grounds of economy, Maria Theresa explicitly ordered sugar figures be replaced by porcelain figurines and real flowers on her tables; this was indeed economical for the Habsburgs, as the WPM was expected to produce the decorations, as well as an extensive array of plates, with no guarantee that the court would compensate the manufactory.[18] Like the other forms of widening aristocratic consumption described above, such feasts created new market opportunities for some, while also driving noble families who sprang for too many "surtouts" to the brink of ruin.[19]

An additional cultural transformation shaping the reception and use of porcelain lies in the alteration of central Europe drinking habits, which seem to have diffused in the opposite direction to the dining customs described above, that is, from the fledgling public urban and middling sphere, into court circles. While wine predominated on noble tables, coffee seems to have first appealed to the commercial classes, especially those oriented to cross-channel trade, which would explain the founding of the first German coffeehouse in Hamburg in 1679 (older histories date the founding of the first central European coffeehouse to 1683, and place it in Vienna where it was furnished, with stores seized from the recently defeated Turks). Quite possibly, here as in England, coffee seemed the right beverage for non-nobles who wished to avoid intoxication and get on with their work. But perhaps as a sign of central Europe's slower integration into the world of "colonial" commerce, coffeehouse culture spread much more slowly here than it did in England, France, or the Netherlands. By 1720, Augsburg had eight, confessionally segregated such that four served Protestant and four Catholic customers. By comparison Paris already counted three hundred coffee shops in 1700, and by 1734—the year of J. S. Bach's "Coffee Cantata," composed for Gottfried Zimmermann's elegant coffeehouse cum recital hall in Leipzig—London could boast 551 licensed shops.[20] German-speaking Europe was even slower to take to tea and chocolate, both of which, like coffee beans, were purchased from Dutch suppliers, but more expensive still. Elite consumers did adopt these commodities, but neither would rival coffee's cultural importance in this part of the world.[21]

By the mid-eighteenth century, however, coffeehouse culture was spreading through central Europe, and coffee could be purchased from grocers, street hawkers, and dealers in overseas specialties in larger cities such as Braunschweig.[22] Cookbooks described its preparation at home. After the dismal failures of the coffee bans of the 1760s and 1770s, proprietors opened pavilions, tents, or "cabarets" to serve coffee to men of different classes.[23] Dresden's "Grüne Bude" dates to 1779, but this shop was little more than a wooden kiosk; there was a more permanent, but perhaps not much more respectable, "Café Bude" in Mannheim. Many public places serving coffee also served alcohol, and as they were frequented chiefly by military officers and nobles of questionable moral character, they were shunned by virtuous women.[24]

Thus perhaps more importantly for the wider population, coffee by the mid-eighteenth century was also becoming part of a newly regularized meal known as "early bit" (Frühstück), prepared and served at home. Rather than consuming gruel or Frederick the Great's beloved "beer soup," urban families especially in the Northwest now organized "breakfast" around the consumption of hot drinks and fresh rolls (Brötchen).[25] As we have seen, Frederick, and other princes, tried to prevent the spread of this practice as they felt it lined the pockets of Dutch traders as well as compromised the health of the working classes; but the upshot of their restrictive measures was simply to hook those who could not obtain or afford the real thing on coffee substitutes made with chicory, roasted barley, or a host of other substitutes and stretchers. Though arriving much later in the South, the custom of starting the day with coffee—or ersatz coffee—and Brötchen spread inexorably. As the habit of breakfasting spread across urban Germandom and to the courts, it would spawn the use of more and more specialized and ornate serving dishes, good news indeed for porcelain makers, who now began to produce a vast array of specialized coffeepots, cups and saucers, milk jugs, and sugar boxes. These items would be the manufactories' biggest-selling items by the eighteenth century's end.

We must not overgeneralize these changes in consumption habits, however, for in central Europe, while prices for "colonial commodities" such as coffee and sugar did fall after about 1780, grain and meat prices tended to increase, and many real incomes stagnated, or, after 1815, actually fell.[26]

Social sanctions, too, depressed the furnishing of homes and favored instead spending on food and drink. "Strict and tight was the budget of the urban citizen," Gustav Freytag wrote; "only a few were sufficiently well-off to be able to give the decoration of their homes and lives a little refinement [*Glanz*] . . . and those who could live well, generally spent little on their households and demonstrated their wealth only on special occasions through additional implements [*Geräte*] and hospitality."[27] Though Freytag may be alluding here to a tendency to purchase tableware—perhaps even porcelain!—to impress guests, we should be wary of envisioning lavish table settings, or big changes in everyday eating habits. Coffee might have become "the nectar of the Germans," but for many that was because it served as an appetite suppressant. Many Germans lived in one or two rooms, sometimes with their animals, and their beds (usually shared) were often their chief assets. Most households had no forks, much less "surtouts." Even in the 1830s, most institutions such as schools, and probably the majority of non-elite housewives, were still serving meals on tin.[28] Breakfast, for most rural dwellers in particular, still consisted of gruel or—Frederick would have cheered!—beer soup. And almost no one ever ate dessert.[29]

The relatively weak participation of central European women in luxury and semiluxury markets may be adduced as an additional factor slowing consumption in this region. The absence of a substantial number of female purchasers is important for us, as from early on the delicacy of porcelain was associated with women as well as with the Orient. Perhaps the connection began with the "Trianon de Porcelaine" at Versailles (1670), built for Louis XIV's rendezvous with the Madame de Montespan; Madame de Pompadour, as we have seen, enhanced porcelain's association with intimate and risqué spaces. Of course, there were some central European female aristocrats who coveted porcelain; previous chapters have mentioned that Augustus II's granddaughters Maria Amalia and Maria Anna Sophia inspired porcelain making in the Two Sicilies and in Bavaria. Holy Roman Empress Maria Theresa bought a significant amount of both imported and home-produced porcelain, but she disapproved of the excessive expenditures of her plenipotentiary Johann Karl Philip von Cobenzl and agreed to pay his debts only "if he gets rid of all the useless porcelain and knickknacks that do not fit his station."[30] In most other cases queens and princesses do not seem to have been the key patrons or porcelain purchasers. Sophia Charlotte, who became queen in Prussia in 1701, was the last Prussian queen for most of the eighteenth century to have significant disposable income (which she used, in part, to commission the Charlottenburg porcelain room). The long reigns of Friedrich Wilhelm I (1713–40) and Friedrich II (1740–86) marked an era in which women, both wives and mistresses, played little role at court, and were kept on absurdly—for the time—short rations.[31] Had Frederick not opted to buy and run his own porcelain factory, it is doubtful that the Prussian court would have done much to further consumption of the new commodity.

Perhaps most importantly, in central Europe, until the century's very end, there seem to have been very few of the "middling" women of the English type who, by the 1760s, were eager to create comfortable, tasteful spaces for the serving of tea, or in the case of central Europe, coffee. "Tea was the catalyst of a momentous reconfiguration of domestic space," writes Amanda Vickery about the ways in which Georgian women's desires to establish a place for their tea parties drove interior design and associated porcelain objects ever more powerfully with women. English men began to complain about their wives' extravagant expenditures on china, failing to mention their own larger investments in horses, alcohol, and silver plate. A highly gendered set of expectations about consumption evolved, with women responsible for textiles and ceramics, and men responsible for major and permanent choices such as exterior architectural design, land, carriages and horses, heavy furnishings, and metalware.[32] Central Europe's elite, its identities so deeply linked to status, developed habits such as the tea party and other forms of strictly gender-segregated consumption and sociability many decades later than did the English. In 1799, we can glimpse the fashion beginning to take hold in one writer's denunciation of women's afternoon visits, in which too much "eating, drinking, gambling, and what is worse than everything else, slandering goes on."[33] Yet this glimpse was a fleeting one; what distressed this writer much more was the moral damage done by a different form of central

European excess: men's drinking and whoring. In general, women's excessive investments in domestic ornamentation was not—yet—a complaint heard widely in the Holy Roman Empire.

Why not? In the early eighteenth century, in many places, German commoners were still constrained by sumptuary laws and social norms, both of which were applied most strenuously to women, who were lectured from childhood on the virtues of thrift, simplicity, and self-denial. Married women, in particular, were far more restricted in their ability to earn a little money of their own than was the case in Britain or the Netherlands. German husbands were known to beat their wives for seeking employment outside the home, and local courts were known to order married women to desist from working independently.[34] Central European women had a great deal to do at home in any case; on top of extensive cleaning routines, wives were expected to do all the child care and cooking, including pickling and preserving fruit and vegetables for the winter, and making clothing for themselves, their children, and even their servants; even urban women typically sewed their own undergarments.[35] There was water to haul—often long distances—and a fire to tend, socks to knit, and bread to bake. Writing in 1790, one Italo-French visitor marveled at the heavy burden of household work, especially washing, carried by married German women.[36]

For women in guild-dominated central Europe, shopping must have been chiefly a chore rather than a pleasure. For bourgeois and lower-class women it entailed unceasing haggling with grocers or craftsmen to get the best bargain. Elite women would have been given license to make everyday household purchases but would have had to consult their husbands for any expensive or durable purchases and had far less access to credit networks than did contemporary Parisiennes.[37] Even for them, casual "shopping" would have been almost inconceivable. By midcentury, some urban shopkeepers were taking a few notable items out of trunks and cabinets to set on a "display table" (*Schautisch*) so that customers could examine them directly;[38] but almost all sales of material goods still necessitated negotiation with a shoemaker, tailor, or other craftsman. Seasonal fairs were about the only opportunity available for impulse purchases, but they too would have entailed haggling, and most noble women would not have felt comfortable buying there, as we may deduce from the fact that in Saxony, Augustus II's mistresses enjoyed shopping at the Leipzig fair, but his queen attended only the opening ceremonies.[39] In any case, such fairs occurred infrequently and did not make for a high level of consumption or sales. Together, values, workload, and restricted purchasing opportunities kept German women's expenditures low. The opening of the market to a large number of female purchasers, it seems, would have to wait for the post-1815 era. Only then, too, would manufacturers begin to take women's tastes and needs seriously.

Court culture, then, shaped porcelain's first uses and associated the commodity, in lasting ways, with display, with women, with intimacy, with elevated status, and with lighter and less vital repasts, dessert and breakfast. Porcelain's affinities with court society would become a powerful part of the manufactories' claim to represent regional refinement even as producers by the century's end—pressed by Wedgwood and the lower-cost German private makers—began to sell to non-elite customers as well. But courtly consumption would also stamp porcelain *producers'* image of their social and artistic functions. Skilled artisans could continue to feel that they belonged, at least partly, to the elegant world, and relish their contributions to the prestige of the princes and their courts as well as their superiority to unskilled workers. Even in making sugar boxes and coffeepots for an expanding urban elite, they could feel that they were producing a commodity valuable chiefly for the purposes of decoration and display, and one purchased by deep-pocketed men rather than women on shoestring budgets. Thus was a certain amount of "nobility" baked into the eighteenth-century porcelain industry. Although transitions were underway as the century closed, porcelain makers' self-image as enablers of elite dining and display would prove difficult to expunge.

Life inside the Manufactory

As we saw in the first two chapters, porcelain making was not an occupation open to all comers, nor was it an individual endeavor. It required access to particular materials, in this case, kaolin clay; wood; and for the glazes, lead, cobalt, and various other minerals. Unlike early modern textile production, most of which was farmed out to rural laborers who spun or wove cloth in their own cottages, porcelain making was a collective endeavor and chiefly had to be done in "factories." At first, too, even the painters worked on site, although a whole industry of cottage decorators known as "Hausmaler"—many of whom had already been occupied in painting faience or glass—also sprang to life (see below). Labor was divided, but by no means was it equal, in prerequisite training, in bodily exertion, or in compensation. Arcanists needed to be good chemists; kiln masters had to understand heat technologies. Unskilled workers who trimmed wood for the kilns or packed items in moss or straw for transport needed brawn but not dexterity or erudition; master painters required both. Long before Adam Smith popularized the efficiencies of the pin factory, porcelain factories were places of divided, specialized labor.

But what did a porcelain factory look like? In the beginning, factories were not purpose-built but rather lodged in unused royal outbuildings or abandoned ecclesiastical properties, such as the hunting lodge at Fürstenberg or Kloster Veilsdorf in Thuringia. Various rooms or areas were then devoted to mixing the clay, modeling, glazing, painting, and so on. Kilns and usually waterwheels or mule- or oxen-powered mills had to be added and were constantly in use, as some of the ingredients used in glazes required upwards of sixty hours to grind into fine powders.[40] As a later view of the Meissen factory suggests, this led to the somewhat incongruous sight of industrial smoke pouring out of medieval palaces and monasteries (fig. 3.1). Many factories, however, were located beyond the gaze of town dwellers in rural, heavily forested areas, beyond, too, the reach of the guilds and near to the all-important resources of wood and clean water. Forests were often places where unskilled labor was cheap and plentiful, but firms with artistic ambitions couldn't be too far from urban centers, which provided skilled laborers such as painters, modelers, and financial overseers. As the customers mostly belonged to the courts, it was also useful to be within easy shipping reach, as was Sèvres, sited conveniently on the road between Paris and Versailles. Locating the factory on a river, as in the case of Meissen (the Elbe) and Fürstenberg (the

3.1. Albrechtsburg, Meissen
Based on an 1821 sketch by Adrian Zingg, this panoramic view of Meissen from across the Elbe River does not omit to depict the smoke rising from the castle complex. Evidently the Meissen porcelain manufactory is hard at work.

Weser), helped, as it was easier to transport both heavy timber and fragile porcelain pieces by water than over central Europe's muddy and rutted roadways.

Very soon, manufactories set up warehouses and retail shops for prospective buyers, and from quite early on, elite customers were allowed to watch the artisans at work[41]—though of course the specifics of the manufacturing process remained trade secrets. Manufactories often included housing for officials and "barracks" for workers, as well as gardens that could be tended and used by employees, according to their place in the pecking order. Instead of picturing them as versions of nineteenth-century textile mills, it might be more useful to see early porcelain factories as the descendants of medieval monastic estates, with the spaces previously dedicated to prayer now set aside for manufacturing, decorating, and sales.

As for the workforce: As in every other sector of the Old Regime economy, elite and non-elite workers received differential treatment and compensation, depending on their precise tasks and skills, their seniority, and their gender. As in the guilded industries, craftsmen carefully guarded their particular tasks and the perquisites that came with each. Every craftsman made a different wage, which was often renegotiated year by year. The salaries of the administrators and master craftsmen ranged far above those of the unskilled workers, but high wages were neither the only, nor the most important, perk employees desired; in this "Society of Orders," status considerations and special privileges often mattered more. The typical costumes sported by each group tell us a great deal; while directors typically wore powdered wigs and courtly dress, skilled painters usually dressed as the bourgeois artisans they believed themselves to be, wearing hats and cravats (plate 5). Turners, who spent the day pushing their wheels with bare feet at workstations layered in porcelain dust, were recognizable in light-colored trousers and shirts; porters, who carried wares to and from firings, and firemen, who fed wood into the kilns, routinely stripped to the waist or soaked their clothes in water to combat the heat. To tour the eighteenth-century factory— culminating in a visit to the courtier-manager's salon—would have been to see Old Regime society in microcosm, with its many different varieties of labor, education, expertise, and dress on vivid display.

At the top of the pyramid was the director and often the inspector, who served as a sort of CFO; in the state manufactories these officials received the title of "Beamter," a privileged, civil service status that entitled one to a good salary, a state pension, a great deal of job security, and often other perks such as a housing allowance or free wood for heating. Many of the directors were, or fancied themselves to be, courtiers; Nymphenburg's Dominikus Auliczek, for example, had served as Bavarian court sculptor before his appointment as director of the manufactory, and, in keeping with his self-conception as a noble personage, had his portrait painted numerous times. To be an "Angestellter" was next best, as this designation put one in the category of the state-employed white-collar workers, chiefly accountants and clerks. Their jobs were relatively secure, though their salaries were often low. For example, at Böttger's death in 1719, Meissen's two *Beamte* (the factory inspector and the director, Dr. Nehmith), made 300 and 360 T per year, respectively, and four *Angestellten* made 144, 120, 96, and 72 T per year; one is registered as making only 36 T, which probably indicates that he was an apprentice or a very junior clerk.[42] At Ansbach in 1791, the arcanist's widow inherited her husband's secret recipe, as well as his high-paying job, and claimed a salary of over 400 T, while the equivalent of the firm's CFO made only about 130 T.[43] Some administrators were diligent and competent men; others paid little attention to the shop floor and had received their positions, as a 1770 report at Meissen baldly states, through "intrigues and illegal favoritism."[44] Like the other classified employees, they were almost impossible to fire.

There were many gradations among the modelers and painters. The highest paid were the masters (usually one of each per manufactory), followed by those who painted human figures, battle scenes, and birds; below them were scenery or flower painters, and lastly those who painted decorations exclusively in blue. In 1766, a master modeler at Fürstenberg earned 720 T, more than double the salary of the court painter, triple the salary of a well-compensated figure painter, and far above the pittance paid to the apprentices (16 T), who probably did the lion's share of the work.[45] At Meissen, where wages were highest, female blue-and-white painters earned just a little more, on average, than unskilled journeymen, at about 62 T per year in 1778. Their male counterparts, by comparison, earned between 122 and 199 T per annum. Other wage data we have shows wild variations and fluctuations, with highly skilled artists earning between 250 and 400 T, and the lesser-skilled ranging between 60 and 150 T per year, the latter an adequate wage, in most years and places, and the former perhaps sufficient for a single person, but not for a family. Wages in the private firms seem to have been lower; at Kloster Veilsdorf, for example, in 1780, the average worker made about 67 T a year, meaning that many families continued to live at subsistence levels, and occasionally had to do without heat, light, or food.[46] Those on the higher rungs expected deference from their inferiors, and even their customers. In 1805, for example, one KPM painter complained bitterly that a customer had left his hat on in his painting studio, an insult to the artisan's bourgeois status.[47]

Operating outside of the factory were independent artisans dubbed "Hausmaler" or "Winckelmaler" (cottage or corner painters), who purchased or pilfered white wares, decorated them at home, and then sold their products below factory rates for decorated vessels. State firms made Herculean efforts to root out this practice, but "Hausmalerei" proved intractable. Meissen stopped selling white goods in 1731 to try to beat this trade, but the problem persisted. In 1761 Frederick Augustus II insisted on jail time for illegal painters, and in 1775 his successor even threatened to lock up their landlords. Nothing worked, not even underglaze trademarks. Forgers and *Hausmaler* scraped them off or covered them with their own. Only the addition of what was called "Schlichte Malerei" or "Ausschussmalerei," blue flourishes painted across the surfaces of white wares, kept outsiders from adding their own decorations.[48] At the end of the eighteenth century, partly as a result of Bavaria's brief promotion of "Kommerz-Freyheit," Nymphenburg gave up efforts to suppress *Hausmalerei* and began trying to hire the good freelancers itself.[49]

At the bottom of the ladder were apprentices, some of them culled from state orphanages. Orphans could be made to work almost for free, but others had to pay for the privilege of their "education," which started at very young ages and entailed five to eight years of paltry pay and often abuse by their masters. Those who survived the ordeal did learn skills that could move them up in the world significantly once they completed their apprenticeships. Less favorable, then, was the lot of the unskilled kiln hands, stable boys, clay crushers, woodcutters, and the like, who might receive 55 T annually, but had no access to education and little prospect of changing their stations in life.[50] Of course, wages for the unskilled also changed over time, dropping by one-third, for example, at Meissen during the Seven Years' War,[51] and purchasing power varied, as food prices rose and fell. When the manufactories' cash flow faltered, they sometimes resorted to the unpopular practice of paying employees in flawed porcelain "seconds." But even at the lower end, persons employed in the porcelain industry seem to have considered themselves more fortunate than many of their contemporaries. In most years, they were certainly better off than the peasant farmers in their areas, who experienced a number of periods of outright starvation in this century; even the average Leipzig craftsman, in the early 1770s, was able to cover only about 65 percent of his family's minimal nutritional requirements (about twenty-four hundred calories a day, per person).[52] Many salaries exceeded the average cloth weaver's income, estimated at 100 T for Berlin in 1780.[53] For this weaver, inhabiting an expensive city, such a wage would have narrowly sufficed for bread, rent, beer, and the occasional cup of chicory coffee or serving of meat, for a family of four;[54] but our porcelain workers were generally located in places with much cheaper rents, and often more perks. There were worse fates than employment in a porcelain factory.

The number of employees engaged by some of our firms puts them among the largest central European manufactories of the age at midcentury. Meissen reached a peak of 731 in 1765; Fürstenberg employed 141 by 1767, and the WPM three hundred by 1775.[55] Meanwhile, in 1750, Prussia had only seventy cotton looms. But by the 1770s, the demand for clothing and bedding had begun to rise, massively outstripping the demand for ceramics in the still-small consumer marketplace. Over the later eighteenth century, the numbers of porcelain employees stabilized or fell, while the numbers in the cloth trades rose greatly; by 1798, for example, Prussia had 2,439 cotton and 3,851 silk looms, and Saxony had many more.[56] In porcelain production, also, the proportion of women and children in the industry rose much more slowly than in textiles, where women and children's entry into the factory signaled the replacement of skilled laborers with cheaper workers and more labor-saving devices. Combining this information demonstrates just how much porcelain making remained, long into the nineteenth and even twentieth centuries, a skilled, semiluxury industry rather than a deskilled and mechanized one.[57]

Perhaps because porcelain making was not guilded labor, the states took a paternalist view of their employees, providing food and skeletal "waiting" wages, for example, during wars and market downturns. Eager to retain skilled workers, some states created institutions similar to those operated by the guilds to ensure the loyalty of these workers. Able-bodied workers paid in, supporting invalids and bereaved families—though often the funds were overdrawn and manufactories themselves had to cover the deficit. In 1736, Meissen established a "death fund" for its artisans, and in 1756, a fund for painters' widows. At the KPM, a similar "death fund" was founded in 1765, and followed in 1789 by a "Versorgungskasse für Erbkranke und Invaliden" (Fund for the Care of Invalids and Victims of Hereditary Disease).[58] Some of the private firms, too, would later adopt this practice. In 1817 and 1819, respectively, the faience makers Nicholas Villeroy and J. F. Boch Buschmann created their own funds to care for those unable to work.[59] At both state and private firms, unskilled workers, including women, were not permitted to become members of these "brotherhoods," yet another way in which a hierarchy of laborers was maintained.

The way in which workers passed the day in eighteenth-century porcelain factories differed greatly from later routinized schedules of labor and leisure time. Böttger, perhaps typically, worked irregularly, interrupting his day for long meals, drinking bouts, walks in the garden, and the pursuit of private projects. Some employees undoubtedly worked very hard; one experienced painter at Fürstenberg, for example, managed to paint more than two hundred items in seventeen days of work.[60] Others kept odd hours and combined work with gossiping, drinking, gambling, or napping. Factories posted enormous rates of breakage or waste ("Brach" or "Ausschuss"), wares with wobbles, uneven glaze, cracks, or improperly attached handles. In 1760, an inspection of the Doccia factory found that of the 72,342 porcelains that should have been made from the clay purchased by the manufactory, more than sixteen thousand had evidently never made it to the kilns, and a further sixteen thousand or more had emerged unsalable, meaning that the factory had thrown away what should have been good profits.[61] Wastage of this sort would not have much troubled courtier-managers such as von Brühl in Meissen's early years, but it began to irritate overseers oriented to efficiency and profits. In 1764, Frederick the Great introduced piece rates and the fining of workers for breakage, arguing that without the necessary discipline imposed by piecework, workers would remain "sloppy and lazy." But Frederick also realized that this form of payment would discourage artistry and so added in special bonuses for good craftsmanship.[62]

Low productivity was addressed in other places by the introduction of piece rates and fines. But in general, eighteenth-century artisans were difficult to discipline and the threat of the most skilled moving elsewhere omnipresent. Looking back on the early period with the nineteenth century's eye for the efficient use of labor, a Meissen director would note that one of the downsides of the possession of the Arcanum was that the manufactory felt obliged to employ everyone exposed to it forever, meaning that the firm was overstocked with lazy and insubordinate workers, and that little technical progress was made.[63] This was certainly unfair but does cover some cases, such as that of Nymphenburg in the 1790s (see chapter 2). While most firms stuck with older labor practices and payments, some added occasional bonuses to incentivize craftsmen who otherwise did not feel the need to overfill their quotas. The many discrepancies in warehouse numbers strongly suggest that, as portrayed in a modern romance novel set in Meissen in the 1740s, some employees were tempted to pilfer from the factory in order to make ends meet or to line their own pockets.[64] In 1770, the Kassel manufactory moved to piece rates, with the result that employees had to put in an additional four or more hours per day to equal their earlier wages. Workers retaliated by allowing the factory itself to go to ruin; a 1778 inspection found the premises littered with shards and excrement.[65]

Working conditions from the first were less than ideal, though perhaps the risks proved no worse than in any other line of early modern employment. The making of porcelain not only requires firing at high temperatures but also generates silicate dust, which clogs the lungs and produces a condition we today call silicosis. By the later eighteenth century lead was known to be a poison, yet this did not prevent its ubiquitous use, in mining, in distilling, and in the making of porcelain glazes. We have seen Böttger's early demise, at thirty-seven, almost certainly brought on by these toxins. Still, thirty-seven was right at life expectancy for Prussian men down to the later nineteenth century, and probably porcelain making wasn't significantly more dangerous than most other occupations, and less so than some, such as mining or sailing. The greatest peril for employees was perhaps the uncertainty of waged work; when sales fell, war came, or the prince needed cash for other projects, employees were furloughed or wages suspended, sometimes for extended periods. That one was kept on the payroll and provided minimal nutrition was comforting, but hardly ideal.

In Prussia, the porcelain makers' average working week was officially eighty-four hours—but where management was weak or absent, which seems to have been many places, some of these hours could be spent in socializing and in sleeping off hangovers. In 1796, the new overseer at Fürstenberg reported "anarchic" conditions on the shop floor: employees hardly worked at all on Mondays or Saturdays, drank schnapps on the job, threw almost whatever came to hand into their clay mixtures, and spent working hours taking care of private business or hunting game for their dinners. One of the kilns had been given over to roasting chicory to make "Prussian" coffee. The factory, he reported, had become a social hub, and the new overseer had felt it necessary to ban Jews, musicians, tradesmen, and beggars from the works so that employees could focus on the tasks at hand. One can understand why this situation had arisen; Fürstenberg was a lonely town, with few public amenities or amusements. Workers, moreover, were regularly gouged by victualers, and their wages were frequently in arrears.[66] They felt no compunction in mixing business with what few pleasures opportunity allowed.

All in all, working in a porcelain factory, whatever one's role, was no picnic but offered more status, skill, and diversions than subsistence farming, the largest occupation of central Europeans into the early nineteenth century. Wages varied radically, from the extravagant to the inadequate; workplace discipline, too, could be oppressive but was often lax. Paternalism favored skilled employees, who looked on their employment as a form of permanent service and, in the absence of consistent management, made their own decisions and ran the works, often with little attention to profits and losses. Workers knew they were making luxury goods beyond their own means and worried little about "the market," whatever that was. But that was a subject that princes, officials, and owners had increasingly to tackle.

Making and Selling

Let us turn now to the actual objects being made, and to those tasked with selling them. Decisions on what to make and how to market one's products were neither self-evident, nor were they always made wisely. Nor could these decisions be made unilaterally; even a commissioning prince had to adapt his demands to the capabilities of the modelers and kiln masters. As for selling non-commissioned craftwares, the industry quickly outgrew the seasonal fair, and the usual artisanal practice—in which makers took orders in advance and kept a very low inventory of unsold goods—was completely unsuited to an industry that increasingly looked to consumers ready to buy finished goods on the spot. Firms would have to invent new means by which to reach an evolving consumer base.

What, exactly, did porcelain makers produce, and how, and to whom, did they market and sell their wares? The answers to these questions are rather complicated, as the industry produced a very diverse set of goods, and its clientele and selling practices changed greatly over time. At the most elite end of the market, we find many one-of-a-kind objects, commissioned or designed with a particular purchaser in mind, and sold together with their own bespoke boxes to prevent breakage or chipping in transit. Next we find "Galantrieartikeln" (articles associated with "gallantry") such as figurines, snuffboxes, scissor cases, fancy clocks, candelabras, and porcelain flowers, the high-end objects that now populate our museums. These were made, of course, almost exclusively for the aristocracy; and yet, they were produced in large numbers and a baffling profusion of forms and styles.[67] A noble lifestyle, after all, required expenditure on many accessories, some of which could come in handy. At the battle of Kunersdorf in 1759, Frederick the Great's own life was saved by a fortuitously placed snuffbox.

Even in the first table services, self-representation and adornment were more significant than daily utility. Although an earlier service may have been made for Augustus II in the late 1720s, the one that attracted the greatest attention was Meissen's two-thousand-plus-piece "Swan Service," modeled by Kändler between 1737 and 1741 for Frederick Augustus's confidant

Heinrich von Brühl. Elaborate services thereafter began to be made for palaces and for diplomatic gifts, at enormous prices. For example, an apple-green service made at Sèvres for presentation to the Habsburgs cost Louis XV more than twenty-six thousand livres.[68] These services, too, were largely meant to be non-utilitarian gifts, for sovereigns were still obliged to use silver services, first introduced by the French in the later seventeenth century, for official banquets. Tsarina Elizabeth, in 1745, seems to have been the first to set a banquet table with porcelain,[69] but for decades afterward, royalty continued to eat off of silver (gold for the king). Gradually, porcelain became acceptable, especially for "simple" garden parties or inferior guests, and by the century's last decades, "picnic sets" (in elegant boxes) and déjeuners for tête-à-tête breakfasts were used for special, informal meals. These smaller sets, too, were often specially commissioned or presented as gifts, which means, of course, that they needed to be splendid works of art.

Yet early on, porcelain makers recognized that while the firm and its masters earned artistic kudos as a result of producing porcelain rhinoceroses or replicas of the Piazza Navona, it was not cost-effective to produce one-of-a-kind artifacts. The ingenuity and craftsmanship that went into creating a design, a mold, and a glaze mixture for just one item was immense, and given the rate of kiln failures and breakage, it was wiser to make multiples. Moreover, elite purchasers did not always pay their bills on time; many regularly overspent their incomes or paid only in installments, and only when constrained to do so.[70] It is estimated that Frederick Augustus II's unremunerated orders cost the Meissen factory almost 400,000 T, or nearly 40 percent of its income, between 1736 and 1747.[71]

In accordance with mercantile practices, porcelain makers first sought to pay their bills by increasing sales abroad. The two markets most hotly pursued at midcentury were the Ottomans and the Russians, both big consumers of hot beverages but lacking functional tableware factories. The Ottomans were eager to purchase handleless cups for their coffee, ordering thousands from Meissen already in the 1730s (see again fig 2.4). The Viennese and the Ansbach manufactory cut into this trade, the latter even adding faked Meissen marks; but then the Thuringians offered even cheaper prices and more attention to Ottoman design requests, and by the century's end the latter dominated the market for "Türkenkoppchen." "For the Turks," wrote Alexander von Humboldt in 1792, "German porcelain is just as much a necessity as ever."[72] Russian nobles proved good customers, as they recognized that their own porcelain products, once available, were no match in quality for those of Meissen, Vienna, and Berlin. There were some sales to England, but its "chinamen" were prohibited from importing and reselling continental porcelains, and those who wanted to order directly "for private use" faced steep duties. The Americas, with no porcelain manufactories of their own, bought little as yet, commerce here hampered partly by British trade restrictions and partly by the lack of a luxury-oriented aristocracy. Still, by 1775 Meissen was working with 105 foreign trading houses,[73] suggesting that its "brand" had acquired as much of a global reach as would have been possible for any retailer of the age.

For decades, factories did not see much promise in domestic, non-noble markets. In the early eighteenth century, this was understandable; few "ordinary" central Europeans would have felt the need to purchase porcelains; their utilitarian tableware needs were fulfilled by the makers of tin, pewter, wood, or earthenware vessels, and their consumption of the newer hot beverages was limited. Moreover, powerful social conceptions of what was "standesmässig," or fitting to one's status, would have made even wealthier townspersons think twice about purchasing costly items whose chief purpose was display. Middle-income women in particular were warned about the moral perils of waste and excess. A popular manual for bourgeois girls awaiting marriage—written by a man—instructed them to grow their own foodstuffs and make household articles so as not to fritter away their children's futures, and not to indulge in too much coffee or sugar for the sake of their health and beauty.[74] Even those who renounced excessive austerity, such as F. J. Bertuch, editor of Germandom's only real fashion magazine, the *Journal des Luxus und der Moden*, were careful to champion the virtues of consumption proper to one's sphere; porcelain was suitable for the Prussian royals' tasteful summer banquets, Bertuch argued in 1787, but upright bourgeois housewives should not indulge themselves in sumptuous French fashions, novels, or makeup, all of which led to moral corruption. Bertuch did not explicitly denounce bourgeois purchases of porcelain, but he was scathing with respect to servants uppity enough to wear silk on Sundays, as if they had noble titles.[75]

But gradually, almost silently, manufactories did begin production of more readily salable items, and comfortably fixed bourgeois families began to buy them. In 1738, Meissen director Samuel Chladni approved the introduction of a modestly priced blue-and-white service, the "Blue Onion" (fig. 3.2), destined to be the most popular (and most regularly imitated) table service in history. Chladni also allowed products graded as "Brac" or "flawed"—as a result of cracks, chips, or imperfections in the painting or glazing—to be distributed to factory officials, and, after 1745, to be sold in a special factory store. In the next decades, Meissen and others also began to expand production of what they termed "Mittelgut" wares, porcelain of a somewhat lower quality of modeling and glazing than the wares labeled "Gut." "Middle-grade" porcelain sold at a correspondingly lower price and at least at first offered a high profit margin. Without much fanfare, and seemingly as a means to support higher-end products, manufactories accordingly began to produce more middle-grade tableware. Already in 1760, Doccia was churning out nearly one hundred thousand pieces of majolica and porcelain per annum, and in 1776, Meissen was able to produce 476,595 items, a total it would not equal until the German industry's "Indian Summer" of 1804–5.[76] Although the figurines attracted connoisseurs' attention then, as they do now, the reality was that already in 1771, figurines formed just over 1 percent of the items fired at Meissen, far behind the blue-and-white, brown, and plain-white cups and saucers, which made up a whopping 89 percent of the wares.[77] The manufactories' practice of featuring the figurines, and selling the soup plates, had already begun.

The meticulously kept record book belonging to the Hamburg schoolmaster Hermann Samuel Reimarus and his wife gives us a glimpse of the sort of consumers who eventually concluded that they, too, could justify investing in porcelains. When the couple set up housekeeping in the 1720s, they purchased chiefly wooden and tin vessels; but in the 1750s, on an increased

3.2. The "Blue Onion"

Designed at Meissen in 1738, the "Blue Onion" was destined to become Meissen's most popular—and most pirated—pattern. This Meissen manufactory sketch of the pattern dates to the later eighteenth century.

budget, they bought some porcelain to serve coffee. In 1775, the family procured twenty "colorful" porcelain plates, though it continued to buy earthenware for daily use down to the time the household's record book ends, in
1780.[78] By this time, however, prices for coffee, tea, sugar, and porcelain itself were falling sharply,[79] and the practice of gathering to drink afternoon
tea had begun to spread, driving up demand for tea sets. This was hardly a
revolution; but it did mean that social sanctions were flagging, to the benefit
of those savvy enough to orient production to tableware for the middling
marketplace.[80]

We know too little, at present, about the business of buying and selling
ceramics in eighteenth-century central Europe. It is clear that the Germanys
did not experience a "retailing revolution" on the scale of the one underway
in Great Britain, where East Asian and domestic ceramics were sold to provincial wholesalers by an army of London "chinamen," some of whom set
up elegant shops in the central city or the West End.[81] By 1717, Thomas
Twining had opened a retail teashop that catered to female buyers; he and
other traders in tea would soon discover the attractiveness of "consumption
bundles" and begin selling sugar, teapots, and other hot drink utensils as
well.[82] The Germanys lacked retailing "chinamen" (on the continent, that
was the Dutch), nor did they have a single fashion center such as London or
Paris where a Twining could capture elite buyers' imagination. Commerce
in the Holy Roman Empire was highly restricted, with very few wholesalers
standing between producers and consumers and sales in city streets limited
to the guilded shops on the specified "high" streets or to annual fairs. Many
localities banned peddlers entirely or licensed only a few to sell specific commodities.[83] So where, and how, did Germans buy their fine ceramics?

The answer to this question is neither clear-cut nor the same over time.
Meissen's first open-market sales took place at the Leipzig fair, which now
occurred thrice each year and, in the elegant formulation of Daniel Roche,
served as "the shop-window of plenty" in an economy of scarcity.[84] This and
other fairs would continue to be important sales points for centuries afterward. Otherwise, early sales were made at the factory itself, which already
had six rooms full of salable goods in 1711 (fig. 3.3). But new marketing

Die Porzellanfabrik zu Meißen : Saal der Maler und Vergolder.

3.3. Meissen factory interior

This sketch of the Meissen modeling studio in the Albrechtsburg just before the move to the new factory shows us masters and apprentices at work while potential customers tour the factory.

mechanisms were in the works. Already in 1710, one trusted merchant had been commissioned to sell Meissen products in Karlsbad—where spa visitors were the target—and soon thereafter additional "factors" were commissioned to sell in other favored locales.[85] Retail outlets (*Niederlage*) were established in larger cities. In 1715 Meissen opened a shop on the New Market Square in Dresden and in 1731 added a second in Warsaw, the Saxon crown's other capital. Meissen's competitors followed suit. The KPM maximized its reach into Prussia by opening twelve shops, but it was outdistanced by the Viennese, who boasted some forty-seven outlets by the 1820s.[86]

But of course not everyone bought directly from the factory. A great deal of porcelain was sold by urban "Galantriehändler," or luxury dealers, who also dealt in silver, crystal, and fine furniture, as well as personal articles such as fans or snuffboxes. By the 1790s, such shops had begun to spread beyond urban entrepôts.[87] At the lower end and in smaller towns, buyers typically made their ceramics purchases at fairs or from itinerant ceramics salesmen, whose poor-quality products and habit of dealing in fakes gave them the worst reputation among traveling salesmen.[88] Many peddlers seem to have been Jewish, which did not raise the Christian public's estimation of the trade. Oversupply led to various ruses for dumping unwanted pieces, including auctions and lotteries, modeled on the Dutch East India Company's wheeze for dispensing with unsalable goods. The first porcelain lottery took place in 1734, in Vienna; Nymphenburg held a lottery in 1758, almost the same year it began production, and in 1767 perfected the art by offering tickets at two price ranges, neatly separating the low- and high-end markets.[89] Auctions became frequent in the age of Wedgwood as a means to clear warehouses of outdated goods. None of these selling venues disappeared entirely over time, as subsequent chapters will illustrate. Long into the twentieth century, porcelain could still be purchased from peddlers, or at fairs, factory shops, or specialty dealerships; only the department store, beginning about 1900, constituted a novel venue. Predictably these giant operations were not welcomed by the luxury dealers and other vendors.

Insofar as something like marketing existing in the century's first half, the favored technique used by princes to plump domestic sales were political ones, beginning with the strong-arming of their local aristocracies to buy local. Early on, Sèvres introduced a Christmas sale where, under the watchful eye of the royal patrons, courtiers felt obliged to buy a present, for their own households or for the monarchs themselves. By the 1760s, perhaps half of the year's sales were made during this season,[90] possibly the first instance of the "Black Friday" phenomenon now so well known to American consumers. Political leaders could also be importuned to implement tariff barriers or even full import bans. But gradually it became clear that buyers needed to be attracted by a means the higher-end manufacturers were loathe to introduce: the open advertisement of fixed prices.

In the mid-eighteenth century, porcelain manufactories adapted a practice in wide use for other goods, the issuing of a "preis courante." Other "going price lists" of the time were created by guilded merchants; they stated, openly, current exchange rates and prices for important commodities (such as grain or herring) in a certain market. From the mid-sixteenth century, "going price lists" of this type had been published in Antwerp, then Amsterdam and London, and had been made available to businesspersons by subscription.[91] In our case, the porcelain "preis courante" were not the result of collaborative agreements but simply advertised the prices offered by each manufactory and in this way formed prototypes of the sales catalog. The first seems to have been issued by the Chelsea factory in 1755, followed by Frankental in 1760.[92] Some were appended to journals or newssheets; the more elaborate type, such as Meissen's first *Preiß Courante* of 1765, would have been available in commissioned shops, or to the individual consumer for a relatively high price.[93]

We should not underestimate the importance or the difficulty of introducing this form of price discipline, for pricing porcelains, as Alessandro Monti has noted, had always been a bit of a shot in the dark. At first, the officials who handled the sales and the books were not privy to the Arcanum and thus did not know how much of which ingredients were needed to make the coveted paste. Costs needed to be covered, but as we have seen, this was a market in which many ordered on commission and paid, it seems, when and how much they cared to pay.[94] Even with the improvement of bookkeeping, the question of how to price porcelains—especially given the very wide range of the pieces' size, quality, and decoration—would never yield stable answers.[95] Meissen's decision to publicize its prices in 1765 signaled that even the market leader recognized the need to embrace this form of transparency, although calculations must have been somewhat arbitrary, and Director Georg Friedrich Helbig was dead-set against competing on price.

Helbig, in fact, took the position that Meissen should stick to a "high price" policy, insisting that if the manufactory catered too much to the lower end of the spectrum, this would lead to the making of poor quality wares and the sullying of Meissen's reputation for refinement.[96] After 1763, his policy had come under pressure from reforming electors, and perhaps the price list was Helbig's attempt to use transparency to show that the manufactory could actually sell to a wide range of consumers. Indeed, the 1765 *Preiß*

Courante offered wares at a staggering 3,087 individual prices, carefully calculated to reflect variations in size, quality, and decoration; soup tureens alone could be had at 118 different prices, ranging from 24 to 75 T.[97] This was an effective means of demonstrating the manufactory's range and was imitated, more elegantly and with images, by Wedgwood, whose catalogs became collectors' items in themselves. Others, such as the Ilmenau factory, used the printed list simply to advertise the cheapness of its wares; at 1 T, 16 groschen, an ordinary urban housewife, after exercising a little frugality, might afford a large blue-and-white coffeepot and a dozen cups and saucers.[98] The Kassel manufactory went one better by placing an ad in the *Casselischen Policey- und Commercien Zeitung* that advertised not only full coffee and tea services, but plates, platters, butter boxes, and the like, "singly or together, to be had for cheap prices; also pieces can be made as you like for services that are missing them. We hereby make this offer publicly and guarantee prompt service."[99] Although relatively few newssheets and circulars from this period survive, these examples suffice to suggest that already by the time Wedgwood entered the German market, the advertising of prices had become part of the porcelain trade.

Fixing prices, however, had consequences, as this allowed commissioned agents a smaller degree of flexibility and—potentially—profit, leading to friction between producers and sellers. Meissen's setting of minimum prices frustrated shopkeepers who were eager to get rid of their items and assumed the risk when customers took goods on credit. Others complained that they had been sent damaged, outdated, or poor-quality goods, or a random selection of wares unsuited to their clientele. Grumblers had to be placated with commissions and kickbacks, and extended credit of their own. One disgruntled salesman commissioned by the Kassel manufactory crafted a twenty-four-page complaint in which he opined: "The fundamental principle must be established that the manufacturer and the worker ought to worry about making the wares and leave the selling of them exclusively to the merchant, as he knows the local market and how to sell goods."[100] In general, however, this advice fell on deaf ears; conceiving themselves as the makers of taste, porcelain makers—aside from a few Thuringian renegades—largely trusted their own visions of what would, or *should*, sell, and how it should be sold.

Even though none of the foregoing amounts to a German "retailing revolution," it suggests that by the 1790s, the luxury market had begun, fitfully, to adjust to a world of competition on price and a widening consumer base, even as it continued to cater mostly to aristocratic tastes. A few new buyers were entering the market; by the century's end, Fürstenberg receipts show that officials, merchants, pastors, and academics were purchasing porcelains.[101] Where means and social strictures allowed, the wives of these middle-class men began to upgrade their tableware. Gustav Freytag, looking back on the period, noted bourgeois women's great pride in their kitchens, outfitted with tin, copper, and, increasingly, porcelain vessels.[102] Despite its aristocratic heritage, porcelain was also becoming an object of middle-class desire.

The Many Styles of the "Golden Age"

Finally in this chapter, let us consider the question of style. Style, in the highly influential analysis of Austrian art historian Alois Riegl, is largely something unconscious, a cultural imprint left by artists and artisans on their products and reflective of the imaginative and technical possibilities and constraints of the day. For Riegl, things of a particular period—whether paintings or shoes—offered a similar sort of insight into the worldview of the times, generally conceived of as unitary, at least within cultural units.[103] This definition will certainly not do for us, as European porcelains never reflected an unconscious or uniform worldview. From the first, European porcelains were deliberately modeled on Chinese and Japanese imports; but by 1711, at least, Meissen was already producing baroque forms as well. Porcelain makers endlessly copied forms, images, and techniques produced by other craftsmen, including terra-cotta and bronze modelers, silversmiths, printmakers, and glassmakers.[104] Certainly by the time Wedgwood came on the scene, all producers had a good understanding of the need to tailor style to "la mode," to offer more than one "look," and to offer goods at varying price points. If not, their experience in trying to compete with the English entrepreneurial genius gave them a painful lesson in realities of modern commerce.

European porcelain, then, never had a single style. And yet, precisely this diversity of styles offers us a fascinating window into the cultural imagination of eighteenth-century central Europe—or at least that of its more elite consumers. In the evolution from chinoiserie to rococo to neoclassicism—with none of these styles fully being eclipsed by its successor—we can see a fascinating progression of tastes, and the importance of certain tastemakers or fads in shaping lines of production. The adoption of foreign styles, from the Chinese to the Italian to the French and English, also tells us an interesting story about the increasing permeability of the central European luxury market with respect to external goods and influences. In the catalogs of figurines we can see these influences reflected, as well as central Europeans' fascination with human diversity, love for animals, and obsession with classical mythology (and, to a much less pronounced degree, its forms of religious devotion). Of course we cannot read eighteenth-century life directly from its tableware: not surprisingly, porcelain makers studiously avoided all-too-real topics such as death in childbirth, malnourishment, and domestic abuse (though child laborers and beggars make appearances). There is a great deal more nakedness and a lot less backbreaking work depicted than we know occurred. But porcelain does have much to tell us about the world of the eighteenth century—or at least the world as central Europeans wished to see it.

On Style and Orientalism

In recent years, many historians have turned to porcelain to illustrate the Eurocentric "orientalism" of the eighteenth and nineteenth centuries. It is certainly the case that porcelain making itself, especially at the outset, was heavily identified with China and Japan, for the obvious reason that everyone knew it had its origins there; Böttger's great ambition was to equal the technical and artistic achievements of the Chinese, and he would have been pleased to hear Frederick the Great refer to Meissen as "Peking de Saxe."[105]

The association of porcelain with the "Orient" was furthered by the use of porcelain vessels for tea and coffee, both "oriental" commodities, though hailing from different "Orients." Before 1750, in particular, European painters eagerly adopted and adapted East Asian patterns, and modelers created figurines that caricatured Asians in a wide variety of ways.

Beyond this, reading "orientalizing" porcelain is treacherous.[106] We might look on the imitation of Chinese wares as a sign of respect for Chinese culture, rather than an indication of contempt for East Asians. We can get wrong Meissen's early "pagodes" for example, as these were modeled directly on Chinese incense burners. But we might well wonder why the grimacing Buddhist figurines—made by many manufactories with varying color schemes and accoutrements—were so popular;[107] some were rendered in ways that at least to our eyes appear to be egregious ethic caricatures (fig. 3.4). "Moors" and Turks, associated with harems, horses, and bizarre headgear, are sometimes more, sometimes less, caricatured. It is also crucial to note that by no means were such "orientalizing" depictions as common as many other types and scenes (see below). We need to put both chinoiserie and "orientalism" more generally in careful context, and to do some rough counting of wares; to do so is to see that "orientalism" in the porcelain industry has both a particular chronology and an important set of contexts that are often overlooked in our rush to identify imperialist worldviews.[108]

As we have seen, Böttger's first creations—like those of the French soft-paste makers before him—were imitations of Asian shapes and decorations. Böttger, like other early manufacturers with access to courtly collections, had many Asian porcelains as well as delftware vessels to use as models. His first red ceramic pieces were modeled on works produced at Yixing, which had been imitated previously by Dutch entrepreneurs.[109] He and his successors then sought to perfect cobalt-blue underpainting so as to imitate Ming wares, and some of Meissen's best-loved early imagery, such as the "Red Dragon" and "Yellow Tiger," copied quite closely favorite scenes in Chinese ceramics. The "Blue Onion" pattern (fig. 3.2) actually meant to depict Mediterranean pomegranates. Moreover, porcelain was scarcely the only "oriental" art form prized in this period; it accompanied Japanese lacquerwares, ornate Ottoman

3.4. "Pagode"

This very early Meissen figurine (1710–20) known as a "pagode" was copied directly from Chinese originals in Augustus II's collection.

weapons, and Chinese silk paintings. Here we have to do, at worst, with a widening ambit of avarice, or at best with a self-conscious embrace of others' good taste.[110]

At first, too, many buyers wanted original East Asian wares and not European imitations, so many, in fact, that in the later 1720s, Meissen works director Hoym and the French luxury merchant Rudolphe Lemaire conspired to place the Meissen mark on the outside of the glaze so that the merchant could scrape it off, and sell the wares as true Japanese porcelain.[111] Yet even as he was selling fake Japanese wares, Lemaire also reported that, at least in France, the style was passing out of fashion. With typically Parisian aesthetic self-confidence, he sent the factory sketches for other styles, made by French craftsmen.[112] As Meissen's master painter Johann Gregorious Höroldt perfected overglaze painting after 1723 (borrowing the technique from glassmakers), the manufactory was able to add new colors to its repertoire and gradually began diverging from Asian imagery. As for the modelers, after Augustus II's death in 1734, Kändler, too, largely left "orientalizing" behind, and by about 1750, *direct* imitation of oriental styles was dead.[113] Craftsmen were now free to elaborate and combine styles; they adopted new colors and imagery to display their virtuosity and to add additional diversity to the marketplace.

The most characteristic style of the next era goes by the name of rococo, referring to the shell-like (*rocaille*) contours it frequently employs. Kändler was the master of this style in porcelain, and in the 1740s he began producing a seemingly endless stream of figurines and sensational decorative objects that made Meissen synonymous with rococo. Kändler's works are deeply imbedded in Saxon court life in ways we can now only partially recover, in its costume parties, in which nobles dressed liked innkeepers and shepherdesses, in its love for Italian comedies, in its obsession with foxes, the hunt, and the garden. The diversity of Kändler's repertoire is notable; he sculpted whimsical monkey orchestras and sober apostles, morally instructive classicizing allegories and teapots shaped like squirrels. Meissen's painters copied Watteau or loosely adapted images from botanical encyclopedias and illustrated works such as Bernard Picart's edition of Ovid's *Metamorphoses*.[114] The same might be said, to a lesser degree, of other manufactories. The variety of subjects and styles would multiply as more competitors joined the market, and factories expanded their repertoire of things to copy.

The figurine generally attracts most attention from commentators seeking to understand "orientalism" in the porcelain trade; in fact, figurines were just as diverse in style as the other wares.[115] If the first porcelain figurines were "pagodes," next came commedia dell'arte figurines. By the 1720s, Meissen was making "dwarfs," birds, figures in national dress (a Pole, a Dutchman, a Janissary), and butter dishes shaped like tortoises.[116] Classicizing mythological or allegorical figures—about which we will have much more to say below—were few until the 1740s, when they began to appear in profusion. By this time—as more central Europeans grew conversant with travelogues, maps, and prints—ethnographic figurines, too, had become popular, sometimes in sets, such as the "street criers of Paris," depicting a wide variety of lower-class tradesmen and modeled on a beloved set of prints.

Most eighteenth-century (and later) figurines portrayed Europeans, the minority "Chinese," "Turkish," or more rarely, Native American or African scenes. As is the case in genre painting, stereotypes, sometimes humorous, dominate, and pieces "read" differently to different viewers. The facial features of the "orientals" sometimes resemble European types, as in Johann Peter Melchior's "Türkenkapelle" of 1775, which depicts a dozen turbaned but otherwise pale-skinned and blond-haired child musicians, or in the strange "Chinese" groups made by the Höchst modeler Johann Peter Melchior, who tended to caricature Asian servants, but to give Chinese nobles white skin and European features (plate 6). We find the Chinese fishing, taking tea in their garden pavilions, or associated with exotica such as parrots or huge artichokes; but Chinese harbors and palaces are also depicted. Turkish men are often paired with horses or musical instruments; Turkish women generally display the luxuriousness of their garments rather than the sensuousness of the harem. Native Americans may exhibit noble or slightly savage-looking features. Africans were rarely depicted but were the most subjected to condescension and exoticization, painted very black with bright red lips and associated with wild animals.

If we now consider the question of "orientalism" in eighteenth-century porcelain, we can see that African, Chinese, and Turkish figurines belong to a much wider repertoire of genre figures, among which there were many variations. Non-Europeans were certainly the most exoticized—after all, Africans, Asians, and Americans *were* least familiar to this audience—but they were not the only ones to be typed or spoofed. If the early eighteenth-century makers modeled turbaned Turks, they also churned out haughty Hussars, boorish Russians, and idle, shoeless Italians by the dozens, echoing the rage for prints depicting varieties of professions or ethnic types. It is impossible to count precisely, but clearly even more frequently represented than any ethnic group were animals, putti, and aristocrats themselves, sometimes in gently parodic

3.5. J. J. Kändler, "Lady and Fox"
Modeled by Meissen's J. J. Kändler, this humorous figurine may have been making an inside joke about a contemporary singer's relationship with a composer named "Fuchs" (fox).

positions (fig. 3.5). We will consider the era's classical repertoire below, but it is surely the case that among eighteenth-century figurines, ancient gods and goddesses far outnumbered Chinese mandarins and denizens of the harem. We do not need to conclude that Europeans did not "orientalize" others; but we do need to understand these portrayals in the context of European consumers' expanding curiosity about the peoples of the world and the widening market's willingness to satisfy them with diverting trinkets of all kinds.

Style in the Age of Neoclassicism

If porcelain is often associated with "oriental" themes, after midcentury it also became inextricably linked with neoclassicism, first of a sweet or "libertine" style." This style, too, has its origins in aristocratic society, and more specifically in the elite men who eagerly participated in the "Grand Tour," an ever more popular custom of gentlemen visiting Europe's great southern cities to commune with classical antiquity and sow their wild oats before marriage. But this was not to be the only style of classicizing porcelain; indeed, by the 1790s the "libertine" style was being replaced by a more austere neoclassicism, more in tune with bourgeois self-conceptions. Even more than in the case of "orientalizing" wares, classicizing porcelains responded to changes in the market and reflect the aesthetic proclivities of their day.[117]

The origins of what I am calling "libertine" neoclassicism lie in the increasing number of northern nobles striking out for Italy on the Grand Tour after about 1720. Here visitors, including the British members of the Society of Dilettanti, learned to admire classical art and architecture and to aspire to bringing more of it home. Like the Italian aristocrats they sought to emulate, these tourists did not fetishize authenticity and preferred baroque restorations to fragmentary originals. Those who could afford monumental sculptures began to buy them from impecunious Italian families or from dealers; but there was also a widening market for reproductions of various sorts. This was perhaps the clientele the Marchese Ginori sought to please with inexact porcelain copies of beloved sculptures such as the Venus di Medici and the Farnese Hercules. But Ginori's sculptures—many of which exceeded fifty centimeters in height—were expensive and difficult to transport. More salable were the smaller figurines that seem to have been first made at Meissen, and then copied by Doccia and all the other European makers. By the 1750s, these white but brightly painted figurines—regularly featuring half-clothed Europas and Sabine women, nymphs playing with satyrs, Bacchus and other lightly risqué subjects—had become all the rage (plate 7).

The sheer number of "libertine" models made at midcentury testifies to Europeans' wide, if not deep, knowledge of classical antiquity, and especially mythology, filtered through the Roman poet Ovid's extremely popular *Metamorphoses*. Between 1710 and 1775, Meissen modeled 240 different classicizing figurines; Venus (twenty-one variations) was the most often featured, with Apollo (eighteen versions) not far behind.[118] Offerings of historical figures, by contrast, were modest; of 173 classicizing figurines made by the

KPM between 1763 and 1786, the only real persons were Solon, Cicero, Diogenes, and Pythagoras.[119] Kändler was again the pacesetter, but artists such as Johann Wilhelm Beyer, model master at the Ludwigsburg factory in Kassel from 1762 to 1768, and the KPM's J. G. Müller, also reveled in this genre.[120] The German antiquarian J. J. Winckelmann, who championed a more austere, purely white, form of neoclassicism, denounced the "ridiculous dolls" made by the porcelain manufactories and blamed them for spreading "childish taste." Were makers instead to copy actual ancient works, this "would contribute more than a little to the furthering of the appreciation for beauty and the elevation of good taste."[121] But the aim of "libertine" porcelain makers was less to elevate good taste than to titillate aristocratic taste buds; this was education in the sense of refinement and *divertissement*, not of *Bildung* or historical understanding, and in Winckelmann's lifetime, this was the form of classicism that sold.

In France, however, an important technical innovation was being pioneered that would begin to transform the ways in which northern Europeans "saw" classical antiquity. This innovation was a bright-white and unglazed mixture known as "biscuit" porcelain, first made in 1751 at the Vincennes royal porcelain factory (soon to be relocated to Sèvres). "Biscuit" was popularized after 1757, when the sculptor Étienne Marie Falconet was tapped to head the French royal manufactory. Falconet adapted this form of porcelain to replicate—in miniature—marble sculptures, including his own widely admired *Nymph Arising from the Bath*. Like the works of the Italian makers, Falconet's surtouts and figurines were made for aristocratic consumers. It is estimated that the reproductions of his *Nymph* at 36.5 centimeters high were sold in 1758 for 144 livres,[122] the equivalent of about four months' wages for an average working man.

Josiah Wedgwood, on the other hand, recognized biscuit's promise to deliver neoclassical style to a much wider clientele. It was essentially biscuit that Wedgwood, the Methodist entrepreneur, adapted to make "Jasperware" cameos, affordable for non-nobles (see the Ilmenau imitation, fig. 2.2); and in his extremely ecumenical list of offerings we also see a more serious and less playful view of antiquity emerge.[123] The 1787 (sixth) edition of his catalog offers a bewilderingly large selection of models, including 151 Roman gods and goddesses, seven illustrious modern men, and 253 popes. What is missing is perhaps more significant: there is no room, here, for Turks with improbable turbans or piano-playing foxes, and the miniaturization of Ovidian scenes tends to desexualize them. There is a seriousness about Wedgwoodian classics that flies in the face of the rococo figurines; these objects were meant to demonstrate the buyer's knowledge, not his or her sense of humor, or willingness to enjoy life's sensual pleasures. This style appealed to some enlightened aristocrats, perhaps especially the Anglophiles and the well-educated, who knew the works of Winckelmann; it also seems to have pleased officials, artists, and schoolmasters, who had their own reasons for disapproving of excessive libertinage and seeking self-representation in a more serious and authentic form of classicism.[124]

At other manufactories, too, biscuit seemed to lend itself to instruction rather than titillation and began to be deployed to create a wider repertoire of new forms, reinforced by princely investment in plaster cast collections, which were increasingly open to local artists and craftsmen as well as scholars and visiting dignitaries. At this time, at least, antiquarian studies and the manufactories seemed to be in tune, and the catalogs began to resemble antiquarian works. The first German maker to adopt biscuit, the Duke of Braunschweig's Fürstenberg manufactory, applied the new medium to the making of affordable mini-busts of classical sculptures and famous modern men.[125] Inspired, apparently, by G. E. Lessing, the neoclassical scholar and playwright who had become the ducal librarian in 1770, Fürstenberg's production began in 1771 with Roman emperors and mythological figures, followed by dynastic portraits, and by 1776, expanding to intellectuals (Voltaire was first). There would eventually be some 135 models, intended at first as table decorations.[126] Fifty-six replicated portions of well-known ancient sculptures, including Winckelmann's favorites, the Dying Gaul, the Medici Niobe, and all three heads of the Laocoön, in different sizes (fig. 3.6). Busts were also made of Lessing, Herder, Goethe, and Winckelmann himself, and of notable Englishmen, including Locke and Alexander Pope.[127] The prices were comparable to Wedgwood rather than Sèvres, with the larger busts

3.6. Laocoön mini-bust

In the 1750s and 1760s, the Vatican's statue of Laocoön and his sons being strangled by snakes played a key role in German aesthetic theory. The Fürstenberg manufactory took advantage of this notoriety by issuing mini-busts of each of the sculpture's three heads.

costing 7 T and the smaller 2 T, the latter comparable to a week's wages for a moderately skilled worker.[128] This put "Kultur" still out of the reach of the journeyman but made it affordable for the middle-income official or merchant. It seems likely that this series of busts—and perhaps all the busts that came afterward—were targeted at the male consumer; very few busts were made of female personages or goddesses. This was, in its way, Winckelmannian classicism embodied: white, desensualized, homosocial; and such trinkets may well have been the way in which most ordinary persons formed their impressions of the classical world.

Winckelmann, together with Wedgwood, Fürstenberg, and the Empire's increasingly ubiquitous plaster cast collections produced a new, whiter, and more austere image of the ancient world, one that was shared by sculptors, architects, artists, and scholars of the post-1780 period, especially but not exclusively in central Europe. More Graeophile than Rome-centered, precise, severe, and blindingly white, this style has been well described by Howard Coutts as "chaste classicism"[129]—as if to draw one's thoughts away from the sensual and toward the ideal. We can see it reflected in the works of many of the next generation's sculptors and architects, Antonio Canova, Bertel Thorvaldsen, Johann Gottfried Schadow, Karl Friedrich Schinkel, and Christian Daniel Rauch, all of whom also provided inspiration and models for the porcelain industry. Schadow's first employment, on his return from Italy, in fact, was as a porcelain painter at the KPM. His romantically tinged neoclassicism soon made him famous enough to receive commissions such as the modeling of sculptures of Hohenzollern princesses and the Quadriga for the Brandenburg gate, but he continued to model occasional pieces for the KPM. Fellow neoclassicists Christian Daniel Rauch and Karl Friedrich Schinkel also made models for KPM, usually to be reproduced in miniature and in biscuit porcelain, very white and unglazed, in tribute to Winckelmann's taste for white marbles.

Already in the eighteenth century, this "chaste classicism" was associated with the rejection of decadent, Frenchified aristocracies, and after the onset of the Napoleonic Wars, with a liberal form of German nationalism. The KPM in particular became identified with this severe style, reflecting, too, the architecture and sculpture Schinkel, Rauch, and Schadow embedded in the Prussian capital, Berlin, and its great boulevard, Unter den Linden. After the wars, the Berlin manufactory in particular capitalized on this identification by commissioning or reproducing works by German artists that combined neoclassical style and nationalist sentiment, and these became enduring money spinners; a classic case was Schadow's sentimental portrait of the very popular Crown Princess (soon Queen) Luise and her sister, Fredericke, made

3.7. Princesses in biscuit

This KPM biscuit porcelain group is a downsized copy of J. G. Schadow's 1797 neoclassical sculpture of Queen Luise of Prussia and her sister Frederike. Such sentimental images of royalty were especially popular in the 1820s.

in marble but eternalized in KPM biscuit miniatures (fig. 3.7). Thereafter, biscuit busts of Goethe and Frederick the Great never left the KPM's lists. It would be this "chaste" nationalist classicism, too, that the KPM conveniently misremembered as its original style in the 1930s (see chapter 8).

This does not mean, however, that such works were the best sellers. If we look beyond the figurines—high profile, but never anything like the majority of sales—to the tableware proper, what sold best, in fact, were always the least costly sets. White was always cheapest, followed by white with cobalt-blue decorations painted under the glaze; until the 1820s, this was the only underglaze painting that stood up to the high heat of firing. In the next costly category were painted cups, coffeepots, and platters, which, once the era of chinoiserie was past, featured, above all, flowers—available in the forms of "German flowers," "Indian flowers," and "strewn flowers," a style invented specifically to spoil plain-white wares otherwise commandeered by the *Hausmaler*. At the next level, involving more colors of paint and sophisticated painters, we find hunting and pastoral scenes and copies (more or less exacting) of paintings after Watteau, Boucher, Greuze, and Angelika Kauffmann. Heroic battle images flourished (at least in Prussia) in the wake of Frederick the Great's wars, and, as Romantic sensibilities swelled, landscapes and lonely castles appeared on plates and platters. "Rousseau cups," memorializing Jean-Jacques, were sold by the Fürstenberg manufactory for 5 T a pair.[130]

A brief fad for porcelains that imitated wood or precious stones—lapis lazuli, or malachite—came and went, as did micromosaic painting. Silhouettes became fashionable in the 1780s, their air of melancholy and mystery furthering proto-Romantic sensibilities. Figurine forms and shapes and sizes of plates, bowls, coffeepots, cups, and serving dishes multiplied, suggesting that the era of historicizing eclecticism, usually dated to the 1820s and after, has deeper roots. At Meissen in the 1790s, customers could order some one hundred different rim and relief designs for plates. In fact, among Meissen's problems in this period was the overabundance of styles offered. This made it difficult for the firm to anticipate demand and resulted in the overproduction of unsalable items when craftsmen filling individual orders made larger batches to economize. No wonder that Goethe, visiting Meissen in 1813, found the number of workers too many, and the warehouses stuffed with outdated goods.[131]

The balance of this section—in which neoclassicism heavily outweighs "orientalism"—is deliberate; it is time, I believe, that we recognize the subordinate, and ambivalent, role the Orient played in eighteenth-century European culture. Unquestionably, Europeans at the century's dawn admired Chinese artistry and technology; in 1800, they were still goggling at reports that the Chinese in "King to cheng" (*Jindezhen*) were operating five hundred kilns and employing one million craftsmen in their porcelain industry.[132] They could afford to admire it less once they had reinvented the secret recipe and began replacing imports with their own products. Midcentury figurines certainly do stereotype grizzled, tea-sipping mandarins and exotically costumed Turks; but then again, they also stereotype wild-eyed Cossacks and improbably coiffed monsieurs. Perhaps the manufactories' post-1760 focus on neoclassical imagery illustrates more forcibly than do their less often depicted Chinese and Turks the diminishing of European regard for Asian cultures; in the end, late Enlightenment Europeans were far more eager to fill their dining rooms with flowers or Venuses than with "orientalized" others.[133]

Although discussions of "golden age" porcelain tend to gloss over stylistic differences, it is clear from our survey that manufactories did not produce goods of a single, rococo, style. There were direct copies of Chinese and Japanese works as well as copies of classical figurines; there were "libertine" and "chaste" classicisms. Although the KPM and Fürstenberg developed something that might be called a Prussian nationalist style in their biscuit wares, by no means was this the only sort of porcelain, or even the only sort of classicism, these firms generated. The Saxon and Bavarian firms, too, cannot be said to have produced uniform "national" or regional styles; the Thuringians, whose output we cannot really survey here, tended to favor genre scenes, landscapes, and flowers, indulging in mythological or religious scenes only for items of the highest value. We must in any case conclude that even in this period, long before the rise of historicism and before the nineteenth century's expansion and stratification of the consumer marketplace,

Germans made porcelains of many different styles, to please many different palates and pocketbooks. A larger proportion of this era's production can be considered "art" than would be the case any time afterward, and a larger portion of it was consumed by a smaller number of persons. But even so, we can see in this period's porcelain something of the diversity of tastes, interests, and worldviews that made up the patchwork culture of "Germany" in the last decades of the Old Regime. We might answer the Tocquevillian question posed at the opening of the chapter by saying that while status distinctions still mattered greatly and income inequality might even have been more exaggerated than before, what had expanded was the range of consumption choices, and that that, perhaps, emboldened at least some non-elites to believe that their tastes were just as good—or better!—than those of the nobleman next door.

The making, selling, and buying of porcelains in the eighteenth century gives life to an economic history that can otherwise seem dry and impersonal. As we have seen in this chapter, European porcelain made its debut in a world still very much dominated by older forms of work, local and limited markets, aristocratic tastes, and mercantile fixations. By no means was the industry willing or able to isolate itself from the wider world, especially as central Europe, after 1750, began to emerge from subsistence and link itself more regularly with foreign markets. Its inhabitants began to expand their information systems, aspirations, and access to consumer goods, and others began to mimic its innovations. As eating habits and tastes changed, so too did porcelain firms—even those supported by princes and blessed by rich commissions—need to adapt their efforts to social and cultural changes whose scope and depth differed very much across the region's many polities. Had a survey of porcelain producers been conducted in 1780, very few would have said that their markets or their customers had remained unchanged since the great founding era of the 1740s to the 1760s. But none, understandably, would have predicted that they were about to enter an age of even greater volatility, one that many would not survive.

Chapter 4

Surviving the Revolutions

Porcelain, as we have seen, was chiefly made for and sup-ported by princes and their courtiers. The logical and, as it turns out, correct inference is that when princes fall on hard times, as they did in France in 1789 and in the Germanys after Napoleon's victories in 1805–6, the porcelain industry suffers. In some cases, as we will see, princely manufactories were shuttered in the wake of revolution and warfare. In others, state subsidies sustained firms across the difficult decade and a half, despite collapsing foreign and domestic sales, in the hopes that when peace returned, production—and consumption!—would return to normal. Regrettably for our manufactories, those hopes would be universally dashed: after the revolutionary and Napoleonic interludes, Europe, and the European porcelain market, would never be the same. For many firms, even those that survived the political and military revolutions, it would be the adjustment to the *postwar* world that would prove most difficult and disappointing of all.

Unquestionably, the French Revolution brought in its wake not only local but pan-European political and economic changes. For our story, the revolution proper mattered most importantly for the French royal manufactory at Sèvres, and the fate of Sèvres mattered for all the other continental manufacturers. But it was the spread of French armies and reforms across central Europe during the Napo-leonic period that made for the deepest transformations in the Ger-man porcelain industry. Napoleon was a formidable foe; in a trivial but telling anecdote, the historian Adolphe Thiers described a meeting between the French emperor and the Austrian foreign minister Count Ludwig Cobenzl in which the former smashed some prized porcelain given to the minister by Catherine the Great, perhaps frightening Cobenzl into ceding Austria's Belgian provinces to France.[1] Much more seriously, French occupation of the Austrian Netherlands, the Rhineland, and subsequently most other German states ushered in the abolition of many of the Old Regime's legal restrictions, including the secrecy of the Arcanum. The wars resulted in severe declines in German princes' expenditures on luxuries; state budgets now had to be devoted to satisfying Napoleon's enormous demands or to waging war against him. Consumers, too, had more urgent needs than the purchasing of saucers and inkwells in a time of war and occupation. If domestic sales plummeted, so too did exports, especially in the wake of Napoleon's empire-wide ban on trade with England (the "Continental System," imposed in 1806) and the cutting off of the Turkish and Russian markets by a series of Russo-Turkish Wars (1787–92; 1806–12), which left hundreds of thousands of "Turkish cups" stranded in warehouses.[2]

But peace, too, brought massive challenges. In 1806, after Austria's defeat at Austerlitz, the Habsburg emperor Francis I formally abolished the Holy Roman Empire. What was reconstituted in 1815 was a German Confederation of about one-tenth the number of Old Regime polities, down from 330-odd to thirty-nine. Some states, Prussia and Austria, in particular, greatly enhanced their holdings; Electoral Saxony, which had sided with the French, lost more than half of its rich territory to its Prussian neighbor. These were still monarchies; but princely expenditures were increasingly subjected to official (if not public) scrutiny. Continuing a process that had begun in the era of enlightened absolutism, most rulers handed over the operation of mercantile manufactories to bureaucrats, many of whom disapproved of excessive luxury spending on the court. Censorship was not abandoned, but information circulated more openly. An era of freer, if not free, trade opened, one that was *not* to the advantage of manufactories born from mercantile dreams.

These political, legal, and economic transformations forced porcelain making, and porcelain selling, to change as well. Declines in princely patronage resulted in new pressures to drop prices, to reduce wages, and to introduce technological and particularly chemical changes into the manufacturing process in order to cut costs. Some firms closed or were sold to private buyers. Those that did survive had to confront challenges to their identity as the producers of artistically impressive "gallantry goods," an identity all the state producers, at least, were loathe to abandon. By about 1830, the "science" side of porcelain making was exerting more force, as firms recognized the crucial importance of employing highly trained chemists, the successors to the eighteenth century's arcanists. The advent of the German Customs Union (Zollverein) in 1834 contributed significantly to the rescuing of several of our manufactories from years of unprofitability in this transitional era.

But the reorganizations, reforms, and new, cheaper recipes of the 1820s also prepared the industry to adjust to an evolving market, one that was still populated by aristocratic buyers, but now also included a growing number of middle-class consumers. By the 1840s, when this chapter ends, even the "survivors" had become leaner, meaner, and more science and market driven than the firms of the 1780s and 1790s. For them, the period between 1815 and 1848 was anything but a "Restoration": it was the Day of Reckoning that prepared them—some better than others—for life in the post-mercantilist marketplace.

This chapter's story is little known; most porcelain connoisseurs pay little attention to the industry after the passing of the eighteenth-century "golden" age. More generally, many German and European historians dash quickly past the 1820s and 1830s to the "Hungry Forties" in preparation for the revolutions that closed that decade. But new work is showing just how fascinating and important are the political, economic, social, and intellectual transformations of the 1820s and 1830s, as an older world attempted to reassert itself and a cadre of new men and women gradually gained the wherewithal to break through barriers and customs, not everywhere and not all at once, but with important long-term consequences.[3] The porcelain industry proves to be a fascinating window through which to examine these changes, as it illustrates beautifully both the impact of political and proto-industrial transformations (examined in this chapter) and the even more remarkable changes in the spheres of culture and consumption (examined in chapter 5). Perhaps more keenly than anyone else, the porcelain makers of this era experienced the long, slow death of mercantilism, intertwined with the equally attenuated and often painful rise of capitalism and industrial society. Their story shows us just how complicated it was for central Europeans to negotiate economies that were neither fully familiar, nor entirely new.

The French Revolution and the Fate of Sèvres

When the revolution commenced in 1789, Sèvres's artistic reputation was still strong, and its royal patrons, Louis XVI and Marie Antoinette, were devoted to its products. Its two-hundred-odd employees worked nine hours a day in winter and eleven in summer. This compared favorably to the thirteen or more hours worked in private factories, of which there were some, despite Sèvres's official monopoly. Pay was relatively good, and conditions more salubrious in small-town Sèvres than in overcrowded Paris.[4] However, the Anglo-French trade treaty of 1786, which Wedgwood had championed, had had disastrous effects, and Sèvres had seen its exports plunge. So serious were the effects of this treaty, combined with the cutting off of other trade and aristocratic emigration after the summer of 1789, that Sèvres's receipts of 380,000 livres in 1787 fell to just 173,000 in 1790.[5]

Louis XVI kept the manufactory open, but in October 1791 he was forced to abolish its royal designation and privileges. When he lost his throne in 1792 the works were put under the control of the minister of public contributions; employees planted liberty trees to demonstrate their loyalty to the revolution. Some skilled workers—who tended to be more loyal to the monarchy—were arrested, and more politicized unskilled workers were emboldened to demand better working conditions. Between 1790 and 1800 the anemic firm churned out neoclassical vases and services to sell abroad and for the domestic market produced cheaper tea sets decorated with typical revolutionary emblems: the tricolor, the lictors' fasces, the Phrygian cap. In 1793, Director Antoine Régnier was ordered to destroy all goods and molds that referred to France's "cy devants tyrans."

He complied in cursory fashion, destroying only wares that featured the royal coat of arms. Though impecunious when the eighteenth Brumaire ushered in the end of the Directory (1795–99), Sèvres—unlike many makers of luxury goods—had survived.[6]

Sèvres survived, in fact, to enjoy new artistic prestige, if not great prosperity, through most of the nineteenth century. In 1800, Lucien Bonaparte, minister of the interior, made what turned out to be a brilliant appointment to the firm's directorship: the young mining engineer Alexandre Brongniart. Brongniart was well connected; his father served as chief pharmacist for Napoleon's beloved Grande Armée, and his own career had blossomed during the Directory, a period of French natural-scientific efflorescence. At the time Brongniart took over the management of Sèvres he was also professor of natural history and zoology at the École Centrale; he would later combine his work at the manufactory with a professorship at the Université de Paris. Together with the natural historian Georges Cuvier, Brongniart was responsible for making an observation on which modern geology, paleontology, and archaeology would rest: that particular fossils are associated with specific geological layers. Even while directing Sèvres, Brongniart continued to work with Cuvier on a grand stratigraphic survey of the region around Paris, which they published in 1811.[7] Brongniart was the first professionally trained natural scientist to take a leadership role in the porcelain industry since Matthias Flurl's ill-starred term at Nymphenburg (chapter 2), but he would certainly not be the last.

Brongniart brought to porcelain making the values of enlightened science, emphasizing, above all, information sharing and what we would call R&D. As soon as Sèvres's budget allowed he invested heavily in scientific experimentation and in market research, which entailed exhaustive polling of local and international firms and extensive travel to study other firms' production and pricing practices. Predictably, he ran into some entrepreneurs who did not share his enlightened attitude toward the sharing of knowledge. For example, in response to Brongniart's request for information, the director of the Valognes manufactory replied: "I will not provide details of the composition of my porcelain pastes, which are based primarily on white clay from the Pieux, because, being father of a large family, I need to retain for a time exclusive use of the important discoveries made in this line."[8] In such statements we see how the Old Regime's forms of artisanal self-protection became the trade secrets of the modern world.

Artisanal habits of secrecy continued, of course. But as Brongniart befriended scholars, local archaeologists, and porcelain makers all over Europe—including Meissen's arcanist (and later director) Georg Frick and Gustav Klemm, cultural historian, state librarian, and curator (after 1833) of Dresden's porcelain collection—he championed the values of scientific exchange, beneficial to the *nation*, if detrimental to individual workshops or localities. We should not forget that as a French official in the age of Napoleon's ascendancy, Brongniart's dedication to science was also part and parcel of his devotion to the French Empire. In his position, at least until 1814, he was able to exert coercive powers beyond the norm, which he used to extract as much information as possible from German makers. Once Napoleon was gone, however, he continued to emphasize the sharing of information across national boundaries. Eventually Brongniart would pour all his knowledge into a general treatise on the art of ceramics, *Traité des arts ceramiques ou des poteries considérées dans leur histoire, leur pratique et leur théorie* (1844), something like the bible for all ceramics makers thereafter.

Brongniart's leadership during his long tenure at Sèvres—ending only with his death in 1848—was instrumental in the placing of chemistry and mineralogy at the center of porcelain makers' concerns and in destroying the culture of Old Regime secrecy. In other ways, too, he was the product of the Napoleonic era, valuing efficiency (though not really profit) and confident of the need for France to take cultural leadership in Europe, if not the world. A newcomer to the porcelain industry in 1800, Brongniart disapproved of Sèvres's paternalist business model, if one could call it that, which permitted officials to help themselves from warehouses and to keep workers on the rolls, even when they had no work to do and the firm had no money to pay them. His first act was to institute a grand-scale warehouse auction; his next was to massively downsize operations, reducing the workforce from 235 to sixty-six employees and pensioning off older workers. He wheedled a fifty-thousand-franc "loan" from the state, which he seems never to have paid back, and his manufactory regularly ran at a deficit, one that reached eighty thousand francs a year between 1814 and 1820, offset, he argued, by unreimbursed royal gifts and a warehouse he valued at more than 420,000 francs.[9] Thanks to his political savvy, Brongniart managed to get Sèvres on the First Consul's *Liste Civile* in 1802 and to prevent the manufactory from being stripped from this state-provided budget for the king's special needs at the time of the very rich Louis Philippe's accession in 1830. Born under the Old Regime in 1770, Brongniart was, nonetheless, a very modern man.

But Brongniart was a scholar and a public servant, not an entrepreneur. His reputation did not depend on Sèvres's bottom line, and profits were never his chief goal, nor that of his ministerial masters. After the revolution Sèvres faced considerable competition from private firms; by one estimate in Paris alone there were twenty-seven porcelain makers operating by 1805.[10] But Sèvres, as the French minister of the interior reported already in 1802, had no interest in making "articles of daily consumption"; if, on the other hand, it did not distinguish itself by being first "in the beauty of its forms, the quality of its pastes, the richness of its colors, [then] it would not merit any longer the government's special protection, and therefore be left to support itself."[11] Brongniart understood clearly his patrons' wishes, writing to the same ministry in 1806: "I am sufficiently well acquainted with the generous and large views of the Emperor to be persuaded that he will require of the Sèvres manufactory only that it continue to be an example of good taste, perfection, and emulation for all porcelain factories."[12]

As we have seen, Brongniart did impose major cost-cutting reforms, but he was also eager to upgrade the artistic quality of French ceramics. Until his time, Sèvres had chiefly made soft-paste porcelains; these products could be gloriously beautiful, but among connoisseurs, soft-paste works lacked the prestige of the German hard-paste wares, as they used cheaper, slightly less plastic clays. Once in office, the new director speedily adopted hard paste for the making of a wide range of wares, permitting the sharpening and purifying of neoclassical forms; he also expanded the firm's color palette by tapping the expertise of chemists and private makers.[13] Throughout his long tenure, Brongniart sought to manufacture "monuments to the history of the arts" and to please not consumers but "men of taste."[14] He said nothing about profits, as indeed was wise; in 1834, a French merchant estimated that the manufactory was receiving some 132,000 francs a year in state subsidies.[15]

This was not, on the whole, a luxury our German firms could afford, at least not in the longer term. In the coming decades they would be expected to compete with Sèvres artistically, but without France's deep pockets. To keep their owners happy, the German firms had to do more than please men of taste; they had to work within limited budgets and conform to the efficiency orientation of their overseers. Increasingly, too, they faced competition for the same consumers from neighboring royal producers and from the private firms, who also suffered from the wars' depredations, but emerged eager to expand their middle-class markets. Even though Sèvres had survived, for the German princely firms, the omens were not auspicious.

The German Firms and the Revolutionary Wars

Perhaps the first "German" firm to feel the revolution's impact was that of Boch Frères, a successful faience factory that had been operating since 1766 at Septfontaines in the Austrian Netherlands.[16] Because they were producing faience rather than porcelain, and perhaps because their operations were located so close to the French border, the Boch brothers were not considered threats to the monopolistic privileges of the Viennese, and Empress Maria Theresa had given the firm the right to display a banner proclaiming its "imperial and royal" status. Standardizing forms without compromising quality, the Boch brothers had prospered and by the mid-1780s were employing upward of three hundred, rivaling the state porcelain makers in sales and size. In 1794, however, the firm's location and successes turned into liabilities. French revolutionary troops, perhaps incensed by that imperial banner, destroyed the works, resulting in losses the owners later calculated at 160,000 T.[17]

After the Terror had passed, one brother (Pierre Joseph) returned to re-build at Septfontaines; Pierre Joseph Boch would run this factory alone. His son, Jean-François, a great admirer of Wedgwood and English commerce, rec-ognized the potential of locating a new manufactory along the Saar River, offering connections to France, the Netherlands, and the western German states. In 1809, this Boch—calling himself Jean-François Boch-Buschmann after his marriage into the prosperous Buschmann family—purchased a ru-ined Benedictine abbey in the town of Mettlach about thirty miles upstream from Saarbrücken and applied to the prefecture in Trier for permission to produce faience. Cooperation and then merger with the French firm of Nich-olas Villeroy would create a larger firm able to create more branches and to survive the fierce competition of the 1820s to the 1840s. As we will see below, thanks to family solidarities, technical innovations, and luck, "Villeroy & Boch" would emerge as one of the most promising "German" ceramics mak-ers by 1850, and a powerhouse by the century's close.

Other firms did not bounce back so easily, or at all. As we saw briefly in chapter 2, having been bailed out in the 1780s, Mainz's Höchst manufactory was still in debt, and its warehouses bursting with outdated goods, when the archbishopric was occupied by the Army of the Vosges in the fall of 1792. Prussian troops besieged and retook the city in the summer of 1793; the French returned to seize a heavily destroyed Mainz in 1795. The deeply indebted fac-tory closed in 1796, an educational lesson, as a nineteenth-century commenta-tor put it, in poor political and economic stewardship.[18] Emboldened by nearby Höchst's travails in the 1780s, Kelsterbach, in Hesse-Darmstadt, re-turned to producing porcelain in 1789, hoping to seize the Hessian market. Picking up some workers laid off at Höchst, Director Friedrich Lay did begin producing, but his debts were so great that no porcelain could be made be-tween 1792 and 1799, when the Landgrave, grudgingly, allowed Lay to sus-pend payments on his loans. When Lay pressed to keep a furniture maker from setting up near his premises, the Landgrave objected to having his "hands tied" but grudgingly gave in. However, when in 1802 Lay admitted that he was still deeply in debt, the enraged Landgrave refused further favors and shut down the works, denouncing his own porcelain as "the worst, and proportion-ally the most expensive I know of."[19]

As in these cases, for many firms, the wars and occupations (not all of them French) simply exacerbated older financial difficulties. After the death, without an heir, of the Bavarian elector Maximilian III Joseph in 1777, Charles Theodore, Palatine Elector and proud owner of the Frankenthal factory, had also become the Elector of Bavaria and master of Nymphenburg manufactory, and moved his collections and court to Munich. Neither factory was flourishing when French armies invaded the Palatinate in 1795. The French seized Frankental and sold the works to a private operator, but it soon landed back in the elector's hands. In 1797, the French declared it national property and leased it out again, but in 1800 the manufactory was closed, and Frankenthal's artists and models were transferred to Munich, thus merging its heritage (and debts) with those of Nymphenburg. The Ansbach factory also fell into Bavarian hands but was sold to a private operator. As war spread across the continent, Royal Copenhagen, too, was affected. Already suffering from financial trouble, exacerbated by factory fires in 1794–5, in 1807 it suffered a further blow, losing its workshops and stocks to English bombardment.[20] French occupation of Italy destroyed aristocratic markets here, and the Neapolitan firm of Capodimonte was sold to a private buyer in 1807. Occupied by French troops, Buen Retiro in Madrid was closed by the French in 1808 and then burned by Wellington in 1812, with the excuse that the French had fortified the buildings.[21] In 1815, turning about unfair play, the Prussians occupied Sèvres and forced workers to destroy all the works and molds bearing Napoleon's image or seal.[22]

The French occupied Braunschweig-Wolfenbüttel and the Fürstenberg factory in 1806. But luckily for this manufactory, the duke, believing the firm in desperate need of reform, had previously hired a French admirer of Wedgwood, Victor Gerverot, as general manager. Whether because he was a Frenchman, or more probably because he was an energetic reformer, Gerverot faced deep difficulties in disciplining his labor force, some members of which were ill, others incompetent, still others surly or overly fond of the bottle. The factory faced threats of closure after Braunschweig became part of the new kingdom of Westphalia, under the rule of Jérôme Bonaparte; it was probably Gerverot's solicitousness of the French court in the city of Kassel that saved it. Gerverot also improved paste quality and to please the king moved production into line with that of Sèvres. Thanks to his efforts, Fürsten-berg received the designation of "manufacture royale" from King Jerôme. But in 1814, when being a Frenchman stopped being a useful thing, Gerverot lost his job (to a German chemist) and had to beg for a pension.[23]

At Meissen, too, as we have seen, the manufactory was in financial trouble even before the revolution began. Its fortunes varied over the period between 1791 and 1805, posting losses more frequently than gains.[24] In 1806, after the collapse of Austria and Prussia, it still employed 515 workers, and it would keep many of them on in good paternalist fashion, despite the drop in sales. Unlike most German states, following Prussia's defeat, Saxony sided with the French and joined the Confederation of the Rhine; Elector Frederick Augustus III now received the title of King Frederick Augustus I, and the man-ufactory officially became the Königlich-Sächsische Porzellan-Manufaktur (having been previously the Churfürstlich-Manufaktur, or Electoral Saxon Manufactory). But allying with the French did not help Meissen's situation, in part because French goods could now freely enter the domestic market, and in part because Saxons, like other Europeans under Napoleonic occupation, had to sacrifice so much of their economic wherewithal to French exactions. Meissen's sales plummeted; the number of workers fell to 395 in 1813, still far too many to produce just 24,378 T worth of salable goods.[25] To keep this workforce fed and production going between 1807 and 1813 the state forked over the enormous sum of 410,000 T. The firm's closure was averted by the winding up of the wars—as it turned out, briefly—in 1814, and the Russian occupation of the manufactory.

This time, at least, Russian occupation did Meissen a good turn. Occupy-ing soldiers—presumably officers—made extensive purchases, and General Repnin-Volkonsky appointed the counselor of mines Carl Wilhelm von Oppel to reorganize the factory.[26] Oppel turned his attention immediately to mak-ing Meissen's wares more marketable, a task made even more difficult after 1815 when, following Napoleon's final defeat at Waterloo, Electoral Saxony lost 58 percent of its land to Prussia. Oppel reduced prices and initiated auc-tions; he obtained molds from Wedgwood's "Etruria" and reduced produc-tion of blue-and-white wares, whose sales had dropped, presumably because so many other makers were offering cheap imitations. Perhaps most importantly, over the protests of older employees, Oppel brought in a chemist, Heinrich Kühn, to serve as technical overseer of the works. When the Russians handed the Meissen factory back to Frederick Augustus I, the king kept both Oppel and Kühn on the job.[27]

The WPM, by contrast, boomed during the early years of the wars. Under the direction of Conrad von Sorgenthal, the manufactory had increased both the artistic and the technical quality of its works and had expanded production. After 1800, sales seem to have been hurt more by the loss of the Turkish market than by the collapse of the Holy Roman Empire. Once again, it helped to have a French-speaking and adaptable director. Sorgenthal's successor Matthias Niedermayr obediently sent paste and finished wares to Sèvres as Brongniart requested. In 1809, the factory was operating at its peak, with 650 workers, when war broke out again, and Napoleonic troops occupied Vienna. The factory itself now had to pay the 666 T per month tribute to the occupiers that had previously been paid for by the state, and when Bavaria sided with the French, the Austrians were cut off from their kaolin supply, located in the area of Passau. As the state teetered toward bankruptcy, sales plunged.

Like Meissen, the WPM was saved from disaster by the war's end, which brought in its train an end to Austrian prohibitions on coffee imports and, more flamboyantly, the Vienna Congress. A glittering array of German, English, Russian, and other nobles set up camp for several months in the city, and those who could afford to do so eagerly purchased tableware to replace the silver they had been forced to melt down.[28] The congress also initiated a new round of diplomatic gift giving and military rewards; the Duke of Wellington proved the biggest winner, receiving lavish Sèvres services from the restored Louis XVIII as well as a 460-piece "Waterloo" service made by the KPM.[29] All seemed in place for the restoration of courtly consumption and the luxury industries that went with it. In 1818, the WPM opened a grand new showroom in honor of its one hundredth anniversary—just at the moment, as it happens, when the market began a cataclysmic downward spiral. Already by 1819, profits had fallen to only 5,771 T, about a tenth of what they had been in 1816.[30]

In the period after Frederick II's death in 1786—the years of Meissen's discontent—the KPM, like the WPM, had prospered, posting good profits. Its successes owed a great deal to the fact that Frederick's successor, Frederick William II, had placed the manufactory under the supervision of a manufacturing commission headed by Friedrich Anton Freiherr von Heinitz, chief of the mining and metallurgy department (Bergbau- und Hüttendepartement) since 1777, and founder of the Prussian Mining Academy, one of Prussia's first technical training schools. An advocate of English-style industrialization and commerce, Heinitz was eager to modernize Prussian porcelain production. He instituted monthly meetings of the commission and pressed for technological improvements with the aim of fiscal independence. On his advice, in 1787–88, the Jewish community was allowed to buy out its obligation to purchase porcelain for 40,000 T, and the free use of wood from royal forests was ended. It was Heinitz who tasked the young Alexander von Humboldt with reporting on the state of the manufactory at Ansbach (which became Prussian patrimony in 1792, when the local Margrave died); from Humboldt's cameralist and scientific insights, Heinitz drew further lessons for reforms both at Ansbach and in Berlin.[31] He purchased the German industry's first steam engine, for mixing the KPM's clay; and he saw that a new line of cheaper white porcelain was produced. On his watch, J. G. Schadow's "chaste classicism" took off, and the manufactory earned a reputation for technical excellence as well as artistic innovation.

But in 1802 Heinitz died, and four years later, the French occupied Berlin and the KPM, staying until November 1808. The cash was seized, and the manufactory forced to make payments to the occupiers, as well as to supply French administrators with items to their taste. The director was compelled to take out loans to cover operations. Then the French simply declared the manufactory in Berlin and its outlet shops in Breslau and Warsaw to be the private property of the emperor, looted the wares, and stabled horses in the buildings. Workers had to be fed at a soup kitchen. The 1810 Prussian Guild Ordinance (Gewerbeordnung), a key part of the Stein-Hardenberg reforms, dissolved guild and corporate privileges in the hopes of opening up the economy; part of the collateral damage—for all reforms, too, have their victims—was the KPM's loss of its monopoly on production and sales. Luckily, the firm now had cheaper white wares to sell, which compensated in part for plummeting high-end sales.[32] In 1815, with the war's end and Prussia's territorial expansion, the firm seemed poised to return to profitability and artistic prominence. In fact, it would be decades before such aspirations would be realized.

From Princely States to Nation-States

The Napoleonic Wars resulted in the dissolution of the Holy Roman Empire and the ravaging of the economies of central Europe. But the French also brought reforms, such as the abolition of serfdom and the tithe, the dissolution of the guilds and older tariff regimes, the emancipation of the Jews (in Prussia), and in many western German states, the adoption of constitutions and some version of Napoleon's Civil Code. These were meaningful changes, and even after the French retreated, many German states embraced some degree of economic or even political liberalization.[33] In the 1820s, some of these reforms were wiped out or tempered as princes and conservatives retrenched; many central Europeans continued to live essentially as serfs. Guilds quickly reorganized as trade associations (*Innungen*), and freedoms given to Jews were never adopted or rescinded. But the Society of Orders had been shaken to its foundations, and no matter how willing, states could not restore all their aristocrats' land or privileges, nor did bankrupt princes have the funds to return to their older mercantile practices. Officially "restored," the Old Regime would not, in fact, return.

Postwar agreements restored some toppled monarchs to their kingdoms, but in the wars' aftermath, monarchs increasingly became ceremonial figureheads with primarily cultural significance. Although there were calls for the unification of the German states from some political liberals and radicals in this postwar period, princes and high officials such as Count Clemens von Metternich, chancellor to Habsburg emperors Francis II and Ferdinand I, tried to stamp them out, and the new German Confederation, like the old Holy Roman Empire, was a largely toothless association of sovereign principalities. But the governance structure of these reconstituted kingdoms underwent a series of transformations as officials and legislative bodies took over more and more of the business of governing and the management of the economy. Where once "Germany" was made up of princely states and free imperial cities, increasingly this abstract entity contained larger-sized nation-states, entities in which all persons are presumed to share a common culture and at least some common interests to be defended by the state's rulers.

This transition to the nation-state does not mean, however, that after the wars, German monarchs became less visible or important to their subjects; in some sense they were needed as icons around which new identities could be formed, and culturally speaking, they probably took on *more* visibility for their subjects, in monuments, prints, and memorabilia.[34] States with newly revised borders such as Saxony, Prussia, and Bavaria tapped the aura of the monarchs and the memory of their courts as a means to anchor their self-definitions as "Kulturstaaten" in glorious and coherent national histories[35] (fig. 4.1). The taste and patronage of the prince, now tempered by a greater seriousness of mind and shared with a wider public, was now to reflect the commitment of the whole nation to culture. Thus was the princely aspiration to exhibit *Glanz* transformed into the national ambition to display *Kultur*.

Chapter 5 will attempt to survey these cultural changes, but it is first necessary for us to grapple with the economic and bureaucratic changes in the post-Napoleonic period, a subject that has received little attention in recent years. The precarious postwar economic situations of the German states— each with its own prince, its particular resources, its idiosyncratic policy makers—shaped the fortunes of the porcelain makers, especially those founded as mercantile enterprises. Again, the porcelain industry did not represent anything more than a small part of the post-Napoleonic economy. But the diverse strategies and fates of its leading firms in this period illustrate nicely just how differently economic and political change looked and felt to those who experienced it, and how impossible it was to foretell what *the* path to modernization might be.

4.1. Frederick William III teacup

During and after the Napoleonic Wars, the "chaste" neoclassical style was used to celebrate monarchs and military leaders.

Navigating the Postwar Economy

Before 1800, some German regions had begun the process historians call early industrialization, characterized by the expansion and coordination of cottage industries and the founding of factories, some of them employing divided labor and small machines. The uneven distribution of industrial enterprises can hardly be emphasized enough; while Saxony, for example, in 1815, had nearly 80 percent of all cotton spindles in German states, territorially larger Bavaria could not muster more than 1 percent of this vital industrial indicator.[36] By keeping English goods out of European markets, Napoleon's Continental System had benefited some fledgling domestic industries, such as cotton weaving and beet sugar refining. But French occupations brought in their train confiscations, exactions, bankruptcies, and, in the wars' last years, inflation unleashed by the forging of banknotes. And when British goods flooded markets once more after 1815, continental manufacturers found it difficult to compete. As if such conditions were not challenging enough, the extreme weather conditions of 1816–17 ("the year without a summer") spread near famine conditions across central Europe; in these years, as in other hardship years such as 1830–31, 1845–48, and 1857, Jürgen Kocka estimates that about half of city dwellers in places such as Hamburg and Cologne needed public assistance to survive.[37] State officials seeking to stabilize and revive their economies had their hands full.

In Berlin, a few reformers committed themselves, and Prussia with them, to moving on from mercantilism. Their championing of a freer market responded to the success of British trade and spread of Smithian ideas; but these early German "liberals" were officials, not men of business. In 1818 these reformers pushed through a remarkably liberal tariff law, dissolving internal customs and radically lowering external duties to encourage trade. The measure was by no means universally popular, as it allowed cheap foreign goods into Prussia, depressing domestic prices, and put terrible strain on manufacturers of exports, who still faced other states' tariffs. For many years afterward, the Prussian economy remained precarious and was saved from bankruptcy only by the machinations of several unusually competent officials and an enormous loan negotiated by Nathan Rothschild. Despised by porcelain makers among others, in the long run, the 1818 tariff, together with the abolition of the guilds, acted as a kind of "shock therapy," forcing weaker competitors out of business, and spurring officials to take a different path to patronizing industry: by promoting technical education and the exchange of information.[38] Once established in 1834, the Zollverein united many of the German Confederation's states in a customs union that did away with most internal tolls to the benefit, in particular, of the larger and more industrially advanced polities.

But Prussia was not "Germany." If officials in other German states saw the need for some forms of economic liberalization, they also feared overly rapid economic and social change. Movement toward liberalization was hampered by competing demands within their states—from guildsmen for example—as well as by large state debts, widespread antipathy toward speculation and industrial concerns, and suspicion of "foreign" (including other German) trading partners. Paternalism continued to inform policy decisions, and particularism to characterize central European development. In Prussia, this took the form of ministerial interventions designed to encourage trade, supply credit, and bring industry to impoverished areas. In Austria, policies were neither so decisive, nor so interventionist. Whereas Prussia abolished its guilds in 1810, Emperor Francis I approved the dissolution of guilds in industries producing for exports, but not those producing for the domestic market, a rather artificial distinction that simply ended in a muddle. Serfdom continued in many places in all but name. Francis periodically imposed bans on new factory building when he felt adequate housing for workers was lacking, not a consideration that worried Prussian bureaucrats. Austria, aside from industrial pockets in Bohemia and Lombardy, was much slower to industrialize and urbanize than the more westerly German states, and never did join the Zollverein.[39] But it can be argued that too much ministerial steering also retarded Prussian industrialization.[40] Mutually distrustful states observed their neighbors closely, but enduring customs, privileges, and uneven resource distributions dictated that they could not have copied one another, even had that been their desire.

One of the things early nineteenth-century German states could not do was to fully resuscitate mercantile policies; for one thing, the wars had left many with deep debts, and for another, liberal officials now considered this an inefficient means to stimulate the economy. But for private persons, too, starting a business in this tumultuous era was difficult. Capital was scarce and credit hard to obtain, as potential investors—often for good reason—found the proto-industrial start-ups worryingly risky. In this situation, even many established producers could not hold on. Jürgen Kocka estimates that even in Saxony, probably no more than 10 percent of entrepreneurs at work before the wars were still in business by the 1830s.[41] By that time, a small group of new, private manufacturers had begun to emerge, pooling family funds and family labor. We can glimpse the expansion of manufacturing in employment figures for Prussia, where the number of "factory workers" expanded from 187,000 in 1816 to 554,000 (plus 100,000 in mining and metallurgy) in 1846. We must keep in mind that these remained mostly very small "factories," with very few machines. In 1846, in all of Prussia, there were only an estimated seven hundred steam engines, or one for every 934 "factory" employees.[42]

While increasing manufacturing made some goods cheaper, it did not necessarily make for "mass" consumption. One of the perplexing statistical findings of economic historians is that in periods of early industrialization, even when average real wages increase, average nutritional standards (measured by adult heights) tend to stagnate or fall. This "Early Industrial Growth Puzzle" has been convincingly explained as the result of widening income discrepancies as well as rising dependence on the market for food, which often made for poorer nutrition for lower-end consumers in particular.[43] In central Europe, sustained rises in real wages are not in evidence until after 1870, and even as coffee, sugar (and porcelain) prices were falling, meat and milk prices remained high. Thus, while some middling urbanites surely could afford to put a pot and teacups on their tables, as an 1836 genre painting (plate 8) suggests, they were no replacement for aristocratic buyers, nor could they possibly absorb the waves of cheaper wares now flooding the market.

This brief sketch of the Germanys' postwar economies offers us a backdrop against which to place the history of the porcelain industry in the Restoration era. The older mercantile firms, in particular, found it hard to accommodate themselves to the hardscrabble early industrial marketplaces of 1815–50. Each manufactory faced a slightly different series of technical and budgetary challenges, but all faced enormous drops in sales. Some did not survive. In addition to the closures described above, Württemberg's royal manufactory (Ludwigsburg) was shuttered in 1824, Korzec closed in 1832,[44] and Royal Copenhagen was sold to a private owner in 1833. Of the thirty-three porcelain makers and painters operating in Paris under the empire, only fourteen survived to see 1819.[45] Even the most prominent struggled. The KPM's gross income fell from 212,000 T in 1819 to 128,000 T just two years later; Meissen posted a more modest but still-painful drop, from 108,500 T in 1819 to 84,700 T in 1822—for a firm whose income had been more than triple that figure (260,500 T) in 1765.[46] The whole of the 1820s would prove sobering, if not disastrous, for all.

Complicating the picture even further was the fact that although much princely patronage—and generosity—had been withdrawn, by no means had these manufactories become autonomous entities. Particularly when they asked for subsidies or loans, the state felt entitled to interfere in hiring, pricing, and marketing practices. Manufactories of this sort were still expected to produce *Glanz*, but with fewer resources and with more exposure to competition based on price. Moreover, they had now to justify their existence to a group of generally less sympathetic patrons than they had found among the princes: the increasingly meddlesome bottom-line minders of the German Confederation's numerous ministries of finance.

Porcelain in the Gimlet Eye of the Finance Ministry

One might say that the 1780s and 1790s, already, foreshadowed postwar antagonisms between manufactories and ministries. It was in this period that states began to put additional cameralist oversight into place and to seriously curtail firms' privileges, most especially their entitlement to wood from princely forests. The KPM, for example, as we have seen, came under the supervision of von Heinitz, who imposed fiscal discipline and introduced modern scientific and industrial practices.[47] But after 1810, the KPM would be more fully subordinated to Prussian bureaucratic management. Taken out of the king's hands, the manufactory was first placed under the administration of the Prussian Interior Ministry. Subsequently, it—like many firms—would be handed off to other ministries, a sign, perhaps, of the bureaucracy's discomfort with managing such an enterprise (see table 4.1).

Ministerial intervention into the manufactory's daily operations was invited by serious losses at a time the state could ill afford subsidies. In the case of the KPM, overseeing ministries did not want to close the factory, but as sales dropped and losses mounted, they doled out funds unwillingly and made the firm promise to reduce costs sufficiently to live within its own budget. In the dark years before 1822, the KPM was kept afloat only by labor

TABLE 4.1. The KPM's Ministerial Minders, 1787–1879

1787	Manufacturing Commission, under supervision of Department of Trade and Manufactures, Customs and Excise Taxes
1810	Ministry of Interior
1815	Ministry of Finance
1817	Ministry of Trade
1825	Ministry of Interior
1834	Ministry of Finance
1835	Office of Trade, Fabrication and Construction
1837	Ministry of Finance
1848	Ministry of Trade
1879	Cultural Ministry

Source: Siebeneicker, Offizianten und Ouvriers, 30–33, 40, 451.

cuts and commissions such as the giant "Waterloo" series and services made to honor Prussia's top military leaders.[48] After that time, it was kept on a short leash and expected to break even, although it was allowed to run occasional deficits, as in 1834–35.[49] This parsimoniousness forced the manufactory to introduce efficiencies, especially at the cost of its skilled workforce, but also restricted its ability to experiment and innovate artistically. Rather like public universities in the United States today, treated as "state" institutions even as the percentage of public support dwindles year after year, the KPM's special status helped it limp along but also prevented it from acting as an autonomous operator and, at least in the manufactory's view, hampered its ability to produce quality products.

The KPM's experience in the brave new world of the "Restoration" typified that of many others. Almost all the other surviving royal firms would be subjected to much more severe budgetary restrictions after 1813, with the exceptions of Sèvres, Nymphenburg, and the St. Petersburg manufactory, which continued to receive lavish royal funding.[50] Paternalism was not dead; but now that fiscally disciplined state bureaucracies rather than (for the most part) profligate princes held the purse strings, the stage was set for new conflicts between luxury producers and patrons: officials dictated strategic directions with an eye to the overall good of the state, while the factory directors made production decisions based on their perceptions of what was good for the factory's prestige.[51] What was good for the factory's prestige, of course, were artistic and one-of-a-kind items, which captured the viewers' attention and displayed the manufacturers' skills. But art and commerce are rarely compatible bedfellows. The making of art requires time, talent, and imagination, and often the "wasting" of supplies, while success in commerce requires speed, flexibility, and economizing on labor and materials. There was no Arcanum to prescribe the perfect way to reconcile these demands, and the insistence on pursuing *both* prestige and profit made for tensions that will accompany us through the next two hundred years of porcelain-making history.

In the case of the private firms, commerce could be prioritized; but this was not the case for the state makers, who were also charged with the maintenance of national *Glanz*. In the absence of direct market discipline, the ministries would try to impose it indirectly, creating a series of running, and unending, conflicts between (state) manufactories and (state) ministerial officials. Nowhere was this combination of new bureaucratic pressure and old-style paternalism more evident than in the affairs of the most venerable of firms, Meissen. The epic tale of the conflict between the manufactory and the Saxon Finance Ministry—won repeatedly by the manufactory—deserves some additional elaboration as it is still going on today (see chapter 9).

Meissen, as we have seen, suffered grievously after 1806 and needed massive subsidies to get through the wars. In 1814, an attempt at cost saving backfired when a yellowish-gray clay damaged the firm's reputation for perfect whiteness.[52] In 1815–16, the firm staged some eighty-five auctions and drastically reduced prices in order to clear warehouses bursting with outdated goods. It managed to sell off almost sixty-five thousand pieces and in that year turned a decent profit.[53] But the ensuing decade was much more difficult; even with serious price reductions, Meissen wares were more expensive than English bone china or French porcelains, not to mention Thuringian ceramics. The Austrians continued to ban Saxon imports, and even when tariffs between Prussia and Saxony were lowered in 1822, huge porcelain duties remained intact.[54] An accounting in January 1820 showed that the manufactory owed the state about 95,000 T, including advances for new buildings and machinery.[55] Warehouses still overflowed with overvalued and unsalable stuff. By 1821, the Finance Ministry had evidently had enough. It instructed the manufactory to stop using the argument of maintaining quality as a means to avoid pleasing modern consumers, and it suggested concrete reforms: the manufactory should immediately drop prices, expand its middle-grade offerings, adopt transfer printing, and institute "the speediest possible introduction of a greater assortment [of goods] in consideration of the latest taste" to increase domestic sales.[56] Not for the last time, the Saxon Finance Ministry told its own manufactory to behave like a proper private enterprise.

Meissen director von Oppel responded, directing his appeal to the Saxon king Frederick Augustus rather than to the Finance Ministry. It was true, he argued, that top-quality goods had not sold in large quantities recently, but increasing production of middle-grade wares would cause those lucrative sales to fall further. Orienting itself to this market, moreover, would force the manufactory to focus on quantity and quick sales rather than on quality: "Commercial interests want a large number of good, middle-quality wares, but in satisfying [such orders], technical proficiency suffers, as it strives only for reducing costs of middle-grade wares."[57] In a follow-up letter written a month later, Oppel reiterated the need to keep up the firm's artistic reputation and issued an ultimatum: "If continuing in this spirit is not desirable then it is better to act at once, to dismiss the artists, to reduce the overall costs, and to devote production to everyday tableware, which would secure and simplify the maintenance of the manufactory."[58]

The ministry was not prepared to go this far, but it continued collecting its own information about the porcelain market and kept up pressure on the firm. By 1828, it had compiled an impressive number of price lists from both private and royal factories, evidently with the purpose of comparing prices and offerings. The manufactory responded to ministerial demands with a 109-page history of the firm, tabulating Meissen's financial benefits to the various princes it had served in its first 108 years. The document concluded that even when more than 700,000 T in subsidies for 1806–27 were subtracted, Meissen had contributed 1,532,946 T to Saxony's finances.[59] Unconvinced, the ministry sent members of the commission to visit the Dresden outlet store and other porcelain shops in the capital and asked several merchants for their opinions. The report from the site visits was scalding; the outlet shop was dank and stocked only with "less salable" items such as heavily gilded vases and biscuit figurines; everything was overpriced and out of style.[60] By comparison, the private emporia were well lighted and offered cheaper and more fashionable items. The merchants, too, were critical of Meissen; one recommended privatization so that the factory could be properly run by a man of business.[61] Everybody recommended further drops in prices.

Predictably, Meissen's management, and especially its artists, found this advice deeply unpalatable, but the manufactory did respond, first of all by lowering prices. By 1830, Meissen's prices had fallen by about 61 percent over the levels of 1804. The manufactory also dissolved its connections with commissioned agents and warehouses, falling from about 105 in 1774 to fewer than ten in 1827. Its production numbers, too, declined precipitously, from over five hundred thousand items made in 1804 to fewer than 264,000 in 1827.[62] As the fiscal wolves closed in, the new king, Anthony, stepped in to offer subsidies amounting to nearly 57,000 T from 1829 to 1832.[63] The revival of eighteenth-century models to satisfy English buyers—a hugely significant turn to self-historicization whose consequences will be discussed in chapter 5—also helped to salvage the firm's bottom line.

Ironically, however, it was the manufactory's extraction from royal ownership and elevation to a national *Kulturinstitut* that saved it. In 1830, Saxony promulgated a constitution, and Augustus II's beloved enterprise became the property of the Saxon people. Given the opportunity to close the porcelain money pit, the new state assembly (Landtag) chose to delay, continuing small subsidies as it awaited the effects of the Customs Union, which went into effect in 1834. The Landtag would be rewarded for its patience: in 1834, for the first time in thirty years, Meissen turned a profit.[64] By 1836, Meissen's profits amounted to 25,000 T, though this fell to an annual average of

13,500 T in the 1840s.[65] But profitability now had to be weighed against national pride. To close the firm after this time would mean much more than the winding up of a royal pet project; it would mean a threat to Saxon tradition and identity itself.

Meissen's reworking of its aims—from the creation of princely splendor to the furthering of national art—ran parallel to efforts elsewhere in the German states. In his campaign to save and renew Nymphenburg, Crown Prince Ludwig had promoted the factory's status as a Bavarian *Kunstanstalt*, a claim reiterated in an 1819 history of the manufactory, written by its technical director. Helpfully, given Nymphenburg's parlous postwar finances, the history asserted that the firm "from its origins had as its goal less the hope of profit than of the advancement of national [*vaterländischen*] art."[66] By 1840, the KPM would also be advertising itself as a national *Kunstanstalt*, in at least implicit competition with others for cultural prestige.[67] This claim to represent a threatened cultural heritage would help the royal firms survive the worst years and provide rhetorical ramparts to protect the manufactories from overzealous finance ministries. But two other significant factors contributed to some of the firms' return to financial solvency: the triumph, we might say, of chemistry, and the embrace of what we would now call "R&D."

The Triumph of Chemistry—and Its Consequences

Chemistry, of course, had always been a critical aspect of ceramics making; but the expansion and professionalization of chemical R&D transformed the porcelain industry in the nineteenth century and put it on the path to mass production. Chemical innovations resulted partly from aesthetic rivalries: since the middle of the eighteenth century, the race had been on to discover new glazes and the whitest paste mixtures. As competition grew, novelty and a diverse range of products and price lines mattered even more. The abolition of the Arcanum and the widening flood of technical journals, manuals, and encyclopedias offering extensive and detailed information about how to produce fine ceramics also fostered innovation.[68] But even more clearly, technical modernization in German industries was the result of increasing competition on price, dating back to the era of Wedgwood's challenge, and the expansion of ministerial oversight we have just surveyed, beginning in the late eighteenth century and accelerating in the post-Napoleonic era. The nearly universal need to cut costs as competition increased resulted in much wider experiments with new kiln design, energy sources, and paste mixtures. Firms searched for locally sourced ingredients and labor-saving devices and adopted transfer printing and then color lithography. Ministry officials also discovered that natural scientists were much easier to work with as factory directors than were the artists, for the scientists, like the officials, valued efficiency over artistry and recognized the impossibility of perpetuating older forms of production in the dynamic new marketplace. And the more science took command, the more quickly the industry moved toward standardization and cost-oriented mass production.

To speak of "science" in the porcelain industry is to refer chiefly to chemistry and mineralogy, not incidentally the special fields of the recipe's founders, Böttger and Tschirnhaus. Mineralogy was involved from the first in the location of proper clays and other essential minerals, including cobalt, feldspar, lead, and alabaster. It would continue to be essential for all the firms in the identification of these minerals close to home, which made them less expensive to procure.[69] But chemistry was even more important, for on it depended the correct assaying of the materials, the identification of workable paste mixtures, and the development of new glazes. In the eighteenth century, this chemistry should be described as "artisanal" rather than research science, for it was undertaken by persons trained as craftsmen, rather than in universities, using the modest tools in their workshops to attempt more or less sophisticated improvisations.[70] Experience was valued over abstract knowledge, and foreign workers (Dutchmen in Prussia, Englishmen in France) continued to be valued as conveyors of craft techniques. The practice of transferring ideas from other crafts continued, perhaps most importantly in imitating the Bohemian invention of poured and molded ("pressed") glass.

Yet porcelain makers recognized, increasingly, the importance of experiments—Wedgwood's success with Jasperware, if nothing else, taught them that. But a more prosaic problem also contributed a great deal to the uptick in experimentation: competition over wood. By the later eighteenth century, heavily populated areas on the continent were suffering deforestation, a fate that had befallen England much earlier. As lands were cleared, populations rose, and small iron forges and glassblowing cottages spread. Competition for wood sources increased; in the face of rising real prices—estimated at 62 percent higher in 1790 than in 1700[71]—German states began to recognize the need to diminish the use of wood as an energy source, and to curtail the founding of firms that lacked independent timber resources. Princes began eliminating forest privileges, an essential perk coveted by all early porcelain makers. When properly prepared and trimmed, wood burns cleanly and thus has always been preferred in the firing of porcelains. But once princes started cutting off free supplies, manufactories had a strong incentive to experiment with the use of other energy sources, and most especially coal.

Wedgwood, famously, had moved production to coal already in the 1770s. Continental producers had some success in adopting it to first firings but found that it spoiled colors and left a sooty residue if used for the second firing. Most state firms gave up and tinkered with kiln design instead. In 1796, the KPM, again at von Heinitz's urging, was first to adopt Wedgwood's round, multishelved kiln, which saved fuel as it allowed wares at different stages of completion to be fired at the same time.[72] The first continental ceramicist to succeed in using coal for both firings would be the private entrepreneur—and great admirer of English technology—J. F. Boch in 1815. After Boch's breakthrough, coal became more and more critical, especially for lower-end producers, so much so that by the 1850s, it became more advantageous to locate a factory near coal deposits than near its customers.[73]

Kiln design was not so much the purview of the chemists, but the all-important mixing of glazes and pastes certainly was, and as the age of "secret recipes" closed, overseeing officials began to turn to men with more abstract scientific training to increase the efficiency of these experiments. In Prussia, once again, von Heinitz played a key role, in 1792 tasking the young Alexander von Humboldt with studying fuel efficiency at Ansbach and then at Tettau. In 1787, he appointed the university-trained chemist Martin Heinrich Klaproth to the inspection committee of the KPM.[74] Klaproth was intrigued by the opportunities for experimenting offered at the manufactory and soon took on a permanent post as the KPM's chemical expert. Once on staff, the chemist devoted himself to the development of pigments for glazes and the training of lab assistants in chemical research methods. As Ursula Klein has shown, Klaproth's work at the KPM was also instrumental in his discovery of the element uranium in 1789.[75] At almost the same time as Klaproth, the less successful chemist Matthias Flurl received an appointment at Nymphenburg (1788); a few years later Brongniart took up his position at Sèvres. By 1810, all the major players were operating full-time "labs," working, for example, on the tricky problem of how to stretch the use of gold leaf as far as possible.

We should not see industrial experimentation as a teleological endeavor, with a single aim and an endpoint after which trials stop. No matter how efficient the manufacturing process, there is always the possibility of perfecting it or of finding cheaper and simpler shortcuts, and the need to keep up with competitors' innovations. Just so in the porcelain industry. Even in 1815, porcelain remained tricky to make, and to fire; some fancy pieces required three or more firings, each one posing a risk that the artists' work would be ruined. Even well-run manufactories recorded a great deal of waste. No one's paste could be exactly the same, as clay contents differed across the continent, and makers never tired of trying new mixtures in the hopes of lowering costs and fuel usage, and of increasing the paste's flexibility and strength. There never was "one" recipe: at Sèvres, for example, Brongniart used 66 percent clay in his mixtures, while his Limoges competitors used 40 percent, and added much more feldspar. Later in the century, the industrial chemist Hermann Seger would up the quartz content of KPM wares to 45 percent (as compared to 25 percent previously), to allow for lower firing temperatures (and a reduction in clay use). English "bone china" mixed 40–50 percent cattle-bone ash into its clay, whitening and strengthening the final product.[76]

One of these experimental pastes would prove crucial to the survival of the KPM in the post-Napoleonic era. Once again this was the brainchild of von Heinitz, who pressed his manufactory to introduce what would be called "Gesundheitsgeschirr" (hygienic wares), in imitation of French "hygioc-erames."[77] "Hygienic wares" were undecorated, easy to clean wares for washing or for serving food and drinks; they were made with a cheaper paste and without lead glazes. Whether because they were lead-free, or, more likely, because they were cheap and useful, "hygienic wares" proved popular even as the postwar market tightened. In 1822, the KPM was able to realize a 32,000 T profit from these items, which were made at a separate factory in Charlottenburg.[78] Profits here would offset losses in the production of artistic porcelains, elaborating a business model for fashionable goods already existing in embryo by the later eighteenth century, in which high-quality, high-cost "runway" items are supported by the simpler, lower-quality wares sold to a wider public.

The KPM's further technical progress awaited the punctuated upward mobility of Georg Frick, who began as an arcanist's assistant in 1797, and was early recognized as a talented chemist. As head arcanist, Frick toured the major German factories with Alexandre Brongniart in 1812 and returned home eager to experiment with colors. In 1814, his experiments with chromium oxide expanded the range of green glazes and made priming with solutions of gold unnecessary; he also pioneered the use of iridium to create new shades of black and gray.[79] As Frick and others expanded the options for coloring rims and surfaces, manufactories began to generate sample plates to entice consumers to customize their wares: few buyers, undoubtedly, understood how many hours of R&D lay behind these alluring advertisements (plate 9).

In 1813–14, as Frick was tinkering with his new glazes, several other manufactories evidently recognized a pressing need to place an expert chemist on staff. For example, both Meissen and Fürstenberg attempted to hire Carl Prössel, a chemist working in Zwickau. Prössel chose Fürstenberg, in part because he was offered 100 T more a year in salary, and in part because the Hessian firm offered him directorship of the entire factory, not just of its technical department. At Fürstenberg, Prössel succeeded in introducing the use of peat for some firings, and he attempted other cost-cutting measures, with little success. His successor increased production of less expensive wares and found a cheaper local source for clay to make Fürstenberg's version of *Gesundheitsgeschirr*. He introduced new round kilns, including a three-chambered, state-of-the-art kiln that was capable of firing three times the number of items with one-half of the wood used in the older kilns. The factory also introduced new drying racks and a more powerful mill for crushing clay, both based on English models. By 1828. Fürstenberg was just one of many firms experimenting relentlessly with techniques to stretch gold, already in 1813 adopting an additive that allowed the gold to bind better with the glazes. It is estimated that by the later 1820s, Fürstenberg had dropped its energy costs by 75 percent and its use of gold by one-half. The ducal cabinet, however, remained unsatisfied as profits were eaten up by an overstaffed, and in their view, overskilled, painting department; privatizing it was yet another sign that the state now valued solvency over artistry.[80]

Failing to entice Prössel, Meissen promoted the technical reforms of Heinrich Kühn. Kühn too moved to introduce shelved kilns that reduced firing time and halved the amount of wood needed.[81] His training in chemistry was evident in Meissen's development of the first non-blue underglaze (green) and, in 1827, of gloss-gilding, in which gold is dissolved in sulfur balsam, allowing it to be spread easily with a brush or mechanically on rims with a "ring machine." This technique used less precious gold and allowed makers to skip the labor-intensive polishing stage.[82] Kühn was elevated to director of the works in 1833, a year before Frick's appointment to the directorship at the KPM. In 1839, Kühn refitted his kilns to fire with coal, though only in 1853 was the tight-fisted Saxon Finance Ministry willing to appropriate the cash to replace his horse mill with steam engines to mix the clay.[83] Meanwhile, private firms such as Pirkenheimer and Klösterle in Bohemia also hired chemists and perfected their pastes and glazes, making the Czechs, blessed with good clay, coal deposits, and cheap, skilled labor, ever more dangerous competitors to the royal firms. They, too, had invested in chemical R&D and were rewarded with market success.

The Perils of Preferring Artistry:
Nymphenburg and the WPM

Two leading firms, the WPM and Nymphenburg, chose to emphasize artistic, rather than technical, reform in the wake of the wars, with sobering consequences. The WPM, in the wars' wake, faced increasing competition not only from French and English goods, but also from the more entrepreneurial quadrants of the Empire—Bohemia, Lower Austria, and Lombardy in particular, though the Poles and Hungarians were also trying their hands at fine earthenware manufacturing. Joseph Hardtmuth, an architect who would go on to great success in the manufacturing of graphite pencils, developed a highly popular lead-free "Wiener Steingut" at his factory near Vienna; by 1820, his enterprise had outlets in Pressburg, Temesvar, Raab, and Pest, and 120 employees.[84] High-tech and high-quality Bohemian glass and porcelain firms such as Schlaggenwald, which employed 250 people as of 1836, cut deeply into the WPM's sales.[85] The WPM, for its part, had to reduce salaries and ask for state subsides every year between 1817 and 1825. A slow revival began in that year, in part, it appears, because the court began to order again, especially expensive sets for diplomatic gifts.[86]

The WPM's response to the postwar crisis was at first to attempt to renew its artistic credentials, hoping to recapture a "restored" high-end market that never materialized—or at least never would be large enough to sustain the firm on its own. As early as 1819, the director announced financial incentives for the devising of innovative new models, and in 1826, the WPM opened a school to train its painters. The Viennese painter Joseph Nigg made a name for himself and gave the WPM a reputation for excellence in flower painting. But none of this helped to contain costs, or to increase sales, or to clear the warehouse backlog. As others hired chemists or introduced labor-saving devices, the WPM began to seem more and more behind the times, though its balance of investments in handwork over technology (97,905 florins spent on labor costs, as against 751 spent on machinery in 1824) was not entirely atypical.[87] By the late 1820s, the firm finally recognized that it needed a scientific upgrade and, in 1827 put Benjamin von Scholz, professor of technical chemistry, in charge. Under Scholz, the factory added, at last, its first steam engine and began to winnow out skilled painters in favor of cheaper labor.

Scholz, however, made a mistake by adopting the use of cheaper clay, which necessitated costly changes in production and also brought the WPM's wares into disrepute, just as its Bohemian competitors upped their game.[88] By the late 1820s, the manufactory was in financial trouble again, and in the wake of the cholera epidemic of 1831–32, the situation was so bad that Scholz and the other officials had to take a salary cut of more than 50 percent.[89] Under Scholz and his successors—a physicist and another chemist—the WPM expanded its line of lower-end wares, and by 1831, only about 12 percent of production was directed at high-end customers.[90] An attempt to brand the firm a *Kunstinstitut*, like Sèvres and Meissen, failed. The WPM managed to limp through the 1830s and 1840s, though its technical improvements were halfhearted and its appeal as a producer of cheaper wares was never established.

The WPM did, however, institute one state-of-the-art practice in this period that would serve Austria, if not the WPM, well in the longer run. At Sèvres, Brongniart had expanded the manufactory's previously existing collection of historical models (including "Etruscan" vases already in the collection since the 1780s) to create a museum of porcelain—at first oriented to contemporary, not historical styles—for his craftsmen to study. With few resources to devote to this, by bartering with ship captains and private dealers he nonetheless managed to form an impressive collection. In Austria, Crown Prince Ferdinand took a page from Brongniart's playbook and in 1819 organized a Technisches Kabinett, which completed 2,775 tests of raw materials by 1829, and which collected, and shared, twenty-eight thousand items from Austrian producers of various kinds.[91] The information-sharing activities of the WPM resembled those of Sèvres and looked forward to the KPM's function as a national ceramics laboratory; after the dissolution of the WPM (see chapter 6), the Technisches Kabinett would become the core of Vienna's forward-looking Museum für Kunst und Industrie, where Alois Riegl learned to curate oriental carpets and other decorative materials, an education that prepared him for pioneering work on the evolution of style.[92]

In 1815, as we have seen, the artistically inclined Crown Prince Ludwig of Bavaria took Nymphenburg under his wing, declaring his wish to reenergize its status as a *Kunstanstalt*. It certainly would not have been recognized as a *Wissenschaftsanstalt*: in 1809, the manufactory had been compelled to send a representative to Paris to reacquire the Arcanum, as no one at the Bavarian firm could remember it. The factory was divided into a white works and a more prestigious branch for creating artistic products; the latter employed a team of forty painters and was headed, from 1822, by the architect Friedrich von Gärtner. First the Finance Ministry and then the mining department were given factory oversight, but Ludwig's eager involvement and patronage, which continued after his accession to the throne in 1825, shielded the manufactory from the same sorts of demands made by the Prussian, Saxon, and Braunschweig ministries. In 1827, Ludwig ordered the manufactory to make copies of the Pinakothek's holdings on porcelain plates, a hugely complex and expensive business meant to preserve a color replica of Bavaria's best paintings, ironically on the eve of revolutions in lithography and photography.[93] The enterprise does not seem to have made money in *any* year of the period after 1815, and by the 1840s, average losses were running at about 10,000 T per annum. More than any other German manufactory, Nymphenburg continued to be run along traditional lines, producing artistic objects almost exclusively for the king and court. Aesthetically, this was admirable; but Nymphenburg's failure to adapt to the liberal-capitalist world would prove disastrous in the decades to come.

The first decades of the nineteenth century posed enormous challenges for mercantile manufactories. Accustomed to thinking of themselves chiefly as master craftsmen working for the prince—even though firms had at least since the 1740s underwritten production with more modest and useful wares—porcelain makers now had to find ways to survive in a newly competitive marketplace. Princely orders helped, but state subsidies became harder and harder to procure. Technical innovations reduced costs, to the detriment especially of painters, while the diversification and historicization of styles expanded elite buyers' choices (see chapter 5). But these established manufactories were increasingly in competition with nimbler private firms, which had fewer bureaucrats to placate—and different consumers in mind.

The Private Firms

Struggling in the eighteenth century, private producers would make significant headway in the last decade of the period anachronistically known as the *Vormärz*, the "pre-March" period that preceded the outbreak of the 1848 revolutions. The conditions for their enhanced viability include the loosening of restrictions on trade, the expansion of the market for modest homes, and the differentiation of function for the rooms in these homes, as well as rising middle-class consumption of a wider array of food and beverages. But in the first years after the war, the private firms, too, faced great challenges. Some lost the vital loans or perks provided by the local princeling and had to close. Established craftsmen and small businesspersons often opposed the founding of new concerns, motivated in part by competition over resources, especially wood, whose real costs rose again by about 25 percent between 1800 and 1810 and perhaps as much as 121 percent between 1810 and 1850.[94] In some places, officials stonewalled efforts at setting up new businesses, protecting their established tradesmen or, paternalistically, seeking to prevent neophyte entrepreneurs from losing their shirts. Even after the abolition of the Arcanum, it was by no means easy to get into the porcelain business—and even harder to persist.[95] The following section sketches the experiences of a few of these private makers, although it will necessarily favor firms that flourished, at least for a time, and obscure the probably larger number that failed without leaving a trace.

The efforts of Carolus Magnus Hutschenreuther to establish a factory are indicative of the hurdles placed in the way of even qualified entrepreneurs. Hutschenreuther had learned to paint porcelain in his father's factory in Böttger's birthplace, Schleiz, a stone's throw from the Bohemian border in the Thuringian forest. Thanks to a fortunate marriage and partnership with a merchant, Hutschenreuther had access to impressive starting capital.

But when he applied in 1816 and again in 1817 to the General Commission in Bayreuth to set up a factory in Hohenberg an der Eger, his applications were rejected. Believing itself obliged, as one commentator puts it, "to protect overly enterprising subjects from losing their capital," the commission put Hutschenreuther's technical skills to the test and determined him unfit to maintain a business.[96] Another—probably major—consideration was Hutschenreuther's access to wood, which iron makers in the region wished to block for the sake of their own supply. After years of endeavor, Hutschenreuther finally received permission to start a factory in 1822. But into the 1830s he faced difficulties in acquiring sufficient wood, limitations on kiln expansions, and technical hindrances, even as his inexpensive wares—pipes, teacups, doll heads—began to sell, in German and Near Eastern markets. When Carolus Magnus died in 1845, leaving the factory to his wife, Johanna, the business was finally beginning to thrive, with fifty to sixty workers,[97] but its rise to this level was punctuated and painful, and it would be only after 1850 that Hutschenreuther would be a name to conjure with. The experience of Heinrich Eichhorn, founder of another later porcelain-making powerhouse, Tirschenreuth, was much the same.[98]

By the later 1820s, however, the numbers of firms and workers had begun to grow. In 1830, according to one estimate, sixty-two private manufactories were operating in the area Bismarck would later unify.[99] By that time, in Upper Franconia, near Hutschenreuther's haunts, the firms of Tettau, Schney, Hausen, and Reichmannsdorf each employed upward of one hundred workers.[100] In the wider Germanosphere, too, entrepreneurs entered the market in large numbers. By the 1840s, there were at least seventy-three ceramics factories in the Habsburg lands, twenty-nine of them in Bohemia alone.[101] The Bohemian industry, in particular, was flourishing, as the Saxon Finance Ministry underscored in caustic communications with Meissen: by 1828, Schlaggenwald employed one hundred, Elbogen sixty, Gießhübel thirty to forty, and Dalwitzer Stoneware nearly ninety; as a price list attached to one of these memos showed, the latter firm had commissioned agents not only in Austria's major cities, but also in numerous smaller towns.[102] Joseph

Hardtmuth (Vienna) and F. A. Schumann (Moabit, near Berlin) would also make their fortunes in this market.

Expansion, of course, was happening outside of central Europe as well. In Limoges, France, home to venerable ceramics workshops and with ready access to kaolin deposits at St. Yrieix, two former employees of Sèvres founded new businesses in the chaotic 1790s. They persevered and by 1804 controlled three-quarters of porcelain production in the region. By 1828, Limoges had become home to upward of nine hundred porcelain workers.[103] Russian production, too, surged, with more than thirty firms founded between 1800 and 1830. Some of these ceramics start-ups endured, though many more swiftly failed, done in by one bad year, insufficient capital, fire, or managerial or technical incompetence.

Earlier in this chapter we described the travails of the Boch Frères manufactory in the course of the revolutionary wars. To take a closer look at the firm and family history of J. F. Boch-Buschmann's future partner, Nicholas Villeroy, is to gain a bit more insight into the little-studied world of the Biedermeier entrepreneur. Now that the secrets of porcelain and fine ceramics making had been divulged and the legal monopolies broken up, the main problem for the would-be founder in this post-mercantile age was capital, which, as Jürgen Kocka noted long ago, was much more accessible to persons than to firms.[104] With little capital available to the ordinary person from private banks, the best way to obtain it was through family connections and lucrative marriages, or through personal connections to state officials. Villeroy, for example, began his career as an official in the state-regulated French salt trade. He made a very fortunate marriage in 1786 and in 1789 purchased shares in a colleague's faience factory. In 1791 he bought out the other (two) shareholders and moved the factory to Vaudrevange in French Lorraine—after 1815 to become Wallerfangen in Prussia.[105] During the Napoleonic period Villeroy also traded in salt, iron, and crystal, and he profited greatly from favoritism shown by the Napoleonic state. Not only did he receive rights from the emperor to operate a factory and extract clay in the occupied Saarland, but he also profited from the French state's willingness

4.2. Villeroy & Boch manufactory, Mettlach

This mid-nineteenth-century drawing illustrates J. F. Boch's brilliance in choosing to refurbish an abbey located directly on the River Saar for his ceramics factory. The crowd of barges and the wisps of smoke rising over the abbey are the only indications of the rising volume of goods being produced at this and other Villeroy & Boch factories by midcentury.

to loan him Napoleonic POWs, some of them former employees of the Staffordshire potteries, to work in his manufactory.[106] Unlike Sèvres's porcelain, his faience sold better in 1800 than in 1788, and he was able to employ fifty workers even in the dismal year of 1815.[107]

Similarly, Boch Frères survived through tumultuous times thanks to the amassing of family capital and know-how; its other secret was Anglophilic technical innovation. As we have seen, during the wars, Jean-François Boch-Buschmann, deploying his wife's fortune, set up a branch factory in a defunct abbey on the Saar River in the town of Mettlach, which, after 1815, belonged to Prussia (fig. 4.2). By 1816, he employed 150.[108] Trained in chemistry and mechanics, Jean-François was a lifelong admirer of Wedgwood, and a founding member of the Verein zur Beförderung des Gewerbefleisses in Preussen (Association for the Promotion of Commercial Development in Prussia) in 1820. There he met Prussia's most important advocate of the new technology, Count Peter von Beuth, whom he would accompany on a study trip to Manchester, London, Chelsea, and other English industrial locations in 1823.[109]

Jean-François used his travels and his training in chemistry and mechanics to good purpose, introducing into his factory labor- and energy-saving devices, though few steam-powered machines, as these remained very expensive. As for most ceramics entrepreneurs, for Jean-François, improving kiln efficiency was a priority, and he succeeded where many previous tinkerers had failed, devising kilns powered exclusively by coal, the first such on the continent. He also introduced copperplate engraving, a machine for shaping plates, and water-powered potters' wheels, which made it possible to employ modelers with less strength and skill. As a result of deploying these devices, by 1841 Boch was able to employ only 60 percent adult men, with the other 40 percent of his thus cheaper labor force divided between women and boys.[110]

But technological modernization and deskilling were not sufficient to keep a *Vormärz* porcelain firm in the black. The vicissitudes of European politics meant that entrepreneurs also needed to change partners, markets, and organizational forms from time to time. Arriving in the wake of the troubled 1820s, the revolutions of 1830s disrupted a great deal of business in a still-precarious market, especially in the western German borderlands. Most problematically for the Boch family, the 1830 revolutions ushered in Belgian independence (and tariff barriers), which cut the Septfontaines factory off from its lucrative Dutch and Belgian markets, isolating it in the ever-shrinking Grand Duchy of Luxembourg. In an 1835 essay, Jean-François Boch blasted Belgian officials and Prussian liberals for allowing in English goods, while denouncing the French for weakening their industry by keeping out foreign competition. What was needed, he insisted, was just enough protection to keep the English out, and just enough free trade to encourage the French and of course the German makers.[111] This intervention—from the pen of an entrepreneur who would later sit in the 1848 Frankfurt Parliament—should remind us of the importance of location and timing in the history of commercial advocacy. It underscores, too, the truth in W. O. Henderson's contention that nineteenth-century German liberal rhetoric was primarily aimed at maximizing the economic advantages of each of the separate states (or separate industries), especially with respect to their British, French (and Belgian) competitors, rather than at forming a German nation.[112] The Thuringians, for example, were also eager to keep out English and French competition so that *their* porcelains—intentionally priced lower than those of the KPM and Meissen—would dominate the German market.[113]

To counter the English threat, Jean-François joined investors in two other local manufactories (which soon went bankrupt). He exploited his family connections with the Belgian liberal statesman (and railway backer) Jean Baptiste Baron Nothomb, who became one of three partners (with his son Eugen and his brother Frédéric-Victor) in the holding company Boch Frères; he oversaw the purchase of both a stoneware factory and the defunct Belgian porcelain factory at Tournai.[114] The firm was saved by the combination of this savvy use of family ties (Nothomb had married one of Jean-François's daughters), Luxembourg's joining of the Zollverein in 1842, and the full merging of the Boch works with the Villeroy operations, cemented by another marriage, between Eugen Boch and Octavie Villeroy. By 1847, sales of wares from the three main factories had reached a quite impressive 303,196 T.[115] By 1850, thanks largely to Villeroy & Boch, the Saar region could boast the most modern and viable ceramics operations on the continent, and a larger workforce (1,825) than the number employed in ironworking (1,368).[116] But the best years, for this firm, were still to come.

For both private and state firms, the post-Napoleonic period was a difficult one, in which experimentation—in chemistry, in labor practices, in management—was vital. Blessed with family members with technical skill, market savvy, political influence, liquid capital, and luck, the Boch and Villeroy firms of necessity had to chart a different path to survival than did Meissen or the KPM. But by 1850, they found themselves in an enviable market position. Other makers had not been so shrewd, nor so fortunate. Although some manufactories continued to cultivate courtly customers and patrons, most did not have the luxury of living this way any longer. On the whole, what made some more successful than others was no longer mercantilist privileges but the discovery of ways to use labor and energy more efficiently. Both private and state firms—nudged by their finance ministries—moved in this direction, transforming in the process their artisanal workplaces even in the absence of new machinery. This critical chapter in the history of the porcelain industry shows us that it was not only textiles that were subjected to the inexorable logic of capitalist competition; ceramics too had to be made in greater numbers, at lower unit costs, for their makers to prosper. Post-Napoleonic consumers wanted a share of princely *Glanz* for themselves, but only at non-luxury prices. And as we will see in the next chapter, what non-aristocratic buyers wanted increasingly had to guide production even of the commodity once celebrated as "white gold."

Chapter 5

The Discrete Charms
of Biedermeier Porcelain

The term "Biedermeier" calls to mind the gentle caricatures of Carl Spitzweg and other nineteenth-century genre painters, in which plump, prosperous, and self-assured bourgeois husbands and wives disport themselves in comfortable salons or provincial gardens. Although this caricature does capture some aspects of the post-Napoleonic cultural world, it can be misleading if taken for the whole. The "Biedermeier" style itself, at least as far as its iconic plain but highly polished furniture is concerned, was not a middle-class invention but began in the courts and only later spread to a slightly wider sector of the upper middle classes. The vast majority of even middling Germans would have been unable to afford more than a single table or desk of the Biedermeier type.[1] As previously, most Germans—and here we are counting German speakers residing in the German Confederation, the successor to the now-defunct Holy Roman Empire—continued to live on the land, and to subsist (often barely) on a combination of agricultural labor and occasional cottage employment. Towns and cities remained small, and, despite the bursts of liberal nationalism unleashed by the Napoleonic Wars, largely inward looking. Many princes had returned to their palaces if not their thrones; many at least attempted to rebuild their courts and to resume old customs. Most ordinary persons remained disenfranchised and relatively poor, though their household inventories were expanding, thanks to falling real prices of minor luxury items such as textiles and ceramics. If evocative for a certain emerging urban elite, "Biedermeier" cannot stand in for the entirety of Restoration-era central European society.

The term "Biedermeier" makes a bit more sense for the subculture of porcelain buyers, however, men and now more prominently women who found themselves eager and sometimes able to outfit a home with new tableware and decorative objects. Here, too, we must be careful; the aristocracy continued to be the major purchasers of high-end porcelains long into the nineteenth century, and, as we have seen, the princes themselves provided the patronage and commissions that enabled firms such as Nymphenburg and the WPM to survive the difficult years of the 1820s and 1830s. Royal banqueting continued to be lavish, and the now-fashionable "service à la russe," in which guests were served on individual plates one course at a time, actually required more, rather than fewer, plates and servers. But middle-level consumption of material goods was also, tentatively, on the rise. Gustav Schmoller's figures for the expansion of craft industries in Berlin between 1784 and 1847 suggest rising investment, especially after 1831, in some household goods, as compared also to the shoes, clothing, and foodstuffs to which earlier disposable income was put: "in 1831," he concluded, "one again built more, one equipped the home better, but one ate, dressed, and shod oneself as of old."[2] New shops, street hawkers, and itinerant salesmen emerged to supply consumers with both handmade and factory-produced goods. As the porcelain industry struggled with patronage cutbacks, falling prices, and parsimonious consumers, catering to more modest needs and tastes became increasingly crucial, even for elite manufacturers. By investigating some of these patterns of production and consumption—without overlooking the persistence of older habits and styles—we can glimpse the gradual widening of the consumer marketplace.

Of course, neither the porcelain makers nor their potential customers could foresee how the post-1815 market would be transformed, and, especially for the state manufacturers, it was painful to realize that they could not simply go back to business as usual. They had been accustomed to producing for nobles and taking care, and often considerable time, with their commissions. In a world of increasingly bureaucratically constrained budgets, however, they were faced with an ever more urgent imperative: staying alive meant selling, and selling meant catering to customers, whether or not customers were men and women of good taste and lofty means. Artisanal employees, too, found it difficult to adjust to new conditions. Skilled porcelain modelers and painters still considered themselves artists, or at least estimable craftsmen, and found the idea of following, rather than instructing, the market unpalatable. They were most disappointed to learn that new customers seemed to want not artistry but historicizing, highly decorated but inexpensive wares, "despite the fact," wrote one knowledgeable Braunschweig merchant, "that the colors can be partly scratched off with a fingernail, as they have evidently been pasted on with glue."[3] Artisanal makers would be even more disappointed to see how much their salaries dropped relative to those of unskilled laborers, on the lower end, and failed to keep pace with the rewards of the chemists and bookkeepers, in the upper income registers. Insofar as the German Confederation was moving in the direction of a "free" market, it is clear that for these mercantile firms, "freedom" was a decidedly mixed blessing.

Adjustments, many of them painful, did occur, however, especially as new private firms joined the market. Although porcelain was by no means yet affordable for every household, by the 1830s and 1840s it was becoming a much more widely available, and universally desired, commodity. Once sold chiefly at fairs, in factories, or by a handful of commissioned agents, by the mid-nineteenth century, porcelain could also be purchased at a large number of luxury haberdasheries as well as from peddlers and at auctions. All firms now printed price lists, offering extensive arrays of standard patterns and forms. While figurines to be used as banquet-table decorations declined in sales, biscuit or plaster busts appeared in middle-class parlors and studies. All firms moved to producing the inexpensive services and tea and coffee wares that sold so well, and in the most diverse and eclectic of patterns.

Perhaps because of their eclecticism, early nineteenth-century porcelains took on new representational powers. For both elite and middling consumers, stylistic choices now seemed to speak from the individual or at least familial heart, and to display the owners' education, taste, character, and national, regional, or communal loyalties. Porcelain was becoming essential not only to *Glanz*, but also to bourgeois *Anständigkeit*, respectability. No "gentle" household could do without it.

This chapter offers a glimpse into Biedermeier and Restoration-era culture by way of its porcelain makers and consumers. It is thus a companion to chapter 3, on porcelain in the cultural world of the Old Regime; to chapter 7, on porcelain at the fin de siècle; and to the portions of chapters 8 and 9 where twentieth-century porcelain cultures are discussed. We begin by surveying the uses of porcelain in the cultural world of mid-nineteenth-century "Germany," focusing most especially on its significance for that most symbolic of Biedermeier spaces: the middle-class home.

From Princely Splendor to Bourgeois Luxury

A series of lifestyle changes underway in the nineteenth century's first half shaped and complemented the ways in which porcelain and other ceramics were made and used. Fashions were changing, at least for those few who could afford to keep up with them, and the varieties and uses of luxury goods were evolving as well. Powdered wigs and some of the more extravagant ornamental wares—including surtouts and figurine sets—were out; plaster busts and sofas were in. Even at the elite level, porcelain usage was shifting ever more distinctly away from its purely decorative functions in favor of much more universal purposes: eating, drinking, and smoking.

Porcelain sellers—still in the early years focused on courtly sales—were quick to note these changes in dining habits and displays, and in a drop in the sale of figurines and other "gallantry items." One Braunschweig merchant dated the change in fashions back to 1814, since when, he claimed, "it is no longer customary to place figurines on tables or fireplaces."[4] In the Biedermeier era, too, figurines lost some of their playful quality, in favor of more serious or sentimental functions. Fewer snuffboxes and ornate scissor cases sold. Porcelain remained a form of ornament, but its evolution from a princely into a bourgeois form of display is important to note and would have a powerful impact on production and sales as well as the cultural connotations of the commodity in the longer term.

In our survey of porcelain consumers we must once again start with the nobility, still the symbolically, if not financially, most important of the industry's customers. Those princes who still owned manufactories—and even those who didn't—continued to commission lavish works for diplomatic or wedding gifts, including the colossal plinth-mounted vases whose intricacy and size became something of a competition among manufactories. These princes also purchased or patronized the making of some art objects such as the many reproductions of masterpieces on porcelain plates made by the elite manufactories at midcentury. But the porcelain "cabinet" and figurines on the table had gone out of fashion, and increasingly the nobility, too, replaced their silver services—many of which had been melted down in the course of the wars anyway—with porcelain and glass. These were not small orders, as the newly fashionable dining "à la russe" called for the serving of many courses, all on separate plates, meaning that tableware sets now needed to be enormous. Czar Nicholas I, for example, regularly commissioned services of five hundred or more pieces.[5] Among the Habsburgs, formal dinners often entailed thirteen courses (a mere "souper" only six to eight courses), and as guests could not help themselves, one servant was assigned to every second diner,[6] meaning that waitstaffs, too, needed to be enlarged. Modern palaces, thus, needed very large stocks of porcelain, now stored in closets. In Hessen, the four princely residences were provisioned with twenty dozen salad plates, sixty-five dozen desert plates, and 172 dozen vegetable plates, among other vessels, just for everyday use.[7] The move from the porcelain cabinet to the porcelain closet is telling; although special pieces were still sometimes displayed on shelves or sideboards, increasingly porcelain was an art for the table, not for the wall, and East Asia pieces, in particular, had largely ceased to count as art at all.

For the non-elite population, however, porcelain was only gradually making its way into everyday existence. The way it entered into everyday consumption habits is also telling. It seems ordinary Germans at first purchased porcelains chiefly for serving coffee and other hot beverages, and for smoking tobacco, rather than for eating meals. This makes sense given what we know about the social history of this period. Historians agree that there was no sustained rise in Germans' real wages until at least 1870, and perhaps 1880, and that food remained the major expenditure for most families.[8] According to one estimate, in Hamburg in the 1830s and 1840s, a typical working-class family spent nearly 50 percent of its income just on bread and potatoes, and a total of 70 percent on food; when rent, heat, and light were subtracted, the family had a measly 2.2 percent for emergencies and extras.[9] Moreover, moralizing handbooks continued to warn non-elite housewives against wasting money on luxurious meals. In 1822, a professor of pastoral theology at the Lyceum in Klagenfurt argued that the good wife would resist the temptation to diverge from standard fare: "Her table is not set with impressively seasoned, oversweetened, expensive dishes but with simple German home-cooking, which suffices to nourish and make one healthy and happy."[10] The fear of overindulging today and starving tomorrow lurks just below the surface of such admonitions to frugality. But if grain and meat prices remained relatively high at midcentury, sugar, coffee, and tobacco costs fell sharply, meaning that even consumers with tight budgets and respectable morals could treat themselves to sweetened ersatz coffee and a pipe. It probably did not hurt that coffee and tobacco were known appetite suppressants.

In spite of moral and financial limitations, however, for some, meals were changing in composition, and in mode of consumption. In a cultural world where women, in particular, felt responsible for teaching moral conduct and proper hygiene to their children and servants, all partakers increasingly got their own plates or bowls, made of tin, wood, or earthenware for those still unable to afford faience or porcelain. Those who could spend more also increasingly ritualized and particularized breakfast and added a late afternoon "fourth meal," at which coffee or tea, fortified with egg yolks, sugar, and spices, was served with buttered bread or cake.[11] Usually this was a meal hosted by women; this offered opportunity for gossip and networking, as well as for sharing treatments for illnesses or tips on good housekeeping. The regularization of this additional meal—one calculated for showing off one's porcelain—and the filtering down of the service *à la russe* to the middle-class table meant a widening market for both everyday and "special" china. As an 1841 report on the state of ceramics production in the Habsburg Empire noted, the tableware industry "has before it an open, wide field, if it succeeds in putting sufficient capital and labor power into its operation to match the greater and greater demand for this sort of tableware which the rising standard of living of the now-numerous middle classes has called forth."[12] Porcelain was well positioned to complement what Anthony Trollope would later depict as "the way we live now."

Regrettably for the porcelain industry in general and the WPM in particular, however, this "open, wide field" was not much in evidence before the mid-1830s. Unlike the Russian czars, local merchants, clergymen, and minor officials who rose into the bourgeois ranks did not need extensive services, for they seem rarely to have hosted dinner parties, and when they did, their guest lists usually did not exceed eight or ten. A few plates, cups, and saucers, along with a coffeepot sufficed for most whist parties or light suppers. After these initial investments, however, families began to feel that everyday ware would *not* suffice for guest visits and holidays. Those occasions should be made special by the use of a "good" set, from which to serve the delicacies offered only on feast days. Plates and cups celebrating special occasions or holiday excursions appeared on salon shelves. As it became more and more conventional for middling households to purchase decorative ceramics, porcelain became a favorite gift, for couples being married, and for friends celebrating anniversaries or birthdays. Of course, this meant an added investment in ceramics, and the mixing of genres in the pantry, as most middling families would have continued to use faience or earthenware for everyday meals.

Over time, then, demand for various types of ceramics slowly expanded. Many households probably ended up with an assortment resembling that of the contemporary state official whose inventory at death showed two-thirds of his dishes to be wood, tin, copper, and stoneware, and the other third—and particularly his cups and saucers—to be porcelain.[13] As the decades passed, the variety of cooking and eating accoutrements available to the non-elite rose exponentially; as an 1852 etiquette manual noted about the multiplication of "crucial" kitchen utensils: "the love of comfort and luxury has promoted the designation of so many things as necessities today which under other conditions would certainly be considered dispensable."[14] For porcelain makers, battered by the travails of the 1820s, the domestic market finally began to look promising. But satisfying it would entail moving away from the aristocratic model toward one we can tentatively label "bourgeois."

Porcelain and the Public Sphere

One of the other novelties of the Biedermeier era was the great expansion of what historians since Jürgen Habermas's pathbreaking study of 1962 have called "the public sphere."[15] The public sphere is both an imagined and a real space, constituted outside of those privileged court settings, clerical institutions, and workshops bound by trade secrets, or for us, between and beyond our places of employment and our private homes. It is a place where persons, at least officially, are allowed to enter at will and to interact as individuals and not as representatives of a particular status group or profession. It encompasses, too, the world of print, where any member of the "public" at least in theory can address his or her fellow members as equals. Its existence as an important space for exchange predates the French Revolution, but the revolution's abolition of so many Old Regime privileges and its championing of the ideas of citizenship, transparency, and the rule of law gave it a great nudge forward. So too was the public sphere enhanced and expanded by the dissolution of clerical institutions and by princely bankruptcies that resulted in "private" collections, parks, and city spaces being given over to the public for upkeep and enjoyment.

In our story, the widening of the public sphere forms the background to the growth of commercial enterprises and the increasing boldness of non-elite consumers and producers to assert their rights and tastes. We can also see this transformation in the increase of public spaces for consumption after the collapse of the Old Regime. We will not appreciate the new functions and social meanings of porcelain without understanding how it fits into a world of persons who increasingly felt entitled to eat, drink, and smoke in public, to claim boulevards and parks for their own, and to offer *their* families and guests a little taste of *Glanz*.

The expansion of coffee drinking is central to this part of our story. Although many central Europeans had learned to drink coffee—or its substitutes—by the end of the eighteenth century, the official bans and monopolies slowed the building of permanent cafés. In 1806, Napoleon's Continental System cut off imports of coffee and cane sugar and thus further delayed the expansion of the coffeehouse culture now entrenched in British and French cities. After 1815, however, establishments selling the hot drink began to proliferate and to attract a wider public. Coffeehouses of the English type, where merchants and bankers congregated and read the latest newssheets, now multiplied, especially in commercially active cities such as Hamburg and Frankfurt. But vendors in the early nineteenth century also experimented with different venues, in part because of restrictive licensing in town centers. More family-friendly "Kaffeegarten" popped up just outside city gates, partly to evade city restrictions and partly to take advantage of the custom of weekend *Ausflüge* (outings). Many central Europeans, and especially women, may have taken their first sip of coffee in a garden rather than a café.

The literary worlds of Berlin and Vienna would eventually give rise to "literary" cafés frequented by poets and composers, many of them with separate rooms for billiards and smoking, and a few with a special "ladies' room" (*Damenzimmer*). Cafés typically stocked newspapers for their customers' edification and quickly became places for political conversation. They were used for meetings of the innumerable social organizations (*Vereine*) that sprang up in the post-Napoleonic era, dedicating themselves to causes as diverse as sharpshooting and prison reform. Some were extremely elegant, such as the café opened in Berlin's Treptow Park in 1822, or Dresden's Café Reale, built in the form of a Greek temple on the city's newly public "Brühl Terrace," overlooking the Elbe (fig. 5.1).[16] Italian, Swiss, and French bakers founded *Konditoreien*, addicting Germans who could afford sweets to an enduring habit of afternoon coffee and cake.[17] We must, however, put this again into perspective and recall that most people drank their coffee at home or at food stalls, workhouses, or factory canteens, where no porcelain was used. Also, even as coffee drinking spread, beer and wine remained the drinks of choice. In 1832, when Dresden might have housed several dozen cafés,

5.1. Café Reale, Dresden

The Café Reale, located on the Brühl Terrace overlooking the Elbe, was a highly fashionable spot for Biedermeier Dresdeners to enjoy coffee and cake.

the city had 660 locales selling wine, beer, and spirits.[18] "Sobering" drinks by no means had outstripped alcoholic ones. The great age of the central European café, not to mention the restaurant and hotel, lay some years in the future. But habits had begun to form that would leave their mark on urban areas in particular, and make for an ever-widening use of porcelain in the public sphere.

Porcelain in the Private Sphere

Beyond the public sphere was, of course, the domestic one, where porcelain's role was expanding alongside the evolution of the Biedermeier family with its carefully defined gender roles. Although the myth of fully separate spheres for men and women was busted some time ago,[19] in this era, middling persons did begin to separate domestic functions more deliberately. When their means allowed, families divided workplaces from living places, cooking spaces from dining spaces, spaces for guests from private spaces for the family, spaces for men from those for women. Male spaces such as the study, smoking room, or, for rich nobles, the hunting lodge took on different sorts of décor than did the more feminine spaces such as the boudoir. Already in the 1780s, one widely reproduced (and translated) architectural manual argued that the male spaces should take on the attributes of Mars, the female spaces those of Venus.[20]

Mars and Venus might have been suitable exemplars for eighteenth-century nobles, but the nineteenth-century middling classes had more sober, respectable values to perform. The images we have of male domestic spaces such as the study or smoking room may feature some military memorabilia or rulers' busts, but more generally emphasize seriousness, learning, and national or local pride; they tend not to contain shepherdesses or crucifixes. After the wars, female purchases and adornments for the salon or boudoir seem to have avoided eroticism and tended instead to the sentimental, their display woven into a family history of gifts or of travel. But they also reflect bourgeois women's roles in creating an orderly, respectable home. The middle-class matron was charged with making the home a place to nurture the family's moral life, protecting its members from dirt, drudgery, and sin, and projecting the family's status as stable and respectable. Her porcelain purchases needed to reflect these cultural and social aims, which were certainly *not* those of eighteenth-century princes and courtiers.

The first and most important domestic place for porcelain in this era was one men and women shared in common, though, at least in the afternoons, it was chiefly a female space: the salon. It was here that bourgeois women, in particular, cultivated the art of friendship, one of the most cherished values of the period. They did so by hosting regular "fourth meals," coffee or tea parties that became known as *Kaffeekränzchen*. These usually took place in the later afternoon; a specially chosen group of guests was typically offered hot drinks and sweets, served on the household's finest china, and expected to engage in friendly, sometimes intimate, conversation.[21] After-dinner parties were usually attended by men as well as women but also featured card games or music and the serving of hot as well as cold drinks, offered to visitors in the "gute Stube" where the best furniture and most valued knick-knacks were displayed. The most revered guests might be invited to sit on the sofa, "the object of every Hausfrau's envy,"[22] and set their drinks on fashionable oval or round polished tables (plate 10). Deep saucers were needed to cool sips of the hot liquids, and sugar boxes and cream pitchers to tailor drinks to individual tastes. Although after the wars the serving of tea or coffee at breakfast time—accompanied by a roll spread with butter, or more commonly fat (Speck)—had become habitual, it is doubtful that the household's best porcelain was used for these meals, unless guests were present. Porcelain's role was to impress and to please one's friends, and accordingly, it was probably most used for these outward-facing occasions.

If porcelain belonged to the guest-oriented culture of the period, we catch another glimpse of Biedermeier culture in the porcelain doll head, produced already in the eighteenth century but manufactured in large numbers after about 1830. This era, as many historians have noted, saw the rise of new attention to children, to their education and their moral formation, and to their play. Specially written and illustrated children's books proliferated as did toys, above all dolls and dollhouses, for girls, and tin soldiers and hobby horses, for boys. Toys belonged to a new culture of sentimentality, in which domestic holidays such as Christmas and birthdays gained new cultural poignancy and purchase. Porcelain's whiteness and delicacy made it ideal for modeling dolls' heads, which could then be sewn into cloth or leather bodies, but the Kahla factory also made whole doll bodies, which could be bathed.[23] Hair was also modeled and painted, or, later, flax or real hair was glued on. Porcelain dolls' skin tones were not as white as the biscuit porcelain used for copies of antique sculpture but were very pale, and many dolls were given heavily rouged cheeks, reflecting the idealized fair complexions of the day. Doll culture was only one way in which young girls were taught domestic habits and virtues, though dolls did not typically scrub stoves or boil laundry, as did real Biedermeier housewives.

Doll heads were some of the first truly mass-produced porcelain items, their production already underway in Thuringia's small workshops in the later eighteenth century. Most were made by lower-end manufacturers, and taken home for finishing by very poorly paid female painters. This does not mean that the dolls were not deeply beloved by their young owners, who appreciated the particularities of their own dolls' features and dress and perhaps saw them as models for the "look" they too wanted to achieve. In this period, porcelain makers also started making child-sized tea sets, for young girls to practice the fine art of pouring and serving guests with elegance and generosity, and without breaking the household's more expensive accoutrements. Manufacturers even created porcelain-peddler dolls, combining both the tiny tea sets and the dolls in one quasi-advertisement for the industry as a whole.

Importantly, porcelain, and especially white porcelain, epitomized health and cleanliness; already in the eighteenth century it had been made for apothecary use, and in the nineteenth century, it was increasingly sought after by domestic consumers for vessels such as washbasins, ewers, and chamber pots. Sickness and death were still omnipresent in this society; cholera and typhus epidemics raged periodically, and tuberculosis was a never-ending threat. Women were expected to do their all to keep illnesses from entering their homes.[24] Perfect cleanliness was prized, especially as gas lighting illuminated previously dark domestic corners, but it was difficult to achieve.[25] Virtually no homes had piped water; it had to be retrieved from common pumps and fountains, or purchased from water haulers. Yet vessels for washing hands and faces, at least, began to appear in every bedchamber. We have noted the rising popularity of "hygienic" porcelain by the 1810s; in the next decades, as other genres stagnated, this type sold briskly. Although only the super-rich, before midcentury, could afford a separate "Badezimmer," eventually, sinks, toilets, tiles, and bathtubs, too, would be made of porcelain, both for practical purposes (porcelain vessels hold hot water without cracking or corroding and are easy to clean) and as a continuation of this conviction in porcelain's intrinsic connection with health.

Finally, porcelain objects increasingly adorned middle-class salons, where these ornaments played a significant role in shaping and spreading Biedermeier sentimentality and local patriotism. The postwar cult of nature found expression in the massive quantities of flowered porcelain purchased for display in the "gute Stube." Though tourism was restricted to the upper elite until after midcentury, porcelain vases and salvers frequently carried images of Italy, France, or castles and cascades closer to home. Romanticized scenes of local monuments, ruins, or scenery—particularly scenes of the Rhineland and Saxon "Switzerland"—appeared on plates and cups, reminding owners of their visits there or stoking their desire to travel. Czech makers operating near Karlsbad made a killing on spa visitors' purchases of inexpensive mementos. Porcelain makers also fueled the cult of the genius, generating busts and pipes displaying the images of Byron, Beethoven, Paganini, and, inescapably, Goethe.

During and after the wars, nationalist porcelain came into fashion, depicting the battle lines at Leipzig, restored monarchs, or the heroic common soldier.[26] Every manufactory produced figurines or medallions of contemporary local princes and often of other notable members of the family. Some "national" figures such as Frederick the Great appeared, but until the Great War, most of these representations seem to have remained local. It is hard to know exactly what it meant to a Hessian merchant to smoke a pipe emblazoned with his grand duke's portrait; perhaps it forged a more empathetic connection between ruler and subject than had previously existed.[27] Although these items were not made at the royals' bequests, they certainly must have ingratiated the manufactories with the court. Issuing such items also linked manufactories to their localities and in this way reinforced a kind of provincial pride that was good at least for local sales, and primed firms to make the many commemorative items for coronations, local festivals, and anniversaries that would be produced particularly in the century's second half. In the production of pictures of the prince *for the people*, we can see how formerly aristocratic manufactories such as Meissen could be made into "Saxon" institutions, and nostalgia for the Old Regime manipulated for the purposes of the new nation-states.

The postwar era also saw a religious revival across the continent, and that too found expression in a much more extensive array of religious porcelains. Most popular here were depictions of the Madonna and child, not surprising given what we have just learned about the new aura surrounding small children. Virtually every manufactory offered versions of that scene, chiefly after models by Raphael and Correggio. Like other makers, Meissen offered Christian themes on Biedermeier pipeheads, including a cross illuminated by the rising sun and captioned "There is the light!"[28] In Catholic regions in particular, manufacturers sold porcelain crucifixes. Of course, all these ideals and fashions found expression in other genres: painting, poetry, needlework, glass. But porcelain provided an affordable canvas on which the period's soul and psyche could be displayed.

By the 1840s, then, porcelain belonged not only to courtly consumers, but to middle-class ones as well, and it had become part of both gender-specific forms of domesticity and an expanding world of public institutions and private businesses. Having associated itself with bourgeois leisure activities, regional patriotism, and sobriety, porcelain proved well suited to the values and habits of an increasingly visible and publicly active middle class. Linked just as intimately with the sentimental world of family and friendships, it also invaded the middle-class home. In some fundamental way, the teapot emblazoned with a Saxon waterfall had replaced the rococo "surtout" as the representative cultural icon of the age. If porcelain had once epitomized aristocratic *Glanz* and frivolity, it was now becoming a quintessentially bourgeois commodity. But to please this market, porcelain producers had to reconcile themselves not only to the new styles consumers demanded, but to the reality that taste making was not in their hands alone.

Learning to Live with Eclecticism

"Eclecticism has become our taste," Alfred de Musset lamented in 1836.[29] Indeed, the massive proliferation of goods appealing to diverse tastes provided both joy and sorrow to Europeans of the century's first half. Ever more conscious of the peculiarities and cultural implications of "empire," "gout grêcque," neo-rococo, or neo-Gothic styles, architects in particular debated the question: "In which style should we build?"—a question made more controversial by the expansion of public spaces, which now needed to represent, in some way, the nation (still Saxony or Prussia; not "Germany"), or at least the locality.[30] In fact, despite many theorists' desire to create stylistic harmony, whether in the growing cities or in domestic interiors, the reality of the Biedermeier era was the coexistence of many forms, signaling that customers and patrons were eager to indulge their own tastes and that the market was large enough to satisfy them. But the revival of older styles, in particular, made artists and craftsmen uncomfortable, as it seemed to suggest that their new ideas were not wanted, degrading them to the status of mere copyists, whose creations, moreover, were increasingly valued according to their price. In a world more and more convinced of its own progress, creators of luxury goods found historicism both a necessary and a bitter pill.

Although reform-minded critics complained—in this era and long afterward—about the horrors of eclecticism, the central European eye was already accustomed to seeing old and new, baroque, medieval, and classical or neoclassical, side by side. Rarely rich enough to pull down habitable buildings, new residents generally patched up or added onto older churches, palaces, and townhouses rather than building new ones. Cities such as Prague and Munich were veritable museums of stylistic variety. Even before the advent of the historicizing sample book we know as the Ringstrasse, the Viennese inhabited a city with a massive Gothic church, an arch-baroque imperial palace, and a neoclassical Theseus Temple, located in the newly public *Volkspark*. In domestic settings, only the very wealthy could afford to make their interior décor match; most people inherited their ancestors' home furnishings and often their linens and clothing as well. It would be wise for historians to resist treating the diverse porcelain offerings of this era as a sign of decadence, as did later purists such as William Morris. Many persons, including women, whose choices in previous centuries had been circumscribed by poverty or by sumptuary laws now had the right, and the wherewithal, to satisfy their own tastes. Can we complain if they spent their pennies on teacups shaped like swans?

Nostalgic purism, moreover, does not fit the historical realities of the German porcelain industry. As we saw in chapter 3, since the 1710s European porcelain makers had produced works in more than one style, baroque side by side with Asian imitations, simple pure-white forms, and complex gilded ones. Among high-end producers, the "libertine" classicism of the 1750s had largely given way to a more "chaste" neoclassicism; this would continue to be popular into the 1820s. But one can also find proto-Romantic landscapes and Egyptizing forms before 1789, and shortly thereafter, porcelains meant to imitate wood, precious stones, or mosaics. Teacups and chocolate sets reflected the eclectic tastes of makers and buyers decades before architects commenced their debates on style. Neither stylistic diversity, nor the imitation of culturally discrete styles, was a nineteenth-century innovation.

What was new for porcelain makers in the 1820s was not eclecticism per se, but recognition that what consumers, and especially English buyers, wanted was not a new look—to be achieved by the combination of available patterns and techniques—but an old one, specifically, rococo, as it had been fashioned in the previous century. While other new styles diffused into the decorative arts from architectural or furniture design, renewed affection for rococo patterns seems to have first been evident in orders for wallpapers and textiles made according to a fashion customers described as "à la pompadour."[31] In fact, Meissen had never entirely given up production in this style, for it had sold well on the British, Russian, and Turkish markets even in the heyday of Wedgwoodian neoclassicism. But after the reduction of British tariffs in the early 1820s, English demand for rococo items surged, provoking even some English craftsmen to seek instruction at Meissen, home to the now nearly forgotten Saxon master modeler J. J. Kändler.[32] What distressed porcelain makers about this development was that they were now being asked to reproduce their own—in their minds—outmoded forms, and models made by deceased artists were now preferred to their own creations. Thus began a battle over the "proper" style for modern porcelain, one which pitted art against income, and theory against market realities.

Financially, for the Saxons, this Old Regime nostalgia proved a godsend. In 1822, when the firm began to return some of the eighteenth-century models to production, Meissen was desperate for income and in need of a branding campaign that would reestablish its status as the first and highest-quality producer. In 1833–44 alone, the year Meissen returned to profitability, sales of what came to be known as "English articles" leapt from 9,661 to 15,091 T.[33] Much to the artists' dismay, retro-production expanded rapidly, such that in a few years' time, the Meissners could generate a "List of China Wares of Old but very pleasant shapes of the Manufactory of H. M. the King of Saxony at Meissen," offering hundreds of items, of first- or second-grade quality, and at all price ranges. The English customer could choose cheap teapots as well as reproductions of Kändler's famous monkey orchestra, small and large versions of Count von Brühl's tailor seated on a goat, and for the hypernostalgic, a king-sized rendering of Augustus the Strong.[34] As they recovered their wherewithal, continental nobles also developed a taste for "Alt-Meissen," and sales boomed especially in the wake of the 1830 and 1848 revolutions. For better and for worse, the manufactory would from now on be powerfully identified with this style.

By no means was retro-rococo production restricted to Meissen. By 1836, Royal Copenhagen and Schlaggenwald had moved in this direction, and the KPM followed shortly thereafter. Nymphenburg, typically, followed later, making the switch in 1848. The private makers, of course, followed suit. As bourgeois consumers accumulated a bit more wealth, they, too, seem to have embraced the style, now associated especially with women (references to "à la Pompadour" tell us a great deal). But rococo revival proved unpopular with another constituency: painters and modelers as well as aesthetic theorists disliked the style and strongly preferred neoclassicism. In their view, there was something more uplifting and dignified about "Greek" than "French" forms and décor, and thus did the (modified) krater and amphora remain the preferred vase shapes for royal gifts and exhibitions of the period.[35] But these were made as "Prunkstücke," as showpieces, and in their everyday production craftsmen were increasingly directed to make the rococo, sentimental, and white wares that sold.

Artisans bitterly resented being told to respond to the retrograde tastes of the market and argued, it turned out rightly, that exhibiting such wares would give the impression "that our firm has absolutely no sense of beauty or progress."[36] Manufactory directors, anxious to revive the factories' artistic prestige, felt they were being bullied by their finance and trade ministries, which indeed, in many cases, they were. When in 1828, some of Meissen's painters complained that a commission they were expected to execute for a customer in Buenos Aires was ugly, the Saxon treasury bluntly instructed them that it was their job to cater to customers of "less developed taste"— you are not, it said painfully, an art institute.[37]

Stung by this realization, our porcelain firms took a variety of steps to upgrade their artistic credentials. Sèvres and Nymphenburg set about a fantastically expensive and technically demanding copying of the paintings in their national galleries onto porcelain plaques, and other firms followed, using the opportunity to demonstrate their artistic virtuosity. Competitors at the high end commissioned artists to create new vase designs—though none, noted the Meissen master modeler Ernst Leuteritz, would accept a commission to create neo-rococo forms.[38] These commissions resulted in showy objects that were expensive and difficult to make. For example, the "antique basket" K. F. Schinkel designed for the KPM for the wedding of Crown Princess Charlotte in 1820 was so intricate that it required over three thousand cuts to be made by hand.[39] Commissioned by Meissen in 1836, the young architect Gottfried Semper designed a neo-Renaissance lidded krater so large and complicated it took fifteen years for the manufactory to figure out how to fire it (fig. 5.2).[40] Even after Meissen managed to produce Semper's masterpiece, it failed to impress the public. Offered the krater at the Crystal Palace Exhibition in 1851, consumers instead admired the smaller neo-rococo works on display and raved about the life-sized porcelain camellia in a pot.[41]

In general, the Saxony manufactory did stop exhibiting "Alt-Meissen" (while making it in huge quantities), and artists took to commenting on the exhibition wares rather than on the entirety of the factory's production. By 1845, Kühn could refute criticisms of gloss-gilding and of rococo knock-offs by noting that since 1835, these had accounted for 50 percent and 28.3 percent of sales, respectively. The critics, he argued, should not compare the factory with an art school, "which has to protect its purity; preferably, instead, [Meissen's] efforts ought to be oriented to producing the truly pleasing, wherever it finds it, and according to the taste of the public. [The manufactory] should

5.2. Semper's Meissen vase

The architect Gottfried Semper designed this vase for Meissen in the 1830s, but its huge size and complex lid meant that it took fifteen years to fire.

not lose sight of the fact that it can only allow itself to cling to noble and ideal beauty insofar as this agrees with reigning tastes."[42] Nor was his firm alone; while Brongniart, early in his tenure at Sèvres, had disdained fashion in favor of subjects "of some historical or literary interest," by 1831 even he had embraced a new eclecticism, including the reuse of rococo models.[43]

It was now apparent that without income provided by the rococo revivals, and the plain-white or blue-and-white middling wares, even the higher-end firms would be forced to close. Hereafter, the survival of the "art" side of the minor arts would be financed by producing an even more diverse set of objects, including things the artists considered tasteless or cheap, and by making luxuries affordable to middle-class consumers. But what did the Biedermeier customer want?

Beyond Art Porcelain: What the Biedermeier Customer Wanted

Biedermeier porcelain producers had to get used to the idea that consumers did not necessarily want "art," and, for good or ill had fallen in love with variety. To compete in this tough market makers had to produce things that were either different, or cheaper, than what their rivals produced, and that appealed to the values that Biedermeier *Bürger* wished to cultivate. When we look at the actual production of the period, as compared to the ideals of its artists, we find a riotous variety of items that range wildly across styles and price ranges, reflecting precisely the "meteoric rise" in the number and diversity of books James Brophy has documented for this era.[44] This very eclecticism, however, makes it impossible to capture the nature of "Biedermeier taste" in a single image or paragraph; collectors and specialists will recognize the limits of my sample. Generalizing broadly, one could say that consumers now favored porcelains that created a "Gemütlich" (cozy) as well as "Gebildet" (cultivated) atmosphere, or which spoke to a kind of local patriotism mixed with a gentle nostalgia for days gone by. "Gallantry objects" such as asparagus-shaped needle cases, for the most part had gone the way of the powdered wig, and more serious biscuit statuettes of Frederick the Great, Aristotle, and John the Baptist had taken the place of playful baroque figurines. No one wanted to see cholera victims or polluted waterways on their tableware. Beyond that, the variety of offerings is stunning, and few holds were barred.

In the following section, I will draw on a considerable number of price lists of the period to compile a sampling of the figurines and painted images offered as standard fare by the manufactories. It should be kept in mind that by far the greatest quantity of porcelain sold was plain white, or blue and white, either Asian style or with "German" or "Indian" flowers. Even hugely popular "colored" flowers usually do not show up in these price lists, so what I am surveying is the repertoire that characterized the relatively small proportion of porcelains that went beyond these plain styles, and were, consequently, more expensive. In the case of the painted pipes, we can be relatively sure we are seeing men's taste reflected; in the case of much of the tableware, we can guess that women were the foremost choosers, especially as shops spread to smaller towns. As for the figurines and busts, some of these seem to be oriented to the male study or smoking room; others seem more likely to have appealed to women, for display in boudoirs or family spaces, but we can't be entirely sure. We also know that factories were willing to cater to individual orders. Consumers could, for example, choose a dinner-plate style, then a rim color and painted decorations, if desired, or order services tailored to their needs.[45] Individualized poems, inscriptions, or portraits could be added, just as the customer wished. Chances are that no two homemakers in Leipzig, for example, had exactly the same tea service.

We should consider, first, the diversity of shapes. Each manufactory offered at least two choices of "forms" for their services, one simple, the other more intricately modeled. In 1826, Gießhübel, near Karlsbad, offered cups in "Chocolate," "Antique and Conical," and "Campagnian and Etrurian" forms; having made this choice, the customer could then opt for blue, multicolor, or white decoration, with or without gold rims. Form fashions changed over time; the sling-handled "Compagnia" cup was popular between about 1800 and 1815, together with delicate, thin-handled conical shapes. The 1820s preferred footed, fluted cup forms. Few ordinary consumers cared for unusual plate shapes such as the twelve-sided Nymphenburg "Pearl" pattern, which was a good thing, as this form was still reserved for the exclusive use of the Wittelsbach family. Gothic style—originally known in some circles as "à la cathedrale"[46]—was available from the 1810s but came of age a decade or two later. Meissen's "Blue Onion" continued in production but was outstripped by the flowered services of Schlaggenwald and Korzec, and by Crown Derby's East Asian imitations, which enjoyed a burst of popularity, though they could not sustain the factory beyond 1848.[47]

Beyond the full services, customers could choose from hundreds of types of teapots and cups. One could buy butter boxes, soup tureens, sugar bowls, inkstands, mirror frames, pitchers, and, of course, chamber pots. Figurines of various sorts were also available, as were a dizzying array of pipe designs (see below). "Lithophanes," too—thin, unglazed porcelain reliefs made to stand in front of lights or windows—proved big sellers for a time and were made by most fine manufactories. All these things could be had in different sizes, at differing levels of quality, and with or without gilding or decoration.[48] Prices also varied widely but, in real and often absolute terms, had fallen sharply since the mid-eighteenth century. Hoping to impress the Finance Ministry, in 1828 Meissen officials noted that a large gilded plate could now be had for less than half its price in 1765.[49]

Falling prices made the accumulation of more and more porcelain possible for those of middling means. At a time in which a well-paid clerk would have made no more than 200 T a year, full, top-quality services remained quite expensive; a 102-piece, twelve-place Meissen white service came to 41 T; a blue service such as the "Onion" pattern came in at just over 52 T. Adding flowers and gold rims brought the cost up to 116 T, or more than a half year's labor for our clerk.[50] Stoneware was a bit less expensive; a fancy service would have cost our buyer only 2.5 months' income.[51] But smaller pieces were much more affordable. In 1828, one (private) factory offered a white coffee service for twelve for a bit under 5 T (9 T with gilding); at about the same time, a stoneware factory in Prague, advertising its Wedgwood-like styles, offered its top-quality coffeepot for a little less than 1 T.[52] One could buy a small KPM teapot for about the same price, and a teacup for five silbergroschen, or about one-sixth of the cost of the pot.[53]

To paint a general picture of decoration, we can note a great uptick in the number of landscapes and verduti, often local; we find more and more tea sets designed for intimate moments, between friends, family members, or lovers, with images or mottos that emphasize the virtues of friendship or familial affection. In the wake of a spate of popular books on "the language of flowers," porcelain makers were flooded with orders for specific floral patterns, and high-quality flower painters, such as the WPM's Joseph Nigg, were in great demand. The hunt continued to be a popular topic. As noted above, public figures were also well represented, especially in busts, with Goethe, Frederick the Great, and Homer topping the list, but other royalty (depending on the location) was also modeled. The usual classical subjects remained in the repertoire—Cupid and Psyche, Venus, Hercules, Zeus—though the more risqué figures—satyrs, nymphs, Europa—flagged; a Biedermeier Priapus seems almost a contradiction in terms. Correspondingly, religious scenes, particularly Madonnas, now flourished. By the 1830s and 1840s, neo-Gothic, neo-Byzantine, and Moorish designs could also be ordered, heralding the full onset of historicism. Extremely popular in the period—and speaking directly to its eclecticism—were mismatched teacups, suitable for placing on display on a mantel or handing out to specially chosen guests. These might feature a special poem or marriage date, a favorite flower or portrait, a beloved landscape or bird. In one 1826 example from the WPM, "Without You, I Can Not Live" was inscribed on the saucer, which accompanied an elegant gilded cup adorned with a flowering coffee plant.[54]

To immerse ourselves fully in the porcelain culture of this age, let us take some additional concrete examples of decorative options offered by the manufacturers, starting with the less expensive wares. In cheapness, after the plain whites, came copperplate-printed and underglaze painted wares. Meissen perfected underglaze green and succeeded in attracting bourgeois customers with its "Old German" vine pattern and with painted relief decorations, adopted from pressed-glass models.[55] The KPM, too, offered green-and-black designs, including lion paws, a memento mori, a wild boar, and Frederick the Great on horseback. Standard inscriptions included "May your hopes and dreams be realized," "For the lady of the house," and "For the good child."[56] The Villeroy & Boch model book for 1831–44 displays a range of available copperplate-printed landscapes, some local, some Italian, including many churches and ruins; some animals (deer, cows, rabbits, donkeys) and soldiers; some gentle jokes (usually involving soldiers); a few Turks on horseback; and two Chinese scenes, one with a figure kowtowing and another featuring a highly "orientalized" mandarin.[57] For fuller purses, Nymphenburg issued plates depicting picturesque Bavarian scenery and folk

5.3. Battle of Leipzig commemorative teacup
This KPM cup commemorates the 1813 battle in which Prussian troops
played a significant role in the victory over Napoleon. The battle plan appears on the saucer.

costumes as well as a set narrating the Nibelungenlied; recognized Romantic
artists such as Wilhelm von Kaulbach and Peter von Cornelius contributed
designs. Fürstenberg expanded its flowered offerings, as well as its military
heroes, holy families, and local landscapes; both the playwright August von
Kotzebue and his republican assassin, Karl Sand, were portrayed in porcelain,
as was the Wartburg, the scene of an important nationalist rally in 1817.[58] The
KPM answered with an elegant cup and saucer commemorating the 1813
Battle of Leipzig, the key turning point in the fight against Napoleon (fig. 5.3).

Figurines had perhaps lost their fashionableness, but they were still made
in astounding varieties, and they give us an even stronger sense of what Biedermeier buyers thought worthy of display in their homes. On the whole we
can say that a combination of seriousness and *Gemütlichkeit* won out over

the eighteenth century's love of playful gallantry and soft porn (though there was still nudity on display, especially in figurines of Venus and Psyche). Real historical personages were now more common than allegorical or perhaps even mythological ones, though the Greek gods and nymphs held their own. An 1828 KPM price list, for example, featured Prussian royals, two czars (Alexander and Nicholas), and four Napoleonic-era generals in biscuit porcelain. Goethe, Schiller, Mozart, and Herder represented the intellectuals, and one could also opt for Christ, Cupid and Psyche, or Bacchus with fauns.[59] Most manufactories made folk figurines, with Russians joining the ranks of the exotic. Schlaggenwald charmed critics with its figurines drawn from Mozart's *The Magic Flute*, while Royal Copenhagen capitalized on small-scale biscuits after the neoclassical sculptures of its native son Berthel Thorwaldsen.[60]

Lithophanes, too, give us insight into the imaginations and self-projections of the world of the 1820s and early 1830s. Patented in France in 1827, these novelties were made by transferring a copperplate engraving to a wax mold, from which a porcelain plate could be made. The result was a semitransparent relief that could be displayed near a window or in front of a lamp to illuminate the scene. An 1828 list from a Paris manufactory included the omnipresent Raphael Madonnas and Thorwaldsen's *Night* and *Day*, as well as Cupid's uncovering of Psyche. There were numerous children, putti, and cats, as well as a drunk and a shepherdess, Charles X, Henry IV, the English politician George Canning, and the Greeks at Missolonghi. An 1830 list added monkeys, a shipwreck, more landscapes, and Susannah bathing. Not to be outdone, the KPM offered Madonnas, castles, and cats, but also the head of John the Baptist, Faust and Gretchen, and the Rape of Hylas—181 different scenes in all. By 1840, this list had expanded to 231 offerings, now including a whole series of Greek (eighteen) and Roman (nine) heads in which Lycurgus, Pericles, and Cicero were included, but interestingly no Caesar or Augustus. By about 1860, the KPM was offering an astounding 554 different lithophanic images, the older models retained but now enhanced by more generals and kings (including Frederick the Great as an idealized child), Romeo, Alexander von Humbolt, and the Indian princess and eponymous heroine of the Sanskrit poem beloved by the Romantics, "Sacontala."[61]

By the 1840s, much of the porcelain intended for domestic use was probably purchased by women, though records are unclear on this.[62] But men, too, were purchasers. Tobacco, which had been cut off by Napoleon's blockade, had become affordable to most men by the 1830s, and pipe smoking was highly popular at least until the 1850s, when cigarettes and cigars came into fashion. Smoking even gained new respectability after the cholera epidemic of 1831 when the rumor spread that smoking kept dangerous miasmas at bay; in that year, Berlin makers alone produced more than one million pipes, half of those painted with colorful enamels.[63] Evidently, as the lists below suggest, men of the period chose or commissioned pipes that expressed something particular about themselves, rather as their wives and daughters expressed themselves in choosing coffee cups featuring sentimental scenes or silhouettes of the beloved. Biedermeier pipes testify, in their own way, to the emergence of a new form of bourgeois self-confidence.

A list of pipe designs offered by Meissen, most of them costing less than 1 T, reflects wild diversity of men's tastes in this eclectic era. The list began by offering probably its most popular images: of the hunt, landscapes and seascapes, military troops on foot or horse; of prominent royals, writers, or musicians; of cities in "interesting" regions; of symbols or scenes pointing to the smoker's employment in a particular trade such as medicine or mining, or his status as a freemason, or both. Standard depictions included a Tyrolian brewer with the ambiguous motto: "My tap/cock serve all comers" and a macabre scales with two skulls and the motto: "Rich or poor, in death the same." For a bit more (2 T 12 groschen) the customer could order Aesclepius, Venus, Bacchus, or Jupiter, alone or in various groups with Leda, Europa, or Danae. Or one could choose a man leaning on the breast of a maiden with the timelessly cheerful motto: "He who dies like this, dies well." The Christian could choose Jesus declaring "I will conquer"; or the sly anti-Semite, Nathan Rothschild, captioned with a line from Schiller's "Ode to Joy": "Millions, let yourself be embraced!" The unrepentant Saxon soldier could contentedly smoke a pipe picturing Napoleon's grave on St. Helena. And the list continues: the literary man could choose scenes from *Macbeth* or from Walter Scott; the history buff, Joan of Arc, Wallenstein, or Wilhelm

Tell. Rogues could purchase pipes depicting girls of all classes, or a scene described as "the Turkish maiden market."[64] Other manufactories, too, produced a similar range of pipes, with the romantic or gently erotic frequently featured (fig. 5.4). One design even twitted men so ignoble as to consume their tobacco in the shape of cigars, picturing the offending items being stuck firmly into life-sized human buttocks. Together with sentimentality and piety, there are indeed, lashings of humor to be found in the consumer culture of this era.

Even this list cannot capture the immense variety of Biedermeier porcelains, however, as it is also in this era that porcelain painting at home became feasible, evidently an attractive way for women to pass their time and to create personalized gifts. The nineteenth century was the great era of women's crafts, ranging from simple embroidery to the creation of intricate shell collages and jewelry made from the hair of the deceased.[65] For middle-class women and girls, the making of gifts for family and friends consumed untold hours and generated powerful emotions.[66] Although embroidery and knitting—taught to girls as young as three years old—played the major role here, porcelain too took part in this almost oppressive cult of the homemade.

Once the Arcanum was out, any number of pamphlets appeared explaining how to make porcelain to would-be entrepreneurial men. But by the 1830s, a new genre of books began to appear offering instructions to women and children in how to paint porcelains of their own. Karl Rottlinger's 1835 *Handbook of Porcelain-Painting, or Basic Instruction in Portrait and Landscape Painting on Porcelain*[67] was one of the first to give laypersons exact details on subjects such as how to mix one's own paints; later manuals, such as X. Froelich's *Secrets of Porcelain-Painting: A Handbook Especially for Those Who Have Some Experience in Drawing and Painting and Who Want for Their Own Purposes to Learn the Art of Durable Painting on Porcelain* (1847), were less technical. Froelich noted that many girls had been taught painting and drawing at school, and some had even learned porcelain painting. But to do it properly, one needed instruction. Porcelain paints, brushes, and glazes, he noted, had long been available to lay purchasers; one Leipzig

5.4. Biedermeier pipe

This intricately painted Meissen pipe bowl from the 1820s to 1830s depicts the most sentimental moment in Goethe's *Faust*—Faust wooing Gretchen in the garden.

vendor had offered sixty-one colors already in 1841! The average amateur, however, could be satisfied with a set of twelve paints, now available for 1 T. Froelich also offered advice about where to take one's painted wares to be fired, how to create a stencil, and how to transfer an engraving to a piece of porcelain.[68] A later handbook included more of the same sort of information, boasting that: "The art of porcelain painting also has the advantage of serving the beautiful as well as the useful and guaranteeing pleasure and profit to a large circle of people." In Dresden in particular, the author contended, every young lady finishes her education by learning to paint porcelain. This writer credited the Egyptians with discovering the art of interior decoration and particularly recommended the imitation of "oriental" painting, renowned for its "glow, sumptuousness, and fire."[69]

All this diversity flies in the face of our assumptions about industrial standardization, and about Biedermeier "feudalization" or homogeneity.[70] Even as "populuxe" items got cheaper, in this industry at least, they also got more diverse. Middling consumers did not necessarily imitate the tastes of their betters but sought domestic items with personal appeal. They did not worry much about things matching, and their souvenirs and gifts made for hodgepodges in their salons. These were the developments that lay behind artists' and reformers' complaints about stylistic incoherence and the overproduction of cheap goods. We might take a sunnier view, and perceive here, too, the opening of a world of self-expressive choices to more persons than ever before. How fully to tap this new market, however, was a difficulty the porcelain industry had not yet really solved.

Marketing and Selling

Some years ago, a historiographical debate raged over when precisely Britain became a consumer society.[71] We do not need to rehearse the controversy for the central European world; in fact, probably few would argue that anything like a consumer society existed here before the 1850s, and perhaps not until the 1950s. But the production of the minor luxury goods one associates with consumer society was certainly increasing across the Biedermeier era, as were the number of venues dedicated to their sale. Restrictions on peddling had been relaxed after the French occupations, and new retailing shops had begun to appear on town high streets, many of them equipped with display windows. Although many housewives continued to make their own clothes and bake their own bread, urban women now had a few more places to buy goods such as coffee and fresh vegetables, or to inspect housewares or lengths of cloth. As Uwe Spiekermann has convincingly argued, the expansion of small-time traders, whether female street hawkers or haberdashers, greatly increased the flexibility of sales and the dynamism of the market. Thanks to these understudied players, he argues, "by about mid-century, the institutional basis of consumer society was, in many places, already in place."[72]

These conditions, however, did not arise overnight, and the picture in the 1820s and early 1830s differs greatly from that in 1850. In the first decades after the wars, periodic agricultural crises crippled the domestic market and slowed the selling of non-necessary items such as toys, clocks, and teapots. The porcelain industry was especially afflicted by the falling off of exports. Prussia, for example, exported only 334 hundredweight of porcelain between 1825 and 1828, while at the same time importing 1,634 hundredweight (stoneware exports, at ten times the figure for porcelain, did, however, outpace imports). The English market helped, but mostly only for the highest-end makers. Only between 1832 and 1836 did Prussia become a net exporter of ceramics once more. Once formed, the Zollverein did much better, with exports exceeding imports by a factor of almost five between 1836 and 1840, and a factor of twenty between 1856 and 1860, though the bulk of the trade here, too, was in undecorated faience and stoneware.[73]

Domestically, in the 1820s and 1830s, would-be merchants and would-be manufacturers faced an array of impediments, from enduring quasi-guild resistance to the ever-present dangers of fire and bankruptcy. In the previous chapter we witnessed the difficulties faced by C. M. Hutschenreuther in starting a porcelain factory; for those who wished to sell his and others' finished products, the business climate was at first equally frosty. The example of J. G.

Hiltl, a Bavarian painter and furniture maker turned omnibus merchant, is revealing. Before the wars, Hiltl had already defied guild restrictions by smuggling foreign-made furniture into Munich to fill elite orders. In the reform years initiated by the powerful Bavarian first minister Maximilian von Montgelas, Hiltl received a privilege allowing him to operate a general furniture business and promising him state assistance to help battle guild opposition. In 1800, he opened the first Bavarian omnibus luxury store, modeled on those operating in Paris and London, from which he sold carpets and decorative items (including, surely, porcelain) in addition to furniture. Courtiers, at this point, were still buying, and receipts sufficed for Hiltl to found a furniture factory of his own. By 1805, reputedly, he employed as many as one hundred workers. But over the next few years Hiltl developed enemies at court, especially as a result of his solicitousness toward the French, and he failed to appease the undying hatred of the guildsmen. In 1810, policemen enforcing Napoleon's ban on imports stripped contraband English wares from his warehouse. Additions to his showroom and the building of a mansion ended in massive debts, and in 1816, Hiltl was forced to liquidate all his holdings and return to making furniture, with only his son Anton to assist him. Anton, as it happens, evolved backward rather than forward according to our sense of economic progress, ending up with a position as "court carpenter and decorator." But even in the Biedermeier era, such a designation ensured Anton a more secure life than that permitted by his father's entrepreneurial career.[74]

Hiltl's experience demonstrates the difficulties faced by central European merchants in the transition to the new consumer society, especially for luxury merchants and manufacturers. In fact, it was not such a bad idea to continue to tap the princes and the court for commissions; the semiluxury market was not yet large or strong enough to provide a reliable stream of orders. This was certainly the case for high-end porcelains, and as mentioned above, many royal porcelain makers still depended on court orders. Recognizing this reality, KPM director Georg Frick sent a sharply worded message to the new Prussian king Frederick William IV on his accession to the throne in 1840. Frick bemoaned the fact that Frederick William III's KPM orders in 1839

(2,292 T) had fallen far below his average annual expenditures in the period 1832–38 (15,200 T per year). This would not do, Frick argued, for a firm that wished to compete for artistic standing with foreign factories—by which he meant Sèvres and perhaps Nymphenburg—"which are all supported by the state. If the stockpiles of the higher quality porcelain do not decrease," he continued, "I will have no choice but to release the artists who have been hired and trained here since 1832. We would then no longer be capable of producing wares of sufficiently high quality for royal orders." If the new king wanted to save the porcelain factory Frederick the Great "so loved and nurtured," he was going to have to buy some stuff.[75] Frick's plea did result in generous commissions from the new king, enough to ensure artists were kept on staff. But the latter's munificence proved in no way sufficient to give KPM the financial security of Sèvres.

The 1820s and early 1830s were certainly difficult for both porcelain makers and sellers, as price wars and weak demand made cost cutting *the* priority. By the mid-1830s, as cities and towns began to grow, business began to improve, but chiefly for lower-end items. We have already witnessed middling households expanding their stocks of consumer goods, and we can postulate something of a knock-on effect. Once one had a salon to decorate, one needed not only tables and sofas, but prints for the walls, curtains, mirrors, glassware, candlesticks, cushions . . . where did it end? Although few could afford all these things at once, and many none of them at all, the desire to inhabit a comfortable house full of things was becoming more and more general.

But how to capitalize on this world of desiring but impecunious consumers? As salesmanship grew more important, traditional workshop-based selling gave way to new forms of retailing based on fixed prices and early forms of advertising. As we have seen, since the eighteenth century, commissioned retailers had been provided with price lists and sample platters; customers were expected to place their orders with the factory and await later delivery. Over time, these price lists gradually became more visually interesting, featuring illustrations of at least some of the items. Omnibus merchants began creating "works folders" containing depictions of items from candelabra to full interiors; halfway between the pattern book and the mail-order catalog, these experimental catalogs would be the proto-form of the mail-order "Versandkatalogen" perfected forty years later by the furniture maker Michael Thonet.[76]

Much more important for our period, however, was the increasing volume of ready-made sales, and the number of shops where porcelain could be procured. As we have seen, the royal firms had already established "outlet" and commissioned shops in the eighteenth century. Now the private firms, too, began spreading their wings. According to one price list of 1828, the Dalwitzer stoneware factory had agents not only in Austria's major cities, but also in the smaller towns of Nachod, Budweis, Temeswar, Szathmar, Eger, and Wadowic.[77] F. A. Schumann, for whom production really began only in 1835, had three shops in Berlin by 1841 and by 1845 had opened outlets in Leipzig and Hamburg and was exporting his wares to Brazil, Indonesia, and Australia.[78] Haberdasheries opened, advertising such mixed wares as "gallantry articles . . . marble vases, porcelain services of different types, Nuremberg toys, hydraulic, optical, and mathematical items . . . wallpapers and borders."[79] Many of these were upscale establishments, eager to win over customers by exhibiting opulence and good taste. They increasingly took care in the decoration of their shops and shop windows. In one striking Austrian image of the later 1830s, a well-to-do family admires a portrait of the emperor, painted on a porcelain plaque, while other ladies, in the company of their husbands, choose teacups. Everyone is immaculately dressed, including the man with the pink waistcoat, who appears to be the shop owner. The shop imagined or depicted here is a very high end one, and the fact that the porcelain is displayed along with fine silver pieces suggests that it probably featured state brands rather than cheaper Thuringian knock-offs (plate 11).

In other ways, too, new forms of retailing were replacing the old. Seasonal fairs continued, though their functions gradually changed. As shops increased their selections of ready-made goods, fairs were less and less vital for household goods such as tinwares and ceramics and began to take on at least a nominal educational function, seeking to instruct visitors in the latest technologies as well as products, something that appealed to the *Bildung*-hungry middling classes. Some offered many products; others were devoted to one specific ware (e.g., the Frankfurt Book Fair). Towns, regions, and states now claimed the commodities produced within and took pride in showing off "their" products.[80] By the 1820s, regional exhibitions had begun to pop up in central European towns and cities; by one estimate more than one hundred of these took place in the German states between 1820 and 1850.[81] The 1851 Crystal Palace Exhibition was as much the culmination of this process as the creation of a new model: the international exhibition. "Porcelain" was there from the beginning and played a major role in promoting both national identities (in 1851, this still meant Saxon, Bavarian, or Prussian identities) and the prestige of brands. The world's fair, in particular, became a key venue for the broadcasting of these ideals (see chapter 7), and a sign that people, words, and things were in motion as never before.

In rural areas peddlers continued to ply the roadways, their number (proportional to the population) actually increasing after 1850. Some now equipped "Wandermagazinen" (wandering-wagon shops) to travel between central Europe's many smaller towns, causing complaints from shopkeepers, who resented their freedom from rent and taxes, and frequently referred derisively to their competitors as "Jews."[82] It is unlikely that anything but the strongest and cheapest stoneware was sold by these itinerant salespersons, for Germany's roads continued to be rough and most rural persons too poor to buy tea services. But the rising number of traders of all kinds tells us much about the ways in which a more dynamic and flexible capitalist marketplace was taking hold.

The new dynamism does not mean, however, that transformations in buying and selling arrived without conflict or costs. As retailers gained more experience and independence, tensions arose between makers and sellers, especially with respect to the minimum prices set by the manufactories. Retailers demanded the right to choose their own stock and especially to offer discounts to reduce backlogs; manufactories insisted on controlling distribution and prices, often, as we have seen, to the consternation of their ministerial minders. These conflicts seem not to have crippled sales in this period, but they were harbingers of battles that would intensify sharply in the early twentieth century (see chapter 8). In the meantime, manufacturers had battles closer to home to fight: on the factory floor.

A Craft Industry in a Class Society

For good reason, the Biedermeier era has long been the focus of social historians interested in the rise of class society. This era saw the transition away from the Old Regime's corporatist society, in which status, as an individual, townsperson, or member of a trade was made manifest in the holding of particular privileges. Class society's hierarchy, instead, ranked individuals on the basis of their property and income. If under the former system what individuals or groups could or could not do was circumscribed by a vast and locally variable series of legal restrictions, under the new, actions were, at least in theory, limited only by what one could afford. This was a seismic, and for many, unwelcome, change. But nowhere did it happen overnight, and in central and southern Europe, the transition occurred more slowly than to the north and west, one of the many reasons why these regions' histories of industrialization and consumption must necessarily differ from those of England or the Low Countries.

If we take as our example the labor market, it is clear that the guilds, here, long retained informal, if not formal power. Guilds were not officially abolished in the Habsburg Empire until 1859, and even after this time, master craftsmen continued to organize looser federations and to attempt to dominate licensing boards; accustomed to the respect of other men of status and relatively high pay (at least for masters), as well as, often, citizenship in one's town or city, they objected fiercely to reforms that threatened to degrade their social standing and to flood the market with cheap, badly made goods. Long into the nineteenth century, thus, central European artisans defended a venerable notion of "skill" that meant mechanical dexterity, but also encompassed financial independence, paternalistic authority in the workshop, and entitlement to the respect of their bourgeois peers.[83] As the privileged position of skilled labor atrophied and the new, more "liberal" marketplace took hold, not surprisingly, many skilled workers felt displaced and dishonored, as, indeed, they were.

In our industry, the degrading of artisanal labor was a much more pronounced aspect of modernization than the introduction of machines. That this was the case in more industries than we had previously recognized is apparent in the newer literature on the Industrial Revolution that emphasizes the way in which production processes were transformed without the sudden introduction of machinery or even the concentration of labor in factories.[84] This is emphatically the case for central Europe, where labor was cheap and machines expensive, and where manufacturers tailored their market niches carefully to avoid competing with their more industrialized British rivals.[85] Manual labor and cottage industries there survived much longer than in Great Britain or the United States; in the 1840s, two in five persons employed in manufacturing still worked according to the "putting out" system.[86] In the porcelain industry, machines were hardly in evidence before 1850, and, although, atypically, many porcelain workers were congregated in "factories" rather than sent home with piecework, some of these factories were actually smaller in the early nineteenth century than they had been in the eighteenth. Even as a few private ceramics makers exceeded one thousand employees in the century's second half, many others remained small. As late as 1907, 78 percent of German ceramics firms had five or fewer employees.[87]

In this period, a deep-seated aspect of fine ceramics manufacture became ever more consequential for labor relations: while half of the workforce saw to preparing the clay and firing the pieces, processes requiring many (anonymous) hands and divided labor, the other half was engaged in forming and decorating, individual tasks assigned to persons who considered themselves artists, or at least respectable artisans.[88] Within the porcelain factories, even though never guilded, in each of these branches, "masters" had always been treated as greatly superior to the rest, and master modelers and painters in particular had been treated as the equivalent of court artists. Their wages and perks had been commensurate, with some paid princely sums, afforded free lodging or firewood, and excused from military service. Over time the kiln masters and clay mixers had lost more relative ground, especially as they were replaced at the top with expert chemists or kiln designers. This left the painters and modelers to be the chief representatives of artisanal values and hierarchies.

Lower-level workers had generally been treated with paternalistic care and oversight, fed in times of dearth, and promised pensions or medical care after long service. Correspondingly, they were subjected to various kinds of moral discipline and expected to accept delays in salary payments or furloughs when the prince was short of cash. J. F. Boch, for example, provided social insurance for skilled men, encouraged saving and sobriety, and insisted on approving male workers who wished to marry before age twenty-five. Later in the century the firm would build housing complexes and recreational facilities, hoping to foster moral probity and diminish radicalization.[89] Of course the application of paternalistic discipline was uneven. Some—like Boch and Frederick the Great—watched workers carefully and kept incisive records. But in other cases, as we have seen, workers drank or snoozed on the job, used factory materials for private commissions, or toasted chicory in the manufactory's kilns.

The nineteenth century, with its freer markets, increased competition, and falling prices put enormous pressure on these older artisanal and paternalist practices. Skilled workers, in general, seem to have lost ground in the century's first half, their real wages fluctuating wildly. They suffered most in the periods 1806–13, 1820–25, 1829–33, and 1846–48, when upsurges in food prices went hand in hand with reductions in orders. Craftsmen were also much more vulnerable to market downturns than were the factories' officials, who generally retained their fixed salaries through periods of hardship.[90] Sometimes, by the factories' own admission, wages fell below the minimum cost of living. But in addition to recognizing the hardships brought on by falling wages, it is important to understand the ways in which the new forms of work discipline and subordination to managerial staff undermined artisans' sense of the respect and autonomy to which they were entitled. It was a further insult to their pride to be replaced by unskilled day laborers, or worse, women.

TABLE 5.1. Women Workers at Meissen, 1765–1876

	Numbers	Percentage of Workforce
1765	15	2%
1806	15	3%
1823	35	10%
1872	66	14%
1876	103	20%

Sources: Barbel Kovalevski, "Frauen in Meissen," in *Kunst oder Kommerz? Meissener Porzellan im 19. Jahrhundert* (Dresden, Sandstein Verlag, 2010), 56–59; Böhmert, "Urkundliche Geschichte," 69, 79, 82.

The great British social and economic historian Maxine Berg long ago alerted us to see the replacement of male labor by the less expensive employment of women and children as a sign of the advance of industrialization. In the porcelain industry, too, we can see a drift in this direction, especially at the private firms, but even at Meissen, for which our records are best (see table 5.1). Very few women were allowed to learn the skills necessary to become modelers, turners, or "multicolor" painters and so largely filled semi-skilled jobs as polishers, glazers, packers, and blue painters. Like part-time laborers and apprentices, they were not allowed to buy into the firms' social insurance programs, and their salaries typically ran at about half those of men. At the KPM in the 1840s, for example, female polishers were paid 93 to 120 T per annum, as compared to male polishers, who made 180–312 T per year; small wonder that in 1848, male coworkers petitioned, with only partial success, for their firing.[91] The proportion of women employed at the private factories was typically higher than at the state firms. While in 1841 the KPM and Meissen employed no more than 10 percent women, at Ville-roy & Boch's Mettlach plant, 19 percent of the workforce was female.[92] This discrepancy is yet another sign of the larger investments in artistry made by the princely factories and the greater cost sensitivity of the private firms.

Another sign of industrialization's advance was the unwelcome recognition that ceramics workers were subject to the lethal ailment that would later be called silicosis. It was already evident in the eighteenth century that porcelain makers were much more likely than others to suffer from lung disease—which in the great age of tuberculosis was saying something. But by the early 1840s, as more statistics began to mount, the pattern became clearer. At Fürstenberg it was recognized that an unusual number of workers were dying young of lung diseases; a study commissioned by the ducal mining and metallurgy department concluded that the cause of these afflictions was bad air, particularly in the lathe operators' rooms, where porcelain dust hung thickly. The effect was exacerbated by the consumption of spirits, which evidently remained a regular practice. Although the report sounded the alarm, it recommended only banning the drinking of spirits on the job and moving the lathe turners to new quarters, where the windows could be opened in good weather.[93] The private maker F. A. Schumann sympathized with the workers' plight and helped fund travel and care for invalids.[94] But not until after 1945 would any serious attempts be made to protect workers from silicosis.

Perhaps we can see the evolution toward new models of production most clearly in the many disputes in the century's first half between factory managers and skilled painters, who wished to preserve their perks and their status as artists. As noted in chapter 4, royal firms in particular were under great pressure to cut labor costs, and as the market increasingly demanded cheaper unpainted or copperplate printed wares, the logical way to do this was to do away with costly artists, though some had to be kept on to satisfy royal commissions and the need for "Prunkstücke" for exhibitions. At the WPM, for example, Director Scholz not only replaced salaries with piece rates but reduced the painting staff severely; by 1830, the firm employed only fifty polychrome and five blue painters, compared to triple that number in 1805.[95] Master modelers, too, lost their positions, and those who remained would figure prominently among the courageous few willing to stand up to factory directors. But as figurines had lost much of their cachet as compared to painted tablewares, master modelers too were no longer so visible as representatives of porcelain artistry and seem to have let the painters take the lead.

Two stories will have to suffice to dramatize the labor conflicts within the manufactories in this period, one from the Fürstenberg manufactory, and the other from the KPM. In the case of Fürstenberg, the tale begins with the efforts of Carl von Marées, the overseer of factory sales and son-in-law of the firm's aging painting director, to tailor production to the changing marketplace. Beginning in 1823, von Marées had gradually assumed more and more of his father-in-law's functions and had begun to butt heads with the painters, who resented what they saw as his high-handed attempts to usurp their privileges. They refused to use the new paints von Marées introduced and resisted giving up their moonlighting endeavors; when he tried to fire one painter for drunkenness on the job, the painter sued the factory. The plaintiff lost, but he was subsequently taken back on for commissioned work, partly out of pity.[96]

Von Marées did, however, have the factory's administrative overseers, the ducal chamber, on his side. In 1827, the chamber commissioned the advice of another businessmen on how to turn around the still-unprofitable enterprise. This adviser suggested that expensive painting not be done on spec, as it only ended up in the warehouse, from which it was auctioned off, usually at a 50–60 percent loss. What was selling were white and gilded single wares; thus, the factory could do away with its skilled painters and outsource special commissions, thereby relieving itself of having to pay high wages and, eventually, pensions.[97] Not surprisingly, the head of the Fürstenberg painting department countered this hardheaded advice with a proposal to revitalize the firm's artistic standing. Von Marées, in response, insisted on the necessity of prioritizing commercial goals, and the orientation of production to cheap and salable wares:

> The commercial circles from which we have up to now received most of our income and to whose tastes and needs I have chiefly catered are comprised of the middling class of citizens. The items which sell most . . . are those with simple gilding as well as individual cups and coffee and table services; here we are able to match the prices of our competitors, the foreign porcelain makers.

Most of the painting, thus, does not need to be managed by artists; [management] lies much more in the commercial sphere, for it is only necessary to use the available workforce properly, to offer the smallest possible painters' salaries, and to watch carefully the consumption of gold. [This plan] also has the advantage that I [as overseer of sales] can satisfy all the wishes of the public and most easily realize them. It is my observation that items over 5 or 6 silver groschen and vases over 10 silbergroschen only rarely sell, and attempts to compete in foreign markets, too, have not succeeded. Thus my goal has remained that of compelling a small workforce to produce the largest possible number of chiefly cheap wares. The successful result is that this workforce is essentially sufficient to sustain a selection that is not too large, and that most of the wares speedily leave the warehouse.[98]

The ducal chamber, predictably, took von Marées's advice and determined that the manufactory could do without skilled painters on staff. In late 1828, the chamber sold the whole department, including its supplies, to von Marées. The disgruntled artists made a brief attempt to form their own brotherhood, but their having no business sense, the endeavor failed, and they had to return to taking commissions from von Marées. One of the most skilled, who had previously earned 400 T a year, had to work so hard that he fell ill, and having five children to support, decided to draw his pension of 150 T per year rather than trying to negotiate the unstable new marketplace.[99]

The conflicts at the KPM in many ways mirror those at Fürstenberg. At the KPM, painters were not loathe to express their grievances and did so in many memos to the ministry. In 1818 they protested fines imposed for allegedly shoddy work; in 1821 they complained vociferously about being shifted to payment by the piece, while the managerial officials continued to draw regular salaries.[100] When rates were lowered again, Director Rosentiel passed their protests on to the ministry, claiming that he had been forced to reduce wages in response to the competition introduced by the new Prussian tariff. But the ministry simply advised him to fire some of the painters to improve the condition of the others. The painters then proceeded to appeal over the heads of both Rosentiel and the ministry to Frederick William III. They reminded him that as they had sworn an oath to the king, it was his obligation to see that they were taken care of, for life. They also asked for an investigation of Rosentiel's practices, which in their view were not furthering sales. Rosentiel received a reproof, and relations between the director and the skilled workers were subsequently poisoned. After workers complained about him again in 1829, blaming him for the latest losses, Rosentiel retired, leaving the fight to the KPM's codirector, the chemist Georg Frick.

By this time, Frick had headed the KPM's painting department for eight years. He had not found the job a pleasant one. Attached to their own mixtures, staff painters disdained Frick's chemical innovations and had to be compelled to use his recipes.[101] Nor did they appreciate his daily shop floor inspections, devoted to—in the words of a later director—"making the painters aware of mistakes and carelessness." Both of these changes, for the painters, diminished their status as autonomous artisans, at the same time as their wages were falling precipitously. Eager to advance the firm's technical modernization and commercial competitiveness, Frick found their resistance exasperating. Insofar as he was able, the new director pensioned off most of the older painters and promoted a couple of lowly green underglaze painters; he also hired twenty-eight girls to do the gold-polishing work previously done by more highly paid men.[102]

Even in nominal terms, porcelain artisans in the Restoration period clearly lost ground. While the average "color" painter at the KPM in 1764 drew 407 T a year, in 1847—a time of exploding food prices—he made only 296 T.[103] Much of this loss was recent; it is estimated that skilled labor costs fell as much as 80 percent between 1822 and 1839.[104] Losses continued into the 1840s. Early in that decade, for example, Frick again reduced piece rates and winnowed the skilled staff; the artisans' situation seemed to be getting worse, even as the economy as a whole improved. These developments provide the context in which to understand artisanal discontent in an era in which little new machinery was introduced: skilled workers experienced proletarianization without actually becoming the classic slaves of the machine portrayed in so many conventional accounts of the Industrial

Revolution. Having experienced such precipitous declines in pay and status, by the spring of 1848, the KPM's porcelain workers had had enough.

In April 1848, emboldened by the spread of Europe-wide revolutions, skilled KPM workers downed tools and petitioned the manufactory to listen to their grievances.[105] They attempted to claw back wage reductions that had been in place since 1842 and insisted on participation in factory decisions (*Mitbestimmung*), fixed wages, protection from being fired, and, for the artists, judgment of their work by artists rather than managerial dilettantes (meaning chiefly Frick himself). Sixty workers crowded into Frick's office and demanded the firing of a particularly oppressive overseer, whom the director narrowly saved from bodily harm. Frick acted quickly to stamp our further protests, summarily firing the ringleaders of the demonstrations. He died—of natural causes—in June 1848, and the KPM shop floor seems to have fallen quiet in the wake of his departure. Meissen saw protests related to wages and lost privileges, but no real political activity.[106] In both cases, events exposed differences in aspirations between skilled workers, who wanted prestige and decision-making responsibility, and unskilled laborers, whose major goal was a wage increase. The former, in particular, did not fail to recognize that in future, organized efforts would be necessary, and the 1850s saw the forming of porcelain workers' societies that transcended individual factories and crossed state borders.[107] A new age was dawning.

In the effort to please connoisseurs and to keep the KPM's artistic credentials intact, Frick, like other directors, had attempted to commission works from independent artists but found this, too, a most frustrating endeavor. As he wrote in retrospect: "None of them had any skill in the art of drawing. They were all arrogant and conceited, riding on their reputations for supposed dexterity. Their education was too one-sided and they were too vain to make the appropriate tests with color. Furthermore, they were not trained to work consistently and on a regular basis."[108] At Meissen, too, there were complaints about the "aristocratic" behavior of the "soi disant artistes." Here too the number of artists as compared to other workers had fallen. While Meissen had employed 441, or about 60 percent of the workforce, in modeling and painting in 1765, in 1833, it employed only 188, or 52 percent in these branches.[109] Director Kühn echoed Frick in his complaints about his painters: "Every artist is, in the main, so completely enamored with his creations that he views every sort of criticism of his sketches as an insult. . . . For what are practical hindrances, whether they lie in technical limitations or in customers' desires, in the eyes of the artists, in comparison to the incomparable achievements of his imagination?"[110] To the managers—now mostly scientists or merchants—the painters' complaints about deskilling were "arrogant" and out of step with market realities; viewing this from the side of the craftsmen, we can see how reconfiguring labor relations threatened their individual and collective rights to control the production process, and rendered their imaginations irrelevant to the work they were to perform. This begins to look very much like the "alienation of labor" described by Karl Marx, not coincidentally a man who came of age in the Biedermeier era.

In many ways, Marxian "alienation of labor" works better in an analysis of the luxury trades than of the many cottage cotton and wool weavers, who probably never really got much aesthetic satisfaction, not to mention prestige, out of their drudgery. In fields such as glassmaking, furniture making, and even dressmaking, the coming of batch-produced wares certainly did mark a new era, one in which their trades became less and less richly rewarded, and the status of even the master makers reached only the level of the "decorative" arts. Not surprisingly, those porcelain "artists" who wanted to retain their imaginations and higher prestige (if not pay) often abandoned ceramics for easel painting; Ludwig Richter, who returned from his study years in Rome to become director of Meissen's drawing school in the late 1820s, is a good example. After several years of what he called "exile," Richter left the factory to paint landscapes, finally landing a professorship at the Dresden academy and escaping his Meissen "exile" in 1841.[111] Not surprisingly given conflicts with its own artists and the art world's increasing disdain for porcelain painting, the KPM actually found it hard to find landscape painters, who now considered working for a state manufactory degrading.[112] Was porcelain making an art at all? That was a question that, as central Europe moved toward mass production, would be ever more urgently posed.

In an extended self-parody, the German Jewish writer Ludwig Börne described to his friend Heinrich Heine the liabilities of his beloved porcelain holdings.

> You have no idea, my dear Heine, how one is curbed by the possession of beautiful porcelain. Look at me, for example, once so wild when I had little baggage and no porcelain at all. With possessions, and especially fragile possessions, come fear and servitude. Unfortunately I recently acquired a beautiful tea service—the pot was so enticingly and sumptuously gilded—the marital bliss of two lovers billing and cooing was painted on it . . . now I am really worried about writing too freely in my stupidity so that I must suddenly flee—how could I pack up all these cups, not to speak of the big pot, in a hurry? . . . Truly, I feel how the damned porcelain hinders me in writing; I am getting so mild, so cautious, so anxious. In the end I am ready to believe that the porcelain dealer was an Austrian police agent and that Metternich saddled me with the porcelain to tame me. Yes, yes, that's why it was so inexpensive and the man was so persuasive. Oh! the sugar bowl depicting marital happiness was such a sweet lure! Yes, the more I examine my porcelain, the more probable it seems that it comes from Metternich.[113]

Börne was of course joking; but his evident affection for his gilded (and inexpensive!) tea service opens a window for us into a Biedermeier world in which even a left-leaning satirist felt the pull of porcelain. Börne did not inquire into how this porcelain was made, and perhaps had he known the travails of the artisans who had produced his tea set he would have been less enchanted by its fragile beauty. The service's sentimental sweetness had enticed him to buy it—evidently ready-made—from a dealer who had persuaded him of its merits. As porcelain became increasingly part of the Germanys' public and private spheres, consumers such as Börne contentedly added it to their "baggage." Most would be loathe to part with items—whether costly or not—that reflected their personal tastes, regional identities, and family histories. They would, instead, simply want *more*.

Chapter 6

Of Capitalism and Cartels

The Glory Days of the Private Producer, 1848–1914

In 1860, the writer Wilhelm Kesselbach looked back at the comfortless, hardscrabble lives of his grandparents as if they belonged to a completely lost and forgotten world. In those days, he wrote, grandfather wore one coat for ten years, and his Sunday clothes lasted his lifetime. Grandmother toiled unceasingly to see that the household was provisioned for the harsh winters. Nowadays, however, Kesselbach averred, households had given up the slaughtering of their own animals, and women had time to read books. "All things considered, Germany has become richer; individuals recognize that they are able to satisfy more of their intellectual and bodily needs than ever before. We consume many more, and much more diverse goods."[1]

When the national economist Gustav Schmoller checked in a decade later, he reiterated Kesselbach's observations, crediting new forms of transport, in particular, with the transformation of Germans' everyday lives: "all is different in the home and at court, at the family dinner table as in the servants' quarters, in the yearly and weekly markets as in the shops of the small towns, in the great exchanges as in the gigantic storehouses, where two worlds exchange their treasures." Schmoller identified so many items being mass-produced—including umbrellas, buttons, hats, soap, pipes, paper, wire, rings, and eyeglasses—that he feared for the survival of the honest German craftsman. He called on the state to limit the damage done by the overly hasty dissolution of the guilds and the unbridled spread of capitalist competition. At precisely the moment that a consumption-oriented bourgeoisie had begun to emerge, Schmoller claimed that the middle class was disappearing, with grave consequences for class relations and the moral fiber of the soon to be united nation.[2]

If in 1870 Kesselbach and Schmoller felt they had already experienced a revolution in their own lifetimes, how much more change, in politics and in everyday life, would their own grandchildren live to see? Between roughly 1850 and 1914, central Europeans experienced such massive social, economic, material, and political changes as to make their lifestyles virtually unrecognizable to individuals born into the world of 1800, or even 1830. Germany became a unified "empire" in 1871, in the wake of Prussia's wars with Denmark, Austria, and France, and began acquiring colonies, and wider global ambitions, in 1884. Habsburg Austria ceded large swathes of prosperous territory to the newly united Italy and, like other European nations, lost millions to transoceanic emigration. Hungary obtained almost full autonomy in 1867, and centrifugal nationalisms made relations between the empire's ethnic groups increasingly contentious. Urbanization across the region surged after 1850, accelerating madly after 1873 as agricultural prices and cottage industries collapsed, sending waves of peasants streaming into cities and towns. Here former peasants found jobs as servants, factory workers, or porcelain decorators. Food prices fell, and real wages increased—but so did working-class organization and strikes. Mechanization, steam-powered transportation, and global competition further endangered craftsmanship and village traditions, resulting in numerous expressions of resistance to "the new." Central European society had never been so dynamic—nor so volatile. Decisions and material goods made here, including Germany's joining the quest for colonies and Alfred Krupp's armaments, would change the course of world history.

As the remarks of our two witnesses suggest, Germany's entry into the age of mass production and consumption arrived quite late—compared to that of the Netherlands and Great Britain—and came on very fast. Nor was this identical with an industrial revolution, as much of what was being mass-produced, Schmoller pointed out, was still being made by hand. Capitalism was triumphing, aided by the freeing up of banking restrictions and of restrictions on the forming of limited-liability corporations in the 1870s; private ownership of businesses and assets had clearly become the norm. But some major operations were still at least partly owned by the states, including the railways and several of our porcelain manufactories, and many who lived through the period, like Schmoller, actually wished the state would do *more* to guide developments. Manchester-style liberalism—which championed free trade on both domestic and international fronts—had some supporters in the 1850s and 1860s, but never much of a German constituency,[3] and by the 1870s, farmers, industrialists, and workers were seeking protections through tariffs or by forming cartels, labor unions, and consumers' collectives. To describe, in this period, the successes of *some* entrepreneurs does not mean that they wholly succeeded in wrestling economic might from kings and landed aristocrats; they did not. Nor did large factories wipe out smaller tradesmen; larger retailers coexisted with local fairs and *Wandermagazinen*, creating a volatile and dynamic mix. Indeed, one of the fascinations of this period is, or ought to be, the ways in which capitalism combined and contended with older forms of mercantilism, paternalism, authoritarianism, and artisanal labor. It did not need to be "pure" to be a potent agent of economic and social change.

Our focus on the porcelain industry offers us the opportunity to view in microcosm many of these social and economic processes. As ever, porcelain is an imperfect mirror, and "high" politics will play little role for us, although this backdrop certainly is important for understanding its history as well. It does matter for us that Bismarck's new state adopted the Prussian king, Wilhelm I, as its emperor and the Prussian residence city, Berlin, as its capital. Crucially, the borders were drawn such that Austrian and Bohemian Germans were excluded, while Alsatians and Silesians received German passports. We will follow these border changes in shifting our focus from wider central European "Germany" to the new Germany proper after 1871, though Bohemian and Austrian producers and markets will remain important to our story.[4] But for us, Bismarck's wars mattered chiefly in the forging of a grand-scale, national market, both for exports and for domestic sales; a new national currency was introduced as well, the mark, which replaced the taler and the florin (at the rate of 3 M = 1 T and 2 M = 1 F). Perhaps surprisingly, Germany's colonial ventures created rather small reverberations in our story. The new colonies did not buy much porcelain; as in other sectors of the economy, the markets of Europe, the Americans, and Australasia were much more important.[5] Wilhelm II's jingoist bluster contributed greatly to the global political insecurities and imperialist rivalries of the fin de siècle. But it made little direct impact on the porcelain industry. Readers will, I hope, not take from my light coverage of such subjects the lesson that those political events were unimportant, but recognize that this is a different kind of German history, one meant only to complement the more familiar accounts of the German Empire's rise to world power.

In this chapter and the next, rather than rehashing familiar political events or engaging in abstract discussions of the liberal—and not so liberal—capitalist—and not so capitalist—Wilhelmine world, we will sample stories about hotels and cartels, railroads and bathrooms, rich men and impoverished child laborers. Making this world concrete by narrowing our focus, this chapter will survey the changes underway in production and the organization of capital and labor in the period after 1850, which has some right to be called porcelain's second "golden age." We give special emphasis, here, to the private producers, especially in the emerging ceramics centers in Silesia, the Saarland, and Upper Franconia, for in this period in particular they were the market leaders and profit makers. At the chapter's end, however, we return to the state firms whose histories we have been following for so long: Nymphenburg and the WPM, Meissen and the KPM, and describe how each of these firms navigated—or failed to navigate—the perilous seas of this age of rapacious capitalist competition. The history of porcelain consumption—mostly told in chapter 7—also reminds us of some home truths that art-historical investigations of the period often overlook, for the good reason that they are focused on original conceptions and virtuoso accomplishments: that what most people liked and bought were wares depicting sentimental landscapes and religious or romantic scenes, very little of it archetypically "modern." Porcelain certainly does not tell us all we need to know about central Europe's "Second Industrial Revolution," which was also, in some ways, its first. But it does tell us a great deal about what it was like to live, work, and shop during the transformational Wilhelmine age, and that is, itself, an interesting tale.

A Second Golden Age?

In general, the period between 1850 and 1914 was one of increasing prosperity for central Europeans, and for the ceramics industry, it brought profits at levels not seen since the mid-eighteenth-century "golden age." The Wilhelmine era witnessed numerous technical advances, greatly expanded production, much more profitable export markets, and a growing workforce. One expert, surveying Germany's fine ceramics industry in 1904, claimed that porcelain making "has now reached its high point."[6] But the "in general" in this paragraph's first sentence, and the boosterism just cited, mask a great deal of change, some of it painful, for porcelain makers in the period. Each manufactory had its ups and downs, and the general trajectory, too, was punctuated by periods of slow growth or even slumps. As in the wider economy, local makers—often with one or two employees—hung on, but they were generally worse off than before.[7] The same could probably be said for small retailers, whose numbers grew even as they became more and more specialized in their offerings and clientele. Statistically, employees in the larger factories were better off than before, enjoying new workplace protections, insurance funds, reduced hours of labor, and wage increases. But anyone reviewing their many complaints about penury, lockouts, filthy conditions, and the treatment of apprentices and female cottage laborers as "slaves" or "animals" would hardly believe that many felt the improvement. The regularity of threats to strike or down tools suggests that the porcelain workforce remained unconvinced that rising national affluence would raise their boats.

Prosperity, moreover, was intermittent and unpredictable. Rises in wealth took time to manifest themselves after the suppression of revolutions in

1848–49. The era of unification (*Gründerzeit*), lasting roughly from 1850 to 1873, saw a great expansion in the domestic market and the founding of many new firms, especially in the boom years of 1865–73. In this period, liberal economic ideas flourished, to the detriment of small manufactories and the surviving mercantile initiatives. Then came the "bust" of 1873, accompanied by the ruination of speculators, the raising of tariffs, and the tightening of credit. Eventually, porcelain sales recovered, and exports, especially to the booming United States, surged—at least until decimated by the banking crisis of 1907. The advent of artistic modernism, too, created a wider gap than ever before between buyers' old-fashioned tastes and critics' expectations. Porcelain making still entailed a great deal of handwork—and in fact homework, performed especially by Thuringian women. But we can definitely say that long before the outbreak of the Great War, the porcelain industry had entered into the era of mass production, with all its wonders and its warts.

This chapter takes on a period in porcelain's historical development in which the literature is much less comprehensive and, it must be said, much less sympathetic to the industry, its overseers, and its employees. Firm histories tend to skate over the period quickly; many don't treat the nineteenth or twentieth centuries at all (albeit because some of our princely firms were by this time leased to private owners), and even the Propyläen history of the European manufactories, which lavishes 212 pages on the period 1700 to 1830, devotes only thirty to the next century. As one writer has noted, collectors and museum curators tend to treat the objects produced in this era—aside from those made by "arts and crafts" reformers or Jugendstil designers—as flea market trash,[8] which, admittedly, much of it has now become. But as noted previously, this book is not about porcelain as a form of art, but rather one that focuses on the industry and its cultural and economic significance for central Europeans. Thus we will now plunge into this little-known territory, exploring in more purely historical terms what might be called—at least financially speaking—the industry's second "golden age."

Statistical Snapshots

One of the things persons of the later nineteenth century liked to do was to record and report statistics. That makes offering an industrial overview all the simpler for us—although after digesting the numbers, we will want to move on to some richer stories. We must also be sure to put porcelain in the context of other consumer goods; public and private consumption of fine (as well as not so fine) ceramics did rise, together with the explosion of public eateries, including cafés, hotels, workplace canteens, *Konditereien* (pastry shops), and restaurants.[9] Yet by no means was porcelain the only semiluxury commodity whose production expanded, or whose export mattered to state officials—there were also toymakers, milliners, and glassmakers asking for backing and favors. And of course, many sectors mattered a great deal *more* to German statesmen and consumers than the luxury trades: grains, steel, coal, textiles, machines, and beer, just for starters, though it was in the realm of finished goods such as porcelain, books, and optical equipment that the later Wilhelmine export market really reveled. Together with the training of the most highly respected scientists and humanists, the production of such sophisticated cultural goods demonstrated to consumers inside and outside the new state that Germany was a land not just of commerce, but of *Kunst* and *Kultur*.

We should not make the mistake of overestimating the size of this industry, or failing to keep up with its changing cultural roles and applications. Even in the areas that counted as porcelain-making centers—Upper Franconia, Saxony, the Saarland, Thuringia, and Silesia—porcelain making was not the only, or even the biggest, trade. In Berlin, for example, where numerous manufactories were located, in 1861, in a population just under 525,000, approximately seventy-five hundred persons were employed in wool weaving and only 1,230 in porcelain and stoneware manufacturing—though this outdistanced makers of furniture (about four hundred) and umbrellas (185).[10] Nor did consumers spend anything like the entirety of their increasing amounts of disposable income on teapots and pipes; porcelain makers operated in a burgeoning world of semiluxury goods, including silk hats, wallpaper, bicycles, picture books, and lace petticoats. And, increasingly, porcelain manufacturers were surviving on the production of things consumers hardly noticed at all: buttons, insulators, doorknobs, floor tiles, false teeth. This period experienced the rise of "technical" and "electrical" porcelains, and their adoption by telegraph offices and railways, creating a branch of the industry that catered to an entirely different set of customers with far more utilitarian needs. We need to be sure to put porcelain in its proper context, rather than assume a continuity of uses, meanings, or economic significance across the long history of this very adaptable commodity.

To note some production and employment statistics, however, is to sense the seismic changes for ceramics makers after the midcentury. While the number of potters seems to have risen very slightly between 1828 and 1858,[11] after this time totals of newly founded firms skyrocketed. We cannot count directly how many ceramics firms went into (or out of) business after midcentury, but the net rise is notable; while there were perhaps 150 fine ceramics manufactories in the German-speaking lands in 1840,[12] the figure by 1882 had reached 1,807. Firm size and the net number of employees also increased rapidly, as table 6.1 shows. Late to enter the market, Upper Franconia, by 1910, was home to sixty-two porcelain manufactories.[13] In the Saarland alone, there was a 398 percent increase in the number of ceramics workers between 1850 and 1913—though this was outpaced by the iron industry, whose numbers swelled by 2,183 percent.[14] Our statistics on the Austro-Hungarian monarchy are less exact, and only for porcelain makers; here, between 1873 and 1890, the number of factories leapt from eighteen to

TABLE 6.1. Firm Size, 1882–1907

	1882	1895	1907
No. of porcelain firms	1,807	1,536	1,579
No. of porcelain workers	23,094	35,914	51,785
Average no. of workers per firm	12.8	24.1	32.8

Sources: Wildner, "Die Porzellanindustrie," 232; Trömel, *Kartell und Preisbildung*, 18; Zimmer, *Die deutsche Porzellanindustrie*, 84. There were, however, still 868 single operators in 1907.

Map 2.

Porcelain manufacturers in central Europe, ca. 1900.

forty-three, and the workforce from 4,896 to 8,975.[15] The expansionary direction, in any case, is clear.

The rapid extension of rail systems after 1850 contributed greatly to economic and social change, transforming a world in which previously an overland shipment might have required four days to travel twenty miles with one in which this distance could be traveled in an hour or less. Transport, as Gustav Schmoller saw already in 1870, had became more and more crucial to giving the bigger firms an edge over the smaller ones.[16] As the rail lines reached beyond the big cities—where labor was relatively expensive—into poorer rural areas, whole "porcelain cities," such as Selb, arose. Located in Upper Franconia in the C-shaped area on the Austro-Bohemian-Silesian border where the magical combination of kaolin, coal, forests, and cheap skilled labor was readily available (see map 2), Selb had once been home to thousands of immiserated cottage textile workers of the sort profiled in Gerhard Hauptmann's dismal play *The Weavers*. In 1857, however, the town was ravaged by fire, destroying looms and leaving inhabitants desperate for work. Seizing this opportunity, Lorenz Hutschenreuther left his father's works in Hohenberg (see the section on C. H. Hutschenreuther in chapter 4) to set up his own factory in Selb. Lorenz's works, as well as those of Philipp Rosenthal, established a bit later, soon made Selb synonymous with ceramics production, just as was true of Limoges in France or Stoke-on-Trent in England. Other German locales also became "porcelain towns": Rehau, Tirschenreuth, Arzberg, and Waldsassen in Upper Franconia; Mettlach and Merzig in the Saarland; Altwasser in Silesia; Kahla in Thuringia. Some regions became almost synonymous with porcelain and glass production. In 1882, in the microstate of Schwarzburg-Rudolstadt in Thuringia there were 383 porcelain firms employing 2,628 workers at a time the state's population could not have exceeded ninety thousand.[17] Bohemia was perhaps even more thickly populated by glass and ceramics workers; in 1902, in porcelain making alone, it hosted fifty-eight factories and 328 painting workshops, occupying about twelve thousand people.[18] Now that labor could move freely—the German Reich had abolished limitations on internal movement in 1871—workers crowded into the industrial towns of the Silesia-Bohemia-Franconia triangle in search of steady, and decently paid, work, and smokestacks rose over what had been "backward" small towns.[19]

Although hundreds, perhaps thousands, of new one- or two-person decorating and finishing workshops were founded, many of them quickly folded again. Larger firms took on more and more employees, especially among the private producers. By 1900, at a time Meissen was flush with eight hundred employees, Rosenthal employed fifteen hundred and Kahla 2,850; by 1913, Villeroy & Boch had exceeded sixty-seven hundred. Capital reserves for all topped two million marks.[20] Increasing factory size was no specialty of the central Europeans; David Haviland, who had visited Limoges in 1842 to explore export possibilities to his native America, by the mid-1860s had built a factory there that employed over one thousand workers, the majority of them women.[21] The concentration of porcelain works and workers made for easier bulk transport and the routinization of production. Some factories installed gas and then electrical lighting so that work could continue around the clock. New efficiencies made it possible for the larger makers to reduce prices, forcing smaller ones to the wall. But concentrating production also made workers' organizations easier to form and sustain and revealed ever more openly the contrast between the living and working conditions of the owners and of their increasingly faceless and interchangeable employees.

The number of pieces produced staggers the mind. Already in 1872, the KPM was producing five hundred thousand pieces of porcelain a year, while the Silesian private firm of Tielsch, with seventeen hundred workers to the KPM's 303, was making twenty million pieces annually.[22] By 1913, the industry's output reached 77,700 tons, nearly double estimates for 1902.[23] So enormous was the need for feldspar and kaolin that German makers became net importers of both from Norway, Sweden, Austria (Bohemia), and England.[24] If in the later eighteenth century exports had chiefly traveled eastward to the Ottoman Empire and Russia, they now went west, and especially to the United States, which by 1913 took 41 percent of its porcelain imports from imperial Germany.[25]

Production numbers were increased, and costs decreased, by a number of factors. Experimental chemistry continued to add to the firms' diverse artistic expressions (see chapter 7), but more importantly for the bottom line, it helped to accelerate casting, shaping, and firing times. At the KPM, the chemist Hermann Seger developed a paste that used less clay and more quartz, allowing it to take more underglaze paints and to be fired at a lower temperature, thus conserving wood or coal. For more goods than ever before, slip casting replaced turning on the wheel; in this process liquid clay, or "slip," is poured into a plaster mold, and the excess water drained off, saving labor time and clay, and allowing for standardization. According to one estimate, a slip-cast coffeepot cost about one-fifth of what it cost to turn one on the wheel. After 1890, slip casting was advanced by adding soda to the slip, which significantly decreased the time necessary for wares to dry before firing.[26]

New technologies also helped. In the 1860s, a machine that had been used to press potatoes was adapted to the making of porcelain insulators, reducing their shrinkage in the kiln and thus insuring greater uniformity.[27] Presses and frames were developed for the swifter production of ceramic tiles, which became a huge money maker for many firms. The introduction of chromolithographic transfer printing ("decalcomania") vastly cheapened the production of vibrantly colored decorated wares. Kiln design continued to evolve, culminating in the "tunnel kiln" (*Kanalofen*), borrowed from the French and introduced into central Europe by the Silesian maker Carl Tielsch. The tunnel kiln greatly shortened firing times, allowing for energy savings of 50 percent as well as reductions in expenditures on capsules and labor.[28] Of course, it was the richer firms that were able to introduce labor-saving devices such as filter presses and mills, and after 1900, to electrify their factories, meaning that the transformation of firms into joint-stock companies with larger capital resources went hand in hand with what now really does count as the industrialization of the porcelain industry.

Another important trend in this period was the steady increase in the making of technical, electrical, and dental porcelains. These new porcelain technologies were far more utilitarian than alluring, but they would prove crucial to many firms' survival, particularly during the twentieth century's wars. In his carefully researched dissertation Heinz-Peter Rönneper described in detail the development of this branch of the industry since the first use of a porcelain insulator for the telegraph lines linking Berlin and Frankfurt in 1849. Insulators were first made in bulk by the KPM's "hygienic wares" factory, expert in producing pipes, doll heads, and other inexpensive, identical items, but its processes were then copied—of course!—by many other factories as well.[29] Expansion of public commissions for these objects would surge as telegraph and then telephone wires were strung across Germany and Europe; and as gas and then electrical lighting spread, utilities services would similarly need both high- and low-voltage insulators.

Porcelain dentures, first made by a French apothecary in the 1770s but always tricky to fit and clean, are another good example of this drift toward invisibility. It took decades to develop the right mixtures for making crowns and single teeth. But by the later nineteenth century, commercial production of dental ceramics had begun.[30] The porcelain crowns and inlays made by the American-born dentist Newell Still Jenkins gave him entrée into a circle of elite nobles and intellectuals—including Richard Wagner and Mark Twain—in his adopted hometown of Dresden in the 1870s and 1880s. Within a few decades, ceramicists were perfecting and cheapening his products for a much wider audience. In the United States, dental ceramics were made in large numbers by companies such as the S. S. White Dental Manufacturing Company, and by 1893, Germany, too, had a manufactory devoted specifically to the making of porcelain teeth.[31]

Despite the expansion of the porcelain marketplace, negotiating its ups and downs in this era was no easy matter. There were feasting days—roughly 1868–72, 1882–84, 1888–90, 1896–1903, 1905, 1909—in which the industry as a whole profited; and, in between these good years, periods of famine, in which the industry sputtered and stalled.[32] When, in the 1880s, output threatened to overwhelm domestic demand, German makers made a major push to break into the export market, targeting especially American consumers. Previously the US ceramics trade had been dominated by the French and the British, who in 1880 together still controlled 70 percent of American imports. But as lower tariffs took effect and German prices fell, American buyers began purchasing German wares. By 1890, British imports to the United

States had fallen to 56 percent; German sales to Britain itself were rising.[33] Alarmed, in 1887 the British passed the Merchandise Marks Act, in which consumer goods produced for export to Britain and its colonies were required to be stamped with the phrase "Made in Germany" in the hopes of dissuading consumers from buying what Britons saw as cheap knock-offs of their own goods. Regrettably for the British, as Maiken Umbach has described, as the Germans improved quality and lowered prices, this stamp took on the opposite sense intended by its instigators. "Made in Germany" increasingly signaled both to buyers abroad and to nationalists at home that Germany had become a producer of high-quality, but affordable, products.[34] By 1897, porcelains valued at thirty-five million marks—or nearly 67 percent of total exports—were traveling overseas, chiefly to the United States and Great Britain.[35] This was, in some way, revenge for Wedgwood.

But as the century turned, German makers were dismayed to find that their exports abroad faced increasingly intense competition from one familiar rival, the Czechs, and a surprise revenant: the Japanese. Not only were Czech goods often of high quality, but they cost much less as Bohemian labor costs ran approximately 30 percent below those across the German border. Wherever the Czechs were able to access export markets, they were a continuing threat. The Japanese producers presented a new, and growing, danger, especially to the US market. In the wake of the Meiji Restoration, Japan invested in the modernization of its fine ceramics industry and by 1901 employed a labor force of 23,904. This number would rise to about fifty thousand by 1920. Japan's share of US porcelain imports in 1912 was already more than 12 percent—compared to a German quotient of 41 percent—and would surge to 63 percent during the war, when the Allied blockade cut off European imports.[36] German exports would recover in the interwar era on the back of the devalued mark, but East Asia's second porcelain-making powerhouse would from now on prove to be a major rival for the German makers overseas.

While all the above suggests accelerated speed, increased competition, and expanded firm size, it must also be said that some things, such as mechanization, changed rather gradually, or gradually at first. The industry's continuing dependence on hand labor, even in the making of standard-sized bricks and pipes, is nicely documented in an English depiction of the different branches of ceramics making from about 1870 (plate 12). In a rundown of exhibitors at the 1873 Viennese International Exhibition, most of the one-hundred-odd German exhibitors claimed to be operating one steam engine, or none; many were still using water or animal power. The KPM, with 303 workers, had only two engines; the largest firms, Tielsch in the Silesian town of Altwasser (seventeen hundred workers) and Villeroy & Boch in Mettlach (1,884 workers), only had seven apiece.[37] As late as 1895, while 131 firms were using steam, gas, or electrical power, sixty-eight still depended on water.[38] Gradually, smaller firms gave up the actual *making* of porcelains, which increasingly did call for expensive machinery. By the century's end, only 12 percent of firms formed and fired their own vessels; the rest devoted themselves to decoration. There was still considerable room for cottage work (3,407 persons in 1895), especially for women, whose share of shop floor employment was also growing. By about 1900, 11,449 women were employed in the industry, 219 as firm owners, of a total of 44,329 workers, making up about 26 percent of the workforce.[39] The rising percentage of female workers is a sure sign that firms were continuing to reduce labor costs, and placing less value on the skills and artistry of the workers as a whole.

The 1873 list of exhibitors does not specifically divide up tableware and figurine makers from firms making utilitarian goods such as insulators, apothecaries' necessities, or stoves and terra-cotta roof tiles, in part because many firms still produced a large range of products and brought only their newest and most presentable to the fair. Again plate 12 nicely captures these different processes, as well as the class-stratification in dress exemplified by the pot-painting artists (central bottom panel) and the kiln builders (middle row, left). Describing all these activities as ceramics making is accurate, but it masks differences in objectives and audiences, as producers of pipes or insulators did not have to care about artistry and catered chiefly to bulk buyers such as other manufacturers and state or municipal procurement offices, while the makers of tableware and accessories had to please retailers, department stores, and individual consumers. Many of the larger firms handled the specialization of products by establishing separate factories for each type of porcelain. Higher fixed costs made it more difficult to enter the technical arena, but once established, the technical makers' sales were usually more stable than those of housewares makers. In the 1873 list it is evident that a shift toward building materials—pipes and flooring—is already underway. This would only accelerate as more shops, eating establishments, and offices opened their doors to a larger, more dirt-conscious public, and more homes acquired running water and dedicated bathrooms.

If mid-eighteenth-century buyers cherished the gallant figurine, and if Biedermeier customers swooned over sentimental coffee cups, fin de siècle consumers worshipped the "hygienic" ceramic tile. In terms of business practices, too, major transformations were underway. For if this was the era of the tile and the washbowl, it was also the era of the cartel and the labor union.

Capital and Labor Get Organized

We should not think that even in liberalism's halcyon years, manufacturers, whether private citizens or civil servants, stopped petitioning the state for help. In general, petitions now took the more general form of pressure exerted by publicists or chambers of commerce rather than private supplications addressed to the prince. To put it schematically, the influential courtier gave way to the interest group. Organization such as the Berlin Association of Colonial Goods Dealers (founded 1869) energetically pressed for subsidies, tariff increases, or quasi-colonial schemes and should not be overlooked, as they often are, in accounts of German imperialist activism. Liberal entrepreneurs, indeed, were some of the strongest backers of overseas interventions. Writing in the *Kölnische Zeitung* in the wake of the Sino-Japanese War, one frustrated entrepreneur praised Japan's methods of opening up the Chinese market: "One cannon shot there is much more effective than endless discussion," he wrote; "Why are the German chambers of commerce asleep?"[40]

For the German and Austrian porcelain makers, however, the main reason to petition the state was not to advocate colonization but rather to obtain assistance in establishing markets abroad, especially through favorable tariff agreements.[41] To exert pressure for help in export markets required working together, and in 1879, by banding together, porcelain makers did succeed in getting porcelain included in Bismarck's tariff, meant chiefly to protect Prussian agriculture. Imposed from outside, the "Made in Germany" stamp bound them together in a common endeavor to advertise and sell "German" goods abroad.

With respect to the domestic market, however, the manufactories remained jealously competitive with one another and looked to their individual "states" to protect their provincial markets and reputations. Bismarck's Reich made no move to create a German "imperial" porcelain manufactory, and the surviving state manufactories had every reason to cultivate their provincial identities and local ties. They continued to enjoy certain perks—freedom from some taxes, cheap or free rent for their facilities, funding for officials' pensions, and state commissions for gifts, or, increasingly, for infrastructure contracts such as provisioning the state telegraph offices with porcelain insulators. Not surprisingly, even after Nymphenburg was leased out to private operators, it made sure to advertise itself as "Bavarian," using the Wittelsbach crest in its trademark. Some private factories, too, were able to capitalize on local contacts, and they, too, frequently advertised their embeddedness in Thuringia, Bohemia, or Silesia. In their porcelain production as in their politics, the Germans remained "a nation of provincials."[42]

In the century's second half, would-be entrepreneurs were hampered not by guild privileges or artisanal secrets but by the need to raise increasingly large capital reserves to *stay* in business over time. Fierce competition and underselling meant that per item costs had continually to be reduced, requiring more and more capital to hire more workers and to purchase labor-saving devices. More credit was now available; thanks to changes in German commercial laws and practices, banks could now extend much larger loans to more individuals and businesses.[43] Increasingly, too, capital was raised by means of forming limited-liability joint-stock companies

(*Aktiengesellschaften*), which replaced the older form of trading partnerships (*Handelsgesellschaften*), in which owners of shares remained responsible for the company's overall debts. After 1870, the forming of an "AG" or a simplified form of the same (*Gesellschaft mit beschränkter Haftung*, or GmbH) became the usual means by which entrepreneurs accumulated capital, though many still depended greatly on family wealth for initial funding or for rescue.[44] Many banks took shares as collateral or bought them outright and, in a few cases, formed special subbanks in order to serve the industry's specific needs, as in the case of the Bank für keramische Industrie, a subsidiary of the Gebrüder Arnhold Bank. By means of holding shares in many related companies, banks spread their risks and forced businesses to cooperate. As one commentator argued in the 1920s, cartels so perfectly suited bankers' desires that if they hadn't previously existed, banks would have had to create them.[45]

The cartel, as David Blackbourn explains, was the quintessential business model of the later Wilhelmine Empire. There were cartels in sugar, cement, and perambulators, created to fix prices, ensure the steady supply of raw materials, or to regulate production levels. Some were more aggressive, some more successful than others.[46] Ceramics makers were early into the game, though efforts to get competitors organized were endlessly fraught with difficulty. We should recall that the whole history of the industry so far was one of secret stealing and imitation, of struggling to stay ahead of others in R&D so that one could create the same products, or at least effects, more cheaply than one's competitors. The idea to band together came precisely at the time that competition, both domestic and foreign, had reached a fever pitch, and makers were scrambling madly to cut costs and vary products so as to attract the widest possible consumer base. For firms to combine forces seemed, to many, absurd, or suicidal. Looking back at the early 1880s, one official at Tielsch, in Silesia, wrote: "the idea that these brother-enemies [the major directors of the Silesian porcelain factories at the time; SM] would have sat at a table together even to drink a glass of wine together, much less to discuss prices and rebates, their most strongly guarded secrets, seemed absolutely grotesque."[47]

But already by 1877, some firms saw their only hope of surviving the now-raging price wars was in banding together, in several regional associations, and/or in a national organization they dubbed Verband der keramischer Gewerke in Deutschland (Cartel of German Ceramics Makers; hereafter referred to as the Manufacturers' Cartel).[48] Their first success, as noted above, was not in price controls, but in the much older pursuit of protection seeking: the inclusion of porcelain in Bismarck's 1879 tariff. Reversing the virtually open market created by the Prussian tariff of 1818, the state now imposed duties of 30 M per one hundred kilograms of decorated porcelain and 14 M on one hundred kilograms of white porcelain.[49] This would protect the home market from Czech, French, and Japanese imports down to the time of the Great War and make possible a boom in domestic sales in the 1880s. But it did nothing to impede the rate and scale of manufacturing, and as production outstripped demand, price wars broke out, causing an industry-wide panic. In 1883, the cartel did manage to agree on minimal prices, at least for domestic sales, leading one commentator to rejoice: "If the cancerous afflictions of the porcelain factories in Germany during the last few years are rooted in the many-sided price wars of the factories, this year, finally, the leading manufacturers have earnestly dedicated themselves to raising prices by making agreements with one another."[50] Free competition—such as it had been from roughly 1850 to 1883—would not really return to the industry until after World War II.

This price agreement came in relatively good times and did not apply to exports, whose prices now often fell to 10–20 percent below domestic prices. Overproduction was not stemmed; many firms, especially the cheapest producers in Thuringia, did not belong to this early cartel and continued underselling. As the US export market became more and more important, larger manufacturers moved to tighten agreements, and smaller makers rushed to join larger entities. In the German Empire proper, over the next decades thirty other subcartels—dedicated to porcelain-painting firms or insulator makers, for example—ranged themselves beneath the umbrella of the Manufacturers' Cartel.[51] A separate cartel of twenty-four members, including the powerhouses Tielsch and Tiefenfurt, was founded in Silesia in 1889; perhaps in response, a Bohemian cartel (also of twenty-four members) was forged later the same year. An Austrian Verband followed.[52] Many of Russia's makers joined the Kusnetzov cartel, which would survive long enough to be nationalized by the Bolsheviks after 1917.[53]

Companies moved to integrate vertically, too, trying to ensure supplies of kaolin against attempts to cartelize clay-mining operations. By about 1904, four big "concerns" had been formed, each composed of a number of companies. Three were named for the major producer: the so-called Kahla group (sometimes referred to as the Strupp concern, for the bank involved); the Rosenthal group; and the Hutschenreuther group. The fourth cartel was named for its controlling (Arnhold) bank.[54] All these "concerns" now employed thousands of workers and made technical porcelains as well as tableware. Villeroy & Boch, producing fine stoneware rather than hard-paste porcelain, similarly became a multibranch operation with thousands of workers in this period, although it continued to be a family-owned firm. Branding themselves as provincial "art institutes," the state firms remained the most visible to the public. Yet these private "concerns" increasingly produced the wares Wilhelmine Germans put on their tables, walls, and floors, and integrated into the infrastructures of their daily lives.

Finally, as the effects of the post-1893 worldwide depression set in, German porcelain makers founded a more powerful empire-wide cartel, the Vereinigung deutscher Porzellanfabriken zur Hebung der Porzellanindustrie GmbH (Union of German Porcelain Manufacturers for the Promotion of the Porcelain Industry; hereafter referred to as the Union of Porcelain Manufacturers). Formed of forty-nine firms in 1900, this new and larger cartel was dedicated to stabilizing prices, promoting the industry abroad, and preventing underselling. Products were divided first into two, and then into four quality categories, ranging from the lowest quality (level 1) to the highest (level 4), and assigned minimum prices. Members also pledged (on pain of stiff fines) to sell only level 4 white wares to *Hausmaler*, who in turn had to consent to sell at a minimum price. Members also agreed not to decorate cheaper white wares, including those made for hotels, and not to sell to dealers who were known to have broken pricing rules or who also sold porcelain made by factories outside the syndicate.[55] Retailers, accordingly, received special prices—usually about 33.3 percent below the sticker price, but sometimes allowing markups of 60 percent[56]—a system known as the *Revers*. This system proved so popular that by 1908, 90 percent of German producers had joined the Union of Porcelain Manufacturers, and these, in turn, had established some eighty-one hundred *Revers* contracts with retailers.

For owners and investors, the Union of Porcelain Manufacturers was relatively successful. It seems to have managed to stabilize prices, though overproduction continued to be a major issue. Downward pressure on wages and frequent furloughing of workers made for falling labor costs, which in turn resulted in higher profits for shareholders. But success was purchased at the cost of both workers, who now had to contend with bouts of un- or underemployment, and smaller and higher-end companies, which had little say in union governance. Seats on the executive board of the cartel were heavily dominated by the big mass producers: Kahla, Hutschenreuther, Rosenthal. That this organization aimed to control production and prices on the lower end—where the biggest market beckoned—is evidenced by the fact that while Meissen and the KPM were initially included in the Union, in 1903 they were allowed to leave and to keep their retail customers. The state-supported firms had their own problems, as we will see, but they could not be solved by joining a cartel, and the Union evidently didn't find them sufficiently worrisome rivals to compel their membership.

Cartelization did provide a mechanism for keeping at least the largest firms from devouring one another entirely, but it was quite clearly a strategy that profited chiefly manufactory owners rather than workers or retailers, both of whom now founded national organizations to champion *their* interests. Retailers who resented being yoked to particular suppliers and having prices imposed on them formed various pressure groups, including the Nuremberg-based Reichsverband deutscher Spezialgeschäfte in Porzellan, Glass, Haus- und Küchengeräte (National Cartel of German Shops Specializing in Porcelain, Glass, Housewares and Kitchenwares, hereafter referred to as the Retailers' Cartel). And then, too, ceramics workers in large numbers began to found and join extrafactory associations. If employers were going to organize, they reasoned, they too needed to present a united front.

Organizing porcelain workers was no easy matter. In the eighteenth century, employers had offered higher wages and perks such as free lodging or kindling or even *Beamter* status to their skilled modelers, painters, and arcanists; these men were also afforded the opportunity to pay into insurance and pension funds, an option not offered to unskilled workers, including women.[57] The industry's low level of industrialization and hierarchy of artisanal laborers kept these traditions alive, even as factory operators in the 1820s through 1840s cut wages and benefits to the bone. The painters in particular continued to think of themselves as a breed apart, dressing in suits, hats, and ties rather than in the whites of the turners (*Dreher*) or the shirt-sleeves and vests of the kiln operators. The revolutionary year 1848–49 had seen numerous protests or work stoppages, though the key issues were wages and privileges, not politics.[58] By the later nineteenth century, many of the skilled artisans employed at Meissen had fathers or even grandfathers who had worked for the manufactory and evinced strong loyalties to the firm, which they expected, reciprocally, to employ them for life. Porcelain workers would form some of their own organizations such as—in Prussia—a Reisegeldverband (Travel Fund Association), an informal network that provided funds for skilled workers to "wander" to a new workplace, for whatever reason.[59] But in general they did not identify their interests with those of other workers, something that would vex socialist agitators and continue to make organizing against management difficult.[60]

In 1869, however, porcelain workers—probably mostly private firm employees—joined in the founding of a more embracive, transregional Gewerkverein in der Porzellan-, Glas- und verwandten Arbeiter (Workers' Association for Porcelain, Glass, and Related Trades). Delegates from seventy-nine locations attended the Workers' Association's first congress in Moabit, a working-class suburb of Berlin, and by 1872, the association had 865 members, by 1890, 4,022. In the same year, the association supported its first strike in Altwasser (Silesia), against wage reductions and the firing of eighteen turners.[61] The strike ended after eight weeks with small concessions from the employer, a workers' victory by contrast with most nineteenth-century strikes. Painters, however, tended to shun the association and in the 1880s founded organizations of their own. After Leo XIII's encyclical *Rerum Novarum* (1891), a series of Catholic workers' organizations also sprang to life; these explicitly renounced social democracy and usually refused to take part in strikes.[62]

The politics of the Workers' Association in its early years were liberal rather than socialist. This was partly pragmatic, as workers caught with socialist publications were regularly fired. But it also reflected the heavy representation of skilled workers, who remained hostile to socialism. But as the proportion of unskilled workers rose, and as dissatisfaction with liberal promises increased, the organization moved leftward. In 1893, the association reorganized and adopted a new name: Verband der Porzellan- und verwandten Arbeiter (Union of Porcelain Workers and Related Tradesmen), and from 1896 it allowed at least some women to join. This was a virtual necessity, as in some factories they now formed nearly 50 percent of the workforce.[63] After the turn of the century, the workers' Verband had many strikes to support, including a wave of actions in the wake of the historic victories of the Sozialistische Partei Deutschlands (SPD; Germany's major social democratic party) in the January 1912 elections. In this case, eighty-five hundred workers either struck or were locked out, and some factories remained closed for more than thirty weeks.[64] An Austrian sister organization was also formed in 1890 and could boast 2,789 members in 1893, many of them at work in Bohemian factories. The Austrian workers' representatives complained that organization of the factories was hampered by the grinding poverty of part-time and domestic workers, the indifference of the self-absorbed, and the painters' "guild-like" snobbery. The latter, they lamented, joined bourgeois gymnastics and choral societies, but not the trade union, and continued to believe, absurdly, in the harmonious relationship of labor and capital. To detail the stupidities of those who clung to their "guild mentalities and artistic conceits" (*Zunft- und Kunststolz*) wrote one organizer, simply made him furious and wasted paper.[65]

TABLE 6.2. Average Wages, 1878 to 1906

	1878 Wages—Meissen	1895 Private Industry	1906 Verband Average**
Turner	965–1,556 M	1,037 M	550–2,400 M
Modeler	1,411–2,160 M	1,450 M	920–1,620 M
Figure, landscape painter	1,110–2,555 M*	1,329 M	470–1,595 M
Female polisher	540–800 M	No data	270–870 M

Sources: Böhmert, "Urkundliche Geschichte," 78–80; Rönneper, "Die Entstehung und Entwicklung," 299; for the Vienna figures, Heckl, *Protokoll des Dritten Kongresses*, 37; Bollmann, *Lohn-Statistik*, 12–15.
*Viennese figures from 1893.
**Based on average weekly wages, for fifty six-day weeks.

The trade unions faced a real challenge in painting a general picture of the porcelain workers' plight, as wages and conditions differed between factories, and for different classes of workers. Of course relative incomes also differed given varying geographies, and fluctuating food prices. At our distance, we have an even tougher job of analyzing these developments, but we can say that wages, for most, remained low, and one income was often insufficient to support a family. In 1878, the average worker at Meissen made only 1,006 M per year—at a time when the minimum costs for a family were estimated at 1,188 M.[66] But then again, our worker was in good or at least multitudinous company, as tax statistics show than nearly 74 percent of Saxon households made 800 M or less a year at the time.[67] Also, as table 6.2 indicates, average wages concealed considerable stratification in pay, both at Meissen and in private industry.

Looking at Meissen's figures here it is noteworthy that male skilled modelers, painters, and turners remained at the top of the scale. Income ranges remained wide; yet in general the distance between pay grades had narrowed since the eighteenth century, when, to cite 1787 statistics, a master turner had made the equivalent of 1,080 M to a clay bearer's 213 M.[68] In general, salaries were higher in the state than in the private sector, as was also the case for railroad employees.[69] It is also notable, however, that the state manufactories continued to take a more paternalist view of their employees and especially their civil service *Beamte*, who received pensions and various additional perks. But often lower-level workers were also a bit better looked after by the state firms than in the private world. In 1876, when sales flagged, for example, the Meissen administration resisted the Finance Ministry's pressure to downsize, arguing that the state had a humanitarian obligation to sustain loyal workers in times of need.[70] This was not a commitment the private firms were willing to make—though periodically private firms also offered paternalist perks, such as meals in times of dearth, or, in 1914, a "marching fee" for men who entered the service of the fatherland.[71]

Our data with respect to the private manufactories is spotty, and once again, averages can be misleading. In 1906, for example, while the paste grinder at Meyer in Bayreuth earned only a bit more than 500 M per year, at Villeroy & Boch, the equivalent worker earned 1,450 M.[72] Working conditions also varied greatly, but nowhere were they very comfortable. In Znaim (Austrian Moravia), turners worked twelve-hour days and were compelled to work in conditions where the clay often froze and without shoes, to better turn their wheels.[73] Wage averages, moreover, depended on constant employment, which seems to have been rare. Compared to salaries in the iron industry these salaries were on the low end, and certainly porcelain workers were outpaced by salaries paid to employees of the chemical company BASF, who averaged wages of 1,723 M per year by 1913. But most ceramics makers were better off than the now-immiserated textile workers of Barmen, who in 1892 could expect to earn only 720 M.[74] There were, indeed, worse jobs than making porcelain.

One of the ways in which the private makers trimmed their costs was in the employment of an increasing percentage of women, especially young, single women, and boys. Women were generally paid one-third to one-half of men's wages, and apprentices earned about the same, or even less; the 1906 statistics show us a range for apprentice turners, for example, of 200–1,000 M per year.[75] Thanks to his early adoption of new machinery, Boch was already employing 40 percent women and boys in 1841; by 1913, at Villeroy & Boch,

1. Porcelain Room, Charlottenburg Palace

Typically for the time, Prussian queen Sophie Charlotte wished to use
East Asian blue-and-white porcelains not to serve coffee but to wallpaper
a special room in her newly built Charlottenburg Palace.

2. Coronation Banquet for Joseph II, 1764

This beautiful painting by Martin van Meytens depicts the banquet following the coronation of Joseph II as Holy Roman emperor in Frankfurt in 1764. At this most sumptuous and politically symbolic meal, the emperor and family dined on gold and the guests on silver tableware; silver and gold is displayed on the walls. But one eighteenth-century innovation has occurred: the tables are set *à la française*.

3. Count von Brühl's fancies

This reimagining of Count Heinrich von Brühl delighting in the Meissen
figurine specially designed for him, and featuring his tailor astride a goat,
was painted by Carl Wilhelm Anton Seiler in 1892. Note that Seiler has
also placed a "pagode" on the count's sideboard.

4. A princely dinner, ca. 1766

The custom of holding less formal dinner parties, where the rank of the guests was equalized by seating all around a circular table, had evidently come at least to the westerly German states by the mid-1760s. The prince of the tiny Rhineland state of Salm-Salm has also commanded that his guests be served *à la française*.

5. Painting department, WPM, ca. 1830

Porcelain painters thought of themselves not as ordinary workers, but as high-status craftsmen, and dressed accordingly.

6. "The Chinese Emperor," detail

"Orientalizing" figurines such as this one by Höchst modeler Johann Peter Melchior (1765–66) employed a wide range of techniques to depict the peoples of East Asia, not all of them racialized.

7. "Sweet" classicism at Meissen

Fashioned in the 1750s, this highly popular version of Europa and her bull
plays down the sexual violence of the myth.

8. A Family Supper, 1836

This 1836 painting by the Berlin painter Eduard Gaertner, who trained as an apprentice at the KPM, depicts coffee time in the conservatory of the prosperous wool merchant C. C. Westfal. Note how simple the porcelain needs were for this quite comfortably off urban household.

9. WPM sample plate and goblet

Even in the early eighteenth century, manufactories eagerly advertised
their willingness to apply colors and patterns according to the customers'
desires.

10. Biedermeier salon, ca. 1830

Well-dressed friends gather for coffee in a typical Biedermeier salon. Note the collection of porcelains—especially mismatched teacups and saucers—on display in the etagere in the foreground.

11. Porcelain shoppers in Vienna, 1838

This 1838 image depicts very well dressed male salespersons helping well-heeled customers choose costly silver and porcelain wares. Note that husbands accompany their wives to consider such expensive purchases.

12. Diversity in the ceramics industry

In this illustration from an English publication, the diverse skills needed to produce ceramics are displayed, from brick and pipe making in the top register to the painting of "Prunkvasen" in the lower one.

13. Wilhelmine dollhouse

This later nineteenth-century dollhouse kitchen overflows with cook-
ware, including, now, a large selection of porcelains. Compare to figure
2.1, in which no porcelain was visible.

14. Wilhelm II on porcelain

During and after the Great War, many manufactories made patriotic
items such as this KPM tribute to Kaiser Wilhelm II.

15. Hitler's train service

Made by the Führer's favorite manufactory, Nymphenburg, this neoclassical service was used for meals in Hitler's special train car.

16. Berlin flea market, today

On a recent visit to the flea market on the Strasse der 17. Juni in Berlin, the author found vast quantities of porcelain for sale, much of it purporting to be Meissen.

6.1. Women tile makers at work

This 1893 photograph from the Villeroy & Boch factory in Mettlach illustrates the degree to which women had replaced men on the shop floor.

72 percent of men and a whopping 92 percent of women were under forty (and 8 percent and 18 percent, respectively, were under sixteen).[76] Many were employed in the semiskilled jobs of tile making or blue-and-white painting, many fewer in color or figure painting (fig. 6.1). In Upper Franconia, where numerous new firms were founded from the 1860s to the 1880s, the substitution of women came a bit later, as factories were able to purchase machines. In 1888, women here composed only 15 percent of the workforce but made up 50 percent in 1912. Apprentices, too, formed a larger than ever percentage of the skilled workers, in 1890 reaching between 30 and 50 percent of the painters and turners; few would end up becoming masters themselves.[77] The percentage of Catholic workers also increased, as impoverished peasants and cottage weavers from Bohemia and Polish-speaking territories moved to industrial towns in search of work. All of this amounted to an

undercutting of the male, skilled workforce, and the exploitation of whole families forced to join the production line to make ends meet.

We know that, overall, conditions for German workers improved in this period, with the proportion of household expenditures on food dropping from 60 to 52 percent between 1850 and 1913, a sure sign that families were moving away from subsistence.[78] We know that children were expected to go to school rather than work, and that the hours of work were generally dropping. Manufactories posted official work rules, establishing hours of work and breaks, and the conditions under which workers could be disciplined or fired.[79] But workers' own accounts of their lives remind us that for some, improvement did not come swiftly, or at all, and that some felt completely left behind in the booming consumer economy.

The individual factory reports given at the 1893 Austrian trade union meeting offer glimpses of the workers' world as they saw it, although here, surely, abuses and worse cases were highlighted, just as the manufactory owners reported best-case scenarios. In the Austrian reports (many of them from Bohemian factories), we hear of filthy workplaces where the wind whistled through broken windows and temperatures ranged from freezing to boiling hot. We hear of harsh "masters," especially in the smaller firms, forcing apprentices to sit up all night finishing commissions. Housing and food costs in industrial cities were often high, and supply limited. One-room dwellings for porcelain- and glass-decorating families were apparently quite normal; those who had an extra bed often took in boarders who could not afford their own rooms. There was no official limit on working hours for men, and kiln workers in particular might work sixty-hour weeks, and up to twenty-eight-hour shifts.[80] Everyone, in fact, worked more than the stated maximum hours when they could; only work, even if poorly compensated, kept the wolf from the door.

Contemporaries recognized that the most exploited were the apprentices, women, and children who painted or made cup handles at home.[81] At midcentury, Bavarian regulations limited the workday of nine-to-twelve-year-olds to ten hours, which suggests longer hours and younger workers had been common. In 1872, Reich-wide legislation prohibited the employment of children under twelve and limited twelve-to-fourteen-year-olds to six-hour days. Violations, however, were common.[82] Those who at fourteen were officially pledged as apprentices were bound by contracts to work at less than survival wages (their parents paid the remaining costs), generally for five to six years. Their hours were very long and living conditions dreadful; they were forbidden from smoking, drinking, and visiting dancehalls, and beatings seem to have been regular occurrences.[83]

The button makers of northern Bohemia, for example, worked twelve-to-sixteen-hour days, for incomes rarely reaching 600 M a year—if, that is, they had constant work. Moreover, the task required looking directly into the fire and breathing petroleum vapors, which imperiled the health of both the workers and their families. "Naturally," wrote the incensed union representative reporting on these conditions, "if a trade minister or the like comes to visit, he is shown a posh, specially furnished [work] room, and thus tricked and duped."[84] Should a vessel be damaged or broken in transporting it to or from these overcrowded hovels, the worker received no pay at all. According to numerous reports, female office staff and servants might just as well lived in a workhouse; their miserable incomes kept them indebted when not starving, and they were regularly subjected to physical brutality and what we would now call sexual harassment or assault.[85] Workers' diets consisted chiefly of potatoes, bread, and coffee, almost certainly *not* served in delicate porcelain cups.

Workplace health and safety was, on the whole, atrocious. Painters and glaze mixers suffered from lead poisoning, and kiln workers, who often doused their clothes with cold water before retrieving items from blazing-hot kilns, regularly contracted rheumatism. Even more than before 1848, susceptibility to lung disease was an open secret, with the average life expectancy of a turner in the 1870s and 1880s only barely exceeding thirty-eight years. The incidence of tuberculosis was seven times higher than that of the average population, heightened both by damp and airless living conditions and by the particles of quartz and feldspar wafting through the manufactory.[86] But the careful studies of "Staublunge" carried out by the Selb doctor Franz Bogner between 1898 and 1907 changed little in the industry. Only in 1927 would Porzellansilikose be identified as an occupational disease.[87] With the immediate feeding of families to worry about, longer-term considerations such as silicosis and lead poisoning remained low on the list of workers' concerns, and expensive fixes low on employers' priority lists. The latter did, however, begin founding more hospital funds and even spa treatments, hoping to palliate the suffering if not address its causes.

Remarkably, given the stresses and strains of the late Wilhelmine economy, both workers and owners would look back on this era as something of a second golden age, one in which prices were relatively stable, work relatively plentiful, and consumers eager to fill their homes with ceramics. Featured in world exhibitions and in arts and crafts movements, porcelain remained estimable as a luxury good, even as at the lower end it became universally affordable and ubiquitous in both the private and the public spheres. The market remained treacherous, above all for workers and operators of the smallest firms. But especially for tough-minded and nimble private makers, it could also be highly lucrative. They had always been best at pleasing non-elite consumers; and now that these buyers could finally afford to stock their china closets and tile their washrooms, it was their time to shine.

The Glory Days of the Private Producer

The 1850s to the 1870s are generally described by central European historians as the period of high liberalism.[88] This does not mean that liberals dominated everywhere—they were most powerful in urban areas and in the West—and where they succeeded they usually did so by uniting with older conservative elites. But some of their signature causes made great strides: nationalism; freer, if not free, trade; equality under the law; (gentle) expansions of the franchise; modernization of transport; expansion of credit; bureaucratic rationality and efficiency. The nobility retained a good deal of its power and wealth, but middle-class officials, professors, entrepreneurs, lawyers, and doctors now also took a share in decision making and in shaping culture. Throughout central Europe non-nobles began building fashionable new townhouses and patronizing museums, theaters, and opera houses;

increasingly they could afford to travel for pleasure and to equip their homes with gas heating, running water, and electric light. Divided gender roles more than ever made women masters of the household and impresarios of the *Kaffeekränzschen*. Wealthy women, including Empress Augusta and her English daughter-in-law Victoria, also engaged in high-profile charitable work and patronage of the arts. Non-noble men and women now regularly ate in restaurants, and on trains and steamships, and tiled their bathrooms. Together with their social and political visibility, their consumer confidence soared.

This was the world that ushered in the massive expansion of the private firms, and enormous increases in the size of porcelain-making operations, though many decorators' shops remained small. Entrepreneurs experienced in other areas of trade recognized that rich profits and dividends were to be had in porcelain making, and investors in one factory glimpsed success in founding new ones, often still relying on family or close associates for capital. In addition to the Saarland, two eastern borderland regions boomed: Silesia and Upper Franconia, in northeastern Bavaria. In both of these areas there had already been a scattering of private firms before midcentury, and both had ready access to coal and cheap Polish, Czech, or German laborers. Table 6.3 offers an overview of the flurry of firm foundings in these regions after 1848. Of course, most start-ups did not last, and older firms—such as Ansbach, Reichsmanndorf, and Regensburg—closed. This list, however, captures the major ventures, most of them postdating the Second Empire's founding.

Specializing in cheap and white wares, and in faking KPM marks, the Silesian firms cut heavily into the KPM's sales of "Gesundheitsgeschirr" and rapidly displaced Berlin makers such as F. A. Schumann, whose labor and coal costs were much higher. By 1855, Silesia was producing more than 40 percent of Prussia's porcelain, and six years later, more than 60 percent. Larger factory size was a feature of the Silesian firms; while by the 1860s, Silesia employed 2,625 in porcelain making, these were distributed across only seven factories. By contrast in Thuringia, 3,778 workers were spread across hundreds of larger and smaller factories.[89] In Upper Franconia, firm

TABLE 6.3. Firm Foundings, Silesia and Bavaria*

Silesian Firms	Bavarian Firms
Karl Krister, Waldenberg, 1831	Tettau, 1793
Franz Prause, Niedersalzbrunn, 1849	C. M. Hutschenreuther, Hohenburg an der Eger, 1814/1822**
Carl Rädisch, Tiefenfurt, 1849	Tirschenreuth, 1832
Graf Franckenburg, Tillowitz, 1851	Lorenz Hutschenreuther, Selb, 1857
Carl Tielsch, Altwasser, 1854	Waldsassen, 1866
Josef Schachtel, Charlottenbrunn, 1859	J. N. Müller, Schönwald, 1879
Königszelt, 1860	Rosenthal, Selb, 1879
Zeh, Scherer & Co., Rehau, 1880	
Carl Schumann, Arzberg, 1881	
Gebrüder Bauscher, Weiden, 1881	
Winterling, Marktleuthen, 1898	
Fritz Thomas, Marktredwitz, 1903	
Seltmann, Weiden, 1910	

*Where firms' names changed over time, I have used the best known; no place name is given for firms named after their localities.

**Hutschenreuther typically dates its founding to 1814 although formal permission to produce was given only in 1822.

foundings surged after the railway opened up access to the territory in the 1860s. These factories produced both white and decorated tableware, as well as industrial and electrical items—and hired as few skilled painters and modelers as possible.

One of these Bavarian enterprises and its founder deserves our special attention, as Philipp Rosenthal was destined to leave a lasting mark on the history of central European porcelain in the decades to follow. The son of a Westphalian china merchant, Rosenthal ran away from home at seventeen to be an American cowboy; he then took odd jobs as an elevator operator, mailman, and dishwasher, before establishing himself as a china buyer in Detroit. When his father, Abraham, died in 1879, Rosenthal came to Selb to negotiate the sale of his father's business. Here he fell in love with a *Hausmalerin* named Mathilde, who, like so many others, bought white china from Hutschenreuther to decorate and sell. Rosenthal began to build the business around Mathilde; nearly bankrupt, they were saved by sales of kitschy ashtrays. By 1884, Rosenthal had hired sixty painters, using transfer printing to ornament services with "galante" names such as "Pompadour" and "Louis XIV."[90] When Hutschenreuther balked at supplying unpainted wares to the successful firm, Rosenthal began making his own porcelain and by 1897 had fifteen hundred employees.[91] Philipp's keen interest in women—he would marry five times—and his desire to associate with contemporary artists would leave a lasting imprint on his manufactory, and a legacy that his son, Philip (one *p*), would resurrect in the post-1945 era. But Philipp also diversified early (in 1900) into "electrical" porcelain, a branch that proved a consistent money maker and very useful when Germany went to war in 1914. By 1925, his workforce of about sixty-two hundred would be second only to that of the Kahla group, at about ten thousand.[92] Rosenthal's advocacy for exports, for minimum prices, and for the upholding of the *Revers* also made him a major player in the many cartels to which his firms belonged, and in German industrial circles more generally. Despite his accomplishments, his ethnicity would make him a victim when the German state turned against its Jewish entrepreneurs in 1933 (see chapter 8).

As space allows us to profile only one more private maker, the choice must fall on Villeroy & Boch, the fine stoneware makers of what had by now become Luxembourg and the Saarland. Having survived the century's first half, Villeroy & Boch now went from strength to strength, wisely expanding into the production of ceramic tiles, drain pipes, washstands, terra-cotta pots, and bathroom fixtures. Some production figures should give us a sense of the magnitude of the firm's growth across the nineteenth century. In 1856, the firm's sales amounted to approximately 647,500 T. By this time, the company had a healthy market, centered in the German states, but extending also to Russian Poland, England, Switzerland, and the Netherlands. The Trier-Saarbrücken rail line was completed in 1860—and Eugen Boch made sure it ran right behind his Mettlach works. This reduced freight costs and eased sales in foreign markets, which now included Turkey, Russia, and

Egypt. Output, correspondingly, soared. In 1868, the value of the company's products surpassed one million taler, a number that nearly doubled again within five years, in the very period in which the KPM was threatened with closure. By 1882–83, Villeroy & Boch was selling products worth the equivalent of 2,930,000 T (now with nearly 1.5 million of this in mosaic tiles) and had become the third-largest employer in the Trier region, after the coal mines and the Stumm ironworks.[93]

After midcentury, Villeroy & Boch greatly enhanced its market position by pioneering, for the continent, the mass production of ceramic tiles. The making of ceramic tiles was a very old industry in Europe, reaching back to the period before the *Reconquista* when Arab craftsmen had decorated Iberian interiors with beautiful tiles. Church floors in late medieval northern as well as southern Europe had been laid with stamped tiles, and since at least the fifteenth century, northern Europeans and Russians had used masonry stoves (*Kachelofen* in German) to hold heat and save wood; there were several in Luther's house (formerly an Augustinian monastery) in Wittenberg. In Spain and Portugal, tile-making traditions continued, and they spread to these nations' colonial territories. But it seems to have been in the Netherlands and England where industrialized production began. If the Dutch perfected the mass production of blue-and-white tiles, it was the English who pioneered the making of medievalizing pressed tiles for use especially in the restoration of churches. After A.W.N. Pugin began designing tiles for the Minton porcelain company, and using them in prestigious projects such as the gloriously neo-Gothic House of Lords (opened in 1847), tastemakers, and other potters, took notice.[94]

What followed were not only technical improvements that made fancy "encaustic" tiles easier to mold and cure but also new printing and glazing techniques, enabling makers to offer a wide range of intricate patterns. Ever attentive to British innovations, Eugen Boch was one of the first on the continent to install tile presses, first at Septfontaines and then at Mettlach. He would later claim that the inspiration for these tiles came from seeing a recently discovered Roman mosaic near his hometown, but that explains little except the marketing name, "Mettlacher Mosaikplatten," which began to roll off the presses in 1852.[95] Villeroy & Boch's imitation English tiles were so successful that the Boch Frères set up a tile-making branch factory in Maubeuge, France, in 1861, and one in Mettlach in 1869, just in time to take advantage of the public and private building boom of the Gründerzeit. Porcelain tiles were colorful and durable, and advertisements touted their adaptability, to simple flooring or elegant bathing (fig. 6.2). For an age ever more interested both in hygiene and in historical restoration, the easy-to-clean tiles quickly became de rigueur for pubs, cafés, hotels, shops (especially those selling foodstuffs), bathhouses, and governmental buildings. Their additional properties—heat and acid resistance—made them useful for less glamorous enterprises such as chemical plants and slaughterhouses. Villeroy & Boch tiles were used in the Hamburg metro, the castle of the Thurn and Taxis in Regensburg, the Bolshoi Theater in Moscow, and the finally completed Cologne Cathedral.[96] By 1883, the firm was selling 1.4 million marks' worth of mosaic tiles, of a total of 7.3 million in sales overall.[97] If the state firms would obtain commissions for some high-profile tiling projects—the KPM for the murals in the Alexanderplatz U-Bahn, Meissen for the dining rooms of the East German Chamber of Deputies[98]—Villeroy & Boch would remain the ordinary customers' go-to firm for this increasingly ubiquitous ceramic product.

Another of Villeroy & Boch's lucrative areas of expansion was that of bathroom fixtures. As most German homes did not have separate bathrooms or running water until after World War I (or even World War II), "fixtures" amounted at first to a mélange of ewers and washbowls, cabinet-fitted toilets or sinks, bidets, and covered chamber pots. Gradually, bathing fixtures evolved from the status of luxury goods to that of middle-class necessities, benefiting the fine stoneware companies in particular. Fixtures made from true porcelain were desirable, but much more expensive and difficult to fire successfully; it was safer, and cheaper, to make sinks, toilets, and bathtubs of stoneware, or ceramic-coated steel. By 1910, Villeroy & Boch were offering thirty-five different models of washbowls, and like other stoneware firms in England and the United States, it would profit greatly as hotels and dwellings added dedicated "bathrooms" and flush toilets.[99] It is this "sanitary"

Autotypie von C. C. Meinhold & Söhne, Dresden.

Fliesen-Badwanne No. 7 mit Wandbekleidung
$\frac{1}{20}$ nat. Grösse.

6.2. Marvelous "mosaic" tiles

As this 1895 advertisement shows, Villeroy & Boch was happy to offer customized bathtubs as well as floor tiles in hundreds of patterns.

porcelain—neither collected by connoisseurs nor dear to art historians—that enhanced this firm's bottom line before the Great War and continues to underwrite its success today.

Much more than the state firms, the private firms made fine ceramics a mass, rather than a high bourgeois or aristocratic, commodity. They put flowered teapots, busts of Bismarck, and ceramic washbowls into the dwellings of at least the middling classes, and they pressed tiles to adorn pubs and cafés. They gave employment to—and exploited—thousands of workers. They were the product of the era of German capitalism at high tide, and they made the most of their new means of financing and transport, and the booming marketplace for consumer goods. The state makers, by contrast—those that had survived the horrors of the Vormärz—would now find that the political and economic winds were more than ever blowing against them.

The State Firm in the Capitalist Age

The private porcelain firms, on the whole, flourished in the era of high liberalism, characterized by a rapidly expanding consumer marketplace, new sources of credit, swifter forms of travel and transport, and an expanding public sphere. For the older state-supported firms, however, the "liberal" marketplace presented a series of new challenges, some of them insuperable. While in Russia and France, governments continued to support the imperial manufactories[100] in central Europe, state officials and liberal and left-leaning deputies balked at the prospect of subsidizing firms that merely contributed to the nation's *Glanz*.

It is useful to remember that state firms faced some barriers to full participation in the fiercely competitive "crockery wars" of the later Wilhelmine era. Given their official status, histories, and reputations, it remained difficult for firms to produce anything other than the highest-quality wares; doing otherwise would have endangered their now-essential "brands," even though, as they endlessly complained, what the public really wanted were cheaply decorated, mass-produced dishes. By accepting so many commissions and keeping so many older models in production, too, the state firms were compelled to keep skilled workers on staff, elevating their labor costs. They could not hire on short-term contracts, take on (cheaper) foreign laborers, or easily downsize when orders flagged; hiring children or too many unskilled women was at least officially taboo. Moreover, when they made a profit, they were generally required to return most of it to the state till, meaning that they often lacked the capital needed to mechanize and accelerate production. While the private firms narrowed their "lines" and simply trashed their molds, the state firms felt obliged to continue offering long-outdated service pieces and figurines. Because they often produced multiples when a single piece was ordered, their warehouses remained eternally overstuffed. They had more reports to write and could not get away with careless bookkeeping. Finally, they were expected to lead others in both artistry and technical perfection. If a century previously there had been advantages in being a mercantile firm, the bloom had now certainly gone off that rose.

In the following sections we trace the trajectories of two manufactories that succumbed to this brave new liberal world, and two that, quite narrowly, survived it. In all cases, serendipity as well as the individual personalities of the directors, princes, and lawmakers mattered, as did branding, technical innovations, and artistic quality. By no means were successes and failures a matter of simple entrepreneurial savvy or aesthetic superiority. For the remaining mercantile firms, it took considerable trading on local tradition, and some luck, to escape the full force of fin de siècle capitalism.

Liberalism's Victims: Nymphenburg and the WPM

When last we examined the workings of the Nymphenburg manufactory, we noted Ludwig I's hefty patronage, which allowed the factory to excel in art and spared it from having to compete with private firms. The consequences were sluggish adoption of technical and chemical improvements and financial losses, averaging about 9,200 T per year in the 1840s. In 1848, Ludwig died, leaving the throne to his more fiscally responsible son, Maximillian II. When Nymphenburg's new director followed Saxon suit and made an effort to claim Nymphenburg as a national *Kunstanstalt*, the king and the Finance

Ministry balked and insisted on closing the separate art branch. The ministry recommended (in vain) that the firm stick to producing the profitable white ware. In 1850, when reorganization failed to end the deficits, the Finance Ministry finally threw in the towel and cut off the subsidies.

Starved for income and unable to compete with cheaper producers, Nymphenburg could not exhibit at the Crystal Palace, and negative reviews of its artistic endeavors multiplied. Its demise was forestalled by large orders from the Bavarian telegraph office, which in 1856 alone purchased sixty-five thousand porcelain insulators. But in that same year, the painting section was fully closed, and in 1859, the state wearied of bothering with the firm at all. In 1862, it was leased to a private owner, Ferdinand Scotzniorsky, who merged it with his brick-making factory.[101] Scotzniorsky put the company in the black again and kept workers on the job; in 1888, he took on a new partner, Albert Bäuml, who was destined to run the business for the next half century. Bäuml, as the Nazis later discovered, was a Jewish convert, probably from Bohemia (see chapter 8); but few objected to his ethnicity when he began renovating Nymphenburg's works and putting the factory's old models back into production. In 1891, a senior Upper Bavarian official visited the factory and completed a report in which he praised Bäuml's new kilns, reissuing of old models, and expanded workforce (now back up to fifty-five). Bäuml, he enthused, had continued to produce insulators and pharmaceutical supplies, keeping the firm in the black, but had also reestablished retail shops in Germany's fashionable cities. He had succeeded in reviving the brand—and now would like a small subsidy. After all, the KPM had received 70,000 M and Meissen a whopping 350,000 M in 1889–90; surely Bäuml deserved 2,400 M?[102] An article in the *Allgemeine Zeitung* similarly sang Bäuml's praises for reviving Nymphenburg's "fabled past," and when Bäuml wrote himself, asking for funds to continue his improvements, what was a ministry to do?[103]

Bäuml received a subsidy, although the sum was modest, and the consequences ugly, for he now had to endure attacks in the press by anti-Semites who complained of giving over state operations to Jews for exploitation.[104] When the time came to renew Bäuml's lease, he offered to raise his payment if he also received 200,000 M to cover renovation costs. After long negotiations, the Bavarian Finance Ministry renewed his lease for twenty years at 3,000 M per annum and paid him 40,000 M.[105] Almost certainly the state felt that it had made a good bargain, and judging by the cost overruns of the other state companies in the era, so it had.

Nymphenburg, technically, remained a state firm; as the Finance Ministry explained in 1923—in the midst of a takeover attempt by the private maker Rosenthal—the buildings and infrastructure of the manufactory belonged to the state, "and on the basis of the contract, the state exerts an influence on how the factory is run, so that it operates according to the fundamental principles of a state manufactory."[106] Like the Fürstenberg factory, leased out already in 1859, by trading on its eighteenth-century history and local traditions, Nymphenburg retained much of its prestige, even under private management.[107] The state also continued to give the manufactory preference for certain commissions. Despite its higher costs, for example, Nymphenburg retained the state's contract for telegraph insulators, for which it received nearly 650,000 M between 1895 and 1910.[108] Bäuml certainly deserves credit for restoring the firm's artistic prestige; but it was probably these commissions that kept this semistate firm's lights on.

The story of the Viennese manufactory (WPM) in the era of high liberalism has some similarities with Nymphenburg's fate. As we have seen, the manufactory suffered grievously in the 1820s and 1830s; it reduced its production of luxury wares, in favor of more salable goods, while also managing to maintain its reputation for excellence in painting. But the state's paltry support on the one hand, and the manufactory's high labor and materials costs—not helped by Austria's exclusion from the Zollverein—on the other, limited the firm's ability to retool and recover. The WPM ran minor deficits again in 1859 and in 1860, allowing liberals in the Finance Ministry and Reichstag to argue that it had been overtaken by private firms.[109] It is perhaps an indication of its desperation to demonstrate its loyalty to the state and affection for the Habsburgs that one of the last products of the WPM was a trompe d'oeil "Kaisersemmel," honoring Franz Josef's favorite breakfast roll and his tradition of distributing them to the public on his birthday.[110]

But even this act of imperial piety—or gently self-critical Viennese humor—left the liberals in the Reichstag unmoved.

In 1862, the Finance Committee of the Austrian Chamber of Deputies voted to close the factory, and production stopped. Debates continued in both houses as representatives bruited the now-familiar proposal to make the WPM a *Kunstanstalt*, or possibly something else. But the finance minister insisted that without a concrete plan it was foolhardy to keep propping up an institution that couldn't compete with private industry, or as another critic noted, give the Austrians the same sort of pride the French had in Sèvres.[111] In 1863, the Reichstag voted to close it, just ahead of Rudolf von Eitelberger's concerted campaign to save and improve Austrian craft traditions.[112] The molds, drawings, and extensive sample collection begun during the Napoleonic Wars were transferred to the ownership of Vienna's Museum für Kunst und Industrie. Although baroque WPM models were put back into use by the Fachschule für Toninudstrie in Znaim after 1890,[113] a successor to the WPM was founded only in 1923. The Wiener Porzellanmanufaktur Augarten is a successor only in that it uses many old models and supplies tableware for official state purposes and for gifts.

Almost simultaneously with Prussia's victory over Austria in the Austro-Prussian War of 1866, the leasing out or closure of Nymphenburg, Fürstenberg, and the WPM marked the further decline of princely power and *Glanz* in central Europe. Kings survived the unification in Bavaria and Saxony, despite their having been on the wrong side of history in this brief conflict, which greased the skids for Bismarck to impose his "small-German" plan for unification, and Saxony, at least, would keep its royal manufactory. But there would be no new "royal" firms founded, and despite the booming economy enjoyed by the Reich in the decades to follow, the two eighteenth-century survivors would find their enterprises difficult to sustain.

The Survivors: KPM and Meissen

Roiled by labor disputes and undersold by private competitors, the KPM in 1848 faced parlous conditions. Like other Berlin manufacturers, its labor costs were a third higher and its coal transport costs three-quarters higher than those recorded by the newer Silesian firms. Asked for a 20,000 T subsidy, the Prussian Trade Ministry requested, in return, a memo on how the KPM might be privatized. After a fierce debate in the Landtag, it was agreed that the KPM branch in the Berlin district of Charlottenburg, which produced "Gesundheitsgeschirr" (the Königliche Gesundheitsgeschirr Manufaktur, or KGGM), at least, should be privatized. The KPM, it was decided, should continue to exist as a "Kunst und Muster-Institut," but also try its utmost to turn profits for the state.[114] In the next few years, however, the KGGM failed to sell, and although its bottom line was helped by major orders from the telegraph bureau for insulators, in 1859 the firm still spent more than 40,000 T over its budget of 74,000 T.[115] After years of negotiation, the KGGM finally sold (for 73,000 T) to a private buyer in 1866.[116] The KPM's wares received scarring reviews at the 1851, 1855, and 1862 world exhibitions, and the manufactory was accused, in the words of a later commentator, of privileging "the technical and the bombastic at the cost of the artistic."[117]

In the late 1860s, the KPM itself came within an ace of closure. Since 1851, the Prussian House of Lords had been meeting in a grand mansion at Leipzigerstrasse 3, previously owned by J. E. Gotzkowsky, who had located his porcelain factory (later to become the KPM) next door, at Leipzigerstrasse 4. The mansion belonged to the Mendelssohn Bartholdy family between 1825 and 1856, when it was sold to the Prussian state. In 1867, the North German Confederation's parliament began to meet here, but space was tight, and after the manufactory's poor showing in the 1867 exhibition the Prussian state opted to seize the land; voices again were heard in favor of closing the factory, including from a liberal representative who argued: "Gentleman, I would like to note that there seems everywhere to be a certain pious regard for the Royal Porcelain Manufactory, perhaps precisely because it dates to the age of alchemy. . . . It must be alchemical reasons—if I may say so—which support its retention, as there can't be chemical or commercial [gewerbliche] reasons."[118]

Liberal opinion was, however, reversed, in part by an intervention made by Jacob Ritter von Falke, the director of the Austrian Museum für Kunst und Industrie, who described the profound regrets even the private makers in Austria now felt for having lost "an ideal model, which prevented [private makers] from sinking into banality and poor quality."[119] Grudgingly, the delegates approved 335,000 T—just slightly more than what the Saxon state paid to move the Meissen works in the previous decade, as we will see—to relocate the KPM to the site of the now-defunct KGGM, in Charlottenburg. The move was hastened by the unification of the German Empire and the new parliament's decision to use Leipzigstrasse 3 and 4 until its new Reichstag building could be finished in 1894.[120] It somehow fits that the KPM, aristocratic by birth, and run by chemists and bureaucrats thereafter, would be replaced first by the House of Lords, and then by Hermann Göring—a fan of both KPM and Meissen porcelains—who commandeered the prime real estate near Hitler's Chancellery in 1934. The building was salvaged after World War II, and used to house the GDR's planning commission and Academy of Sciences.[121] Today Leipzigerstrasse 4 is occupied by the Bundesrat, a non-elected representative body that reviews legislation affecting the federal states. In a city teeming with historical markers, no plaque commemorates the manufactory's original home.

Even after the factory's move, the status of the KPM remained precarious, especially as the firm began to lose money again in the wake of the banking crisis of 1873. Desperate for buyers, sellers cut costs, engaging in what one manufacturer called "suicidal competition."[122] Berlin makers, with higher labor and transport costs, were hit hard, and workers were laid off. In 1874 there were 1,941 ceramics workers in Berlin; three years later there were only 1,067.[123] A commission was appointed to investigate the KPM's circumstances, and Director F.H.G. Möller produced a memo, suggesting the creation of something like a ceramics trade school, such as those the Austrians had been busily creating, that would help bridge university and practical chemistry and give the whole of the German industry a leg up.[124] When the Trade Ministry suggested further lowering prices instead, Möller responded angrily not only that this would cause financial ruin for the factory, but that to devote itself purely to money-making mass production "is unseemly and damaging to a state model institute."[125]

The question became urgent when, in 1877–78, the firm lost more than 50,000 M, and once more threats of closure resounded.[126] A six-day conference was held on the manufactory's future, resulting in a long, printed memo. Noting that there remained considerable conflict on what the goal of the manufactory actually was, the memo compared the KPM to Sèvres, with a budget of 567,000 francs, and income of 130,000 francs, meaning that the manufactory was losing approximately 150,000 M, on top of which the state paid for pensions and the upkeep of buildings. Meissen was making money (250,000 M in the last year), but only by producing outdated artistic forms, with increasingly less skill. The KPM, for its part, was certainly falling short in the artistic department. Its warehouses contained works whose flaws were concealed with ridiculous overdecoration, the worst being porcelain imitations of early modern Rhenish beer steins. The fault lay in too much effort to suit the public in order to turn a profit, the commission concluded, and it advised the KPM to devote itself to wider ceramics experimentation for the good of the nation—presumably now Germany, and not exclusively Prussia, was meant—as well as to appoint a commission of artistic advisers.[127]

In the end, the Prussian state accepted the commission's plan and in 1878 permitted the creation of a Chemisch-Technische Versuchsanstalt (Institute for Chemical-Technical Experiments), to be operated as part of the KPM, but to share its findings with private industry. Its director, chemist Hermann Seger, almost immediately demonstrated the virtues of this form of R&D by developing a new paste that contained only 25 percent kaolin (as compared to the usual 50 percent for hard-paste porcelain), 45 percent quartz, and 30 percent feldspar. "Seger Porzellan" could be fired at slightly lower temperatures and thus take new underglaze paints in a range of colors beyond the traditional cobalt blue and the green developed in the early nineteenth century. Seger's experiments ran parallel with those at Royal Copenhagen and made possible the production of high-quality works that imitated the simple elegance of East Asian masterworks; European chemists were especially proud of their ability to make, at long last, vessels in "ox blood" red and "celadon" green.[128] It is worth noting that precisely in the era of high imperialism, as Germany was establishing its own quasi-colony in Tsingtau, some central European artists and chemists exulted in the beauties and technical excellence of East Asian art.

At the fin de siècle, and afterward, the KPM certainly did not give up on rococo; financially, it simply could not do so, no matter what the critics said. The manufactory did not go as far as did Royal Copenhagen in adopting a naturalistic Japanese style, or as far as Sèvres in developing art nouveau. It was, consequently, punished by critics for its Paris 1900 displays, which, as one wrote, "lack true artistic progress and a clear creative goal. One has the impression that interest in chemical and technical experiments stand in the foreground, without these being put to the highest possible artistic ends."[129] When Theo Schmuz-Baudiss, known for his art nouveau styles, took over the manufactory's direction in 1908, the firm tried to introduce more modernism but ran into opposition from another quarter: Kaiser Wilhelm II, who did not hesitate to try to impose his historicist tastes on the empire's artistic institutions.[130] But the firm remained in the black, and in business, down to the time of the war's outbreak. It had weathered the liberal storm, but only narrowly, by relocating—symbolically—to the Prussian capital's periphery, and by emphasizing science over art.

Meissen, Fin de Siècle

As a careful chronicler of the firm's history wrote in 1880, despite Meissen's better record of profits than most state firms, throughout the nineteenth century, the Saxon state remained ambivalent about the fate of its porcelain manufactory, viewing it both "as the spoiled child of art-crazed princes and as a gem in the rich crown of a bustling nation's industrial enterprises."[131] Like the KPM, Meissen was expected both to lead artistically and to turn a profit, a combination that mass production and fierce competition made almost impossible. That Meissen was able at least in part to square this circle can be chalked up to the enduring respect buyers exhibited for the first manufactory's reputation for high quality, to its successful branding campaign, reinforced through the endless reproduction of eighteenth-century models, and finally to the fact that the state did, in the end, come through.

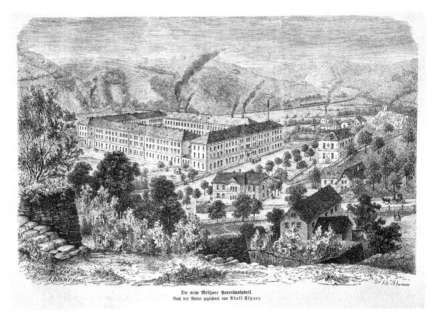

Die neue Meißner Porcellanfabrik.
Nach der Natur gezeichnet von Adolf Eltzner.

6.3. Meissen's new factory

The new Meissen factory in 1869. After 160 years of manufacturing on the Albrechtsburg, thanks to state subsidies and loans the firm could now move to a purpose-built factory on the outskirts of town, directly on the rail line.

In the revolutionary years 1848–51 Meissen ran in the red. The longtime technical manager, Heinrich Kühn, finally elevated to director, was compelled to submit monthly reports to his Finance Ministry as well as to endure the halfhearted advice of a committee of artists contemptuous of the manufactory's products. In 1853, the state gave him a meager 8,000 T to replace his horse mill with a steam engine.[132] Gradually, thereafter, the firm began to cash in on rising domestic consumption, averaging nearly 18,000 T in profits between 1855 and 1863.[133] Producing "English Articles" helped, but what underwrote Meissen's success in this era was a decision taken by the Saxon Landtag to pay for the building of a new Meissen factory at a location on the outskirts of the ancient town (fig. 6.3). The request for new premises did not come from the manufactory itself, but from the Saxon Heritage

Association, which was agitating for the historical preservation of the Albrechtsburg Castle, where porcelain mixing, firing, modeling, and painting had been done since the days of Böttger. The association made its pitch in 1854, at a time the Finance Ministry was exploring selling the factory to a private buyer.[134] Then King Johann entered the fray, using his bully pulpit to express his desire to see 300,000 T invested in moving the factory. The Landtag waffled, its liberals expressing concern about the economic viability of the manufactory in ways that closely resemble debates in Berlin, Munich, and Vienna. In the end, in this case, the argument for the maintenance of "patriotic honor" and local employment won out, and the Landtag approved the grant, which, as one commentator has pointed out, would have taken forty years to pay back had it simply been a bank loan.[135]

Although the transition took time and 1866—when Saxony again chose the losing side in the Austro-Prussian War—was painful, after the forming of the North German Confederation in 1867, profits boomed. By 1878, the factory was producing nearly twice the quantity of 1869, and reeling in 235,000 M in annual profits. It could now afford to add new kilns and machinery, as well as workers, whose numbers jumped from 365 to 603.[136] In the 1880s, profits returned to the state averaged almost 400,000 M a year, and by 1900, Meissen employed upward of eight hundred workers, finally topping its previous high of 751, achieved in 1763.[137]

In the Bismarckian era, Meissen's sales, if not its artistic standing, benefited greatly from another wave of nostalgia, generating public admiration for what was known as the "third" rococo and rising taste for this abroad, especially in America, England, and France. Meissen was able to trade on its reputation for high quality and obtain premium prices from customers eager to have a showy piece for their salons. Even more important for the bottom line, however, was an enormous expansion in blue-and-white sales, which increased from 51,000 M in 1863 to an impressive 556,000 M in 1879, amounting to about one-third of total sales.[138] So popular did the Blue Onion become that scores of other factories imitated it, forcing Meissen to engage in a series of lawsuits to protect its pattern (see fig. 3.2). But financial success had artistic costs, for Meissen was slow to introduce art nouveau and

Jugendstil forms. Even as the KPM developed high-temperature glazes and the Parisians perfected "paste on paste" techniques, Meissen emphasized its status as the oldest of the porcelain firms and played to its eighteenth-century, rococo, strengths. Its huge selection of historical models nicely illustrates the blend of local and national patriotism exhibited by Germans of the period: along with busts of Bismarck, Wotan, and the kaisers, one could purchase painted works featuring Saxon landscapes, kings, miners, and figures in regional costume. The manufactory won lasting appreciation from the Saxon monarchy and residents of Dresden by restoring the tiled frieze of the Procession of the Wettin Princes. So popular were its wares that in 1890, Josef Hellmesberger Jr., the conductor of the Vienna Philharmonic, composed a ballet titled "Meissen Porcelain" and featuring characters from its eighteenth-century repertoire. As we will see in chapter 7, the manufactory did experiment with some contemporary designs. But in the end "modern" was not the look most Meissen customers were after.

Yet, tastes, and more importantly, the market, were changing, and perhaps Wilhelmine "china" closets could hold no more. As the worldwide depression set in after 1893, Meissen's profits began to decline, sinking to 11,031 M in 1900, though rebounding to 146,900 M in 1901.[139] Moreover, the state had received complaints that orders took six to twelve months to fill, and that customers for cheaper wares were treated poorly in commissioned shops. Retailers complained that the manufactory was not sending them salable items, and insisting on charging exorbitant prices. Painters complained that they couldn't make a proper living on their wages. Warehouses were filling up with outdated "art" items, at an estimated value of almost two million marks in 1902. The manufactory increased prices, which had not happened for nearly fifty years, but which raised eyebrows. Meissen was, once again, on the hot seat.

A Saxon Landtag committee had already begun investigating (and criticizing) in 1903, eliciting a defensive report by Director Gesell.[140] The committee was not satisfied and kept up pressure to improve sales, reduce costs, and fill the vacant job of art director with a first-class artist. In the spring of 1906, it presented an extremely detailed report on the manufactory's expenditures, practices, and products to the Landtag. The report recommended that the manufactory save money (partly by hiring non–civil servants who didn't have to be promised pensions), that it pay more attention to consumers' desires, and that it not spend so much on exhibition wares that ended up as warehouse white elephants.[141] The Saxon finance minister then presented the report to the Landtag for debate.

Mirroring debates in Berlin about the KPM, and those that ended with the leasing of the Viennese and Bavarian firms several decades earlier, this 1906 debate tells us a great deal about the enduring contradictions in the old mercantilist business model. Meissen, as one delegate said, had been subjected to more criticisms and condemnations than virtually any other institution.[142] As another put it, the finance minister, like Goethe's Faust, harbored two souls in one breast, one of which embraced Meissen's historical reputation for artistic excellence, while the other insisted on the production of profitable modern wares.[143] All were aware that the manufactory was the victim, like no other, of forgeries and cheaper imitations, and that the market for luxury goods had largely evaporated. Defenders criticized the crude taste of American buyers ("gold, gold, and more gold") that dragged down Meissen's artistry, and they championed the "world renown" of "vieux Saxe."[144] And yet, the politicians vociferously denounced the manufactory's decision not to sell unpainted porcelains, its poor treatment of customers, and its failure to keep up artistically: and why not commission the works of *Saxon* artists? one local patriot asked.[145] The SPD objected to allowing the factory too much budgetary freedom and accused the firm of tricking painters into taking reduced salaries.[146] Except for the publicly voiced criticisms from the Left—made possible by Saxony's widened franchise—this was the same set of complaints that had dogged the manufactory for at least one hundred years. *Are we to pursue art or commerce?* Meissen director Kühn had asked pointedly in 1851.[147] And the unhelpful answer remained: both.

This time there was no question of closing the manufactory; as even the Saxon Finance Minister agreed, they were now dealing with "a piece of history . . . a venerable Saxon institution."[148] Meissen's director Gesell—who had formerly served as sales manager—was adamant, too, that it was his business to please not the retailers but the consumers, and especially the Saxon "educated" classes, including: "officers, officials, scholars, the poorer nobility, and so forth." It was in defense of these consumers that the director proudly, and rather repetitiously, declared that the manufactory, "based on cultural considerations, regards it precisely as its duty not to allow the bastion in the battle against the monied interests, which the royal manufactory has down to today represented, to be shaken by the assaults of purely monied interests."[149] But he did have to soothe the Faustian soul of his paymasters. Accordingly, the manufactory tried to assuage critics with a few modern commissions, while expanding production of its "Alt-Meissen" models, slathered in "gold, gold, gold." Gesell increased production of tourist and commemorative wares and in 1909 introduced an annual "Christmas plate," creating a tradition whose popularity continued into the 1970s.[150] His efforts were rewarded with an upsurge in exports to the United States, which reached 30 percent of the firm's intake by 1909.[151]

In 1910, Meissen celebrated its two-hundredth anniversary with considerable fanfare, featuring the factory singing club performing Felix Mendelssohn's arrangement of Schiller's ode "to the artists" and rococo tableaux enacted by actors dressed as Kändler figurines. In his directorial address, Gesell did not fail to note that the firm had experienced "great curves" in its history; the only constant had been "the wise and benevolent care which the august wearers of the Saxon royal crown and the government since the constitution, especially the royal ministry of finance . . . have dedicated, often under difficulties and in connection with sacrifices, to the weal of the royal china factory." In exchange, the director argued,

> the royal porcelain factory has not only created lasting ideal works, depopulating Olympus in order to reconcile men with the rough realities of life; it has not only written a full and rich page in the history of art; it has not only spread the fame of Saxon art and industry all the world over and been the pioneer of Saxon industry in general: it has, besides all of this, been of material benefit to its country. Between 1863 and 1909, [the Meissen manufactory] has brought a profit of about 14 millions to the royal treasury.[152]

Meissen had navigated the perilous seas of fin de siècle capitalist competition, but its managers were well aware that its perennial endurance was by no means assured. They had learned to expect "great curves" in the market and in political support. Even so, neither they nor any of the guests at the festivities could envision the cataclysm that would befall them just four years on.

In celebrating their two hundred years of production, the Meisseners, understandably, did not reflect broadly on the changes the porcelain industry as a whole had undergone in the course of two centuries, or even the last four or five decades. The luxury producers had lost a great part of their market share, something that was even more clearly the case for the two remaining fully state-owned producers. By moving increasingly to organization in joint-stock companies and cartels, the industry had joined the world of advanced capitalism; its workers increasingly joined the organized and politicized labor movement. As the proportion of skilled workers and small firms dwindled, owners, managers, and workers increasingly faced one another as members of different, and often hostile, classes. More than ever before, competition raged in both the domestic and the export markets and focused chiefly on offering the lowest prices, something that in turn put downward pressure on wages and drove innovations in energy saving and the use of alternative materials and forms of decoration. Machines and the rationalization of labor practices contributed to massive increases in production capacity, though not to standardization and uniformity of styles. Mass production and mass consumption had come to the porcelain industry, but not in the same way, or at the same time, exactly, as they came to other industries.

As is the case in all moments of major economic and political transformation, some people win, and some people lose. The era of capitalism triumphant was good for some porcelain makers—for those near rail lines and cheap labor, for those who had sufficient capital to increase in size, for those whose chemists and artists guessed right about next year's fashions. They were not so good for impoverished domestic workers, or for small producers with little access to capital. Nor was the period so good for older luxury producers, a number of which failed to negotiate high capitalism's rocky seas. For the two state firms that did survive, there was still some official patronage to be had, in the form of telegraph office concessions or the tiling of subway stations and post offices; but direct subsidies were harder than ever to extract from the state and now exposed the manufactories to close public scrutiny and fierce legislative debates. Artistic critics, too, could voice their reservations about the manufactories' lines of production in a press ever more critical of established institutions. If German porcelain making was undergoing a transition from craft industry to big business, it was doing so in the context of a still-monarchical state moving in the direction of democracy. Neither porcelain, nor the Wilhelmine Empire, would ever fully complete these transitions; their "modernities," nonetheless, give us a fascinating snapshot of the diversity of intertwined political paths, cultural trajectories, and economic pursuits that characterized central Europe as it rushed across the threshold of the new century.

Chapter 7

Porcelain, the Wilhelmine Plastic

*I*n its social and cultural as well as in its economic life, the Wilhelmine Empire exhibited fantastic contrasts and strange combinations of modern and medieval. Many persons continued to live in class- or regionally segregated worlds, the experiential reality of the deeply Catholic Bavarian peasant contrasting sharply with that of the avant-garde Berlin artist, or Rhenish steelworker. Down to the nineteenth century's end, or even beyond, the classical gymnasium served as the gateway to university education and the free professions. But there were more advocates than ever before for science, technology, and modern history; railways linked inward-looking villages with bustling cities. No one woke up one morning fully 'modernized,' especially as numerous central Europeans found embracing such an identity not to their tastes.

In this world of contrasts, art academies persisted, but secessionist movements surged and brought their visions to wider publics. Similarly, historicizing novels and popular travelogues persisted even as Thomas Mann, Franz Wedekind, and Rainer Maria Rilke innovated. The Protestant and Catholic churches remained full (especially of women) and continued to shape moral norms; but there were also people who now identified themselves as Buddhists, Monists, or nudists.[1] The imperial courts continued to function, and in fact royal figures increasingly honed their images to appeal to at least a high-bourgeois public.[2] But this, too, was a world of mass politics, in the wake of Bismarck's great expansion of the franchise in 1879 and the rise of socialist and Catholic parties in succeeding decades—and a world of mass consumption. Germany had been united; but the Wilhelmine Empire was by no means a world in which all Germans were alike.

As we saw in the previous chapter, porcelain by the final third of the nineteenth century had become a mass-produced commodity. By the same token, it had become an item of mass *consumption*, as its purchase in some form had now come within the reach of most. Virtually all porcelain by this time was ready-made, though special orders were still taken; it was sold not directly from factories but by luxury retailers or, increasingly, department stores or haberdashers of one sort or another. Mass production did not diminish the variety of ceramic objects produced; by 1885, a price catalog showed that Villeroy & Boch was producing 7,062 ready-made items, including toast racks, beer steins, and decorative plates, the latter featuring, among many other choices, Bismarck on horseback, a gnome raising a glass, a shepherd and shepherdess, and a view of the Wartburg.[3] And then there were the more invisible uses: the tiles, teeth, and telegraph insulators. And yet, porcelain making remained a relatively high-profile art, one featured at trade exhibitions and world fairs, and one cultivated by champions of the arts and crafts movement as essential to tasteful modern living. Fierce arguments continued within manufactories and in the public press over the extent to which production should be guided by artists, or by the backward-looking and banal tastes of the general public. But the manufactories stuck to their commitment to variety and, in doing so, flourished in this world of so many contrasts and consumer identities. Without losing entirely its reputation for *Glanz*, porcelain also became the Wilhelmine era's plastic.

Simply to invoke "mass production" is to blanket over a host of new procedures and processes that are not as self-evident as they may seem; something similar can be said about "mass consumption." While the first term typically denotes the standardization of ready-made wares and the imposition of Taylorist work discipline, the second suggests the widening of the social spectrum of buyers and the national and international distribution of like goods. Where these two meet is difficult to pinpoint and differs from industry to industry, and from place to place. Harmonicas were surely easier to standardize than shoes, and meat extract was easier to ship long distances than porcelain. This chapter begins by sketching what these concepts meant in terms of technologies and practices for the porcelain industry before turning to a more general discussion of porcelain's place in the cultural world of fin de siècle central Europe. We then travel a bit further up the aesthetic ladder to discuss the place of porcelain at that crucial occasion for national and brand self-promotion, the world's fair, where we reencounter the much older tension between porcelain as a form of art and porcelain as a means of making profits. Following this excursus the chapter considers the relationship between the arts and crafts movements and modern design, on the one hand, and the porcelain industry on the other. The chapter ends, as did the Wilhelmine Empire, with the Great War, during which the manufactories largely forsook debates about "art" and turned their attention to producing the technical porcelains vital to the war effort. In the making of field telephones and hand grenades, the industry found yet another set of uses for its "plastic."

Mass-Producing Luxury

For a luxury industry built on pleasing diverse consumer tastes, mass production could not simply mean mechanization and standardization; even Thuringian manufacturers of doll heads prided themselves on offering many looks, sizes, and shapes. In German porcelain factories, labor was organized around batch production, in which a few skilled journeymen oversaw their own "teams"—mixing, modeling, firing, decorating—rather than subjecting production to a single centralized command or model of through-put.[4] Machines were present, but not yet dominant. The larger producers introduced machines for mixing, grinding, and a few specialized shaping and decorating tasks, such as forming plates or painting rims. But even at Kahla and Rosenthal, workers were needed at every turn to add ingredients, pour slip, apply decals, paint flourishes, load and unload drying racks and kilns, and pack finished items for shipping. The game was to substitute as many unskilled laborers as possible for master modelers and painters, not to do away with workers as such. In central Europe, labor remained very cheap, and

machines relatively expensive; when German workers' salaries rose, manufactories simply looked east for impoverished workers who would accept
lower wages. The Fürstenberg factory, for example, sent agents to Poland to
recruit young girls, promising them free dormitory housing and wages of
1.3 M per day (meaning penurious wages of about 400 M per year); this
practice continued until 1927.[5] The fully automated factory was by no means
a Wilhelmine reality.

If mass production means, too, the reduction of variety in order to reduce
the cost of both materials and labor, we see only the beginnings of this in
the Wilhelmine era. Some of the factories producing the cheapest goods did
reduce the variety of their production in order to push costs down, and the
state firms, with the largest repertoires, suffered from their inability to do
this. Most firms, even the state ones, reduced their production of the finest-
quality, one-of-a-kind wares even further. But it is still remarkable just how
many objects and decorative schemes the manufactories continued to offer,
with Villeroy & Boch, as we saw above, listing more than seven thousand
items in its catalog. Others too demonstrated remarkable ecumenicism. One
could buy, still, the full range of items offered to the Biedermeier customer—
including trinket boxes, clocks, candelabra, shaving mugs, and tea sets—
plus newer items such as ashtrays, name plates, and developing trays for
photographers. A thriving public sphere ordered porcelains for hotels, spas,
railroad and steamship dining rooms, and the now-ubiquitous cafés and bak-
eries. Multitudes of vases were made, probably more often to be used as objets d'art than to hold flowers; one could choose the newer art nouveau forms,
Wedgwoodian or "third rococo," Gothic or "Moorish," or some mixture of
any of the above.[6] The souvenir market boomed, as visitors clamored for
scenes from the Rhine, the Alps, Rome. After 1900, German makers brought
out their own versions of the French oven-safe ceramics, giving them exciting new names such as Luzifer Feuerfest and Walküre.

Figurines had become a less important market as the century wore on,
and many lower-end makers dispensed with making them entirely. Others
trimmed their lists, reducing the number of classical figures, and adding some
modern ones. But what is remarkable for this age of mass production is just

how many different models continued to be offered for sale. Emperors and military leaders remained popular, but some manufactories now also produced busts of non-noble political figures such as Daniel O'Connell and Lajos Kossuth. Offerings at the higher end tended to be more conservative and backward looking. In its catalog of 1900, Meissen was still offering hundreds of figurines, including the Crieurs de Paris, multitudes of peasants, fauns and nymphs, Cupid in numerous poses and costumes, Parsifal, the Four Seasons, and children with cats. Customers could choose from seventy-three different species and sizes of birds. And then came the biscuit porcelains, almost all classicizing and heavy on Venus, Cupid, and allegorical forms. Living persons, in this list, were limited to Bismarck, the king and queen of Saxony, Emperor Wilhelm I (not II), and Helmuth von Moltke.[7] This was, after a fashion, production for the masses—but with a full understanding that "the masses" were composed of many different sorts of buyers, with many different needs, tastes, and incomes.

To make so many objects at affordable prices manufactories worked hard to reduce their materials costs. Officials tinkered endlessly with kiln design, finding ever-new ways to fire more pieces simultaneously, with a higher degree of consistency, and smaller uses of energy. Most introduced slip casting (see chapter 6), a much speedier and therefore cheaper method than turning pieces on the wheel. Chemical experimentation continued to be crucial. Although exact recipes for pastes and glazes could now be found printed in any number of handbooks, encyclopedias, and professional journals, manufactories still competed to be the first to pioneer a new technique or recipe. One such was the new form of biscuit known as "Parian" porcelain, designed to imitate the famously white Greek marble quarried on the island of Paros, and to be used chiefly for miniaturized classical or classicizing sculptures such as Hiram Powers's hugely popular, and semipornographic, *The Greek Slave*, and the old favorite, the Medici Venus. Developed first by the Copeland factory in about 1843, "Parian" porcelain also resisted dust and could be cleaned with soap and water, essential in an era in which homes were heated with smoky coal. By the later 1840s, other British firms were also making "Parian"—though continental makers largely stuck to older biscuit recipes, which eventually triumphed, because they were cheaper to make. Both Parian and biscuit figurine makers profited from new techniques of miniaturizing, using, for example, Benjamin Cheverton's reducing machine, patented in 1844 and shown at the Great Exhibition, which allowed the mechanical copying of originals on a smaller scale.[8]

Other techniques made decoration cheaper and more diverse. Again the English led the way in the development, in 1863, of the acid gold process, which entailed the etching of patterns on a biscuit porcelain surface by controlled immersion in acid; these patterns were then gilded and polished, leaving behind layers of matt gold intaglio and glossy relief. Lithographic color printing had been possible in the first half of the century but remained expensive and unreliable. Only in the 1880s did German manufacturers improve color chromolithographic transfer and the printing of decals that could be affixed to cheaper wares (the aesthetic inferiority of the transferred image, however, meant that the higher-quality producers still spurned this process). The "printing and filling in" technique developed in the United States improved the aesthetics and variety of painted motifs but required the largely female painting staff to decorate by hand.[9]

But technical innovation was also seen as the means to create new forms of art, especially designed to impress judges and critics at exhibitions and trade fairs. The technique of pâte-sur-pâte, for example, developed at Sèvres and first exhibited at the Crystal Palace, was a time-consuming process, requiring a skilled craftsperson to patiently brush thirty to forty layers of liquid slip onto the vessel, allowing each to dry before sculpting the material, and then glazing and firing the pot. The result was a cameo-like relief with contrasting opaque and translucent shades, and intricate masterpieces that earned the manufactory many kudos and prizes.[10] Inspired by East Asian technical virtuosity, as we have seen, chemists at Royal Copenhagen and the KPM perfected a series of new underglaze paints, known to the Germans as *Scharffeuerfarben*, for their avant-garde lines.[11] These techniques were widely imitated, especially for the production of animal and bird figurines and the making of Jugendstil and faux East Asian wares. Indeed, more than one commentator has argued that the new glazes themselves made possible the industry's break from neo-rococo styling and its embrace of more abstract and "modern" decorative repertoires.[12]

As in previous centuries, both technical processes and styles diffused quickly. Information about how to make and sell porcelain had never been so readily available; industry-wide journals such as *Sprechsaal* (founded 1868) and *Tonindustrie Zeitung* (founded 1876) now shared techniques and recipes openly. Perhaps the culmination of this trend was the 1922 book *Anlage, Einrichtung und Betrieb einer Porzellanfabrik*, which offered a fulsome account of how to set up and operate a manufactory, down to how to calculate prices and keep personnel statistics.[13] And yet, the higher-end firms in particular were also eager to protect their patterns and trade secrets, and they rejoiced at the passage of a trademark protection law in 1874, and an addendum protecting patterns and models in 1876. But, as usual, legal protections were only moderately successful against the ever-ingenious borrowers.[14] In 1905, Rosenthal's great success with its "Donatello" service led to its close copying by several manufactories; in this case, unusually, Rosenthal sued and forced the mimics to desist.[15] Meanwhile, forged or imitated Sèvres, KPM, and especially Meissen wares proliferated.

In the midst of mad modernization, being "old" took on nostalgic appeal as well as monetary value. Everyone who had an "ancient" porcelain manufactory returned as many rococo models to service as possible, advertising them explicitly as Alt-Meissen, Vieux Sèvres, Alt-Nymphenburg; following suit, the now-private Fürstenberg greatly expanded its production of older models after 1902 and began marketing them directly as "Alt Fürstenberg."[16] So lucrative, in fact, was the designation "Alt" that even the Thuringians, renowned for producing cheap goods for ready-made buyers, fought over it. In 1910, the Thuringian firm descendant rather vaguely from the Rudolstadt manufactory, and now proudly calling itself Älteste Volkstedter Porzellan, sued the nearby firm of Unterweissbach for calling itself "Älteste Volkstedter Porzellanfabrik."[17] Evidently even in Thuringia—notorious for its cheap knickknacks—it was crucial to be not the most modern, but the "oldest" porcelain factory.

One area in which mass production had certainly come to our industry was in the making of technical, or "electro-technical" porcelains. The increasing use of machines and the extension of railroad and subway lines created an ever-greater need for porcelain parts to prevent friction from starting fires. Industrial orders from public agencies and private businesses surged as German laboratories and dye works demanded more acid-resistant, impermeable crucibles and beakers than ever before. Here, the need to make identical items in these "technical" and "electro-technical" branches was much stronger than in the tableware branch, meaning that the firms making this sort of porcelain adopted machines such as the dry press, which reduced the shrinking of pieces during firing. They also did not need to worry about style or even about consumers' tastes, as orders for these utilitarian items came from the state or from businesses.

By 1910, porcelain was being used for sinks as well as for molds for rubber gloves and mouthpieces for musical instruments. The larger private firms retooled to produce these porcelains, and the percentage of workers devoted to this form of production, compared to luxury or tableware production, would steadily increase. Gradually, a whole separate branch, with its own cartels and workers' organizations, would emerge. "Technical" porcelain would prove a vital part of the industry, and of munitions making, during the First and the Second World Wars. More than any other portion of the industry, this almost invisible part of the porcelain-making universe fits our traditional understanding of mass production. But it was not this sector that most people imagined when they heard the word "porcelain," nor is it the form of mass production artists complained about. Most consumers and artists, and most historians and museum curators too, have essentially ignored this branch of ceramics making. But for the porcelain *industry*, "technical" porcelain would from this time forward form an essential part of doing business, and of economic survival.

Mass Consumption

If mass production is hard to define exactly, mass consumption, too, is a tricky term. On the one hand, we can consider the affordability of goods and the opportunity to purchase them, and on the other, the various ways in which the goods were actually "consumed." With respect to affordability, we can certainly say that even though Germans' average income by 1914 still lagged considerably behind that of the Britons and Belgians,[18] porcelain was within the reach of many more of the kaiser's subjects than ever before. Absolute as well as relative prices for simpler goods plunged in the later nineteenth century; in 1863, for example, a small "English-style" KPM coffeepot that had cost twenty-five silver groschen in 1828 could be had for twenty, and a teacup for four rather than five.[19] Real prices fell again in the 1870s and 1880s, stabilizing a bit in the next decade thanks largely to the interventions of the Manufacturers' Cartel. But a few years on, prices began to fall again, and shortly after the century's turn, one could buy a teacup at three pfennigs, equal to about .75 of the now-defunct groschen. One economic historian of the period estimated that one could buy a coffee service for 39 percent less or a decorated cup for 60 percent less in 1907 than in 1895, and that selection had quadrupled in these years.[20] Prices this low encouraged middling-level customers to demand better quality and more highly decorated vessels, while allowing even working families such as the one pictured in fig. 7.1 to cram cabinets with simpler wares. There had been less-expensive porcelains in the eighteenth century; but now producers vied especially for lower-end sales—understandably, as the table services under 50 M outsold those at higher prices by more than a 3 to 1 ratio.[21] It was more possible than ever before for families to purchase at least some "good" china, for Sundays or holidays, though we can safely assume that many still took their daily meals from sturdier and cheaper earthenware, faience, and tin.

By no means was it easy to sell to everyone, even if everyone had access to the same goods and services, which was emphatically not the case. Sales venues were diverse and increasingly segmented by class. By the 1890s, porcelain was being sold by peddlers and in department stores, in older haberdasheries and bazaars,[22] in elegant luxury-goods establishments and pawn shops, at layaway emporiums and stores featuring "colonial wares," at annual fairs and by telegraph or mail order. Commissions such as those of Ferdinand of Saxe-Coburg-Gotha and his Portuguese queen Maria II for the

7.1. Working-class interior, Berlin, 1913

This 1913 photograph of a working-class one-room apartment shows that despite shortages of income and space, this family owned a considerable ceramics collection, some of which appears to be porcelain.

furnishing for their "Sala Saxe" were surely negotiated directly with the Meissen factory. Those buying for business purposes could consult special catalogs made for "hotel porcelain," which would also be suitable for cafés; these customers were cultivated by factory owners themselves or by traveling salesmen, bearing sample trunks and price lists. For the larger exporters, the commissioning of local dealers gave way to dedicated brand stores in places such as New York and Chicago. Selling porcelain was by no means the same operation as the selling of hats or sewing machines, and the enormous variety of grades and uses of this "plastic" made for a hugely complicated and diverse set of retailing practices, which no one has fully mapped for the German-speaking world.[23] But clearly no single mass-marketing strategy fit all.

There were, however, dramatic changes in the retail landscape in central Europe in the 1880s and 1890s, as the first department stores opened their doors in the larger cities. Department stores had been founded in France, the United States, and Great Britain already by the 1840s; it is another sign of central Europe's relative "belatedness" in the sphere of consumption, and the power of its small merchants, that these arrived in the East forty or more years later, though after that time they spread quite quickly, and there were some five thousand or more by 1914.[24] In some ways German department stores such as Tietze and Wertheim were larger versions of earlier haberdasheries and bazaars; but the new "cathedrals of consumption" surrounded their goods with a new aura, making self-indulgence rather than thrift respectable.[25] Elaborately decorated establishments such as Budapest's six-floor Párisi featured elaborate displays of massed wares and gas or electrical lighting, making for a sharp contrast with the often dark and dusty older urban shops. Featuring fixed prices and encouraging buyers to browse, rather than having a clerk attend customers with the expectation of a sale, the new department stores made shopping for pleasure an urban habit, especially for women, who were now the target audience. They were lured in with seductive window displays, low prices for specialty foods such as jam and canned goods, and cafés where friends could meet.

Naturally, not everyone greeted the advent of the department store with glee. Small shopkeepers in particular saw them as quality-destroying capitalist monstrosities, tempting good German housewives to ruin their families, reducing all goods to mere commodities, and obviating the expertise of the knowledgeable salesperson. That many of the largest stores were owned by Jewish entrepreneurs further provoked illiberal opposition.[26] Their cultural impact, in fact, was out of proportion with their economic significance; by one estimate, even in 1913 only 2.3 percent of Germany's retail sales took place in department stores.[27]

It is appropriate that one of the greatest of the early department stores, Wertheim, occupied its most impressive premises in Berlin's Leipzigerstrasse, across the street from the original site of the KPM manufactory. Porcelain was, indeed, one of the department stores' most beloved offerings, often filling up large sections of the higher floors. At first the stores chiefly stocked goods the factories considered "damaged" or "rejects," previously offloaded to fair salesmen or the lowliest of peddlers. This led to complaints from the smaller luxury dealers who resented being undersold and losing the opportunity to shape customers' tastes. It was the sellers' responsibility, in the words of the Retailers' Cartel, "to educat[e] even the least sophisticated woman not to set her table with worthless and ugly shards, but only with proper (*anständig*) dishes."[28] The department stores did gradually improve the quality of their offerings, and those bound by the *Revers* had to give up selling flawed pieces. But in general they were content to ingratiate themselves with the penny-pinching public, no matter how poor their taste, and to leave higher-end sales to the specialty shops, which continued to offer personalized customer service and advice. Unlike earlier advocates of frugal simplicity, the department store managers recognized, in Deborah Cohen's words, that "the customer had come to expect flattery and a wide selection, rather than criticism and restraints."[29]

By the later nineteenth century, it is clear that porcelain marketing was directed chiefly at women, for household purposes. Etiquette guides and cookbooks instructed homemakers on how to equip their kitchens and impress their guests with appropriate table settings for every meal. The values to be cultivated were now "taste" and "comfort" rather than "frugality" and "simplicity."[30] The number and type of "necessary" items continuously expanded; already by 1868, one guide highly recommended stocking the kitchen with the following things made of porcelain: dessert plates, molds for puddings, egg cups, oil and vinegar bottles, coffeepots and teapots, plates, salad plates, sauce boats, platters, vegetable plates, sugar boxes, and milk pitchers.[31] Instructions were given for buying good-quality items as well as for washing and repairing tableware. It seems to have been generally understood that no respectable home would lack a healthy selection of porcelains; to serve meals on tin, or from a single pot, unless absolutely necessitated by poverty, was out of the question.

But if porcelain was increasingly identified with everyday tasteful living, it also remained centrally linked to holidays and to gift giving. Manufacturers understood this and already by midcentury were producing special Christmas items.[32] Production and marketing targeted to this holiday only increased thereafter. All the manufactories added extra hours in November and December for workers to fulfill Christmas orders; special Easter items followed. This was, in its way, the systematization and monetization of Biedermeier sentimentalism, and the regularization of middle-class gift exchange. In the eighteenth century, princes had presented services as diplomatic gifts, and often on the occasion of royal weddings. Already by the early nineteenth century, the practice of giving porcelain as a wedding gift had evidently begun to trickle down to the bourgeoisie.[33] In the early 1890s, the American entrepreneur Walter Scott Lenox launched a campaign to advertise the appropriateness of porcelain for weddings, and other porcelain makers and glassmakers quickly followed suit. If the department store wedding registry dates only to the 1930s, the tradition of preparing a prenuptial ceramic trousseau has its roots in late nineteenth-century middle-class culture.[34]

Where did potential customers learn about porcelain for sale? By the later nineteenth century, the sources of product information were much more diverse and widely circulated, though catalogs (now often with photographs!) were largely directed at retailers, not at individual consumers, or at the booming hotel and restaurant market, which was also served by traveling salesmen. Urban dwellers could scrutinize shop windows, and more and more rural inhabitants too came to the cities to marvel at the now electrically illuminated shops. Exhibitions and fairs featured the manufactories' most elaborate or recent pieces but nonetheless served as education for would-be buyers. Peddling persisted. Many factories offered tours in the hopes of inspiring sales. Visiting Meissen became so popular that the manufactory could charge an entrance fee and in 1904 alone netted 8,000 M in proceeds for its factory tours.[35]

But for the individual consumer, surely most effective were personal conversations, especially among women, and visits to others' homes, where porcelain pieces might be on view in etageres or cabinets, or used for the serving of coffee and tea. One early description of cross-class envy and imitation has vegetable-selling girls from the provinces goggling at the interiors

7.2. International Women's Congress meeting, 1914

If, by 1914, workers had some porcelain, the middling classes had much more, even when they subscribed to radical political notions. In this picture of a meeting of the International Women's Congress in Berlin, porcelain covers the walls and the mantelpiece.

of their betters, and resolving to copy them;[36] how much more common this would have been in the later nineteenth century, as rural populations flooded into the cities, and the number of domestic workers surged! Judging by this depiction of a meeting of feminist activists in Berlin in 1914, porcelain consumption and display was common across the political spectrum (fig. 7.2). We can imagine conversations between Wilhelmine mothers and daughters, or established hostesses and brides to be, about what sort of porcelain to buy, where to purchase it, and how many pieces would be necessary or desirable. Although it is difficult to document directly, we can be sure that a great deal of porcelain "marketing" went on, informally and inadvertently, not in public shops, but in the comfort of the bourgeois home.

Porcelain in the High-Bourgeois Home

What role did porcelain play in the Wilhelmine and late Habsburg home? We have previously surveyed its uses in aristocratic courts and castles, where unique items or impressively large and highly decorated services were part of the mise-en-scène for princes exhibiting their ability to command the production of masterpieces. In the Biedermeier era, we saw porcelain used to externalize sentiments, to create an ambience of quiet domestic *Bildung*, guest friendship, and measured *Gemütlichkeit*. For the second half of the century, the first and most general observation we can make about porcelain in domestic settings is its ubiquity. The homes of the expanding middle and above-middling classes now featured porcelains in almost every room: in addition to the tableware displayed in the dining room, there were "china" dolls and tea sets in the nursery, dressing-table sets in the bedroom, inkstands and biscuit busts in the study, elaborate vases and touristic souvenirs in the parlor. Even the maids' rooms generally featured a faience or "hygienic ware" wash basin and ewer. Specially decorated or costly porcelains filled display cabinets or adorned holiday tables; "electrical" porcelains, formed into gas jet insulators or lampshades, served entirely utilitarian functions. Porcelain had become an essential component of the middle-class home.

Not surprisingly, it is the least-useful and least-used ornamental porcelains that are most often depicted or described in nineteenth-century art and literature. Paintings and photographs of domestic interiors usually depict not the more "private" and "utilitarian" rooms of the house such as the bedrooms or kitchens, but the sacred space of the parlor, often used by the family only when guests came to visit. In these images we are confronted with profusions of decorative objects, in which porcelain vases, figurines, or ornamental plates are part of a rhetoric of consumerist excess, meant by the homeowners to show the breadth and richness (if not the refinement) of their taste (see again fig. 7.2). Porcelains appear on walls, alongside books and clocks, mirrors and framed pictures, inhabiting rooms furnished with clunky furniture, oriental carpets, gilt wallpapers, heavy curtains, and the increasingly indispensable piano. In contrast to Biedermeier interiors, relatively uncluttered and with painted, rather than papered walls, these parlors seem dark and overcrowded; biscuit porcelains and other objets d'art are often covered with glass bells to prevent their smudging with fireplace soot or coal dust. Contemporary novelists, understanding their rhetoric better than we do, evoked these porcelains as symbols of absurd bourgeois exhibitionism; they are epitomized by the Sèvres inkwell, made in the shape of a black-spotted hunting dog, that graces the family salon in Thomas Mann's *Buddenbrooks*.

All across Europe, families frequently spent as much on furnishings for the special guest spaces—the parlor and the dining room—as they did for equipping the rest of the house.[37] Similarly, a family might spend a great deal of money on an elaborate porcelain service, but this, like the "good" silver, would be used only on special occasions. A Hungarian novelist nicely sketched the fin de siècle bourgeois family's reverent tending of its fine tableware: "The silver was kept in a cupboard, like the scrolls of the Torah in their ark. The silver was never used on ordinary occasions, just as the damask tablecloths and the best porcelain weren't either. Everything was saved up, according to the household's secret code, for use on some unfathomable, unimaginable special feast-day, when the table would be laid for twenty-four." When the silver and porcelains were used, the novelist continued, the specialness of the objects actually cast a pall over proceedings, leading guests to worry about their table manners rather than enjoying the company and the meal.[38] Prohibited from playing in parlors, children were endlessly warned about touching items displayed in etageres and taught to be very careful with their teacups. The very fragility of porcelain acted as a means to "civilize" and discipline the middle-class body.

The other great space for Wilhelmine porcelain to show itself was the dining room. As Claudia Kreklau has argued, food was an essential means for middle-class Germans to demonstrate their class status,[39] and in this period, their meals diverged more than ever before from those of the working class, who subsisted on diets of bread, beer, potatoes, and coffee, with meat (often horse) and butter and milk being additional luxuries. The working classes increasingly had their own pubs, canteens, and *Würst* peddlers, but they had no dining rooms, and little use for cookbooks, as soups were made from what was in the larder. For the middling classes, on the other hand, meals had become more extravagant, ingredients more various, and concerns about nutritious preparation and tasteful presentation more pressing. Many more people now ate dessert or served afternoon cake and coffee. Already in 1852, one cookbook included more than twenty pages of instructions on carving animals from *Auerhuhn* (wood grouse) to *Ziege* (goat),[40] and the sixth edition (1872) of Henriette Davidis's enormously popular *Die Hausfrau: Praktische Anleitung* offered recipes for twenty-one kinds of soup, twenty-three vegetable dishes, twenty-one sorts of fruit juices and jellies, and eight flavors of pancakes.[41] Naturally, most people did not eat multicourse meals every day, but when they did, or when guests appeared, setting a good table to show off these comestibles would have been essential. Everyone's plates would need to match throughout multicourse meals served *à la russe*. This is the porcelain Germans would later remember as inextricably linked with family life and special occasions, and with the mothers and grandmothers who made the meals (or commanded the servants) and saw that the table was properly set. Family memories were made in these dining rooms, memories in which porcelain became intrinsic to the middle-class idea of "home."

The great domestic spaces for porcelain, then, were the salon and the dining room. Porcelains seem to often have been stored in the kitchen and categorized as "Küchengeräte" (kitchenwares), as wonderfully depicted in one gloriously overequipped Wilhelmine dollhouse kitchen (plate 13). But this was not the context in which Wilhelmine porcelain truly belonged. Where servants worked, or the lady of the house slaved over a hot stove, was no place for display, nor for fragile vessels; what was needed here were iron and copper pots, stoneware jugs, tin utensils. Kitchens, too, it has been shown, were often the last place in the house to be redecorated or modernized, especially because labor in central Europe remained very cheap, and there was little incentive to install labor-saving devices, or to beautify them.[42] All of this presumes that homeowners had separate kitchens to cook in, which was not the case for the many who rented one-room dwellings or rural cottages, some still with open hearths. Although some makers experimented with ovenproof porcelains, for the most part, porcelain did not belong to the work of cooking, but to the joy of sipping, feasting, and display.

Moving on to the more private spaces of the home, we can note the continuing gendered segregation of porcelain forms and styles. In the study, the private preserve of the paterfamilias, and off-limits to those who spent the most hours at home, the wife, children, and servants, one would be more likely to find items intended exclusively for male pursuits, such as pipes or writing accoutrements, or "educational" porcelains: biscuit busts of Greek philosophers or German poets, for example. Here, in keeping with the ideals of the male-only classical gymnasium, Renaissance and classical styles dominated, and men were told to choose dark, serious colors,[43] against which white porcelain gleamed all the more brightly. The feminine and "emotional" space of the bedroom would certainly hold items to be used in grooming—brushes, makeup containers, washbasins, and chamber pots—the toilette, as it were, of "Venus." For this room, couples were advised to choose rococo, with its feminine "curves," rather than classical or modern styles. It was Saxon porcelain—meaning "third rococo"—specifically that a leading vendor recommended for the perfectly outfitted modern German boudoir.[44]

As we have seen, even as it took on more and more utilitarian functions, porcelain for the Wilhelmine consumer remained connected to display if not to artistry, to refinement, and to domestic bliss. Purchases of ornamental wares, in particular, took on private significations, connected deeply with family life and middle-class respectability. For some, owning items made by the local manufactory, or by the KPM and Meissen, which now functioned as something like national brands, added a layer of patriotic pride to bourgeois sentimentalism. These emotional and patriotic associations helped to keep the higher-end makers in business, even as lower-end mass producers engaged in rapacious underselling. They also reinforced the traditional firms' belief in their duty to reflect the nation's (or the region's) refinement and to prevent mass production from destroying public taste. But how to get these messages out, and how to pay for taste-instructing masterpieces now that princely patronage was largely gone, and the courts were no longer the places taste was made? The art of porcelain would need another raison d'être, and another public venue. The best option was the most prominent international showcase of the age, the world's fair.

Porcelain Goes to the (World's) Fair

When I gaze, amazed, at "porcelain,"

Its great tradition fills me with pride!

For even apart from Baroque etiquette

It is a noble art of true distinction.

Only perhaps today at Sèvres

Is the craft so "royal" as in the firms

That spread our fame across the seas.

Ah, that makes me think of the proud days

Of the long-forgotten Napoleonic age

Whose elegance no longer pleases!

That we paint much better than in previous times

I have, to my joy, learned here.

But I will stick with cheaper faience

In a friendly *belle alliance*

As our potters even in the far, far North

Have themselves become "artists."[45]

—*Max Rusticus (aka Max Bauer), light verses composed in
honor of the 1896 Berlin Industrial Exhibition*

The title of this section is a bit misleading: since its reinvention, European porcelain had *always* gone to the fair—indeed, one can almost say that the European porcelain industry was *born* at the fair, as it was at the Leipzig fair in 1710 that Augustus the Strong announced the founding of the Royal Saxon manufactory. The Leipzig fair—held three times a year—was the great showplace and wholesale emporium for porcelain for most of the eighteenth century, although it soon could be purchased at factory shops, at outlets, and from commissioned merchants and peddlers, at auctions, and finally in department stores. Of course, there were also many more local and regional fairs that brought together producers and wholesalers or retailers, and that continues to be the case down to the present day. But the nineteenth-century international exhibitions added a new wrinkle to porcelain promotion. For one thing, these were visited by many more people, most of them—as the poem above suggests—just admiring the beautiful pieces rather than buying them. The world exhibitions were much more important for the advertising of national achievements, and for the individual firms, for the reiteration of their artistic bona fides, than for the selling of products (for which the Leipzig fair remained crucial).[46] But these less tangible functions were no trivial matter, and firms continued to care deeply about their showings at the world's fair even though marketing, for the most part, took place elsewhere.

For the manufacturers, the fair was an opportunity to demonstrate not what sold most, but their latest models and designs, and their "Prunkstücke," or special display pieces. As one image of the KPM booth at the 1900 fair shows (fig. 7.3), the items displayed were often large and complex, pieces such as elaborately ornamented vases too enormous to hold any real flowers, or figurines too large for any normal vitrine. Although many manufactories made few figurines or services with modernist designs, a disproportional number of these were shown at the fairs. The intent, here, was to document the manufactories' commitment to principles beyond pure sales, something especially crucial for the state firms that billed themselves as *Kunstanstalten*. As exhibits were judged by expert juries and discussed extensively in newspapers and magazines, those who won prizes or acclaim could feel justified in their commitment to aesthetic principles and modern design even if these items failed to sell. Of course, there was risk here as well, as a poor showing at an exhibition usually meant additional heat from one's finance ministry and local arts community. Even Sèvres, treated to terrible reviews at the

7.3. KPM booth, 1900 World Exhibition
Every manufactory's exhibition booth sought to demonstrate the firm's artistic and technical mastery. State makers such as the KPM (whose 1900 World Exhibition space is depicted here) were under additional pressure to demonstrate their nation's talents and taste.

1889 exhibition, faced parliamentary refusal to renew its funding; although a vigorous artists' campaign saved it, the manufactory had to promise to reorganize.[47] Royal Copenhagen enjoyed the opposite experience, as its 1886 exhibits elevated its reputation far above its earlier status.[48] In any event, the fair played a crucial role in the industry's self-understanding as well as in maintaining, for the state institutions, the public image that made continued official support viable.

Pressed to emphasize money making rather than artistry, our German manufacturers generally found the nineteenth-century world's fairs mortifying.

Organized by Prince Albert, the Crystal Palace Exhibition of 1851 was meant to show off *British* goods and *British* progress, as indeed it did. It did not do much for German and Austrian manufacturers, who ended up chastened at having their "backwardness" exposed. Though Meissen received high marks for the whiteness of its paste, its artistry was criticized, both by connoisseurs and by the Finance Ministry. The KPM fared even worse. Thanks to their financial travails, Nymphenburg and the WPM were unable to mount exhibits; Sèvres and the English maker Minton carried off the prizes. Meissen showed poorly, too, at an 1854 trade show, but reviews were more positive in 1862 and 1873. One observer judged the KPM's 1873 assortment "stupid"; the official report more gently suggested that they were overly classicizing and lacked the imagination of the French.[49] At the Philadelphia World's Fair in 1876, an official German observer deemed all his nation's products "cheap and bad" as well as ridiculously militaristic. Judging by this exhibit, he wrote, Germany's contribution to the decorative arts amounted to a great number of "marching Germans, Borussians, emperors, Crown Princes . . . in porcelain, in biscuit, in bronze, in zinc, in iron, formed up precisely in battalions."[50]

Thus, just as the industry's sales soared, the critics sharpened their quills, carrying over exhibition critiques into more general attacks on German ceramic artistry. In 1879, Friedrich Jaennicke, writing a comprehensive history of ceramics that he billed as "a reliable guide for Connoisseurs, Collectors, Manufacturers, Modelers, and Trade Schools," attacked Germanic majolica imitations, which were characterized by "a very striking dullness and insipidity in form and color, qualities which together with great tastelessness still in many ways characterize German decorative arts as a whole." This is not a secret within many workshops, the author argued; "although such comments are mostly avoided as their expression in the press and in public forums in general is considered unpatriotic, and to the detriment of our industries, the truth is partly silenced, and partly whitewashed." As concerns the porcelain industry specifically, Jaennicke argued, the Germans had preferred mass production and technical improvements to the tastefulness pursued by, for example, Sèvres. "That tasteless cannot be replaced by patriotism,"

Jaennicke continued, "does not need further elaboration here." But he admitted that other than Sèvres, French porcelain too was unimpressive; the 1878 Paris Exhibition had comprised too much sappy stuff, paintings after the sentimental academician William-Adolphe Bouguereau or rehashings of Watteau and Boucher, and female biscuit nudes, "depicted in more or less coquettish, self-conscious positions, which even in the most exemplary sculptures so clearly separate them from the antiquities which they otherwise resemble."[51] The critic was more generous to German faience makers, bearing out our poet's observation that the wise consumer might just as well buy the cheaper stuff.

One of the sensations of the 1873 Vienna Exhibition—aside from the cholera epidemic that ruined its attendance—was the display of Japanese decorative arts. Japanese influence on the fine arts had commenced in the 1860s, in France, where writers and artists praised the simplicity and technical refinement of Japanese woodcuts, textiles, lacquer, and ceramics. The Vienna Exhibition played an important role in the spread of Japonisme, inspiring manufactories to seek a more naturalistic style and deeper, richer colors. The KPM took to it relatively quickly and earned praise for East Asian–inspired glazes in 1889 (though afterward its artistic fortunes dipped again until restored somewhat under the leadership of the Jugendstil designer Theo Schmuz-Baudiss after 1908). Meissen was largely untouched by Japonisme, and in any case it could not exhibit between 1885 and 1900, the period in which KPM and Royal Copenhagen impressed the judges. Meissen exhibited 1,239 items in Paris in 1900, only about fifty of them modern in design.[52] Alongside its Jugendstil works it featured *Prunkstücke* of a different sort: a four-meter-tall mirror adorned with Apollo and the muses, more Kändler reproductions, and a crucifixion scene. Naturally, the critics denounced the firm for its backwardness. "However," as a savvy commentator remarked, "the then-director resignedly confirmed the timeworn practicality that the Meissen factory, still today, has to attend more closely to the wishes of its customers and patrons than to those of the critics, who in general never buy anything."[53]

There were, however, benefits to the obligation to exhibit. The need to produce *Prunkstücke* and to make a good showing meant that for these occasions manufactories could invest some extra time and money in artistic and technical innovation—or at least in trying to catch up with the other firms' innovations. Exhibitions, more than anything else, nudged central European firms to respond to the dawning of various antihistoricist movements: art nouveau, Jugendstil, and modernism. They also played an important role in cross-pollinating the decorative arts and disseminating across them a passion for the creation of *Gesamtkunstwerken*, unified arts programs and living spaces, in which textiles, paintings, ceramics, and metalwork combined to form harmonious living spaces. By no means accepting that tableware had to be cheap and banal, Josef Hoffmann and Joseph Maria Olbrich, founders of the Viennese Secession and then the Wiener Werkstätte, designed ceramics as well as buildings, furniture, and silverware, as did the inhabitants of Darmstadt's fin de siècle colony. Even as we emphasize the increasing importance of utilitarian wares for the porcelain industry in the later chapters of this book, it is important to remember the alternative story underlined in so many museums and catalogs: that ceramics making remained an art, and that exciting innovations continued—and today continue!—to be made. Although this section must necessarily be brief—particularly as so many real experts in the ceramic arts have written specialized monographs on the subject—we cannot overlook the fact that even as it took on the malleability and affordability almost of today's plastic, porcelain remained, as well, a form of art.

The Advent of Avant-Garde Ceramics

The need to demonstrate artistic innovation at the fair and to critics led to the widening of practices employed earlier in the century, in which well-known artists were commissioned to make models for the manufactories. These commissioned works were now explicitly credited to the artist-designer, though they were not necessarily one-of-a-kind pieces. Some were made to be mass-produced; others were made in small batches. To extend the market for artists' pieces, at Royal Copenhagen carefully trained women were tasked with copying high-end artistic creations. These were sold at a more modest price than the original, which was distinguished by the artist's signature.[54] Collaborations between artists and the manufactory were never easy, but they did result in some splendid works for display and in fodder for art historians of the future.

Space allows the invoking of just a few examples of this collaboration, which was attempted by all the high-profile manufacturers, and some of the middle-range producers as well. Founded in 1881, Gebrüder Bauscher Porzellan had profited from selling to hotels, railroads, and shipping lines and by 1900 employed 294 workers. By this time, the firm had in fact hived off its hotel branch, opening a works in Weiden. This factory developed a partnership with several important Jugendstil artists, including Peter Behrens and J. M. Olbrich, who were experimenting with interior design at the artists' colony on the Mathildenhöhe in Darmstadt. More industrially oriented than many, this group had some commercial success, for example with Behrens's six- and eight-sided saucers, which lent themselves to use as hotel ashtrays.[55]

Less commercially successful were the Jugendstil animals made under KPM director Alexander Kips, many of which languished in the warehouse.[56] But the KPM had its most embarrassing experience with modernism in the Wedding Procession group commissioned from Adolf Amberg, and intended for display at the nuptials of Prussian Crown Prince Frederick William and Duchess Cecilie of Mecklenburg-Schwerin. The kaiser rejected the elaborate twenty-piece set of figures, which, apart from its Jugendstil flavor, featured too much nudity for his taste; admittedly, the father of the groom might have found the (topless) depiction of the bride as Europa riding a bull a bit racy for a wedding table.[57] But Wilhelm II disapproved of artistic modernism in general—preferring history and genre paintings—and harbored a wider set of animosities toward KPM art director Theo Schmuz-Baudiss. The kaiser remained a relentless critic of his own manufactory's attempts to innovate. In 1916, he insisted that the KPM return to historical models and remove modernist pieces from its Leipzigerstrasse showroom. As it happens, Schmuz-Baudiss got the last laugh. He kept his job longer than did Wilhelm II, and his successors were, first, a champion of art déco, and then a founding member of the Werkbund.[58]

7.4. Van de Velde chocolate service

Belgian art nouveau master Henry van de Velde designed this service for Meissen, but it proved to be difficult for the manufactory to make and unpopular with customers, who preferred "Alt-Meissen."

In surveys of the history of art porcelain, the most often featured artistic-industrial coproduction are Henry van de Velde pieces made for the Meissen manufactory. Just after the turn of the century, Meissen commissioned the Belgian art nouveau designer with the modeling of a modern service that, it hoped, might replace the now universally imitated Blue Onion pattern. Although van de Velde's resulting designs are often displayed in museums and art catalogs, descriptions here usually do not dwell on the original difficulties and disappointments of this partnership. After two years of development and wrangling over artistic control, van de Velde's service was released—to the critics' disappointment and the public's disapproval; the spare, linear decoration may please connoisseurs now, but at the time simply looked like cheap, machine-generated printing[59] (fig. 7.4). Critics, accurately, attacked the service for failing the test of truth to materials: the plates were so difficult to fire properly that three dozen had to be fired in the hopes that one dozen would be salable.[60] A new commission given to Richard Riemerschmid in 1903 achieved somewhat better success. But the experience discouraged the Meisseners from inviting more outside commissions, as, its administration explained,

> the resources of the manufactory are greatly burdened by these experiments and too many unsalable products are created. We must also mention in this connection that normal production and commercial operations are encumbered by an overabundance of artistic experiments and by the introduction of all too many foreign elements, particularly when the experimenting artists are familiar neither with the fundamental properties of the materials nor with the methods of manufacturing.[61]

For Meissen, making modern art, in short, did not pay.

A final example of collaboration between art and industry points up the evolution of some new dimensions of this relationship. In this case, our focus falls on a private firm, now officially known as Porzellanfabrik Ph. Rosenthal & Co. AG, headquartered in the Franconian town of Selb. The firm's founder, Philipp Rosenthal, whom we met in chapter 5, had from the first aspired to the production of at least relatively good quality decorated wares and paid close attention to consumers' desires. As a leading member of the makers' cartel, he was instrumental in obtaining pricing agreements and in imposing the *Revers* on dealers. But Rosenthal was also ahead of other private producers in adopting Jugendstil models and high-temperature glazes, for which the firm was praised at the 1900 Paris World's Fair.[62] Between 1900 and 1908, the restless entrepreneur made several contradictory moves: on the one hand, he established an "electro-technical" department ("E") and purchased Thomas, a maker of inexpensive household porcelain located in Marktredwitz, near Selb. On the other, he established an art studio, which was to employ artists—though not the most famous ones—in the designing of high-profile models.

Rosenthal was deeply serious in his desire to cultivate porcelain as an art, and he was willing to undertake losses in this department for the sake of giving his firm a modern face and restoring its artistic credentials. But it is part of Rosenthal's genius that he also recognized the usefulness of the art department as a form of PR and made its products central to his advertising campaigns of the interwar era. The work of this department rarely, if ever, met its costs; but he had Thomas and the electrical porcelains to cover that. While commissioning modern artworks, he continued to produce neo-rococo services with names such as Versailles, Pompadour, and Sanssouci. In a way, Rosenthal had finally squared the porcelain manufacturers' circle, and made possible the marriage of *Kunst* and *Kommerz* by foregrounding the artistic pieces while making money on humdrum sales. In Rosenthal's wake, others would extend and embellish his practices, none more successfully than his son, Philip (with one *p*), who would repossess and revive Rosenthal Porcelain in the post-1950 period (see chapter 9).[63]

One might say that what Rosenthal pioneered was something like an early form of corporate image advertising, using the more idealistic branch of his business to stand for, and in part to cover over, the more mundane sides of its operations, as do many high-fashion designers today.[64] Rosenthal's design investments occluded not only the making of electrical parts, but also the strong-armed sales techniques the entrepreneur exerted, both as president of the Manufacturers' Cartel and as director of his own firm. Even in the making of his art line, Rosenthal drove a very hard bargain; he was no fan of artistic autonomy and certainly was not willing to kowtow to self-important artists. He was also uncompromising with respect to advertising and marketing, to the dismay of retailers. To ensure his art items were properly displayed, Rosenthal insisted that sellers feature his wares in shop windows, separating clearly the utilitarian and the artistic items. In some cases he tried to force stores to call themselves "Niederlage der Porzellanfabrik Rosenthal & Cie.," and to sell nothing but his products. If the shop owners refused, he threatened to stop supplying the business, and instead to set up his own competing outlets nearby.[65] It is sad, though perhaps telling, to note that the squaring of art and commerce, at least in this case, also required a considerable amount of coercion.

The Porcelain Industry and the
Arts and Crafts Movement

We are in a good position now to understand some of the complexities of the relationship between the porcelain industry and the various arts and crafts organizations that made the struggle against mass production and the return to craftsmanship and truth to materials their rallying cry in the second half of the nineteenth century. Naturally, a great deal has been written about these movements in their particular contexts, but rarely, if ever, has the story been told from the perspective of their antagonists, the mass-producing manufacturers. For our purposes, we will have to lump together movements led by the architect and theorist of ornament Gottfried Semper, and the architects, artists, and theorists of the German Werkbund and Austrian Wiener Werkstätte, something that does not do justice to the particular criticisms of these reformers and their considerable artistic achievements, or to the excellence of the many art historical works dedicated to each of them. But as far as the industry was concerned, all these reform movements posed the same sort of threat, as well as inspiration.

Opinions varied among these theorists on the extent to which artists could and should work with industry to improve the objects of everyday existence. Like Semper, most art reformers of the fin de siècle emphasized the importance of basic forms, defined by usefulness as well as truth to materials and "honest" methods of fabrication.[66] A unified style was, in their view, the sign of a healthy, organic culture, one that eschewed the vulgarities of mere historicism and the miscegenation of materials (in porcelain wares painted to look like malachite, for example). They were not opposed to working with the state to create craft training schools or artistic institutes that would improve the nation's taste and manufactures—mercantilism with a modern twist. Some were eager to partner with industry; but they largely envisioned coproductions as ones in which the artists made the designs to be carried out and marketed by the manufactories, which would, presumably, then stop making and selling vulgar goods in retro styles. Already in his extensive discussion of ceramics in volume 2 of *Der Stil in den technischen und tektonischen Künsten* (1863), Semper made a number of these key points. He championed the Greek vase, its utility, form and decoration in harmony, and derided the products of the modern factories, their gloss-gilding, for example, "so superficial that one can lick it off with the tongue." He protested the manufactories' adoption of inferior materials, the discounting of handwork in their attempts to trim costs, and the use of technical advances merely to enable "blind imitation" of past models.[67] And he lamented that in his day, porcelain certainly "did not arise from the people and had no influence on them."[68]

Aside from this curious last statement, to which we will return, we can now see how much Semper's comments reflected the true state of the porcelain factories, without any appreciation, however, of the financial constraints that had forced them into precisely this situation. His views were entirely reflective of the worldview of the artists the manufactories had once employed, and now commissioned, to create masterpieces that they hoped would restore the makers' claims to artistic value—not surprisingly, as the young Semper himself had been just such an artist (see chapter 5). His critiques were entirely representative, too, of those artists' failures to take seriously customers' actual tastes and the limitations imposed by the materials and technical capacities of the factories. Small wonder, then, that Georg Kolbe, director of the KPM, was deeply vexed by Semper's critiques of his industry in *Der Stil*. What Semper did not understand, Kolbe wrote in 1863, was that "the real state of things"—that is, the modern economy—made mockery of Semper's organic ideal of art. Decorative arts producers, and especially ceramics makers, could not possibly follow Semper's rules and still please the public; and without pleasing the public, the KPM and others could not continue to produce, among their wares, the artistic works that Semper championed. Were his factory to seek a unified style, and to produce only Greek or Chinese forms, Kolbe wrote, "almost the entirety of the whole modern porcelain art-world would fall into ruins."[69] The artists might turn up their noses at historicism; but if the public wanted it, the manufactories, including the state *Kunstanstalten*, were going to have to give it to them. Only after pleasing the customers could they afford to patronize "art."

Semper's critique of faux luxuriousness, style eclecticism, and lack of truth to materials, then, was on the mark as far as the ceramics industry of his day, and criticisms of this sort continued to be voiced in slightly varying forms down to at least 1914. But Semper and later arts and crafts reformers seem never to have appreciated something the manufacturers kept trying to tell them: "the people" *desired* diversity, and *wanted* to buy pieces that appeared luxurious, even if the gloss-gilding could be licked off. The manufactories had not directed taste in this direction; indeed, many of them had tried to resist consumers' demand for "English articles" and "Alt-Meissen" figurines. Since at least the 1830s, state producers in particular had been engaged in a desperate attempt to maintain their mercantile and aesthetic values, and to raise the level of public taste, at the same time as financial necessities forced them to adapt older craft techniques to new cost-saving means of production and to produce a wide array of choices for price-sensitive consumers. Their bookkeepers and ministerial minders, at least, had realized relatively early on that they could go on producing exemplary works of art, such as Semper's own neo-Renaissance vase (fig. 5.2), only if they produced a large number of gloss-gilded baroque tea sets and doll heads as well. Semper, as a theoretician, could ignore the market, but the manufacturers could not—and nor should we ignore it, if we are to understand why *Der Stil* and other reformers' treatises struck men like Kolbe and even Rosenthal as idealistic, rather than practicable, treatments of the decorative arts.

Founded in 1907, the Deutscher Werkbund was formed by artists willing to work with industry in the service of improving modern German design. Its work—possibly because it received state patronage—did result in the production of some exquisite modern products and in the upgrading of the prestige of the "made in Germany" label. But the Werkbund, too, pursued a grand-scale design-reform program, championing the redemption of art and culture from the fallenness of the modern age by the overcoming of stylistic diversity. As for Semper, the idea was to recreate the conditions of spiritual harmony and cultural unity that had (allegedly) prevailed in the era before historicism fractured the modern soul. As Hermann Muthesius, one of the founders, wrote in 1902: "Earlier there had been no styles, merely a single predominant artistic tendency to which everything was subordinated in a perfectly natural way. Not until the nineteenth century was mankind banished from this artistic paradise, having eaten from the tree of historical knowledge. Then people divided themselves into supporters of the *different* styles."[70] In arguing for *Sachlichkeit*, a concept that embraced truth to materials and the avoidance of unnecessary decoration, the Werkbund hoped to drive out cheap imitations and teach consumers to appreciate functionality and elegant design. Aesthetically Muthesius's disdain for "parvenu taste" and overly ornamented "pretentious junk"[71] may have been fair enough—and generally art historians have sympathized with his abhorrence of historicist mass production. But, like Semper, Muthesius could not convince even Meissen or Rosenthal, much less Tielsch or Kahla, to devote themselves exclusively to one, modern style. Rather than instigating a return to artistic paradise, to do so, they knew all too well, would have resulted in financial suicide.

The manufactories could travel some distance with the Werkbund and its later offshoots, such as the Bauhaus. As we have seen, they did on occasion commission works from these artists.[72] Partnerships worked somewhat better in the 1920s, when some artists embraced the idea of making mass-producible forms, and a larger number of consumers embraced modern, functional design. But manufacturers could not share artists' contempt for consumers' desires or allow the artists to dictate production. Long experience, the tutelage of the finance ministries, and the punishing experience of the ever-changing market had taught even the state firms to accept the "fallen" conditions of the present.

There was no going back to the artisanal world artists idealized. Indeed, the eclecticism that had always been part of porcelain production became even more crucial as the consumer marketplace widened. It was inspiring to be urged to develop a unified, modern style; but it would never be possible for modern manufactories to implement such a thing in a capitalist marketplace. Competition and the relentless search for new buyers had created what the great English design critic Charles Eastlake called "the lust of profusion that is the bane of modern design."[73] Ironically, perhaps, the lesson of mass production was the persistence of the diversity of tastes. Ultimately, then, it was less artistic modernism that transformed the porcelain industry than an event that most workers and employers, focused on more proximate problems, could not have foreseen: the outbreak of the Great War.

The Great War

From the perspective of just a few years onward, of course, these prewar conflicts over style came to seem quaint and insignificant, for by early August 1914, Europe had thrown itself headlong into world war. The greatness of the Great War lay not only in the colossal quantities of suffering inflicted on so many populations and individuals, but also in its empire-shattering effects, bringing down, as it eventually did, the Russian, German, Austrian, and Ottoman imperial regimes. The war also had a tide-turning effect on the world economy; Great Britain, which had been losing market share since the 1880s or 1890s but was still the commercial world leader in 1914, by 1918 had became a debtor, as were all the other European nations. Germany, which had been advancing impressively in industrial output, quite suddenly was plunged into terrible financial straits, exacerbated by heavy reparations payments. The upstart United States emerged as the most powerful of the creditors; Russia collapsed in communist revolution. It is impossible, in a few sentences, to capture the experience and impact of these long, terrible years of starvation, privation, pain, anger, and grief on the German population; it will have to suffice, here, to quote Sigmund Freud, who, only six months into the conflict, observed that the war "hurls down in blind rage whatever bars its way, as though there were to be no future and no peace after it is over."[74] At the time Freud made this sorrowful comment he could have no inkling that the war had almost another *four years* to run.

Quite apart from its devastating impact on central European lives and political regimes, the Great War had a series of powerful cultural and economic effects, but in the porcelain industry, as elsewhere, it chiefly accelerated earlier trends rather than creating a full break with past practices. Most obviously, with so many men called up for service, a severe shortage of skilled labor set in, and the female labor force swelled. Domestic sales dropped, and the Allied blockade, so painfully effective in limiting imports of foodstuffs, also cut off access to the all-important American export market. The state took over control of coal supplies and not surprisingly gave preference to those producing technical porcelains for military purposes, perhaps most urgent of which were fittings for field telephones.[75] Raw material costs rose. Manufacturers tried to offset dramatic falls in consumer purchases by producing patriotic plates and figurines, or, more lucratively, by retooling for technical and munitions production. Hutschenreuther, for example, willingly took up war production in order to keep some of its skilled workers on hand, and to be ensured a proper supply of coal; Rosenthal opened a chemical-technical department ("C") in 1915 and made mine covers, cartridge boxes, and parts for hand grenades.[76] The KPM contributed its share for the armaments industry; Waldsassen made sanitary wares for hospitals.[77] By the war's end, Nymphenburg had put 75 percent of its capacity into war work.[78] Meissen, whose sales immediately fell by half, pursued quite a different tack and took the opportunity of slumping orders to complete its three-floor museum, shoring up for the future the historical reputation of the firm, and its indispensable contributions to regional tourism and cultural pride.

All the manufactories, but perhaps especially the state manufactories, saw the war as an opportunity to advertise their patriotism and to capitalize on the loyalties of their consumers. Myriad commemorative plates and cups were made saluting the Austrian and German kaisers or depicting Iron Crosses and oak leaves; Germania and the German "Michael" also appear (plate 14). Some of this commemorative work would continue after the war itself, when manufactories had more materials to work with. It is doubtful that these items were great sellers during the war itself—and certainly were no replacement for the tourist wares and commemorative items made for local associations whose activities were suspended during the war. But patriotic endorsement gave the manufactories a means to contribute to the war effort and to revive, for a new market, their long-standing tradition of celebrating monarchs and military leaders.

For workers, the war spelled disaster, especially in its first months, before retooling for war production occurred. Military service depleted the ranks;

at Lorenz Hutschenreuther, the proportion of male to female employees fell from 53 to 36 percent in the war's first two years—though this would climb back steeply after 1918.[79] Women were compelled to fill positions requiring heavy labor; by one estimate, women employed in the capsule-making departments might have found themselves lifting as much as 33,530 pounds a day.[80] But the larger story is the winnowing of the workforce overall. Firms that had already been operating on a very thin margin struggled to keep skilled employees on the payroll even when shortages in raw materials halted production.[81] A report on employment conditions in the northern Bavarian region in January 1915, for example, described industry conditions as ranging from full stoppage to cuts in hours and pay averaging about 50 percent.[82] Rosenthal, which had employed 1,336 workers in 1913, paid only 1,056 in 1916; Lorenz Hutschenreuther's workforce fell from 913 to 531 in the same period.[83] Many smaller plants closed, at least temporarily, or severely cut back working hours, both calamitous for families dependent on full-time wages.

The factories complained loudly and asked the war ministry to come to the aid of their suffering workers, as well as to release from service badly needed skilled craftsmen and bookkeepers. The military bureaucracy was occasionally willing to oblige, agreeing, in one memo, to substitute porcelain for stoneware in hospitals and garrison houses. "The continuation of these factories should be supported by the state not only for the good of the war effort, as they employ many workers and officials but also in light of the position this industry has achieved, with great difficulty, in the world market," wrote one obliging War Ministry official.[84] But of course it was war matériel, not tableware, the ministries really cared about, and most factories prioritized, and it was really only by shifting production in this direction that many were able to survive the war.

War conditions naturally also cut deeply into domestic demand, especially for luxury items, putting pressure on retailers to lower prices. The situation exacerbated preexisting tensions between sellers and the Manufacturers' Cartel, which, we must remember, had insisted on price floors for its members' goods before the war. In 1915, however, wartime pressures led to a fierce conflict between the Retailers' Cartel (Reichsverband deutscher Spezialge-schäfte in Porzellan, Glas, Haus-, und Küchengeräte) and the Union of Por-celain Manufacturers.[85] In August of that year, the Retailers' Cartel an-nounced that the *Revers* was no longer tenable; non-cartel suppliers, they argued, offered the same goods for half of the *Revers* price. The department stores were already cheating on *Revers* agreements and trading with these makers, too, allowing them to undersell the small merchants. Moreover some smaller factories, they claimed, wanted out of the cartel (now com-posed of sixty-four members), so that they could lower their prices, and compete with the larger firms. Positioning themselves as the advocates of small businessmen and consumers, the retailers now set their sights on break-ing up the cartel.

By the year's end the situation had grown critical; 1,150 (of a total of about fifteen hundred) dealers had renounced the *Revers*, though Rosenthal, as the cartel's head, had refused to negotiate until the war was over, and threatened legal action. While the sellers claimed to be taking the part of the consumer, the cartel charged the sellers with endangering the wartime "civil peace." Infuriated by this assault on their patriotism, the retailers responded:

> consideration for the common good here is deployed as a slogan, which the P.Z. [Porzellanverband] is using only to cloak its obviously *purely ego-centric interests*. If one wants to speak at all about the destruction of a branch of the economy, then it is better to refer to the more than distressed situation of the *dealers*, who, in order to have possibility of continuing to exist and to be able even to barely maintain their competitiveness with the department stories, *are compelled to do away with minimum prices*.... To see in this desire a *disruption of the civil peace* is more than frivolous; in any case the civil peace has been disrupted: But *only* by the selfish ac-tions of the Porzellanverband and its president. [86]

This fierce fight would continue throughout the war, resulting in a new se-ries of complaints not only by sellers, but by Meissen, Nymphenburg, and the KPM, backed by the Prussian Trade Ministry, in the last months of the war.[87] The retailers did not succeed in fully dismantling the Manufacturers'

Cartel, but the battle deeply embittered market relations and made the cartel's policies difficult to enforce once the war had ended.

In fact, as the war ground on and manufactories severely curtailed production for the consumer market, shortages began to be felt and sales increased. Perhaps by 1916–17 women were eager to buy something that reminded them of the days before self-sacrifice for the national good became a way of life; perhaps precisely because foodstuffs were so rigorously rationed, some measure of income could now be diverted into the purchasing of household durables. As the Waldsassen director commented in early 1917, "Demand grows every day. A great volume of painted wares are now being sold, which were never desired before."[88] Factories began adding more hours, and some to show healthy sales. In the year of the third battle of Ypres and the Russian revolutions, Fürstenberg—now under private management—made 60,000 M, its largest profit in fifty years.[89] Schönwald, to give one more example, having lost significant sums in 1914–16, turned a small profit in 1917, and a much larger one in 1918.[90]

But as sales recovered, pressure on wages and the expression of workers' pent-up grievances created chaotic conditions on shop floors. With so many men dead or fighting at the front, skilled workers were in ever shorter supply, forcing up wages. In the war's last stages, women, in particular, tired of food shortages and rationing practices, fueling episodes of unrest in various porcelain-producing towns and huge increases in the membership of workers' associations.[91] In May 1918, industry leaders and porcelain workers began negotiating their first pan-industrial contractual agreement on minimum wage levels, the length of the workweek, policies on termination, and fines for damaged wares; the agreement came into force in December and resulted in a 25 percent pay increase for workers, one of the few triumphs of the workers' association.[92] But these gains were wiped out by wildly increasing food prices, which in one of the porcelain-producing centers amounted to rises of 132 percent for bread, 160 percent for potatoes, and a whopping 250 percent for beef and pork over prices paid in 1914.[93]

Motivated by new demand as well as by rising labor, energy, and raw materials costs, firms began to increase prices exponentially, resulting in complaints to state officials about profiteering, a minor worry but one that echoes the much more volatile conspiracy theories circulating in the war's final years.[94] When the Reich's Economics Ministry was asked to investigate price gouging in the ceramics industry, it found that by 1918, the Theodor Paetsch Stoneware Company (Frankfurt an der Oder) had lifted prices 390 percent above those in 1914, and that its 1917 profit was already double that of 1913.[95] Dealers also began to complain about massive price rises as well, and state officials took this seriously enough to pursue extensive investigations into "real" production costs. Their inquiries, however, yielded a torrent of factories' angry denunciations of the daily rises in costs and fluctuations in coal supply, and claims that such calculations were impossible to make.[96] As *national* officials now sought to regulate the industry, another chapter in the fraught relationship between porcelain and the state bureaucracies begins; for the Weimar period, at least, it was not to be a happy one.

When the war ended at last on November 11, 1918, the prospects for the peace looked relatively rosy, even though all industry participants—workers, dealers, artists, small and large makers—regarded one another with more suspicion and perhaps hostility than ever before. The Wilhelmine world, with all its diversity, its hierarchies, and its conflicts, had been washed away in torrents of blood, sweat, toil, and tears, to borrow Winston Churchill's accurate prediction for what the next war would cost. The fin de siècle's "plastic" was still desired and needed, for electrical fixtures and explosives canisters as well as for coffeepots. But despite the efforts of the arts and crafts movement, the porcelain industry's reality, if not its advertised identity, had been divorced even further from the craft tradition. The political and economic volatility of the Weimar period would simply expose this reality, making evident to all the fact that porcelain, too, had become "big business." Returning to what in retrospect—*pace* Muthesius—now looked like a prewar "paradise" would prove to be more difficult than anyone could have imagined.

Porcelain's "second golden age" brought big profits, especially for private producers, who churned out an ever more diverse selection of goods. Although the increasingly industrialized techniques used to make ceramic vessels more and more affordable offended critics, the industry believed that its survival, not to mention its flourishing, depended on pleasing middle- or even lower-class buyers, in America as well as at home. As porcelain appeared in more and more forms, from doorknobs to insulator tubes, consumers began to look on this former delight of princes almost as a banality—as we today view plastic. Some private manufacturers were able to take this in stride, but state makers, in particular, could not. Meissen, the KPM, and Nymphenburg, in particular, faced political pressure to create modern artistic masterpieces, while also confronting a market that demanded they stick to old models. The Great War would put an end to this "golden age," but by no means resolve any of the contradictions inherent in the endurance of this mercantile luxury good in the age of capitalist mass production.

Chapter 8

The Fragility of Interwar Porcelain

The historical narrative of the Weimar Republic is often divided into three parts, with the first stretching from the proclamation of the republic in Weimar (and, simultaneously, in Berlin, of a workers' state) on November 9, 1918, to the implementation of the Dawes Plan, which ended the hyperinflation of 1922–23. These first postwar years were marked by the terrible suffering of widows, orphans, and veterans, and the equally palpable bitterness directed at Wilhelmine elites, Allied "peacemakers," "war profiteers" (including especially Jews), and Weimar officials who were blamed for their failure to make everyone whole.[1] The second period runs generally from 1924 to 1929 and features the stabilization of the economy and the flourishing of the literary and artistic movement known as the Neue Sachlichkeit ("The New Objectivity"), as well as of the architecture and design of the Bauhaus, the flowering of the raucous humor of the cabaret, and the advent of expressionist film. The final chapter begins quite suddenly, with the collapse of the American stock market on Black Tuesday (October 29, 1929) and finishes just as abruptly, with Hitler's swearing in as Reich chancellor, on January 30, 1933. As this very schematic overview suggests, political and economic history in this era go hand in hand, and both reveal an era of extreme pressures and painful experiences, as well as one of artistic experimentation, culminating in a cataclysmic political, economic, and cultural "revolution from the Right"—which did not, however, change everything, either.

This periodization helps us to organize our interwar story, and indeed porcelain's fate reflects rather well the extremes and uncertainties of this era. But we should also note longer-term trends and parallels. In fact, the era offers fascinating similarities to the other postwar era we studied closely in chapter 4: the Biedermeier era. Again in the 1920s producers had to deal with a radically changed marketplace, one in which the state could not afford to subsidize money-losing art institutes. This time it was the middling classes, and not the aristocracy, whose buying power was curtailed, especially during and after the hyperinflation. Even when customers were able to buy, too, trends over the 1910s and 1920s make clear that luxury consumption was changing its shape, just as it had done in the 1820s. This time—as many porcelain makers noted with regret—buyers were dispensing with domestic servants and elaborate dinners; those who still had means increasingly devoted them to travel, radios, or automobiles rather than to tableware. Market expansion downward was hampered by the weak buying power of the working classes as well as the industry's bourgeois orientation. When prices fell in the later 1920s, making porcelain affordable as never before to the working classes, as a Meissen employee noted, those consumers were still unlikely to invest in twelve-piece services; quite apart from their different dining cultures, there was no room in their tiny apartments for such things.[2] But manufactories—especially Meissen and the KPM—could not throw out all their "Alt" models in favor of purely functionalist wares. Once again, the industry would have to learn how to please many palates with budgets that did not allow for waste.

A number of other aspects of this market are reminiscent of that of the 1820s. Once again, domestic consumption could not keep up with production, and exports proved essential. But tariff walls and competition in the export market put downward pressure on prices and resulted in new rounds of cost cutting and underselling, forcing some smaller competitors out of the market. The number of porcelain businesses shrank—from about sixteen hundred in 1907 to 1,313 in 1925—while the number of employees rose, from a little under 51,500 to a little over seventy-one thousand.[3] For once, workers made gains in wages, at least until 1928; but as machines grew

TABLE 8.1. Expansion of Administrative Staff, Meissen, 1765–1930

	1765 (Total 731)	1913 (Total 928)	1930 (Total 774)
Administrative staff	31 (including commercial Beamte) (4%)	92 (10%)	150 (19.4%)
Production staff (kiln and machine operators, paste mixers, etc.)	222 (31%)	250 (27%)	243 (31.3%)
Artisans (painters, modelers, turners)	478 (65%)	586 (63%)	381 (49.3%)

Sources: Landtag debate, 51 Sitzung, July 2, 1931, p. 2041; Böhmert, "Urkundliche Geschichte," 62.

relatively cheaper and labor more expensive, the numbers of workers began to fall, even as output increased. Although the higher-end manufactories felt obliged to commission works of art to maintain the prestige of the brand, it was once again the art departments that took the hardest hit. Meissen itself trimmed its art output from approximately 33 percent in 1920 to 13 percent in 1927.[4] It is perhaps even more telling to examine the growth of factory administration with respect to other staff, and particular with respect to artisans. As table 8.1 shows, whereas in 1765 there had been about 15 artisans for every official, by 1913 this ratio had fallen to a little over 6 to 1. By 1930 the proportion hovered at about 2.5 to 1, and less than 2 to 1 for the production staff. The age of managerial capitalism had come to the porcelain industry.[5]

Another, almost invisible, continuity in industrial development deserves note: the expansion, begun in the 1850s, of "technical" porcelain. While the number of luxury porcelain firms remained the same between 1913 and 1927 (forty-six) and the tableware firms rose in number only slightly in the same period (from 108 to 112), the number of electrical firms jumped from thirty-two to fifty-seven.[6] Or, to put this another way: whereas before the war, only 7 percent of the industry's output had been in technical porcelains, by 1928, as tableware sales declined, the share of this industry would rise to 22 percent.[7] Of course this commodity was vulnerable, too, as cheaper substitutes replaced it—steatite, Bakelite, and then plastic—what Victor Hugo said of the successive displacement of one art form by another, "ceci tuera cela" (this will kill that) is even more true of technology than of aesthetic genres. But until these substitutes arrived on the market, and for some purposes even afterward, for the ceramics entrepreneur, technical porcelain was an increasingly good bet, or at least backstop to fund the higher-profile, but usually money-losing, artistic branch of the business.

The increasing importance of technical porcelain, then, is a story we could, and should, begin in the nineteenth century. But its widening importance, as compared to that of tableware and "Galantrieartikel," also underlines the new dimensions of our story, in which the making and selling of porcelain became, to state the obvious, big business, with firms now managed neither by artists nor by chemists but by engineers or men with business savvy. As most firms now took the form of joint-stock companies, management concerned itself with expanding its capital and making shareholders happy as well as with sales. Internally and quietly the larger firms expanded their technical sides, while for the consumer-oriented branch, advertising departments became essential. Black-and-white "preis courantes" gave way to glossy posters and magazine ads, in color when possible. Soon radio and film ads followed. In a way, the director's role had not changed since the days of Sorgenthal and Kühn: while managing costs internally, externally he was expected to cultivate big clients and enhance the brand's public image. But political and economic contexts had been transformed; princely *Glanz* had evolved into PR.

This chapter surveys porcelain's fate in this new postwar era, taking the story into the first years of the Nazi regime. It emphasizes the economic fortunes of firms and their workers, but it also discusses consumption and stylistic developments in two sections, one on the Weimar era and the other on the Nazi period. We investigate developments at the two remaining state manufactories, Meissen and the KPM, and confront the possibility that it may well have been the Nazi period that restored to them some of their "national" representational power and *Glanz*—this was certainly true, at least briefly, for Nymphenburg, Hitler's favorite manufacturer. We engage here one of the most closely studied periods of German history, into which porcelain, once again, gives us a revealing, but hardly complete, view.

Porcelain's Postwar Discontents, Redux

As in the post-Napoleonic era, porcelain makers in the interwar era quickly learned that there was no going back to the good old days, in this case, the days of Wilhelmine-style mass production. Politically, the porcelain manufactories faced several immediate challenges as the western front collapsed, and revolutions swept out kaisers and threatened to expropriate capitalists. The two remaining state firms had to agree to name changes: the KPM was rebaptized the Staatliche Porzellan Manufaktur Berlin, and Meissen redubbed Staatliche Porzellan-Manufaktur Meissen. Both, however, got to retain their trademarks, and for the sake of simplicity we will continue to refer to them as the KPM and Meissen. Nymphenburg, whose trademark included a crown and version of the Wittelsbach family shield, also successfully defended its right to retain historical iconography. Had any of the communist takeovers lasted, the private firms would have been nationalized, as happened in Russia, and in East Germany after 1945 (see chapter 9). That would have suited many porcelain workers, once liberals, who now joined the SPD or in places, the KPD (Communist Party), although according to one source, the Meissners belonged mostly to the Christian parties and trade unions.[8] Even the painters, by now, generally recognized themselves as industrial workers rather than artisans. In fact, factory owners were fortunate that they had agreed to higher wages already in 1918, so that this did not become a rallying cry among activists once the war ended. Many workers, perhaps most, now regarded management as the enemy and were prepared to join workers' organizations and, if necessary, to strike.

By the war's end, like all but the most fanatical right-wing Germans, both porcelain factory owners and their employees were eager for peace. Employees could look forward to the better working conditions they achieved thanks to the labor shortages at the war's end and the prolabor policies of the Weimar Republic, which included the institution of the eight-hour day (forty-eight-hour week). Owners were confident that the return to peace would unleash pent-up domestic demand and were impatient to recover their export markets. But restarting production was not such a simple matter. The first, most pressing problem was the shortage of coal, essential for the firing of ceramic wares. Coal had already been rationed during the conflict, but with the dissolution of the Habsburg monarchy and independence of the new state of Czechoslovakia as well as the French occupation of the Saarland, supplies collapsed. Many factories could not reopen, and those that did operated with shorter hours and only gradually could resume prewar levels of production. One official estimated that in 1919 northern German factories received only about 20 percent of their prewar coal allotments, and the Bavarians—previously so dependent on Bohemian coal—got one-third less than this.[9]

Once factories did reopen, domestic demand was not as robust as producers might have wished. Inflationary pressures hit everyone hard, as labor and coal costs rose, and too much devalued paper money chased too few foodstuffs and durable goods; a severe shortage of coins and small bills made small-scale commerce difficult. The thin silver lining for Meissen was that in 1920, the Saxon state commissioned the firm to make "emergency money" (*Notgeld*) out of the now rarely used Böttger red stoneware. Other localities—including Guatemala—followed suit, though the currencies were always temporally and regionally limited, and in the end, Meissen's *Notgeld* was probably more attractive to collectors than useful in the everyday economy.[10]

The border changes imposed by the treaties of Versailles and St. Germain posed a third set of difficulties for the postwar porcelain makers. Villeroy & Boch, two of its major factories located in the Saarland, fell under French administration until a decisive plebiscite returned the region to Hitler's Reich in 1935. As mentioned above, the Franconian firms were hard hit by the creation of the new Czechoslovakia, which was unwilling to send its coal and kaolin across the border as cheaply as before the war. Although the Silesian firms remained within German borders, they faced severe challenges once again in coal supply; their lucrative prewar markets in the East, too, were cut off by the Russian Revolution, the Russo-Polish War, and the creation of new, tariff-wielding, states. In 1920, the once-booming Tielsch factory (in Altwasser, Silesia) was taken over by C. M. Hutschenreuther, and the next year, Rosenthal purchased another prewar giant, Krister Porzellan (Waldenburg), though both firms continued to produce under their own names, in the latter case until 1971. Sophienau and Königzelt merged and were purchased by the Strupp banking house, which since the later nineteenth century had specialized in ceramics.[11] By 1925, this region was producing only 6 percent of Germany's porcelain, as compared to 10 percent in 1895.[12]

Nor did it prove to be so easy to reestablish Germany's highly profitable porcelain export trade. Great Britain, so important for Meissen's revival after 1820, and a major importer of "Dresden china" before 1914, put up stiff tariff barriers of 60–70 percent, as did several other former trading partners.[13] Manufacturers set their sights on the American market, where German porcelains had sold so well before the war. But the Japanese, who had already captured 14 percent of this trade by 1914, by 1920 controlled 33 percent of American imports and were not inclined to give up their share; in fact by 1929, they had captured 39 percent of this market, compared to 34 percent for Germany.[14] The Czechs, too, reentered the fray, able, like the Japanese, to offer lower prices because of their lower labor costs. The German brands, however, remained popular abroad; and as the mark lost in value, making them more affordable, exports rebounded. Prices at home had to be elevated in order to offset underselling in exports, and then the industry took to pricing pieces in dollars, which led to (just) accusations that the industry was favoring the foreign consumer. Though sales were brisk, and the manufactories generally posted profits in the period between about 1919 and 1922, we must recall that these profits were enumerated in inflated marks and were not necessarily a sign of health, either of the industry, or of the German economy as a whole.

The war saw the end of the "civil peace," if such it was, between the porcelain producers' cartel and the retailers. The retailers won a minor victory in getting the cartel to lower prices on flawed wares by 30 percent in 1920. But they still felt they had had a "Diktatfrieden" (dictated peace) imposed on them in the cartels' refusal to lower other prices, to allow weaker firms to leave the cartel, or to exempt sellers from the *Revers*. Price minimums were reimposed by the 127-member Verband Deutscher Fabriken für Gebrauch-, Zier-, und Kunstporzellan (Cartel of German Makers of Utilitarian, Decorated, and Art Porcelain, successor to the prewar Manufacturers' Cartel) in the inflationary year of 1922—but of course prices were rising anyway. Chaos reigned in 1923, when several billion and then trillion marks were needed to buy a teacup or a loaf of bread. The introduction of the rentenmark in late 1923 and the new reichsmark (RM) in the summer of 1924 stabilized the currency, and the Dawes plan allowed American short-term loans to flow to Germany, making possible a return to quasi-normality. The Manufacturers' Cartel survived the hyperinflation, and in 1925, renewed complaints about its profiteering and the exorbitant fines it imposed on small factories forced the republic's Economic Ministry to investigate again. The ministry concluded that prices for ordinary wares were being kept artificially high, to offset cheaper prices on the export market as well as to support the money-losing luxury wares. Smaller manufacturers and dealers were being pressured to close by the cartel's strong-armed operations.[15] The ministry undertook to force reforms and price reductions on the Manufacturers' Cartel, for the sake, it said, of the public good.

Ministerial intervention reaped outraged resistance from manufacturers. The Rosenthal manufactory remonstrated vociferously, arguing that the economic crisis faced by the whole country could partly be blamed on the Reich's pricing policies, which had inclined potential customers to delay their purchases in the hopes of getting ever cheaper prices.[16] The makers' cartel collectively objected that first of all, what they were selling was not a daily necessity—precisely the language necessary to prevent failing under wartime laws against profiteering—and thus regulating it to protect the public weal made no sense. Secondly, were the minimum price calculations to fall away, the industry would return to prewar conditions, in which firms immiserated workers in order to undersell one another. Doing away with domestic minimum prices would immediately result in illegal exporting, undercutting that market as well.[17] After months of battling, the makers' cartel grudgingly agreed to modest price reductions and a few changes to the *Revers*.[18] The Bavarian Bureau on Prices (Bayerische Landespreisstelle) concluded that the cartel was complying with this order in what could only be described as "a disloyal way,"[19] which was indeed true; but the republic had few instruments at its command with which it could steer the economy, much less "bust" the cartel.

Downward pressure on prices was less the result of state intervention than the fact that during the hyperinflation many firms had purchased new machines, extending production capacity. In the aftermath, neither the domestic nor the export market could absorb all this output, leaving makers desperate to sell at almost any price. When, in the later 1920s, the Manufacturers' Cartel attempted to reimpose minimum prices or the voluntary limitation of production or both, it found this largely ineffective. Too many firms had huge backlogs to liquidate, and it was increasingly difficult to paper over the divergent interests of smaller and larger, luxury and utilitarian, electrical and tableware makers.[20] Porcelain could be purchased in more places than ever before; department stores such as Berlin's luxurious Kaufhaus des Westens offered whole floors of tableware for customers to choose from (fig. 8.1). But lower prices—some coffee, tea, and margarine merchants even gave away individual pieces or full services[21]—meant that selling large quantities was more vital than ever before.

Thus, like other consumer-oriented firms, porcelain makers and dealers in the 1920s put more emphasis than ever before on advertising and customer service, both directed, now, especially at women. Coached by the industry journal *Die Schaulade*, retailers invested great effort in designing eye-catching window displays, in which porcelains often climbed the walls in ways reminiscent of early modern displays of silver (fig. 8.2; compare plate 2). Dealers now made extra efforts, too, at customer service, though most had given up repair work and replacements even before the war in the hopes buyers would simply purchase something new. It was important, the sales professionals insisted, to train employees to give good service; all should have clean fingernails and greet every customer individually, no matter his or her dress. Ideally, women should serve men, and men women, and clerks should refrain from sneezing or yawning. Staff were to be instructed to treat

8.1. Porcelain department, Kaufhaus des Westens, 1932

In the 1920s and early 1930s, department stores offered whole floors of porcelain for customers to choose from. This image shows the expansive offerings of Berlin's most elegant department store, the Kaufhaus des Westens.

accompanying children kindly and to avoid making buyers feel badly for being unable to afford high-end goods.[22] More than ever before, the customer was queen; what was important was that she bought something to *her* taste, not something that met sellers' or makers' standards of refinement.

All these efforts did certainly result in sales, and we might hazard a guess that if more than 50 percent of Wilhelmine households owned at least one porcelain item, in the Weimar period this number was closer to 80 percent. But production capacity still outstripped demand, and by the end of the 1920s, prices fell once more as both makers and sellers turned to the working classes, the last unconquered porcelain continent. By 1929, they were offering prices so low, as the cartel put it, that their soup plates were now cheaper than soup and coffee cups cheaper than the coffee they contained.[23] But then the Depression hit, and soup and coffee became commodities not all could afford, and porcelain a luxury all could forego. By 1933, Germans

GEORG MÜLLER

8.2. Rosenthal shop window

This image of an elaborately decorated Rosenthal outlet window appeared in the ceramics and glass industry's trade magazine *Die Schaulade* as an example of how to stimulate Christmas sales. Note the great variety of styles and objects designed to offer viewers a wide choice of possible gifts for purchase—though the text warned that "only high-priced items—deliberately—were exhibited."

on average were spending 43 percent less on household articles than they had done in the already troubled year of 1928.[24]

Labor relations, as we have seen, had never been harmonious in the porcelain industry, but the interwar period witnessed louder complaints from workers, who were increasingly concentrated in large factories and willing to make common cause to obtain pay raises and rights. Employers had already made some concessions during the Great War; and in the tumultuous months after its end, in which revolutions not only spread across Russia and Hungary but rocked several German cities as well, employers realized they would need to make more. Food prices had risen more than wages; the Spanish flu had decimated porcelain workers, whose lungs were already weakened by silicosis. Yearly renegotiations of the 1918 agreement on wages and conditions followed in the subsectors of the industry, resulting in gradual rises in minimum pay as inflation set in. In the fall of 1921, as negotiations threatened to break down, employers threatened a lockout and in Franconia were greeted in return with a strike that at its peak involved as many as fifteen thousand workers.[25] In this case, the employers largely gave in, though wage rises were quickly wiped out by spiraling inflation. Statistics show that pay increases continued through the mid-1920s, such that by 1928, German workers were making as much as 58 percent more than in 1924; even the Czech workers were also improving their pay, although at lower rates.[26] But this meant little in real terms. Judging by cost-of-living estimates for the Bavarian workforce, only the best-paid workers, in the market's best years, earned salaries above the subsistence minimum.[27] In the 1920s, porcelain workers joined unions by the thousands; in the dark hour of 1923, the Verband der Porzellan- und verwandten Arbeiter und Arbeiterinnen Deutschlands counted an astonishing 72,500 members, though this fell to almost half in the improved circumstances of 1925.[28] There were more strikes in the region in 1924, and in 1927, after another threatened lockout, a major, if short, walkout affected some five thousand at Selb and threatened to spread to the entire industry.[29]

In the middle of the decade, many firms did make money and paid handsome dividends.[30] The industry reached peak production in 1926, at one hundred thousand tons, more than double the amount produced by the next-largest manufacturers, the Czechs.[31] Market pressures once again resulted in the closing or merging of smaller firms, and the increasing size and market share of the larger producers. Whereas in 1907 only fourteen manufacturers employed more than five hundred workers, by 1925, thirty-six surpassed this figure.[32] Taking advantage of others' hardships and seeking to shore up their fortunes in uncertain times, the largest of the private firms engaged in new rounds of both horizontal and vertical integration. Rosenthal, for example, wisely signed a ninety-nine-year partnership with the electrical company and design innovator AEG in 1921, giving the company a stable source of income from making electrical parts as tableware sales fluctuated widely.[33] A series of mergers created a "big three": the Kahla concern, the Arnhold concern (grouped around the Gebrüder Arnhold bank and led by Lorenz Hutschenreuther), and Rosenthal, all of which also looked to buy up kaolin works, printing houses, and lumber mills as well as smaller porcelain makers. The Thuringian Strupp cartel fell apart in 1927, and its associated factories—including C. M. Hutschenreuther and Gebrüder Bauscher—were sold to other large firms. Consolidation in the making of technical porcelain was especially noticeable; by 1928, 90 percent of sales of this commodity went to the four largest producers, with Kahla and Rosenthal alone accounting for 69 percent of the market.[34]

Ominously, too, as the decade closed, the workforce began shrinking in size. By November 1928, the number of employees in the industry had fallen to 57,762 from 72,899 in 1925.[35] Also, firms had begun to sharply favor the hiring of young, single workers—nearly 21 percent in 1928 were under eighteen—and to dismiss apprentices just as they finished their terms and were entitled to full salaries.[36] That the market was already soft in 1928–29 is illustrated by a long report sent by the Bavarian cartel to the Bavarian Foreign Ministry in July 1929. The report noted that unemployment in the industry had topped 11 percent, exports were falling, and consumers were spending money on movies, radios, and motorcycles rather than on fixing up their homes. Twenty-two firms with more than four thousand workers had already closed.[37] Even as the fifth year of "stability" ended, the signs, for the porcelain industry, were not propitious.

The Ravages of the Great Depression

And then, on October 29, 1929, the American stock market crashed, and short-term loans, many of them made to German companies in the wake of the Dawes Plan, were called in. Banks ran short of currency and refused to issue new loans. Industry wide, in 1930 porcelain sales dropped by 40 percent, and by 1933, sales had dropped 51 percent from 1928 levels. In early 1931, the Manufacturers' Cartel gave up on its attempt to impose minimum prices, causing another downward spiral in tableware prices.[38] Whereas the Reich's Porcelain Week slogan in 1928 had been "Porcelain Is Culture," the slogan for 1932 says it all: "Porcelain, Cheaper Than Ever Before!"[39]

Porcelain workers, who numbered almost seventy-two thousand in 1925, by 1933 totaled just over thirty-seven thousand, and unemployment in the industry was running at 43 percent.[40] Wages for those lucky enough still to be employed fell radically. A Bavarian turner who had made 2,592 RM a year in 1928 by 1930 was making only 1,530 RM and by 1933 only 408 RM.[41] By 1933, rent—which had cost about 10 percent of the turner's income in 1905 and the 1920s—was now absorbing 64–70 percent of his wages.[42] An exposé in the *Münchner Neueste Nachrichten* in late 1932 lamented the continuing exploitation of female decorators, who could now be expected to earn no more than 1–3 RM a week (adding up to at most 150 RM a year) for sixty and more hours of work, and frequently enrolled their children in production.[43] The whole industry was in crisis; as the cartel put it in a plea for state assistance: "A centuries-old industry, one that has made Germany highly respected on the world market, stands before its collapse."[44]

The Weimar state had made some efforts to increase the industry's exports, the Economics Ministry producing in 1928 a series of reports on market conditions and sales opportunities in markets across the world, from Sweden to Chile and the Dutch East Indies; the Foreign Ministry reported that its embassies were working hard to try to improve German porcelain sales abroad.[45] As the Depression set in, more and more firms turned to national and regional officials for help. Already in November 1929 the Manufacturers' Cartel was asking for new tariff protections, against increasing sales of Japanese and Czech wares in the vital US market, but also in Holland, England, and South America, and even in Germany itself.[46] The Seltmann Porzellan manufactory begged the minister president of Bavaria for a bailout in mid-1931, as the bank was calling in its loans; not only would hundreds of thousands of reichsmarks invested in equipment and materials be forfeited, the director lamented, but employees would have to be laid off. But the government neither would nor could help the smaller firms, many of which went under, making for further consolidation in the industry. The larger concerns, backed by big banks, could afford to take several years of losses by extending their credit and cutting jobs. They limped along into the Nazi era and by 1935 began once again to turn profits. But in the meantime, terrible damage had been done, both to their workers' lives and to everyone's trust in the market, and in the Weimar Republic. In the March 1932 elections for Reichspräsident, Selb, a town of radicalized porcelain workers and reactionary middle management, chose Hitler, with the communist Ernst Thälmann taking second place.[47] Understandably, given the horrors of the era, many voters had lost confidence in the "free" market, and with it, regrettably, in liberal government and democracy. The porcelain industry, too, longed for a strong man who would bring order and stability to the market and, they hoped, rule in *their* favor. This was, of course, the mistake so many made in voting for Hitler and other authoritarian rulers in the interwar era: the Nazis, for their part, had their own aims and ambitions, some of them genocidal, to pursue.[48]

Mercantile Survivals in a Democratic Age

To trace the histories of Meissen and the KPM in the interwar period is to recognize that while still politically and culturally prominent, these manufactures were definitively not the market leaders. As 1928 figures showed, Meissen's percentage of sales amounted to just 2.64 percent of total porcelain sales, as compared to Rosenthal's 15.5 percent and C. M. Hutschenreuther's 13.4 percent.[49] Nymphenburg in the same year sold less than a third as much as Meissen.[50] And yet, after 1918 the state manufactories found themselves and their budgets, once again, uncomfortably in the public eye. Prussian Landtag debates on the circumstances of the KPM—now under the supervision of the Prussian Trade Ministry—took place regularly in the first half of the 1920s, with both the liberals and the socialists insisting that the manufactory make a profit. SPD delegates argued that in addition to cultivating its artistic reputation, the manufactory should "do justice to the middle classes in reduced circumstances and make provision for the aspirations of the rising working classes, who are hungry for culture. Art must not be reserved only for the few from the upper classes who can afford to pay for it; art must be applied and cultivated for the people."[51] Other interest groups expressed their own views on how the manufactory should operate. The trade journal *Keramische Rundschau* contended that the duty of the state manufactory was "to give objective counsel and encouragement to private industry with the help of the special advantages which it enjoys, and to test new processes, which would be risky for private industry, and to put them on a suitably firm basis for industrial use."[52] The *Vossische Zeitung*, on the other hand, complimented the firm for finally waking from its artistic "Cinderella sleep," which had rendered it unable to compete with the Danes and the English, but berated the Leipzigerstrasse outlet for showing no desire to please customers. The conservative manufactory, it charged, lacked the private firms' eagerness "to take up the fight with success."[53]

Despite disappointing all these parties, the KPM once again managed to survive privatization attempts in the early Weimar era. To help the bottom line, it received commissions for electrical fittings for Berlin's radio tower and metro system, as well as for thread guides for textile mills and other industrial parts. Yet by the later 1920s, it was once again requiring subsidies of nearly 500,000 RM per year, triggering new calls for its closure, and the replacement of its director. Appointed to head the institute in 1929, Günther von Pechmann, a founding member of the Werkbund and champion of functionalist design, undertook new cost-cutting measures and reduced prices in the hopes of pleasing socialist critics as well as selling the firm's wares. Pechmann did commission a series of more utilitarian and "popular" lines, though the KPM's Urbino service still cost more than double compared to wares made by the Arzberg factory.[54] In general, the Weimar era was not kind to the KPM. As we will see, the Prussian manufactory, if not its director, would actually profit from the Nazi takeover, which allowed it to reiterate its function as a "state" manufactory, and return to producing the Schinkelian wares for which it was famed.

Meissen: Rococo Cannot Die

Just before the war's outbreak in 1913, Meissen's sales had, for the first time, reached three million, and although it reduced its output by 60 percent during the war, trimming in particular its artistic creations, it had still managed to issue 109 new models between 1914 and 1917, complementing its offerings of 675 eighteenth-century forms.[55] In the immediate postwar period, the firm's sales resumed briskly, and Meissen seemed in good financial health, despite having lost even more of its mercantile perks; it now had to pay for its officials' pensions, as well as for taxes and interest on loans from the state. Orders flooded in from abroad, and especially from the United States, and in 1920, the firm turned a profit of 2.37 million M. The year 1922 was even better, leaving the manufactory 12 million M in the black (though 1 M was now worth about $.003, whereas in 1918 it had been valued at about $.25). The *Neue Leipziger Zeitung* cheered, calling the new general director, Max Pfeiffer, "a reverse alchemist": "he sought porcelain, and found gold! This can only be a pleasure for the Saxon Finance Ministry!"[56] Indeed, the Saxon Finance Ministry was, for a change, pleased; but this did not mean that it allowed the firm to keep more than a small share of these profits, which the manufactory put into building projects, including improved housing and public spaces for workers.

Nor did Meissen's relative economic stability shield it from other critics, in whose comments we can further appreciate just how much public pressure, from multiple perspectives, the state manufactories had to endure in this period. While critics lampooned Meissen's devotion to the rococo, when designers moved in functionalist directions, the manufactory's traditional consumer base rejected the new work as insufficiently "meissentypisch."[57] One writer in the *Dresdner Neueste Nachrichten* criticized Meissen's cavalier attitude toward sales, claiming that while Rosenthal and other private firms kept their booths at the Leipzig fair continuously staffed with eager salesmen, Meissen closed its booth from one to three in the afternoon: "the state firm does not find it necessary to temporarily inconvenience itself for so incidental an event as the Leipzig fair."[58] Another more left-leaning journalist commented that the profits were nice, but the prices still too high, and most average citizens still could not afford such "luxurious frivolities": "Brown bread is still more vital than brown Böttger-stoneware."[59] Even further to the left, *Der Kämpfer* denounced Meissen as typical of an industry that produced decorations for bourgeois apartments: "But no one notices how much poverty and misery, hunger and bloody tears are involved in the making of these things."[60] A half-mercantile, half-capitalist enterprise, Meissen, not surprisingly, caught flak from all sides.

The hyperinflation of 1922–23 did increase Meissen's sales, but not its profits. The manufactory was compelled to follow the government's price regulations, and raw materials and labor costs soared. Ominously, some buyers seem to have invested in Meissen as a means of storing real value against the economy's wholesale collapse. "Many [buyers] apparently calculate that Meissen porcelain's real value makes it cheaper than currency,"[61] a journalist commented in late 1922. But what followed the next year was much worse. The mark's complete loss of value wiped out the firm's operating capital, and the Saxon state forced the firm to take out a 2.7 million RM loan from its own state bank at 6 percent interest to replace this capital. Worse, the hyperinflation ravaged middle-class savings, rather in the way the Napoleonic Wars had emptied princely purses, and sales slumped. As the firm explained, "the people who up until now had the necessary culture and the necessary understanding of art to possess high-quality wares have now, for the most part, lost the means to satisfy their desires of this kind."[62] The Saxon Landtag voiced a wider set of complaints, attacking the firm's high prices, its bursting warehouses, and its lack of business acumen, but in the end it grudgingly agreed to subsidies. Workers—some of the highest paid in the industry—had no choice but to accept furloughs and layoffs. The firm promised to pay more attention to sales and advertising, to lower prices, and to clear the warehouse backlog—an exceedingly difficult endeavor, as we have seen in previous attempts to winnow down unsold wares without undermining the value of newer ones. Although 1927 and 1928 were somewhat better, by September 1929, sales had fallen another 7 percent.[63]

In the latter year, the state loans—swollen by interest added—also fell due. Backed this time by the Finance Ministry, Meissen asked to convert its loan into investment capital of about 3 million RM. This, it argued, would save the manufactory from further punishing interest payments and allow it to operate in the red until the year's end, when Christmas buying would enhance its bottom line. Under considerable political pressure, the Finance Ministry composed an extensive, secret memorandum defending the manufactory but also recommending a series of measures to goose sales and to reduce costs. Overproduction of unsalable goods had to cease, and the firm's management should work hard to increase its customer base, and to keep big customers happy, as did the private firms. The ministry denounced Meissen's inattention to advertising and advised it to increase its visibility by advertising on the radio and in cinemas. The firm had already squeezed down its tableware varieties from approximately seven hundred to fifty but could cut back further, to reduce fixed costs. It should also take better stock of modern tastes, which was important for sales outside of Saxony.[64] Once again, as in the 1820s, the Finance Ministry berated its own porcelain manufactory for failing to act like a private firm, and the manufactory could only restate the obvious: for reasons it had patiently reiterated and defended since at least 1820, it was, in fact, *not* a private firm.

At the manufactory, reforms were tried, and advertising expanded and improved; the making of cheaper wares increased. Tellingly, the advertisements emphasized Meissen's historic reputation for quality, but also that pieces were available "in all price ranges." Artists' hours were cut by 25 percent and other workers' hours by 15 percent. But dealers' margins could not be decreased much, as recommended, as otherwise salespersons simply advised customers to buy other firms' wares instead. Nor could the Saxon "Kunstanstalt" simply stop producing new models or those money-losing figurines: "Even when they sell only with difficulty," an official report concluded,

> they are an especially significant means of advertising which the state porcelain manufactory can't do without. If [the manufactory] gives up the making of new items of artistic value because of the difficulty of selling

such creations, it will also give up its status and cultural importance and thereby lose precisely the particularities for which the state supported it through previous periods of economic hardship.[65]

In some ways, this was *1829* all over again: it would take a new "prince," and a new Zollverein, to save the day.

The year 1930 proved disastrous, and the firm lost upward of 2 million RM.[66] The year 1931, too, began poorly and culminated in losses of nearly 800,000 RM.[67] A special Landtag committee was formed to investigate the manufactory once more, and to give advice on its continuation. The committee reiterated most of the Finance Ministry's suggestions for cost cutting, and defenses of current practices.[68] Debate in the chamber was vigorous, as representatives of the Communist Party (KPD) denounced cuts made to workers' pay and the protection of management. Everyone decried Meissen's poor salesmanship and the bloatedness of the warehouse, which now housed approximately 15 million RM worth of goods. No one advocated the immediate closure of the manufactory, but more than one delegate acknowledged that eventually this would have to happen; this was absolutely the last time, a Nazi representative stormed, that his party could stomach such subsidies. Several delegates called for the firing of firm director Max Pfeiffer. Weary of the constant repetition of the same debates, one veteran cut to the chase: "Certainly the porcelain manufactory is a problem child, not only for the directors, officials, clerks, and workers, but for everyone. Why? Because in today's difficult times the factory simply cannot be made economically viable. Despite that, however, we are proud that we in Saxony can call such a great cultural entity our own." Thus they would vote to keep Meissen in business, he argued, based only on the hope that next year's sales would be brisk and the factory would not need further subsidies. "Oh what an optimist!" one colleague interjected. "That's a pious wish!" shouted another.[69] The subsidy passed, and Meissen continued production. Losses for 1932 were less than for 1931, but still considerable at 468,689 RM.[70]

Thanks to Nazi state patronage and a rebound in domestic sales, Meissen did not need hefty subsidies long beyond 1933. Had it done so, however, we have every reason to believe that the Nazi delegate would have eaten his words, and voted to maintain the manufactory. Meissen's status at home as well as abroad made it a major instantiation of German excellence in design, and a fixture in the Saxon cultural landscape. Even when the "problem child" caused grief for all, its symbolic and emotional value was too precious to throw away.

Style: The Age of Functionalism?

In an age of bitter social and economic contestation, it is not surprising that debates about style, too, carried strong whiffs of political sentiment. The Werkbund's vision took on a more democratic as well as utilitarian tint and embraced more enthusiastically industrial materials: steel, aluminum, glass, even plastic. The drive for transparency and geometric rationality as well as hygiene made basic colors, especially black and white, fundamental to the new style, and the appeal of pure, white form, not surprisingly, gave porcelain a special role in articulating this new vision. More than that, too, the interwar campaigns undertaken especially by left-leaning municipal governments to address the severe housing shortage by building grand workers' housing projects helped to forward discussions about modern, affordable living spaces, including the rational kitchen. We often forget just how utopian some of this thinking was: the new art was to shape the new man.[71] But how much porcelain did the new man—or the new woman—need? The unhappy answer for the porcelain industry seemed to be "not much," and especially, not much at the luxury prices that could sustain the artistic or even artisanal side of the industry. Functionalism, in fact, did not do the porcelain industry any favors—at least until the state began ordering it in large quantities after 1933.

Of course, functionalism, too, was a style championed by artists, and as Paul Betts has noted, its champions were typically deeply skeptical about consumer capitalism, often to the point of antiliberalism; fundamentally, they wanted to tell consumers what they *should* buy, whether or not customers found "pure form" attractive. Weimar buyers, however, were not necessarily ready or willing to adopt their "rational" kitchens and utopian visions.

Recognizing this, the higher-end porcelain manufactories were willing to go some distance with the functionalists of their day but remained skeptical about their grand dreams for the transformation of living spaces. (The lower-end manufacturers were already, of course, making utilitarian "hotel" and everyday wares.) A number of services were commissioned from artists related to the Bauhaus and Werkbund, especially by the KPM, and for the first time, female ceramicists were among those commissioned. For the first time in decades, Meissen produced tableware and figurines in pure white, including Max Esser's stylized animals—though the production of inexpensive white tableware probably had more to do with the Saxon Landtag's long-standing demand for the manufactory to produce cheaper wares than with admiration for functionalism.[72] Philipp Rosenthal, who had perceived the power of artistic modernism for advertising his brand before the war, now built on that reputation, commissioning works from the Bauhaus-educated industrial designer Wilhelm Wagenfeld. The newly opened Porzellanfabrik Augarten AG, claiming succession from the WPM, won critical acclaim for its "Melon Service," designed by the great industrial designer of the Wiener Werkstätte, Josef Hoffmann.[73] Once the founding member of the Werkbund Günther von Pechmann rose to the directorship of the KPM, that manufactory arranged to collaborate with two former Bauhaus artists, Gerhard Marks and Marguerite Friedlaender-Wildenhain, whose functionalist "Hallesches Form" was especially widely praised. Another female artist, Trude Petri, succeeded even better with her rotund "Urbino" service, which remains in production today.[74]

But here again we obtain an unrepresentative understanding of what the industry made and sold if we examine only the artworks featured in advertisements and museum catalogs. In addition to making functionalist ware, Rosenthal also continued to make services with the retro names "Pompadour" and "Sanssouci." In addition to featuring Josef Hoffmann, Augarten also put older WPM patterns back into production and had its biggest figurine success not with modernist works but with a series of models based on performers from the Spanish Riding School. Both at the KPM and later at Meissen, the most popular of modelers, Paul Scheurich, made figurines that can be said to have looked back to Kändler, or ahead to the age of Nazi classicism rather than continuing the Jugendstil or symbolist lines of the prewar era; his most popular figurines included "Lady with Moor," "The Garter," and putti supporting a clock; he also made a critically praised "Europa" and a "Drunk."[75] Meissen, like other manufactories, also made numerous Great War commemorative pieces, including regimental services, and various sorts of advertising medallions and anniversary pieces for businesses and social organizations.[76] Pfeiffer was very careful to limit external commissions and even developed a new funding strategy by which subscriptions from collectors—rather than the manufactory's operating funds—paid for the making of a small number of signed pieces.[77]

The whole functionalist aesthetic, in fact, was rather hard to pass off as "art" in an industry where the highest-value objects were expected to be the most heavily ornamented. As Wilhelm Wagenfeld later remarked with respect to the reception of functionalist products in the Weimar period: "dealers and manufacturers laughed over our products. . . . Although they looked like cheap machine production, they were in fact expensive handicrafts."[78] More successful were the designers such as Hermann Gretsch at Arzberg, who had, from the first, very low prices as well as pure form in mind. Gretsch's 1931 model "Arzberg 1382" was destined to be one of the best-selling patterns ever (fig. 8.3)[79]—though Gretsch, who became the director of the Nazified Werkbund, would defend it and Arzberg's other functionalist wares not as modernist creations but as *völkisch* forms, articulated against the age of liberalism, in which imitation of the court prevailed.[80]

Fürstenberg, too, made functionalist styles as well as continuing its "Alt" lines. With the onset of the Depression, it also made a bid, as did others, to design tableware for buyers who wanted to buy only one service for all purposes. Its advertisement for a new pattern, "630 Rhinegold," offers useful insight into the ways in which manufacturers were trying to please as many customers as possible, and to square modernism and nationalism:

Powerful in its basic form like the waters of the Rhine, capricious and inspiring in its lines like sparkling wine, tasteful in the gold detail work

8.3. Arzberg advertisement, Form 1382

In a Depression era characterized by fierce competition, falling prices, and impoverished customers, the success of Arzberg's inexpensive Form 1382 made it stand out. Not surprisingly, the manufactory took to boasting to wholesalers that 1382's simple (*schlicht*) elegance made for easy sales to a broad public.

of all the pieces, so that the noble material qualities of porcelain are happily emphasized, this is the new tableware of the Fürstenberg Porcelain Factory. . . . "Rhinegold" is equally suited for holiday tables and for everyday meals, for modern interiors as for dining rooms of the older style. This creation offers the long-sought after standard tableware for the German household.[81]

Regrettably, for Fürstenberg, "630 Rhinegold" did not prove any more attractive than other interwar innovations. When the republic ended in early 1933, no one had found a way to bring all Germans to the table.

The "New Woman" and the
Politics of Weimar Porcelain

The Weimar period famously saw the advent of "the new woman," a figure often depicted as a sexually liberated habituée of cafés and cabarets or as a soulless American, in either case not at all a person likely to possess a twenty-six-piece KPM service.[82] Figurine designers in the 1920s devoted much attention to this figure, featuring especially modern dancers, from flappers to Josephine Baker, the American performer who scandalized Europe with her risqué banana skirts.[83] But these, like most figurines, did not sell in large numbers, and we can speculate that rather few of them sold to the typical female porcelain purchaser. For them, the image of modern womanhood needed to be somewhat toned down. It is worth noting that most of the women featured in the period's advertisements were sleekly dressed modern women, but clearly homemakers and not working women, or even "new women." The industry, as ever, was trying to please as many customers as possible, but they believed, probably rightly, that real dangers lay in dissociating porcelain from the prewar—often romanticized—bourgeois home.

Of course the Weimar era did usher in a new age for many women, who could now vote and pursue higher education in larger numbers. The war had opened new career opportunities, even though many married women were displaced when men returned from the front. Urban areas tolerated shorter haircuts and skirts. But by no means had central European gender relations transformed overnight, and maintaining a respectable, hygienic, and harmonious home was still an emphatically female duty. "New women" were surely outnumbered by conservative women and impoverished, overworked war widows, who had no time or money for cabarets. Left-wing reformers, in particular, touted the benefits of "the rational kitchen," supplied exclusively with efficient modern shelving and utilitarian utensils. Undoubtedly these designs pleased many eyes, and they could be implemented in the new housing developments planned and built in the interwar era. But how many women threw away their breakfronts and their grandmothers' mismatched teacups in favor of functionalist home furnishings?[84]

8.4. Dollmaking in Thuringia, 1927
Here a 'Hausmalerin' and her female helpers paint and assemble dollheads
in a spare living space. This, too, was a "modern" workplace.

Once again, our porcelain story reminds us of the endurance of older
forms of everyday life and work. A 1927 image of a Thuringian woman
and her daughters decorating doll heads reminds us of the endurance of
outsourced household labor, the continuity in female dress from the nineteenth century through the interwar era, and even the ongoing demand
for cheap dolls (fig. 8.4). The bourgeois family Christmas depicted in a
photograph taken in 1930 is similarly unmarked by modern elements
(fig. 8.5). Making merry for this family entails music, a decorated tree, and
Stollen and coffee served on the "good" china, in this case a Rosenthal service imitating the Biedermeier-era Meissen "green vine" pattern. In this case,
we know that the violin player was Georg Knorr, a watchmaker injured in
the Great War who worked from his own apartment; he would predecease
his wife Irene (seated to his right) by forty years.[85] The doll makers and the

8.5. Christmas, 1930

This classic Christmas photo taken in Chemnitz in 1930 captures the importance of porcelain for bourgeois holiday celebrations.

female Knorrs, too, were Weimar Germans, but they were not by any means "new women."

Such images and the lives of the persons depicted in them demonstrate forcibly both the association of porcelain with "home," and the tensions looming behind the assumption that the German home was a place exclusively for leisure and comfort; contemporaries knew very well that it also remained a place for work and a location where deprivations were marked and felt. Producers and dealers understood that for various reasons, which they tended to stigmatize as lack of taste or decaying morals, the era of well-appointed family feasts had gone, and with it the need for porcelain. As one of the organizers of the first porcelain dealers' exhibition in 1928 lamented in the introduction to the catalog: "After the war, a form of superficiality has been spreading into our family life which makes external appearances the only goal, and thus more and more threatens to destroy the culture of the home itself. Earlier it was the German family's pride to own and use the most

8.6. Weimar-era sales tactics

In the 1920s, porcelain manufacturers experimented with advertising of all sorts. Here two salesmen attempt to lure wholesalers to the Bareuther booth at the Leipzig fair.

beautiful porcelain. This comprehensive show aims to reawaken and develop this sensibility, which is in danger of being completely lost."[86] As our images suggest, it was less superficiality than poverty that accounted for the failure of Weimar women to fill their homes with new consumer goods. We might, indeed, wonder if the conception of the perfectly outfitted "home" wasn't in part the invention of those with excess housewares to sell.

Cementing the relationship between porcelain and the respectable home was a major goal of the industry's Weimar-era advertising. Advertising had become a much bigger part of firms' budgets, and funds were sunk into placards for train cars as well as magazine pages; at the Leipzig fair, all manner of gimmicks were tried to attract the interest of wholesalers (fig. 8.6). For the individual consumer—now universally assumed to be female—ads reiterated at every turn the connection between porcelain and good, tasteful housekeeping. Shop windows—so important a means of attracting women shoppers that female designers were often hired to decorate them[87]—endlessly reiterated this point. These elaborate displays massed porcelains together, sometimes in playful ways, but endlessly linking the product to weddings and holidays as well as to the housewife's duty to tend and perfect the home. When firms banded together to celebrate the first "National Porcelain Week" in 1927, and again in 1931, they chose as its slogan "Your Home—Your World, Its Ornament: Porcelain!" The 1928 theme struck a bourgeois note: "Porcelain Is Culture."[88] The industry was now well aware that it would live and die by the ordinary female consumer and her attachment to nineteenth-century norms.

Nostalgia was a powerful marketing force, operating through prewar bourgeois ideals as well as in the many "Alt" items made by the manufactories. But the past was not necessarily a healthy country, either. Already before the war porcelain use, especially by men, could be associated with decadence; in Thomas Mann's "The Blood of the Walsungs"—written before but published after the war—the neurasthenic Herr Aarenhold eats at a table adorned with two orchids at each place, and eats only the blandest of foods, including bouillon served in tiny cups of translucent porcelain.[89] The old-fashioned bureaucrat Franz Spineder in Hugo Bettauer's 1922 *Die Stadt ohne Juden*, keeps a portrait of Franz Josef over his desk and inhabits a sitting room decorated with nineteenth-century furniture, two authentic Waldmüller genre paintings, and "Altwiener" porcelain; he commits himself to toleration and the new (Austrian) Republic, but in the end gives in to anti-Semitism.[90] Perhaps the most telling of the hypernostalgic short stories published in 1922 by the popular nationalist (and later Nazi) author Will Vesper features a highly sympathetic French prince who reluctantly parts with an early eighteenth-century Meissen figurine to buy his beloved wife a few last comforts before her guillotining. Vesper clearly meant the smashing of the figurine by the prison warden—who sees the figurine as "yet another sign of the decadence of this despicable class"—to underline the unsuitedness of the barbaric underclasses for rule, but we can see, too, his understanding of the political implications Meissen, in particular, conjured in the minds of his contemporaries.[91]

Porcelain can have many political valences. Modernist art pieces can and do challenge conservative styles; functionalism can be harnessed to promote the equalization of consumers. During the 1920s, Russian makers produced revolutionary porcelains, just as German makers produced medallions honoring Hindenburg or commemorating the end of the French occupation of the Ruhr. It is a dubious proposition to try to find signs of the catastrophe to come in Weimar ceramics. As the Katz-Ehrenthal Collection held by the US Holocaust Museum demonstrates, an extensive array of anti-Semitic porcelain was already being made in the nineteenth century, by British, American, and Czech as well as German and Austrian ceramicists.[92] Almost certainly porcelains were made commemorating the Weimar Republic and championing the new democracies of central Europe; as we have seen, virtually everything was depicted on porcelains. But these are very hard to find. Perhaps contemporaries simply couldn't find much heroism, sentimentality, patriotism, or even sensuality in the republic and its leaders. And that, one might say in retrospect, was an ominous sign.

Nazi Porcelain: "Alt" and "Modern"

The Nazi rise to power brought mostly gradual, rather than sudden, change to the benighted porcelain industry. A few artists lost their positions, and as we will see, some Jewish entrepreneurs were attacked and a few eventually expropriated. The Nazis championed porcelain as a prestigious "German" art form, and a potential source of foreign hard currency. Manufacturers, almost universally, were eager to produce for the state, whose patronage was welcome at a time of economic chaos and was more dependable than that of the fickle market. Recovery from the Depression came slowly, but by 1936 many firms that had sustained large losses and engaged in major layoffs in the period 1928–33 were once again able to turn profits and to hire workers. Real wages, however, lagged; in 1935, by one estimate, they stood at only about 75 percent of the value of 1928 wages.[93] Not surprisingly, technical porcelain in particular benefited from Hitler's rearmament campaign, and especially from the war effort after 1939. The trend toward functionalist styles continued, though "Alt" porcelains continued to be marketed widely through the period and favored by the elite; the "new woman" definitively lost out to the family-oriented *Hausfrau*. State manufacturers rebounded, aided by official commissions and now shielded, like other state bodies, from public criticism. The Kaiser Wilhelm Institute for Labor Physiology concerned itself briefly with silicosis, but only to find that some workers' nasal hairs more efficiently filtered out silica dust. Its recommendation for treating the problem was to advise employers to test workers' noses and hire those with the highest filtering capacity.[94] Even in the ignoring of this major industrial affliction there was continuity, of a sort, across the Nazi era.

Most historians now agree that the German economy was already on the eve of a recovery when Hitler became chancellor in January 1933,[95] though real improvement was not in evidence until about 1935. This pattern is partly borne out by statistics for porcelain, glass, and other kitchen utensils collected by the Reich, which show a further dip from 1932 levels in 1933, and a slow recovery thereafter (see table 8.2). If we look at some individual firms, we can see a gradual return to profitability. C. M. Hutschenreuther, for example, sustained losses of over 200,000 RM in 1932 and 1933, and of about 75,000 RM in the period 1934–36. But by 1937, domestic sales had risen 22 percent and exports 12 percent, and the company was able to post profits of 22,700 RM; in 1940, these amounted to 290,000 RM.[96] Kahla lost nearly 2 million RM in 1931, and a further 2.3 million RM in 1932 and 1933, but managed to turn a small profit (2,700 RM) in 1934. Its winnings were modest for its size until the war began.[97] Having lost more than 800,000 RM in 1931 and 1932, Rosenthal gradually climbed out of its hole, posting profits of more than 200,000 RM for most of the rest of the 1930s, and over 500,000 RM in 1941.[98] Two of the traditional firms bounced back quickly. After losses in 1933 of 465,520 RM, in 1934, Meissen snatched a narrow victory, reckoning a profit of 243.67 RM.[99] By 1935, Fürstenberg, under the direction of a Nazi Party member, was able

TABLE 8.2. Relative Increase and
Decrease of Sales of Porcelain,
Glass, Etc. (1932 Baseline)

1932	100
1933	98.5
1934	113.8
1935	121.7
1936	134.4

Source: SJfDR 1937:375,
http://www.digizeitschriften.de.

to expand its workforce from two hundred to three hundred workers, although its profits remained small.[100]

Why fortunes turned is partly a matter of speculation, but what did *not* happen was a direct state bailout of the industry or the manipulation of the market in favor of the smaller businessmen, who, demographically, were among Hitler's most ardent supporters.[101] To prevent underselling by the larger concerns, after Hitler's ascent to power the Jaeger & Co. and Walküre firms demanded price controls, with jail time for offenders, and limits on production; Paul Meyer, of Walküre, even suggested the appointment of a porcelain industry commissar.[102] The new regime did curtail the spread of chain stores and promoted (low) price stability, which helped those who could not afford to undersell. But instead of shuttering department stores—a major demand of small shop owners—the Nazis simply seized the largest from their Jewish owners. It did more or less bust the Manufacturers' Cartel, in 1934 subordinating porcelain manufacturers to the Reichsstelle für Glas, Keramik, und Holzverarbeitung, one of the many offices tasked with controlling raw material supplies, prices, and labor in the manufacturing sector. But it does not seem that this agency intervened very much, at least until the war commenced, and by no means did small businesses profit from its restrictions.

Instead, what we find is, in some sense, salvation engineered by a new "prince" and a new "Zollverein." After 1933, makers could look to a powerful, centralized state making huge orders of simple tableware for Labor

Front canteens, technical porcelain for the Wehrmacht, and non-utilitarian luxury porcelains for party members and representational purposes, one might even say a new form of *Glanz*. Moreover, the Nazi regime in its first years encouraged the production of Germanic babies as well as the consumption of household goods by instituting a marriage loan program. These loans enabled young couples—many of them deprived of private space by the Weimar era's housing shortages and starved of consumer goods by the Great Depression—to set up homes, and to outfit them with modest, "homey" goods. The rational kitchen, where working women could make efficient meals, gave way to the glorification of the family dinner table, something that suited the industry's efforts to emphasize the home, and pleased bourgeois critics who had disapproved of this form of "Americanization."[103] Together, incentives, the return to full employment, and the emphasis on female homemaking did restore health to the household goods industry, which rose 58 percent over 1932 levels by 1938. Porcelain sales, at least on the lower end, profited from this initiative. According to a 1937 survey, some 95 percent of upper-class homes, 88 percent of middle-class homes, and 48 percent of workers' homes now contained porcelain tableware of some kind. Thanks to rising sales, workers too recovered ground. By 1938, an industry journal rejoiced, the average porcelain worker's income had increased 61 percent over 1933 levels.[104] Thus did the Nazis buy political loyalty not only by putting consumer goods makers back to work, but by allowing many to equip—modestly—their "gemütlich" new homes.[105]

Encouraging the consumption of inexpensive household durables was a means to emphasize both Germany's return to prosperity, and the sanctity of the Aryan family home. As Paul Betts has brilliantly noted, in addition to their grandiose military and political ambitions, the Nazi elite, including Hitler himself, also longed to reenchant commonplace objects of consumption, "as a living witness of cultural rebirth, social reconstruction, racial victory, and private pleasure."[106] And what better than good German porcelain—its excellence acknowledged throughout the world—to perform this reenchantment? After all, as advertisers had put it in the 1920s: "Porcelain Is Culture." Manufacturers were happy to reinforce this Germanic vision. As a wordy advertisement paid for by several makers, including Meissen, explained in 1935, porcelain was essential to German happiness, no matter one's income level or tastes. Since the eighteenth century, it had graced both great halls and small salons:

> And it is the same for us too, who more than ever are concerned with the culture of our immediate surroundings, with the comfortable beauty of our home; we have taken porcelain ever more to heart. *Our* porcelain. The porcelain of our age. In grandmother's old-fashioned living room we happily drink guest-coffee from rounded, Alt-Meissen flowered cups—at home, surrounded by the couch, the cupboard, and steel chair we prefer the modern forms, the simple band decoration, the [coffee] pot, which stands on steady feet. Fine porcelain, pale, shimmering wonders on the whitest damask—does it not almost determine the style of dinner conversation? Colorful dishes with garden flowers on the balcony—don't they make one happy, even when the sun is not shining?

Like rococo consumers, the ad concluded, surely we too experience "happiness through beauty, joy through good form?"[107]

The theme of the German made joyful by beautiful forms, whatever the political "weather," was one the manufacturers could underscore without hesitation. Regrettably for them, however, this was not a motto that worked for the export market, which was not pleased by aggressive and autarkic Nazi policies. According to one carefully researched article of September 1939, porcelain exports had fallen 45 percent since 1928, at the same time as the amount of ordinary tableware had risen appreciably. Decorated porcelain, in particular, had fallen off the table; accounting for 65 percent of exports in 1928, by 1939 it had plummeted to just 17 percent.[108] We must be careful not to overinterpret our statistics, however, as some of the softness in this market was undoubtedly the result less of political than economic conditions, as the Great Depression lasted far beyond 1933 in some of Germany's large export markets such as the United States and Great Britain. Moreover, the industry continued to do well with exports to fascist-sympathizing or neutral nations, Italy, Hungary, Switzerland, and some South American countries. At least until the outbreak of the war, there were, regrettably, plenty of people willing to do business with the Nazi regime.

8.7. Nazi mass consumption

The Nazi state purchased utilitarian porcelain in great quantities for uses such as this: a 1940 outing for the Union of German Girls (Bund der deutsche Mädel).

In any event, as the 1939 article continued: "the extensive collective needs of the Wehrmacht, the Party, the Labor Front, the work cafeterias and the 'Strength through Joy,' none of which existed previously or not on this scale, have filled in for this decline in exports. Naturally, a lively trade has also come with the greater buying power of many parts of the population." The massive expansion of the military and the state sector, and the desire to control these organizations down to the coffee cups they drank from, had indeed opened the way to major orders of mass-produced, identical goods, suitable for events such as the outing of the Union of German Girls captured in a 1940 photograph (fig. 8.7). These orders were most welcome at a time when exports and domestic sales remained soft, and they also offered firms the opportunity to grease up to state patrons who might have future commissions in their gift.[109] Yet as Albrecht Bald has shown, this was not the hoped-for panacea either; although some firms profited from making terrines for the meat-saving "one dish meals" the party advocated, this was hardly an enduringly lucrative market, and the "beauty of work" services made by many manufacturers were never ordered in the colossal quantities manufacturers dreamed of. A final section in this article must have been worrying, rather than encouraging for producers: "The rise in sales has also been accomplished by great sacrifices in the matter of prices. Today in Germany much more porcelain is used, but considerably less is paid for it." The author then made a calculation that would have horrified eighteenth- or even nineteenth-century makers: the cost of porcelain *per kilo* had fallen from 1.58 RM per kilo in 1928 to 1.17 RM per kilo in 1938.[110] This meant that labor and production costs would need to be squeezed even more, were profits to accrue; this was by no means a return to an artisanal paradise.

If Nazi aggression cut into porcelain exports, it proved a boon to the German industry in other ways, annexing whole enterprises and filling state pockets with confiscated resources. The Saarland plebiscite, won by the Germans in a surge of hypernationalism, brought the main factories of Villeroy & Boch "home to the Reich," and the *Anschluss* incorporated Austria, with all its customers as well as its manufactories. But most important, for this industry, was surely the occupation of the Sudetenland and then the swallowing up of the Czech state in 1938–39.[111] All this annexing resulted in the expansion of Germany's porcelain-producing capacity by at least 30 percent, as well as the elimination of pesky Czech competitors and costly coal and kaolin imports.[112] Experiments using inferior German clays could be stopped as Czech kaolin now flowed freely into the Reich. Most egregiously, Himmler's Allach manufactory commandeered the recently modernized "Bohemia" factory near Karlovy Vary (formerly Karlsbad) and tasked it with making dinnerware for the Wehrmacht, as well as symbolic gifts for loyal SS men. During the war, female inmates of the Flossberg concentration camp and foreign forced laborers were compelled to work here, and in the kaolin mines nearby.[113]

The Nazis seem to have spread their porcelain patronage rather widely, and makers seem to have continued, in many ways, pre-1933 stylistic trends.

Such a wave of pro-Nazi memorabilia—including Führer busts and eggcups—greeted the *Machtergreifung* that by mid-March 1933 propaganda minister Josef Goebbels felt compelled to promulgate a law to control the flood of kitsch, in which porcelain makers had their share.[114] Manufactories, like many public officials, "worked towards the Führer" in the well-known formulation of Ian Kershaw,[115] cooperating with the Labor Front, the navy, and the SS to produce canteen ware as well as plaques, commemorative medals, and the like. As a brief survey of items for sale on the internet confirms, many, if not all, porcelain firms produced items for Nazi organizations. This includes Rosenthal, Villeroy & Boch, and Mitterteich; the modernist firm Bauscher, which had worked with the Darmstadt modernists, made tableware for the SS. Meissen issued commemorative plates for the paramilitary Stahlhelm.[116] The extent of this production, however, remains to be studied, and one suspects that much of what now is now sold as Nazi porcelain—yes, even that!—is faked.

None of this tells us very much about what exactly went on in these manufactories, another subject that awaits closer study. Like other businesses, porcelain makers were, for the most part, willing to go along with the Nazis and in some cases collaborated eagerly, as in the cases surveyed below. Once again they could make the (accurate) claims that they kept workers employed, and that except in the case of Allach, they did not produce exclusively Nazi wares. The stylistic latitude of the Nazi regime permitted the porcelain firms and German designers to retain a good deal of international respectability, and to emerge after World War II relatively unscathed by association with the murderous regime.[117]

As usual, figurine making has caught the eye of those (few) who have examined the industry in this period, and their attention has been drawn to Himmler's manufactory, founded initially in the Munich suburb of Allach in 1935 with a 45,000 RM subsidy from the SS Reichsführer. Figurine-making operations moved in 1937 to a larger location near the Dachau concentration camp, from which, after the war's outbreak, laborers would be drawn to help make figurines and plaques for SS purposes. Some of these, such as the SS "Flag Bearer" and the SS "Rider"—modeled by an artist who had worked for Rosenthal until 1935—Himmler reserved for special gifts for his men and were not available for purchase, although a factory store did open in 1938, at Leipzigerstrasse 13, a stone's throw from the original KPM site, and virtually next door to Göring's Air Ministry.[118] The factory made mawkish Hitler Youths and half-naked Aryan fencers, "Jul-lights" and "Jul-plates" to celebrate Himmler's invented Aryan Winter Solstice holiday, figurines dressed in traditional Germanic costumes as well as horses, dogs, and "innumerable animal forms from our forests."[119] There was a terrible "Girl after the Bath" that would have made Falconet shudder, and a bear slicing its chains with a massively oversized sword. Hitler commissioned one hundred figurines of Frederick the Great on horseback. Strikingly, one aim of the manufactory was to revive that dream of stylistic unity dreamt by so many reformers, "to introduce *one* direction into china design—to contrast those very many models made only for success measured in hard cash, with those that possess enduring cultural value."[120] Allach could afford to do this, of course, only because it was, in modern guise, a wholly mercantilist enterprise, founded by a "prince" and wholly dependent on orders from his "court." And in fact, after steep losses between 1936 and 1939, it was lucky to be able to annex the tableware-producing "Bohemia," whose products could be sold to the Waffen SS, Wehrmacht, and Red Cross to balance losses in the figurine department.[121]

If Himmler, characteristically, was most crude and deliberate in his efforts to instill Aryan culture, other leading members of the regime turned to the "traditional" state firms to make their commissions. After the *Anschluss*, the Führer—Austrian by birth—took on the protection of the reopened WPM (now Augarten) and commissioned a rococo service for the Reich Chancellery.[122] But Hitler was much more partial to Meissen; he loved his "Red Dragon" service[123] and used it regularly at his summer palace at Berechtesgaden. He was delighted by the retro figurines issued by the manufactory (fig. 8.8). Meissen also produced items for Göring, including a hunting "surtout" to grace his birthday celebrations.[124] A catalog issued in November

8.8. Hitler and Himmler admire Meissen figurines
As this image shows, Hitler and Himmler were evidently charmed by
Meissen's old-fashioned military figurines.

1938—the month of Kristallnacht—expressed pleasure at the turn of political events, saying in the "Forward":

> At the State Porcelain Factory, Meissen, artistic porcelain modeling has al-
> ways been cherished and cared for. Even in times of economic collapse
> and cultural decline, the manufactory has devoted itself to only using the
> most suitable models to render in porcelain. The economic revival that has
> set in since the National Socialist revolution and the recollection of the ar-
> tistic powers unique to our race have created receptive foundations for
> taking porcelain modeling seriously once more.[125]

Interestingly, this catalog incorporated figurines made between 1919 and
1938, thus including many that would, from the Nazi standpoint, have been

made during the period of republican "cultural decline." Meissen's prices remained high, and its offerings various and largely backward looking. It almost certainly benefited from the "flight to real assets" many Europeans made in uncertain times.[126] The firm returned to profitability very quickly after Hitler's ascent to power, and it remained in the black, astonishingly, even through 1944 (see chapter 9). For Meissen, at least, Nazi "mercantilism" was a blessing rather than a curse.

The Nazis trifled little at first with the former KPM, lodging it under the Reich's Economics Ministry until 1937 (when it was once again moved to the Prussian Finance Ministry's ledger). Günter von Pechmann was allowed to continue on as director until 1938, despite his connections to the now-defunct Bauhaus and his wife's status as a "half-Jewess." But on the eve of the firm's 175th anniversary, Pechmann was finally replaced by Max Pfeiffer, who brought Paul Scheurich with him from Meissen—replaying on a smaller scale Frederick the Great's extractions from the Saxon manufactory during the Seven Years' War. With Pechmann gone, the manufactory used the occasion to present itself as the legitimate and logical heir of Frederick the Great, fulfilling Prussia's artistic destiny.[127] The manufactory issued a self-commemorating service ("Arkadia") adorned with Schinkelian biscuit medallions, conveniently forgetting that Frederick's tastes had remained thoroughly rococo. Hitler's great affection for the grandiose neoclassicism of Paul Ludwig Troost and Albert Speer might also have inclined the manufactory to take this philhellenic turn. Paul Scheurich's elaborate all-white table tableaux "The Birth of Beauty," made for Nazi foreign minister Joachim von Ribbentrop in 1942, went in quite a different direction, combining rococo design with a disturbingly fascistic form of nudity.

The most favored of the manufactories under Nazi rule, however, was Nymphenburg, which had enjoyed more financial success under its private leaseholder Albert Bäuml than it had ever done under the Bavarian monarchy. Bäuml had taken control of the lease in 1888 and made Nymphenburg profitable, on a small scale, even during the later 1920s. He died in 1929, but not before renewing the lease so that his sons could take over production. In 1935, Erich Geldner, the leader of the Nazi trade group devoted to glass and ceramics, opened an inquiry into Bäuml's ancestry and determined that according to Nazi racial laws, Bäuml had been a Jew; he had married a Bavarian Catholic, meaning that his sons were, at best, *Mischlinge*. But there the inquiry was stonewalled. The Finance Ministry seized an opportunity for plausible deniability, as Albert, upon arriving in Munich, had given his father's name as "Ignaz" (his more honest brother Josef, a coal dealer, had recorded "Isaac" as his father's name and had acknowledged that his religion was "Mosaic"; as a result, Josef had lost his citizenship). The ministry noted instead that two of Bäuml's sons had volunteered for service at the front in World War I, and that Geldner, on the other hand, had had ties with the "Jewish" firm of Rosenthal, which had tried to buy Nymphenburg in the early 1920s. Undoubtedly more important in the protection of the firm, however, was a fact that the Bavarian minister president let slip in correspondence with the Finance Ministry: the Führer had just ordered a dinner service for thirty-six from Nymphenburg.[128]

The tale behind Führer's order is an instructive one. It begins with an artistic friendship between the sculptor Joseph Wackerle, who had worked at Nymphenburg since at least 1907 and became its artistic director in the 1920s, and Paul Ludwig Troost, Hitler's favorite architect, who had designed shop interiors for the firm before the Great War. Troost, like Wackerle, revered the "chaste" classicism of the Napoleonic era, and in the 1920s, the two pioneered what we might call fascist classicism. Troost, for his part, had designed Munich's "Temple of Honor" for the Nazis killed in 1923 and its Haus der deutschen Kunst, where the "Degenerate Art" exhibition was staged in 1937. Wackerle, meanwhile, created oversized, classicizing figure groups, including Nazi eagles and the sculptures for the 1936 Olympic stadium. Both Troost and Wackerle were friends of Bäuml; and Troost, along with his wife Gerdy, a designer and interior decorator in her own right, helped to throw commissions Nymphenburg's way. This was even more the case after Hitler's rise to power; although Troost died in 1934, Gerdy Troost became Hitler's personal adviser for the decoration of his homes and office spaces, including his railcar (plate 15), his apartment in Munich, and his Reich Chancellery. For these, she ordered heavily from Nymphenburg, and as in the era of the rococo princes, where Hitler led, his "nobles" followed.[129] Accordingly, Nymphenburg became, in the words of one commentator, "the purveyor-in-chief for the political elite of the 'Third Reich'"[130]—and proudly produced porcelains for the state's highest offices and officers.[131] It was Gerdy, probably along with another heavy consumer of Nymphenburgia, Albert Speer, who protected the Bavarian manufactory from an attempted takeover by Himmler, and Bäuml's sons from persecution later in the period, when at one point they were in danger of deportation to a concentration camp. In 1941, as the regime's need for self-monumentalization faded in favor of its need for war matériel, Nymphenburg converted chiefly to military production, employing eight of its own forced laborers.[132]

Much more than most German leaders, at least since the eighteenth century, the Nazis cared deeply about style and symbolism, though functionalism in tableware as in architecture also suited a regime whose ideals rarely trumped its commitment to militaristic efficiency.[133] Despite Hitler's strong preference for what was described above as "chaste classicism," and Meissen's hopes for a racially proper artistic Renaissance, in general, for everyday wares the functionalist aesthetic of the end of the Weimar period prevailed, as in, for example, Werkbund artist Wilhelm Wagenfeld's simple 693 form, made and lightly decorated for the Wehrmacht by Fürstenberg; or Tirschenreuth's Form 100, sold to the Labor Front for its canteens.[134] The industry's output of luxury porcelain continued to decline.[135] In part this was the result of price controls, and of restrictions on the use of gold, which had begun already in the mid-1930s (for domestic porcelains) and became full prohibitions by 1943. The Nazis, too, faced a market characterized by a shrinking number of ceramics connoisseurs, and customers more inclined to invest their cash in appliances or other durable goods.

But if we sketch Nazi styles and forms beyond the functionalist, we can certainly see patterns. The most obvious is the return to pure white, already heralded by the animals of Esser and neoclassical nudes. As we know well from other artistic genres, the Nazis favored sharp white/black contrasts and oversized, classicizing male nudes, along the lines of the sculptures made by Arno Breker and Joseph Wackerle and the architecture of Troost and

Speer. Leni Riefenstahl's photography, too, fits this mode precisely, especially if one thinks of her film "Olympia," replete with images of seminude athletes, shot from below and against vast, empty skies. This aesthetic orientation lent the regime an air of gravitas and eternity and paid homage to its cult of the pure Aryan body. The Nymphenburg commissions Hitler ordered and the KPM's assertive issuing of "Arcadia" testify to the regime's commitment to this fascistic form of *Glanz*. It comes as little surprise that Himmler specifically instructed his SS manufactory at Allach that most of its figurines be made in white, and that the firm's first catalog claimed: "White porcelain is the embodiment of the German soul."[136]

If we try to put together a list of common, or at least valued, items made for the regime to compare with "preis courante" lists from previous chapters, we find many fewer models, and, not surprisingly, little in the way of ethnographic or even modern figurines. Very likely the most widely sold figurines were those of Aryan children, and of animals, and especially of horses, particularly valued by the party leadership.[137] Figures from the forest continued to appeal, especially to fanatical hunters like Göring, but also to those whose German nationalism included the rapturous invocation of the Germanic "Wald." Replicas of paintings by Dürer, whose Germanness had made him a nationalist hero for some time, increased in popularity. Then there were figurines of oversized, underdressed, heroes, mostly not identified with specific Greek or Roman gods, but now anonymized, and female nudes, whose nakedness has a particularly prurient quality to it. Hutschenreuther, Nymphenburg, and of course Allach made busts of Hitler himself; Fürstenberg made memorial cups for the Olympics of 1936.[138] Meissen's 1938 catalog offers Venuses and putti, a Turk with a pipe, bears and birds, painted or plain white. Only three real persons merited statuettes: Henry the Lion (Duke of Saxony and Bavaria and founder of Munich), Frederick the Great, and war hero and former *Reichspräsident* Paul von Hindenburg, now safely dead. Ideologically, this was rather tame; not even the Hindenburg bust would need to be smashed when the genocidal regime and its supporters faced their reckoning after 1945.

Porcelain was not a medium suitable for depicting one's enemies, and though anti-Semitic figurines certainly were produced, especially by smaller factories, their numbers do not seem to have increased during the Nazi era.[139] But of course the Nazis did apply their racial laws to many living porcelain makers and owners, including the Jewish Simson family, which had operated the Gotha porcelain manufactory since 1883.[140] The most notorious case was that of Philipp Rosenthal, the founder of that most "modern" of ceramics concerns, Rosenthal Porcelain. Before 1933, Philipp Rosenthal had been a very important person indeed. In 1918, he had received the title "Geheimrat" and soon thereafter had been offered membership in the powerful Reichsverband der deutsche Industrie. In addition to having served as president of the Manufacturers' Cartel, he had been a vocal spokesman for German exports and had played a crucial role in saving the Leipzig trade fair. On the occasion of the fiftieth anniversary of his involvement in the porcelain industry in 1929, even Weimar president Hindenburg had attended the party to present his compliments. In that year, the newspapers praised this German "self-made man" who now operated eight factories employing nearly seven thousand workers; Rosenthal's friends and coworkers compiled a hagiographic biography, which failed to mention his wartime fights with the dealers or his aggressive attempts to take over other firms.[141]

Rosenthal took heavy losses in the years 1929–33, including 800,000 RM in 1932, but that was the case across the industry, and by 1934, the manufactory was already back in the black.[142] But by this time, Rosenthal himself was becoming a liability; not only was his Jewishness well known, but the Geheimrat was approaching eighty. To ward off the Aryanizing of his firm, in November 1933 he attempted to bequeath his shares to his playboy "Aryan" stepson, over the heated objections of his board, and two of his grandsons, who claimed he had lost his reason.[143] In 1934, now packed with party members, the board forced Rosenthal to take a "vacation" and confronted rumors about the firm's Jewishness by advertising their own Aryanness in the Nazi press. Their ad concluded by turning the tables on the firm's critics, and asking for help in rooting out the saboteurs who were endangering the jobs of nearly four thousand hardworking *Volksgenossen* by besmirching the Rosenthal brand.[144]

In 1936, a psychiatrist confirmed that Rosenthal had been mentally incompetent since March 1934. The family was now stripped of its voting rights and forced to sell its shares at rock-bottom prices; soon thereafter, Philipp died in a sanatorium in Bonn, and Maria (wife number 5) fled to the South of France.[145] The board accused Rosenthal of having nearly run the business into the ground, which further legitimated his ouster—though it was best, the Trade Ministry said, not to sue him directly, so as not to damage the brand.[146] Directed by NSDAP members, the company continued production through World War II, focusing especially on technical porcelain. Thanks to the support of Reich economic minister Hjalmar Schacht, Rosenthal kept its original name, despite complaints about its Jewishness; doing so was critical to continuing sales abroad.[147] During the war itself, one thousand forced laborers were at work in Selb, six hundred of them employed in Rosenthal's electrical works.[148]

Of course, it was not just Jewish factory owners who suffered from Nazi depredations. Many Jewish owners of valuable (and not so valuable) porcelains also were stripped of their possessions, as images from Nazi warehouses of looted goods show.[149] Many readers know about the expropriation of the Ephrussi family in Vienna, thanks to Edmund De Waal's elegiac *The Hare with the Amber Eyes*; in this case, the family's netsuke collection alone was saved, thanks to the brave actions of a maid. The heirs of Gustav von Klemperer, chairman of the Dresdner Bank and a great collector of porcelain, were deprived of a collection of over eight hundred pieces after the family was forced to flee Germany (fig. 8.9). Once in Nazi hands, the collection was packed into twenty-five crates and thought to have been destroyed in the bombing of Dresden. Many years after the war, four of the crates were discovered, and in 1991 the recovered pieces, many of them broken, were finally returned to the heirs, who donated most of them back to the Dresden Porcelain Museum. A further restitution of some shards took place around 2010, with a portion of these being auctioned at Bonhams for nearly £550,000.[150] The Arnhold family's collection suffered a much less tragic fate.

8.9. The Klemperer family collection
Taken about 1911, this photo of the Klemperer clan posing in front of their
priceless collection of Meissen figurines demonstrates the pride this Dresden
Jewish family took in their porcelains.

After her husband's death in 1935, Lisa Arnhold managed to flee Germany
with their enormous Meissen collection, selections of which were displayed
at the Frick Museum in 2008.[151]

The stories we know are just the most famous stories, of the largest and
most valuable collections; they represent only the very tip of an iceberg of
family histories involving the salvaging or the loss of special porcelain pieces,
their travel into exile, their survival or destruction, together with the lives of
individuals. Many of these pieces would have already been heirlooms, handed
down by earlier generations of German and central European women who
had so lovingly dusted them on salon shelves or placed them on holiday tables.
Because of its special attachments to middle-class respectability, to display, to
feasts and special guest visits, porcelain embodied an emotional world that
was largely, but not wholly, destroyed by World War II and the Holocaust. As

the original users and those who remember these pieces die out, we are in danger of losing a great expanse of family memory that is much more precious than any of the shepherdesses and soup tureens those women held so dear.

The recent literature on consumption during the Nazi era agrees that the Nazis' greatest trick was to take credit for the ending of mass unemployment,[152] and to maintain, even into wartime, a hopeful vision of the happy, healthy, mass-consumer society "Aryan" Germans had only begun to enjoy. The "surface normality" that allowed members of the race to go back to working and consuming distracted ordinary Germans from the regime's violent repression of its enemies and its preparations for world war.[153] The porcelain industry played a relatively minor role in making the racial state, though it did profit, at least at first, from the policies of the new "prince," and did not hesitate to oust Jewish entrepreneurs or serve its new masters. The maintaining of brand product names as well as of sentimental associations with the Wilhelmine bourgeois home would ease porcelain's transition to yet another regime when the Nazi war machine came crashing down in 1945.

Chapter 9

From Cold War Wonder to Contemporary White Elephant

Does the Story End Here?

Like German history proper, porcelain's later twentieth- and early twenty-first-century story teems with disasters as well as new beginnings. Remarkably, the years 1945–49 did not prove so very disastrous for this industry, as in many places production was able to resume almost immediately after the war's end. The ensuing period of Germany's division into two states, one integrated into the capitalist marketplaces of the West, and the other into the planned economies of the communist East, actually proved to be something of a third "golden age" for porcelain makers on both sides of the Iron Curtain. Functionalism, at least in theory, carried the day; in practice, porcelain makers never gave up on stylistic diversity, even as machines came into increasing use, especially in western manufactories. One state maker survived on each side of the Berlin Wall, the KPM in (West) Berlin, and Meissen in socialist Saxony. In fact, the Cold War treated Meissen remarkably well, once, that is, officials recognized its potential for harvesting hard currency by exporting wares (chiefly rococo models) to the West.

Already by 1989, however, western, and to a lesser degree, eastern, porcelain markets and labor forces were contracting, as customers once again changed their patterns of luxury consumption. The fall of the wall brought many socialist producers to their knees, without doing any obvious favors for their once-again-brothers in the West. But the real sting in our story's tail is what has happened to the porcelain industry after the 2008 economic downturn. The KPM has finally been privatized (though correspondingly, Nymphenburg has returned to princely administration), and hundreds of firms have closed. If we have seen firms come and go in the past, we have not before confronted the possibility that the whole *industry* will disappear, at least in Europe, and only individual porcelain artists will survive;[1] but at this writing, this appears a likely prospect. German porcelain's story may, indeed, end here.

Porcelain Survives a Second World War

Whether war is good or bad for business depends, of course, on the war and on the business. For our porcelain makers, the Second World War in general brought headaches, especially for smaller firms and those dedicated mostly to tableware production. For those with the capacity to produce technical porcelains and armaments, however, business was not all that bad, except that everyone was subjected to greater and greater squeezes put on by the state. This is another area that needs considerable research, but we can gather scattered testimonies to suggest trends across the period from 1939 to 1943, and the fallout afterward of what became quite suddenly in 1944 a serious on-the-ground conflict for German and Austrian workers and factories.

As we have seen, porcelain sales rose across the mid-1930s and were quite healthy in 1939, thanks especially to state orders. Some intervention into personnel and management on the basis of racist policies occurred, as in the cases of Rosenthal and the KPM, and some manufactories were patronized more than others. Prices were not allowed to rise, and in fact fell steeply. But, aside from Allach, the state did not operate any of these factories directly nor intervene extensively in the market. In April 1941, two months before the invasion of the Soviet Union, however, that began to change. At this point, the Economics Ministry invoked its July 1933 act allowing for the creation of forcible cartels to insist that all tableware and art makers accede to the measures imposed by the Verband Deutscher Porzellangeschirr-Fabriken, to which 117 factories officially belonged.[2] The effect of this order is hard to gauge, but it seems to have resulted chiefly in tighter regulation of exports and the severe limiting of non-war-related production and of the use of precious substances, such as gold. Hutschenreuther, for example, had to report quarterly on its stocks of palladium and platinum, which it received from the Wehrmacht, and which, it complained, were retrieved with difficulty because they came chiefly from "smashed teeth,"[3] presumably from the regime's victims.

Business in the industry remained good enough that in August 1941 both the Winterling concern and Rosenthal were planning to open new works, each employing 100–150 workers. Reports collected by the Bavarian trade ministry in 1942–43 indicated that manufactories in this area, including Zeh, Tettau, Kahla, and Waldsassen, were still operating, and showing profits. In 1942 Kahla posted profits of over 1 million RM.[4] As of 1943, demand began to outstrip supply, and porcelain was added to the list of rationed commodities; rumors circulated that even in Thuringia, supplies were so short that in larger families all the children had to drink from one cup.[5] On May 1, 1944, manufactories were ordered not to make decorated ceramics of any kind.[6] But even in 1944, many firms, like Fürstenberg, were still posting small gains,[7] and requisitions remained high. A summer 1944 report estimated the Reich's ceramics needs at seventy-nine million pieces, of which the industry had managed to make 94 percent; as far as porcelain was concerned, by November, nearly the full quota of seventeen million pieces had been made.[8] Small wonder that on its one hundredth anniversary in 1944, Kahla employed nine thousand, some of whom were surely foreign forced laborers. The much smaller works at Kloster Veilsdorf alone employed more than two hundred of these, mostly from the USSR and Poland.[9] Of course firms were not just making tableware but, even more than between 1914 and 1918, focused production on munitions, metal substitutes, and hospital supplies.

How did porcelain makers' physical facilities fare in the course of this total war? Our information is piecemeal, but suggestive. One apprentice employed by Augarten (successor to the WPM) remembered spending most of his time fixing windows, shoveling snow, and chopping wood for other employees to take home to heat their dwellings; he was injured when the factory was struck by a bomb.[10] But most factories appear to have suffered relatively little damage from the fighting. Kahla seems to have remained fully intact until seized by Soviet soldiers at the war's end. The Waldsassen factory escaped damage until April 1945, when it was the site of a German-American fire-fight and suffered the destruction of about one-third of its plant.[11] Oscar Schaller & Co. was occupied by the Americans also in April 1945 but was in sufficiently good shape to wish to start production again in August.[12] Tirschenreuth, also in Bavaria, also escaped destruction and rapidly restarted production of wares to sell to US servicemen.[13] The Silesian firms, too, were protected from bombing and continued producing until the collapse of the eastern front in early 1945; many were able to begin production again after V-E Day in early May. Like Kahla and Meissen, their difficulties would come after the war, with their occupation by Soviet troops.[14]

The state firms, in fact, suffered more physical destruction than most of the private firms. Late in the war, the Nymphenburg factory sustained considerable damage from aerial bombardment, estimated by the leaseholders (still the Bäuml brothers) at a bit over 250,000 RM—though the works were sufficiently intact to still employ 102 workers in February 1946. Though it acknowledged that the buildings and machines were its responsibility to repair, the Bavarian government, facing more pressing problems, dragged its feet, finally forwarding the leaseholders 83,000 DM in 1952.[15] Bombers struck the KPM in November 1943, but it was able to resume production in January 1944 at about 50 percent capacity. In June, operations vital to the war effort were moved from Berlin to Selb, where production resumed, but no decorated porcelains were made. In the confusion after the war's end, the painting department fell into Czech hands, and the return of materials from Selb (under British occupation) to the manufactory in the American sector of Berlin was difficult. In 1946, the courts ruled in favor of the continuation of the KPM under the name "Berlin Porcelain Manufactory" and placed the factory under the authority of the municipality of Berlin.[16]

In Saxony, Meissen continued production—including bazookas—and still employed 712 (including at outlet shops) in 1943.[17] Sales in 1944 amounted to an astonishing 3.5 million RM, down only about 60,000 RM from the previous year, and netting a profit of 200,000 RM.[18] Late in the war, the Meissen works also provided quarters for Hungarian members of the Wehrmacht as well as space for a firm making radio equipment. The museum's showpieces were boxed up and placed in Böttger's old haunts, the cellars of the Albrechtsburg.[19] The buildings remained unscathed until the final year of the war, when the Wehrmacht destroyed two bridges over the Elbe in a fruitless attempt to prevent the invasion of the Soviets. When on May 6, 1945, the town's residents were asked to stage a last-ditch defense of the city, some of them chased out the Nazi town council instead.[20] No one could have known then what the future for Meissen—the town or the factory— would hold.

Life after Nazism?

The Nazi period, and even the Second World War, were not disastrous for the porcelain industry; in fact, one might say that many firms did quite well out of this devil's bargain. But *after* 1945 came difficulties, for both private and state firms, and especially for those with the misfortune to fall into Soviet hands. In Silesia, occupied by the Russians and then incorporated into the new Polish state, the German population either fled or was forced out after the war's end. The Poles did move to restart the industry and even retained many of its old trademarks, including Altwasser and Königszelt. Weisswasser, which fell on the East German side of the Oder-Neisse line, was nationalized after the founding of the German Democratic Republic in 1949.[21] Similarly, Kahla fell into East German hands once the Soviets retreated from Thuringia and in 1952 was nationalized under the title VEB (Volkseigener Betriebe, or People's Enterprise) Porzellanwerk Kahla.[22]

The transition from war to peace was neither perfectly smooth nor agreeable to the factories in the West, either. Occupation officials controlled coal supplies, and they had more pressing uses for this precious material than making porcelain. Occupiers also seized unoccupied edifices, using parts of the Schönwald factory, for example, to intern more than two thousand civil and military prisoners.[23] The Allies found that they too needed porcelain, for their own purposes. In early 1946, the Bavarian Economics Ministry complained to the occupation government that the US Army had seized the porcelain stocks of the factories in the region, and was refusing even to help supply local hospitals and canteens or desperately needy refugees. Eight major factories, including Nymphenburg, Rosenthal, Lorenz Hutschenreuther, and Arzberg, the minister reported, "have already become pure U.S. army factories and are, therefore, not allowed to supply the civil population." The complaint was accompanied by a request to turn distribution over to local authorities, and a Standard Operating Procedure was suggested, and apparently approved, for the release of china for sale in the area.[24]

At Meissen, the war's end and Russian occupation took a considerable toll. In the wake of the Nazis' defeat, local leaders tasked Herbert Neuhaus, a former painter and SPD activist who had been dismissed in 1933, with heading the manufactory, but he could not prevent the Russians from seizing the Albrechtsburg treasures and dismantling most of the works.[25] Just as seriously, the firm's bank accounts had been blocked, taking away its liquid capital.[26] There was, moreover, a coal shortage—something that afflicted all the firms in the immediate postwar period, as had happened at the Great War's end. Nonetheless, Neuhaus and workers desperate to keep their jobs restarted production in September 1945, with painters decorating white works that had somehow escaped destruction in the course of the war and its wake. But the Soviets had not finished their expropriations and began requisitioning porcelain and stoneware, including two hundred complete table services, valued at 284,000 RM, specifically from the Meissen factory.[27] In July 1946 the Red Army ordered the creation of a liquidation committee to seize all the works' assets.[28] On its way to dissolution, Meissen was folded into a firm known as Sowjetisch Staatlich Aktien-Gesellschaft für Baustoffe "Zement." In 1948, when the future of the manufactory was still unclear, the Saxon Finance Ministry estimated that in seizing the factory, the USSR had taken assets valued at 2.17 million RM.[29] What they would do with the Saxon porcelain manufactory was still anyone's guess.

At the factory itself, Neuhaus and his German workforce tried to forestall liquidation, taking the inventorying process slowly and objecting to

Soviet demands to fire workers in order to commandeer their salaries. In late 1947, a fed-up Director Neuhaus unleashed his frustration with the Liquidation Committee and detailed the unfolding of events at Meissen since the war's end, beginning in May 1945:

> There was no longer any governing force. There was also no authority who could have given any instructions on the continuation of the factory. Under the dictates of the occupation powers the mayor of the city of the Meissen was given local authority with command powers. The manufactory too was temporarily entrusted to the city of Meissen. Meissen requested that Mr. Herbert Neuhaus take over the leadership of the manufactory as business director, under his own charge. During the time that the manufactory was being nearly 100% disassembled, it continued production, not because clever measures were used to cling onto cash, which the Russian army fully controlled, but in order to save the manufactory's cultural heritage of models and forms, artistic artifacts, valuable paintings, drawings, and the like. That this [rescue operation] succeeded we have only the full dedication of the workforce to thank. Through the idealistic efforts of [Meissen's] craftspersons the manufactory has survived the greatest crisis of its history.[30]

This is why, Neuhaus explained, the firm did not fire its workers, and the Russians, too, should be thankful to them, rather than calculating their cost. "Those responsible for the manufactory have acted as Germans and done their duty, and all of their efforts were made in the best interests of the factory and its workforce." Go ahead and discipline us, he concluded, if you must!

As it happens, however, Meissen managed to escape liquidation, perhaps because it did keep workers employed and producing, perhaps because its Soviet codirector N. D. Nikotin was sympathetic to the cause.[31] Another commentator claims that the Soviet elite coveted Meissen's coffee services—the older patterns, of course.[32] In any event, the Saxony manufactory rode out this storm as well, and in 1950 its operations were handed over to a new state, the German Democratic Republic, and it received a new name: VEB Staatliche Porzellan Manufaktur Meissen. By this time, it could claim a whopping 918 employees.[33] It would now have to face the challenge of finding customers for its luxury goods in a seemingly hostile communist context; and not surprisingly, until at least 1955, it operated, once more, in the red.[34]

We will return to find Meissen in better circumstances. Let us now briefly survey the fate of the other surviving state manufactory, the KPM, in the immediate postwar era. After 1945, the KPM, its works still located in the western suburb of Charlottenburg, had been placed in the hands of the (West) Berlin city government. But in 1948, as West Berlin itself was struggling to stay out of the hands of the Soviets, the North-Rhine Westphalia government attempted a takeover. Only after the British-American airlift saved the western portion of the city did British military officials restore the works to Charlottenburg by decree. The relocated works in Selb were still operating, however, and it took energetic negotiations for the Berliners to get the Bavarians to stop "KPM" production, which only occurred in 1955 (and the technical works continued there until 1960). The newly refurbished factory reopened in Charlottenburg in 1955, at a cost of about 4 million DM. But the restoration story was not over. During the war, the KPM's historical molds had been sent to a cave near Eisleben for safety and then fell into the hands of the Russians, who eventually sent them to the Märkisches Museum in East Berlin. The KPM was allowed to use them but then had to send them back and forth to the East until they paid 15,000 DM to purchase them outright. The firm's archives remained in the East and were not restored to the KPM until 1981, as part of a deal for the West's return of Karl Schinkel's sculptures for the Unter den Linden castle bridge.[35] Like Berlin itself, the KPM's postwar history was largely shaped by Cold War machinations beyond its control and not particularly conducive to its flourishing.

Porcelain in a Divided Germany

In 1949, the Germany that Bismarck had united and Hitler had first expanded and then destroyed officially became two Germanys, divided along the lines that divided Allied and Soviet occupation zones. Berlin, too, was divided into zones, though separated by the fearsome wall only in 1961. Each state acquired a new political and economic ideology, democracy and capitalism in the West, and communism and state planning in the East. After 1949, two new currencies appeared: the deutschmark (DM) and the ostmark (OM). Ostmarks, like other Soviet-bloc currency, were not pegged to the price of gold, nor were they officially exchangeable for western currencies, beyond very small amounts for travelers' use. In the first years of both states' existence, efforts went chiefly into disentangling and rebuilding each economic unit, and integrating them into each side's political-economic "bloc." At least fourteen million Germans had lost their homes to air raids during the war, and millions more were displaced from eastern zones; many German soldiers did not return from Soviet captivity until the early 1950s. Both Germanys faced terrible food, heating, and housing shortages; in the East Nazi collaborators were much more harshly treated than in the West, where many senior businessmen, scholars, and even military officers were given a pass in the interests of fighting the new, "cold," war. West Germans received Marshall Plan assistance; East Germans did not. In the eastern zone, when Soviet troops retreated, they took a great deal of industrial as well as cultural booty with them. A centrally planned socialist economy was put in place and private enterprises dissolved in favor of nationalized firms. In the West there was more continuity, but also chaos as firms assessed war damage, negotiated with occupiers, sought to reestablish workforces and supply chains, and battled a flourishing black market.

One of the difficulties the industry had to face in the immediate postwar era was—as in 1815 and in 1918—the impoverishment of many of its would-be customers. At the war's end and for several years thereafter, the whole of central Europe was awash with displaced persons—Jews and other survivors of concentration camps, foreign forced laborers, Germans who had fled or been ejected from the eastern regions Hitler had ravished, and "Trümmerfrauen," women whose homes had been destroyed by bombing and now subsisted in the ruins. Of course the first priority for all these individuals was food and shelter; but the upside of their predicament, for our industry, was that a very great number of people longed to set up house again, and to equip those homes with tableware (not to mention toilets). In a way, too, perhaps the industry was lucky that its female consumer base had not been as thoroughly decimated as the middle-aged male population; in 1950, in the Federal Republic, women between twenty-five and thirty-nine outnumbered men by 1,400 to 1,000, and nearly one-third of households were headed by widows or single women. But 15 percent of the population also still lived in dwellings averaging three persons per room.[36] The market was potentially a vast one, at least on the lower end; but again the question was: what would consumers buy? And would they buy enough to keep the industry alive? These questions were even more complicated for those makers who ended up on the communist side of the German border: what would they be allowed to make, and sell?

Initially, the return to sales was hampered by another postwar reality: the ubiquity of the black market and the permeability of the never entirely "iron" curtain. In Germany itself, food and even consumer durables were widely available until the very end of the war; but in the last months, as armies converged from all sides, order collapsed. Especially in the zones occupied by the Red Army, extensive looting (as well as the raping of perhaps two million women) took place, and food, cigarettes, and other valuables—such as watches and Meissen porcelain—became items of significant worth. After the Nazis capitulated in May 1945, millions of Germans surged back into our porcelain regions, Silesia, Bohemia, Thuringia, and Saxony, heading for the West, and a great deal of porcelain appeared on the black market. American occupiers in the region evidently sent large porcelain parcels home to the United States.[37] In the fall of 1949, the Franconian ceramics maker Rudolf Pech complained to officials that huge numbers of figurines from Russian-occupied Thuringia were appearing in shops in Munich, Heidelberg, and Frankfurt. Unscrupulous merchants, he claimed, were taking advantage of devalued currency and of desperate sellers and were offering prices far below his own. His firm's existence—and that of its workers, 80 percent of whom were Silesian and Sudeten refugees—was in peril.[38]

Now deploying Cold War rhetoric, western porcelain firms once again asked for state protection. In April 1950, the *Nordbayerische Zeitung* published an article entitled "A Serious Danger: Smuggling and Dumping from the Eastern Zone," in which it was alleged that the communist states were trying to undermine West German capitalism by secretly dumping cheap wares, including electrical and building materials, in the western zone; a porcelain factory owner in Selb sent a copy of the article to the Bavarian Ministry of Economics, together with a plea for protection against these "black imports."[39] Another owner of a technical firm complained, similarly, about a German entrepreneur's plans to start production of electrical porcelain in Pausa, on the eastern side of the "curtain," and to dump his wares in the West.[40] These complaints continued into the early 1950s, alongside requests for tax breaks to subsidize further mechanization and measures to prevent silicosis, which government officials, at last, were attempting to enforce. Unable to offer tax breaks, the Bavarian government retreated to making silicosis remediation not binding, but a recommendation.[41]

State officials would be wise to pay attention to the ceramics industry, one interested party advised the Bavarian Economics Ministry; porcelain, he claimed "is the Bundesrepublik's Number 1 hard currency supplier." Bavaria itself, he argued, had made more than 6 million DM in 1949 alone, and the *Süddeutsche Zeitung* had recently described it as "Bavaria's Nibelungen Hoard."[42] This was certainly an extravagant claim, but ceramics sales were indeed healthy in the immediate postwar era. The Waldsassen firm, restarted by Oskar Bareuther's wife while he was undergoing de-Nazification, had 266 workers at the war's end, and 360 by 1947; sales in 1947 were already 1.7 million RM and improved greatly after the introduction of the DM in 1949.[43] In western Germany in 1950, there were some 1,517 ceramics businesses, employing 62,406 persons (25,303 of them women and 14,108 of them "Heimatsvertriebene" Germans driven out of their "homelands" in eastern Europe), more than employed in all of Germany in 1928.[44] Exports of stoneware and porcelain stood at 15 million DM in 1950 and 39 million DM in 1951. It would be hard to estimate the full value of electrical and technical porcelains, but they clearly played a significant role in the "electrotechnical products" that accounted for 659 million DM in exports in 1951.[45] The United States took the largest share of the 61.2 million DM worth of stoneware and porcelain exported in 1952, followed by Italy, the Netherlands, and Belgium.[46]

9.1. Rosenthal studio house, Düsseldorf

Interior of the hypermodern Rosenthal "Studio Haus" in Düsseldorf.
There were eighteen of these in West Germany by 1980, and a further
thirteen in other European cities.

A few Jewish factory owners had their property returned to them. The Freiernola firm in Thuringia, for example, was returned to its owners in 1948 and continued to produce under the communist regime.[47] The most notable case, however, was that of Rosenthal Porzellan, which, as we have seen, was forcibly extracted from its owners in 1935. Philipp Rosenthal's son, Philip, had joined the Hitler Youth in 1931, not realizing that according to Nazi racial standards, he was a Jew. This he recognized only after being sent to Oxford in 1934 for safety. At the time of the war's outbreak he was in France, organizing an expedition to Mongolia; as a non-citizen he could not join the French army and thus joined the French Foreign Legion, which he despised. He was interned for desertion but eventually returned to England, where he waited out the war as a baker's apprentice.[48] In 1948 Philip returned to Bavaria and launched a campaign for the return of his father's company; with the help of Ludwig Erhard (later FRG president) he recovered 11 percent of the firm's shares. In 1951 he went to work as head of the firm's advertising department, and in 1958 he became president of the board.[49]

From the first, Rosenthal Jr. had his eye on the US market; he also retained, and elaborated, his father's dedication to patronizing artists, if for no other reason than to lend the firm *Glanz* and prestige. When, in the 1950s, the KPM and other traditional makers were profiting greatly from reissuing rococo models—substituting rich American and Rhineland industrial consumers for lost Pomeranian elites—it was rather risky to plunge production into modern design.[50] But Philip's wager earned him excellent publicity, including a largely complimentary cover story in *Der Spiegel*. In the mid-1950s, he worked successfully with the American designer Raymond Loewy, whose Form 2000 was one of the few modernist commercial success stories, selling 132,000 services between 1954 and 1956, and helping Rosenthal take second place in imported European porcelains in the US market, behind the German industry's traditional rival, Wedgwood.[51] He also patronized an international array of artists such as the Danish designer Bjorn Winblad, the Finnish artist Tapio Wikkala, and even Salvador Dalí, and in 1960, he established "Studio Line," a special, limited-edition line of artistic products that were sold in hypermodernist boutiques (fig. 9.1).

As we will see below ("Style and Postwar Identity"), however, Rosenthal was not willing to devote the whole of his production to modern art, and artists who worked for him had to follow his commands, and not vice versa. "Studio Line" projects were created in Selb, under Rosenthal's watchful eye, and with his sometime heavy-handed input. In America alone Rosenthal consented to allowing department stores to sell his wares, and at home luxury retailers complained about his strong-arm tactics in insisting that only his factory's products be featured in their shop windows. Other sellers, especially Lorenz Hutschenreuther, threatened lawsuits. As if reprising the elder Rosenthal's combat with the dealers during the Great War and interwar period, Philip refused to back down in what he himself described as "a hell of a fight with the retailers in Germany." In the end, Rosenthal made a deal with the retailers, and first Hutschenreuther, and then Villeroy & Boch, responded by opening their own boutique outlets.[52]

Artistry made for good advertising. But for all manufacturers now, pleasing the bourgeois housewife remained critical. As the West German economy recovered and boomed in the mid-1950s and 1960s, women invested heavily in rebuilding and redecorating their homes. The family meal took on renewed symbolic value as women sought to recover what they had lost in the war and occupation period: "familial integrity, physical and spiritual health, economic stability, and material well-being."[53] Holidays—previously tempered by rationing and wartime anxieties—could again become festive family occasions, characterized by material abundance and rich food; Christmas plates and Easter decorations returned to the market. New home-decorating magazines appeared—in the East as in the West—to tout modern living, which did finally catch on. Customers bought small appliances such as electric irons, clad in heat-resistant porcelain.

The emphasis on domesticity and family did not, of course, halt the reopening of cafés, restaurants, and hotels, all of them in need of ceramic services. The ubiquity of cigarette smokers—all of whom required an ashtray—also gave the industry a wide range of new customers, especially as ashtrays became a common means of advertising other products. Even the fashion for fresh flowers helped the industry, which devised hundreds

9.2. Worker shoveling porcelain, Selb, 1960

The porcelain industry has always produced a great deal of flawed or unsalable excess.

or perhaps thousands of new vase forms, chiefly in basic white, in the
postwar era.

The 1950s and 1960s, one might say, constituted something of a third
"golden age" for porcelain makers, though overproduction and waste remained perpetual problems (fig. 9.2). Many firms engaged artists to pioneer
modernist designs, profits were steady, and workers enjoyed what were generally speaking well-paying jobs. The design palate remained wide, ranging
from continued prewar patterns to chic asymmetrical forms.[54] By 1958,
Schönwald employed twelve hundred, exceeding its post-Depression peak of
1,015, though not its 1928 zenith (1,340). It continued to be successful,
thanks to its investment in the production of "hotel" porcelain.[55] Despite the
fact that many firms' profits were ploughed back into plant modernization
and machinery, overall in the industry employment numbers remained high
in 1970, with an estimated seventy-nine thousand working in fine ceramics

in West Germany alone. But in 1971 that number fell to seventy-five thousand, employed by 319 firms; by 1981, the last year for which statistics keepers separated out this category of workers, this number had dropped again, to 153 businesses and fifty-four thousand employees.[56]

The reasons are not far to seek and lie partly in lifestyle changes in the later 1960s, as women began to challenge domestic roles, and dining manners gradually lost their formality. Plastics and cheaper ceramics could be substituted for some household purposes. But the drop in employment owed more directly to new cost calculations, for as labor became relatively more expensive in the postwar period, manufacturers increasingly substituted machines. At Tirschenreuth, for example, much of the work was done by hand into the 1950s; but in 1958, the firm put three new tunnel kilns into service, increasing production from 70 to 110 tons of porcelain per month and reducing the need for workers. In the 1970s, the firm added partially automated rolling machines with plasticizing units (*Plastifizierungsanlage*) to replace grinding drums and filter presses, once again saving labor. New technologies such as the use of natural gas rather than generators finally—in 1988!—removed all the poisonous gasses from production.[57] Waldsassen, which had 889 employees in 1970, had only 679 in 1980, and 466 in 1990, a year in which sales were the same (32 million DM) as in 1981.[58]

As consumption and production patterns shifted once again, the porcelain industry in the West adjusted to a now more or less "free" marketplace. The remaining fully state owned enterprise, the KPM, limped along, as did Nymphenburg, still leased to the Bäuml brothers; artistic leadership had passed to private owners, especially Rosenthal. Ironically, it was not in the capitalist West but in the communist East that many of the industry's traditions were not only continued but in some sense reborn.

Making "White Gold" in a Communist State

The story of porcelain production in postwar East Germany is a particularly intricate one, as here manufacturers had to deal not only with the hardships of the 1940s and 1950s, but also with the ideological discomfort of producing a luxury good, heavily associated with the rococo princely courts, in a workers' state. It was also much harder to return to "business as usual," as the East German state controlled even more thoroughly than had the Nazi regime the supply of materials, the disposition of the workforce, and the lines of production. As in the case of the Nazis, however, the highly centralized workers' republic had a great deal of patronage in its gift; even a communist state needed self-promoting tea sets, railway services, canteen dishes, insulators. And, at least after 1956, the East Germans did not want to be seen as lagging behind the West in providing at least a minimum of consumer satisfaction, either.

Of course, the ardently communist German Democratic Republic would not allow entrepreneurial business to go on as usual. Industrial production was to be planned and directed by the state, in the interests of all workers, rather than for the sake of capitalist profits. Thus, after the founding of the new state, larger firms were nationalized and rebaptized VEB, Volkseigener Betriebe, or People's Enterprise. Many smaller firms were forced into combines (*Kombinat*) led by larger ones.[59] The interwar giant Kahla, for example, became first a VEB and then a Kombinat, grouping together in the period 1968–74 the firms of Triptis, Könitz, Volkstedt, and others; by 1977 the Kahla Kombinat employed 4,828.[60] VEBs Colditz (previously chiefly a stoneware factory) and Henneberg (the successor to the Ilmenau works) also prospered, employing in the same year 3,372 and 2,365, respectively.[61]

Meissen, as always, was a special case. In 1950, the "royal" factory became the property of the people of the GDR, not all of whom were sure that a luxury industry of this sort was worth sustaining (but then again, there had long been disagreement on this point). To meet its budget, the factory introduced new machines, and the not entirely socialist measure of pegging salaries to workers' productivity. Meissen began exporting again in 1952, though this was complicated by the lack of trade treaties between the GDR and the capitalist West. The factory blamed rumors that Meissen's quality had plunged on enemies of the socialist state. But once agreements were made, sales with the Soviet Union and the United States contributed to returning the factory, at last, to the black, in 1955.[62] By 1959, exports, at just

16 percent of sales in 1952, had reached 51 percent, and in response to the GDR's new seven-year plan, the manufactory articulated a business strategy that could have been devised on the Iron Curtain's other side:

> The offerings of porcelain figurines and tableware with the blue swords must be carefully considered and put together, from fair to fair, from exhibition to exhibition, from nation to nation, through preparatory research into each market situation and taste-trend. Nonetheless, [the wares'] chief character should remain unshakably and enduringly Meissen, so that the public retains its admiration [for its products] and this most important export operation of the German Democratic Republic retains its world renown.

The factory would refrain from creating cultural works designed only to shock the public but could play a role in modernizing its taste: "In presenting, in exhibitions, a truly prestigious selection of modern figurines in Böttger Stoneware and white porcelain we have the possibility of guiding the public through controversial new developments in vase and plate forms."[63] To do so it needed to be free to produce not just the ever-salable rococo, but new, artistic models as well. At its 250th anniversary in 1960, Meissen once again reiterated "national" prestige, exports, and taste leadership as its raisons d'être.

But these were insufficiently good reasons for GDR officials to allow the continuation of business as usual, and in 1960 Meissen was told to stop using its old, aristocratic models and instead to produce for the people of the GDR. This disastrous policy—a Marxist variation on the Semperian ideal—made Meissen little more than an overpriced producer of ordinary ceramics, and a luxury maker of money-losing curiosities such as its Young Pioneer figurines—not surprisingly of no interest to western buyers—and a twenty-seven-piece group entitled "Communist Revolution" for the Museum of Combat Glory.[64] Exports, which had amounted to 80 percent of sales in 1959, fell to only 58 percent by 1969. The firm was headed for bankruptcy and political trouble once again when, in 1969, a new director, Karl Petermann, took over, and reinstated . . . the eighteenth-century models.[65]

Petermann and other East German porcelain makers profited greatly from a change in GDR ideology and economic practices in 1975, when party officials decided that for the sake of desperately needed hard currency, the state needed to increase its exports, both to the other communist countries and to the West. Reacting to the GDR's reputation for producing cheap, poor-quality wares and taking no interest at all in customers' desires, the Economics Ministry launched a campaign to push high-tech exports in which porcelain, as well as glass and optical equipment, was to play a major role.[66] Targets were set for exports to the communist and the non-communist world. For 1975, for example, Kahla managed to produce 26.8 million OM in communist world exports, and 19 million VM, or "valutamark" (the fictional equivalent of the deutschmark) in western sales.[67] The fact that Kahla, like the others, nearly met its target meant that in subsequent years, the expectations simply rose, and in 1978 the firm was expected to export 42.6 million OM and 22.4 million VM worth of goods.[68] Meissen was projected to produce less overall, but to send its products exclusively to western markets. It fell short of its plan for 1976, exporting only 17 rather than 21 million VM,[69] but amounts did rise afterward, and after all, this was valuable hard currency. By 1980, the plan was to export as much as 115 million OM to the communist bloc, and 69 million VM to the West, and the industry was instructed to strengthen its "political-ideological work" to realize these goals, "as particularly the *fulfilling of the export mission* in the NSW [*nichtsozialistische Wirtschaften*] is an absolute focal point for the glass and ceramics industry."[70] In 1979, in 1982, and again in 1989, the GDR demonstrated its pride in its porcelain heritage by featuring Meissen porcelain pieces on its postage stamps (fig. 9.3). Mercantilism, reconfigured once more, had returned to the porcelain industry.

Communist mercantilism seems to have made life much more comfortable for porcelain factory managers and workers. Kahla was thriving and providing steady employment for Thuringians, as the region's porcelain manufacturers had promised for centuries. Sufficient proceeds were returned to the Meissen factory that it increased its workforce, from 1,102 in 1975 to 1,696 in 1989, and this town, too, flourished. Kilns were repaired, and new

9.3. GDR Meissen stamps

So proud were the East German communists of their Meissen porcelains—produced chiefly to be sold to western buyers for hard currency—that they issued several series of commemorative stamps.

buildings were added, including an apartment house for single workers; a day-care center opened.[71] New apprentices were hired, and trained for jobs they *would* get, and get to keep. Some attempts were at last made to prevent, rather than simply palliate, silicosis. Factories formed singing and sports clubs and sponsored Socialist Youth picnics and rallies. It is hard to reconstruct what it was like to work in these communist-era manufactories, but it seems clear that wage differences, at least, between workers and management had greatly narrowed; when Meissen reported on this in 1989, the difference between "Arbeiter und Angestellte" and "Leitungs- und Verwaltungspersonal" was only 571 OM a year, or about 15 percent.[72] Officials probably received additional perks; but they always had done. Making porcelain in the GDR, and especially at Meissen, made for a good life, for the unskilled workers in particular, probably a relatively better and certainly more stable life than ever before in the history of the industry. Communist paternalism, too, had its upsides.

Naturally, marketing and selling practices too were controlled by the East German state. Given the barriers imposed by the Cold War, the great opportunity to reach western wholesalers directly was the Leipzig fair, to which representatives of western as well as eastern nations continued to flock. These were very important opportunities to show off products and to make deals, and the manufactories reported on them faithfully to the Ministry for Glass and Ceramics. In the early 1980s, they expressed worries, rightly, about the falling off in buyers—though Kahla savored a little schadenfreude in reporting, in 1982, the news that in the West, Hutschenreuther and Westerwald stoneware were floundering.[73] The other means to sell high-value wares in the West was to contract with official dealers in art and antiquities, who took the goods, and returned about half of the proceeds to the factory.[74] The Kunst und Antiquitäten GmbH Mühlenbeck, founded as a subsidiary of the State Security Ministry in 1973, was especially active here. This official dealership, dedicated to redressing the regime's hard-currency deficit by selling off museum treasures and antiquities confiscated from "enemies of the state," also did a brisk trade in high-quality porcelains. It supplied Meissen works in particular to western dealers as well as to Interhotels, where highly placed travelers or party members could shop using hard currency.[75]

In two documents outlining five-year plans for socialist and non-socialist regions for the years 1981–85 we can see remarkable continuities in conceptions of how best to market porcelain, at least in the western zones. Here, diversity and branding were key, "to secure the necessary exports through corresponding innovations in forms and stronger coordination with current fashion trends (at least one new form per factory and per year)." Marketability was to be increased by moving away from services toward the production of individual articles, with offerings changing every four years for individual consumers, and every two years for hotel porcelains. Advertising was to be increased, at fairs and exhibitions, and catalogs published in German, English, French, and Spanish. The key was to advertise the GDR as a producer of quality wares, and to emphasize "the line of tradition of today's products, organically arising from the high-quality Saxon-Thuringian porcelain of past centuries." In the hopes of realizing yearly exports in excess of 93 million VM by 1985, Meissen was to advertise its leadership role, its tradition of excellence in handwork, and its continuation "of the tradition of Böttger, Höroldt und Kändler."[76] As for the socialist markets, the aim was, quite bluntly, a minimum of financial expenditure on marketing; the few advertisements needed were to emphasize industrial rationality and socialist brotherhood.[77] Presumably, neither fashion, nor tradition, nor quality, mattered here.

Through the 1970s and into the 1980s, these firms seem to have been reasonably healthy, though as revolutions began to break up the Soviet bloc, strains were showing. In the first quarter of 1989, Meissen reported that it was lagging a bit behind export targets; the one part of the plan it was overfulfilling was in doctor's visits and unpaid vacations.[78] In September 1989— as GDR citizens stormed embassies and rallied for reform—Kahla reported that it had fallen short of planned production by more than 19 percent, and that several of its branch factories were running over budget. Worryingly, too, its warehouses were overfull (of course there was a "plan" for this as well), always a sign, as we have seen in previous centuries, of overproduction and flagging sales.[79] The political revolution that pulled down the Berlin Wall and the GDR itself would come on the heels of this already ominous report.

Style and Postwar Identity

The end of Nazism and the division of Germany made for acute identity crises for central Europeans, as well as massive displacement and the longing to establish new "homes." With so many dislocated, bombed-out, and homeless persons seeking shelter, politicians in both Germanys were under great pressure to provide places to live. Both in the West and in the East, needs were great and funds tight, and there was considerable pressure to normalize designs and furnishings; in addition, there were ideological reasons in both East and West to develop universally applicable norms and types, and to provide affordable spaces in which Germans could build modern lives. Yet even in this atmosphere, porcelain would be one of the goods that resisted norming; even in the East, the Cold War could not kill the stylistic diversity the industry had cultivated from the first.

As Karin Zachmann has argued, the kitchen proved an especially important space for working out what those "new days" would look like, and how women, in particular, would fit into new democratic or communist futures. In the West, an anticonsumerist idealization of stylistic simplicity was championed by the former Bauhaus designer Wilhelm Wagenfeld, now head of the Department for Norm and Type Creation at the Institut für Bauwesen (1947–49).[80] Wagenfeld's functionalist kitchen designs fit well with feminist support for minimalizing housework. But more importantly, as Paul Betts has argued, the rational, functional style, inherited from the Werkbund and Bauhaus, had not been sullied by Nazi usage and could be embraced as something essentially "German," in contradistinction, too, to Anglo-American ornamental excess. The pursuit of "good form" was a means to resurrect the positive connotations of the label "made in Germany," and to help West Germans reconceive the purpose of their state from that of "racist mission and collective sacrifice to that of individual choice and material well-being."[81] Thus the functionalist kitchen served as a site to display both anti-Americanism

9.4. Reform kitchen

Designed by the furniture maker August Siekmann in 1953, this rational-
ized kitchen still offered a small display window for the household's
porcelains.

and postfascist German individuality, often expressed in its tablewares. For
example, the furniture maker August Siekmann's "reform kitchen" of 1953
cleared away the clutter but left a display space for the homemaker's—not
necessarily modern—porcelain (fig. 9.4).

Industrial design, one could say, now came into its own, and many of the
most striking of the new wares featured form over decoration. Asymmetrical vases, such as the fat-bellied "Pregnant Louise," designed by Fritz Heiden-
reich for Rosenthal in 1950, had a brief cachet. As noted above, Rosenthal
also enjoyed great success with its futuristic "2000" service, designed by Raymond Loewy—though by 1978, its allure had evaporated.[82] Porcelains were
also made in bold, flat colors, or with modern geometric patterns; often innovation came in the form of oddly shaped handles or pouring spouts rather

than in ornament, very little of which was now hand-painted. We are a long way from the Ovidian scenes of the eighteenth century, or even the Romantic landscapes of the nineteenth. Leading makers now fashioned very few figurines, chiefly for art connoisseurs, leaving the making of Zeuses and chubby children to producers for Greek and Italian tourist shops or to the Fritz Goebel factory, which has been producing sentimental "Hummel" figurines based on the drawings of Berta Hummel (Sister Maria Innocentia) since 1935, mostly for the American market.[83]

Functionalism, then, was the style featured in outlet shop windows, advertisements, and of course, exhibitions. But we can be sure that Wagenfeld's wares were not what everyone wanted, and certainly not all that was sold. In fact, what many buyers in the 1950s wanted, one historian has written, was something else. "With respect to interiors, the decorative style popular among the bourgeoisie since the late nineteenth century—ornate, representational, including furniture in imitative styles made from dark, highly polished and often noticeably grained wood—found its continuation."[84] In the 1950s, Tante Emma Läden micro-haberdasheries spread across the country, selling a variety of foodstuffs, gifts, and tablewares; it is likely that these matronly owner-operators stocked almost anything but functionalist wares. Ever a telling straw in the market's countervailing winds, the porcelain industry quietly continued producing versions of older orientalizing, rococo, and "chaste" neoclassical services alongside modern patterns. As ever, stylistic diversity remained essential to porcelain's survival.

This clash between market demand and modernist design was epitomized by negotiations initiated in 1953 between the Werkbund and the Rosenthal manufactory, which, as we have seen, had a soft spot for functionalist works and was eager to work with modern designers. But talks broke down when the Werkbund insisted that the manufactory desist from producing decorated porcelains and "kitsch" alongside its pure-white, functional forms. Its members accused Rosenthal of using the Werkbund for publicity for the firm, while devoting only a part of the manufactory's production to its designs. This was aesthetically and ethically unacceptable, it argued, to which Rosenthal simply replied that the consumers wanted choice.

The argument continued in trade journals and among critics, but the reality, as ever before, was the same: consumers, in Rosenthal's words, "did not want a single, unitary form of white porcelain, made according to one particular canon of beauty."[85] Rosenthal was willing to invest, and often lose, money to create avant-garde works; in the 1950s and 1960s he served on numerous committees dedicated to investment in and improvement of German design. He himself was no fan of historicism but took the position, increasingly, that artistic progress could be achieved only from the top down. For the consumer market at large, the idea was to strive for a middle ground, which did not give up on decoration in pursuit of a unitary and utopian "pure form." In his simultaneous promotion of his "Studio Line" and of this "middle ground," Philip followed his father's lead and perhaps came closest of any maker of his era to squaring the art/industry circle that had brought so many porcelain makers—and far more artists—to grief over the preceding 150 years.

In the East, as noted above, refurbishing homes was delayed after the war's end by the fledgling socialist regime's focus on agriculture and heavy industry rather than consumer goods. But by the mid-1950s, state officials recognized that consumers had become impatient with frugality, and with continuing housing shortages. As the GDR began rolling out a massive project of erecting prefabricated apartment buildings, planners realized that the chemical industry—concentrated in the German East—might help by producing plastic substitutes for expensive imports. As Eli Rubin recounts, the GDR was enormously successful in making plastic furnishings and housewares that appealed to the population; it was far less successful in making *enough* of these commodities to satisfy demand. Like the porcelains made in the West, plastics chiefly took on functionalist forms, as these suited its qualities as well as the objects' chiefly utilitarian purposes, but they could also be playful and were often brightly colored. As their quality improved and their variety increased, plastics were used as substitutes for wood, cotton, glass, leather—and of course for ceramics. As everything new was rare, and plastics were more durable, East German consumers satisfied their demands for household luxury with this commodity and learned to live with, if not love, the modernist aesthetic.[86]

9.5. GDR supper, 1955

Undoubtedly staged to demonstrate the high living standards of this farming family under the conditions of communism, this image shows that porcelain—on the table and in the breakfront—remained an essential part of respectability.

And yet, even in the GDR, makers such as Graf von Henneberg continued to produce old-fashioned decorated wares. It was for sale in "Industry Shops" in big cities and in department stores, at premium prices, and remained a coveted good, of whose manufacture Germans were proud. When propagandists wished to document the prosperity of a rural family in the mid-1950s, they could think of no better scene than that of the family taking their evening meal from porcelain vessels, with a well-stocked figurine cabinet in the background (fig. 9.5). Even in a purportedly classless society, porcelain still stood for affluence and respectability.

No one knew better the limits of modernism's appeal than Meissen's postwar artists. Writing in 1960, Otto Walcha begged for patience as the manufactory tried out new designs, noting that there had been many experiments in the factory's history "which were treated with the wringing of hands, and even regularly described in official reports of the manufacturing commission as stylistic fiascos." We must be willing to take some risks! he pled. But, in the midst of ideological challenges to the "Alt" traditions, Walcha also emphasized the danger of too much deviation from Meissen's "old haunts."[87] Meissen, like the other socialist makers, had learned that the old, no matter how feudal, could not be sacrificed for the new.

We must return again, then, to our previous observations about the impossibility of reducing the porcelain industry's output at any time in its history to a single style. Even in the age of functionalism triumphant, production remained eclectic. Figurine production continued to drop but could not be cancelled altogether, at least by the higher-quality makers, as it provided such excellent advertising for its studio lines. Many "Alt" patterns continued or were revived, though manufactories cut down significantly on the choices they offered, both in shops and in catalogs. Some patterns continued from the Weimar and Nazi years, including the KPM's "Urbino" and "Arkadia," first produced in 1931 and 1938 respectively. Communist makers made clunky utilitarian wares, including mugs for the Volkspolizei and members of various party organizations, and fancier but cheap tourist wares, whose gilding would have sent Semper into a furious rage. West German makers also tried to suit modern tastes and needs, producing in the 1950s kidney-shaped dishes to complement kidney-shaped sofas and couches, and "mod," boldly colored items for the 1960s. Most continued to offer at least one Jugendstil pattern. Perhaps typical was Tirschenreuth, which, for its 150th anniversary, both reissued "Fortuna," a fancy fin de siècle service, and advertised a new, very plain, stoneware service, "Murnau," for contemporary uses.[88] Today, although the number of items each firm offers has plummeted, the diversity of styles remains. The dream of creating one service to appeal to all seems to be dead, even among art critics, most of whom have probably given up on the idea of uniting art and industry for good.

A final look at a recent Augarten catalog (one of the last print offerings before online catalogs took over) gives us, again, a partial but telling overview of what the high-quality porcelain makers still believe their customers might buy and sums up nicely some of the trends we have been following. The full-color catalog for 2014 offered smoking utensils, collectors' teacups, decorative platters, vases, and office accessories, as well as table services, in patterns with names such as Habsburg, Mozart, and Belvedere; customers could purchase versions of Josef Hoffmann's Mocha service, and Secession-style decorative objects. Augarten proffered a yearly plate, Easter rabbits, and Christmas decorations; one could still order Franz Josef's favorite breakfast roll in porcelain. The manufactory also presented some more modern artistic items, including a series of "Pinocchio" vases, which can be painted to look like billiard balls with long necks. The catalog dedicated considerable space to the remarkable range of figurines still on offer, from Viennese types to cats, from "exotic" figures (three Chinese and one "Moor") to figurines depicting horses and riders from the Spanish Riding School. There were very few renderings of real persons—the list included only Mozart, Johann Strauss, Schubert, Goethe, Franz Josef, and his queen "Sisi"; Prince Eugene of Savoy and George Washington appeared on horseback. There were seventeen different birds on offer, as well as a seductive Susannah in the Bath, and a horrendous "Indian Putto." One could still have special messages inscribed, or family crests added on.[89]

Postwar porcelain continued many older stylistic traditions, functionalist as well as rococo, adding in, of course, new models that generally—like those of the early modernists—did not last more than a season or two. Perhaps making porcelain purchases helped to link women, in particular, to older Germanys and family members they had lost or allowed them to make a fresh start. Certainly, in the 1950s and 1960s, porcelain had not lost its associations with women, with special occasions, and with the respectable, middle-class "home." Choices of styles or makers might reiterate local loyalties, or political positions; in one case I know of, a staunchly liberal Hamburg family chose Wedgwood, partly to assert its *resistance* to "old German" traditions. For others, nostalgia inclined the purchasing of older-fashioned sets, now thoroughly identified with grandmothers and forfeited Heimats. Inge Behrens (b. 1925), a woman who grew up in a skilled working-class household in Erfurt using blue-and-white Kahla "Strewn Flowers" for everyday meals and Rosenthal "Maria White" for Sundays, provided her postwar family with Royal Copenhagen "Blue Flowers" and Rosenthal's all-white "Variation," neither very far from her family's traditional tastes.[90] A sociological study of porcelain, or other luxury goods, for this period would surely tell us a great deal about families' self-conception and the ways in which they wished to connect, or disconnect, themselves from their pasts. Until we have such a study, we can only surmise—based on sales, catalogs, women's magazines, and a few families' stories—that porcelain, into the 1960s at least, remained an essential part of homemaking, of guest friendship, of what it was to be German. But culture, like industry, has undergone far-reaching changes since then, and it seems quite clear—again on the evidence of sales, magazines, and personal stories—that porcelain no longer plays its former roles. Whether it is valued at all in our fast-paced world of takeout meals, dispersed and smaller families, working women, and electronic *Glanz* is the question the industry confronts today.

The German Porcelain Industry Today

At this writing, in late 2019, the German porcelain industry is a shadow of its former—at least its Wilhelmine or 1950s—self. It faces enormous competition from cheap Chinese imports, as well as from huge discounters such as Ikea. Lifestyles and eating habits have changed: "People eat and live differently today than they did 20, 30 years ago, and they have other requirements for their porcelain. Many makers have failed to recognize this and simply continue to produce 36-piece coffee services," argued Kahla's director in 2014.[91] But in fact many porcelain makers *do* realize this; it is simply hard to know what to do about it. In a world of Styrofoam takeout plates and paper coffee cups, there is not nearly as much scope for porcelain as there once was. Family and holiday meals, when they happen, are not nearly so elaborate as once they were—or the focus is on the gourmet food, not the tableware. The *Kaffeekränzschen* seem to have largely moved to cafés. Exacerbating the situation, the post-2008 global economic crash had devastating effects, as we will see below. Most of the specialty porcelain and glass shops—once the pride of every middle-sized town—have closed; few have need for anything new, in any case, as there are acres of much cheaper, used porcelain available from eBay, Replacements Limited, flea markets, and antiques stores. Younger persons seem not to want their mothers' and grandmothers' sets; who, after all, wants to make room for even one, much less three or four, one-hundred-piece services?

To take a quick survey of firms and their fates in this period is to paint a sorry picture. A not very merry television story broadcast on Christmas day 2016 claimed that some 190 German firms making fine ceramics had closed between 2006 and 2014; most of these were said to be small firms, with fewer than ten employees, and the cause was put down, in part, to lifestyle changes and partly to competition from East Asian firms and overproduction by the biggest makers.[92] But larger firms have also closed, consolidated, and/ or sold their brand names to others. In Upper Franconia, for example, of thirty-four firms still producing in 1989, by 2001 only eighteen remained[93]— and since then, many of these have closed; the industry's regional employment statistics tell the story (see table 9.1). One of the towns most afflicted was the once-flourishing Arzberg, former home to four factories; now they are all in ruins, and Arzberg is depopulated and depressed.

TABLE 9.1. Porcelain Workers, Bavaria, 1925–2016

Year	Porcelain Workers, Bavaria
1925	30,410
1959	31,118
1963	27,500
1977	19,000
1988	18,000
2016	3,400

Source: Wolfgang Schilling, "Die nordostbayerische Porzellanindustrie seit dem Zweiten Weltkrieg," in Wüst, Industrialisierung einer Landschaft, 170–83.

The same, to a lesser degree, can be said for Rosenthal's Selb. In financial straits, in 1997, Rosenthal, ironically, agreed to merge with one of the German industry's oldest rivals: the Waterford Wedgwood Group. Philip died in 2001—Wikipedia states that his ashes are interred in a Rosenthal porcelain vase—and in 2009, Waterford Wedgwood collapsed, causing Rosenthal AG, too, to declare bankruptcy. The brand name was sold to an Italian entrepreneur and made a part of the Sambonet-Paderno Group. A restaurant and hotel line still bears the name Rosenthal, and some production continues at Selb. But the giant, art-promoting firm is no more. Fittingly, an elegiac article at the time of the firm's bankruptcy was titled: "With Rosenthal, Part of Bourgeois Identity Dies."[94]

In general, in the former western zone, the firms that survive are those that cater to the market's lower end, or specialize in the less visible "sanitary" or ordinary porcelains; they are now in competition not with Wedgwood but with the Swedish omnibus discount retailer Ikea. BHS Tabletop, which includes older brands such as Bauscher and Hutschenreuther, is the largest German porcelain maker today, employing 1,012 in 2018, and managing a €1.18 million profit on over €92 million in sales.[95] Reflecting the general trend, tableware sales are down at Villeroy & Boch, but the stoneware company is thriving, thanks to its "sanitary" department and increasing sales to China.[96]

The firms of the former GDR, perhaps kept artificially robust by lower levels of mechanization and by exports to the West, suffered grievously from the post-1989 "turn" to capitalism. Already in late December 1989, Kahla reported a deficit of 25 million OM and told the Ministry for Glass and Ceramics: "Negotiations with the state bank have concluded that financing with additional credit is not possible."[97] Privatized in 1991, Kahla declared bankruptcy in 1993; a successor named Kahla/Thüringen Porzellan GmbH was founded in the same year and over the next decade received some €79 million in state support. In 1999, it was sued by the European Commission for receiving aid incompatible with the principles of the common market, and in 2002 it was ordered to repay €15.7 million. An appeal in 2010 failed.[98] In 2017 one factory was operating, but with only three hundred workers. As of 2012, Volkstedt was losing money; Sitzendorf began liquidation in 2013, throwing much of its unsold produce into the Schwarze River, where a friend of mine fondly fished out souvenirs.

As for the former state manufactories: In the 1970s and 1980s, the KPM again fell into financial difficulties and was subjected once more to bruising discussions of privatization. In 1988, the Berlin Senate took the monumental step of finally voting to privatize the business, reasoning that "a company acting and operating in a market and having to confront competitors" needs more flexibility than public ownership permits. It stipulated, however, that an advisory board of international artistic and cultural experts be appointed to protect the traditional firm's artistic standards.[99] Under those conditions, the firm did not sell and was still hemorrhaging tens of millions of euros in 2004, when the Berlin banker Jörg Woltmann got wind of rumors that Chinese investors were interested in purchasing the manufactory. "I did not want that!" he said in a 2014 interview. "The KPM belongs in Berlin, and not in Beijing or Shanghai." He mustered sufficient credit to finance a holding company of investors that included the Prussian crown prince. When the prince pulled out, Woltmann himself purchased the KPM for €13.5 million. Between 2006, when the purchase was completed, and 2014, Woltmann sunk some forty million euros in the manufactory, which he insists on giving its full, traditional name: Königliche Porzellan-Manufaktur Berlin. He also insists on running the operation royally: offering no discounts, selling no "junk" (*Ramsch*). When asked in this interview when the KPM would finally find itself in the black, he responded, "Soon, very soon!"[100] As of 2016, when the firm lost an additional €2.2. million, that fervent hope had not come true.[101]

The others share the KPM's fate. Hungary's Herend—which seems to receive significant state commissions—alone appears to be doing relatively well.[102] Schlaggenwald has closed. Fürstenberg has been regularly losing more than €3 million a year and in 2017 lost more than €4 million; employee numbers are down.[103] Nymphenburg had cost overruns of more than €18 million in 2011, when it returned to its royal Bavarian owners and its old name, "Königliches Porzellan Manufaktur Nymphenburg."[104] The reinvented

Höchst improved its position in 2015 but remained €425,000 in the hole, and in March 2018 the company filed for bankruptcy.[105] In 2003, Augarten gave notice to all its employees and then was purchased by the foreclosure expert Ehrhard Grossnigg, who also owns a football club; these are the only two businesses Grossnigg operates "from pure passion and without interest in profits,"[106] in the words of one journalist. It is good that he has the passion; as for the profits: there aren't any. By 2016, the Viennese manufactory, which now employs only sixty (including fifteen painters), was carrying forward losses topping €710,000.[107] The surviving firms make beautiful ceramics, using time-honored methods, thereby keeping artisanal skill sets alive. But how long will their patrons wait for profits, particularly as there is now so little *Glanz* to be had in porcelain making?

By one accounting, a fine ceramics industry that still employed twenty-five thousand in 1991 by 2014 had fallen to about five thousand, and sales of tableware and decorative porcelains fallen from about €550 million to about €302 million.[108] Department stores offer fewer and fewer patterns; and in any case, department stores themselves are facing an uncertain financial future, part of a more general, global "retailing revolution," whose results we cannot yet foresee. As families shed their porcelain heirlooms, treasures regularly feature on the TV program *Kunst & Krempel* (Art and Junk), the German equivalent of the British and American *Antiques Roadshow*, and flea markets teem with brand-name offerings (plate 16). Thuringia, Saxony, and Franconia, such famous porcelain-making places, have built museums to celebrate the industry, and organized "preservation societies" (*Schutzvereine*) and tours to awaken interest in this part of their cultural heritage. Despite the ravages of time and the horrific events of the twentieth century, as beautiful exhibition catalogs demonstrate, museums and private collectors still own enormous collections of German porcelain. Factory tours at Meissen and elsewhere emphasize the traditions of handwork, implicitly when not explicitly defending the manufactory's high prices. Will "musealization" save the industry, however? The prospects are not auspicious.

And Then, Again, There Was One

The final chapter of our story must bring us back, once more, to Meissen, the original German porcelain firm, and the only remaining state-funded one at this writing in fall 2019. At its height, the factory employed as many as eighteen hundred workers, and at one time as many as six hundred painters,[109] a success story that continued down to communism's collapse in 1989–90. Evidence suggests that in the heady and chaotic months before the abolition of the ostmark and the reunification of the states, Meissen's sales surged; a great deal of porcelain, too, including a fifteen-thousand-piece collection of Thuringian masterworks, was transferred into the hands of the state's official dealers, perhaps to feather the nests of panicking party officials.[110] On November 22, 1989, in fact, the GDR officially stopped exports of antiquities, hoping to curtail the pillaging of cultural heritage the state itself had overseen since 1973. But it did not dissolve the official plundering body, the Kunst und Antiquitäten GmbH Mühlenbeck, and in the summer of 1990, millions of DM in Meissen porcelains passed from this firm to Sabatier Antiquitäten in Verden, the official "liquidator" of Meissen's warehouse.[111] We can only guess how many individuals, desperate to survive the *Wende* or eager to profit from it, sold their porcelains to the western antiquities dealers who fanned out across the East in search of treasures in those tumultuous times.

At the time of the monetary union with the West in 1990, the firm possessed a credit of 11.2 million OM in the Berliner Kreditbank, which was adjusted to 6 million DM.[112] The agency entrusted with privatization (Treuhand-Anstalt) was prevented from selling the firm by the intervention of Kurt Biedenkopf, the Saxon minister president, who steered it into the hands of the Saxon state government. Sales seem to have been healthy for a time thereafter; in 1997 Meissen sold 80 million DM worth of goods. Careful readers of this book will not be surprised to learn that four-fifths of these sales are estimated to have been of eighteenth- and nineteenth-century models, and included, of course, the Blue Onion. Meissen had a very good year in 2001, selling €44.7 million worth of porcelains, but then, as if to remind the manufacturer of the perils posed by the elements, in 2002 the flooding of the Elbe River did considerable damage to the factory, and to the number of visitors to its museum, which had become a popular tourist attraction from the time the Russians restored its contents in 1958. Revenues plunged, 160 workers were fired, and the firm took to producing buttons and decorative tiles for swimming pools.[113]

From this time forward, the skies over Meissen have darkened. The firm managed to withstand a takeover attempt by the Japanese firm Mitsubishi, but in 2008 a scandal involving its longtime director, Hannes Walther, broke, in which Walther, who had worked for the firm for thirty-four years, was accused of bribing the Saxon minister president to make his Stasi files disappear.[114] And then the global financial crisis arrived. In 2008, Meissen lost €6 million, and the new director Christian Kurtzke's attempts to make it into a "Saxon Gucci" by producing branded jewelry, clothing, and pillowcases failed to attract younger buyers, or any buyers at all. In 2010, employees were ordered to smash €2.6 million worth of backlogged items in a single "Polterabend" (wedding fest); perhaps this seemed the right way to finally deal with the very old problem of the overstuffed warehouse, but media coverage was scathing.[115] Layoffs followed, and while the larger metropolises of Dresden and Leipzig began to boom, Meissen, like other small towns in the former East, began to take on the grim bitterness of an American rustbelt town. Out of office, Biedenkopf blamed the Saxon finance minister for failing to follow through on his promises to provide "unlimited" support for the firm's growth strategy.[116]

It was to be, once again, the Saxon Finance Ministry that raised the warning flag, albeit quietly, in 2014. After another punishing year of losses, the manufactory's debts stood at €20 million, and reform was urgent. Kurtzke was forced out, and cost cutting ensued. But the manufactory still needed funds, and, without Landtag approval, the ministry (led by a member of the conservative CDU, or Christian Democratic Union) in the same year also approved two €5 million state loans for the factory, which SPD delegates later suggested amounted to trickery.[117] In 2015, the firm lost €12.1 million (on sales of €39.2 million), and rumors circulated that the firm would cut 30 percent of the firm's 660 jobs, causing the SPD to charge that the reform of the manufactory was coming out of workers' hides; the party calculated that Saxony had now invested €49 million in Meissen since 2009.[118]

In June 2016, Sebastian Scheel, representing Die Linke, the post-1989 leftist party to which many former communists belonged, broke protocol and insisted on an open discussion of Meissen's budget in the Saxon Landtag. Scheel did not call for the privatizing of the manufactory—only the extreme right-wing party Alternative für Deutschland (AfD) suggested a "partial" privatization—but deplored the manufactory's business practices. He was greeted with a barrage of criticism for having sullied the name of the manufactory. A CDU delegate went so far as to call him an "elephant" who did not belong in a porcelain manufactory, and a reactionary who wanted to retreat to the days in which he washed dishes by hand, and perhaps tried to use a knife and fork—a lightly veiled reference to the "barbaric" days of the GDR. The Greens complained about plans to outsource production and replace hand painting with machine decoration, but they defended the firm and its budget. Even the SPD delegates expressed their patriotic support for the manufactory: "It embodies Saxony, it is an image-bearer for Saxony, it is our Saxony," declared Mario Pecher. As debate in the Landtag raged, the AfD leader Frauke Petry commented: "Who would have thought that a debate over 'old dishes'—you will excuse my quotation marks—could be so lively?" But the end result was foreordained: "The Meissen porcelain manufactory has belonged for 300 years to the cultural heritage of the free state [of Saxony]," the finance minister concluded at the debate's end. "It is a part of Saxony's identity and ought to remain in future a Saxon business that we can all be proud of."[119]

What comes next for Meissen is anyone's guess, but as our delegate stated in 1906 (chapter 7), the "problem child" is too precious to Saxon cultural identity to be easily detached from the state purse. In 2016, hopes for lucrative sales in a now-booming China were dashed when a much too large Beijing outlet had to be shuttered; the majority of sales continue to come from Germany itself. After many loans, in 2017, Saxony gave the manufactory a one-time subsidy of €28 million to rebuild its capital, but by fall 2018, debts of about €52 million had accrued, and managers refused to release details of where all the money had gone.[120]

Although the manufactory in 2015 still employed three hundred skilled painters, the town's economy began to falter further, and its mood to darken. In this year, there was an arson attack on a planned camp for refugees, and in recent elections, one-third of Meisseners voted for the AfD.[121] In November 2019, the manufactory announced further job cuts, reducing the workforce from 619 to 418, and the closing of "non-profitable" locations. It hopes in this way to spend no more money than it makes, and thus "to survive well into the future despite challenging market conditions."[122] But these hopes begin to sound rather more desperate than confident.

If Meissen does close or privatize, that will mark a turning point, in many ways signaling the final victory of capitalism over mercantilism, and mass production over artisanal craftwork. Perhaps in a few years' time, production will be entirely returned to East Asia, where porcelain making first began. But it is hard to believe that this is the end of the story we have followed over the course of more than three hundred years. European porcelain began with an alchemical miracle in the heart of central Europe, and it will take some advanced magic to bring the industry back to life. But one never knows: even now, in a basement in Dresden or Kahla, a modern Böttger may be tinkering with a new recipe for *Glanz*.

Notes

Note on Currencies and Other Abbreviations

1. In circulation were also Dutch rijksdaaler, Danish rigsdaler, and in the Austrian Netherlands kronenthaler, all with slightly different silver values.
2. Gerhard and Kaufhold, "Einleitung," 26.
3. Pierenkemper and Tilly, *German Economy during the Nineteenth Century*, 35–36.

Introduction

1. Just to cite a very few: Bald et al., *Porzellan für die Welt*; Wittwer, *Refinement and Elegance*; Wolff-Metternich and Meinz, *Die Porzellanmanufaktur Fürstenberg*; Siemen, *Königstraum und Massenware*.
2. Here I am in agreement with Frank Trentmann's critique of commodity histories, which tend to the triumphant, "with one exotic food conquering all before it." Trentmann, *Empire of Things*, 165.
3. Finlay, *Pilgrim Art*; Rappaport, *Thirst for Empire*.
4. See, e.g., the discussion of this topic, with extensive references, in "AHR Conversation."
5. Roche, *Culture of Clothing*, 502; Auslander, *Taste and Power*, 425.
6. There are, of course, exceptions, such as Hartmut Berghoff's *Zwischen Kleinstadt und Weltmarkt*; Sudrow, *Der Schuh im Nationalsozialismus*; and most importantly for my purposes, Paul Betts's wonderful *Authority of Everyday Objects*. Uwe Spiekermann's extraordinary *Basis der Konsumgesellschaft* should have accelerated the longitudinal study of German commerce and consumption more than it seems to have done. For the Nazi and postwar periods, this is indeed underway; see, e.g., Wiesen, *Creating the Nazi Marketplace*; Rubin, *Synthetic Socialism*; Swett, *Selling under the Swastika*. German advertising could use more investigation, but there are a few recent studies, including Lamberty, *Reklame in Deutschland, 1890–1914*; and Ciarlo, *Advertising Empire*. There are also a few global histories of consumption that include interesting examples from Central Europe, including Stearns, *Consumerism in World History*; and Trentmann, *Empire of Things*.
7. Swett, *Selling under the Swastika*, 6.

8. Of course this would include the very many excellent studies not only of Marx and his milieu, but of Frankfurt School critics of capitalism and bourgeois culture. Warren Breckmann's "Disciplining Consumption," for example, frames this important debate but doesn't investigate in detail what kinds of luxury goods were being marketed and purchased. Much literature on the arts and crafts movement tells us a great deal about the reformers' dreams of overcoming the evils of mass production, but little about what was actually being made or how it was sold. Even studies of the German department store, such as Paul E. Lerner's *The Consuming Temple*, introduce the "consumer revolution" only to focus chiefly on its critics. All the works cited certainly deal with crucial aspects of German history, from socialism to anti-Semitism. But now we need well-researched works of the quality of Michael B. Miller's classic *The Bon Marché* and Regina Lee Blaszczyk's *Imagining Consumers* (which treat France and the United States, respectively) to take the next step in this field.

9. Kreklau, "'Eat as the King Eats'"; Treitel, *Eating Nature in Modern Germany*; Giloi, *Monarchy, Myth, and Material Culture in Germany*; A. Green, *Fatherlands*; Schramm, *Konsum und regionale Identität*.

10. Almut Spaulding and Paul S. Spaulding's intensive study of the consumption habits of the Reimarus family is extremely detailed and revealing, but of course this is only one, unusual middle-class household, and the account books on which it is based end in 1780. See Spaulding and Spaulding, *Account Books of the Reimarus Family*. Daniel L. Purdy's intriguing *Tyranny of Elegance* made the important observation that much German consumption in this era was more imagined than real; but we need to know much more about which goods were purchased, and when. For foodstuffs we can turn to Ellerbrock, *Geschichte der deutschen Nahrungs- und Genussmittelindustrie*, and the many essays of Hans J. Teuteberg and Günter Wiegelmann, including their joint *Unsere tägliche Kost*; but there is still much to learn. James M. Brophy's forthcoming book on the German book trade will help us fill in gaps in our knowledge about the consumption of printed materials. For a taste of his pathbreaking findings, see Brophy, "Second Wave." There are scattered works on silk production or glasswares cited in the pages below, and probably more that I have missed. But in general, one can say that this remains a rich field for future historians to plow.

11. Flanders, *Inside the Victorian Home*; Cohen, *Household Goods*.

12. For example, one major study of Meissen's history devotes 165 pages on the history of the firm to 1815, and only thirty-one on the period 1815 to 1970, despite the fact that the author actually worked for the manufactory in the period after WWII. See Walcha, *Meissen Porcelain*.

13. Krueger, "Einführung," 7.

Chapter 1: Reinventing the Recipe

1. It is estimated that the *White Lion* was carrying between six hundred and eight hundred kilograms of porcelain, most of it probably Dutch East India Company property, but some perhaps also purchased by individual crew members for lucrative resale in Europe. Pijl-Ketel, *Ceramic Load of the "Witte Leeuw,"* 25.

2. For an explanation of the differences between "faience" and "hard-paste" porcelain see below.
3. Quoted in Röder, *Das Kelsterbach Porzellan*, 67.
4. Hofmann, *Das Porzellan der europäischen Manufakturen*, 52.
5. Gillette, *China's Porcelain Capital*, 16.
6. Finlay, *Pilgrim Art*, 158–66.
7. Cf. de Waal's discussion of this in *White Road*, 113–65.
8. Pijl-Ketel, *Ceramic Load of the "Witte Leeuw,"* 28.
9. Trentmann, *Empire of Things*, 57; De Vries, *Industrious Revolution*, 130.
10. Alessandro Monti, *Der Preis des "weissen Goldes,"* 65. De Vries argues that by the end of the eighteenth century, Europeans had imported more than seventy million pieces of porcelain, virtually all of it produced in Jingdezhen. De Vries, *Industrious Revolution*, 130–31.
11. Finlay, *Pilgrim Art*, 258–60; Gillette, *China's Porcelain Capital*, 23.
12. Sometimes this genre of ceramics is also called "frit" porcelain, because it was often made using "frit," ground-up glass that stabilized the toxic materials in the mix.
13. Quoted in Jaennicke, *Grundriss der Keramik*, 592.
14. Dutch tiles were in use even in humble abodes in the Netherlands in the later seventeenth century; De Vries, *Industrious Revolution*, 55.
15. De Vries, *Industrious Revolution*, 131; DuPlessis, *Transitions to Capitalism*, 232. DuPlessis doesn't say how many workers constituted a "large" workshop, but we can probably assume twenty-five to fifty workers here.
16. De Vries, *Industrious Revolution*, 131.
17. Le Corbeiller, "German Porcelain of the Eighteenth Century," 6.
18. Sponsel, *Kabinettstücke*, 9.
19. Zeh, *Hanauer Fayence*, 10–12.
20. Herzfeld, *Preussische Manufakturen*, 36.
21. Jaennicke, *Grundriss der Keramik*, 459–647; Herzfeld, *Preussische Manufakturen*, 36.
22. Klaus-Peter Arnold, "Meissener Porzellan und Kaffee," in Arnold, Heise, and Ropers, *Ey wie schmeckt der Coffee süsse! Meissner Porzellan und Graphik*, 25.
23. Even in the late eighteenth century, the use of a full complement of silverware—knife, fork, spoon—was restricted to the elite. Kuczinski, *Geschichte des Alltags des deutschen Volkes*, vol. 2, *1650–1810*, 291.
24. Cf. W. Smith, *Consumption and the Making of Respectability*.
25. Dolan, *Wedgwood*, 13.
26. Quoted in Sheehan, *German History*, 72.
27. Louis also owned a great deal of East Asian porcelain, including fifteen-hundred-odd pieces presented to him by the king of Siam in 1686. J.V.G. Mallet, "European Ceramics and the Influence of Japan," in Ayers, Impey, and Mallet, *Porcelain for Palaces*, 49.
28. The porcelain room seems to have been completed only in 1703. Pietsch, "Meissen Porcelain," 12.
29. On Saxon fox-tossing, see Tim Blanning, *Pursuit of Glory*, 403.

30. Sponsel, *Kabinettstücke*, 9.
31. Expenditures fell for the larger states after 1750—especially in Austria and Prussia, where Joseph II and Frederick II, both of whom loathed courtly rituals, cut back severely. By one estimate, the Viennese were spending only 9 percent of the state budget on the court, down from 12.4 percent in 1700. V. Bauer, *Hofökonomie*, 33, 46.
32. Roche, *History of Everyday Things*.
33. This point is made clearly by Kaufhold, "Gewerbelandschaften in der frühen Neuzeit (1650–1800)," 112–202.
34. DuPlessis, *Transitions to Capitalism*, 223; Sarti, *Europe at Home*, 86.
35. Kisch, "Prussian Mercantilism," 4.
36. Berg describes the ways in which these industries, in the English context, formed a central piece of what she has called "a national project to create quality consumer goods." Berg, *Luxury and Pleasure*, 92.
37. DuPlessis, *Transitions to Capitalism*, 230.
38. Krenn and Hirsch, *Zoll im Wandel der Zeit*, 412.
39. One example is Frankenthal, founded in 1755 by Karl Hannong, bankrupt by 1762, it continued production thereafter under the patronage of the Elector of Bavaria. Schnorr von Carolsfeld, *Porzellan der europäischen Fabriken*, 185. For other examples, see chapter 2.
40. Ogilvie, "Consumption, Social Capital, and the Industrious Revolution," 292; Ellerbrock, *Geschichte der deutschen Nahrungs- und Genussmittelindustrie*, 51–52.
41. Ogilvie, "Consumption, Social Capital, and the Industrious Revolution," 295.
42. On Linnaeus, see Koerner, *Linnaeus*; on Prussian silk, Henderson, *Studies in the Economic Policy of Frederick the Great*, 35, 58.
43. Henderson, *Studies in the Economic Policy of Frederick the Great*, 138.
44. Jaennicke, *Grundriss der Keramik*, 647.
45. Siegfried Ducret gives a breakdown of various chemical mixtures used by some of the major firms in Ducret, *Zürcher Porzellan des 18. Jahrhunderts*, 1:42–43.
46. Saxony's collection was begun by Elector Christian I, who acquired some porcelains from the Duke of Florence in 1590. Pijl-Ketel, *Ceramic Load of the "Witte Leeuw,"* 28.
47. Böttcher, *Böttger*, 13–28.
48. See Nummedal, "Practical Alchemy and Commercial Exchange."
49. This story is told in greater detail in Böttcher, *Böttger*; and in English, in Gleeson, *Arcanum*.
50. Chatwin, *Utz*, 111–12.
51. Gleeson, *Arcanum*, 11.
52. Böttcher, *Böttger*, 56–70.
53. De Waal, *White Road*, 130–65; Watanabe-O'Kelly, *Court Culture in Dresden*, 222–23; Walcha, *Meissen Porcelain*, 5; Jaennicke, *Grundriss der Keramik in Bezug auf das Kunstgewerbe*, 701.
54. Böttcher, *Böttger*, 94–95, 108–9.
55. Klein, "Apothecary Shops, Laboratories, and Chemical Manufacture in Eighteenth-Century Germany."

56. For more on the technical side of Böttger and Tschirnhaus's experiments, see Goder et al, "Die technische Entwicklung."

57. Böttcher, *Böttger*, 95; Wolff-Beckh, *Johann Friedrich Böttger*, 43.

58. Böttcher, *Böttger*, 125, 127. Feldspar and quartz would later replace alabaster in most mixtures.

59. Quoted in Gleeson, *Arcanum*, 78.

60. Christine A. Jones stresses this point with respect to French soft-paste porcelain in *Shapely Bodies*, 3–14. Berg also emphasizes the overall importance of "invention as imitation" for eighteenth-century luxury manufacturing. Berg, "New Commodities, Luxuries, and Their Consumers in Eighteenth-Century England," in Berg and Clifford, *Consumers and Luxury*, 76–82.

61. Goder and Walter, "Die Anfänge der Porzellanmanuktur Meissen," 140, 134–38.

62. Böttcher, *Böttger*, 112–91.

63. Gielke, *Meissener Porzellan des 18. und 19. Jahrhunderts*, 17.

64. On the variations in plans over the years see Wittwer, *Die Galerie der Meissener Tiere*, 32–53.

65. Kenzelmann, *Historische Nachrichten*, 18–20; Röntgen, *Book of Meissen*, 30.

66. Augustus quoted in Kenzelmann, *Historische Nachrichten*, 24.

67. Steffen Förster and Mike Huth, "Eine Manufaktur—was ist das?," in M. Fischer, Förster, and Huth, *Manufakturisten als Bürger der Stadt Meissen*, 9–27; "Katholische Manufakturisten als Urzelle der Pfarrgemeinde St. Benno," in M. Fischer, Förster, and Huth, *Manufakturisten als Bürger der Stadt Meissen*, 36–39.

68. Cf. Mack Walker's classic study *German Home Towns*.

69. Walcha, *Meissen Porcelain*, 33–34.

70. Gleeson, *Arcanum*, 142.

71. Pazaurek, *Deutsche Fayence- und Porzellan-Hausmaler*, 1:145.

72. Gleeson, *Arcanum*, 143–49. Stöltzel would return to Meissen in 1723.

73. At Nymphenburg, in Bavaria, for example, arcanists swore "not to divulge the secret of the mixture to anyone, until death, except on the basis of a command from the sovereign [eines höchsten Befehls]." Hofmann, *Geschichte der Bayerischen Porzellan-Manufaktur Nymphenburg*, 1:135.

74. Hofmann, *Geschichte der Bayerischen Porzellan-Manufaktur Nymphenburg*, 1:3–4, 7–43. Wolff-Metternich and Meinz, *Die Porzellanmanufaktur Fürstenberg*, 1:42.

75. Röder, *Das Kelsterbach Porzellan*, 11–14. There remains some suspicion that Böttger himself played a role in spreading the secret to Vienna. See Böttcher, *Böttger*, 183–84. On Ringler, see Hofmann, *Geschichte der Bayerischen Porzellan-Manufaktur Nymphenburg*, 1:40–45; quotation 44.

76. Suttner, *Zur Geschichte*, 3.

77. Böhmert, "Urkundliche Geschichte," 62.

78. See the documents in Wittwer, *Galerie der Meissener Tiere*, 262–63.

79. Throughout this book I have given nominal prices and wage data when available to give readers a ballpark idea of how much things cost at the time. Because these varied over time and place, and because other essential commodities such as bread and rent also varied enormously, it is difficult to estimate the full "real" value of

commodities or wages, and even more tricky to compare them across space and time. Readers will, I hope, appreciate the complexity of these calculations and comparisons and simply take these figures as estimates. See also the note about currencies at the front of the book.

80. Gielke, *Meissener Porzellan des 18. und 19. Jahrhunderts*, 18.

81. Walcha, *Meissen Porcelain*, 149; Röntgen, *Book of Meissen*, 116.

82. Böhmert, "Urkundliche Geschichte," 47. Alessandro Monti's figures for cash profits are little higher than Böhmert's. See Monti, *Der Preis des "weissen Goldes,"* 471.

83. Röntgen, *Book of Meissen*, 196–99. It is possible that Höroldt stole the enamel recipe from another artisanal experimenter, David Köhler, who died in 1723. Röntgen, *Book of Meissen*, 200.

84. Hofmann, *Das Porzellan der europäischen Manufakturen*, 138. The price per dozen of these decorated cups in the first printed price list (1765) varied from 1 T, 9 groschen to 10 T per dozen. *Preiß-courante über Türcken-Copgen bey der Churfürstl. Sächs. Porcellain Manufactur zu Meissen* (Meissen, 1765).

85. Röntgen, *Book of Meissen*, 143. The Viennese, too, by the mid-1730s, were moving away from chinoiserie toward rococo forms. Schnorr von Carolsfeld, *Porzellan der europäischen Fabriken*, 108.

86. Wittwer, *Galerie der Meissener Tiere*, 81–100.

87. For more on Kändler's style, see chapter 3.

88. Walcha, *Meissen Porcelain*, 97–99; Ducret, *Zürcher Porzellanmanufaktur des 18. Jahrhunderts*, 2:25.

89. "Übersicht der Geld-Einnahme für verkäufte Porzellan-Waaren," [1828] in SHStAD, FA 10036, loc. 41908, Rep. IXb, Lit A, Nr. 1.

90. Wittwer, "'King of Prussia,'" 140.

91. T.C.W. Blanning, *Frederick the Great*, 283.

92. Monti, *Der Preis des "weissen Goldes,"* 176–77. Frederick subsequently raised the lease to 5,000 and then 7,000 T per month.

93. Böhmert, "Urkundliche Geschichte," 48.

94. Übersicht der Geld-Einnahme für verkäufte Porzellan-Waaren," [1828] in SHStAD, FA 10036, loc. 41908, Rep. IXb, Lit A, Nr. 1.

95. Hufbauer, *Formation of the German Chemical Community*, 47; Schepkowski, *Johann Ernst Gotzkowsky*, 270–71.

96. Wilckens, *Krepon, Kredit und Porzellan*, 50–54; 58–61; Wegeley quotation (1751), 59.

97. Wilckens, *Krepon, Kredit und Porzellan*, 58.

98. Siebeneicker, *Offizianten und Ouvriers*, 146.

99. Henderson, *Studies in the Economic Policy of Frederick the Great*, 30.

100. On Gotzkowsky, see Wilckens, *Krepon, Kredit und Porzellan*; Henderson, *Studies in the Economic Policy of Frederick the Great*, 17–37; and Schepkowski, *Johann Ernst Gotzkowsky*.

101. Samuel Wittwer, "Interior Decoration and War Trophies: The Porcelain Table Services of Frederick the Great of Prussia," http://www.haughton.com/system/files/articles/2009/05/22/45/ceram_cat_pp36–47.pdf, 37.

102. Schepkowski, *Johann Ernst Gotzkowsky*, 271–76, 298–99.

103. Neuwirth, *Porzellan aus Wien*, 27, 37. By the 1780s, more than half of the WPM's exports were going to the Ottomans. Still, in 1762, Maria Theresa asked her commercial advisers to discuss the pros and cons of privatizing the manufactory. Maria Theresa to Graf Hatzfeld, May 6,1762, in ÖVA, AT-OeStA/FHKA, Fasz. 144, Box 452.

104. I have converted the local currency, gulden or florins, here, to taler, at the rate of 1 florin = .66 T.

105. Krueger, "Die Geschichte," 89–98.

106. Hofmann, *Geschichte der Bayerischen Porzellan-Manufaktur Nymphenburg*, 1:9–12.

107. A similar case is that of Ludwigsburg, which boasted 154 workers in 1766. But when the Württemberg court moved back to Stuttgart the next year, the number fell to eighty-one. Schnorr von Carolsfeld, *Porzellan der europäischen Fabriken*, 203.

108. Hofmann, *Geschichte der Bayerischen Porzellan-Manufaktur Nymphenburg*, 1:40–61, 97–98. Again here I am converting florins to taler.

109. Hofmann, *Geschichte der Bayerischen Porzellan-Manufaktur Nymphenburg*, 1:99–112.

110. Röder, *Das Kelsterbach Porzellan*, 21.

111. Röder, *Das Kelsterbach Porzellan*, 14–66.

112. Upon the death of the last of the Medici line in 1737, the grand duchy passed into the possession of the Habsburg prince Francis Stephen, who had just married Maria Theresa, soon to be Holy Roman empress.

113. On Doccia, see Liverani, *La Manifattura di Doccia nel 1760*; Monika Poettinger, "From Aristocracy to Business and Back: The Ginori Family and Porcelain, 1735–1896," paper for European Business History Association, Twenty-First Annual Congress, 2017, https://www.academia.edu/34395276/THE_GINORI_FAMILY_AND_PORCELAIN_1735–1896.

114. Hofmann, *Das Porzellan der europäischen Manufakturen*, 130.

115. Guida, "Business Organization of the Bourbon Factories," 5.

116. Popow, *Russisches Porzellan aus privaten Manufakturen*, 7; Ross, *Russian Porcelains*, 38–40.

117. Gwilt, *Vincennes and Early Sèvres Porcelain*, 20–22; Hofmann, *Das Porzellan der europäischen Manufakturen*, 64.

118. Whitehead, *Sèvres sous Louis XVI*, 16, 25.

119. Hofmann, *Das Porzellan der europäischen Manufakturen*, 64.

120. For the full story see C. Jones, *Shapely Bodies*, 198–212.

121. Sandon, *Worcester Porcelain*, 7–13; Lippert, *Eighteenth-Century English Porcelain*, 172.

122. Collini, *Lettres sur les Allemands*, 148.

Chapter 2: The Challenge of Wedgwood and the Rise of the Private Firm

1. In 1701, the great elector's successor, Frederick I, finagled the title king in Prussia from the Holy Roman emperor, Leopold I. The titular promotion meant that Frederick was considered to be a king in Prussia, although in the empire he remained an

elector, a dignity he shared with the Elector of Saxony, the prince-bishop of Mainz and six others, and thus formally subordinate to the emperor, a Habsburg, who resided in Vienna.

2. Hagemann, *Revisiting Prussia's Wars*, 42.

3. Henderson, *Studies in the Economic Policy of Frederick the Great*, 125; DuPlessis, *Transitions to Capitalism*, 223.

4. His investment in silk making, however, did spur the success of some entrepreneurs, especially Mennonites, in the area around Krefeld. These manufacturers employed thousands of cottage laborers and made their own fortunes in a luxury industry not dissimilar to the porcelain trade. Kisch, "Prussian Mercantilism," 9–19; investment estimates, p. 13. To put Frederick's industrial investments in perspective, he also spent about 15.5 million T per year on the army. Herzfeld, *Preussische Manufakturen*, 15.

5. Fairchild, "Production and Marketing of Populuxe Goods."

6. Lindemann, *Merchant Republics*, 265–96.

7. Blackbourn, *History of Germany*, 20.

8. DuPlessis, *Transitions to Capitalism*, 220, 222.

9. Kellenbenz, *Deutsche Wirtschaftsgeschichte*, 2:331.

10. Frederick, for example, leased out the state wool works and left the risk taking in the mining sector to others. Herzfeld, *Preussische Manufakturen*, 14. For a discussion of the reciprocal workings of the state and private enterprise in the later eighteenth century, see Straubel, *Kaufleute und Manufakturunternehmer*, 397–437.

11. Pollard, *Peaceful Conquest*, 61–63, has a concise summary of efforts made to restrict guild powers in the eighteenth century.

12. Schubert, "Daily Life, Consumption, and Material Culture," 371.

13. Philips, "Art and Politics in the Austrian Netherlands," 68, 108, 171. Of Tournai, Cobenzl once stated: "j'aime et suis attaché à cette manufacture comme à une maitresse." Philips, "Art and Politics in the Austrian Netherlands," 108.

14. We can see this, for example, in the expanding range of goods purchased by the Reimarus family in Hamburg. See chapter 3.

15. Harold Perkin long ago argued that Britain's semiluxury economy was spurred by a distinctive form of "social emulation" in which consumers at all levels of the social pyramid emulated those just above them. In central Europe, emulation seems to have occurred chiefly within status groups (lesser nobles imitating greater ones, for example), rather than across them. Bourgeois consumers wanted to display their wealth, but not in the same way as their noble betters. See Perkin, *Origins of Modern English Society*. Many thanks to Margaret Anderson for this reference.

16. Ellerbrock, *Geschichte der deutschen Nahrungs- und Genussmittelindustrie*, 79. These statistics end, however, just before Frederick's restriction of coffee consumption, on which see below.

17. Ellerbrock, *Geschichte der deutschen Nahrungs- und Genussmittelindustrie*, 79, 66.

18. Evidence suggests that Germans had increased their ownership of clothing over time. For example, in seventeenth-century Württemberg, one peasant village averaged three and another twelve articles of clothing per person; by about 1750, a century later,

the average was sixteen and twenty-seven; fifty years on, this number had doubled again. By this time, too, brightly colored cottons could be found among Germans' possessions—decades after their Dutch, English, and French counterparts had acquired them. Trentmann, *Empire of Things*, 42. On the French clothing trade, see Roche, *Culture of Clothing*.

19. Weatherill, *Consumer Behaviour*, 26. Tin kitchenwares diversified enormously and fell in relative price as new means of working tin developed. Pennell, *Birth of the English Kitchen*, 83.

20. Discussion of the "consumer" or "retailing" revolution for England had already begun with the publication of Neil McKendrick's pioneering article "Josiah Wedgwood: An Eighteenth-Century Entrepreneur in Salesmanship and Marketing Techniques" but accelerated after the publication of the volume McKendrick edited together with John Brewer and J. H. Plumb, *The Birth of a Consumer Society* (1982). The subject has been elaborated by many British and some French historians since, but the consumer worlds of the Holy Roman Empire need much further study.

21. Simonis, "How to Furnish a Palace." Thanks to Dror Wahrman for this reference.

22. Sponsel, *Kabinettstücke*, 11.

23. Treue, "Sozialgeschichte des Handwerks," 221.

24. Treue, "Sozialgeschichte des Handwerks," 220.

25. According to Susanne Netzer, the glassmaking firm Zechliner Weissglashütte had eight sales points in Prussia already by 1784. Netzer, *Von schönen und necessairen Künsten*, 35. In Weimar, Gustav Klauer built a successful business retailing plaster casts, garden sculptures, and other home furnishings. See "Gipse bei Hr. M. G. Klauer in Weimar," in *Journal des Luxus und der Moden*, June 2, 1787, xliv–xlv, https://zs .thulb.uni-jena.de/receive/jportal_jparticle_00085899.

26. "Memoir," sent to Baron von Alversleben by his cousin, March 22, 1788, in KPM Archive, Box 282. By my calculations, thirty écus would have been about 20 T.

27. A. Green, *Fatherlands*, 81–82.

28. Günter Wiegelmann, "Zucker und Süsswaren im Zivilsationsprozess der Neuzeit," in Teuteberg and Wiegelmann, *Unsere tägliche Kost*, 141.

29. De Vries, *Industrious Revolution*, 161.

30. Albrecht, *Braunschweig und der Kaffee*, 346–47.

31. Henderson, *Studies in the Economic Policy of Frederick the Great*, 72; Teuteberg, "Die Eingliederung des Kaffees," 191; Ellerbrock, *Geschichte der deutschen Nahrungs- und Genussmittelindustrie*, 126n11.

32. Collini, *Lettres sur les Allemands*, 132–33.

33. Ellerbrock, *Geschichte der deutschen Nahrungs- und Genussmittelindustrie*, 128.

34. Netzer, *Von schönen und necessairen Künsten*, 142.

35. Netzer, *Von schönen und necessairen Künsten*, 23–27, 55–57.

36. If there is one area in which historians, as well as connoisseurs and art specialists, have explored the history of the ceramics industry, it is this one. Pioneered by Neil McKendrick, studies of Josiah Wedgwood's artistic, scientific, and entrepreneurial accomplishments have become extensive. See McKendrick, "Josiah Wedgwood"; and more recently Kate Smith, *Material Goods*.

37. I am invoking here some of the classic analyses of the social and technological back-drop to the British industrial revolution, as portrayed, for example, by Joel Mokyr, in his *The Enlightened Economy*.

38. Hilary Young, "Introduction. From the Potteries to Saint Petersburg: Wedgwood and the Making and Selling of Ceramics," in Young, *Genius of Wedgwood*, 10.

39. Dolan, *Wedgwood*, 45, 51–55.

40. Dolan, *Wedgwood*, 60, 116, 92, 113, 184.

41. Davidoff and Hall, *Family Fortunes*.

42. Cf. Vickery, *Behind Closed Doors*, 207–30.

43. Berg, *Luxury and Pleasure*, 53.

44. Young, "Introduction," 16.

45. Dolan, *Wedgwood*, 179. On the Society of Dilettanti, see Kelly, *Society of Dilettanti*.

46. He stocked his manufactory's library with volumes of Montfaucon, Caylus, Passeri, and d'Harcanville (plus of course Hamilton). Gisela Bungarten, "Vasen aus der Manufaktur Wedgwood & Bentley," in Bungarten and Luckhardt, *Reiz der Antike*, 149.

47. Robin Reilly, "Josiah Wedgwood: A Lifetime of Achievement," in Young, *Genius of Wedgwood*, 52. See chapter 3 for more on neoclassical styles in porcelain. In this Wedgwood may have also been imitating the blue and white medallions the Doccia factory had been selling to Grand Tourists, including members of the Society of Dilettanti, since the 1750s.

48. The Portland Vase was a masterpiece of Roman glass purchased by Hamilton in Italy; Hamilton lent this rarity to Wedgwood, who spent years in the effort to copy it properly. The vase itself subsequently became one of the best-loved treasures of the British Museum.

49. Reilly, "Josiah Wedgwood," 53; Young, *Genius of Wedgwood* (catalog entry), 42–43.

50. Wedgwood's virtuoso salesmanship is the theme of McKendrick's famous 1960 essay "Josiah Wedgwood."

51. Quoted in Vickery, *Behind Closed Doors*, 99.

52. McKendrick, "Josiah Wedgwood," 410–12, 429, 431.

53. Wedgwood letter of 1772, quoted in Berg, *Luxury and Pleasure*, 143.

54. Quoted in McKendrick, "Josiah Wedgwood," 428.

55. By 1858 only one of these was left, De Porceleyne Fles. In 1849, this factory—destined to be renamed Royal Delft in 1919—was saved from closure by adding the production of fire bricks (for lining fireplaces). Exhibition material, Royal Delft Museum, Delft.

56. The relationship between philhellenism and the porcelain industry is explored in chapter 3.

57. This service is on view at the Friedenstein Palace, Gotha.

58. Umbach, "Visual Culture," 136.

59. His tastes stuck resolutely in the rococo era, Frederick the Great did not approve of neoclassicism, and the KPM's full embrace of this style had to wait until after his death in 1786. Schnorr von Carolsfeld, *Porzellan der europäischen Fabriken*, 142.

60. Wedgwood, *Catalogue of Cameos, Intaglios, Medals, Bas-Reliefs, Busts, and Small Statues*, 92.

61. Dick Syndram, "Die schönen Künste als Wirtschaftsfaktor: Dresden und seine Sammlungen," in "Sachsen zwischen 1763 und 1813," special issue, *Dresdner Hefte* 31, Heft 114, no. 2 (2013): 47–50.

62. Quoted in Jörg Feldkamp, "Wie Phönix aus der Asche: Die neuen Wissenschaften und der Beginn der industriellen Revolution in Sachsen," in "Sachsen zwischen 1763 und 1813," special issue, *Dresdner Hefte* 31, Heft 114, no. 2 (2013), 57–62; quotation, 62.

63. By comparison, just a bit later, Royal Doulton employed 160; in 1790, Wedgwood employed only 279. K. Smith, *Material Goods*, 55, 102.

64. Monti, *Der Preis des "weissen Goldes,"* 434.

65. Monti, *Der Preis des "weissen Goldes,"* 395; Syndram, "Die schönen Künste als Wirtschaftsfaktor, 51.

66. See Sponsel, *Kabinettstücke*, 215–17.

67. Monti, *Der Preis des "weissen Goldes,"* 191.

68. It also strikes me that this transformation has much in common with the contemporary revolution underway in aesthetic philosophy, exemplified especially in Kant's *Critique of Judgment* (1790), which identified beauty not as something intrinsically possessed by certain objects but as a judgment made by the individual viewer. In both cases, value is detached from the material world and given over to anonymous and perhaps inexpert judges to determine.

69. Böhmert, "Urkundliche Geschichte," 49.

70. Monti, *Der Preis des "weissen Goldes,"* 193–215.

71. Böhmert, "Urkundliche Geschichte," 49.

72. Walcha, *Meissen Porcelain*, 177.

73. See Monti's table, *Der Preis des "weissen Goldes,"* 472.

74. Berling, *Meissen China*, 71.

75. Wolff-Metternich and Meinz, *Die Porzellanmanufaktur Fürstenberg*, 1:91; Ducret *Fürstenberger Porzellan*, 1:98–101.

76. By 1773, employee numbers were down to eighty-nine. Wolff-Metternich and Meinz, *Die Porzellanmanufaktur Fürstenberg*, 1:130, 125, 91.

77. Ducret, *Fürstenberger Porzellan*, 1:119.

78. For example, there is a long discussion of porcelain in *Eröffnete Akademie der Kaufleute oder vollständiges Kaufmanns-Lexicon* by Carl Günther Ludovici (professor of Vernunftlehre at the Hohe Schue in Leipzig and archivist and member of Prussian Academy of Science), part 4, *R to S*, 2nd ed. (Leipzig: Bernhard Christoph Breitkopf und Sohn, 1768). In 1771, the *Neues Hamburgisches Magazin* translated the two-part essay by M. Macquer from the 1769 issue of the *Journal des Sçavans*. See *Neues Hamburgisches Magazin*, vol. 49 (1771), 166–92, 183–92. At the end of this essay, Macquer provided a list of forty-four of the most important writings on porcelain.

79. Ingrao, *Hessian Mercenary State*, 98.

80. Winstone, *Royal Copenhagen*, 19. It did, however, rebound, evidently by copying French works at a fraction of the price and by 1800 was supplying the Danish crown with an estimated 40,000 T a year in profits. *Neu eröfnete Academie der Kaufleute*, 348–49.

81. Hofmann, *Das Porzellan der europäischen Manufakturen*, 65.

82. Monti, *Der Preis des "weissen Goldes,"* 364.

83. Röntgen, *Book of Meissen*, 120.

84. Hofmann, *Geschichte der Bayerischen Porzellan-Manufaktur Nymphenburg*, 1:123–29.

85. Sorgenthal quoted in Lehner-Jobst, "For Emperor and Connoisseur," 28.

86. Lehner-Jobst, "For Emperor and Connoisseur," 29. In a letter to Sorgenthal, the floral painter Joseph Kastner commented: "I have made various observations about the reform of the porcelain factory and have found that His Grace is having much the same experience as the Emperor has had with his religious reforms."

87. T.C.W. Blanning, *Frederick the Great*, 457–58.

88. Rückert, *Schloss Lustheim*, 81.

89. Schade, *Berliner Porzellan*, 110.

90. Tobias Schenk, "Einleitung: Gegenstand, Hintergrund und Aufbau der Datensammlung zu Rechts- und Sozialgeschichte der Juden in friderizianischen Preussen (1769–1788)," and Schenk, "Porzellanverkäufe der preussischen KPM an Juden (1769–1788)," http://quellen-perspectivia.net/de/judenporzellan/introduction, accessed May 15, 2018. Thanks to Christopher Mapes for this citation.

91. Jean Nordhaus's poem "The Porcelain Apes of Moses Mendelssohn" is only one of many invocations of this story. Nordhaus, *The Porcelain Apes of Moses Mendelssohn* (Minneapolis: Milkweed Editions, 2002), 55–56.

92. Quoted in Siebeneicker, *Offizianten und Ouvriers*, 25.

93. Schade, *Berliner Porzellan*, 105.

94. Siebeneicker, *Offizianten und Ouvriers*, 28, 458.

95. Siebeneicker, *Offizianten und Ouvriers*, 34, quotation, 35.

96. Schade, *Berliner Porzellan*, 119–20.

97. Quoted in Hülsenberg and Schwarz, *Alexander von Humboldt*, 20.

98. Zais, *Der Kurmainische Porzellan-Manufaktur zu Höchst*, 38–45; also *250 Jahre Höchster Porzellan, 1746–1996*, 18. For the fate of this manufactory during the revolution, see chapter 4.

99. Christ, *Ludwigsburger Porzellanfiguren*, 44–45.

100. Coutts, *Art of Ceramics*, 194.

101. A sprinkling of new businesses also graced Upper Franconia and the Pfalz in this period. See Günter Dippold, "Frühe bürgerliche Gründungen," in Bald et al., *Porzellan für die Welt*, 10–16.

102. Many years later, the novelist Gustav Freytag offered a lovely evocation of these respectable members of his grandparents' generation: "The old fascination with alchemy had not been snuffed out. Still did sensible and honorable men labor, earnestly seeking the great secret, though something always intervened that hindered the final triumph. Such efforts were undertaken secretly, but the towns well knew that Mr. Official or His Honor, the Secretary, 'pursued the dubious Henry'—that is, heated the stove—to make gold." Freytag, *Bilder aus der deutschen Vergangenheit*, 442.

103. One of these teacups remains on display at Friedenstein castle in Gotha. Augustus was also the author of a novel about homosexual love, *Ein Jahr in Akadien: Kyllenion* (1805), and the maternal grandfather of England's Prince Albert.

104. *Die Gothaer Porzellan-Manufaktur*, 5–12.

105. On Macheleid, see Baur, "Porzellan zwischen Okident und Orient," 73.

106. Greiner, *Lebenserinnerungen von Johann Gotthelf Greiner*, 146–47.

107. Fleischer, "Porzellan aus Sitzendorf und Volkstedt," 25–34; Stieda, *Die Porzellanfabrik zu Volkstedt*, 84, 107–17, 391–95.

108. Quoted in Fleischer, "Porzellan aus Sitzendorf und Volkstedt," 36.

109. Stieda, *Die Porzellanfabrik zu Volkstedt*, 1–44. After several more bankruptcies and changes in name and ownership, the firm eventually became part of the cartel connected to the Arnhold bank and adopted the title Älteste Volkstedter Porzellanfabrik. See Fritzsche, "Die wirtschaftliche Entwicklung," 147–55.

110. For Johann Gotthelf's biography, see Kühnert, "Greiner, Johann Gotthelf."

111. Greiner, *Lebenserinnerungen von Johann Gotthelf Greiner*, 125–48.

112. Schroeder, "Vom Rokoko zum Klassizismus—Fürstliche Leidenschaft und bürgerlicher Gewerbefleiss," 135.

113. Stieda *Die Anfänge der Porzellanfabrikation*, 71–97, also Stieda, *Die Porzellanfabrik zu Volkstedt*, 78–87.

114. See Stieda, *Die Anfänge der Porzellanfabrikation*, 101–2, 108; Küstner, *Die Thüringer Porzellanstrasse*, 93.

115. Lange, "Das Thüringer Porzellan in der Wirtschafts- und Technikgeschichte," 15.

116. This is all very hazy. See the very brief description in Scherf, *Thüringer Porzellan*, 7.

117. Stieda, *Die Anfänge der Porzellanfabrikation*, 176–90; Stieda, *Die Porzellanfabrik zu Volkstedt*, 390.

118. Fleischer, "Porzellan aus Volkstedt und Sitzendorf," 34; Scherf, *Thüringer Porzellan*, 58.

119. Szkurlat, *Porcelain and Faience Manufactory*, 12–13.

120. Szkurlat, *Porcelain and Faience Manufactory*, 34, quotation, 36.

121. WPM Director to K u. K Directorium, February 28 and July 28, 1793; and WPM Director to K. K. Hofkammer, June 7, 1799, in ÖVA, AT-OeStA/FHKA, Fasz. 122, Box 147a.

122. Poche, *Böhmisches Porzellan*, 10–27.

123. See "Porzellanfabrik in Klösterle," Tourismus Portal der Region Karlovy Vary, http://cestovani.kr-karlovarsky.cz/de/pronavstevniky/Zajimavosti/Krajemporcelanu/Seiten/PorcelaankavKlasterci.aspx, accessed August 16, 2017.

124. Poche, *Böhmisches Porzellan*, 29–32.

Chapter 3: Making, Marketing, and Consuming in the "Golden Age"

1. For an example of the critique of luxury, see the anonymous *Mode und Luxus, oder über die Armuth und ihre Quellen* (Elberfeld: Comptoir für Litteratur, 1799).

2. It is hoped that this will help us get past the problem that in discussions about early modern luxury, both in the primary source literature and in the secondary sources, we often lack discussions of the actual objects in question. Maxine Berg and Helen Clifford, "Introduction," in Berg, and Clifford, *Consumers and Luxury*, 5. The German diatribe (*Mode und Luxus*) cited above, for example, specifies only Indian spices among the corrupting foreign imports nobles should abandon.

3. Tocqueville, *Ancien Régime and the Revolution*, 85–102. This famous passage has provided the jumping-off point for many "revisionist" historians seeking to understand the transformations of absolutism that preceded the revolution itself. For example, see Furet, *French Revolution*, 9–10.

4. I am alluding here to Roche, *History of Everyday Things*.

5. Saalfeld, "Lebensverhältnisse der Unterschichten Deutschlands im Neunzehnten Jahrhundert," 215.

6. Pfister, "Consumer Prices and Wages," 3. Rent is excluded from these calculations because of lack of data.

7. Lemire, *Global Trade and the Transformation of Consumer Cultures*, 18.

8. Saalfeld, "Die ständische Gliederung," 465.

9. Styles, "Enlightened Princesses," 45.

10. See Ulinka Rublack's beautiful *The First Book of Fashion*.

11. Quoted in Styles, "Fashion and Innovation," 42.

12. Styles, "Fashion and Innovation," 46.

13. Roche, *Culture of Clothing*; Rublack, *Dressing Up*.

14. Roche, *History of Everyday Things*, 213 ("pursuit"), 116, 104.

15. Roche, *History of Everyday Things*, 67.

16. Katherine Norberg emphasizes the importance of courtesans' home furnishings for the shaping of taste in eighteenth-century France; porcelain pieces, especially for the boudoir or intimate déjeuner sets, belonged very much to this milieu and were often decorated accordingly. See Norberg, "Goddesses of Taste: Courtesans and Their Furniture in Late Eighteenth-Century Paris," in Norberg and Goodman, *Furnishing the Eighteenth Century*, 97–114.

17. Wiegelmann, "Zucker und Süsswaren im Zivilisationsprozess der Neuzeit," 145.

18. Haslinger, *Küche und Tafelkultur am kaiserlichen Hofe zu Wien*, 51. Haslinger estimates that the Hofzuckerbäckerei alone kept about six thousand florins' (4,000 T) worth of porcelain in its cabinets in the eighteenth century.

19. Mosshuchina, "Die Tischkultur am Zarenhof und in russischen Adelskreisen," in *Fragile*, 71–72. This was particularly the case in the Russian Empire, where the expectation for nobles to offer balls or "public lunches" open to all respectably dressed persons bankrupted more than a few urban magnates.

20. Schubert, "Daily Life, Consumption, and Material Culture," 365; Wills, "European Consumption and Asian Production," 141; Cowan, *Social Life of Coffee*, 154.

21. Statistics show that as late as 1834, Germans were consuming only one pound of tea per person per annum, at a time the British average was forty pounds a year. Rappaport, *Thirst for Empire*, 91.

22. Albrecht, *Braunschweig und der Kaffee*, 344–45.

23. Cosimo Alessandro Collini, an Italian nobleman in the service of the Bavarian court, describes these "Cabarets" as central to German (male) sociability in 1790. Collini, *Lettres sur les Allemands*, 185–89.

24. Them, *Kaffeehausgeschichten aus dem alten Dresden*, 31.

25. W. Smith, *Consumption and the Making of Respectability*, 183–87.

26. Ewert, "Biological Standard of Living on the Decline," 66, 79. Again note the fragmentary nature of this data.
27. Freytag, *Bilder aus der deutsche Vergangenheit*, 445.
28. In 1836, Prussia alone still had 940 tin-vessel masters operating. By 1849, however, this number had fallen to 135, perhaps suggesting a strong movement in the direction of ceramics. Stieda, *Die Anfänge der Porzellanfabrikation*, 2.
29. Dessert came in first as a Sunday or holiday treat; it took a long time before ordinary folk could afford to serve sweets on weekdays. Günter Wiegelmann, "Zucker und Süsswaren im Zivilisationsprozess der Neuzeit," in Teuteberg and Wiegelmann, *Unsere tägliche Kost*, 149.
30. Quoted in Philips, "Art and Politics in the Austrian Netherlands," 68.
31. Frederick did renovate his mother's Monbijou Palace and permitted her a prominent social role until her death in 1757. See here T.C.W. Blanning, *Frederick the Great*, 64–65, 467–68.
32. Vickery, *Behind Closed Doors*, 208–12; 272–303; quotation, 274.
33. *Mode und Luxus*, 15.
34. Trentmann, *Empire of Things*, 76.
35. See R. Habermas, *Frauen und Männer*, 43–50; Spiekermann, *Basis der Konsumgesellschaft*, 219.
36. Collini, *Lettres sur les Allemands*, 171.
37. Ogilvie, *Bitter Living*, 135–38; 192–205; Trentmann, *Empire of Things*, 42–43; Crowston, *Credit, Fashion, Sex*.
38. Spiekermann, *Basis der Konsumgesellschaft*, 142.
39. Karl Czok, "August der Starke und die Leipziger Messe," in Rodekamp, *Leipzig*, 82.
40. This process is wonderfully detailed in the Porzellanikon museum in Selb.
41. Böttcher, *Böttger*, 158; K. Smith, *Material Goods*, 49–60.
42. Böhmert, "Urkundliche Geschichte," 47.
43. Hülsenberg and Schwarz, *Alexander von Humboldt*, 23.
44. Quoted in Röntgen, *Book of Meissen*, 120.
45. Ducret, *Fürstenberger Porzellan*, 1:101–2.
46. Scherf, *Thüringer Porzellan*, 9. Again prices in florins have been translated into taler.
47. Siebeneicker, *Offizianten und Ouvriers*, 387–88.
48. Röntgen, *Book of Meissen*, 226, 199.
49. Pazaurek, *Deutsche Fayence- und Porzellan-Hausmaler*, 1:1, 2:440.
50. The lowest-paid female workers made only 20 T per year. Böhmert, "Urkundliche Geschichte," 69. Wages were comparable, but a bit higher, at the KPM. See Siebeneicker, *Offizianten und Ouvriers*, 474. At Höchst, in 1764, the director earned 400 F per year, the model master 480 F, the painter in charge of "galante Figuren u. Viehstücke" 480 F, a blue painter 192 F, and a kiln stoker (Brenner) 144 F. Zais, *Der Kurmainische Porzellan-Manufaktur zu Höchst*, 82.
51. Röntgen, *Book of Meissen*, 117.
52. Ewert, "Biological Standard of Living on the Decline," 78–79.
53. Kellenbenz, *Deutsche Wirtschaftsgeschichte* 1:330.

54. Herzfeld, *Preussische Manufakturen*, 129.

55. Wolff-Metternich and Meinz, *Die Porzellanmanufaktur Fürstenberg*, 1:191.

56. Herzfeld, *Preussische Manufakturen*, 14.

57. Cf. Berg, *Age of Manufactures*, 160–78.

58. Herzfeld, *Preussische Manufakturen*, 244. The Meissen works provided extra grain and salary subsidies to its workers when wheat prices soared in 1771–72, and again in 1770–84, and in 1805. Böhmert, "Urkundliche Geschichte," 68, 70.

59. Banken, *Die Industrialisierung der Saarregion*, 1:452.

60. Ducret, *Fürstenberger Porzellan*, 1:157.

61. Liverani, *La Manifattura di Doccia nel 1760*, 21–24. More than thirty-five thousand of the projected ninety-six thousand (!) pieces of majolica, similarly, never reached the firm's warehouse. Liverani, *La Manifattura di Doccia nel 1760*, 23.

62. Quoted in Ducret, *Zürcher Porzellanmanufaktur*, 1:33.

63. Kühn's report cited in Böhmert, "Urkundliche Geschichte," 67.

64. The novel depicts both systematic pilfering and fraud on the part of a senior official, and a trivial theft on the part of a woodcutter, which plunges his family into destitution. Jasmund, *Das Geheimnis der Porzellanmalerin*.

65. Ducret, *Die Landgräfliche Porzellanmanufaktur Kassel*, 152, 154.

66. Ducret *Fürstenberger Porzellan*, 1:175–86.

67. By one estimate, each modeler could be expected to design twenty to twenty-five new figurines a year; Kändler alone designed at least nine hundred over the course of his career. Ducret, *Zürcher Porzellanmanufaktur*, 2:21.

68. Hofmann, *Das Porzellan der europäischen Manufakturen*, 209.

69. Pietsch, "From the 'Yellow Lion' to 'Blue Band,'" 102.

70. This has been wonderfully demonstrated for Parisian aristocrats by Crowston, *Credit, Fashion, Sex*. Archival account books show that Meissen and other manufactories made regular, but rather halfhearted, attempts to collect. Frederick the Great, who insisted on seeing the factory's books every month, was one of the few to insist on collecting payments promptly, emphasizing the need "especially to recapture foreign debts." Hofmann, *Das Porzellan der europäischen Manufakturen*, 130.

71. Peter Braun, "Meissen Porcelain and Porcelain Diplomacy: Concluding Remarks," in Cassidy-Geiger, *Fragile Diplomacy*, 305.

72. Quoted in Hülsenberg and Schwarz, *Alexander von Humboldt*, 64.

73. Hofmann, *Das Porzellan der europäischen Manufakturen*, 132.

74. Ewald, *Die Kunst*, 37, 180.

75. F. J. Bertuch, "Ueber Luxus in Berlin," *Journal des Luxus und der Moden*, December 1787, 399–416, uni-jena.de.

76. Monti, *Der Preis des "weissen Goldes,"* 169–71, 477.

77. Monti, *Der Preis des "weissen Goldes,"* 210, 480. Similarly, what sold most at Fürstenberg were white-and-blue and white wares. Wolff-Metternich and Meinz, *Die Porzellanmanufaktur Fürstenberg*, 1:391.

78. These cost ten Hamburg marks, while the six wooden plates purchased in 1728 had cost only a bit over ten schillings. Spaulding and Spaulding, *Account Books of the Reimarus Family*, 2:1023–24.

79. Statistics suggest that while general standards of living rose between 1770 and 1849, so too did the gap between rich and poor, rural and urban; owing to increasing prices for necessary foodstuffs, rural populations seem to have actually experienced poorer nutrition (measured by falling average adult heights) across this period of early industrialization. Ewert, "Biological Standard of Living on the Decline," 53–64. The downward trend is especially notable for those born after 1800. As Ewert notes, this evidence is fragmentary, based on estimates for three regions, Saxony, Württemberg, and Bavaria.

80. This was in fact Alexander von Humboldt's advice to the Ansbach manufactory in 1792: rather than producing intricate, heavily decorated items to sit unsold in warehouses, the factory should make simple, salable items in larger batches. Hülsenberg and Schwarz, *Alexander von Humboldt*, 62.

81. It is estimated that there were some 519 "chinamen" in England by 1780, some repackaging items for resale in Ireland, the American colonies, and the Caribbean. Weatherill, *Consumer Behaviour*, 86; Sloboda, *Chinoiserie*, 40, 47–48.

82. Rappaport, *Thirst for Empire*, 47, 56.

83. Spiekermann, *Basis der Konsumgesellschaft*, 30–37.

84. Roche, *History of Everyday Things*, 48.

85. Walcha, *Meissen Porcelain*, 29.

86. Hofmann, *Das Porzellan der europäischen Manufakturen*, 131–32.

87. *Mode und Luxus*, 35.

88. Schubert, "Daily Life, Consumption, and Material Culture," 366.

89. Ducret, *Zürcher Porzellanmanufaktur*, 1:125–26.

90. The Christmas sales are described in the Louvre's audio guide, 2017.

91. McCusker, "Demise of Distance," 301–3.

92. Hofmann, *Das Porzellan der europäischen Manufakturen*, 135.

93. In 1800, for example, Meissen's twelve-page "price current" cost a hefty 1 taler. *Neu eröfnete Academie der Kaufleute*, 355.

94. In 1734, for example, Meissen recorded the cost of the animals and vessels produced for the Japanese Palace in that year as 21,543 T and 19 groschen, but despite its specificity, this was merely an estimate of what the materials and labor cost, and a wishful reckoning of what the sovereign might like to pay. Sponsel, *Kabinettstücke*, 57. The Margrave of Ansbach had to fire his own manufacturing deputation in 1770 because they refused to lower prices, even though they were too low to cover production costs. Hülsenberg and Schwarz, *Alexander von Humboldt*, 21.

95. For more on pricing at Meissen, see Monti, "Moderne Unternehmen."

96. Monti, *Der Preis des "weissen Goldes,"* 175, 181.

97. *Preiß-Courante von denen bunten Porcellainen mit Vergoldung und feiner Mahlerey, nebst angefügten Galanterien bey der Churfürstl. Sächs. Porcellain-Manufactur zu Meissen* (Meissen, 1765), 8–9.

98. Ilmenau price list in *Journal des Luxus und der Moden* 2 (August 1789): lxiv–lxvi.

99. Ducret, *Die Landgräfliche Porzellanmanufaktur Kassel*, 213.

100. Ducret, *Die Landgräfliche Porzellanmanufaktur Kassel*, 220.

101. Wolff-Metternich and Meinz, *Die Porzellanmanufaktur Fürstenberg*, 1:391.

102. "Especially in elegant Saxony," he wrote, "rarely did a well-heeled housewife lack for porcelain cups, pitchers, and knickknacks [Nippesfiguren]." Freytag here greatly overstates the quantity of porcelains owned by non-nobles in the eighteenth century, but he is right to date the desire for such things to this era. Freytag, *Bilder aus der deutschen Vergangenheit*, 446.

103. On Riegl, see Olin, *Forms of Representation*; and Reynolds-Cordileone, *Alois Riegl in Vienna*.

104. For close studies of Meissen's use of prints in its first years, see Cassidy-Geiger, "Graphic Sources for Meissen Porcelain"; and Möller, "Meissen Pieces Based on Graphic Originals."

105. Hofmann, *Das Porzellan der europäischen Manufakturen*, 55.

106. As Rappaport says, context is all: "Depending on context, chinoiserie could represent refinement, beauty, elite social status, and politeness or signify pretentiousness, licentiousness, and the feminizing effects of luxury and foreignness." Rappaport, *Thirst for Empire*, 25.

107. Between 1724 and 1728, some 1,846 of these in various sizes were made by the Meissen factory alone. Kunze-Köllensperger, "Pagode," 170. Note that one appears on the mantel in the portrait of von Brühl (plate 3).

108. This section is meant to warn readers against interpreting this material along the lines of Edward Said's analysis in his very important, but overly schematic and condemnatory *Orientalism*.

109. Sloboda, *Chinoiserie*, 36, 10.

110. Sloboda, *Chinoiserie*, 27.

111. See Pietsch, "Meissen Porcelain," 24–25.

112. Berling, *Meissen China*, 17

113. J.V.G. Mallet, "European Ceramics and the Influence of Japan," in Ayers and Mallet, *Porcelain for Palaces*, 52.

114. Cassidy-Geiger, "Graphic Sources for Meissen Porcelain," 113. On Sèvres's use of prints, see Gwilt, *Vincennes and Early Sèvres Porcelain*, 33.

115. It is rarely pointed out that the making of figurines long predates the origins of European porcelain. For centuries, small porcelain sculptures had been made in China, and in Europe, especially in Italy, figurines had been made in terra-cotta, in bronze, in wood, in faience, in wax, and in sugar. The Neapolitans specialized in making religious figurines for crèches. After 1708, European porcelain makers simply took over the genre and made it their own.

116. Kunze-Köllensperger, "Meissen. Dresden. Augsburg," 56–57.

117. For a deeper investigation of this topic, see S. Marchand, "Porcelain."

118. Herzog, "Mythologische Kleinplastik," 4–6, 13–65.

119. "Archivalische Tabellen," in Köllmann and Jarchow, *Berliner Porzellan*, 24–28.

120. Beyer worked at Ludwigsburg for six years and subsequently designed the garden sculptures for the Viennese Versailles, Schönbrunn. On Beyer, see Schnorr von Carolsfeld, *Porzellan der europäischen Fabriken*, 208. A later KPM director would denounce J. G. Müller's insipid putti and saccharine goddesses: "His figurines are bloodless creatures with expressionless, wooden movements and heads like dolls." Schnorr von Carolsfeld, *Porzellan der europäischen Fabriken*, 154.

121. J. J. Winckelmann, *Anmerkungen über die Geschichte der Kunst des Alterthums: Texte und Kommentar*, ed. Adolf H. Borbein and Max Kunze (Mainz: Philipp von Zabern, 2008), 34.

122. "A Bather," V&A Search the Collections website, http://collections.vam.ac.uk/item /O99105/a-bather-figure-falconet-etienne-maurice/. In a few cases, after 1765, when the first externally oriented price list was produced, we have prices for the figurines; Kändler's nineteen-centimeter-high "the drunken Silenus," for example, was priced at 30 T, and an Apollo with chariot at 43 T. Herzog, "Mythologische Kleinplastik," 98, 66.

123. Wedgwood, *Catalogue of Cameos, Intaglios, Medals, Bas-Reliefs, Busts, and Small Statues.*

124. I am speculating to some extent here, but this reasoning would be in keeping with the arguments about the transformation in styles set out in Evans, *Pattern*, 115–28; and Howard, *Antiquity Restored*, 154–68.

125. Alfred Walz, "Bildnisse berühmter Persönlichkeiten: Gelehrte und Dichter und Ihre Nachbildungen," in Bungarten and Luckhardt, *Reiz der Antike*, 64–70.

126. MacLeod, "Sweetmeats for the Eye," 58.

127. Walz, "Bildnisse," 64, 67.

128. MacLeod, "Sweetmeats for the Eye," 68, 64n43 (prices).

129. Coutts, *Age of Ceramics*, 222.

130. Wolff-Metternich and Meinz, *Die Porzellanmanufaktur Fürstenberg*, 1:70.

131. Walcha, *Meissen Porcelain*, 173, 180.

132. *Neu eröfnete Academie der Kaufleute*, 344.

133. One can find striking parallels here with the "disenchantment" of the Orient Jürgen Osterhammel places in the later eighteenth century. See Osterhammel, *Unfabling the East*.

Chapter 4: Surviving the Revolutions

1. Heine, *Ludwig Börne*, 7.

2. Schilling, "200 Jahre Porzellan der bayerischen Fabriken," 23.

3. See, e.g., Brophy, "Bookshops, Forbidden Print and Urban Political Culture in Central Europe"; Daston and Most, "History of Science and History of Philologies"; Johnston, "Time and the Place to Network."

4. Dahlberg, "France between the Revolutions," 17.

5. Whitehead, *Sèvres sous Louis XVI*, 78–86, 102. The livre was also losing value in 1789–90, so the conversion for 1790 is probably a high estimate.

6. Whitehead, *Sèvres sous Louis XVI*, 104–26; Dahlberg, "France between the Revolutions," 16.

7. Sepkoski, "Earth as Archive," 57–60.

8. Quoted in Béatrice Pannequin, "Clay, Pedagogy, and Progress: The History of the Enquête des Préfets, 1805–1810," in Ostergard, *Sèvres*, 160.

9. Tamara Préaud, "Brongniart as Administrator," in Ostergard, *Sèvres*, 44–48.

10. Monti, *Der Preis des "weissen Goldes,"* 430.

11. M. Chaptal, "Rapport du Ministre de L'Interior sur la manufacture à Sèvres," 9 Thermidor, Year 10 (August 10, 1802), in KPM Archive, Box 282.

12. Préaud, "Brongniart as Administrator"; and Préaud, "The Nature and Goals of Production at the Sèvres Manufactory," in Ostergard, *Sèvres*, 43–61, 75–80, quotation, 75.

13. Winfried Baer, "Die Porzellankunst des Empire," in Hofmann, *Das Porzellan der europäischen Manufakturen*, 214–15.

14. Quoted in Préaud, "Nature and Goals," 80.

15. Untitled, undated memo, in French, in SHStAD, 10036 FA, Loc. 36342, Rep. IX, NR. 4425g.

16. This firm had been originally founded by François Boch, a French cannon maker, in the Duchy of Lorraine in 1748. When France annexed Lorraine in 1766, François's three sons did not want to compete in the crowded French marketplace and moved operations across the border to the Austrian Netherlands (now Luxembourg), setting up shop on an estate called Septfontaines. Thomas, *Die Rolle der Beiden Familien Boch und Villeroy*, 65–79; *Villeroy & Boch*, 9–27.

17. Der Landräthliche Kommissarius [Werner] to Royal Prussian administration in Trier, January 12, 1817, about the faience factory of Herr Boch-Buschmann (from Staatsarchiv Koblenz, Abt. 442, nr. 4788), Mappe 250a, V&B Archive.

18. Zais, *Der Kurmainische Porzellan-Manufaktur zu Höchst*, 41–48.

19. Röder, *Das Kelsterbach Porzellan*, 82–91. The further history of the Kelsterbach faience factory, which continued to operate until 1840, was also one of periodic bankruptcies and recriminations.

20. Winstone, *Royal Copenhagen*, 28.

21. Hofmann, *Das Porzellan der europäischen Manufakturen*, 62; José de Vicente González, *Antiguas boticas españolas y sus recipientes* (San Salvador: TresCtres, 2009), 391.

22. Faÿ-Hallé and Mundt, *Porcelain of the Nineteenth Century*, 26.

23. Wolff-Metternich and Meinz, *Die Porzellanmanufaktur Fürstenberg*, 2:271–79.

24. See Monti's table, *Der Preis des "weissen Goldes*," 473.

25. Monti, *Der Preis des "weissen Goldes*," 472–73; Böhmert, "Urkundliche Geschichte," 62. In 1774, 606 workers had made 143,205 talers' worth.

26. Böhmert, "Urkundliche Geschichte," 51.

27. Berling, *Meissen China*, 82.

28. Lehner-Jobst, "For Emperor and Connoisseur," 27.

29. Lehner-Jobst, "For Emperor and Connoisseur," 38–44; Feuchtmüller and Mrazek, *Biedermeier in Österreich*, 81.

30. Otruba, *Vom Steingut zu Porzellan*, 83. Figure in florins (8744) converted to taler.

31. Humboldt's report has now been carefully edited, and the editors' careful introduction offers deep insight into the technical side of the production process at the time. See Hülsenberg and Schwarz, *Alexander von Humboldt*.

32. Siebeneicker, *Offizianten und Ouvriers*, 37–41; Wittwer, "Betwixt Vienna and Paris," 55–57.

33. See Brose, *Politics of Technological Change in Prussia*, esp. 27–132; and Brophy, *Capitalism, Politics, and Railroads in Prussia*, 24–30.

34. Cf. Giloi, *Monarchy, Myth, and Material Culture in Germany*, 23–104.

35. Cf. A. Green, *Fatherlands*.
36. Ewert, "Biological Standard of Living on the Decline," 71.
37. Kocka, *Lohnarbeit und Klassenbildung*, 59.
38. Henderson, *State and the Industrial Revolution*, 76–147; on the 1818 tariff, p. 91; also Treue, *Wirschafts- und Technikgeschichte Preussens*, 285–304.
39. Macartney, *Habsburg Empire*, 161–203.
40. This is essentially the view of Eric Dorn Brose. See his *Politics of Technological Change in Prussia*.
41. Kocka, *Unternehmer in der deutschen Industrialisierung*, 32.
42. Treue, *Wirtschafts- und Technikgeschichte Preussens*, 317, 339.
43. Ewert, "Biological Standard of Living on the Decline," 52–54, discusses this puzzle and cites extensive literature on the question with special attention to the German states.
44. The faience factory was sold, but not reopened until after 1850, when it began to produce porcelain as well. Falling into Bolshevik territory, this factory was nationalized after the October Revolution of 1917.
45. Baer, "Porzellankunst des Empire," 218.
46. Siebeneicker, *Offizianten und Ouvriers*, 459; Monti, *Der Preis des "weissen Goldes,"* 472–74. These amounts are not, of course, strictly comparable as buying power changed over this long period, but the nominal amounts give us some sense of the firm's fall in income.
47. Heinitz, as we have seen, also attempted to do this at Prussia's newly acquired manufactory at Ansbach, commissioning an extensive report from Alexander von Humboldt. See Hülsenberg and Schwarz, *Alexander von Humboldt*.
48. Himmelheber, *Kunst des Biedermeier*, 46. The WPM made 195 pieces, and Meissen 134.
49. Georg Frick to Trade Ministry, October 26, 1835, GStAB, Rep. 120 Nr. 13, vol. 1.
50. Faÿ-Hallé and Mundt, *Porcelain of the Nineteenth Century*, 112.
51. Siebeneicker, *Offizianten und Ouvriers*, 44.
52. Röntgen, *Book of Meissen*, 124.
53. Berling, *Meissen China*, 147; Monti, *Der Preis des "weissen Goldes,"* 379, 407.
54. Bülow to Bernstorff (State and Cabinet Minister), and to Ministry of Trade and Finance, September 19, 1822, GStAB, III HA II, Nr. 3504.
55. "Cassen Bestand," January 1820, in SHStAD, 10036 FA, Loc. 41911, Rep. IXb, Nr. 205u.
56. Finance Ministry to Meissen Director June 11, 1821, in SHStAD, 10036, FA, Loc. 41911, Rep IXb, Nr. 205f; and Finance Ministry Report, to Meissen Director, October 30, 1821, SHStAD, 10036 FA, Loc. 36342, Rep. IX, Nr. 4425c, quotation in June document.
57. Oppel to king, December 8, 1821, SHStAD, 10036 FA, Loc. 36342, Rep. IX, Nr. 4425c.
58. Oppel to king, January 23, 1822, SHStAD, 10036 FA, Loc. 36342, Rep. IX, Nr. 4425c.
59. This handwritten document can be found in SHStAD, 10036 FA, Loc. 41908, Rep. IXb, Lit A, Nr. 1.

60. Reports of Holm von Egidy, October 16 and 17, 1829; in SHStAD, 10036 FA, Loc. 36342, Rep. IX, Nr. 4425f.

61. J. G. Uhmann [private dealer selling Meissen goods] to Saxon Financial Adviser Schechler in Dresden, October 31, 1829, and December 8, 1831. "Vorschläge zu kaufmännischer Benutzung der Königl. Sächs. Porcelaine Fabrik zu Meissen," by Julius Louis Sehmieder [businessman], to Geheimrat and Interior Minister von Lindenau, in SHStAD, 10036 FA, Loc. 36342, Rep. IX, Nr. 4425f.

62. Monti, *Der Preis des "weissen Goldes,"* 504, 502, 477–78.

63. Böhmert, "Urkundliche Geschichte," 53.

64. Its profit amounted to 1,500 T. Röntgen, *Book of Meissen,* 124.

65. Berling, *Meissen China,* 147–48; Röntgen, *Book of Meissen,* 128.

66. Hofmann, *Geschichte der Bayerischen Porzellan-Manufaktur Nymphenburg,* 1:168; quotation from Schmitz, *Grundzüge,* 2.

67. Frick uses this language in his 1840 appeal to Friedrich Wilhelm IV. See I. Bauer, "Pinnacle," 89–90.

68. See, e.g., the entry on "Porzellan" in *Dr. Johann Georg Krüntz's ökonomisch-technologische Encyklopädie* (vol. 115, 1810), which ran 283 pages (plus extensive pictures). Full books also soon appeared, such as Ludwig Friedrich Schumann, *Die Kunst durchsichtiges Porzellan und weisses Steingut mit durchsichtigen Glasur anzufertigen* (Weimar: Berhn. Friedr. Voigt, 1835). The culminating masterpiece, as we saw above, was Brongniart's own *Traité des arts céramiques, ou des poteries considérées dans leur histoire, leur pratique, et leur théorie* (1844).

69. For a fascinating discussion of how minerals were located and exploited in the premodern era, see Felten, "History of Science."

70. Treue describes how little university chemistry had to do with industry before 1815. Treue, *Wirtschafts- und Technikgeschichte Preussens,* 179–80.

71. Pfister, "Consumer Prices and Wages," 6.

72. Siebeneicker, *Offizianten und Ouvriers,* 93; Baer, "Porzellankunst des Empire," 224, 221. Meissen introduced the "Etage-Ofen" in 1816, the WPM only in 1829. In 1828, Fürstenberg's director claimed that he had reduced energy costs to one-fourth of the earlier figures. Wolff-Metternich and Meinz, *Die Porzellanmanufaktur Fürstenberg,* 2:364.

73. Siebeneicker, "Weisses Gold aus Moabit," 44.

74. On Humboldt, see Daum, *Alexander Von Humboldt,* 26.

75. Klein, "Chemical Experts in the Royal Prussian Porcelain Manufactory"; Klein, "Klaproth's Discovery of Uranium." On Humboldt, Daum, *Alexander von Humboldt,* 26.

76. Mundt, "Vom Biedermeier bis zur neueren Zeit," 226–27.

77. Plinval de Guillebon, *La Porcelaine à Paris,* 114.

78. Siebeneicker, *Offizianten und Ouvriers,* 466.

79. Siebeneicker, *Offizianten und Ouvriers,* 115.

80. Wolff-Metternich and Meinz, *Die Porzellanmanufaktur Fürstenberg,* 2:293, 367–68, 291, 365. See chapter 5 for the full story.

81. Mields, "Die Technik der Porzellan-Manufaktur," 143–46.

82. Himmelheber, *Kunst des Biedermeier*, 46; Faÿ-Hallé and Mundt, *Porcelain of the Nineteenth Century*, 144.

83. Walcha, *Meissen Porcelain*, 186.

84. Otruba, *Vom Steingut zu Porzellan*, 88.

85. Figures from "Region of Porcelain," tourist portal of Karlovy Vary Region, http://cestovani.kr-karlovarsky.cz/en/pronavstevniky/Zajimavosti/Krajemporcelanu/Pages.

86. In 1810, for example, the WPM ran a deficit of 40,000 F. Graft von Chroinsky to Hofkammer, January 24, 1821, ÖVA, AT Fasz 12, 4.486.

87. "Vorantschlag der kaiserl. königl.-Porzellan Manufaktur für das Jahr 1826," in ÖVA, AT Fasz 12, 4.486.

88. Faÿ-Hallé and Mundt, *Porcelain of the Nineteenth Century*, 136.

89. Lehner-Jobst, "For Emperor and Connoisseur," 49.

90. ÖVA, AT FHKA MHK Fas 12, Sub.2, 4.488. Factory records for 1831 give the following breakdown: 95,209 pieces of white, 48,773 pieces of blue and white; and 58,924 pieces of middle-grade porcelain, and 25,811 of fine-grade porcelain in 1831, in addition to 1,930 art pieces, for a total of 230,647 pieces.

91. Otruba, *Vom Steingut zu Porzellan*, 86. In 1841, imperial statistics showed that there were 12 state-privileged (*landesbefugte*) and 45 private (*einfach*) stoneware factories in the Empire, and 11 state-privileged and 3 private porcelain manufactories. By 1873, there were 18 porcelain factories in the Monarchy, by 1880, 26, by 1890, 43. Otruba, *Vom Steingut zu Porzellan*, 101, 125.

92. On Riegl, see Olin, *Forms of Representation*; and Reynolds-Cordileone, *Alois Riegl in Vienna*.

93. Hofmann, *Geschichte der Bayerischen Porzellan-Manufaktur Nymphenburg*, 1:163, 169–72. Between 1842 and 1848, Ludwig I spent nearly 61,000 F (40,626 T) on this project. Copies of paintings on porcelain plates were also made, in smaller quantities, at Sèvres, Meissen, and elsewhere. Hofmann, *Geschichte der Bayerischen Porzellan-Manufaktur Nymphenburg*, 1:188.

94. Laufer, "Der Handwerks goldener Boden?," 45. On wood prices, Pfister, "Consumer Wages and Prices," 7.

95. One case of bankruptcy that we know about is that of Moritz Georg. By 1837, Ebers's porcelain factory was losing so much money that it threatened to undermine his successful banking business as well; these anxieties triggered Ebers's sudden death (probably suicide) just weeks before the birth of his fifth child, the future Egyptological novelist Georg Ebers. See Suzanne Marchand, "Georg Ebers," 21, n.9.

96. Vershofen, *Tat und Vorbild*, 12.

97. Vershofen, *Tat und Vorbild*, 28.

98. Eichhorn was at first denied permission to found a factory on the grounds that it would use too much wood and compete with local stoneware firms; moreover, his already existing kilns were too close to the road and created a fire hazard. Eichhorn received a permission to set up a firm in the town of Waldsassen only after he hired a lawyer; but even then it took five years to build a proper kiln and begin production. Tirschenreuth would go on to become one of the major producers of inexpensive porcelain in the German Empire until 1927, when it was taken over by Lorenz

Hutschenreuther, a branch of the ceramics empire founded by Carolus Magnus. *150 Jahre Porzellanfabrik Tirschenreuth*, 4–6.

99. Siebeneicker, *Offizianten und Ouvriers*, 52.

100. Zehentmeier, *Leben und Arbeiten*, 30.

101. Otruba, *Vom Steingut zu Porzellan*, 108.

102. "Nachrichten über die Porzellan und Fayenze-Fabriken in Böhmen" July 28, 1828; also "Preis Liste über die in der k. k. privilegirten Dalwitzer Steingutfabrik nach Wedgwood erzeugten Tafel- und Kaffe-Service dann Dessert," in SHStAD, 10036 FA, Loc. 41911, Rep IXb, 205o.

103. Merriman, *Red City*, 27–29.

104. Kocka, *Unternehmer in der deutschen Industrialisierung*, 66.

105. Banken, *Die Industrialisierung der Saarregion*, 1:432, 436.

106. August 13, 1904, in V&B Archive, Mappe 288; and Gerald E. Brennan, "Villeroy & Boch AG," in *International Directory of Company Histories*, vol. 37, ed. Tina Grant (Detroit: St. James, 2001), 416.

107. Banken, *Die Industrialisierung der Saarregion*, 1:433.

108. *Villeroy & Boch*, 23, 30–32, 41.

109. Banken, *Die Industrialisierung der Saarregion*, 1:453.

110. Banken, *Die Industrialisierung der Saarregion*, 1:449–51.

111. J.-F. BB [Boch-Buschmann] *Comparison entre la fabrication des poteries en Angleterre et sur le continent, pour server de base aux modifications à apporter au tariff des douanes concernant cette industrie* (Luxembourg: J. Lamort, 1835), 17; V&B Archive, Mappe 242, 17a.

112. Henderson, *Zollverein*.

113. Junghanns, *Die Fortschritt des Zollvereins*, 110–11.

114. *Villeroy & Boch*, 61–63.

115. "Übersicht der Beiträge der versandten Wären," V&B Archive, Mappe 435.2.

116. Banken, *Die Industrialisierung der Saarregion*, 1:459–61.

Chapter 5: The Discrete Charms of Biedermeier Porcelain

1. See Ottomeyer, "Von Stilen und Ständen, 100–104.

2. Schmoller, *Zur Geschichte der deutschen Kleingewerbe*, 56.

3. Quoted in Wolff-Metternich and Meinz, *Die Porzellanmanufaktur Fürstenberg*, 2:294.

4. Quoted in Wolff-Metternich and Meinz, *Die Porzellanmanufaktur Fürstenberg*, 2:294.

5. Mosshuchina, "Die russische Tischkultur des 19. Jahrhunderts," in *Fragile*, 150.

6. Haslinger, *Küche und Tafelkultur*, 19.

7. Wolff-Metternich and Meinz, *Die Porzellanmanufaktur Fürstenberg*, 2:379.

8. Pierenkemper and Tilly, *German Economy during the Nineteenth Century*, 14; Pfister, "Consumer Wages and Prices," 8, 25.

9. W. Fischer, Krengel, and Wietog, *Sozialgeschichtliches Arbeitsbuch I*, 170.

10. Eigl, *Die würdige deutsche Hausfrau im täglichen Leben*, 55.

11. Kreklau, "'Eat as the King Eats,'" 64–69.

12. Quoted in Otruba, *Vom Steingut zu Porzellan*, 102.

13. Wolff-Metternich and Meinz, *Die Porzellanmanufaktur Fürstenberg*, 2:392.

14. Berndt, *Das Buch der Hausfrau*, 315.

15. Habermas's original title was: *Strukturwandel der Öffentlichkeit: Untersuchung zu einer Kategorie der bürgerlichen Gesellschaft*. The literature on "the public sphere" is now legion; for some relevant synthetic studies, see Van Horn Melton, *Politics, Culture, and the Public Sphere*; and La Vopa, "Conceiving a Public."

16. Them, *Kaffeehausgeschichten aus dem alten Dresden*, 39.

17. Schmoller estimated that the number of pastry shops in Prussia rose 72 percent between 1831 and 1861. Schmoller, *Kleingewerbe*, 394.

18. Them, *Gasthausgeschichten aus dem alten Dresden*, 40. Fifty-two of these were hotels and *Gasthöfen*, 443 were *Gastwirtschaften*, and 165 were *Victualienhändler* who were allowed to sell alcoholic beverages.

19. R. Habermas, *Frauen und Männer*, 315–25.

20. Rossberg, "Zur Kennzeichnung," 107–8.

21. R. Habermas, *Frauen und Männer*, 164–65.

22. Ottomeyer, "Von Stilen und Ständen," 101.

23. A collection of these are on view at the "Porcelain Experience" museum in the Leuchtenburg castle near Kahla.

24. R. Habermas, *Frauen und Männer*, 166–68.

25. See Judith Flanders's wonderful description of the battle against dirt in *Inside the Victorian Home*, e.g., 43–47, 100–116.

26. Famously, the "Gurjewski" service, commissioned by Russian finance minister D. A. Gurev in 1809, jarringly encased idealized pictures of Russian commoners in classicizing rims. Klaus Klemp, "Porzellan im Kontext: Eine Einführung in die Austellung," in *Fragile*, 30.

27. See Eva Giloi's insightful analysis in her *Monarchy, Myth, and Material Culture in Germany*, esp. 23–32.

28. "Preis-Courant von Tabacksköpfen und Abgüssen in der Königl. Sächsischen Porzellan Manufactur in Meissen und in deren Niederlagen zu Dresden und Leipzig" (undated), in SHStAD 10036 FA, Loc. 41911, Rep IXb, Nr. 205q.

29. Quoted in Ottomeyer, "Von Stilen und Ständen," 112.

30. Cf. Hubsch et al., *In What Style Should We Build*.

31. Ottomeyer, "Von Stilen und Stände," 110.

32. Jedding, *Meissener Porzellan*, 8–9.

33. Kunze, "Die Kritik Dresdener Künstler," 105.

34. SHStAD, 10036 FA, Loc. 419ii, Rept IXb, Nr. 205s.

35. Faÿ-Hallé and Mundt, *Porcelain of the Nineteenth Century*, 140–54.

36. Quoted in Katharina Schulze, "Die Beteilungen der Meissener Porzellanmanufaktur an den Weltausstellungen 1851–1893" (MA thesis, University of Hamburg, 1992), 22.

37. Röntgen, *Book of Meissen*, 204.

38. Schulze, "Die Beteilungen der Meissener Porzellanmanufaktur," 22.

39. See the KPM's website, https://de-de.kpm-berlin.com/kpm-berlin/manufaktur/designer/?L=2%252F. This form is still being manufactured—but in plain white, without the luxurious decorations Schinkel added.

40. Nor did Semper's "Rimini Vases," designed for Sèvres in 1849, sell well, and again the production costs were exorbitant. Orelli-Messerli *Gottfried Semper*, 66, 163.

41. Faÿ-Hallé and Mundt, *Porcelain of the Nineteenth Century*, 47.

42. Kühn quoted in Kunze, "Die Kritik Dresdener Künstler," 112–13.

43. Préaud, "Nature and Goals," 80.

44. Brophy, "Bookshops, Forbidden Print and Urban Political Culture in Central Europe," 406; and Brophy, "Second Wave."

45. The Steingutfabrik in Altrohlau bei Karlsbad, for example, stated on its price list for 1826: "Consumers may omit anything from these pre-arranged services according to their liking, or substitute items according to the list below; accordingly, the price will rise or fall." "Preis Liste" for k. k. priv. Steingutfabrik in Altrohlau bei Karlsbad (1826), in SHStAD, 10036 FA, Loc. 41911, Rep IXb, 205o.

46. Jedding, *Meissener Porzellan*, 63.

47. The molds would later be sold and the old name recycled as Royal Crown Derby after 1890.

48. "List of China Wares of Old but very pleasant shapes of the Manufactory of H. M. the King of Saxony at Meissen," in SHStAD, 10036 FA, Loc. 419ii, Rept IXb, Nr. 205s.

49. The 1828 price was 1 T, 2 groschen; the 1765 price was 2 T, 8 groschen. "Vergleichung der Porzellan-Preise verschiedenen Artikel von Jahr 1765 und der von Jahre 1828," in SHStAD 10036 FA, Loc. 41908, Rep. IXb, Lit A, Nr. 1.

50. "Preis Nota" in SHStAD, 10036 FA, Loc. 41911, Rep IXb, Nr. 205o.

51. The Bohemian Altrohlau works, for example, charged 47 F (31 T) for its "common" twelve-piece service, but 81 F (53.5 T) for its blue-painted "Viennese" tableware set. "Preis Liste" for k. k. priv. Steingutfabrik in Altrohlau bei Karlsbad" (also 1826), in SHStAD, 10036 FA, Loc. 41911, Rep IXb, 205o.

52. "Preis Verzeichniss der Porcellan-Fabrik zu Althaldensleben 1828," in KPM Archive, Box #157; "Preis Liste über die in der k. k. privilegirten Dalwitzer Steingutfabrik nach Wedgwood erzeugten Tafel- und Kaffe-Service dann Dessert," in SHStAD, 10036 FA, Loc. 41911, Rep IXb, Nr. 205q.

53. "Vergleichende Preis Nachweisung für Kaffee- und Thee-Geschirr," [1863], comparing 1863 prices with those of 1828. KPM Archive, Box #157.

54. Ahrens and Lehner-Jobst, *Augartenmuseum*, 69.

55. Faÿ-Hallé and Mundt, *Porcelain of the Nineteenth Century*, 139, 145. Note the Rosenthal version of this on the table in figure 8.5.

56. "Preis Courant der KPM über grün und schwarz unter der Glasur bemalte Porzellan Geschirre," 1828, KPM Archive, Box #157.

57. *Musterbuch 1831–1834*, in V&B Archive.

58. Wolff-Metternich and Meinz, *Die Porzellanmanufaktur Fürstenberg*, 2:333.

59. Preis-Courant der KPM in Berlin über diverse weisse Porzellan-Geschirr, 1828 in KPM Archive, Box #157.

60. Faÿ-Hallé and Mundt, *Porcelain of the Nineteenth Century*, 151, 155.

61. "Prix des Produits de la manufacture de Lithophanie, Paris," July 1828; "Prix Courans de Produits Lithophaniques," 1830; "Preis-Courant der KPM in Berlin über

porzellanen transparente Lichtschirmplatten," 1828; "Preis Courant der KPM über transparente Lichschirmplatten," ca. 1860; all in KPM Archive, Box #157.

62. Etiquette manuals describing how to stock one's kitchen with the proper cooking and serving ware—including extensive warnings against purchasing items with toxic glazes—now address themselves exclusively to women. Cf. Berndt, *Das Buch der Hausfrau*, 320–25.

63. Bernhard, *Das Biedermeier*, 245; "Fabrikwesen Berlin," 20; in B Arch, A Rep. 200-01, #879.

64. "Preis-Courant von Tabacksköpfen und Abgüssen in der Könlig. Sächsischen Porzellan Manufactur in Meissen und in deren Niederlagen zu Dresden und Leipzig" (undated), in 10036 FA, Loc. 41911, Rep IXb, Nr. 205q. A KPM list for 1823 offered a similar set of options (196 in all): military and mythological figures, images of the hunt and of Berlin's new buildings, landscapes, sentimental figures of hope and harmony, Masonic symbols, drunken sailors, Frederick the Great (of course), Diogenes, and a mule. "Preis-Note der Königlichen Porzellan-Manufaktur in Berlin über bemalte Tabaksköpfe und Abzüge," in KPM Archive, Box #157.

65. Schaffer, *Novel Craft*.

66. R. Habermas, *Frauen und Männer*, 55–61.

67. Karl Rottlinger, *Handbuch der Porzellan-Malerei oder gründlicher Unterricht im Portraitiren und Landschaft-Malen auf Porzellan* (Quedlinburg: Goltfr. Basse, 1835).

68. X. Froelich, *Die Geheimnisse der Porzellanmalerei: Ein Handbuch inbesondere für Diejenigen, welche bei einigen Vorkenntnissen im Zeichnen und Malen sich der Kunst, haltbar auf Porzellan zu malen, aneignen wollen* (Graudenz: Julius Gaebel, 1847), iv, 20, 73–75.

69. A. Kühn, *Praktische Anleitung zur Ölmalerei, Aquarell-, Miniatur-, und Fresko-Malerei, der Malerei auf Porzellan . . . etc.* (Berlin: S. Mode's Verlag, n.d.).

70. Deborah Cohen makes a similar case for the British middle classes' pursuit of individuality in their midcentury home furnishings. See Cohen, *Household Goods*, 125–44.

71. See the essays in Brewer and Porter, *Consumption and the World of Goods*, and in Berg and Clifford, *Consumers and Luxury*.

72. Spiekermann, *Basis der Konsumgesellschaft*, 50–78, quotation, 73.

73. Probst, "Die Deutsche Porzellan- und Steingutindustrie," 15, 18.

74. Details on Hiltl in Moll, "Zwischen Handwerk und Unternehmen," 57–70.

75. Frick quoted in I. Bauer, "Pinnacle," 89–90.

76. Parenzan, "Schöner Wohnen in Biedermeier und Vormärz," 33.

77. "Preis Liste über die in der k. k. privilegirten Dalwitzer Steingutfabrik nach Wedgwood erzeugten Tafel- und Kaffe-Service dann Dessert," in SHStAD, 10036 FA, Loc. 41911, Rep IXb, 205o.

78. Siebeneicker, "Weisses Gold aus Moabit," 22–24.

79. Quoted in R. Habermas, *Frauen und Männer*, 73.

80. In 1836, for example, Villeroy & Boch's Mettlach factory sold 78 percent of its produce in Prussia, and an additional 19 percent in other German states, leaving only 3 percent of sales abroad. Banken, *Die Industrialisierung der Saarregion*, 1:455.

81. J. Davis, "Representation, Rivalry and Transfer," 166.

82. Schmoller, *Kleingewerbe*, 219–49. Schmoller's rough estimates show the number of peddlers in Prussia doubling between 1852 and 1858, and in Saxony rising from 131 peddlers per one hundred thousand people to 383 by 1861. Schmoller, *Kleingewerbe*, 246, 243, 247.

83. Farr, *Artisans in Europe*, 284–85.

84. E.g., Farr, *Artisans in Europe*, 276–97.

85. Herrigel, *Industrial Constructions*, 42.

86. Blackbourn, *History of Germany*, 142.

87. Trömel, *Kartell und Preisbildung*, 18, 28.

88. This insight was made by the economic historian Werner Sombart in his *Der moderne Kapitalismus*, vol. 1 (Leipzig: Dunckler & Humblot, 1902), 40–42.

89. Gorges, *Der christlich geführte Industriebetrieb*, 105–16.

90. Siebeneicker, *Offizianten und Ouvriers*, 329.

91. Siebeneicker, *Offizianten und Ouvriers*, 311–13.

92. Banken, *Die Industrialisierung der Saarregion*, 1:452.

93. Wolff-Metternich and Meinz, *Die Porzellanmanufaktur Fürstenberg*, 2:371–72.

94. Siebeneicker, "Weisses Gold aus Moabit," 36–38.

95. Faÿ-Hallé and Mundt, *Porcelain of the Nineteenth Century*, 138.

96. Wolff-Metternich and Meinz, *Die Porzellanmanufaktur Fürstenberg*, 2:326–27.

97. Gutachten from summer 1827; Wolff-Metternich and Meinz, *Die Porzellanmanufaktur Fürstenberg*, 2:326–27, 362–63.

98. Quoted in Wolff-Metternich and Meinz, *Die Porzellanmanufaktur Fürstenberg*, 2:356. On von Marées's career, 326–28, 356–65.

99. Wolff-Metternich and Meinz, *Die Porzellanmanufaktur Fürstenberg*, 2:328–30.

100. Siebeneicker, *Offizianten und Ouvriers*, 388, 405.

101. Baer, "Veduta Panting, "Veduta," 72.

102. I. Bauer, "Pinnacle," 86.

103. Siebeneicker *Offizianten und Ouvriers*, 332, 474.

104. Siebeneicker, "Weisses Gold aus Moabit," 33; Schade, *Berliner Porzellan*, 122.

105. In 1848 Meissen workers also petitioned for some of the same reforms, including reduction of the proportion of wages paid by the piece. Böhmert, "Urkundliche Geschichte," 72–74. Yet even the factory history written during the GDR had to admit that the revolutions of 1830 and 1848 did not find much of an echo among Meissen's workers. Walcha, "Die Geschichte der Meissner Manufaktur," 80.

106. Scholz, "Soziales Herkunft und soziales Milieu," 39.

107. Siebeneicker, *Offizianten und Ouvriers*, 407–21.

108. Frick quoted in Kolbe, *Geschichte*, 393–94.

109. Figures from Böhmert, "Urkundliche Geschichte," 62. The complaints were voiced in a memo written for the ministry by a French merchant, in the spring of 1834. SHStAD, 10036 FA, Loc. 36342, Rep. IX, NR. 4425g.

110. Quoted in Kunze, "Die Kritik Dresdener Künstler," 118.

111. Neidhardt, *Ludwig Richter*, 15–31.

112. Kolbe, *Geschichte*, 275.

113. Börne quoted in Heine, *Ludwig Börne*, 7–8. Thanks to Brendan Karch for recommending this source.

Chapter 6: Of Capitalism and Cartels: The Glory Days of the Private Producer, 1848–1914

1. Wilhelm Kesselbach, "Drei Generationen" *Deutsche Vierteljahrschrift* 1860, Heft 3, 14–32; quotation, 32.

2. Schmoller, *Kleingewerbe*, 175–83, 209, 677–78, quotation, 175.

3. Pierenkemper and Tilly, *German Economy during the Nineteenth Century*, 139.

4. The Wars of Unification themselves made little dent in exports. Although 1871—the year that saw the Franco-Prussian War's end and Germany's unification—proved a dismal year for German porcelain sales abroad, in 1872, the united state was able to double exports over the figures previously posted by the North German Confederation. Probst, "Die Deutsche Porzellan- und Steingutindustrie," 22. The private makers Utzschneider and Villeroy & Boch, despite being headquartered near the French border, saw profits of 29 percent and 24.4 percent respectively in 1871. Banken, *Die Industrialisierung der Saarregion*, 2:566.

5. Cf. Blackbourn, *History of Germany*, 253.

6. Wildner, "Die Porzellanindustrie," 231.

7. Cf. Schmoller, *Kleingewerbe*, 671. Schmoller's statistics reach only to 1869, but the plight of the Thuringian industry after this time suggests that small makers continued to suffer through the later Wilhelmine years.

8. Krueger, "Einführung," 7.

9. To take just one example: of the household expenditures of a six-person household of a Frankfurt carpenter, coffee made up 9 percent of the total grocery costs, more than was spent for butter, vegetables, or even potatoes. H. Fischer, *Konsum im Kaiserreich*, 216–17.

10. "Fabrikwesen Berlin," 38. B Arch, A Rep 200-01, #879.

11. Schmoller estimates that there were 4,981 ceramics masters at work in Prussia in 1828 and 5,090, only about one hundred more—despite a huge jump in population—in 1858. Schmoller, *Kleingewerbe*, 274.

12. This generous estimate is based on Probst, "Die Deutsche Porzellan- und Steingutindustrie," 16–17.

13. Information from Porzellanikon Museum, Selb.

14. Banken, *Die Industrialisierung der Saarregion*, 2:553.

15. Otruba, *Vom Steingut zu Porzellan*, 125. We know from another less exact source that there were at least seventy-nine ceramics factories in the empire in 1883, and 174 in 1896, of which fifty were in Bohemia. *Addressbuch der keramischen Industrie* (Coburg, Müller & Schmidt, 1883); *Addressbuch der keramischen Industrie* (Coburg: Müller & Schmidt, 5th ed., 1896).

16. Schmoller, *Kleingewerbe*, 166–70, 264.

17. Probst, "Die Deutsche Porzellan- und Steingutindustrie," 27.

18. Trömel, *Kartell und Preisbildung*, 20.

19. On the permeability of this borderland, see Murdock, *Changing Places*, 33–56.

20. Figures from Rönneper, "Die Entstehung und Entwicklung," 341; *Villeroy & Boch, Mettlach, Sonderdruck aus* Die freiwilligen sozialen Fürsorge- und Wohlfahrtseinrichtungen in Industrie, Handel, und Gewerbe im Deutschen Reiche (Halle: Carl Marhold Verlagsbuchhandlung, 1913), http://webopac.hwwa.de/PresseMappe20/PM20 .cfm?T=F&qt=153110&CFID=4036887&CFTOKEN=78722948.

21. Merriman, *Red City*, 81.

22. Siebeneicker, *Offizianten und Ouvriers*, 80.

23. Schilling, "Der Export, 1814–1914," 30.

24. Probst, "Die Deutsche Porzellan- und Steingutindustrie," 6–7.

25. Werner, "' Goldenen Zeiten?,'" 125.

26. Lux, *Studien über die Entwicklung der Warenhäuser*, 46.

27. Rönneper, "Die Entstehung und Entwicklung," 197, 359.

28. Probst, "Die Deutsche Porzellan- und Steingutindustrie," 8–9.

29. See Rönneper, "Die Entstehung und Entwicklung," e.g., 12–15, 30, 41, 138.

30. D. Jones, "Development of Dental Ceramics," 630, 642.

31. Taylor, *History of Dentistry*, 96–97, 143–48; Rönneper, "Die Entstehung und Entwicklung," 120.

32. Zehentmeier, *Leben und Arbeiten*, 24.

33. See Blaszczyk, *Imagining Consumers*, 55–82. On the expansion of the French export trade, see Jaennicke, *Grundriss der Keramik*, 833; Merriman, *Red City*, 81.

34. Umbach, "Made in Germany," 407.

35. Wildner, "Die Porzellanindustrie," 235.

36. Trömel, *Kartell und Preisbildung*, 54.

37. "Thonwaaren," *Wiener Weltausstellung: Amtlicher Katalog der Ausstellung des Deutschen Reiches* (Berlin: Königliches Geheim Ober-Hofbuchdrückerei, 1873), 368–75.

38. Wildner, "Die Porzellanindustrie," 234.

39. Wildner, "Die Porzellanindustrie," 235, 232–33. This was, however, lower than in Limoges, where women in 1901 formed 35 percent of the workforce. Merriman, *Red City*, 168.

40. "Das moderne China und seine Bedeutung für Deutschland," *Kölnische Zeitung*, December 11, 1895, in SHStAD, 11497, #130.

41. This was listed as point 1 in the statutes of the Verband keramischer Gewerke in Deutschland, formed in 1877. Rönneper, "Die Entstehung und Entwicklung," 312.

42. This phrase invokes Celia Applegate's pathbreaking book of 1990, which demonstrated that even as Germans developed a sense of their Germanness, they retained, or even further developed, their sense of belonging to their provincial homelands. Applegate, *Nation of Provincials*.

43. On changes in the banking industry, see Brophy, *Capitalism, Politics, and Railroads in Prussia*, 87–106.

44. Most companies still had few shareholders. When, for example, Oskar Bareuther's Waldsassen manufactory in 1904 became an AG, capitalized at one million M, it still had only five shareholders, and it was these men—mostly family members and longtime partners—who enjoyed its 12–15 percent yearly dividends. Schilling, "Die Porzellanfabrik Waldsassen," 32–37.

45. Trömel, *Kartell und Preisbildung*, 47.

46. Blackbourn, *History of Germany*, 244.

47. Quoted in Trömel, *Kartell und Preisbildung*, 61.

48. There had evidently been an attempt at forming a cartel in the porcelain industry in 1814, when seven Thuringian firms signed a contract to set prices and to adopt a common trademark: but this was surely only possible as most of the owners belonged to the Greiner family. In any event, the agreement never seems to have gone into force. Stieda, *Die Anfänge der Porzellanfabrikation*, 6–9.

49. Trömel, *Kartell und Preisbildung*, 53.

50. Quoted in Trömel, *Kartell und Preisbildung*, 62.

51. Rönneper, "Die Entstehung und Entwicklung," 33.

52. It is also possible that the Bohemian Verband predated this time; a notice of intent to form such an organization was published in 1886. Trömel, *Kartell und Preisbildung*, 57.

53. Popow, *Russisches Porzellan aus privaten Manufakturen*, 9.

54. Perhaps the most well known of the firms here was the successor to the Rudolstadt firm founded by Macheleid, the Älteste Volkstedter Porzellanfabrik.

55. Probst, "Die Deutsche Porzellan- und Steingutindustrie," 43.

56. Lechelt, *Die Porzellanmanufaktur Fürstenberg*, vol. 3, *Von der Privatisierung im Jahr 1859 bis zur Gegenwart*, 25.

57. At Villeroy & Boch, for example, joining such a fund became imaginable for such workers only after 1874, just five years before Bismarck's national insurance plan was passed. Banken, *Die Industrialisierung der Saarregion*, 2:561. Domestic workers, women, apprentices, and many others continued to be excluded from such provisions long after this time. See Heckl, *Protokoll des Dritten Kongresses*, e.g., 17, 25.

58. Scholz, "Soziales Herkunft und soziales Milieu," 65.

59. Siebeneicker, *Offizianten und Ouvriers*, 421–22.

60. Scholz, "Soziales Herkunft und soziales Milieu," 52, 63. As early as 1874 one socialist propagandist denounced porcelain workers for joining their own particularistic unions and throwing money away on workers' funds that solved none of their problems. R. Meyer, *Der Emancipationskampf des vierten Standes*, vol. 1 (Berlin: Aug. Schindler, 1874), 280.

61. Siebeneicker, *Offizianten und Ouvriers*, 421–28.

62. Zehentmeier, *Leben und Arbeiten*, 237–38, 260–62, 273.

63. Bald, *Porzellanarbeiterschaft*, 28. See also Zehentmeier, *Leben und Arbeiten*, 197–200.

64. Bald, *Porzellanarbeiterschaft*, 62; Zehentmeier, *Leben und Arbeiten*, 278–79.

65. Heckl, *Protokoll des Dritten Kongresses*, 32, 40, 18–19; quotation, 18.

66. Kellenbenz, *Deutsche Wirtschaftsgeschichte*, 2:309–10; Walcha, *Meissen Porcelain*, 200.

67. W. Fischer, Krengel, and Wietog, *Sozialgeschichtliches Arbeitsbuch I*, 133.

68. Böhmert, "Urkundliche Geschichte," 69.

69. In 1869, a signalman in the private sector averaged 516 M per year as compared to 627 in the state's employ. W. Fischer, Krengel, and Wietog, *Sozialgeschichtliches Arbeitsbuch I*, 159.

70. Meissen to Finance Ministry, December 17, 1877, in SHStAD, 10704 OK 99/1.

71. Hanold, *Geschichte der Porzellanindustrie in Schönwald*, 73.

72. Bollmann, *Lohn-Statistik*, 16.

73. Heckl, *Protokoll des Dritten Kongresses*, 29.

74. Kellenbenz, *Deutsche Wirtschaftsgeschichte*, 2:309–10. Schmoller (1871) gives the wages for a small town tailor at 600 M, an urban one at 1,200 M. Schmoller, *Kleingewerbe*, 647.

75. Bollmann, *Lohn-Statistik*, 14.

76. *Villeroy & Boch, Mettlach, Sonderdruck aus* Die freiwilligen sozialen Fürsorge- und Wohlfahrtseinrichtungen in Industrie, Handel, und Gewerbe im Deutschen Reiche (Halle: Carl Marhold Verlagsbuchhandlung, 1913), http://webopac.hwwa.de/Presse Mappe20/ PM20.cfm?T=F&qt=153110&CFID=4036887&CFTOKEN=78722948.

77. In 1871 Schmoller estimated that no more than five of seven apprentices in the current economy overall were likely to achieve masterdom; the actual success rate for the later Wilhelmine era was almost certainly less than this. Schmoller, *Kleingewerbe*, 337.

78. Kellenbenz, *Deutsche Wirtschaftsgeschichte*, 2:211.

79. Several of these have been preserved in StAR Mappe 1732. "Arbeits-Ordnung für die Porzellanfabrik und Malerei von Beyer und Bock in Schmarza u. Volkstedt" (1896), and "Arbeits-Ordnung für das Personal Ilmenauer Porzellanfabrik" (1896).

80. Rönneper, "Die Entstehung und Entwicklung," 496, 408.

81. Cf. Rönneper, "Die Entstehung und Entwicklung," 240–41.

82. This was also true of the toy industry. See Hamlin, *Work and Play*, 77.

83. Zehentmeier, *Leben und Arbeiten*, 45, 97–116.

84. Heckl, *Protokoll des Dritten Kongresses*, 17.

85. Heckl, *Protokoll des Dritten Kongresses*, 19.

86. Rönneper, "Die Entstehung und Entwicklung," 484–92.

87. Bald, *Porzellanarbeiterschaft*, 42–44.

88. The classic account is Sheehan, *German Liberalism in the Nineteenth Century*.

89. Schmidt-Stein, *Schlesisches Porzellan vor 1945*, 19–24.

90. "Rosenthal Porzellan: Der Bedarfsweckungstour," 19–20.

91. Kerr, *Rosenthal*, 8; Hilschenz, *Rosenthal*, 6.

92. Rönneper, "Die Entstehung und Entwicklung," 354.

93. Mappe 435.2, V&B Archive; *Villeroy & Boch*, 70; Reiter, *Handelsgesellschaft Villeroy & Boch*, 23.

94. Graves, *Tiles and Tilework of Europe*, 112–21.

95. *Villeroy & Boch*, 71–72.

96. *Villeroy & Boch*, 77–79, 117–19.

97. "Übersicht der Beiträge der versandten Wären," in Mappe 453.2, V&B Archive.

98. On the importance of tiles, see Röber, "Repräsentation & Experiment vs. Funktion & Wirtschaftlichkeit," 29–44, here 34–40.

99. Röber, "Repräsentation & Experiment vs. Funktion & Wirtschaftlichkeit," 13–29.

100. Sèvres did, however, face serious attempts to slash its budget in 1850, 1871, and 1891. Mundt, "Vom Biedermeier bis zur neueren Zeit," 233.

101. Hofmann, *Geschichte der Bayerischen Porzellan-Manufaktur Nymphenburg*, 1:186–200.

102. Travel diary excerpt in BHStA, Mwi 7790.

103. "Das Porzellan und die Porzellanmanufactur Nymphenburg," *Allgemeine Zeitung*, September 17, 1891, BHStA, MF 68639 Ny 1895–1907.

104. "Königlich bayerisches Porzellan?," *Bayerisches Landeszeitung* 18, no. 2. (1898), BHStA, Mwi 7790.

105. See the lease document in BHStA, MF 68630.

106. Finance Ministry to Bäuml, November 21, 1923, in BHStA, MF 86112.

107. On Fürstenberg in the post-1859 era, see, Lechelt, *Die Porzellanmanufaktur Fürstenberg*, vol. 3, *Von der Privatisierung im Jahr 1859 bis zur Gegenwart*; and Krueger, *Sammellust*, 98–101.

108. Telegraph construction department to Transport Ministry, December 14, 1910, in BHStA, MF 68630.

109. Suttner, *Zur Geschichte*, 4, 10.

110. Ahrens and Lehner-Jobst, *Augartenmuseum*, 83.

111. Suttner, *Zur Geschichte*, 4–13.

112. Eitelberger was an eminent art historian and influential adviser to Franz Josef who cofounded Vienna's Museum für Kunst und Industrie and spearheaded the founding of the Habsburg Empire's extensive network of schools for applied art.

113. Neuwirth, *Wiener Keramik*, 4–6.

114. Siebeneicker, "Weisses Gold aus Moabit," 44–45, 34; Siebeneicker, *Offizianten und Ouvriers*, 62–63.

115. Von der Heydt to Crown Prince, March 26, 1859, in GStAB, I HA Rep 89, Nr. 27921.

116. Trade Ministry to Wilhelm I, March 13, 1865, in GStAB, I HA Rep 89, Nr. 27921.

117. Schade, *Berliner Porzellan*, 177.

118. Siebeneicker, *Offizianten und Ouvriers*, 74–78; quotation, 75.

119. Quoted in Suttner, *Zur Geschichte*, 14. Suttner also claims that Falke's essay also helped to prevent the Saxons from thinking about privatizing Meissen. Suttner, *Zur Geschichte*, 15.

120. Siebeneicker, *Offizianten und Ouvriers*, 75–78.

121. "Leipziger Strasse," Verein für die Geschichte Berlins, e.V., https://www .diegeschichteberlins.de/geschichteberlins/berlin-abc/stichwortehn/829-2015-06-08 -08-06-33.html.

122. Quoted in Siebeneicker "Weisses Gold aus Moabit," 52.

123. Siebeneicker, *Offizianten und Ouvriers*, 81.

124. Möller, "Denkschrift betreffend die in Anregung gebrachte Umgestaltung der Königliche Porzellan-Manufaktur zu einer Musteranstalt für das ganze Arbeit der Keramik," in GStAB, I HA Rep. 10 F, Nr. 53.

125. Möller to Aschenbach (Trade Min.) in GStAB, I HA Rep. 120, F, 53.

126. Siebeneicker, "Weisses Gold aus Moabit," 54.

127. Bericht über die am 3. bis 8. Juni 1878 stattgehabte Sachverständigen-Conferenz in Betreff der Verhältnisse der Königlichen Porzellan-Manufaktur zu Berlin (printed; Berlin: Kayssler & Co., 1878), in GStAB, I HA Rep 85, Nr. 27922.

128. Treskow, *Die Jugendstil-Porzellan der KPM*, 15–27.

129. Quoted in Treskow, *Die Jugendstil-Porzellan der KPM*, 55.

130. Schade, *Berliner Porzellan*, 185.

131. Böhmert, "Urkundliche Geschichte," 60.

132. Walcha, *Meissen Porcelain*, 186–88.

133. Böhmert, "Urkundliche Geschichte," 54.

134. In 1851–52, the ministry undertook close investigations of the factory's budget and demanded a full inventory of the warehouse. See the documents in SHStAD, 10036 FA, Loc. 41911 Rep. IXb, Nr. 2051; and Gustav Fischer (Finanzrat) to Finance. Ministry, October 15, 1853, in Dresden SHStAD, 10036 FA, Loc. 36340 Rep. IX, Nr. 4421.

135. Röntgen, *Book of Meissen*, 128.

136. Böhmert, "Urkundliche Geschichte," 58, 62.

137. Zoeller-Stock, "All Nations Are Welcome," 112.

138. Böhmert, "Urkundliche Geschichte," 59; Schramm, *Konsum und regionale Identität*, 190.

139. Director Gesell's report of March 2, 1904, reprinted in "Bericht der Finanzdeputation A der zweiten Kammer," Nr. 178 (February 13, 1906), p. 4, in SHStAD, 10704 OK 99/1.

140. Director Gesell's report of March 2, 1904, 4–8.

141. Director Gesell's report of March 2, 1904, 1–25.

142. Abg. Hofmann, in 60. Sitzung February 19, 1906, 1470, landtagsprotokolle.sachsendigital.de. Hereafter cited as sachsendigital.de.

143. Abg. Goldstein, 60. Sitzung, February 19, 1906, 1478, sachsendigital.de.

144. Dr. Naumann, 30. Sitzung, March 1, 1906, 414; Abg. Edler von Querfurth, 60. Sitzung, February 19, 1906, 1468, sachsendigital.de.landtag.

145. Abg. Andrä, 60 Sitzung, February 19, 1906, 1473, sachsendigital.de.

146. Abg. Goldstein, 60. Sitzung, February 19, 1906, 1478, sachsendigital.de.

147. Zoeller-Stock, "All Nations Are Welcome," 92.

148. Dr. Rüger (Finance Minister), in 60. Sitzung, February 19, 1906, 1474, sachsendigital.de.

149. Gesell to Finance Ministry, March 16, 1906, SHStAD, 10701 AM, Nr. 6671.

150. Sandon, *Meissen Porcelain*, 100. Another of Gesell's ideas—modernizing and naturalizing Kändler's "Monkey orchestra"—proved disastrous; critics ridiculed it, and consumers far preferred the eighteenth-century version. Sandon, *Meissen Porcelain*, 101.

151. Röntgen, *Book of Meissen*, 130.

152. Gesell quoted in Berling, *Meissen China*, 161,160.

Chapter 7: Porcelain, the Wilhelmine Plastic

1. See M. Green, *Von Richthofen Sisters*.
2. Cf. Giloi, *Monarchy, Myth, and Material Culture in Germany*.
3. Post and Thomas, *Mettlacher Steinzug*, 270.
4. The same holds for British and US potteries. See Blaszczyk, *Imagining Consumers*, 77, 56.
5. Lechelt, *Die Porzellanmanufaktur Fürstenberg*, 3:57, 88.
6. In 1890, C. M. Hutschenreuther alone offered 812 models! May, "Die bayerische Porzellanindustrie," 67.
7. *Prix-Courant de la Manufacture Royale de Porcelains de Saxe à Meissen et de ses dépôts à Dresde et Leipzig* (Meissen, C. C. Kurtz, 1900). The catalog was also available in English, and of course in German.
8. Atterbury, "Porcelain of the Victorian Era," 161–62.
9. Blaszczyk, *Imagining Consumers*, 77.
10. Busch, "'Modern Renaissance,'" 80; Atterbury, "Porcelain of the Victorian Era," 174–75, 169.
11. Winstone, *Royal Copenhagen*, 85–89.
12. Zoeller-Stock, "All Nations Are Welcome," 111.
13. Oskar Georgi, *Anlage, Einrichtung und Betrieb einer Porzellanfabrik* (Coburg: Verlag von Müller & Schmidt, 1922).
14. Here see May, "Die bayerische Porzellanindustrie," 92–94.
15. Lechelt, *Die Porzellanmanufaktur Fürstenberg*, 3:62.
16. Lechelt, *Die Porzellanmanufaktur Fürstenberg*, 3:64–65.
17. Legal complaint, dated April 6, 1910, in StAR, Mappe 6250. The solution was that the firms—both controlled by the Arnhold bank, were fused, creating an entity called Älteste Volkstedter Porzellanfabrik und Porzellanfabrik Unterweissbach. Fritzsche, "Die wirtschaftliche Entwicklung," 154.
18. Pierenkemper and Tilly, *German Economy during the Nineteenth Century*, 15–16.
19. *Vergleichende Preis Nachweisung für Kaffee- und Thee-Geschirr*, KPM Archive, Box 157.
20. Lux, *Studien über die Entwicklung der Warenhäuser*, 50, 53.
21. Lux, *Studien über die Entwicklung der Warenhäuser*, 54.
22. Invented by the British just after the Napoleonic Wars, the bazaar was a sort of permanent covered market in which individual dealers leased stalls to sell their wares. The first of these in the German states appeared in the late 1860s. Cohen, *Household Goods*, 47; Spiekermann, *Basis der Konsumgesellschaft*, 233–36.
23. There are some fine discussions of selling practices in May, "Die bayerische Porzellanindustrie," 94–101; and for the postwar era, Werner, "'Goldenen Zeiten?,'" 165–96, among others; but a synthetic survey on the model of Regina Blaszczyk's *Imagining Consumers* would be most welcome.
24. Spiekermann, *Basis der Konsumgesellschaft*, 237.
25. Lamberty, *Reklame in Deutschland, 1890–1914*, 65–75.
26. Lerner, *Consuming Temple*, 21–55.

27. Crossick and Jaumain, "World of the Department Store," 6.
28. Lux, *Studien über die Entwicklung der Warenhäuser*, 49–72; quotation (1908), 62.
29. Cohen, *Household Goods*, 34.
30. E.g., Berndt, *Das Buch der Hausfrau*, 241–56.
31. Kranich and Maier, *Die wohlberathene Haus Frau in Stadt und Land*, 193–95, 526–33.
32. Them, *Alltagsgeschichten aus dem alten Dresden*, 34–35.
33. R. Habermas, *Frauen und Männer*, 186.
34. Blaszczyk, *Imaging Consumers*, 47–49, 257–58.
35. "Bericht der Finanzdeputation A der zweiten Kammer," Nr. 178 (February 13, 1906), p. 151 in SHStAD, 10704 OK 99/1.
36. *Mode und Luxus*, 36.
37. Gyáni, *Parlor and Kitchen*, 100. Also Flanders, *Inside the Victorian Home*, 214–52.
38. Quoted in Gyáni, *Parlor and Kitchen*, 88.
39. Kreklau, "'Eat as the King Eats'"; also R. Habermas, *Frauen und Männer*, 68–73.
40. Berndt, *Das Buch der Hausfrau*, 266–84.
41. Henriette Davidis, *Die Hausfrau: Praktische Anleitung*, 6th ed. (Leipzig, E. A. Seemann, 1872).
42. Gyáni, *Parlor and Kitchen*, 100.
43. Rossberg, "Zur Kennzeichnung," 111.
44. Carl Behr, "Ueber Dekoration und Möblierung unserer Wohnräume. II: Das deutsche Haus und seine Räume," in *Illustrierte Kunstgewerbliche Zeitschrift für Innen-Dekoration* 1, Heft 13 (July 1890): 103.
45. Max Rusticus [Max Bauer], untitled poem about the Berlin Industrial exhibition of 1896 in *Heiteres und Weiteres von der Gewerbe-Austellung: Skizzen in Knittelversen* (Berlin: Lenz, 1896), 12. Thanks to David Ciarlo for this reference.

> Wenn ich am "Porzellan" bewundernd staune,
> Erfüllt mit Stolz mich schon die Tradition,—
> Denn selbst im Zuschnitt von barocker Laune
> Liegt edler Kunst vornehme Distinction . . .
> So königlich, wie die Manufactur,
> Die übers Weltmeer unsern Ruhm getragen,
> Arbeitet man vielleicht in Sèvres nur—
> Allein, mich dünkt dass nach den stolzen Tagen
> Der längst vergessenen Napoleoniden
> Man mit der Eleganz nicht mehr zufrieden!
> Dass wir viel besser malen, als vor Jahren,
> Hab' ich zu meiner Freude hier erfahren
> Ich bleibe auch mit billiger fayance,
> In einer freundschaftlichen belle alliance,
> Und unsre Töpfer selbst in hohen Norden
> Sind in der Form zu "Künstlern" schon geworden!

46. On Prince Albert's orders, at the Crystal Palace exhibition there were to be no sales.

47. Faÿ-Hallé and Mundt, *Porcelain of the Nineteenth Century*, 223.

48. On Royal Copenhagen's East Asian experiments and achievements, see Reto Niggl, "Den Kongelige Porcelainsfabrik København/Manufacture Royale de Copenhague/ Königliche Porzellanmanufaktur Kopenhagen/Royal Copenhagen," in *Porzellan: Kunst und Design*, 386–88, 385–486.

49. *Amtliche Bericht über die Wiener Weltausstellung im Jahre 1873*, vol. 2 (Braunschweig: Friedrich Vieweg und Sohn, 1874), 453.

50. Zoeller-Stock, "All Nations Are Welcome," 109; quoted in Gert Selle, *Die Geschichte des Design in Deutschland von 1870 bis Heute* (Cologne: DuMont Buchverlag, 1978), 28.

51. Jaennicke, *Grundriss der Keramik*, 827, 832, 835.

52. Just, *Meissen Porcelain of the Art Nouveau Period*, 44.

53. Jedding, *Meissener Porzellan*, 12.

54. Frederich Deneken, "Dänisches Porzellan," [1898] reprinted in *Porzellan: Kunst und Design*, 409.

55. Karl H. Bröhan, "Porzellanfabrik Gebr. Bauscher, Weiden," in *Porzellan: Kunst und Design*, 63.

56. Trade Min. to Kaiser's Cabinet, November 28, 1916, GStAB, I HA Rep. 85, Nr. 27922.

57. Treskow, *Die Jugendstil-Porzellan der KPM*, 108.

58. Karl H. Bröhan et al., "Königliche Porzellanmanufaktur Berlin," in *Porzellan: Kunst und Design*, 79.

59. Just, *Meissen Porcelain of the Art Nouveau Period*, 65–68, 126.

60. Marusch-Krohn, *Meissener Porzellan*, 12.

61. Quoted in Just, *Meissen Porcelain of the Art Nouveau Period*, 81.

62. May, "Die bayerische Porzellanindustrie," 74.

63. Siemen-Butz, "Philip Rosenthal," 47–48, 86; Rosenthal: *Hundert Jahre Porzellan*, 8–9.

64. The great book on this subject is Roland Marchand, *Creating the Corporate Soul*.

65. "Memo betreff. Porzellanindustrie," dated Munich, 1918, in BHStA, MHIG 298.

66. Payne, *From Ornament to Object*, 46.

67. Semper, *Der Stil*, 2:182, 185.

68. Semper, *Der Stil*, 2:182n2, 187.

69. Kolbe, *Geschichte*, 250.

70. Muthesius quoted in Schwartz, *Werkbund*, 19.

71. See Schwartz, *Werkbund*, 13–14; Muthesius quoted, 43.

72. For some lovely examples see May, "Die bayerische Porzellanindustrie," 50–62.

73. Eastlake, *Hints on Household Taste*, 19.

74. Quoted from Freud, *Reflections on War and Death* (1915), trans. Anna Gouveia (n.p.: CreateSpace, 2017), 5. There are, of course, many fine books on this subject, including Chickering, *Imperial Germany and the Great War*; and B. Davis, *Home Fires Burning*.

75. Rönneper, "Die Entstehung und Entwicklung," 373–74.

76. *Philipp Rosenthal: Sein Leben und sein Porzellan*, ed. by his friends and coworkers (Leipzig: Klinkhardt & Biermann Verlag, 1929), 16. This tribute to Rosenthal also boasted that the manufactory employed many POWs.

77. Schilling, "Die Porzellanfabrik Waldsassen, 41.

78. "Memo betreff. Porzellanindustrie," dated Munich, 1918, in BHStA, MHIG 298.

79. Zehentmeier, *Leben und Arbeiten*, 30.

80. Rönneper, "Die Entstehung und Entwicklung," 470.

81. Vereingte Steingutfabriken GmbH to Volkwirtschaftliche Abteilung des Reichs-ernährungsministerium (hereafter VadRM), September 23, 1918 in B Arch, R 3101 12788.

82. "Die am 17. Januar 1915 zu Marktredwitz tagende Arbeitskonferenz," in BHStA, MH9955.

83. Zehentmeier, *Leben und Arbeiten*, 30.

84. War Ministry to (Bavarian) Royal and Foreign Ministry August 27, 1915, in BHStA, MH 9955.

85. A Berlin branch of this organization had existed since 1900, its purpose to unite smaller and more elite dealers against the threat of the department store. Lamberty, *Reklame in Deutschland, 1890–1914*, 132–34.

86. See Theodor Wieseler, "Porzellankartell und Abnehmerschaft," in *Deutsche Handels-Korrespondenz: Mitteilung zur Deutsche Wirtschaftspolitik*, February 21, 1916, 12–14; Reichsverband deutscher Spezialgeschäfte in Porzellan, Glas, Haus- und Küchenräte (hereafter RdS) memo, Streng vertraulich! October 1915; "Gutachten über den Streit zwischen dem Verband Deutscher Porzellanfabriken zur Wahrung keramischer Interessen, GmbH, Berlin-Friedenau und den Händler Verbänden" written by Fr. P. Martini for the Nord & Süd Einkaufsgenossenschaft (one of the 3 major sellers' unions), undated; and RdS to Verband, November 25, 1915, all in BHStA, Mwi 7794; quotation in Reichtsverband to Verband, November 25, 1915.

87. "Wirtschaftliche Rundschau," in *Münchner Neueste Nachrichten*, 13 July 1918, in BHStA, MHIG 298.

88. Quoted in Schilling, "Die Porzellanfabrik Waldsassen," 43.

89. Lechelt, *Die Porzellanmanufaktur Fürstenberg*, 3:59.

90. Hanold, *Geschichte der Porzellanindustrie in Schönwald*, 25–27.

91. Rönneper, "Die Entstehung und Entwicklung," 574–83.

92. Gewerberat für Oberfranken to [Bavarian] Royal and Foreign Ministry, May 18, 1918, in BHStA, MH 9955; Rönneper, "Die Entstehung und Entwicklung," 407–15.

93. Rönneper, "Die Entstehung und Entwicklung," 571.

94. Booksellers were also accused of profiteering. See Walther Dietz, *Die Preisbildung des deutschen Buchhandels im Lichte der Kriegswucherverordnungen* (Berlin: R. Stein, 1919).

95. VadRM, "Aktenvermerk" April 22, 1919, in B Arch R3101 12787.

96. See, e.g., Nürnberger Bund (wholesalers' union) to VadRM, June 27, 1919, (Reich) Interior Ministry to Saxon Interior Ministry, War Profiteering Office, September 8, 1918, and Villeroy & Boch to VadRM, September 20, 1919, as well as other correspondence in B Arch R 3101,12788.

Chapter 8: The Fragility of Interwar Porcelain

1. See the wonderful treatments of this issue in B. Davis, *Homes Fires Burning*; and Whalen, *Bitter Wounds*.

2. "Überfullung der keramischen Berufs: Die schlechte Lage der Porzellanindustrie— Warnung an Eltern und Erzieher," in *Volkszeitung für Meissen*, August 27, 1929, in SHStAD, 10702, SKN, Nr. 877.

3. Marusch-Krohn, *Meissener Porzellan*, 27. Yet especially in Thuringia, the tradition of small firms persisted; of the 1,274 porcelain-making and decorators operating in that year, 684 employed ten or fewer, and 331 no more than fifteen. Zimmer, "Die deutsche Porzellanindustrie," 31–32.

4. Marusch-Krohn, *Meissener Porzellan*, 30.

5. Dr. Voigt in Landtag debate, 51 Sitzung, July 2, 1931, p. 2041; Böhmert, "Urkundliche Geschichte," 62. Cf. Alfred Chandler's classic work *The Visible Hand: The Managerial Revolution in American Business*.

6. Zimmer, "Die deutsche Porzellanindustrie," 68.

7. Rönneper, "Die Entstehung und Entwicklung," *Entstehung und Entwicklung*, 243.

8. Zehentmeier, *Leben und Arbeiten*, 201. "Schwarzweissrotgoldene Areiterfreundlichkeit," in *Der Kämpfer*, February 3, 1925, in SHStAD, 10702, SKN, Nr. 877.

9. Schilling, "Die Porzellanfabrik Waldsassen," 44.

10. Marusch-Krohn, *Meissener Porzellan*, 41–44.

11. Schmidt-Stein, *Schlesisches Porzellan vor 1945*, 28.

12. Zehentmeier, *Leben und Arbeiten*, 51.

13. Marusch-Krohn, *Meissener Porzellan*, 28.

14. "Die deutsche Porzellanindustrie auf dem Weltmarkte," by Kurt Ludwig, *Frankfurter Zeitung*, March 20, 1926, in SHStAD, 10702, SKN, Nr. 877; Werner, "'Goldenen Zeiten?,'" 125.

15. Unterlagen zu einem Vorgehen gegen den Verband Deutscher Fabriken für Gebrauch-, Zier-. und Kunstporzellan," December 14, 1925, in B Arch, R 3101 12789.

16. A. Zoellner (Rosenthal directorship member) to Trade Ministry, December 11, 1925, in BHStA, MHIG 6363.

17. Verband to (Reich) Economics Ministry, April 7, 1926, in B Arch, R 3101 12789.

18. RWM, "Vermerk" December 5, 1926, in B Arch, R 3101 12789.

19. Bayerische Landespreistelle to Trade Ministry, November 30, 1925, in BHStA, MHIG 6363.

20. Schilling, "Die Porzellanfabrik Waldsassen," 52.

21. Werner, "'Goldenen Zeiten?,'" 126.

22. See, e.g., *Das Porzellan- und Glasgeschäft heute und Morgen* (Bamberg: Verlag "Die Schaulade" 1928).

23. "Denkschrift über die überaus ungünstige Lage der deutschen, inbesondere der Bayerischen Porzellan-Industrie," sent by Verband Bayerischer Porzellan-Industrieller e.V. to Bavarian Foreign Ministry July 8, 1929, in BHStA, MHIG 6358.

24. *Statisches Jahrbuch für das Deutsche Reich* (SJfdDR), 1934, 333.

25. Zehentmeier, *Leben und Arbeiten*, 268; see also documents in BHStA, MHIG 6362.

26. Zimmer, "Die deutsche Porzellanindustrie," 59. Zimmer estimates that in Czech factories, skilled men in 1928 were making up to 24 percent more than in 1924, and unskilled workers and women at least 5 percent more.
27. Rönneper, "Die Entstehung und Entwicklung," 305–8.
28. Rönneper, "Die Entstehung und Entwicklung," 600.
29. Labor Office Selb to Upper Franconian Chamber of Internal Affairs, March 28, 1927, in BHStA, MHIG 6362.
30. For a table of dividends, see Zimmer, "Die deutsche Porzellanindustrie," 92.
31. Lechelt, "Art Déco," 559.
32. Data from Rönneper, "Die Entstehung und Entwicklung," 242.
33. *Philipp Rosenthal: Sein Leben und sein Porzellan*, ed. by his friends and coworkers, 19.
34. Rönneper, "Die Entstehung und Entwicklung," 327, 340.
35. Zimmer, "Die deutsche Porzellanindustrie," 41.
36. Rönneper, "Die Entstehung und Entwicklung," 479, 481–82.
37. "Denkschrift über die überaus ungünstige Lage," in BHStA, MHIG 6358.
38. "Die Preisschutzpläne der Porzellangeschirr-Industrie," *Kölnische Zeitung*, July 20, 1932, in SHStAD, 10702, SKN, Nr. 877.
39. Werner, "'Goldenen Zeiten?,'" 186.
40. Jarchow, *Berliner Porzellan*, 36; Marusch-Krohn, *Meissener Porzellan, 1918–1933*, 31.
41. Zehentmeier, *Leben und Arbeiten*, 133.
42. Zehentmeier *Leben und Arbeiten*, 370.
43. "3 Mark Wochenlohn: Das Elend der Heimarbeit" in *Münchner Neueste Nachrichten*, December 25, 1932, in MHIG 6263.
44. Quoted in Marush-Krohn, *Meissener Porzellan*, 32.
45. See the correspondence in B Arch, R3101, 4703.
46. Dr. Warnke, Verband keramischer Gewerke in Deutschland to Bavarian Foreign Ministry, November 23, 1929, in BHStA, MHIG 6357.
47. Zehentmeier, *Leben und Arbeiten*, 206; for more detail on the coming of Nazism to Selb, see Bald, *Porzellanarbeiterschaft*, 171–254.
48. Cf. Adam Tooze's brilliant discussion of the "partnership" between Nazism and industry in the early 1930s in *The Wages of Destruction*, 99–134.
49. "Denkschrift des Finanzministeriums über die wirtschaftliche Lage der Staatlichen Porzellanmanufaktur Meissen und die zu ihrer Besserung zu ergreifenden Massnahmen" (December 1929) (Vertraulich), in SHStAD, 10701, SKN, Nr. 312.
50. Meissen's sales amounted to 3,140,000 RM; Nymphenburg's to only 809,983 RM. See files in BHStA, MF 86112.
51. Quoted in Jarchow, *Berliner Porzellan*, 29–30.
52. Quoted in Jarchow, *Berliner Porzellan*, 31.
53. "Die Porzellanmanufaktur auf neuen Wegen" in *Vossische Zeitung*, January 24, 1924, in SHStAD, 10702 SKN, Nr. 877.
54. Jarchow, *Berliner Porzellan*, 107–8, 38–62.
55. Marusch-Krohn, *Meissener Porzellan*, 21.
56. "Der Goldmacher von Meissen," by Ehm Welk, December 23, 1922, *Neue Leipziger Zeitung*, in SHStAD, 10702, SKN, Nr. 877.

57. Lechelt, "Art Déco," 580.

58. Untitled, in *Dresdner Neueste Nachrichten*, March 10, 1922, in SHStAD, 10702, SKN, Nr. 877.

59. "Zu Besuch in der Meissner Manufaktur," *Dresdner Neueste Nachrichten*, December 23, 1922, in SHStAD, 10702, SKN, Nr. 877.

60. "Schwarzweissrotgoldene Areiterfreundlichkeit," in *Der Kämpfer*, February 3, 1925, in SHStAD, 10702, SKN, Nr. 877.

61. "Zu Besuch in der Meissner Manufaktur," *Dresdner Neueste Nachrichten* December 23, 1922, in SHStAD, 10702, SKN, Nr. 877.

62. Quoted in Marusch-Krohn, *Meissener Porzellan*, 29.

63. "Denkschrift des Finanzministeriums" (December 1929), SHStAD, 10701, SKN, Nr. 312.

64. "Denkschrift des Finanzministeriums" (December 1929), in SHStAD 10701, SKN, Nr. 312.

65. "Denkschrift des Finanzministeriums" (December 1929), in SHStAD 10701, SKN, Nr. 312.

66. Landtag report; SHStAD, 10693 Volkskammer 1919–33, Film #15741, p. 51.

67. "Staatl. Porzellan-Manufaktur Meissen, Bericht über das Geschäftsjahr 1931," in SHStAD, 10851, MF 12308.

68. Landtag report; SHStAD, 10693 Volkskammer 1919–33, Film #15741, pp. 30–52.

69. Abg. Lasse, in 51. Sitzung, July 2, 1931, in SHStAD, 10693 Volkskammer Nr. 3003, Film #15741, 2033.

70. Finance Ministry to (Saxon) State Treasury, November 24, 1933, in SHStAD, 10851 MF,12308.

71. "Introduction," in Buddensieg, *Berlin 1900–1933*, 31.

72. Marusch-Krohn, *Meissener Porzellan*, 15; see discussion of 1906 Landtag debates in chapter 7.

73. Ahrens and Lehner-Jobst, *Augartenmuseum*, 87, 117.

74. Angela Schönberger, "It's a Joy to Live—Spirits Are Rising"/"Es ist eine Lust zu leben, die Geister bewegen sich . . ." in Buddensieg, *Berlin 1900–1933*, 114–16.

75. In Karl Bröhan et al., "Königliche Porzellan Manufaktur," in *Porzellan: Kunst und Design*, 193–95; Walcha, "Die künstlerische Entwicklung, 200.

76. Jedding, *Meissner Porzellan*, 25–28, 106–39.

77. Walcha, "Die Geschichte der Meissner Manufaktur," 84.

78. Quoted in De Waal, *White Road*, 344.

79. See the exhibit at the Porzellanikon, Hohenberg an der Eger.

80. Advertisement in *Die Schaulade* 8 (1932), 122–23.

81. Lechelt, *Die Porzellanmanufaktur Fürstenberg*, 3:96.

82. On the "new woman," see Nolan, *Visions of Modernity*, 120–27.

83. For one example, see Lechelt, "Art Déco," 605.

84. As Nolan notes, many bourgeois reformers thought such housing "soulless" and lacking in the true qualities of a home. The new apartments, too, were affordable only for the highest-paid workers. Nolan, *Visions of Modernity*, 119, 126.

85. Information thanks to personal communication from the owner of the photograph, Ortwin Knorr.

86. Quoted in Werner, "'Goldenen Zeiten?,'" 174.

87. Swett, *Selling under the Swastika*, 21.

88. Werner, "'Goldenen Zeiten?,'" 126, 164–83.

89. Thomas Mann "The Blood of the Walsungs," trans. Helen Tracey Lowe-Porter, in Mann, *Death in Venice, Tonio Kröger and Other Writings*, ed. Frederick A. Lubitsch (New York: Continuum, 2003), 164–65.

90. See Hugo Bettauer, *Die Stadt ohne Juden* (Vienna: R. Loewit Verlag, 1922), especially chapter 7.

91. Will Vesper, "Zu späte Liebe," in Vesper, *Novellen* (Leipzig: H. Haessel Verlag), 247.

92. The collection can be viewed at https://collections.ushmm.org.

93. Bald, *Porzellanarbeiterschaft*, 193.

94. Proctor, *Nazi War on Cancer*, 69–70.

95. E.g., Wiesen, *Creating the Nazi Marketplace*, 13.

96. For Hutschenreuther's corporate reports in this era, see http://webopac.hwwa.de /PresseMappe20E, Hutschenreuther, docs. 29–41. Also, "Porzellanfabrik CMH, AG," in *Reichsanzeiger*, July 14, 1937, and "Porzellanfabrik C. M Hutschenreuther AG, Hohenberg" in *Münchner Neueste Nachrichten*, July 20, 1938, in BHStA, MHIG 6357.

97. Corporate reports and clippings in http://webopac.hwwa.de/PresseMappe200, Hutschenreuther docs. 15–161.

98. See reports online at http://webopac.hwwa.de/PresseMappe20, Rosenthal docs. 16–26.

99. Finance Ministry to (Saxon) State Treasury, June 29, 1934, and "Staatl. Porzellan-Manufaktur Meissen, Bericht über das Geschäftsjahr 1935," in SHStAD, 10851, MF 12308.

100. Lechelt, *Die Porzellanmanufaktur Fürstenberg*, 3:145–47. Reports online at http:// webopac.hwwa.de/PresseMappe20, Fürstenberg, docs. 14–21.

101. This echoes the general findings of other historians that Nazi policies were better for larger than smaller "Aryan" businesses. Wiesen, *Creating the Nazi Marketplace*, 15.

102. "Aufruf zur Staatshilfe: Wie kann der deutschen Porzellangeschirrindustrie geholfen werden?," produced by Porz. Fabrik Marktredwitz Jaeger & Co., April 13, 1933, and Siegmund Paul Meyer (at Walküre) to (Reich) Economics Ministry, July 21, 1933, in BHStA, MHIG 6359.

103. Betts, *Authority of Everyday Objects*, 225.

104. "Das Jahr 1938," in *Keramos* 18, no. 1 (1939): 1, in BHStA, MHIG 6361.

105. Betts, *Authority of Everyday Objects*, 225–31, 69, 71.

106. Betts, *Authority of Everyday Objects*, 72.

107. "Verzauberung durch Porzellan," in *Dresdner Neueste Nachrichten*, November 11, 1935, in SHStAD, 10702, SKN, Nr. 877.

108. "Wandlung der Porzellanindustrie," in *Frankfurter Zeitung*, September 21, 1939, in BHStA, MHIG 6361.

109. Bald, "'Porzellan für die Welt'?," 210–16.

110. "Wandlung der Porzellanindustrie," in *Frankfurter Zeitung*, September 21, 1939, in BHStA, MHIG 6361.

111. A self-congratulatory memo written for Saxon officials claimed that the Sudeten ceramics-makers and glassmakers had undergone severe hardships of their own during the Depression, and now rejoiced at the prospect of joining the German market. "Vergrösste deutsche Porzellanherstellung: Zur Eingliederung der sudetendeutschen Glas- und Keramikindustrie," October 22, 1938, in SHStAD, 10702, SKN, Nr. 877.

112. "Wandlung der Porzellanindustrie," in *Frankfurter Zeitung*, September 21, 1939, in BHStA, MHIG 6361.

113. Bald, "'Porzellan für die Welt'?," 206–9.

114. Bald, "'Porzellan für die Welt'?," 200.

115. Kershaw, "'Working Towards the Führer.'"

116. One of these is on display at the Deutsches Historisches Museum, Berlin.

117. Betts, *Authority of Everyday Objects*, 11, 64. This is also a point made for other brands by Swett, *Selling under the Swastika*, 259.

118. Dennis R. Porell, *Allach Porcelain, 1936–1945*, vol. 1 (Atglen, PA: Schiffer Military, 2010), 6–9, 34–36; Bald, "'Porzellan für die Welt'?," 208.

119. Untitled essay in *Das Schwarze Korps*, July 14, 1938, in BHStA, MHIG 6361.

120. Quoted in De Waal, *White Road*, 353.

121. Bald, "'Porzellan für die Welt'?," 208.

122. Ahrens and Lehner-Jobst, *Augartenmuseum*, 135.

123. Porell, *Allach Porcelain* 1:470.

124. "Meissner Porzellan auf Görings Geburtstagstisch," *Meissner Tageblatt*, January 14, 1937, in SHStAD, 10702, SKN, Nr. 877.

125. "Vorwort," in *Staatliche Porzellan-Manufaktur Meissen: Figuren und Gruppen aus den Jahren 1919–1938* (Katalog 379) (Meissen, 1938), n.p.

126. Bald, "'Porzellan für die Welt'?," 224.

127. Jarchow, *Berliner Porzellan*, 64–66. Arcadia remains in production today.

128. Erich Geldner, Leiter der Reichsfachgruppe Glas und Porzellan, March 20, 1935, to the Führer's representative for economic questions in Munich, in BHStA, MH 6369, and further correspondence in BHStA, MF 86112. For Josef's fate, see Fuchsberger and Vorherr, *Schloss Nymphenburg unterm Hakenkreuz*, 164. If this is the same service mentioned by Bald, it was in fact a service for five hundred. Bald, "'Porzellan für die Welt'?," 205.

129. Annelies von Ribbentropp, for example, ordered thirty vases from the manufactory for the refurbishing of the German Embassy in London. Lechelt, "Art Déco," 578.

130. Fuchsberger and Vorherr, *Schloss Nymphenburg unterm Hakenkreuz*, 166–69, quotation 169.

131. In 1942, Nymphenburg proudly described its relationship with Gerdy von Troost in Ludwig Deubner, ed. *Staatliche Porzellan-Manufaktur Nymphenburg: Ihre Entwicklung von der Gründung bis zur Gegenwart* (Munich: Bayerland-Verlag, 1942), 35–63.

132. Fuchsberger and Vorherr, *Schloss Nymphenburg unterm Hakenkreuz*, 165, 169.

133. Cf. Barbara Miller Lane's wonderful analysis in her *Architecture and Politics in Germany, 1918–1945*.

134. Lechelt, *Die Porzellanmanufaktur Fürstenberg*, 3:153; *150 Jahre Porzellanfabrik Tirschenreuth*, 7.

135. "Wandlung der Porzellanindustrie," in *Frankfurter Zeitung*, September 21, 1939, in BHStA, MHIG 6361.

136. Quoted in De Waal, *White Road*, 356.

137. Images in Lechelt, *Die Porzellanmanufaktur Fürstenberg*, 3:172–77.

138. Krueger, "Die Geschichte," 104.

139. This, however, remains a topic that requires study.

140. After the war, this manufactory would later be nationalized by the East German government rather than returned to the family. *Die Gothaer Porzellan-Manufaktur*, 6–10.

141. E.g., "Philipp Rosenthal: Der Förderer des deutsch Exports," in *Dresdner Neueste Nachrichten*, August 30, 1929, in SHStAD, 10702; Siemen-Butz, "Philip Rosenthal," 45. The biography is titled: *Philipp Rosenthal: Sein Leben und sein Porzellan*, ed. by his friends and coworkers.

142. "Rosenthal Porzellan" (*Frankfurter Zeitung*); "Erstmals Gewinn bei Rosenthal" in *Frankurter Zeitung*, April 25, 1935, in BHStA, MHIG 6369.

143. "Rosenthal Porzellan: Die Bedarfsweckungstour," 21–22.

144. "Zur Abwehr!" (n.d.) in BHStA, MHIG 6369. Also Lillteicher, *Raub, Recht, und Restitution*, 180–81. Swett describes a similar series of anti-Semitic denunciations and responses during the early Nazi years. See Swett, *Selling under the Swastika*, 71–74.

145. Lillteicher, *Raub, Recht, und Restitution*, 182–83.

146. [Trade Min.] to Amtsgericht Starnberg, March 25,1937, in BHStA, MHIG 6369.

147. Even trade associations defended this decision. See Aussenhandelsstelle für Nordbayern und Südthüringen to government of Oberfranken, etc., June 10, 1941, in BHStA, MHIG 6369.

148. Bald, "Die Porzellanindustrie in Nordostoberfranken, 258.

149. Images of these warehouses run by the Einsatzstab Reichleiter Rosenberg (Special Forces of Reich Leader Rosenberg) can be found, for example, in the Bundesarchiv's photographic collection. See, for instance, https://www.bild.bundesarchiv.de/dba, image B 323 Bild-0 311-063, from a warehouse in Paris.

150. The full story is told in: Anette Loesch, "Das Schicksal der Porzellansammlung Gustave von Klemperers," *Keramos* 184 (2004): 75–90. One of the heirs has written a moving account of the story: Michaela Howse, "Breaking Porcelain: A Journey in the Curatorship of Inherited Meissen Shards" (master of visual arts thesis, Stellenbosch University, South Africa, March 2017), http://artdaily.com/news.

151. "The Arnhold Collection: From Dresden to New York," Frick Collection website, https://www.frick.org/sites/default/files/archivedsite/exhibitions/meissen/arnhold .htm.

152. Ludwig Eiber argues that the Nazis' success in the porcelain industry was not to increase the number of workers but to reduce those working only part time. Their real hourly wages did not necessarily increase, as food prices rose and many worked longer weeks after 1933. Eiber, *Arbeiter unter der NS-Herrschaft*, 170–71, 181–82.

153. I am synthesizing, here, the findings above all of Wiesen, *Creating the Nazi Marketplace*; and Swett, *Selling under the Swastika*.

Chapter 9: From Cold War Wonder to Contemporary White Elephant: Does the Story End Here?

1. Many younger designers are featured in Katia Baudin, *Utopien des Alltags: Künstler und Designer experimentieren mit Porzellan*, vol. 3 of *"Königstraum und Massenware"* catalog (Hohenberg an der Eger: Deutsches Porzellanmuseum, 2010).

2. "Anordnung über den Absatz von Geschirr- und Ziergegenständen aus Porzellan," *Deutscher Reichsanzeiger*, April 18, 1941, in BHStA, MHIG 6361.

3. C. M. Hutschreuther to Reichsstelle für Edelmetalle, June 2, 1944, in B Arch R 8-X 154.

4. *Porzellanfabrik Kahla: 55 ordentliche Hauptversammlung*, http://webopac.hwwa.de /PresseMappe20/PM20.cfm?T=F&qt=153110&CFID=4036887&CFTOKEN =78722948.

5. Bald "Die Porzellanindustrie," 259.

6. *Deutscher Reichsanzeiger*, April 19, 1944, in BHStA, MHIG 6361.

7. *Fürstenberger Porzellan, Geschäftsberichte, 1944*, http://webopac.hwwa.de/Presse Mappe20/PM20.cfm?T=F&qt=153110&CFID=4036887&CFTOKEN=78722948.

8. "Kriegsauflagenprogramm für Porzellan, Steinzug und Feinsteinzug," July/September 1944, and "Kriegsauflageprogramm Porzellan," November 1944, in B Arch R3101 11784.

9. Dieter Högermann, "Porzellanfarik Kahla, Kahla i. Thür," in *Porzellan: Kunst und Design*, 375; on Kloster Veilsdorf, see the Wikipedia entry for "Porzellanwerk Kloster Veilsdorf," https://de.wikipedia.org/wiki/Porzellanwerk_Kloster_Veilsdorf; documents from the Arolsen archive substantiate that the manufactory did have forced laborers, https://collections.arolsen-archives.org/search/?s=Kloster%20Veilsdorf.

10. "Augarten Porzellan Homestory," https://www.theguesthouse.at/blog/wien/augarten -porzellan-homestory/.

11. Schilling, "Die Porzellanfabrik Waldsassen," 58–59.

12. Oscar Schaller & Co. to government of Oberpfalz, February 8, 1945, in BHStA, Mwi 14867 Porc 1945-8.

13. *150 Jahre Porzellanfabrik Tirschenreuth*, 8.

14. Schmidt-Stein, *Schlesisches Porzellan vor 1945*, 32–33.

15. Nymphenburg to (Bavarian) Economics Ministry, February 11, 1946, in BHStA, Mwi 14867 Porc 1945-8, and Nymphenburg to (Bavarian) Finance Ministry, January 5, 1950, and other documents in BHStA, MF 86113.

16. Jarchow, *Berliner Porzellan*, 74–81.

17. "Kurzfristige Erfolgsrechnung der Staatlichen Porzellan-Manufaktur Meissen für Monat Dez. 1944," in SHStAD, 11384, LSMfWuA, #838.

18. "Bericht über das Geschäftsjahr 1944," January 19, 1946, signed Director Neuhaus, in SHStAD, 11384, LSMfWuA, #838.

19. Schrauber, "Die Entwicklung," 91.

20. Walcha, *Meissen Porcelain*, 208–9.

21. Schmidt-Stein, *Schlesisches Porzellan vor 1945*, 32–33.

22. Dieter Högermann, "Porzellanfarik Kahla, Kahla i. Thür," in *Porzellan: Kunst und Design*, 375.

23. Hanold, *Geschichte der Porzellanindustrie in Schönwald*, 141–42.
24. Bavarian Economics Ministry to Headquarters of Bavarian Military Government (in English and German), February 18, 1946, in BHStA, Mwi 14867.
25. In the account offered in the 250th anniversary volume of 1960, the manufactory excused the plunderings, saying that this "Wiedergutmachung" was not only a matter of monetary justice, but also a proof that the firm recognized the "serious consequences of its past." Schrauber, "Die Entwicklung," 96.
26. "Staatliche Porzellan-Manufaktur Meissen: Geschäftsbericht für das Jahr 1945" (March 1946), in SHStAD, 11384, LSMfWuA, #838.
27. Popow (deputy for economic questions for the Soviet military administration in Saxony) to Minister-President of Saxony, Seydewitz (undated, ca. 1946), in SHStAD, 11376, LSMfWuA, 0175, film #F 15193; "Aufstellung der an der Durchführung des Befehlsauftrag 1/440," September 30, 1947, in 11376, LSMfWuA, Nr. 107; film #F15284.
28. Chief of the USSR military organization for the occupied Saxony, July 19, 1946, Befehl, in SHStAD, 11376, LSMfWuA, 0175, film #F15193.
29. Saxon Finance Ministry to Office of the Ministerpräsident, December 21, 1948: from the Schätzungsprotokoll of October 14, 1947, in SHStAD, 11376, LSMfWuA, 0175, film #F15193.
30. Neuhaus to Liquidation Commission, November 7, 1947, in SHStAD, 11382 Liquidationskommission, Nr. 82.
31. This is the view of Otto Walcha, but we must recall that Walcha was Meissen's archivist beginning in 1957, and his history (1973) for obvious reasons overemphasized Soviet-German brotherhood at the factory. Walcha, *Meissen Porcelain*, 210.
32. Röntgen, *Book of Meissen*, 10.
33. Walcha, *Meissen Porcelain*, 210.
34. Röntgen, *Book of Meissen*, 11.
35. Jarchow, *Berliner Porzellan*, 82–83.
36. Castillo, "Domesticating the Cold War," 269–70, 279.
37. Fritz, "Vom Ende des Zweiten Weltkrieges," 232.
38. Rudolf Pech to Arbeitsamt Kronach, September 9, 1949, and November 8, 1949, in BHStA, Mwi 13424.
39. Adolf Heinrich to Bavarian Economics Ministry, April 29, 1950, in BHStA, Mwi 13424.
40. Schwarzfärber & Co. to Bavarian Economics Ministry, July 21, 1950 in BHStA, Mwi 13424.
41. (Bavarian) Finance Ministry to Chief Finance Directors in Munich and Nuremberg, April 5, 1951, and other correspondence in BHStA, Mwi 13424.
42. Eduin Klatte to Bavarian Economics Ministry, September 21, 1950, in BHStA, Mwi 13424.
43. Schilling, "Die Porzellanfabrik Waldsassen," 58.
44. This was about the same number as employed in the rubber (Gummi) industry, but only about one-ninth as many as employed in machine building. *Statistisches Jahrbuch für die Bundesrepublik Deutschland* (SJfdBD), 1953, 157.

45. SJfdBD 1953, 240, 243.

46. SJfdBD 1953, 253.

47. Porcelain factory Freienorla (Thürignia) to Bavarian Economics Ministry, April 30, 1948, in BHStA, Mwi 14867.

48. "Rosenthal Porzellan: Die Bedarfsweckungstour," 22.

49. Siemen-Butz, "Philip Rosenthal," 55–56; Hilschenz, *Rosenthal*, 15–16. In addition to serving a variety of leading roles at Rosenthal Porzellan for the next three decades, Philip Rosenthal would also have a significant, if unusual, career, as a politician. Elected in 1968 as a delegate to the Bundestag, Rosenthal would go on to serve as cabinet minister in the Economics Ministry and later on various committees and advisory boards, including the Rat für Formgebung and the Bauhaus-Archiv. Siemen-Butz, "Philip Rosenthal," 166–237.

50. "Rosenthal Porzellan: Die Bedarfsweckungstour," 25.

51. Kerr, *Rosenthal*, 10; "Rosenthal Porzellan: Die Bedarfsweckungstour," 26.

52. Siemen-Butz, "Philip Rosenthal," 72–83, 91–97; Rosenthal quoted (in English), 96.

53. Alice Weinreb, "Matters of Taste: The Politics of Food in Divided Germany, 1945–1971," *Bulletin of the German Historical Institute* 48 (Spring 2011): 71–72.

54. For an excellent overview of designs in the Bavarian industry in this era, see Fritz, "Vom Ende des Zweiten Weltkrieges," 227–90.

55. Hanold, *Geschichte der Porzellanindustrie in Schönwald*, 105, 111–12, 228.

56. SJfdBD 1973:200, and SJfdBD 1983:167.

57. *150 Jahre Porzellanfabrik Tirschenreuth*, 8–15. For more on technical changes in the postwar era, see Fritz, "Vom Ende des Zweiten Weltkrieges," 258–60.

58. Schilling, "Die Porzellanfabrik Waldsassen," 62–64.

59. A few smaller ones did manage to survive as well. In 1975, West German statisticians estimated that there were thirty-eight businesses devoted to "fine ceramics" in the GDR. SJfdBD, 1983, 588.

60. "Staatliche Planauflagen zum Jahresvolkswirtschaftsplan 1977 für den Exportförderbetrieb Kahla," in B Arch, DG6, 975.

61. "Staatliche Planauflagen zum Jahresvolkswirtschaftsplan 1977 für den Exportförderbetrieb Colditz" and "Staatliche Planauflagen zum Jahresvolkswirtschaftsplan 1977 für den Exportförderbetrieb Henneberg," in B Arch, DG6, 975.

62. Schrauber, "Die Entwicklung," 105–7.

63. Plan quoted in Schrauber, "Die Entwicklung," 111–12.

64. Sandon, *Meissen Porcelain*, 108.

65. Röntgen, *Book of Meissen*, 12–17.

66. "Arbeitsgruppe für Organisation und Inspektion beim Vorsitzenden des Ministerrates der DDR," May 28, 1976; "Information über Reklamationen bei der Realisierung von Exporten in das nichtsozialistische Wirtschaftsgebiet 1975–1976," in B Arch DG6, 974.

67. "VEB Kahla Planjahr 1976 Exportförderbetreib 12.11.1975," in B Arch DG6, 975.

68. Staatliche Plankommission, "Exportförderbetriebe VEB Porzellankombinat Colditz und VEB Porzellankombinat Kahla," December 18, 1978, in B Arch, DG6, 975.

69. "Mindestziele für die Exportförderbetriebe 1976 gemäss Ministerratsbeschulss vom 20.6.1975" and "VEB Staatliche Porzellanmanufaktur Meissen Planjahr 1976: Exportförderbetreib 12.11.1975" in B Arch, DG6, 975.

70. Min. für Glas und Keramik, October 3, 1980, "Führungsplan" and "Bericht über die Ergebnisse der Leipziger Frühjahrsmesse 1980 im Bereich des Ministeriums für Glas- und Keramikindustire, 20 März 1980" (quotation in latter document), in B Arch DG6, 1080.

71. "VEB Staatliche Porzellanman Meissen Planjahr 1976 Exportförderbetrieb," November 12, 1975, in B Arch, DG 975; "VEB SPM Meissen Quartalanalyse für das I. Quartal 1989," April 24, 1989, in B Arch, DG 2184, pt. 2; "Berichterstattung über die Entwicklung des Exportes des Exportförderbetriebes VEB Staatliche Porzellan-Manufaktur Meissen am 15 Juni 1977," in B Arch, DG6, 974.

72. "VEB SPM Meissen Quartalanalyse, für das I Quartal 1989," 24 April 24, 1989, in B Arch, DG 2184, pt. 2.

73. VEB Kombinat Feinkeramik Kahla [incl. VEB Henneberg and Ilmenau] to Min. für Glas und Keramik, September 9, 1982, in B Arch DG6, 1080.

74. E.g., "Vereinbarung zwischen dem VEB SPMM und den AHB Kunst und Antiquitäten GmbH Berlin," June 26, 1985, in B Arch DL210, 1888.

75. Blutke, *Obskure Geschäfte*, 20.

76. "Langfristige marktstrategische Konzeption für den Export in das NSW 1981–1985," October 15, 1981, in B Arch, DG6, 1080.

77. "Langfristige marktstrategische Konzeption für das sozialistische Wirtschaftsgebiet, 1981–1985," October 14, 1981, in B Arch, DG6, 1080.

78. "VEB SPM Meissen Quartalanalyse für das I. Quartal 1989," April 24,1989, in B Arch, DG 2184, pt. 2.

79. VEB Kombinat Kahla, "Stand der erreichten ökonomischen Ergebenisse," September 30, 1989, in B Arch DG6, 2184, pt. 2.

80. Karin Zachmann, "Küchendebatten in Berlin? Die Küche als Kampfplatz im Kalten Krieg," in *Konfrontation und Wettbewerb: Wissenschaft, Technik und Kultur im geteilten Berliner Alltag (1948–1973)*, ed. Michael Lemke (Berlin: Metropol Verlag, 2008): 181–205.

81. Betts, *Authority of Everyday Objects*, 4–10, 262.

82. Fritz, "Vom Ende des Zweiten Weltkrieges," 252.

83. On the appeal of Hummel figurines, see Chaimov, "Hummel Figurines."

84. Quoted in Siemen-Butz, "Philip Rosenthal," 60. Quoted from Hermann Glaser, *Die 50er Jahre: Deutschland zwischen 1950 und 1960* (Hamburg: Ellert & Richter, 2005), 54.

85. Siemen-Butz, "Philip Rosenthal," 67–70, Rosenthal quoted, 69.

86. Rubin, *Synthetic Socialism*, shows that some consumers did, and others did not, love their plastic goods.

87. Walcha, "Die künstlerische Entwicklung des Meissner Porzellans," 203, 205.

88. *150 Jahre Porzellanfabrik Tirschenreuth*, 18.

89. *Augarten Porzellan: Manu factum est* (Vienna: Augarten, ca. 2014), https://issuu.com/augarten/docs/gesamtkatalog_feb2014/368.

90. Budde, "Porzellan und Lifestyle."

91. "Thüringer Konkurrenzlos: 170 Jahre Porzellan aus Kahla," *Nordwest Zeitung*, June 7, 2014, https://www.nwzonline.de/wirtschaft/170-jahre-porzellan-aus-kahla_a _15,0,658924145.html.

92. Sophie Rohrmeier, "Gutes Design allein reicht nicht: Einzelteile sind des Porzellan-Service Tod," N-tv Nachrichtenfernsehen, December 25, 2016, https://www.n-tv.de /wirtschaft/Einzelteile-sind-des-Porzellan-Service-Tod-article19398606.html.

93. Hanold, *Geschichte der Porzellanindustrie in Schönwald*, 17.

94. Peter Dittmar, "Mit Rosenthal stirbt ein Stück Bürgerlichkeit" in *Die Welt* online, https://www.welt.de/lifestyle/article3012007/Mit-Rosenthal-stirbt-ein-Stueck -Buergerlichkeit.html. There is still a Rosenthal at work in the business, however; in 1993, Philip's son Turpin purchased a piece of the Kahla works from the Treuhand-anstalt (the bureau charged with the privatization of formerly state owned proper-ties after the fall of communism) and pulled Könitz Porzellan out of bankruptcy by firing 96 of 104 employees. Könitz has now acquired two more ceramics firms, in-cluding Weimar Porzellan, founded in 1790, and nearly killed off first during the Vormärz and again after the Wende, and the Waechterbachters Keramik company, into which Wolfgang-Ernst, prince of Ysenburg and Bündigen, simply couldn't pour any more money. In 2018, testifying to the founder's marketing savvy, the company won a Promotional Marketing Award. "Unsere Geschichte," on Könitz Porzellan's site, https://www.koenitz.com/unternehmen/unternehmensgeschichte.

95. "BHS Tabletop Geschäftsbericht 2018," 115, 125, https://www.bhs-tabletop.de/en /investor-relations.

96. Bilanzpressekonferenz, February 8, 2018, https://www.villeroyboch-group.com /fileadmin/user_upload/images/Investor_Relations/Publikationen/Praesantationen /VilleroyBoch_BPK_2018_Handout.pdf.

97. VEB Kahla to Min. für Glas und Keramik, December 28, 1989, in B Arch DG6, 2184, pt. 2.

98. Dieter Högermann, "Porzellanfabrik Kahla, Kahla i. Thür," in *Porzellan: Kunst und Design*, 375; Eva Valle, "Aid in Favour of Kahla Porzellan GmbH and Kahla/Thürin-gen Porzellan GmbH, *Competition Policy Newsletter* 1 (Spring 2003), 105, https://ec .europa.eu/competition/publications/cpn/2003_1_105.pdf.

99. Jarchow, *Berliner Porzellan*, 96–98.

100. Erwin Koch, "Der Bankier mit der Königserbe," in *Cicero: Magazin für politische Kultur*, May 5, 2014, https://www.cicero.de/stil/koenigliche-porzellan-manufaktur -berlin-unternehmer-joerg-woltmann-der-banker-mit-dem-koenigserbe/57514.

101. "KPM Königliche Porzellan-Manufaktur Berlin GmbH, Jahresabschluss zum Ge-schäftsjahr vom 01.01.2016 bis zum 31.12.2016," https://www.unternehmensregister .de/ureg/result.html;jsessionid=97A4B51B4788AD5286CB937B7AAE58C1 .web01-1?submitaction=showDocument&id=20537435.

102. The *Budapest Business Journal* reported that 2017 domestic sales had fallen 7 percent, but the firm still posted a pretax profit of HUF 300 million, or about €966,500. "Her-end Porcelain Manufactory Reports Lower Profit," *Budapest Business Journal*, Febru-ary 7, 2018, https://bbj.hu/business/herend-porcelain-manufactory-reports-lower-profit _145091.

103. "Porzellanmanufaktur Fürstenberg GmbH, Jahresabschluss 31.12.2017," https://
www.unternehmensregister.de/ureg/result.html;jsessionid=C62726428439E280C40
81F0225E573D8.web02-1?submitaction=showDocument&id=23360413.

104. "Königliche Porzellan Manufaktur Nymphenburg GmbH, Jahresabschluss zum 30
September 2011," https://www.unternehmensregister.de/ureg/result.html;jsessionid=
97A4B51B4788AD5286CB937B7AAE58C1.web01-1?submitaction=showDocument
&id=9749345.

105. "Höchster Porzellan-Manufaktur Gesellschaft, Jahresabschluss zum Geschäftsjahr
vom 01.01.2015 bis zum 31.12.2015," https://www.unternehmensregister.de/ureg
/result.html;jsessionid=C88896D792538FA931FAF101D9404140.web01-1
?submitaction=showDocument&id=18735093; "Höchster Porzellan-Manufaktur
Gesellschaft, Veränderungen, 14.03.2018," https://www.unternehmensregister.de/ureg
/result.html;jsessionid=C62726428439E280C4081F0225E573D8.web02-1
?submitaction=showDocument&id=21327228.

106. Quoted in Daniel Nutz, "Erhard Grossnigg: Der Sanierer," https://www.zeit.de/2016
/45/erhard-grossnigg-firmen-sanierung/komplettansicht.

107. "Justiz Firmenbuch: Republik Österreich, Jahresabschluss," December 31, 2016, www
.firmenbuchgrundbuch.at. Augarten today employs only 60, 15 of them painters;
"Augarten Porzellan Homestory," https://www.theguesthouse.at/blog/wien/augarten
-porzellan-homestory/.

108. "Thüringer Konkurrenzlos."

109. Doreen Reinhard, "Männer in Porzellanladen," *Zeit Online*, July 29, 2017, https://
www.zeit.de/2017/31/porzellanmanufaktur-meissen-bilanz-geschaeftsmodell.

110. Blutke, *Obskure Geschäfte*, 21.

111. See receipts from Sabatier Antiquitäten for July 23 and August 7, 1990, and others
in B Arch DL210 1938.

112. Pietsch and Ufer, *Mythos Meissen*, 81–84. Evelyn Hauser, "Staatliche Porzellan-
Manufaktur Meissen GmbH," in *International Directory of Company Histories*, vol.
131 (2012), 370–75, esp. 374.

113. Hauser, "Staatliche Porzellan-Manufaktur Meissen GmbH," 374.

114. Pietsch and Ufer, *Mythos Meissen*, 77.

115. Hauser, "Staatliche Porzellan-Manufaktur Meissen Gmbh," 374–75. For example,
Steffen Fründt, "Schwerter zu Scherben," in *Welt*, October 19, 2014, https://www.welt
.de/print/wams/wirtschaft/article133427687/Schwerter-zu-Scherben.html.

116. Reinhard, "Männer in Porzellanladen."

117. Peter Anderson, "Umstrittene Finanzspritze für Manufaktur Meissen," *Sächsische
Zeitung*, August 19, 2016, https://www.saechsische.de/umstrittene-finanzspritze-fuer
-manufaktur-meissen-3471173.html.

118. Quoted in Uwe Kehr, "Scherben bringen Meissen-Porzellan kein Glück," in *Freie
Presse*, June 23, 2016, https://www.freiepresse.de/nachrichten/wirtschaft/wirtschaft
-regional/scherben-bringen-meissen-porzellan-kein-glueck-artikel9555938.

119. "Aktuelle Debatte: Die staatliche Porzellanmanufaktur Meissen," Sächsiche Landtag,
6. Wahlperiode, 36. Sitzung, June 22, 2016, 2921–30, https://www.landtag.sachsen
.de/de/aktuelles/sitzungskalender/protokoll/859.

120. Jan Keuchel, "Porzellan-Manufaktur Meissen bekommt Steuergelder trotz Millionen-Verlusten," *Handelsblatt*, November 22, 2018, https://www.handelsblatt.com/untern ehmen/mittelstand/mittelstaendler-porzellan-manufaktur-meissen-bekommt-steuer gelder-trotz-millionen-verlusten/23668492.html?ticket=ST-59151882-qA7zVNbq 5BRZwPZurqhP-ap6.

121. Christoph Eisenring, "Die letzte Chance für Meissener Porzellan," *Neue Zürcher Zeitung*, July 25, 2018, https://www.nzz.ch/wirtschaft/die-letzte-chance-fuer-meissener -porzellan-ld.1406191.

122. "Press Release: Further Measures to Be Adopted to Ensure the Future Viability of Meissen State Porcelain Manufactory," November 14, 2019, https://www.meissen .com/pub/media.

Bibliography

150 Jahre Porzellanfabrik Tirschenreuth: 1833–1988, Tirschenreuth: Porzellanfabrik Tirschenreuth, 1988.

250 Jahre Höchster Porzellan, 1746–1996. Frankfurt: Höchster Porzellan-Manufaktur, 1996.

"AHR Conversation: Historians and the Study of Material Culture." *American Historical Review* 114, no. 5 (December 2009): 1355–404.

Ahrens, Annette, and Claudia Lehner-Jobst. *Augartenmuseum: Porzellan.* Vienna: Augarten, 2011.

Albrecht, Peter. *Braunschweig und der Kaffee: Die Geschichte des Röstkaffeemarktes von den Anfängen bis in unsere Tage.* Göttingen: Wallstein Verlag, 2018.

Applegate, Celia. *A Nation of Provincials: The German Idea of Heimat.* Berkeley: University of California Press, 1990.

Arnold, Klaus-Peter, Ulla Heise, and Michael Ropers, eds. *Ey wie schmeckt der Coffee süsse! Meissner Porzellan und Graphik.* Dresden: Porzellansammlung, 1991.

Atterbury, Paul, ed. *The History of Porcelain.* London: Orbis, 1982.

———. "Porcelain of the Victorian Era." In *The History of Porcelain*, ed. Paul Atterbury, 155–78. London: Orbis, 1982.

Auslander, Leora. *Taste and Power: Furnishing Modern France.* Berkeley: University of California Press, 1996.

Ayers, John, Oliver Impey, and J.V.G. Mallet, eds. *Porcelain for Palaces: The Fashion for Japan in Europe, 1650–1750.* London: Oriental Ceramic Society, 1990.

Baer, Winfried. "*Veduta* Painting at the Royal Porcelain Factory Berlin (KPM) after 1786." In *Along the Royal Road: Berlin and Potsdam in KPM Porcelain and Painting, 1815–1848*, ed. Derek E. Ostergard, 67–83. New York: Bard Graduate Center, 1993.

Bald, Albrecht. "Die Porzellanindustrie in Nordostoberfranken, 1933–1945." In *Industrialisierung einer Landschaft—der Traum von Textil und Porzellan: Die Region Hof und das Vogtland*, ed. Wolfgang Wüst, 247–60. Erlangen: Lehrstuhl für Bayerische und Fränkische Landesgeschichte, 2018.

———. *Porzellanarbeiterschaft und punktuelle Industrialisierung in Nordostoberfranken: Der Aufstieg der Arbeiterbewegung und die Ausbreitung des*

Nationalsozialismus im Bezirksamt Rehau und in der kreisfreien Stadt Selb, 1895–1936. Bayreuth: C. u. C. Rabenstein, 1991.

———. "'Porzellan für die Welt'? Bayerisches Porzellan und Nationalsozialismus: Schwerpunkte und Diskussionsanstösse." In *Porzellan für die Welt: 200 Jahre Porzellan der bayerischen Fabriken*, ed. Albrecht Bald et al., 197–226. Hohenberg/Selb: Staatliches Museum für Porzellan, 2014.

Bald, Albrecht, et al., eds. *Porzellan für die Welt: 200 Jahre Porzellan der bayerischen Fabriken.* Hohenberg/Selb: Staatliches Museum für Porzellan, 2014.

Banken, Ralf. *Die Industrialisierung der Saarregion, 1815–1914.* 2 vols. Stuttgart: Steiner, 2000.

Bauer, Ilse. "The Pinnacle of Achievement: Veduta Painting at the Royal Porcelain Manufactory, Berlin (KPM), 1832–1848." In *Along the Royal Road: Berlin and Potsdam in KPM Porcelain and Painting, 1815–1848*, ed. Derek E. Ostergard, 85–96. New York: Bard Graduate Center, 1993.

Bauer, Volker. *Hofökonomie: Der Diskurs über den Fürstenhof in Zeremonialwissenschaft, Hausvaterliteratur und Kameralismus.* Vienna: Böhlau Verlag, 1997.

Baur, Désirée. "Porzellan zwischen Okident und Orient: Die Erfindung des 'Weissen Goldes' in Thüringen in der Epoche der Rokoko." In *Porzelland Thüringen: 250 Jahre Porzellan aus Thüringen*, 71–79. Jena: Städtische Museen, 2010.

Berg, Maxine. *The Age of Manufactures, 1700–1820: Industry, Innovation, and Work in Britain.* 2nd ed. London: Routledge, 2005.

———. *Luxury and Pleasure in Georgian Britain.* Oxford: Oxford University Press, 2005.

Berg, Maxine, and Helen Clifford, eds. *Consumers and Luxury: Consumer Culture in Europe, 1650–1850.* Manchester: Manchester University Press, 1999.

Berghoff, Hartmut. *Zwischen Kleinstadt und Weltmarkt: Hohner und die Harmonika, 1857–1961.* Paderborn: Schöningh, 2006.

Berndt, Heinrich. *Das Buch der Hausfrau: Eine Mitgabe für Frauen und Töchter gebildeter Stände.* Leipzig: Otto Spamer, 1852.

Bernhard, Marianne. *Das Biedermeier: Kultur zwischen Wiener Kongress und Märzrevolution.* Düsseldorf: ECON Taschenbuch Verlag, 1983.

Betts, Paul. *The Authority of Everyday Objects: A Cultural History of West German Industrial Design.* Berkeley: University of California Press, 2004.

Berling, K. *Meissen China: An Illustrated History.* New York: Dover, 1910; reprint 1972.

Blackbourn, David. *History of Germany, 1780–1918: The Long Nineteenth Century.* 2nd ed. Malden, MA: Blackwell, 2003.

Blanning, T.C.W. *Frederick the Great: King of Prussia.* New York: Penguin Books, 2016.

Blanning, T.C.W. *The Pursuit of Glory: The Five Revolutions that Made Modern Europe, 1648–1815.* New York: Penguin Books, 2007.

Blaszczyk, Regina Lee. *Imagining Consumers: Design and Innovation from Wedgwood to Corning.* Baltimore: Johns Hopkins University Press, 2000.

Blutke, Günter. *Obskure Geschäfte mit Kunst und Antiquitäten: Ein Kriminalreport.* 2nd ed. Berlin: Ch. Links Verlag, 1994.

Böhmert, Victor. "Urkundliche Geschichte und Statistik der Meissner Porzellanmanufaktur von 1710 bis 1880." *Zeitschrift des K. Sächsischen Statistischen Bureau's* 26 (1880): 44–93.

Bollmann, Georg. *Lohn-Statistik für das Jahr 1906.* Charlottenburg: Otto Goerke, 1906.

Böttcher, Hans-Joachim. *Böttger: Vom Gold- zum Porzellanmacher.* 2nd ed. Dresden: Dresdner Buchverlag, 2014.

Breckmann, Warren. "Disciplining Consumption: The Debate about Luxury in Wilhelmine Germany, 1890–1914." *Journal of Social History* 24, no. 3 (Spring, 1991): 485–505.

Brewer, John, and Roy Porter, eds. *Consumption and the World of Goods.* London: Routledge, 1993.

Brophy, James M. "Bookshops, Forbidden Print and Urban Political Culture in Central Europe, 1800–1850." *German History* 35:403–30.

———. *Capitalism, Politics, and Railroads in Prussia, 1830–1870.* Columbus: Ohio State University Press, 1998.

———. "The Second Wave: Franco-German Translation and the Transfer of Political Knowledge, 1815–1850." *Archiv für Geschichte des Buchwesens* 71 (2016): 83–116.

Brose, Eric Dorn. *The Politics of Technological Change in Prussia: Out of the Shadow of Antiquity, 1809–1848.* Princeton, NJ: Princeton University Press, 1993.

Budde, Elisabeth. "Porzellan und Lifestyle." In *Porzellan in Architektur, Design, Lifestyle,* ed. Andreas C. Röber et al., vol. 2 of *Königstraum und Massenware: 300 Jahre europäisches Porzellan,* 182–200. Hohenberg an der Eger: Deutsches Porzellanmuseum, 2010.

Buddensieg, Tilmann, ed. *Berlin 1900–1933: Architecture and Design.* New York: Cooper-Hewitt Museum; Berlin: Gebr. Mann Verlag, 1987.

Bungarten, Gisela, and Jochen Luckhardt, eds. *Reiz der Antike: Die Braunschweiger Herzöge und die Schönheiten des Altertums im 18. Jahrhundert.* Petersberg: Michael Imhof Verlag, 2008.

Busch, Jason T. "'Modern Renaissance': Revival and Progression in Decorative Arts at the World's Fairs." In *Inventing the Modern World: Decorative Arts at the World's Fairs, 1851–1939,* ed. Jason T. Busch and Catherine L. Futter, 50–91. New York: Skria Rizzoli, 2012.

Cassidy-Geiger, Maureen. *Fragile Diplomacy: Meissen Porcelain for European Courts ca. 1810–63.* New Haven, CT: Yale University Press, 2007.

———. "Graphic Sources for Meissen Porcelain." *Metropolitan Museum Journal* 31 (1996): 99–126.

Castillo, Greg. "Domesticating the Cold War: Household Consumption as Propaganda in Marshall Plan Germany." *Journal of Contemporary History* 40, no. 2 (April 2005): 261–88.

Chaimov, John. "Hummel Figurines: Molding a Collectible Germany." In *Journal of Material Culture* 6, no. 1 (2001): 49–66.

Chandler, Alfred. *The Visible Hand: The Managerial Revolution in American Business.* Cambridge, MA: Belknap Press of Harvard University Press, 1971.

Chatwin, Bruce. *Utz.* New York: Penguin, 1988.

Chickering, Roger. *Imperial Germany and the Great War, 1914–1918.* 3rd ed. Cambridge: Cambridge University Press, 2014.

Christ, Hans. *Ludwigsburger Porzellanfiguren.* Stuttgart: Deutsche Verlags-Anstalt, 1921.

Ciarlo, David. *Advertising Empire: Race and Visual Culture in Imperial Germany.* Cambridge, MA: Harvard University Press, 2011.

Cohen, Deborah. *Household Goods: The British and Their Possessions*. New Haven, CT: Yale University Press, 2006.

Collini, Cosimo Alessandro. *Lettres sur les Allemands*. Hamburg: n.p., 1790.

Coutts, Howard. *The Art of Ceramics: European Ceramic Design, 1500–1830*. New Haven, CT: Yale University Press, 2001.

Cowan, Brian. *The Social Life of Coffee: The Emergence of the British Coffeehouse*. New Haven, CT: Yale University Press, 2005.

Crossick, Geoffrey, and Serge Jaumain. "The World of the Department Store: Distribution, Culture and Social Change." In *Cathedrals of Consumption: The European Department Store, 1850–1939*, 1–35. London: Ashgate, 1999.

Crowston, Claire Haru. *Credit, Fashion, Sex: Economies of Regard in Old Regime France*. Durham, NC: Duke University Press, 2014.

Dahlberg, Laurie. "France between the Revolutions, 1789–1848." In *The Sèvres Porcelain Manufactory: Alexandre Brongniart and the Triumph of Art and Industry, 1800–1847*, ed. Derek E. Ostergard, 15–24. New York: Bard Graduate Center, 1997.

Daston, Lorraine, and Glenn Most. "History of Science and History of Philologies." *Isis* 106, no. 2 (June 2015): 378–90.

Daum, Andreas W. *Alexander Von Humboldt*. Munich: C. H. Beck, 2019.

Davidoff, Leonore, and Catherine Hall. *Family Fortunes: Men and Women of the English Middle Class, 1780–1850*. London: Hutchinson Education, 1987.

Davis, Belinda. *Home Fires Burning: Food, Politics, and Everyday Life in World War I Berlin*. Chapel Hill: University of North Carolina Press, 2000.

Davis, John R. "Representation, Rivalry and Transfer: The German States and the 1862 Exhibition." *Journal of the Decorative Arts Society 1850–the Present*, no. 38 (2014): 162–77.

De Vries, Jan. *The Industrious Revolution: Consumer Behavior and the Industrial Economy, 1650 to the Present*. Cambridge: Cambridge University Press, 2008.

De Waal, Edmund, *The White Road: Journey into an Obsession*. New York: Farrar, Strauss, and Giroux, 2015.

Die Gothaer Porzellan-Manufaktur: Geschichtliche Entwicklung und künstlerische Eigenart. Museen der Stadt Gotha, 1975.

Dolan, Brian. *Wedgwood: The First Tycoon*. New York: Viking, 2004.

Ducret, Siegfried. *Die Landgräfliche Porzellanmanufaktur Kassel, 1766–1788*. Braunschweig: Klinkhardt & Biermann, 1960.

———. *Fürstenberger Porzellan*. 3 vols. Braunschweig: Klinkhardt und Biermann, 1965.

———. *Zürcher Porzellan des 18. Jahrhunderts: Seine Geschichte und seine Erzeugnisse*. 2nd ed. 2 vols. Zurich: Fretz & Wasmuth, 1945.

DuPlessis, Robert S. *Transitions to Capitalism in Early Modern Europe*. Cambridge: Cambridge University Press, 2004.

Eastlake, Charles. L. *Hints on Household Taste in Furniture, Upholstery, and Other Details*. London: Longmans, Green and Co., 1868.

Eiber, Ludwig. *Arbeiter unter der NS-Herrschaft: Textil- und Porzellanarbeiter im nordöstlichen Oberfranken, 1933–1939*. Munich: Stadtarchiv München, 1979.

Eigl, Mathias. *Die würdige deutsche Hausfrau im täglichen Leben.* Klagenfurt: Anton Gelb, 1822.

Ellerbrock, Karl-Peter. *Geschichte der deutschen Nahrungs- und Genussmittelindustrie, 1750–1914.* Stuttgart: Franz Steiner Verlag, 1993.

Evans, Joan. *Pattern: A Study of Ornament in Western Europe from 1180 to 1900.* Vol. 2. Oxford: Clarendon, 1931.

Ewald, Johann Ludwig. *Die Kunst eine gutes Mädchen und eine gute Gattin, Mutter und Hausfrau zu werden.* 4th ed. Vol. 3. Frankfurt am Main: Friedrich Wilmans, 1807.

Ewert, Ulf Christian. "The Biological Standard of Living on the Decline: Episodes from Germany during Early Industrialisation." *European Review of Economic History* 10, no. 1 (April 2006): 51–88.

Fairchild, Cissie. "The Production and Marketing of Populuxe Goods in Eighteenth-Century Paris." In *Consumption and the World of Goods,* ed. John Brewer and Roy Porter, 228–48. London: Routledge, 1997.

Farr, James Richard. *Artisans in Europe, 1300–1914.* New York: Cambridge University Press, 2000.

Faÿ-Hallé, Antoinette, and Barbara Mundt. *Porcelain of the Nineteenth Century.* New York: Rizzoli, 1983.

Felten, Sebastian. "The History of Science and the History of Bureaucratic Knowledge: Saxon Mining, circa 1770." *History of Science* 56, no. 4 (2018): 1–29.

Feuchtmüller, Rupert, and Wilhelm Mrazek. *Biedermeier in Österreich.* Vienna: Forum Verlag, 1963.

Finlay, Robert. *The Pilgrim Art: Cultures of Porcelain in World History.* Berkeley: University of California Press, 2010.

Fischer, Hendrik K. *Konsum im Kaiserreich: Eine statistisch-analytische Untersuchung privater Haushalte im wilhelminische Deutschland.* Berlin: Akademie Verlag, 2011.

Fischer, Martina, Steffen Förster, and Mike Huth, eds. *Manufakturisten als Bürger der Stadt Meissen.* Meissen: Druckerei Thieme, 2011.

Fischer, Wolfram, Jochen Krengel, and Jutta Wietog. *Sozialgeschichtliches Arbeitsbuch I: Materialen zur Statistick des Deutschen Bundes, 1815–1870.* Munich: C. H. Beck, 1982.

Flanders, Judith. *Inside the Victorian Home: A Portrait of Domestic Life in Victorian England.* New York: W. W. Norton, 2003.

Fleischer, Horst. "Porzellan aus Sitzendorf und Volkstedt." In *Porzellanland Thüringen: 250 Jahre Porzellan aus Thüringen,* 25–40. Jena: Städtische Museen, 2010.

Fragile: Die Tafel der Zaren und das Porzellan der Revolutionäre; Porzellan als Kunst und Instrument in Diplomatie, Wirtschaft und Gesellschaft. Bad Homburg: Museum für Angewandte Kunst Frankfurt, 2008.

Freytag, Gustav. *Bilder aus der deutschen Vergangenheit.* 1859. N.p.: Wentworth, 2019.

Fritz, Bernd. "Vom Ende des Zweiten Weltkrieges bis zur deutschen Wiedervereinigung (1945–1989)." In *Porzellan für die Welt: 200 Jahre Porzellan der bayerischen Fabriken,* ed. Albrecht Bald et al., 227–90. Hohenberg/Selb: Staatliches Museum für Porzellan, 2014.

Fritzsche, Christoph. "Die wirtschaftliche Entwicklung der Porzellanmanufaktur Volkstedt und ihre Besitzverhältnisse im 19. Jahrhundert." In *Porzellanland Thüringen: 250 Jahre Porzellan aus Thüringen*, 147–56. Jena: Städtische Museen, 2010.

Fuchsberger, Doris, and Albrecht Vorherr. *Schloss Nymphenburg unterm Hakenkreuz*. Munich: Allitera Verlag, 2014.

Furet, François. *The French Revolution, 1770–1814*. Translated by Denis Richet. London: Weidenfeld and Nicolson, 1970.

Gerhard, Hans-Jürgen, and Karl Heinrich Kaufhold. "Einleitung: Preismaterialen—Gedanken und Anmerkungen" In *Preise im vor- und frühindustriellen Deutschland: Nahrungsmittel, Getränke, Gewürz, Rohstoffe und Gewerbeprodukte*, 17–44. Göttingen: O. Schwartz, 1990.

Gielke, Dieter. *Meissener Porzellan des 18. und 19. Jahrhunderts: Bestandskatalog der Sammlung des Grassi Museums Leipzig*. Leipzig: Grassi Museum, 2003.

Gillette, Maris Boyd. *China's Porcelain Capital: The Rise, Fall, and Reinvention of Ceramics in Jingdezhen*. London: Bloomsbury, 2018.

Giloi, Eva. *Monarchy, Myth, and Material Culture in Germany, 1750–1950*. New York: Cambridge University Press, 2011.

Gleeson, Janet. *The Arcanum: The True Extraordinary Story of European Porcelain*. London: Bantam, 1998.

Goder, Willy, et al. "Die technische Entwicklung von Böttgersteinzeug und Böttgerporzellan." In *Johann Friedrich Böttger: Die Erfindung des europäischen Porzellans*, 99–127. Stuttgart: Verlag W. Kohlheimer, 1982.

Goder, Willy, and Hannes Walter. "Die Anfänge der Porzellanmanuktur Meissen." In *Johann Friedrich Böttger: Die Erfindung des europäischen Porzellans*, 128–50. Stuttgart: Verlag W. Kohlheimer, 1982.

Gorges, Karl-Heinz. *Der christlich geführte Industriebetrieb im 19. Jahrhundert und das Modell Villeroy & Boch*. Stuttgart: Franz Steiner Verlag, 1989.

Graves, Alun. *Tiles and Tilework of Europe*. London: V&A, 2002.

Green, Abigail. *Fatherlands: State-Building and Nationhood in Nineteenth-Century Germany*. Cambridge: Cambridge University Press, 2001.

Green, Martin. *The Von Richthofen Sisters: The Triumphant and Tragic Modes of Love*. Albuquerque: New Mexico University Press, 1974.

Greiner, Johann Gotthelf. *Lebenserinnerungen von Johann Gotthelf Greiner, 1732–1797*. Edited by Rudi Greiner-Adam. Sondershausen, Thür: Starke Druck & Werbeerzeugnisse, 2014.

Guida, Silvana Musella. "The Business Organization of the Bourbon Factories." *California Italian Studies* 3, no. 1 (2012): 1–31. https://escholarship.org/uc/item/8c25c6gt.

Gwilt, Johanna. *Vincennes and Early Sèvres Porcelain from the Belvedere Collection*. London: V&A, 2014.

Gyáni, Gábor. *Parlor and Kitchen: Housing and Domestic Culture in Budapest, 1870–1940*. Budapest: CEU, 2002.

Habermas, Jürgen. *Strukturwandel der Öffentlichkeit: Untersuchung zu einer Kategorie der bürgerlichen Gesellschaft*. Neuwied: Luchterhand, 1962.

Habermas, Rebekka. *Frauen und Männer des Bürgertums: Eine Familiengeschichte (1750–1850).* 2nd ed. Göttingen: Vandenhoeck & Rupprecht, 2002.

Hagemann, Karen. *Revisiting Prussia's Wars against Napoleon: History, Culture, and Memory.* New York: Cambridge University Press, 2015.

Hamlin, David D. *Work and Play: The Production and Consumption of Toys in Germany, 1870–1914.* Ann Arbor: University of Michigan Press, 2007.

Hanold, Andrea. *Geschichte der Porzellanindustrie in Schönwald.* Edited by Wilhelm Siemen Selb: Deutsches Porzellanmuseum, n.d.

Haslinger, Ingrid. *Küche und Tafelkultur am kaiserlichen Hofe zu Wien.* Bern: Benteli Verlag, 1993.

Heckl, Rudolf, ed. *Protokoll des Dritten Kongresses aller keramischen und verwandten Arbeiter von Oesterreich-Ungarn in Wien.* Vienna: Rudolf Heckl, 1893.

Heine, Heinrich. *Ludwig Börne: A Memorial.* Translated by Jeffrey L. Sammons. Rochester, NY: Camden House, 2006.

Henderson, W. O. *The State and the Industrial Revolution in Prussia, 1740–1870.* Liverpool: Liverpool University Press, 1967.

———. *Studies in the Economic Policy of Frederick the Great.* London: Cass, 1963.

———. *The Zollverein.* Cambridge: Cambridge University Press, 1939.

Herrigel, Gary. *Industrial Constructions: The Sources of German Industrial Power.* Cambridge: Cambridge University Press, 1996.

Herzfeld, Erika. *Preussische Manufakturen: Grossgewerbeliche Porzellan-, Gobelin-, Seiden-, Uhren- Tapeten-, und Waffenfertigung in 17. und 18. Jahrhundert in und um Berlin.* Berlin: Verlag der Nation, 1994.

Herzog, Katharina Christiane. "Mythologische Kleinplastik im Meissener Porzellan, 1710–1775." PhD diss., University of Passau, 2008.

Hilschenz, Helga, ed. *Rosenthal: Hundert Jahre Porzellan.* Austellung Kestner-Museum Hannover; Stuttgart: Union Verlag, 1982.

Himmelheber, Georg. *Kunst des Biedermeier, 1815–1835.* Munich: Prestel Verlag, 1988.

Hofmann, Friedrich H. *Das Porzellan der europäischen Manufakturen.* Propyläen Kunstgeschichte. Frankfurt am Main: Propyläen Verlag, 1980.

———. *Geschichte der Bayerischen Porzellan-Manufaktur Nymphenburg.* 3 vols. Leipzig: Karl W. Hiersemann, 1921–23.

Howard, Seymour. *Antiquity Restored: Essays on the Afterlife of the Antique.* Vienna: Irsa, 1990.

Hubsch, Heinrich, et al. *In What Style Should We Build? The German Debate on Architectural Styles.* Los Angeles: Getty Research Institute, 1996.

Hufbauer, Karl. *The Formation of the German Chemical Community, 1720–1795.* Berkeley: University of California Press, 1982.

Hülsenberg, Dagmar, and Ingo Schwarz, eds. *Alexander von Humboldt: Gutachten und Briefe zur Porzellanherstellung, 1792–1795.* Berlin: Akademie Verlag, 2014.

Ingrao, Charles W. *The Hessian Mercenary State: Ideas, Institutions, and Reform under Frederick II, 1760–1785.* Cambridge: Cambridge University Press, 1986.

Jacobeit, Sigrid, and Wolfgang Jacobeit. *Illustrierte Alltagsgeschichte des deutschen Volkes, 1810–1900.* Leipzig: Urania Verlag, 1987.

Jaennicke, Friedrich. *Grundriss der Keramik in Bezug auf das Kunstgewerbe: Eine historische Darstellung ihres Entwickelungsganges in Europa, dem Orient und Ost-Asien von den ältesten Zeiten bis auf die Gegenwart.* Stuttgart: Verlag von Paul Neff, 1879.

Jarchow, Margarete. *Berliner Porzellan im 20. Jahrhundert/Berlin Porcelain in the 20th Century.* Berlin: Dietrich Reimer, 1988.

Jasmund, Birgit. *Das Geheimnis der Porzellanmalerin: Historischer Roman.* Berlin: Aufbau Taschenbuch, 2017.

Jedding, Hermann. *Meissener Porzellan des 19. und 20. Jahrhunderts, 1890–1933.* Munich: Keyser, 1981.

Johnston, Jean-Michel. "The Time and the Place to Network: Werner Siemens during the Era of Prussian Industrialization, 1835–1846." *Central European History* 50, no. 2 (2017): 160–83.

Jones, Christine A. *Shapely Bodies: The Image of Porcelain in Eighteenth-Century France.* Newark: University of Delaware Press, 2013.

Jones, Derek W. "Development of Dental Ceramics: An Historical Perspective." *Dental Clinics of North America* 29, no. 4 (1985): 621–44.

Junghanns, Carl. *Die Fortschritt des Zollvereins.* Leipzig: Weidmannsche Buchhandlung, 1848.

Just, Johannes. *Meissen Porcelain of the Art Nouveau Period.* Translated by Edward Larkey. Cincinnati: Seven Hills Books, 1985.

Kaufhold, Karl-Heinrich. "Gewerbelandschaften in der frühen Neuzeit (1650–1800)." In *Gewerbe- und Industrielandschaften vom Spätmittelalter bis ins 20. Jahrhundert,* ed. H. Pohl, 112–202. Stuttgart: F. Steiner, 1986.

Kellenbenz, Hermann. *Deutsche Wirtschaftsgeschichte.* 2 vols. Munich: C. H. Beck, 1981.

Kelly, Jason M. *The Society of Dilettanti: Archaeology and Identity in the British Enlightenment.* New Haven, CT: Yale University Press, 2009.

Kenzelmann, M.C.B. *Historische Nachrichten über die königliche Porzellan-Manufaktur in Meissen und deren Stifter, Johann Friedrich Freiherr von Böttger.* Meissen: Ignaz Jackowitz, 1810.

Kerr, Ann. *Rosenthal: Excellence for All Times: Dinnerware, Accessories, Cutlery, Glass.* Atglen, PA: Schiffer, 1998.

Kershaw, Ian. "'Working Towards the Führer': Reflections on the Nature of the Hitler Dictatorship." *Central European History* 2, no. 2 (July 1993): 103–18.

Kisch, Herbert. "Prussian Mercantilism and the Rise of the Krefeld Silk Industry: Variations upon an Eighteenth-Century Theme." *Transactions of the American Philosophical Society* 58, no. 7 (1968): 3–50.

Klein, Ursula. "Apothecary Shops, Laboratories, and Chemical Manufacture in Eighteenth-Century Germany." In *The Mindful Hand: Inquiry and Invention from the Late Renaissance to Early Industrialisation,* ed. Lissa Roberts et al., 246–76. Amsterdam: Koninklije Nederlandse Akademie van Wetenschappen, 2007.

———. "Chemical Experts in the Royal Prussian Porcelain Manufactory." *Ambix* 60 (2013): 99–121.

———. "Klaproth's Discovery of Uranium." In *Objects of Chemical Inquiry,* ed. Ursula Klein and Carsten Reinhardt, 21–46. Sagamore Beach, MA: Waton, 2014.

Kocka, Jürgen. *Lohnarbeit und Klassenbildung: Arbeiter und Arbeiterbewegung in Deutschland, 1800–1875*. Berlin: J.H.W. Dietz Nachfolger, 1983.

———. *Unternehmer in der deutschen Industrialisierung*. Göttingen: Vandenhoeck & Ruprecht, 1975.

Kolbe, Georg. *Geschichte der Königlichen Porcellanmanufactur zu Berlin*. Berlin: Königlichen Geheimen Ober-Hofbuckdruckerei, 1863.

Köllmann, Erich, and Margarete Jarchow. *Berliner Porzellan*. Vol. 1, *Textband*. Munich: Klinkhardt & Biermann, 1987.

Koerner, Lisbet. *Linnaeus: Nation and Nature*. Cambridge, MA: Harvard University Press, 2001.

Kranich, Margarethe, and Mechtilde Maier. *Die wohlberathene Hausfrau in Stadt und Land, oder: Vollständige und zuverlässige Belehrung über Alles, was eine Hausfrau, ausser Besorgung der Küche, wissen soll und muss, wenn sie ihr und der Ihrigen Wohlseyn und Glück begründen will*. 2nd ed. Lindau: Johann Thomas Stettner, 1868.

Kreklau, Claudia. "'Eat as the King Eats': Making the Middle Class through Food, Foodways, and Food Discourses in Nineteenth-Century Germany." PhD diss., Emory University, 2016.

Krenn, Walter, and Heinz Hirsch. *Zoll im Wandel der Zeit: Unter besonderer Berücksichtigung der österreichischen Zollgeschichte*. Vienna: Hubert Krenn Verlag, 2004.

Krueger, Thomas. "Die Geschichte und das Sammeln von Porzellan aus Fürstenberg—ein Einführung." In *Sammellust: Einführung in das Sammeln von Porzellan aus Fürstenberg*, 89–127. Holzminden: Verlag Jörg Mitzkat, 2011.

———. "Einführung." In *Sammellust: Einführung in das Sammeln von Porzellan aus Fürstenberg*, 7–9. Holzminden: Verlag Jörg Mitzkat, 2011.

———, ed. *Sammellust: Einführung in das Sammeln von Porzellan aus Fürstenberg*. Holzminden: Verlag Jörg Mitzkat, 2011.

Kuczinski, Jürgen. *Geschichte des Alltags des Deutschen Volkes*. Vol. 2, *1650–1810*. Cologne: Pahl-Rugenstein Verlag, 1981.

Kühnert, Herbert. "Greiner, Johann Gotthelf." *Neue Deutsche Biographie* 7 (1966): 38–39.

Kunze, Joachim. "Die Kritik Dresdener Künstler an den Meissener Porzellanen nach 1830." *Staatliche Kunstsammlung Dresden: Beiträge und Berichte* 15 (1983): 104–28.

Kunze-Köllensperger, Melitta. "Meissen. Dresden. Augsburg. Meissen Porcelain Sculpture before Kirchner and Kändler." In *Triumph of the Blue Swords: Meissen Porcelain for Aristocracy and Bourgeoisie, 1710–1815*, ed. Ulrich Pietsch and Claudia Banz, 52–59. Leipzig: E. A. Seemann, 2010.

———. "Pagode." In *Triumph of the Blue Swords: Meissen Porcelain for Aristocracy and Bourgeoisie, 1710–1815*, ed. Ulrich Pietsch and Claudia Banz, 170–71. Leipzig: E. A. Seemann, 2010.

Küstner, Elke. *Die Thüringer Porzellanstrasse: Die 40 lohnendsten Ziele zwischen Kahla und Kloster Veilsdorf*. Erfurt: Sutton, 2015.

Lamberty, Christine. *Reklame in Deutschland, 1890–1914: Wahrnehmung, Professionalisierung, und Kritik*. Berlin: Duncker & Humblot, 2000.

Lane, Barbara Miller. *Architecture and Politics in Germany, 1918–1945*. Cambridge, MA: Harvard University Press, 1968.

Lange, Peter. "Das Thüringer Porzellan in der Wirtschafts- und Technikgeschichte." In *Porzellanland Thüringen: 250 Jahre Porzellan aus Thüringen*, 15–24. Jena: Städtische Museen, 2010.

Laufer, Ulrike. "Der Handwerks goldener Boden? Meister, Gesellen, Arbeiterinnen, Pfuscher und Unternehmer zwischen Zunft und Industrialisierung." In *Biedermeiers Glück und Ende . . . die gestörte Idylle, 1815–1848*, ed. Hans Ottomeyer, 44–55. Munich: Münchner Stadtmuseum, 1987.

La Vopa, Anthony. "Conceiving a Public: Ideas and Society in Eighteenth-Century Europe." *Journal of Modern History* 54, no. 1 (January 1992): 79–116.

Lechelt, Christian. "Art Déco: Glamour und Nüchternheit zwischen den Weltkriegen." In *Von den Ursprüngen des europäischen Porzellans bis zum Art Déco*, ed. Isabelle von Marshall et al., 543–622. Hohenberg an der Eger: Deutsches Porzellanmuseum, 2010.

———. *Die Porzellanmanufaktur Fürstenberg*. Braunschweig: Appelhans, 2016.

Le Corbeiller, Clare. "German Porcelain of the Eighteenth Century." *Metropolitan Museum of Art Bulletin*, n.s., 47, no. 4 (Spring 1990): 1–56.

Lemire, Beverly. *Global Trade and the Transformation of Consumer Cultures: The Material World Remade, c. 1500–1820*. Cambridge: Cambridge University Press, 2018.

Lerner, Paul E. *The Consuming Temple: Jews, Department Stores, and the Consumer Revolution in Germany, 1880–1940*. Ithaca, NY: Cornell University Press, 2015.

Lehner-Jobst, Claudia. "For Emperor and Connoisseur: Vienna Porcelain between Classicism and Biedermeier." In *Refinement and Elegance: Early Nineteenth-Century Royal Porcelain from the Twinight Collection, New York*, ed. Samuel Wittwer, 27–54. Munich: Hirmer Verlag, 2007.

Lillteicher, Jürgen. *Raub, Recht, und Restitution: Die Rückerstattung jüdischen Eigentums in der frühen Bundesrepublik*. Göttingen: Wallstein Verlag, 2007.

Lindemann, Mary. *The Merchant Republics: Amsterdam, Antwerp, and Hamburg, 1648–1790*. New York: Cambridge University Press, 2015.

Lippert, Catherine Beth. *Eighteenth-Century English Porcelain in the Collection of the Indianapolis Museum of Art*. Bloomington: Indiana Museum of Art, 1987.

Liverani, Giuseppe. *La Manifattura di Doccia nel 1760: Secondo una Relazione inedita di J. de St. Laurent*. Florence: L'arte della Stampa, 1970.

Logan, Thad. *The Victorian Parlour: A Cultural Study*. Cambridge: Cambridge University Press, 2001.

Lütteken, Anett. "'Minna' auf der Zuckerdose: Porzellan des 18. Jahrhunderts als literaturgeschichtliche Quelle betrachtet." *Das Achtzehnte Jahrhundert* 27 (2003): 217–34.

Lux, Käthe. *Studien über die Entwicklung der Warenhäuser in Deutschland*. Jena: G. Fischer, 1910.

Macartney, C. A. *The Habsburg Empire, 1790–1918*. London: Wiedenfeld and Nicolson, 1969.

MacLeod, Catriona. "Sweetmeats for the Eye: Porcelain Miniatures in Classical Weimar." *The Enlightened Eye: Goethe and Visual Culture*, ed. Evelyn K. Moore and Patricia Anne Simpson, 41–72. Amsterdam: Rodopi, 2007.

Marchand, Roland. *Creating the Corporate Soul: The Rise of Public Relations and Corporate Imagery in American Big Business.* Berkeley: University of California Press, 1998.

Marchand, Suzanne L. "Die Alten Ägypter zum Leben erwecken: Georg Ebers, Herodot und die Weltoffenheit eines Orientalisten im 19. Jahrhundert." In *Jüdische Wissenschaftler, Träumer, Abenteurer und Agenten zwischen Orient und Okzident*, ed. Julius H. Schoeps and Thomas Gertzen, 16–33. Leipzig: Hentrich & Hentrich, 2020.

———. "Porcelain: Another Window on the Neoclassical World." *Classical Receptions Journal*, https://doi-org/10.1093/crj/clz026.

Marusch-Krohn, Caren. *Meissener Porzellan, 1918–1933: Die Pfeifferzeit.* Leipzig: Edition Leipzig, 1993.

Mattl-Wurm, Sylvia. "Die Industrialisierung in der Metropol." In *Biedermeier in Wien: 1815–1848*, 41–46. Mainz: Philipp von Zabern, 1990.

May, Ellen. "Die bayerische Porzellanindustrie, 1871–1918, von der Reichsgründung zur Weimarer Republik." In *Porzellan für die Welt: 200 Jahre Porzellan der bayerischen Fabriken*, ed. Albrecht Bald et al., 35–120. Hohenberg/Selb: Staatliches Museum für Porzellan, 2014.

McCusker, John J. "The Demise of Distance: The Business Press and the Origins of the Information Revolution in the Early Modern Atlantic World." *American Historical Review* 110, no. 2 (April 2005): 295–321.

McKendrick, Neil. "Josiah Wedgwood: An Eighteenth-Century Entrepreneur in Salesmanship and Marketing Techniques." *The Economic History Review* 12 no. 3 (1960): 408–33.

McKendrick, Neil, John Brewer, and J. H. Plumb, eds. *The Birth of a Consumer Society: The Commercialization of Eighteenth-Century England.* London: Europa, 1982.

Merriman, John M. *The Red City: Limoges and the French Nineteenth Century.* New York: Oxford University Press, 1985.

Mieck, Ilja. *Preussische Gewerbepolitik in Berlin, 1806–1844.* Berlin: Walter de Gruyter, 1965.

Mields, Martin. "Die Technik der Porzellan-Manufaktur von der Erfindung bis zur Gegenwart." In *250 Jahre Staatliche Porzellan Manufaktur Meissen*, 115–64. Meissen: Staatliche Porzellanmanufaktur, 1960.

Miller, Michael B. *The Bon Marché: Bourgeois Couture and the Department Store, 1869–1920.* Princeton: Princeton University Press, 1981.

Mokyr, Joel. *The Enlightened Economy: An Economic History of Britain, 1700–1850.* New Haven: Yale University Press, 2009.

Moll, Christian. "Zwischen Handwerk und Unternehmen—das Leben des Johann Georg Hiltl (1771–1845)." In *Biedermeiers Glück und Ende ... die gestörte Idylle, 1815–1848*, ed. Hans Ottomeyer, 57–76. Munich: Münchner Stadtmuseum, 1987.

Möller, Karin Annette. "Meissen Pieces Based on Graphic Originals." In *Triumph of the Blue Swords: Meissen Porcelain for Aristocracy and Bourgeoisie, 1710–1815*, ed. Ulrich Pietsch and Claudia Banz, 84–93. Leipzig: E. A. Seemann, 2010.

Monti, Alessandro. *Der Preis des "weissen Goldes": Preispolitik und- strategie im Merkantilsystem am Beispiel der Porzellanmanufaktur Meissen, 1710–1830.* Munich: Oldenbourg Wissenschaftsverlag, 2011.

———"Moderne Unternehmen in der vorindustriellen Zeit: Das Beispiel der Porzellan-manukatur Meissen." *Jahrbuch für Wirtschaftsgeschichte* 2012, no. 2, 63–91.

Mundt, Barbara. "Vom Biedermeier bis zur neueren Zeit: 1830–1930; Technische Voraussetzungen." In *Porzellan der europäischen Manufakturen*, ed. Friedrich H. Hofmann, Frankfurt am Main: Propyläen Verlag, 225–54.

Murdock, Caitlin E. *Changing Places: Society, Culture, and Territory in the Saxon-Bohemian Borderlands, 1870–1946.* Ann Arbor: University of Michigan Press, 2010.

Neidhardt, Hans Joachim. *Ludwig Richter.* Leipzig: E. A. Seeman Verlag, 1991.

Netzer, Susanne. *Von schönen und necessairen Künsten: Glasproduktion und Glasveredelung in Preussen zwischen 1786 und 1851.* Berlin: Duncker & Humblot, 2017.

Neu eröfnete Academie der Kaufleute, oder encyclopädisches Kaufmannslexicon alles Wissenswerthen und Gemeinnützigen in den weiten Gebieten der Handlungswissenschaft und Handelskunde überhaupt. Edited by Johann Christian Schedel, part 5. Leipzig: Breitkopf und Härtel, 1800.

Neuwirth, Waltraud. *Porzellan aus Wien: Von Du Paquier zur Manufaktur im Augarten.* Vienna: Jugend & Volk, 1974.

———. *Wiener Keramik: Historismus, Jugendstil, Art Déco.* Braunschweig: Klinkhardt & Biermann, 1974.

Nolan, Mary. *Visions of Modernity: American Business and the Modernization of Germany.* New York: Oxford University Press, 1994.

Norberg, Katherine, and Dena Goodman, eds. *Furnishing the Eighteenth Century: What Furniture Can Tell Us about the European and American Past.* London: Routledge, 2010.

Nummedal, Tara E. "Practical Alchemy and Commercial Exchange in the Holy Roman Empire." In *Merchants and Marvels: Commerce, Science, and Art in Early Modern Europe*, ed. Pamela H. Smith and Paula Findlen, 201–22. New York: Routledge, 2002.

Ogilvie, Sheilagh. *A Bitter Living: Women, Markets, and Social Capital in Early Modern Germany.* Oxford: Oxford University Press, 2003.

———. "Consumption, Social Capital, and the Industrious Revolution in Early Modern Germany." *Journal of Economic History* 70, no. 2 (June 2010): 287–325.

Olin, Margaret Rose. *Forms of Representation in Alois Riegl's Theory of Art.* University Park: Pennsylvania State University Press, 1992.

Orelli-Messerli, Barbara von. *Gottfried Semper (1803–1877): Die Entwürfe zur dekorativen Kunst.* Petersberg: Michael Imhof Verlag, 2010.

Ostergard, Derek E., ed. *The Sèvres Porcelain Manufactory: Alexandre Brongniart and the Triumph of Art and Industry, 1800–1847.* New York: Bard Graduate Center, 1997.

Osterhammel, Jürgen. *Unfabling the East: The Enlightenment's Encounter with Asia.* Translated by Robert Savage. Princeton, NJ: Princeton University Press, 2018.

Otruba, Gustav. *Vom Steingut zu Porzellan in Nieder-Österreich.* Vienna: Bergland Verlag, 1966.

Ottomeyer, Hans, ed. *Biedermeiers Glück und Ende . . . die gestörte Idylle, 1815–1848.* Munich: Münchner Stadtmuseum, 1987.

———. "Von Stilen und Ständen in der Biedermeierzeit." In *Biedermeiers Glück und Ende . . . die gestörte Idylle, 1815–1848*, ed. Hans Ottomeyer, 91–128. Munich: Münchner Stadtmuseum, 1987.

Payne, Alina. *From Ornament to Object: Genealogies of Architectural Modernism*. New Haven, CT: Yale University Press, 2012.

Parenzan, Peter. "Schöner Wohnen im Biedermeier und Vormärz." In *Biedermeier in Wien, 1815–1848: Sein und Schein einer Bürgeridylle*, ed. Patricia Rochard, 31–40. Mainz: Philipp von Zabern, 1990.

Pazaurek, Gustav E. *Deutsche Fayence- und Porzellan-Hausmaler*. 2 vols. Leipzig: Karl W. Hiersemann, 1925.

Pennell, Sara. *The Birth of the English Kitchen, 1600–1850*. London: Bloomsbury Academic, 2016.

Perkin, Harold. *The Origins of Modern English Society, 1780–1880*. London: Routlege and Kegan Paul, 1969.

Pfister, Ulrich. "Consumer Prices and Wages in Germany, 1500–1850." *Center for Quantitative Economics Working Papers* 15/2010:1–45.

Philips, Catherine Victoria. "Art and Politics in the Austrian Netherlands: Count Charles Cobenzl (1712–70) and His Collection of Drawings." PhD thesis, University of Glasgow, 2013.

Pierenkemper, Toni, and Richard Tilly. *The German Economy during the Nineteenth Century*. New York: Berghahn Books, 2004.

Pietsch, Ulrich. "From the 'Yellow Lion' to the 'Blue Band': Famous Eighteenth-Century Meissen Dinner Services." In *Triumph of the Blue Swords: Meissen Porcelain for Aristocracy and Bourgeoisie, 1710–1815*, ed. Ulrich Pietsch and Claudia Banz, 95–105. Leipzig: E. A. Seemann, 2010.

———. "Meissen Porcelain: Making a Brilliant Entrance, 1710 to 1763." In *Triumph of the Blue Swords: Meissen Porcelain for Aristocracy and Bourgeoisie, 1710–1815*, ed. Ulrich Pietsch and Claudia Banz, 10–33. Leipzig: E. A. Seemann, 2010.

Pietsch, Ulrich, and Claudia Banz, eds. *Triumph of the Blue Swords: Meissen Porcelain for Aristocracy and Bourgeoisie, 1710–1815*. Leipzig: E. A. Seemann, 2010.

Pietsch, Ulrich, and Peter Ufer. *Mythos Meissen: Das Ersten Porzellan Europas*. Dresden: Sächsische Zeitung, 2008.

Pijl-Ketel, C. L. van der, ed. *The Ceramic Load of the "Witte Leeuw" (1613)*. Amsterdam: Rijksmuseum, 1982.

Pinkard, Susan. *A Revolution in Taste: The Rise of French Cuisine, 1650–1800*. Cambridge: Cambridge University Press, 2011.

Poche, Emanuel. *Böhmisches Porzellan*. Prague: Artia, 1956.

Post, Anton, and Thérèse Thomas. *Mettlacher Steinzug, 1885–1905*. Saarwellingen: Buchbunderei Schäfer, 1976.

Plinval de Guillebon, Régine de. *La Porcelaine à Paris sous le Consulat et L'Empire*. Genève: Droz, 1985.

Pollard, Sidney. *Peaceful Conquest: The Industrialization of Europe, 1760–1970*. New York: Oxford University Press, 1981.

Popow, W. A. *Russisches Porzellan aus privaten Manufakturen.* Leipzig: E. A. Seemann Verlag, 1984.

Porzellan: Kunst und Design 1880 bis 1939; Vom Jugendstil zum Funktionalismus. Berlin: Bröhan Museum, 1993.

Porzellanland Thüringen: 250 Jahre Porzellan aus Thüringen. Jena: Städtische Museen, 2010.

Probst, Friedrich. "Die Deutsche Porzellan- und Steingutindustrie: Ihre technischen Grundlagen, ökonomische Entwicklung, und heutige volkswirthschaftliche Bedeutung." PhD diss., Friedrich-Universität Halle-Wittenberg, 1909.

Proctor, Robert. *The Nazi War on Cancer.* Princeton, NJ: Princeton University Press, 1999.

Purdy, Daniel L. *The Tyranny of Elegance: Consumer Cosmopolitanism in the Era of Goethe.* Baltimore: Johns Hopkins University Press, 1998.

Rappaport, Erika. *Thirst for Empire: How Tea Shaped the Modern World.* Princeton, NJ: Princeton University Press, 2017.

Reiter, Hans J. *Die Handelsgesellschaft Villeroy & Boch von der Gründung 1836 bis zum Jahr 1878.* Frankfurt am Main: Peter Lang, 1992.

Reynolds-Cordileone, Diana. *Alois Riegl in Vienna, 1875–1905: An Institutional Biography.* London: Taylor and Francis, 2017.

Röber, Andreas C. "Repräsentation & Experiment vs. Funktion & Wirtschaftlichkeit—die Bedeutung von Porzellan gegenüber keramischen Alternativen in den Bereichen Sanitär, Architektur und Möbel ab 1850." In *Porzellan in Architektur, Design, Lifestyle,* ed. Andreas C. Röber et al., vol. 2 of *Königstraum und Massenware: 300 Jahre europäisches Porzellan,* 10–71. Hohenberg an der Eger: Deutsches Porzellanmuseum, 2010.

Roche, Daniel. *The Culture of Clothing: Dress and Fashion in the "Ancient Régime."* Translated by Jean Birrell. Cambridge: Cambridge University Press, 1994.

———. *A History of Everyday Things: The Birth of Consumption in France, 1600–1800.* Translated by Brian Pearce. Cambridge: Cambridge University Press, 2000.

Rodekamp, Volker, ed. *Leipzig: Stadt der wa(h)ren Wunder: 500 Jahre Reichsmesseprivileg.* Leipzig: Stadtgeschichtliches Museum, 1997.

Röder, Kurt. *Das Kelsterbach Porzellan: Werden und Vergehen einer deutschen Porzellanmanufaktur.* Darmstadt: Gesellschaft Hessischer Bücherfreunde, 1931.

Rönneper, Heinz-Peter. "Die Entstehung und Entwicklung der Produktion von technischer Keramik, inbesondere elektrotechnischen Porzellan- und Steatitartikeln in Bayern und Thüringen bis in die 1920er Jahre." PhD diss., FernUniversität-GHS-Hagen, 2006.

Röntgen, Robert E. *The Book of Meissen.* Eaton, PA: Schiffer, 1984.

"Rosenthal Porzellan." *Frankfurter Zeitung,* August 18, 1933, n.p.

"Rosenthal Porzellan: Die Bedarfsweckungstour." *Der Spiegel,* May 9, 1956, 18–28.

Ross, Marvin C. *Russian Porcelains.* Norman: University of Oklahoma Press, 1968.

Rossberg, Anne-Katrin. "Zur Kennzeichnung von Weiblichkeit und Männerlichkeit im Interieur." In *Building Gender: Architectur und Geschlecht,* ed. Dörte Kuhlmann and Kari Jormakka, 105–24. Vienna: Edition Selene, 2002.

Rubin, Eli. *Synthetic Socialism: Plastics and Dictatorship in the German Democratic Republic.* Chapel Hill: University of North Carolina Press, 2008.

Rublack, Ulinka. *Dressing Up: Cultural Identity in Renaissance Europe*. Oxford: Oxford University Press, 2012.

———. *The First Book of Fashion: The Book of Clothes of Matthaeus and Veit Konrad Scharz of Augsburg*. London: Bloomsbury Academic, 2015.

Rückert, Rainer. *Biographische Daten der Meissener Manufakturisten des 18. Jahrhunderts*. Munich: Bayerisches Nationalmuseum, München 1990.

———. *Schloss Lustheim: Meissner Porzellan-Sammlung, Stiftung Ernst Schneider*. Munich: Bayerisches Nationalmuseum, München, 1991.

Saalfeld, Diedrich. "Die ständische Gliederung der Gesellschaft Deutschlands im Zeitalter des Absolutismus: Ein Quantifizierungsversuch." *Vierteljahrschrift für Sozial- und Wirtschaftsgeschichte* 67, no. 4 (1980): 457–83.

———. "Lebensverhältnisse der Unterschichten Deutschlands im neunzehnten Jahrhundert." *International Review of Social History* 29, no. 2 (1984): 215–53.

Said, Edward. *Orientalism*. New York: Viking, 1978.

Sandon, John. *Meissen Porcelain*. Oxford: Shire, 2010.

———. *Worcester Porcelain*. Oxford: Shire, 2009.

Sarti, Raffaella. *Europe at Home: Family and Material Culture, 1500–1800*. Translated by Allan Cameron. New Haven, CT: Yale University Press, 2002.

Schade, Günter. *Berliner Porzellan: Zur Kunst- und Kulturgeschichte der Berliner Porzellanmanufakturen im 18. und 19. Jahrhundert*. Leipzig: Koehler & Amelang, 1978.

Schaffer, Talia. *Novel Craft: Victorian Domestic Handicraft and Nineteenth-Century Fiction*. Oxford: Oxford University Press, 2011.

Schepkowski, Nina Simone. *Johann Ernst Gotzkowsky: Kunstagent und Gemäldesammler im friderizianischen Berlin*. Berlin: Akademie Verlag, 2009.

Scherf, Helmut. *Thüringer Porzellan: Geschichte, Fabriken, und Erzeugnisse*. Kahla: Kreisheimatsmuseum Leuchtenburg, 1992.

Schilling, Wolfgang. "200 Jahre Porzellan der bayerischen Fariken—der Anfänge." In *Porzellan für die Welt: 200 Jahre Porzellan der bayerischen Fabriken*, ed. Albrecht Bald et al., 17–28. Hohenberg/Selb: Staatliches Museum für Porzellan, 2014.

———. "Der Export, 1814–1914." In *Porzellan für die Welt: 200 Jahre Porzellan der bayerischen Fabriken*, ed. Albrecht Bald et al., 29–34. Hohenberg/Selb: Staatliches Museum für Porzellan, 2014.

———. "Die Porzellanfabrik Waldsassen Bareuther & Co.—Zur Geschichte eines mittelständischen Unternehmens." In *125 Jahre Bareuther Porzellan aus Waldsassen (1866–1991)*, ed. Wilhelm Siemen, 22–66. Hohenberg an der Eger: Museum der Deutschen Porzellan Industrie, 1991.

Schmidt-Stein, Gerhard. *Schlesisches Porzellan vor 1945*. Würzburg: Bergstadtverlag Wilhelm Gottlieb Korn, 1996.

Schmitz, Karl Franz Ludwig. *Grundzüge zur Geschichte der königliche-bayerischen Porzellan-Manufactur zu Nymphenburg*. Munich: Kunst- und Gewerbe-Blatte, n.d.

Schmoller, Gustav. *Zur Geschichte der deutschen Kleingewerbe im 19. Jahrhundert*. Halle: Verlag der Buchhandlung des Waisenhauses, 1870.

Schnorr von Carolsfeld, Ludwig. *Porzellan der europäischen Fabriken des 18. Jahrhunderts*. Berlin: Richard Carl Schmidt, 1920.

Scholz, Trude. "Soziales Herkunft und soziales Milieu: Herkunfts- und Patenschaftsbeziehungen der im Jahre 1872 in der Porzellanmanufaktur Meissen beschäftigten Arbeiter." *Jahrbuch für Wirtschaftsgeschichte* 4 (1982): 33–66.

Schramm, Manuel. *Konsum und regionale Identität in Sachsen, 1880–2000: Die Regionalisierung von Konsumgütern im Spannungsfeld von Nationalisierung und Globalisierung.* Stuttgart: Franz Steiner Verlag, 2002.

Schrauber, Erich. "Die Entwicklung der Porzellan-Manufaktur von 1945 bis zur Gegenwart." In *250 Jahre Staatliche Porzellan-Manufaktur Meissen*, 89–114. Meissen: n.p., 1960.

Schroeder, Susanne. "Vom Rokoko zum Klassizismus—Fürstliche Leidenschaft und bürgerlicher Gewerbefleiss." In *Porzellanland Thüringen: 250 Jahre Porzellan aus Thüringen*, 131–38. Jena: Städtische Museen, 2010.

Schubert, Ernst. "Daily Life, Consumption, and Material Culture." In *Germany: A New Social and Economic History*, ed. Sheilagh Ogilvie, vol. 2, *1630–1800*, 350–76. London: Arnold, 1996.

Schwartz, Frederic J. *The Werkbund: Design Theory and Mass Culture before the First World War.* New Haven, CT: Yale University Press, 1996.

Semper, Gottfried. *Der Stil in den technischen und tektonischen Künsten.* Vol. 2. Frankfurt: Verlag Kunst u. Wissenschaft, 1863.

Sepkoski, David. "The Earth as Archive: Contingency, Narrative, and the History of Life." In *Science in the Archives: Pasts, Presents, Futures*, ed. Lorraine Daston, 53–83. Chicago: University of Chicago Press, 2017.

Sheehan, James J. *German History, 1770–1866.* Oxford: Oxford University Press, 2008.

———. *German Liberalism in the Nineteenth Century.* Chicago: University of Chicago Press, 1978.

Siebeneicker, Arnulf. *Offizianten und Ouvriers: Sozialgeschichte der Königlichen Porzellan-Manufaktur und der Königlichen Gesundheitsgeschirr-Manufaktur in Berlin, 1763–1880.* Berlin: De Gruyter, 2002.

———. "Weisses Gold aus Moabit: Die Porzellanmanufaktur F. A. Schumann: Eine Firmengechichte." In *Die Porzellanmanufaktur F. A. Schumann in Moabit bei Berlin*, ed. Dietmar Jürgen Ponert, 11–72. Berlin: Scherer Verlag, 1993.

Siemen, Wilhelm, ed. *Königstraum und Massenware: 300 Jahre europäische Porzellan.* 4 vols. Hohenberg an der Eger: Deutsches Porzellanmuseum, 2010.

Siemen-Butz, Alexandra. "Philip Rosenthal, M.A.: Ein innovativer Unternehmer und politischer Mensch." PhD diss., Eichstätt-Ingolstadt University, 2013.

Simonis, Ruth Sonja. "How to Furnish a Palace: Porcelain Acquisitions in the Netherlands from Augustus the Strong, 1716–1718." *Journal for Art Market Studies* 2, no. 3 (2018). https://www.fokum-jams.org/index.php/jams/article/view/52/115/.

Sloboda, Stacey. *Chinoiserie: Commerce and Critical Ornament in Eighteenth-Century Britain.* Manchester: Manchester University Press, 2014.

Smith, Kate. *Material Goods, Moving Hands: Perceiving Production in England, 1700–1830.* Manchester: Manchester University Press, 2014.

Smith, Woodruff. *Consumption and the Making of Respectability, 1600–1800.* Hoboken, NJ: Taylor and Francis, 2012.

Spaulding, Almut, and Paul S. Spaulding. *The Account Books of the Reimarus Family of Hamburg, 1728–1780.* 2 vols. Leiden: Brill, 2015.

Spiekermann, Uwe. *Basis der Konsumgesellschaft: Entstehung und Entwicklung des modernen Kleinhandels in Deutschland, 1850–1914.* Munich: C. H. Beck, 1999.

Sponsel, Jean Louis. *Kabinettstücke der Meissner Porzellan-Manufaktur von Johann Joachim Kändler.* Leipzig: Hermann Seemann Nachfolger, 1900.

Stearns, Peter. *Consumerism in World History: The Global Transformation of Desire.* New York: Routledge, 2006.

Stieda, Wilhelm. *Die Anfänge der Porzellanfabrikation auf dem Thüringerwald.* Jena: Gustav Fischer, 1902.

———. *Die Porzellanfabrik zu Volkstedt im achtzehnten Jahrhundert.* Leipzig: S. Hirzel, 1910.

Straubel, Rolf. *Kaufleute und Manufakturunternehmer: Eine empirische Untersuchung über die sozialen Träger von Handel und Grossgewerbe in den mittleren preussischen Provinzen (1763 bis 1815).* Stuttgart: Franz Steiner Verlag, 1995.

Styles, John. "Enlightened Princesses between Germany and Britain." In *Enlightened Princesses: Caroline, Augusta, Charlotte, and the Shaping of the Modern World*, ed. Joanna Marschner, 31–52. New Haven, CT: Yale University Press, 2017.

———. "Fashion and Innovation in Early Modern Europe." In *Fashioning the Early Modern: Dress, Textiles, and Innovation in Europe, 1500–1800*, ed. Evelyn Welch, 33–55. Oxford: Oxford University Press, 2017.

Sudrow, Anne. *Der Schuh im Nationalsozialismus.* Göttingen: Wallstein Verlag, 2010.

Suttner, Gustav Freiherr von. *Zur Geschichte der Auflösung der k. k. Porzellanfabrik in Wien.* Vienna: Als Manuscript gedruckt, 1887.

Swett, Pamela E. *Selling under the Swastika: Advertising and Commercial Culture in Nazi Germany.* Stanford, CA: Stanford University Press, 2014.

Szkurlat, Anna. *The Porcelain and Faience Manufactory in Korzec.* Warsaw: Publishing House of the Royal Castle, 2011.

Taylor, J. A. *History of Dentistry: A Practical Treatise for the Use of Dental Students and Practitioners.* Philadelphia: Lea and Febiger, 1922.

Teuteberg, Hans J. "Die Eingliederung des Kaffees in den täglichen Getränkenkonsum." In *Unsere tägliche Kost: Geschichte und regionale Prägung*, 2nd ed., ed. Hans J. Teuteberg and Günter Wiegelmann, 185–201. Munster: F. Coppenrath, 1986.

Teuteberg, Hans J., and Günter Wiegelmann. *Unsere tägliche Kost: Geschichte und regionale Prägung.* 2nd ed. Munster: F. Coppenrath, 1986.

Them, Andreas. *Alltagsgeschichten aus dem alten Dresden.* Dresden: SAXO'Phon, 2012.

———. *Gasthausgeschichten aus dem alten Dresden.* Dresden: SAXO'Phon, 2010.

———. *Kaffeehausgeschichten as dem alten Dresden.* Dresden: SAXO'Phon, 2011.

Thomas, Thérèse. *Die Rolle der beiden Familien Boch und Villeroy im 18. und 19. Jahrhundert.* Saarbrücken: Saarbrücker Druckerei, 1974.

Tooze, Adam. *The Wages of Destruction: The Making and Breaking of the Nazi Economy.* New York: Viking, 2007.

Thümmler, Sabine. *Die Geschichte der Tapete: Raumkunst aus Papier.* Kassel: Staatliche Museen, 1998.

Treitel, Corinna. *Eating Nature in Modern Germany: Food, Agriculture, and Environment, c. 1870–2000*. New York: Cambridge University Press, 2017.

Tocqueville, Alexis de. *The Ancien Régime and the Revolution*. Translated by Gerald Bevan. London: Penguin Classics, 2008.

Trentmann, Frank. *Empire of Things: How We Became a World of Consumers, from the Fifteenth Century to the Twenty-First*. London: Penguin, 2017.

Treskow, Irene von. *Die Jugendstil-Porzellan der KPM*. Munich: Prestel Verlag, 1971.

Treue, Wilhelm. "Sozialgeschichte des Handwerks im Übergang zur privatkapitalistischen Industriewirtschaft: Anmerkungen zu einem Buch über europäische Möbelkunst im 18. Jahrhundert." *Zeitschrift für Unternehmungsgeschichte* 28 (1983): 214–22.

———. *Wirschafts- und Technikgeschichte Preussens*. Berlin: De Gruyter, 1984.

Trömel, Werner. *Kartell und Preisbildung in der deutschen Geschirr- und Luxusporzellanindustrie*. Jena: Gustav Fischer, 1926.

Umbach, Maiken. "Made in Germany." In *Deutsche Erinnerungsorte*, vol. 2, ed. Étienne François and Hagen Schulze, 405–38. Munich: C. H. Beck, 2001.

———. "Visual Culture, Scientific Images and German Small-State Politics in the Late Enlightenment." *Past and Present* 158 (February 1998): 110–45.

Van Horn Melton, James. *Politics, Culture, and the Public Sphere in Enlightenment Europe*. Cambridge: Cambridge University Press, 2001.

Vershofen, Wilhelm. *Tat und Vorbild: 125 Jahre C. M. Hutschenreuther Hohenberg, 1814–1939*. Bamberg: Bamberger Verlagshaus, 1939.

Vickery, Amanda. *Behind Closed Doors: At Home in Georgian England*. New Haven, CT: Yale University Press, 2009.

Villeroy & Boch: 250 Years of European Industrial History, 1748–1998. Mettlach: Villeroy & Boch, 1998.

Walcha, Otto. "Die Geschichte der Meissner Manufaktur von 1710 bis 1945." In *250 Jahre Staatliche Porzellan-Manufaktur Meissen*, 53–87. Meissen: Staatliche Porzellan-Manufaktur, 1960.

———. "Die künstlerische Entwicklung des Meissner Porzellans." In *250 Jahre Staatliche Porzellan-Manufaktur Meissen*, 167–205. Meissen: n.p., 1960.

———. *Meissen Porcelain*. New York: G. P. Putnam's Sons, 1981.

Walker, Mack. *German Home Towns: Community, State, and General Estate, 1648–1871*. Ithaca, NY: Cornell University Press, 1971.

Watanabe-O'Kelly, Helen. *Court Culture in Dresden: From Renaissance to Baroque*. Houndsmills, Hampshire: Palgrave, 2002.

Weatherill, Lorna. *Consumer Behaviour and Material Culture in Britain 1660–1760*. 2nd ed. London: Routledge, 1996.

Wedgwood, Josiah. *Catalogue of Cameos, Intaglios, Medals, Bas-Reliefs, Busts, and Small Statues*. 6th ed. with additions. Etruria, 1787.

Werner, Petra. "'Goldenen Zeiten?' Zwischen Inflation und Weltwirtschaftskrise, 1918–1933." In *Porzellan für die Welt: 200 Jahre Porzellan der bayerischen Fabriken*, ed. Albrecht Bald et al., 121–98. Hohenberg/Selb: Staatliches Museum für Porzellan, 2014.

Whalen, Robert Weldon. *Bitter Wounds: German Victims of the Great War, 1914–1939*. Ithaca, NY: Cornell University Press, 1984.

Whitehead, John. *Sèvres sous Louis XVI et la Révolution: Le premier apogée*. Paris: Éditions courtes et longues, 2010.

Wiesen, S. Jonathan. *Creating the Nazi Marketplace: Commerce and Consumption in the Third Reich*. Cambridge: Cambridge University Press, 2010.

Wilckens, Friedrich. *Krepon, Kredit und Porzellan: Vom steilen Aufstieg und tiefen Fall der Unternehmerfamilie Wegeli aus Diessenhofen im Berlin des 18. Jahrhunderts*. Frauenfeld: Verlag des Historischen Vereine des Kantons Thurgau, 2008.

Wildner, Paul. "Die Porzellanindustrie." In *Handbuch der Wirtschaftskunde Deutschlands*, 3:223–44. Leipzig: B. G. Teubner, 1904.

Wills, John E., Jr. "European Consumption and Asian Production in the Seventeenth and Eighteenth Centuries." *Consumption and the World of Goods*, ed. John Brewer and Roy Porter, 133–47. London: Routledge, 1993.

Winstone, H.V.F. *Royal Copenhagen*. London: Stacey International, 1984.

Wittwer, Samuel. "Betwixt Vienna and Paris: The Royal Porcelain Manufactory Berlin in the Grand European Context." In *Refinement and Elegance: Early Nineteenth-Century Royal Porcelain from the Twinight Collection, New York*, ed. Wittwer, 55–95. Munich: Hirmer Verlag, 2007.

———. *Die Galerie der Meissener Tiere: Die Menagerie Augusts des Starken für das Japanische Palais in Dresden*. Munich: Hirmer Verlag, 2004.

———. "'The King of Prussia Has Requested the Rapid Completion . . .': Friedrich the Great and Meissen Porcelain." In *Triumph of the Blue Swords: Meissen Porcelain for Aristocracy and Bourgeoisie, 1710–1815*, ed. Ulrich Pietsch and Claudia Banz, 139–50. Leipzig: E. A. Seemann, 2010.

———, ed. *Refinement and Elegance: Early Nineteenth-Century Royal Porcelain from the Twinight Collection, New York*. Munich: Hirmer Verlag, 2007.

Wolff-Metternich, Beatrix Freifrau von, and Manfred Meinz. *Die Porzellanmanufaktur Fürstenberg: Eine Kulturgeschichte im Spiegel des Fürstenberger Porzellan*. 2 vols. Munich: Prestel Verlag, 2016.

Wolff-Beckh, Bruno. *Johann Friedrich Böttger, der deutscher Erfinder des Porzellans*. Berlin: Max Brodek, 1903.

Wüst, Wolfgang, ed. *Industrialisierung einer Landschaft—der Traum von Textil und Porzellan: Die Region Hof und das Vogtland*. Erlangen: Lehrstuhl für Bayerische und Fränkische Landesgeschichte, 2018.

Young, Hilary, ed. *The Genius of Wedgwood*. London: V&A Museum, 1995.

Zais, Ernest. *Der Kurmainische Porzellan-Manufaktur zu Höchst: Ein Beitrag zur Geschichte des deutschen Kunstgewerbes*. Mainz: J. Diemer, 1887.

Zeh, Ernst. *Hanauer Fayence: Ein Beitrag zur Geschichte der deutschen Keramik*. Hanau: Werner Dausien, 1978.

Zehentmeier, Sabine. *Leben und Arbeiten der Porzelliner in Nordostbayern (1870–1933)*. Hohenberg an der Eger: Deutsches Porzellanmuseum, 2001.

Zimmer, Harry. "Die deutsche Porzellanindustrie und ihre neuere Entwicklung." PhD diss., University of Würzburg, 1929.

Zoeller-Stock, Bettina. "All Nations Are Welcome." In *Kunst oder Kommerz? Meissener Porzellan im 19. Jahrhundert*, 85–114. Dresden, Sandstein Verlag, 2010.

Zühlicke, Sabine. "Warenzeichneiss als Quelle der Formalanalyse." In *Westerwälde Gebrauchsgeschirr von der Mitte des 19. Jahrhunderts bis in der 1960s*, ed. Christine Dippold et al., vol. 1, *Texte und Firmzeichens*, 41–69. Nuremburg: Germanisches Nationalmuseums, 2008.

Digital Collections

Pressemappe 20. Jahrhundert: Digitalisierung der Pressearchive von HWWA und IfW, webopac.hwwa.de

Sächsische Landtag, www. Sachsen.landtag.de

Statisches Jahrbuch für das Deutsche Reich (SJfdDR), https://www.digizeitschriften.de

Statisches Jahrbuch für die Bundesrepublik Deutschland (SJfdBD), https://www .digizeitschriften.de/dms/toc/?PPN=PPN514402342.

Unternehnmens-Register (Bundesanzeiger Verlag), www.unternehmensregister.de

Archival Abbreviations

B Arch   Bundesarchiv Lichterfelde (Berlin)

BHStA   Bayerisches Hauptstaatsarchiv (Munich)

(MF = Ministerium der Finanzen; MHIG = Ministerium für Handel, Industrie und Gewerbe; Mwi = Ministerium für Wirtschaft)

GStAB   Geheimes Staatsarchiv, Berlin

KPM Archive   KPM Archive (Charlottenburg, Berlin)

ÖVA   Österreiches Verwaltungsarchiv (Vienna)

SHStAD   Sächsisches Hauptstaatsarchiv, Dresden

(AM = Aussenministerium; FA = Finanzarchiv, LSMfWuA = Landesregierung Sachsens, Min. f. Wirtschaft u. Arbeit; MF = Ministerium der Finanzen; OK = Oberrechnungskammer; SKN = Staatskanzlei, Nachrichtenstelle)

StAR   Staatsarchiv Rudolstadt

V&B Archive   Villeroy & Boch Archive (Merzig)

Image Credits

Figure 1.1. Gift of R. Sténuit, Brussels; Inv. #: NG-1978-127-9508-W. Rijksmuseum, Amsterdam.

Figure 1.2. ©Schlösserland Sachsen.

Figure 2.1. ©Germanisches Nationalmuseum, Foto: Monika Runge.

Figure 2.2. ©GoetheStadtMuseum Ilmenau; Foto: Thomas Wolf.

Figure 2.3. ©Museum Eisfeld, Germany, Inv. MuE.A2.8027.

Figure 2.4. Rijksmuseum, Amsterdam, Inv. #BK-15115-A.

Figure 3.1. Photo by Historic Maps/Ullstein Bild via Getty Images.

Figure 3.2. Staatliche Porzellan-Manufaktur Meissen GmbH, Unternehmensarchiv.

Figure 3.3. ©Schlösserland Sachsen.

Figure 3.4. The Metropolitan Museum of Art, New York; the Lesley and Emma Sheafer Collection, Bequest of Emma A. Sheafer, 1973; Inv. #: 1974.356.506; www.metmuseum.org.

Figure 3.5. The Metropolitan Museum of Art, New York; Gift of Irwin Untermyer, 1964; Inv. #: 64.101.125; www.metmuseum.org.

Figure 3.6. Landeshauptstadt Hannover, Museum August Kestner, Foto: Chr Tepper.

Figure 3.7. INTERFOTO/Alamy Stock Photo.

Figure 4.1. ©Porzellanikon-Staatliches Museum für Porzellan Selb/Hohenberg an der Eger Dauerleihgabe Oberfrankenstiftung, Bayreuth, Foto: Helmut Groh.

Figure 4.2. Villeroy & Boch Unternehmensarchiv, Bestand Fotoalben Nr. A1.1, Alte Abtei vor 1900.

Figure 5.1. Kupferstich-Kabinett, Staatliche Kunstsammlungen Dresden, Foto: Herbert Boswank.

Figure 5.2. ©Staatliche Porzellan-Manufaktur Meissen GmbH, Unternehmensarchiv.

Figure 5.3. J.G.A.N. de Vries Bequest, The Hague; Rijksmuseum Amsterdam, Inv. #: BK-NM-13875-B.

Figure 5.4. Wiki commons; https://commons.wikimedia.org/wiki/File:Gustav _Heinrich_Naeke_(1785–1835),_Faust-Szene_im_Garten,_Porzellanmalerei, _Pfeifenkopf,_D2152.jpg.

Figure 6.1. Villeroy & Boch Unternehmensarchiv, Bestand Fotoalben Nr. A11, Mosaik-fabrik 1893.

Figure 6.2. Villeroy & Boch Unternehmenssarchiv, Fabrik Dresden.

Figure 6.3. Wiki commons; https://de.wikipedia.org/wiki/Mei%C3%9Fner_Porzellan# /media/Datei:Die_Gartenlaube_(1869)_b_109.jpg.

Figure 7.1. bpk Bildagenteur/Heinrich Lichte/Art Resource, NY.

Figure 7.2. bpk Bildagenteur/Art Resource, NY.

Figure 7.3. From A. J. Meier-Graefe, *Die Weltausstellung in Paris 1900 mit zahlreichen photographischen Aufnahmen, farbigen Kunstbeilagen und Plänen* (Paris/Leipzig, 1900), p. 119.

Figure 7.4. INTERFOTO/Alamy Photo Services.

Figure 8.1. bpk Bildagenteur/Staatsbibliothek zu Berlin/Art Resource, NY.

Figure 8.2. *Die Schaulade* 12, Heft 12 (1936), Ausgabe B, 480.

Figure 8.3. *Die Schaulade* 12, Heft 12 (1936), Ausgabe B, 456.

Figure 8.4. bpk Bildagenteur/Kunstbibiothek SMB/Phototek Willy Römer/Art Resource, NY.

Figure 8.5. Knorr Collection; by permission of Ortwin Knorr.

Figure 8.6. Bundesarchiv, Bild 102–13204/Photo: Georg Pahl.

Figure 8.7. bpk Bildagenteur/Liselotte Purpur (Orgel-Köhne)/Art Resource, NY.

Figure 8.8. bpk Bildagenteur/Bayerische Staatsbibliothek/Archiv Heinrich Hoffmann/Art Resource, NY.

Figure 8.9. Photo and permission thanks to Michaela Howse and the von Klemperer Family.

Figure 9.1. ©Porzellanikon, Rosenthal-Archiv Selb, Dauerleihgabe Oberfrankenstiftung, Bayreuth, Foto: Rosenthal-Archiv.

Figure 9.2. INTERFOTO/Alamy Stock Photo.

Figure 9.3. Author's collection.

Figure 9.4. Reproduced by permission of the August Siekmann Company.

Figure 9.5. Bundesarchiv, Bild 183-29989-0002/Photo: Klein.

Plate 1. Stiftung Preussischer Schlösser und Gärten Berlin-Brandenburg/Hans Bach.

Plate 2. Bundesmobilienverwaltung, Foto Edgar Knaack.

Plate 3. ©Victoria and Albert Museum, London.

Plate 4. *Dinner in the Ballroom of the Palace of the Princes of Salm-Salm*, oil on canvas. Photo: Mairie de Raon-l'Ètape, Vosges, France.

Plate 5. INTERFOTO/Alamy Stock Photo.

Plate 6. GDKE Rheinland/Pfalz, Landesmuseum Mainz, Foto: U. Rudischer.

Plate 7. Mr. and Mrs. Drucker-Fraser Bequest, Montreux; Rijksmuseum, Amsterdam, BK-16578.

Plate 8. Eduard Gaertner, "The Family of Mr. Westfal in the Conservatory," Metropolitan Museum of Art, New York; In. # 2007.70; www.metmuseum.org.

Plate 9. INTERFOTO/Alamy Stock Photo.

Plate 10. Wiki commons; https://commons.wikimedia.org/wiki/File:Salon,_ca._1830.jpg.

Plate 11. Photo by Oxford Sciene Archive/Print Collector/Getty Images.

Plate 12. Photo by DeAgostini/Getty Images.

Plate 13. ©Germanisches Nationalmuseum, Foto: Monika Runge.

Plate 14. INTERFOTO/Alamy Stock Photo.

Plate 15. INTERFOTO/Alamy Stock Photo.

Plate 16. Author's photo, 2018.

Index

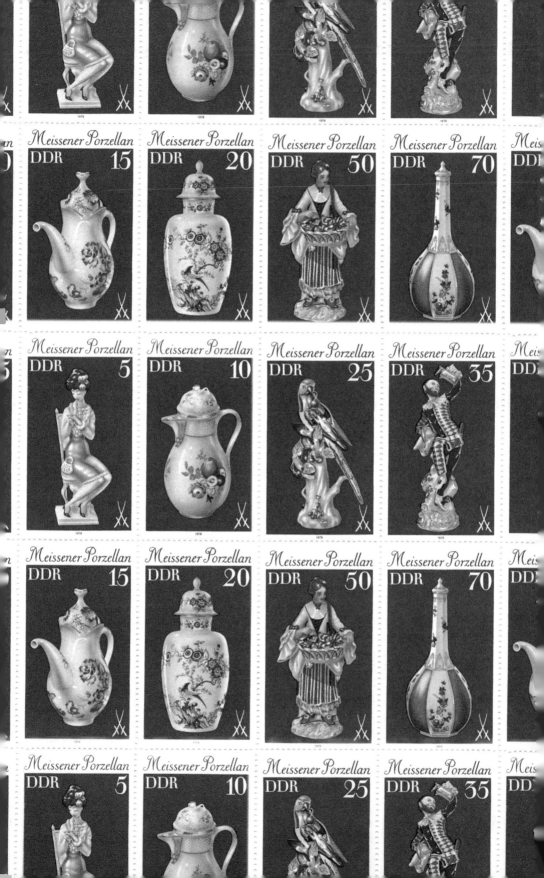

Meissener Porzellan DDR 15
Meissener Porzellan DDR 20
Meissener Porzellan DDR 50
Meissener Porzellan DDR 70
Meis DDR

Meissener Porzellan DDR 5
Meissener Porzellan DDR 10
Meissener Porzellan DDR 25
Meissener Porzellan DDR 35
Meis DDR

Meissener Porzellan DDR 15
Meissener Porzellan DDR 20
Meissener Porzellan DDR 50
Meissener Porzellan DDR 70
Meis DDR

Meissener Porzellan DDR 5
Meissener Porzellan DDR 10
Meissener Porzellan DDR 25
Meissener Porzellan DDR 35
Meis DDR